Schweizer Anglistische Arbeiten
Swiss Studies in English

Begründet von Bernhard Fehr
Herausgegeben von Andreas Fischer (Zürich), Henri Petter (Zürich), Werner Senn (Bern)

Band 128

Yvonne Studer

Ideas, Obsessions, Intertexts

A Nonlinear Approach to Russell Hoban's Fiction

francke verlag

Cover picture: Fractal figure (from Heinz-Otto Peitgen and Peter H. Richter, *The Beauty of Fractals. Images of Complex Dynamical Systems*, Berlin: Springer Verlag, 1986; reproduced by kind permission of the authors).

This thesis was accepted as a doctoral dissertation by the Faculty of Arts of the University of Zürich in the winter semester 1998/99 on the recommendation of Professor Dr. Henri Petter.

Published with support of the Swiss National Science Foundation.

Die Deutsche Bibliothek – Cataloguing in Publication Data

Studer, Yvonne:
Ideas, obsessions, intertexts : a nonlinear approach to Russel Hoban's fiction / Yvonne Studer. – Tübingen ; Basel : Francke, 2000
(Swiss studies in English ; Bd. 128)
Zugl.: Zürich, Univ., Diss., 1999
ISBN 3-7720-2440-8

Printed by Müller + Bass, Tübingen
Bound by Gogl, Reutlingen
Printed in Germany

ISSN 0080-7214
ISBN 3-7720-2440-8

TABLE OF CONTENTS

Part II: Through a Garden of Forking Paths to the Brink of the Abyss

Abbreviations

Abbreviations in parenthetical references refer to the following texts by Russell Hoban (for detailed publication information see the Bibliography; a chronological list of Hoban's fiction and essays including examples of his children's fiction precedes the Bibliography):

BB	"The Bear in Max Ernst's Bedroom or The Magic Wallet" (1987)
BR	"Blighter's Rock" (1989)
CC	"With a Choked Cry" (1991)
CL	"The Colour of Love" (1990)
CO	"Certain Obsessions, Certain Ideas" (1985-6)
CY	"Thoughts on a Shirtless Cyclist, Robin Hood, Johann Sebastian Bach, and One or Two Other Things" (1971)
DK	"The Devil's Kitchen" (1992)
DO	"Dark Oliver" (1989)
DW	"Dream Woman" (1985)
EH	"Some Episodes in the History of Miranda and Caliban: An Entertainment in Two Acts" (1990)
FL	"Fragments of a Lament for Thelonious Monk" (1983)
FP	"Footplacers, London Transport Owls, Wincer-Boise" (1982)
FR	*Fremder* (1996)
GH	"The Ghost Horse of Genghis Khan" (1987)
HT	"Household Tales by the Brothers Grimm" (1976)
IC	"'I, that was a child, my tongue's use sleeping...'" (1984)
KL	*Kleinzeit* (1974)
LN	*The Lion of Boaz-Jachin and Jachin-Boaz* (1973)
MC	*The Mouse and his Child* (1967)
MD	"The Man with the Dagger" (1989)
MF	*The Medusa Frequency* (1987)
MM	"Masada One Morning" (1990)
MT	"Mnemosyne, Teen Taals, and Tottenham Court Road" (1982)
MUM	*The Moment under the Moment* (1992)
NH	"North" (1989)
NL	"My Night with Léonie" (1991)
PG	*Pilgermann* (1983)
PK	"Portknockie" (1981)
PL	"Pan Lives" (1983)
RC	*Mr Rinyo-Clacton's Offer* (1998)
RV	"The Raven" (1989)
RW	*Riddley Walker* (1980)
RWE	*Riddley Walker*. Expanded Edition (1998)
SZ	"Schwartz" (1988; 1990)
TB	"Thoughts on Being and Writing" (1975)
TD	*Turtle Diary* (1975)
TS	"Time Slip, Uphill Lean, Laminar Flow, Place-to-place Talking and Hearing the Silence" (1972)
VS	"A View from the Soup" (1975)
WP	"Word Pix" (1991)

Illustrations

The illustrations on the title page and on the pages introducing parts I to IV are from Heinz-Otto Peitgen and Peter H. Richter: *The Beauty of Fractals. Images of Complex Dynamical Systems* (Berlin: Springer Verlag, 1986).

Acknowledgements

I am most grateful to Professor Henri Petter for his steady encouragement and for his patient, open-minded and diligent supervision throughout the time it took to complete this study. Not only do I owe him many turns of phrase and hints about relevant publications but also many escapes from error. I am also grateful to Professor Brian Vickers, who let me listen to the tape recording of Russell Hoban's 1983 reading in Zürich and who generously provided me with early essays on and by Russell Hoban that would have been beyond my reach at the beginning of my explorations. Further, I wish to thank Professor Elisabeth Bronfen for bringing theory to the English Department in Zürich and for reading parts of my manuscript.

Professors Heinz-Otto Peitgen and Peter H. Richter kindly allowed me to embellish my study with computer graphics from their intriguing book *The Beauty of Fractals*. I therefore want to give my thanks to them, too.

I am deeply grateful to my former colleagues at the English Department of the University of Zürich for their friendship and support: to Marianne Dada-Büchel for ever so often boosting my morale and giving me advice on the art of producing an attractive layout, to Christa Knellwolf for numerous stimulating discussions, and to Petra Lott and Viviane Müller for their cheerfulness and sympathy. My thanks are also due to my friends Tom Whalen and Susan Bernofsky for reading parts of the manuscript and giving me stylistic advice. Moreover, I thank my husband Dani, my parents Ursula and Paul Wüthrich, and my mother-in-law Susanne Weber for their unfailing support.

Finally, I would like to thank Russell Hoban for kindly answering many of my questions, but above all, for having raised even more.

For Dani and for my parents, Ursula and Paul Wüthrich

Introduction

The story of this study is the story of a continual, fractal branching out. One might also put it differently and say, it shows my effort to regain distance from a theme which has preoccupied me for more than a decade. The story began in November 1983, when Russell Hoban came to Zürich for a reading in Professor Brian Vickers's lecture course on "Contemporary Writers" at the Eidgenössische Technische Hochschule. Although I was a student in her beginnings, hardly capable of understanding what Hoban was reading, my interest was aroused and I decided to read all his novels. In 1987 I began working on Russell Hoban's fiction. Collecting material for the thesis I was supposed to submit as part of my university degree at the University of Zürich (the so-called "Lizentiatsarbeit"), I found that there were only a few reviews, essays and interviews available. Russell Hoban's English publishers, i.e. Jonathan Cape and Pan Books, generously provided me with reviews of *The Medusa Frequency*, which had just been published, but otherwise I had to feel my own way through the jungle. The title of the thesis which I eventually submitted to Professor Henri Petter in May 1989 was "Russell Hoban's Novels: '... the next time you look there's something different about it'" – its subtitle being a quotation from Pilgermann (128). What was then meant to be a self-ironical commentary on the impossibility of describing once and for all the work of a writer, has also proved to be true for the next phase. After my final exams, Professor Petter encouraged me to continue my explorations of Hoban's fictional world. So I began working on my doctoral thesis in 1990, blissfully ignorant of the reading adventures, occasional blocks, tortuous paths, and fights for time to write that were ahead.

In the meantime, the situation of secondary sources on Hoban's texts had changed considerably: the jungle turned out to be quite crowded (cf. Bibliography). Particularly *Riddley Walker* had elicited the greatest range of responses and been discussed in terms of its style, of its examplarity as nuclear fiction, of its affinities with deconstruction, of its mysticism and its being the nightmare of history, etc. Owing to the success of *Riddley Walker*, Hoban's name also began to appear in general studies of postmodernist literature such as Brian McHale's *Postmodernist Fiction* (1987) and *Constructing Postmodernism* (1992), or in literary histories such as Marcus Cunliffe's *The Literature of the United States. Fourth Edition* (1986) and, underscoring the difficulty of locating Hoban within a national tradition, also in David Punter's contribution to *The British and Irish Novel Since 1960* (1991). I now had to make sure not to bump into other Hobanians. On the other hand, not all the studies I would have liked to respond to were available to me, or available in time, e.g. Elizabeth Dipple's "Russell Hoban: This Place Called Time" (1988). The insight that many other Hoban scholars had found more interesting paths than myself was fortunately balanced by the recognition that everything I had found out in my "Lizentiatsarbeit" need not be buried. Still, it was obvious that I had to learn to leap high enough, and later, to grow theoretical wings, so as not to lose my sense of orientation altogether and, worse, get stuck in soft ground.

In 1989 Christine Wilkie published the first book-length study of Hoban's work, i.e. *Through the Narrow Gate. The Mythological Consciousness of Russell Hoban*. She examines not only the novels from *The Mouse and his Child* to *The Medusa Frequency*, but also addresses their adaptations for the screen (*Turtle Diary*) and the stage (*Riddley Walker*, *The Carrier Frequency*); moreover, there is a chapter on Hoban's children's literature as well as the transcript of an interview with Russell Hoban conducted in 1982. Wilkie's approach is Jungian, as she points out – an approach I myself find useful only for Hoban's early novels, but too limiting for the novels and short stories Hoban has published after *Turtle Diary*. The "collective unconscious" is too immobile and ideologically questionable as a reference grid to describe what Hoban is up to when he tries to enlarge the limited-reality consensus by means of his predominantly nonrealistic fiction. Moreover, many of Wilkie's analyses are not particularly extensive and therefore create the impression that readings should actually begin where she stops.

Barbara Herkommer's doctoral thesis *Das Muster in Bewegung. Die Romane Russell Hobans*, published in 1994, is characterized by a hermeneutical approach, that is, it is based on careful step-by-step close readings in which narratology, philosophy, theology, Jungian analytic psychology, Freudian psychoanalysis, myth criticism, Capra's New Age meditations on science and culture as well as the paradoxical genre conventions of the postmodern novel are brought into play to underline specific themes and methods used in Hoban's novels. Herkommer traces Hoban's gradual turning into a postmodernist writer, but this is not her only trajectory. While studying his work, she discovers that there are only intermediate vantage points to be reached ("Gehpunkte", 251), i.e. vantage points which never offer a full picture. Clearly Herkommer presents a greater variety of aspects and a more thorough introduction to Hoban's novels than Christine Wilkie. Occasionally, I will simply refer the reader to her interpretations rather than to repeat work she has already done, having come to understand that it is a privilege rather than a disadvantage to be in the position of a later explorer. There are also respects in which I disagree with her, of course. I think, for instance, that terms from non-literary disciplines have sometimes been applied too uncritically; they then serve as mere labels whose mutually exclusive underlying presuppositions go unnoticed because the terms are too readily integrated with the textual analysis (e.g. Freudian and Jungian notions of the unconscious). It is clear that different approaches can result in irreconcilable positions, but these must be addressed rather than suppressed.

Neither Wilkie nor Herkommer addresses from a feminist perspective the way Hoban represents women and men in their problematic dealings with each other and their definitions of subjectivity. It cannot be overlooked how deeply unsettling the theme of the uncanny, unstable relations between sex, gender, and mortality has always been for Russell Hoban; these points have indeed been addressed by both of my predecessors, but not with the approach developed specifically to examine this subject. A feminist psychoanalytical approach has an advantage over Jungian analytic psychology or gender-blind deconstruction because it reflects the patriarchal (oedipal) presuppositions which inform not only the majority of texts in our culture but also the language and the theories used to describe that culture (e.g. philosophy, psychology, psychoanalysis). A good deal of attention will therefore be paid to this aspect of Hoban's fiction: I want to show how Hoban has tried to define conditions for better relationships throughout his career, despite, or perhaps because of, his increasing awareness of irreconcilable differences between subjects and also within subjects themselves. His first impetus was to call into question received notions of masculinity, especially virility myths; reconsiderations of femininity inevitably followed.

Although the feminist psychoanalytical approach has coloured all my perceptions, this colouring is not the only thing that will be discussed and given emphasis. Stylistics and narratology will be applied to draw attention to the linguistic construction of Hoban's narratives, and to describe the various means of creating meaning (or confusion) at different levels of textual organization. My interest in mysticism and ethics will manifest itself on various occasions. Finally, the blind spots of a Barthesian structural analysis (as applied to *Turtle Diary*) will be implicitly contrasted with the advantages of the Derridean post-structuralist notion of open systems (see the analysis of *Riddley Walker*). Terry Eagleton, for whom critical pluralism appears to be a rather suspect evasion of commitment, writes in *Literary Theory* that "Those critics who parade their pluralism are usually able to do so because the different methods they have in mind are not all that different in the end" (198). He is not wrong. The question of the relation between sex, gender and mortality in Hoban's fiction is indeed related to the discussion of the relationship between mysticism and ethics, or to the investigation of stylistic particularities, because what will be looked at in all these cases are breakdowns of systems, or transgressions of laws and boundaries (sex/gender norms, religious laws, conventional morality, grammar, etc.), and assertions of difference and novelty. And the generic investigation of Hoban's magic realistic assaults on the limited-reality consensus will present a further facet of this theme. The adoption of different approaches nevertheless does make sense, though; it is not simply an expression of the belief that "there is a little truth in everything" (Eagleton 199), because their possible mutual incompatibility can actually be used to show conflicting evaluations of the outcome of a story or of the development of a character which, perhaps, would not emerge so clearly by a strict adherence to only one method.

Hans-Georg Gadamer's hermeneutical idea of a manifold exchange between text and reader in which understanding is a productive process in both directions is an attitude I can also subscribe to. However, I do not agree with the underlying assumptions of hermeneutics which Eagleton has spelled out: e.g. the idea of a "mainstream tradition" in which all "valid" works participate, which is related to the view that "history forms an unbroken continuum, free of decisive rupture, conflict and contradiction" (Eagleton 72); I also reject the assumptions that the "alien is *always* secretly familiar" (73; emphasis added), and that failures of communication are merely ephemeral (rather than, in certain cases, systematic and unbridgeable) (73). Finally, a notion such as the "hermeneutical circle" may still be helpful to explain what happens in *Kleinzeit* and what is satirized in *Riddley Walker* when Goodparley interprets the *Legend of St Eustace*, but it cannot deal with the fragments, ruptures and obscurities of *Pilgermann*, *The Medusa Frequency*, or *The Moment under the Moment* because, as Eagleton writes, "Hermeneutics does not generally consider the possibility that literary works may be diffuse, incomplete and internally contradictory, though there are many reasons to assume that they are" (74). I have therefore called my approach *nonlinear*, to signal that I do not wish to reconcile my different approaches in a totalizing gesture. I might have called myself a selective pluralist, but this would have suggested that all my choices had always been altogether deliberate, which is not the case. Just as statisticians know that their discipline is not nearly as "objective" as it is generally taken to be, working on my doctoral thesis has made me very much aware of subjective influences, e.g. the importance of both coincidental finds and unpredictable crises, on the way I went about my readings.

The term nonlinear acknowledges the fact that the idea of presenting a multifaceted study of Hoban's fiction did not come from reading hermeneutical or other theories but from seeing pictures of the Mandelbrot Set, those weird and strangely attractive forms of fractal, i.e. nonlinear, geometry. Their variety and yet self-similarity at different scales, the proximity as well as interpenetration of order and chaos which makes those still shapes seem to flicker, the calling into question of the idea of boundaries, and the sudden transitions between areas which seem empty and others which are intricately laced: these seemed to be the perfect metaphors for those aspects of Hoban's fiction I found most interesting. Nonlinearity also suggests indirection: By means of comparing Hoban's fiction to texts by other writers, i.e. by looking at them out of the corner of the eye, certain features emerge more clearly than they would otherwise. Literary intertexts range from short stories and novels by Borges, Hemingway, Nabokov, Golding and Burgess to novels by Aldiss, García Márquez, Morrison, D. M. Thomas, Pynchon, Coetzee, Carter and Rushdie.[1]

Doing research on this study often felt like looking into the magic wallet of the Fool described in "The Bear in Max Ernst's Bedroom or The Magic Wallet" (1987): "... it's heavy with the past, present, and future of the universe; in it is a jumble of unformed words and images, of colours and sounds and strangeness, continually arranging itself in new combinations wanting to be worlds" (MUM, BB 197).[2] To present my finds, however, I had to impose a certain order on chaos: the Greek word "thesis" means "a placing", after all. I will therefore end by briefly explaining how the eleven chapters of my thesis have been arranged:

"Part I" opens different "Doors to the World of Russell Hoban's Fiction". Chapter "1. Metamorphoses", is a biographical essay which will situate Hoban's fiction in a personal context. In chapters "2. The Mouse and his Child (1967)" to "5. Turtle Diary (1975)" I will look at individual aspects of the four novels published between 1967 and 1975. I have abstained from comparing them to novels by other writers *here*, so that a dynamic picture of Hoban's fictional world, of its genres, themes, characters, moods, settings, narrative structures, stylistic particularities, and a sense of Hoban's ongoing development can begin to take shape.

In "Part II: Through a Garden of Forking Paths to the Brink of the Abyss", which is concerned with the novels from "6. Riddley Walker (1980)" to "8. The Medusa Frequency (1987)", diverse theories and texts by other

---

1 By "intertexts" I neither mean sources, i.e. texts which demonstrably influenced Hoban's writing, nor do I want to go into the subtleties of Julia Kristeva's semiotic definition of intertextuality (cf. "Revolution in Poetic Language", 111). Intertext here simply refers to a text chosen for comparative and contrastive analysis on the strength of formal or thematic qualities.

2 For a key to the abbreviations used in parenthetical references see the list inserted directly after the Table of Contents. Stories and essays from *The Moment under the Moment* will be identified both by reference to the book and to their own title to avoid confusion with possible earlier publications. A Chronology of Russell Hoban's texts precedes the Bibliography.

writers will be consulted to deepen aspects outlined earlier. Chapter "8.4. Vermeer Girl into Medusa: The Repressed Returns", for example, is the "place" where my hitherto implicit feminist approach will be applied explicitly. It is here, too, that Hoban's early novels will become engaged in comparisons from which they were exempt in Part I. The chapter is deliberately bulky, for what has been "repressed" usually gets distorted; but sections have been given titles (and that practice will also be followed in other long and/or comparative chapters) to make the reading easier.

"Part III: The Two Sides of the Reality Membrane" will take a leap to two of Hoban's latest publications. Chapter "9. The Moment under the Moment (1992)", is concerned with his only collection of stories, fragments and essays. It will be examined mainly in terms of Julia Kristeva's notion of the semiotic as a deliberate exposure to the influence of the death drive. In chapter "10. Fremder (1996)", on the other hand, I will present the novel published four years later as the counterpoint to *The Moment under the Moment*, that is as a conscious affirmation of life despite its drab and horrifying aspects. Rather than to adopt a new approach I will here return to close reading, relating *Fremder* to the ideas presented in its predecessors.

Finally, "Part IV: Enlarging the Limited-Reality Consensus", will end my study in a manner which will, I hope, open up new doors and engender a whole host of further readings: chapter 11 is entitled "Magic Realism – Realism Unrestrained". From working out a definition of "magic realism" in chapter "11.1. Towards a Definition", I will proceed to a series of comparisons between diverse magic realists in chapter "11.2. A Magical Mystery Tour from Borges to Rushdie", and eventually conclude in chapter "11.3. Certain Obsessions: The Semi-Transparent Screens of Russell Hoban's Magic Realism", by describing the special features of Hoban's use of the genre.

There are still plenty of undiscovered areas in Hoban's fictional world, e.g. his latest novel *Mr Rinyo-Clacton's Offer*, published in February 1998, while I was writing the last sentences of my study. Or one might take a close look at the afterword, the notes and the glossary Hoban added to *Riddley Walker* in the Expanded Edition published in 1998. But "The fires col / My storys tol" (RW 19). It is for others to make new connections and add further colours and shades to the discussion of the work of this fascinating writer.

Part I:

Doors to the World of Russell Hoban's Fiction

1. Metamorphoses

> My life has a very discontinuous feel. It feels as if it's had bursts of being here and there, but not as if there is a continuous accumulation of experience that led up to my writing. It was a sort of jungle, and eventually I broke through to a clear space where I could write. (Hoban and Kincaid 7)

In this excerpt from an interview, Russell Hoban points out what to him is the predominant feature of his life: a lack of continuity that has strongly influenced both his personal philosophy of life as well as the topics and the style of his writing. Especially the year 1969 marks a major split in his career; it was the year when the American writer's first marriage broke up. Soon after leaving the USA with his family, Hoban had moved in with another woman in London. His wife and the four children went back home to Connecticut while he stayed in England, convinced that London was the only place that could provide sufficient inspiration for him to continue writing. He left behind the existence of a successful author of cosy and didactic books for little children to take on the more demanding identity of a writer of novels for adults and of emancipatory books for eleven to twelve-year-olds.

Most of his American background faded away in the process:

> Since the beginning of my unlimited writing took place here, the beginning of my writing about men and women, it seems all of my people in one way or another originate either in England or out of my present experience since I've been here. I don't find myself able to use any of my childhood or my growing up, except indirectly. (Hoban and Kincaid 7)

The Moment under the Moment, however, a collection of short stories and essays published in 1992, offers a few glimpses of his early years. In "'I, that was a child, my tongue's use sleeping...'" (1984), Hoban talks about the house of his childhood, his parents and his sisters (MUM, IC 157f.). In "With a Choked Cry" (1991), he recalls the moment when he threw his favourite children's books down an incinerator chute:

> In March 1943, just before I left for the army, I opened that flap and down the chute went *Treasure Island, Robin Hood, The Arabian Nights*, and some lesser favourites, all books that I loved and had read several times. I was eighteen and going off to the war, maybe I wasn't coming back; I was presiding over the death of my childhood as I burned those books and when I got to the induction centre I gave my civilian clothes to the Red Cross. (MUM, CC 172)

Russell Hoban was born in rural Lansdale, Pennsylvania, on 4 February 1925. His parents were Jewish immigrants from Ostrog, in the Ukraine:

> They're both dead now and my two sisters and I continue their outward journey from that town we've never seen. They were both young when they came to America. My father had been poor in Russia, he told me how once outside a bakery he had seen a boy with a freshly-bought cheese pastry take out the cheese and throw away the crust which he, my father, then picked up and ate. (...)
>
> My mother came to America before my father, in 1911 I think, when she was seventeen. She came with her sisters and she worked as a seamstress to earn my father's passage. He became a newsboy in Philadelphia, he had a dog who sat on the back of his bicycle. ... I am named after Dr Russell Conwell who gave a famous lecture called 'Acres of Diamonds' in which a man travelled the world in search of wealth and then found it in his own backyard. (MUM, IC 157)

Both his mother and his father, who eventually became an advertising manager of the *Jewish Daily Forward* and an amateur theatre director, supported their son's flair for drawing. After Russell had graduated from High School in 1941, he therefore became a student at the Philadelphia Museum School of Industrial Art. During his first year he met Lillian Aberman. They married in 1944 before he was sent to Italy, where he served as infantry messenger. Although he was awarded the Bronze Star Medal in 1945, World War II had taught him forever to distrust the glorification of war, and he subsequently tried to pass this on to his readers.[1]

After the war, Hoban took on several jobs before he joined an advertising agency in New York where he worked himself up to the post of a TV art director. Traces of this particular "burst of being" can be found in his second novel *Kleinzeit* (1974). In 1956, his ambition to work as a freelance illustrator was gratified. He designed front-covers for several American magazines, among them *Time* and *Life*:

> Risk-taking was a big thing in my mind at the time. Only a year before that I'd left my TV art director job at J. Walter Thompson to become a freelance illustrator. That was a risk I'd hesitated to take: I had a wife and three children[2] and a mortgage, I was a responsible citizen with a lot to lose. One evening coming home on the train I'd said to my friend Harvey Cushman, who worked at another advertising agency, 'When I have $10,000 in the bank and a couple of steady accounts I'll do it.'
>
> 'You'll never do it then,' said Harvey. 'I've heard lots of guys say the same thing and somehow the time never comes. If you're going to do it you'll do it without the $10,000 and the steady accounts.'

---

1 Cf. e.g. "Time Slip, Uphill Lean, Laminar Flow, Place-to-place Talking and Hearing the Silence" (1972), p. 38.

2 The dating of events is not quite consistent. In "The Bear...", Hoban is actually talking about the time around 1958, when he did not have any children yet. Perhaps different moments at which similar decisions had to be made have been condensed into one memory.

> So I did it and I prospered and I was confirmed in my belief that the human animal is a hunting and finding and risk-taking animal. (MUM, BB 187-188)

At home, he also kept a folder with drawings of horses, wagons and construction vehicles. When friends of his saw them, they suggested that he turn them into a children's book. Hoban added a text to his illustrations, and the result was published under the title *What Does It Do and How Does It Work* in 1959.

Ever since school, where he had won several poetry and story writing competitions, Russell Hoban had felt attracted to writing. This activity had never been poisoned by the pressure to succeed as had his other talent, drawing, which his parents encouraged so vehemently. After the publication of his first book, he therefore decided to write further children's books. He collaborated with Lillian Hoban, who did the illustrations, on a series of books about Frances the Badger, the first of which, *Bedtime for Frances*, was published in 1960. Later on, they developed a series of picture books on the Brute Family, little ill-mannered creatures.[3]

In 1963, Hoban started working on *The Mouse and his Child*, his first longer book, which took him about three years to finish. It marks an important preliminary stage of his career as a writer of fiction for adults: although the book grew famous as a children's "classic", it contains issues that betray Hoban's wish to address his own age group. Neither the animal characters nor the happy ending of the novel can disguise the many passages where philosophical, social and ethical subjects are treated with adult humour and irony. Besides writing, he read a lot of Conrad, Dickens, Melville and writers of supernatural stories, but the eight years between the publications of *What Does It Do and How Does It Work* and *The Mouse and his Child* were not only productive, they also exhausted his financial, physical and mental resources. After giving up his free-lance work as an illustrator in 1965, he had to go back to copy writing to earn a living for his family, which had increased by three daughters and a son between 1959 and 1963.

Only after 1967 did the royalties from his children's books enable him to write full-time, but then it was discovered that he suffered from diabetes and from dysfunction of the gall bladder. Moreover, he experienced writer's block for the first time. When it had lasted two years, Hoban decided to "shake things up and move to London for a change" (Hoban and Toomey 20), as he explained in an interview later on. Still, he could not find the desired inspiration for a

3 For discussions of Hoban's children's books, see ch. 11 of Christine Wilkie's *Through the Narrow Gate* (88-97); the essays "A Narrow Pavement says 'Walk Alone'" (1976) by Gillian McMahon-Hill and "The Fantasy World of Russell Hoban" (1980) by A. Joan Bowers particularly explore bridges between Hoban's writing for children and for adults.

sequel to *The Mouse and his Child*, not even after Lillian and the children had gone back to the United States in March 1970. Hoban suffered from a serious mid-life crisis:

> I felt this tremendous pull to be with my children, where I could see them, but somehow I found I couldn't leave London. It had a lot to do with all kinds of things beyond needing a change, or my career, or anything like that, and for the first year after the break up, I kept trying to write, but couldn't get anything down on paper at all. I did finish the last Frances book *Egg thoughts and other songs*, but that was all. I couldn't start that old groove again that had been so profitable with the illustrated books, and I couldn't get anything new going. (Hoban and Toomey 20)

Eventually, the theme of his first "real" adult novel *The Lion of Boaz-Jachin and Jachin-Boaz* evolved out of his difficulty in dealing with his teenage son, who was angry about his father's giving up the family. Hoban started working on the book in April 1971; two years later, it was published and reviewed very favourably by most critics. The lion got into the story because Hoban had been interested in Mesopotamian art and mythology for a while and had been planning to write a supernatural story about a lion. The preoccupation with the link between fathers and sons, however, biased his writing so much that the lion was turned, above all, into a personification of their mutual feelings. By writing about his problem, Hoban found a way of coming to terms with it, which in turn opened up a door for another go at life. In the summer of 1970, he had met Gundula Ahl, a German woman who worked in a London bookshop. They got married in 1975, after Hoban had gained a formal divorce from his first wife. The couple has three sons, born between 1972 and 1978.

His second life has enabled Hoban to reconsider quite many things. Although he wrote books for children again,[4] he could no longer figure himself making up stories about cuddly animals that would predictably sell well. In an interview given in 1975, he rebelled against the "crime of the [publishers'] syndicate" that was "out to consensify children" (Hoban and Hamilton 8). Instead of passing drab social conventions on to children, he would rather help them to liberate their radical spirit and gain independence, as he pointed out in several essays published in the early seventies.[5] In *Turtle*

---

4 According to the "Biographical Notes" from Jonathan Cape Ltd. he had published 51 by 1987; I admit having given up counting them. One of Hoban's latest children's books is *The Trokeville Way*. Its protagonist is a boy harassed by a school bully until he encounters Moe Nagic. Since 1989, school bullies have also haunted the protagonists of his fiction for adults: see "The Man with the Dagger", "Dark Oliver" and *Fremder*.

5 E.g. "Thoughts on a Shirtless Cyclist, Robin Hood, Johann Sebastian Bach and One or Two Other Things" (1971), "Time Slip, ..." (1972), or "Thoughts on Being and Writing" (1975).

Diary (1975), his third novel, he created in Neaera H. a character whose thoughts about children's literature can easily be identified with his own. Thus, the books for children and adults have been showing more and more resemblance in matter and style over the years. At the beginning of his second life, Hoban also began to make "friends with Death" (Hoban and Kincaid 6) when, during a stay in hospital to make tests because of his diabetes, he was lying next to terminal patients and could not help thinking about the fragile borderlines between life and death, sanity and madness, or freedom and imprisonment. Comically distorted, this experience reappears in *Kleinzeit*.

Apart from borrowing the material for his novels from his own life, Hoban often turns to the myths of fairy-tales and legends to redefine matters such as growing up or dying, looking, it seems, for a minimal amount of stable elements within a life of constant change. He does not object to the fantasy elements that characterize many of these tales:

> The fantasy of our legends, myths and stories helps with those new definitions. It is as close as we can get to the thingness of things through the appearance of things. Fantasy isn't separate from reality; it is a vital approach to the essence of it. (CY 13)

Psychoanalytical ideas have influenced the novels as well as elements from several religions. Thus, the figure of Punch in *Riddley Walker* (1980), his fourth and most successful novel as yet, is the artist's answer to certain repressed tendencies in human beings, i.e. to the Freudian "id" or the archetype defined by C. G. Jung as the "shadow".[6] Philippa Toomey's account of the books on Hoban's shelves is quite revealing: "... on the shelves are Freud, Jung, Laing, Zen and Montaigne, mythologies, dictionaries, books on navigation and Folkestone (*Folkestone*?)" (Hoban and Toomey 20). Her italicized question can be answered retrospectively: the books on Folkestone might have been a source for *Riddley Walker*, for the place is one of the settings of the novel though its name has degenerated into "Fork Stoan".

Riddley's initiation and other cultic ceremonies, on the other hand, must have been influenced by Mircea Eliade's studies on religious history, for in *Turtle Diary*, the novel preceding Hoban's post-holocaust tale, William G. reflects on a book on shamanism by Eliade (TD 61). In *Pilgermann* (1983), the fifth novel, which is dominated by the symbolism of Islamic patterns and issues relating to Judaic, Islamic and Christian theology, Hoban even documents his sources in an appendix. It almost follows from these premises that he does not consider himself the creator of his stories; he rather feels like a

6 Also see Hoban's remarks on, and views of, Punch in *Riddley Walker*. Expanded Edition (1998), pp. 224-227, 232.

mediator between his readers and reality as he experiences it: "I am not in the business of making clockwork novels which go from A to B when you wind them up, I'm at the service of the material that enters me. It takes me where it wants to go, and I might not know why I'm going there" (Hoban and Haffenden 132). He does not object to being called a "free-lance mystic" (Hoban and Myers 12) or a "religious writer", that is "a writer who is always examining the position of one's self in the universe" (Hoban and Bodmer 2).

The material that "entered" him varied from time to time. Although his main concerns have remained nearly the same over the years, his settings range from contemporary London (the tunnel system of the tube or the zoo) to devastated Kent in more than 2500 years' time, from picturesque Polperro to Germany and Antioch in the eleventh century. Realistic descriptions alternate with dream landscapes that can turn into nightmarish scenes any time. Except for *The Medusa Frequency* (1987), there has also been a development from introversion to extroversion regarding Hoban's authorial focus. As he said in an interview in 1984, "it's been a process of getting out of myself and into the world a bit more all the time" (Hoban and Myers 8) ever since *Turtle Diary*, with its two narrators who join for a common aim, i.e. setting turtles free.

However, the four years between the publications of *Pilgermann* and *The Medusa Frequency* did not allow him to pursue this line of development. Hoban's increased popularity since the publication of *Riddley Walker* brought on reading engagements all over the world, and the bustle about his person made him turn back to himself and his difficulty to write. In 1984, he also started working on two theatrical projects. One of them was a performance project with the Impact Theatre Cooperative, *The Carrier Frequency*, which one critic has described as a "startling juxtaposition of speech and image working simultaneously on many levels" (Hoban and Chaillet 95). Christine Wilkie presents more detailed information:

> *The Carrier Frequency* was first performed at Leeds in November 1984 ... and has since been performed in Manchester, Reading ..., Cardiff, and London (1984); Holland, Belgium, Spain, and Italy (1985); and in Switzerland, Italy, Warsaw, and London (The Place) (1986).
>
> *The Carrier Frequency* ... is a rich, poetic, and enigmatic experience that in its rhythm and movement evokes, at once, pathos and tension, humor and terror. Any form of description about it, anything that is *not* the experience, is reductive. The action happens in one thousand gallons of water and with several tons of reinforced concrete. It is organized on two strata in a submerged world that explores the spectrum of sound and experience and which might or might not be regarded as a literal romp around the inner world of the unconscious, its personal and its collective aspects – the underworld of Orpheus and Eurydice. (Wilkie 85)

The other play was a stage version of *Riddley Walker* for the Manchester Royal Exchange Theatre. Wilkie has described the difference between the novel and the stage adaptation, which was first performed on 20 February 1986:

> ... the important single difference between the novel and the reworking for the stage of *Riddley Walker* has been the erosion from the stage narrative of the heuristic facility by which readers of the novel make connections, draw conclusions from inferences, solve riddles, and make their own deductions from, in this case, the confusions that have arisen from folklore etymologies. The reading process has been simplified. And the necessary work to make meaning in reading the novel has been dispensed with in the stage narrative by the use of explanations, articulations, actualizations, and by the clever use of dialogue between characters. (...)
>
> Little if anything, of the plot has been lost in translation from the novel. Hoban has managed to condense all its major themes. But details have been added. There are some different and additional characters with names bearing the same, if not greater, invention as the already familiar names from the novel. ... And, as part of the How Fents community, more women appear as named characters: Gerty Rundl, Minsy Wattl, Tangy Sasser. There are many more singing rhymes, and in this three-dimensional discourse they lend themselves to dance set to music. (Wilkie 67, 69)

Both dramatical experiments met with mixed criticism. Only the critics who had enjoyed the poetic qualities of the novels' languages, with their puns and songs and their rhythmical prose, could thoroughly appreciate the plays; for their plot was of even lesser importance than it had been in the novels.

Like the eponymous hero of *Pilgermann* who finds it difficult to tell the events of his life as a story, that is as a "coherent sequence of picture cards" (PG 38), the author has recognized that traditional plots are inconvenient for his messages. Hence, he usually has to make a real effort to find ways of connecting his ideas:

> There are lots of other people who have a much stronger sense of story than I do. Mostly what I'm concerned with is the strangeness of consciousness, that there should *be* such a thing as consciousness, that we should all be members of it. So story is not the first thing in my mind, and I have to work hard to find a story to hook into. (Hoban and Bodmer 2)

At the time Hoban gave this interview, in November 1983, a draft of what was to be *The Medusa Frequency*, more precisely parts of chapters four and five, were already in his travelling baggage. Yet, at that stage, he was convinced that the text with the title "A Conversation with the Head of Orpheus" was not fit for being turned into a novel. Thus, he first used it as an inspirational source for *The Carrier Frequency*.

Although he spends ten hours a day and seven days a week behind his desk when he is at home in Fulham, the draft had to wait four years until new elements caused a "novelistic necessity"; Hoban's term implies that "you start out with characters and circumstances, and the characters do things, and the circumstances change, and a new action is generated, and one thing leads to another, and it's got to keep moving" (Hoban and Bodmer 1). It was a series of personal concerns such as a heart attack and writer's block, the creative possibilities inherent in playing around with an Apple II computer (the apple of knowledge?), a certain disgust at commercial writers, and the continued effort to understand the relationship between males and females that provided the impetus to finish the novel. The result for the first time resembles one of the previous novels. Both the setting of *The Medusa Frequency* in contemporary London and the recurring theme of Orpheus and Eurydice establish a link with *Kleinzeit*. In terms of the relationships represented in the novel, however, *The Medusa Frequency* documents the progress in Hoban's thinking about sex and gender since *Kleinzeit*. Reviewers were split: Paul Bailey was too disgusted with the protagonist Herman Orff to enjoy the novel:

> It's the quality of Herman's mind, of Herman's aspirations that worries me. Beyond all the mythologising, much of it elegantly expressed, there is a hole that is Herman. Philip Roth's Zuckermann registers as a genuine writer, as does the Calvino-like narrator of 'If On a Winter's Night a Traveller...,' but Orff does not even seem the equal of L. Ron Hubbard. (Bailey 23)

Boyd Tonkin, on the other hand, voiced his approval:

> Since the Renaissance, plotless authors have always turned for succour to that data-base of ready made narratives known to us ... as Greek mythology. In modern fiction what follows is usually a stilted effort to dress a frail anecdote in the robes of universality.
>
> Russell Hoban knows about these traps and knows how to dodge them. (...)
>
> Short, smart and fizzy, the novel seeks out the roots of creativity with none of the solemnity that phrase implies. (Tonkin 27)

What both reviews manifest is a reaction to Hoban's gradual reduction of story and character in favour of a more playful style. This playfulness also extended beyond the realm of literature. Besides writing for the stage he began to experiment with other media: two short films, "Deadsy" and "Door" resulted from collaborations with the director David Anderson; and his fascination with opera eventually sparked the desire to write libretti.

In his next book, *The Moment under the Moment* (1992), he presented his ideas in a mixture of fiction, i.e. stories and story fragments, and nonfiction, i.e. essays and descriptive sketches. Having always admired the fragmentary quality of Rainer Maria Rilke's *The Notebooks of Malte Laurids Brigge*, "the fragmentation of consciousness as it's happening" (Hoban and Bodmer 14), he now put into effect what had been in his mind as early as in 1983:

> ... it conceivably could happen that there will come a time when certain ideas won't want to go the full distance of a novel and won't want to be resolved even as little as my novels get resolved, but will just want to leave themselves hanging.... (Hoban and Bodmer 14)

At the centre of *The Moment under the Moment* is the libretto for the opera, "Some Episodes in the History of Miranda and Caliban" (1990), which underlines his interest in the musicality of his own texts and the ability of music to convey ongoing processes. These processes, as sketched out by the stories and essays grouped around the libretto, include moments of both bliss and rupture: there is no holding on to either, just a letting go. While "Some Episodes...", with music by Helen Roe, did not draw much attention, though, his collaboration with the composer Harrison Birtwistle proved to be a success: the première of their opera "The Second Mrs Kong", performed by the Glyndebourne Touring Opera on 21 October 1994 was even reviewed in Zürich's local newspaper *Tages-Anzeiger* and praised as a masterpiece (Meyer 85).

Another two years passed until the novel *Fremder* (1996) was published, nine years after *The Medusa Frequency*. Its setting is the twenty-first century: dilapidated space stations as well as an overpopulated and polluted London define the realms between which the protagonist Fremder Elijah Gorn commutes. While I earlier characterized Hoban's novels as moving from introversion to extroversion and back, *Fremder* encompasses both. Fremder goes almost too far both into and out of himself, flickering across the Fourth Galaxy on his thirtieth birthday and again a few weeks later. He has become entangled in a plot designed by an uncanny half-organic "Data Evaluator (Autonomous Response)" called Pythia (FR 72). But instead of flickering to the other side of the reality membrane with "her", he succeeds in liberating himself.

Where will we find the next protagonist? It is not for me to say. An eighth novel, *Mr Rinyo-Clacton's Offer*, was published in February 1998, but the copy has not arrived at my bookshop yet. However, it is good to know that Hoban is still under way, travelling, thinking, and adding further facets to his fiction.

2. The Mouse and his Child (1967)

2.1. The Transition from Children's to Adults' Literature

Choosing *The Mouse and his Child* as the first of Russell Hoban's books for discussion is not an altogether arbitrary decision. Hoban often calls it "my first novel" (Hoban and Kincaid 5) and admits in the interview with John Haffenden, "To be honest, I thought I was writing an adult book at the time. I didn't make any concessions" (Hoban and Haffenden 125).[1] In fact, his aim was no less than to draw a "world picture that was an attempt to see the thingness of some things in a very narrow compass, a microcosm" (CY 13). What mainly induced his publishers to treat the novel as a children's book was the use of speaking animals and clockwork-toys (reminiscent of Kenneth Grahame's and Hans Christian Andersen's) as protagonists, moreover the absence of adult sexuality: "Most adult novels are about clockwork dolls who copulate. Mine happens to be about clockwork mice who walk, and therefore it is a children's book" (CY 13-14).

In fact the book should never have been labelled, though, except, perhaps, with a term like "family novel". For certain critics, anxious to preserve the genre limits, did not fail to accuse it, above all, for those qualities which appeal to adult readers:

> For 65 pages I thought I'd found a classic.... But then the author starts over-the-shouldering like mad, with a crow drama workshop called the Caws of Art and many sly digs at Beckett and Existentialism. The book never really recovers for the rest of its 200 pages. (Hildick 640-642)

Even though children may be unable to appreciate or understand certain elements of the novel when they encounter them for the first time, these may provide new pleasures for them as adolescents or as adults, perhaps when they re-read the book to their own children. One might also say that *The Mouse and his Child* is a book to grow up with, offering itself differently at each new reading. "... the next time you look there's something different about it", says brickmaster Tower Gate in *Pilgermann* about the pattern designed by the

1 Barbara Herkommer and Christine Wilkie's studies of Hoban's works begin with a discussion of *The Mouse and his Child*, too (cf. Herkommer 10; Wilkie 21). For A. Joan Bowers, there are two further "transitional" books, i.e. *Ugly Bird* (1969) and *The Sea-Thing Child* (1972): "These are transitional not because they represent a midpoint between 'low art' – writing for children – and 'high art' – writing for adults – but because they reveal Hoban struggling with themes he had previously hinted at but not explored" (85); though both books have been published after *The Mouse and his Child*, they are shorter and less complex (88).

novel's protagonist (128). This quality, which is to be found in all of Hoban's works, already manifests itself in *The Mouse*. I shall therefore analyze its literary qualities, its language and style, its plot and its characters without carrying on the discussion of its suitability for children. "It may not be a Children's Book," as an anonymous critic for the *Times Literary Supplement* wrote, "but, my goodness, it is a *Book*" ("What toys endure", 357).

The book's hybridity mirrors Hoban's ambivalent position at the time he was writing it. Tired of simplifying the world and its phenomena for the sake of young readers, he occasionally allowed himself to satirize art, science, and philosophy, to attack war, and to explore the nature of freedom and death. But he was not bold enough yet, maybe too inhibited to liberate his thinking from conventional restraints, just as he was inwardly letting go of his family while making outward efforts to preserve the idyll. The decisive step was taken in 1969, i.e. two years after the publication of *The Mouse and his Child*, but many typical "Hobanian" concerns and stylistic features may be traced back to this work. Transitional though it may be in terms of genre, it decidedly marks the starting point of the author's development as a writer of adult fiction.

2.2. The Plot

The plot of *The Mouse and his Child* is characterized by a clear-cut structure. The beginning and the end of the book are marked by the appearances of a tramp, which form a frame around a quest story composed of short episodes. There is no personal narrator: the adventures of the two mice are told as a third-person narration with many dialogic scenes and descriptions both of the landscape and of the characters' actions and external features; the protagonists' thoughts and perceptions are represented only occasionally, when their mental life must be known for their actions or their passivity to become intelligible (e.g. 23, 41, 124f., 180, 186). A summary might be helpful.

During the Christmas season a tramp looking through the window of a toyshop sees how a pair of clockwork mice are placed among other toys next to a huge dolls' house. At night they make the acquaintance of a clockwork elephant and a seal. The mouse child dreams of their becoming a family. Already the next day, though, they are sold to a human family and used as Christmas ornaments. The fifth time they are dancing in a circle under the Christmas tree, the mouse child suddenly notices a small dolls' house among the presents and begins to cry, breaking an iron clockwork law. Alarmed by his sobbing the cat leaps on a table, causing a heavy vase to fall on the mice.

The crushed toys are thrown away, but the tramp finds them in the dustbin. He repairs them, and sets them free outside the town. They are to be tramps like himself. Although dancing in a circle is no longer possible for them, the mouse father can now walk straightforward if someone winds him up.

Their freedom does not last. Manny Rat takes them to his trash empire in the dump where they have to work for him as food carriers like other discarded windups. Their first job is to accompany Manny's assistant Ralphie to the Meadow Mutual Hoard and Trust Company, where he is to steal treacle brittle. On their way, a bullfrog tells their fortune. Since Frog feels that his and their fates are linked, he secretly follows them. When Ralphie is killed by the bank's badger guard, Frog offers to accompany the mice. The mouse child defines the aim of their quest: he is determined to find the elephant, the seal and the big dolls' house from the toyshop. They decide to go to the pine woods first because Frog remembers having seen a seal there two years earlier. She was with a group of travelling actors. A bluejay meanwhile spreads the news of the failed bank robbery. Manny instantly takes up their pursuit. In his wake, there is a new acquisition: the clockwork elephant he has just found and repaired.

The two mice and Frog become witnesses of a cruel war between shrews. Although they succeed in escaping from the battlefield, Frog is abducted by a horned owl while they are crossing a frozen stream. Before Manny can catch up with them, the mouse and his child are taken up by the Caws of Art, an experimental theatre group rehearsing the absurd play "The Last Visible Dog" at an amphitheatre nearby. Unfortunately, the seal is no longer a member of the group. After helping to defend the players against a weasel attack during the evening performance, the windups suddenly find themselves face to face with Manny. Instead of recoiling they induce the audience to mob him. While Manny is struggling to save his life, Euterpe the parrot carries the two mice to the beaver pond, the home of Muskrat. He is a gifted tinkerer although pure thought now fascinates him more than its application. When they arrive, he is busy inventing a machine for felling trees. He also knows the seal: she was living at his place before she went away with a kingfisher. Muskrat promises to make the mice self-winding in exchange for their assistance: their walking in a circle will be the motor of his machine. Toiling for several months, the mice are eventually found by Manny and the elephant. The rat's curiosity is stronger than his desire to smash the windups: he wants to see the tree fall and therefore speeds up the mice's pacing. The consequences are disastrous: the tree falls in the wrong direction and the two mice are catapulted into the water. Since the beaver dam has been destroyed, too, they are swept downstream into C. Serpentina's pond. Manny can do no more than watch them disappear.

C. Serpentina is a monstrous turtle philosopher who lives at the bottom of the pond. He turns out to be the author of "The Last Visible Dog". Merely interested in contemplating infinity and in uttering grand-sounding but meaningless phrases, he refuses to help the mice. While the father despairs, the mouse child makes friends with Miss Mudd, a tiny nymph who will later metamorphose into a dragonfly. She helps the mouse child to think about infinity and backs up his opinion that there is more to life than mud. When the child finally devises a plan by which they can be hauled out of the pond, she takes great risks to execute it. Their efforts are crowned by success: after months spent in murky water, the mice emerge into the sunlight again. Yet, new problems instantly present themselves. When a bittern tries to wind them up, the father's motor turns out to have gone rusty. Then they hear the bluejay report Muskrat's death. Before they can begin to worry about their situation, however, a hungry marsh hawk picks them up. Noticing that they are heading for the dump the mouse child induces the hawk to drop them. Once more they are shattered.

Their flight has not passed unnoticed. Both Frog, who has survived his abduction by the owl, and the seal have lived near C. Serpentina's pond for some time. When they realize what has happened, they ask the bittern and the kingfisher to follow the marsh hawk. Manny Rat, too, learns of the windups' return to the dump. Before his new assistant Iggy can find them, however, Frog and the seal succeed in taking the broken mice to an oak tree where they repair them. From the tree, the mouse child suddenly spots the old dolls' house. Manny has turned it into his new head quarters. The mice and their friends devise an ingenious plan to conquer the dolls' house and defeat the rats for good. Manny's spare-parts can contains most of the ingredients they need, among them a motor for the mouse child. After they have killed most of the rats and liberated the elephant and other clockwork slaves, the dolls' house becomes the home of the newly founded mouse family and their friends. Later, it will acquire fame as a hotel for migrating birds, and a cultural centre for the whole area. Even toothless Manny Rat eventually becomes integrated into the family – after failing to blow up the house –, and his genius adds many comforts to their lives. When the tramp peers through the windows of the dolls' house at Christmas, he draws up a new guideline: they are now to be happy.

Incidentally, the noun phrase, "the tramp" opens as well as closes the novel so that the frame describes a genuine circle that structurally contradicts the linear development of the quest just as the word "tramp" suggests a way of life diametrically opposed to the aim achieved by the two mice. For Wilkie, their quest is circular, too, though:

> The mouse and his child move in their circular quest for self-winding and territory from their high point of relative comfort and security in the toyshop to a low point of mud and despair at the bottom of the pond to arrive by progressions of experience at their dolls' house hotel. (22)

Considering that they move from dolls' house to dolls' house, this argument is right. But when the development of the mice is compared to the invariability of the tramp, who returns each Christmas as if he were one of the attributes of the season, or an alter ego of Santa Claus, the linear aspect of the two mice's quest will become visible: They are no longer owned by anyone but have become owners of the dolls' house; instead of one toy they are now two separate subjects, not altogether independent and self-winding, for perpetual motion is impossible, but no longer as dependent on each other and on friends to wind them up as at the beginning; their experiences have left indelible traces on their bodies: certain damages cannot be repaired; finally, there is absolutely no way back to the toyshop. Perhaps, then, their quest should really be described in terms of a three-dimensional helix, a figure which combines the linearity of progress with the circular recurrence of certain elements. In the novels from *The Lion of Boaz-Jachin and Jachin-Boaz* to *Turtle Diary*, Hoban's plots will focus more on the protagonists' need to overcome stagnation and advance; he will examine the conditions that must be fulfilled for action cycles (individual events) to take place and be superseded by others. But in *Riddley Walker*, where the tensions between different ways of life are an important theme, "way of life" designating the totality of all action cycles performed by an individual, the helix will again mediate between the need to advance from one action cycle to a new one and the need to hold on to, or the impossibility of letting go of, certain traditions and limitations.

The two clockwork toys' journey is told chronologically, without any flashbacks or major digressions from the beginning to the happy ending. Although Manny Rat's pursuit forms an important parallel narrative strand, it does not interrupt the main story except in those phases when the mice are either immobile (e.g. 65-66: directly after the battle of the shrews) or engaged in some prolonged action (e.g. 104-105: the tree-felling project). Occasionally, information about other characters is added in the same places to that about Manny (e.g. 105: about animals in and around the beaver pond and about Frog), but there are no separate chapters about the mice's antagonist or their friends.

The central story can be divided into three parts. Chapters 1 and 2 provide an exposition. The contrasts between the idyllic toyshop, the place under the Christmas tree, and the dump make the mice dissatisfied with their situation;

tired of being pushed around by various owners they seek the company of their equals and try to find a place where they can live together in peace.

On their journey, described in chapters 3 to 8, they come in contact with war, art, science, and philosophy. Chapters 5 and 6, which cover their prolonged stays with Muskrat and C. Serpentina, are the centre of the novel. By chance rather than by their own skills, the mice get very close to achieving their aim, for Muskrat promises them self-winding in exchange for their work, gives them a hint about the whereabouts of the seal, and they also see the elephant again for the first time. But because Manny intervenes shortly before they can fulfil their contract with Muskrat, they are unexpectedly sent to the nadir of their journey. Their return to the dump and the conquest of the old dolls' house must be planned and earned step by step.

To begin with, both a mental leap and a literal leap are necessary. A. Joan Bowers has pointed to the essential transformation the two mice undergo at the bottom of the pond, reduced to utmost external immobility: it is the "philosophical acceptance of their own ultimate 'aloneness' which provides the impetus for the mouse and his child to find a way up and out of the pond and to continue their quest" (91). Her reference to the novel's epigraph, the excerpt from W. H. Auden's poem "Leap Before You Look", is crucial (88): "*The sense of danger must not disappear: / The way is certainly both short and steep, / However gradual it looks from here; / Look if you like, but you will have to leap*" (MC 9). Even without knowing *Riddley Walker* at the time she was writing her essay (both were published in 1980), she nevertheless felt the centrality of such moments for all of Hoban's later texts. Not only the recreative leaps made by the characters of *Lion*, *Kleinzeit*, and *Turtle Diary* are subsumed by the last line of Auden's poem but also the leaps leading from Riddley and Pilgermann's mystical moments to Fremder Gorn's daring escape from the clutches of Pythia.

A typical fairy tale happy ending then seems to ensue, with the mouse father marrying the clockwork elephant after the battle described in chapter 8. But the novel does not end here yet, as a fairy tale would. Manny's return to the house in chapter 9, which culminates in his relapse into hostile behaviour in chapter 10, introduces an element of instability. And an outlook on the family's future (the only deviation from the novel's otherwise strictly chronological development) particularly enhances the point that stories do go on after the last page of a book.

Yet, as all the prospects of the mouse family are happy, a false note accompanies the outcome of the novel. The protagonists are allowed to enjoy final happiness in spite of the first line of novel's epigraph, that is "The sense of danger must not disappear" (9). The prospect of eternal happiness does not only disagree with what they have experienced throughout the book but also with episodes such that of the bass who is doomed to die at a moment of exultation (138f.). Two reasons induced Hoban to turn *The Mouse and his Child* into a success story:

> At the time I was wary of attempting validation through tragedy, which I think the inexperienced writer too frequently attempts – on the premise that if you make it heavy, maybe it will be good. I don't necessarily believe that an unhappy ending is to be taken more seriously than a happy ending. It also coincided with a time in my life when I was trying hard to put things together. I'd left my wife and stayed away for about three months. We got back together and built a brave new house, and I was on for seeing things being resolved by a determined putting-together of elements that had exploded before and might explode again. (Hoban and Haffenden 125)

Except for this fundamental inconsistency, he tried to ensure the coherence of the novel. One critic found the plotting "as intricate and as carefully fitted together as the works of a clock" (Anonymous, "Paperbacks: New and Noteworthy", 31). Especially the dog motif connects all parts of the story: Bonzo, the tramp's little black-and-white spotted dog (16) resembles the dog on the label of BONZO dog-food cans that are standing and lying around everywhere in the book. Manny uses one of them for spare parts of clockwork toys and tools (34), and so does Muskrat (94). Another specimen, which is standing half-buried in the mud of C. Serpentina's pond, has inspired him to write a play called *The Last Visible Dog*. This play is performed by the "Caws of Art" with disastrous results at the beginning (73ff., 104), but later turns out to be a great success (193). In various battles, BONZO cans serve as armour (e.g. 66) whereas the label is used as a sign for the dolls' house that has been converted into a hotel. Its name – who would not anticipate it? – is "The Last Visible Dog" (190). Frog's prediction of Manny's future, "A dog shall rise; a rat shall fall" (54) is not only connected with his own travelling in a BONZO can carried by a kingfisher in the battle against Manny (161ff.), but also with the trajectory of Sirius, the Dog Star, which thus becomes the guiding star of the two mice's odyssey (31, 103f., etc). The network of references is almost too tightly woven. A motif that is so much foregrounded invites interpretation. Yet, what does this "too-muchness of dogs" (74) stand for? Is it loyalty, as the tramp's dog suggests? But then the allegory has been anchored in a very threadbare "character". Or did Hoban think of the idiom "it's a case of dog eat dog" when he decided to represent infinity by means of a BONZO dog-food label? But how could all the other uses of the motif be accounted for?

The plot thus reveals most clearly that Hoban was at the beginning of his career when he wrote *The Mouse and his Child.* On the one hand, he counteracted the logic inherent in the story by letting his personal situation influence the story's outcome; on the other hand, the persistent use of one motif to connect all the parts of the novel is reminiscent of advertising techniques – all the more considering that the motif lends itself to various interpretations which, however, seem to be unintended side-effects rather than intentional messages.

2.3. Language and Style

The next feature I want to look at is Hoban's use of language. In every sentence, he shows great skill in handling the material that calls for expression, whether it is something as prosaic as a dump, a special sound effect, or a metaphysical idea. Sound is by no means of secondary importance in the process of composition:

> I do a lot of revising as I write. I read all the pages aloud and keep changing them to get the sound I want, and as the story moves forward and the idea shows itself more and more I have to rewrite most of what was done earlier. For *The Mouse and his Child*, apart from the ordinary running page and chapter revisions, I did four complete rewrites. (CY 16)

A comical effect is created in a scene where pure sounds are more meaningful than words; the graphic quality of words conveys information too:

> KLOP! C. Serpentina rose up from the mud and snapped his jaws. 'Nothing!' he said. 'Absolutely nothing! Accretions and abstractions of annotated nothing. Bafflements of nothing. Charismas, demiurges, and epiphanies of nothing. *Note well. See above. See below.* Nothing.' SCRUNCH! CHOMP, CHOMP, CHOMP. ULP. ULP. He had snapped up the snake that had eaten the tadpoles, and was a long time in swallowing it. (125)

While the noises in capital letters indicate that C. Serpentina has done something "substantial", i.e. provided himself with food, the alphabet of abstract terms is no more than a melodious extension of "nothing". The parody of scholarly works in which well-phrased sentences often disguise a lack of contents is obvious. This effect is enhanced by reference words in italics that do not refer to anything in particular.

Rhythms support certain actions. Muskrat, for instance, needs the two mice's regular pacing in order to be able to construct a machine to fell a tree:

> 'I can't pace right any more,' he said. 'My best Much-in-Little thinking was done before I lost my leg in the trap; I can't reason as I did when I was

> whole. There's a universal rhythm that the mind must catch. I used to feel it; now I don't. My mental powers are hobbled, like my gait.' (93)

It is a small step from rhythms to songs. They always help the characters to bear situations that put an emotional strain on them. Thus, Manny Rat's foragers sing a song to ease their slavery: "*Who's that passing in the night? / Foragers for Manny Rat! / Make your move and take your bite / After us, or stand and fight / Manny Rat!* " (33). Simple as such songs may be, they illustrate Hoban's belief that art "evokes vital resources in us" (TB 71). In his opinion, many contemporary works of literature "are not essentially literary" because they "simply communicate experience, and that of itself is not art" (TB 71).

Apart from using musical forms (in later novels, poems will occasionally substitute for the songs), Hoban ensures the literariness of his texts by means of carefully adapting the style of his prose to the subjects he writes about. In *The Mouse and his Child*, he not only parodies scholarly language but also the languages of newspaper headlines and advertisements: "'ARE YOUR EYES LOSING THEIR REDNESS?' boomed the voice. 'HAS THE SNAP GONE OUT OF YOUR TAIL? NATURE'S REMEDIES AND RESTORATIVES SOLD HERE. LOVE POTIONS AND MAGIC CHARMS.'" (37). A sober account of the battle between shrews, with its military jargon and its unheroic description of dying characters (61), contrasts with the poetical representation of the arrival of spring (107).

Frog's prophesy allusively summarizes the events of the two mice's quest: "*Low in the dark of summer, high in the winter light; a painful spring, a shattering fall, a scattering regathered. The enemy you flee at the beginning awaits you at the end*" (41-42). The evocative use of vowels in this passage (assonances, dark vowels for the desperate situation, high ones for the promise of happiness), of internal rhymes ("shattering" / "scattering"), and of a pun upon "spring" and "fall" confirm A. Joan Bowers' analysis of Hoban's prose: "... the rich humorous prose which seems to come most easily to him ... often achieves lyricism without any apparent effort" (87).

Hoban also toys with possibilities inherent in syntactic structures. Tension is often created by removing the most significant element of a sentence as far from the sentence's beginning as possible:

> And in another part of that world beyond the pond, high in a hickory tree, in a leafy squirrel nest into which he had providentially fallen when he slipped out of his woollen glove and the horned owl's talons, *the frog,* under a kind of polite duress that amounted to house arrest, told fortunes night and day, and begged the squirrels to help him down and on his way. (105; emphasis added)

In another example, the inversion of the sentence's subject and predicate imitates the movement that is described: "Onward walked the mouse child, backwards..." (107).

Whether he translates meaning into sound patterns or visible (syntactic or graphic) structures, Hoban always tries to be concrete and precise. The same intention is apparent in those passages where he uses figurative expressions in their literal sense, e.g. when the "voice of swamp and pond" C. Serpentina ponders on his situation: "'One has no need to get out of here,' said Serpentina. 'One is *at home* on the bottom. One *sees below the surface* of things. One *thinks in depth* and *acquires profundity...*'" (118; emphasis added).

Hoban's talent for substituting images for abstract concepts cannot be denied. Representing eternity by means of the label of a dog-food can instead of having recourse to the hackneyed image of two mirrors reflecting each other *ad infinitum* is original. The image is excellent for another reason: it allows Hoban to explore both the quality of infinity and an individual's reaction to its recognition. Although one "can't swallow infinity" (126), i.e. understand it and make it disappear, and though one might have to admit that "Nothing is the ultimate truth" (125), the mouse child insists on finding out what is "on the other side of nothing" (125). He is looking for a viable alternative to resignation and finally finds it in himself: "'Ah,' he said, 'there is nothing on the other side of nothing but us.'" (126). Is there in literature a simpler illustration of what is meant by "existentialism"?

However, not all of the novel's images work equally well, especially when they are used repeatedly and commented on by the characters. Thus, the image of the "balance of nature" is at first impressive and awful in its merciless consequence:

> 'I know you'll like this place,' said the female [weasel] to her mate. 'I came here the other night, and it's really a darling little hollow. There's always something good. Mmm! Smell those shrews!' (...)
>
> ... Below them both armies were dragging off the wounded and the dead....
>
> 'Oh, all right,' said the male. 'Let's have shrew then. I don't want to argue about it.'
>
> The weasels flowed like hungry shadows down into the hollow, and once among the shrews, struck right and left with lightning swiftness, smiling pleasantly with the blood of both armies dripping from their jaws. (...)
>
> 'It's not bad,' said her mate. 'Not a bad little territory at all. I could see us making a home here.' They nuzzled each other affectionately as they ran, and their heads were so close together that when the horned owl swooped down out of the moonlight his talons pierced both brains at once. (63-64)

Since this scene is so self-explanatory, the explicitly commented variation of the image three chapters later sounds flat: "'... Naturally the hawk eats up the mice and the chipmunks. That's how it is. I eat and you get eaten.'" (134). This example illustrates why one critic found the style of *The Mouse and his Child* "garrulous and ... even laboured" (MacKillop 58) compared with the style of Hoban's later novels. Indeed, Hoban continually reduced the amount of explicit passages ever after. Gillian McMahon-Hill reports that at a writers' workshop in 1974, he "stressed the need to let the reader draw his own conclusions: some work must be left for him; everything should not be explicitly expressed" (46).

Hoban's style at this early stage thus unites the following features: it is successful on the linguistic level because he uses all the means of expression offered by language, graphic, phonological, syntactic, and semantic. It equally succeeds in drawing upon various stylistic registers, from sober to parodistic or poetical. But when the text is looked at as a medium of interaction between a writer and a mature reader, *The Mouse and his Child* gives away its transitional status.

2.4. Characters

The Mouse and his Child could be called a fable but for its length. A certain didacticism is perceptible, for instance, with regard to those characters who represent but one human trait that is exposed to laughter and criticism. The characters' being toys and animals capable of speech is another obvious though less essential feature. Hoban particularly attacks characters who act mechanically and mindlessly, e.g. the original inhabitants of the dolls' house, whose heads are filled with newspaper headlines instead of ideas of their own (18-21), the shrews who go to war like machines (55-62), Muskrat, the ambitious scientist, who wastes his skills imitating beavers and consequently "MEETS DEATH IN BEAVER DAM RECONSTRUCTION PROJECT" (132), or the stupid and predictably aggressive bass, whose death scene has been mentioned earlier (MC 138f.; cf. above, ch. 2.2).

C. Serpentina, at first the caricature of a narrow-minded and pedantic scholar and just as flat as the characters I have mentioned above, is given a chance to expand. The turtle is described as a creature that unites the animate with the inanimate, a symbol of the origin of time, space and life: "He was very old and ponderously fat, and the eye that watched them seemed the very eye of time itself, set like a smoky gray jewel in some old and scaling rock" (116). Since his authority is merely based on old age and immobility, however, it is doomed to crumble before the mouse child's determination to get out of the pond (127). The stern philosopher who initially denies that leaving the pond makes sense, because "other mud is like this mud" (117), eventually not only accepts the invitation to "The Last Visible Dog". He also initiates an annual "Deep Thought Symposium" (196), leaving behind both his narrow-mindedness and his intellectual arrogance. The more the characters develop, that is, the rounder they are, the less do they belong to the realm of the fable. The main characters, who survive their exploits unlike most of the minor characters, are capable of learning a lesson from the minor characters' mistakes as well as from their own experiences. Their potential for development in fact contributes to the production of a novelistic coherence that distinguishes *The Mouse and his Child* from an otherwise very similar classic, *The Wind in the Willows* by Kenneth Grahame.[1]

There are considerable differences between the main characters regarding the scope of their characteristic features, their psychological depth and their function in the novel. The seal and the elephant are the least attractive creations. I am not even convinced that the seal should be counted among the main cast for she neither really develops nor contributes anything essential to the story. I think she has been introduced for no other purpose than to supply the family with a second female, which makes the group symmetrical and average-sized. The elephant develops in so far as she gives up part of her arrogance through her suffering (cf. 20, 43, 110). But even at the end of the novel, she is mostly concerned with appearances. It is not her knowledge of electricity that prevents the house from being blown up in the first place, but her housewifely disgust at the gunpowder on the floor (187). The clichéd representation of females continues after this episode. Of all the things that are organized at "The Last Visible Dog", the elephant and the seal achieve no more than to guide the "Fashion Forum and Homemaker's Clinic" (194). That this kind of characterization is sexist will be felt more keenly nowadays than at the time the book was published. In the meantime, Hoban has become sensitized to stereotypes, too, and made an effort to clear his writing of them.[2]

Here, however, the male characters are the ones who do the tinkering and the thinking, who move things and are creative while the female characters do no more than support them in their efforts. Miss Mudd in chapter 6 may serve as another illustration of this principle. Yet, her assistance counts more than that of any other character since it is thanks to her risky manoeuvres that the two mice find a way out of the pond in which they are stuck. Moreover, she is a crucial personification of renewal and transcendence, themes which will

1 Barbara Herkommer has pointed out another important distinctive feature: the characters of Grahame's book are not exposed to cruelty, bloodshed and falls as dangerous as those shown in *The Mouse and his Child* (41, n. 35).

2 The stages of his development will be discussed in ch. 8.4.

become prominent in later novels: "'... I just can't believe that I'm this muddy thing you see crawling about in the muck. I don't *feel* as if I am. I simply can't tell you how I feel inside! Clean and bright and beautiful – like a song in the sunlight...'" (122). Unlike people who overrate their abilities from a lack of self-knowledge, Miss Mudd rejects her appearance because she knows herself well. Utmost exhaustion precedes her rebirth as a dragonfly:

> 'I feel so odd!' she said. 'I can scarcely catch my breath, and my eyes are growing dim. Perhaps I'm dying, and my little muddy life is finished, and I never was meant to be anything but what I was.'
>
> Miss Mudd began to cry, and as her body heaved it split down the back. 'Oh!' she said, and felt the life stir in her wet and wrinkled wings that were already stiffening for flight. 'It was so difficult to be sure!' (128-129)

As the book's title suggests, the two clockwork mice are the most important characters in the novel. Their complementarity constitutes a central aspect worth looking at in some detail. The two mice start out dancing in a circle with joined hands. Nothing can change their situation until they are crushed flat by a falling vase. Paradoxically, this accident enables them to become "round" characters in the figurative sense because their repair adds new elements to their features and removes those that have kept them from moving on. After the tramp has mended them, they walk straightforward in one direction, and the mouse child no longer needs to be lifted up by his father but is capable of walking on his own, though backwards.

At the beginning the father has the leading part. It is he who decides about their direction even though the child is the dreamer who suggests ways to go. They represent the duality of consciousness and the unconscious as well as of body and soul: "'... Our motor is in me. He fills the empty space inside himself with foolish dreams that cannot possibly come true'" (48). However, the son soon turns from the baby who cried in the toyshop into an encouraging partner. On stage, threatened by Manny Rat, he prevents the father from losing his nerves: "The audience laughed, anticipating new comic variations in the toy-mouse act. The irony was too much for the child; it made him giddy. 'Just let it happen,' he said to his father. 'Your line.'" (80). At the bottom of C. Serpentina's pond, finally, when the father is standing with his back to the BONZO can, the son willy-nilly has to take the initiative – his imaginative power saves them from destruction: "'The child is father to the mouse,' said the child. 'I'll do it'" (120). Thus, their relative strength becomes reversed. The division of space into three distinct realms, i.e. the landscape around the dump, the stage, and the underwater world, recalls a laboratory situation. Hoban exposes his complementary couple to conditions which correspond to confrontations with reality, art and the mythic realm of origins, the site at which the distinction between animate and inanimate is being made. On firm ground, the soul seems to be unable to exist without the encasement of the body, the unconscious seems to be inferior to consciousness; art, on the other hand, activates both components: creative action is the result of balance and cooperation; in the primal mud, finally, only an irrational spark of life can prevent consciousness from giving up and thus turning the body over to the soothing inanimateness of the mud.

While the mouse child gains mental strength, realising that his role is vital, the father despairs in the pond because there is nothing that could give him new impetus within the range of his vision. Pessimistic since they took up their journey, "'... the whole idea of such a quest is impossible...'" (48), he starts getting used to the thought of being buried in the mud and returning to the inanimate state all life came from. His pains are soothed in turn:

> ... he found himself thinking that the mud, once one got used to it, was not uncomfortable; the motion of the water was soothing. The startling, sudden, lightning-bright image of the elephant in the mist of that departed morning was sharp within his memory, and it was painful to him, as if a spring within his mind were wound up aching tight. Powerless to act, he could not convert that coiled energy to motion, and his determination faded as he settled deeper in the mud. (124)

Caught by a hawk after their spectacular escape from the pond, he gives himself up completely (133). Yet, the son has grown strong enough to hold him and is so clever that he can induce the hawk to drop them over the dump. Their bodies are smashed on the ground, their hands are separated, but the son's hope is rewarded as Frog finds them at last.

Once more, loss means gain for the two mice because Frog not only repairs them but equips the son with a motor of his own. The father becomes rejuvenated and plucks up new courage; not even the sight of Manny Rat can deter him any more. He is resolved to fight him in order to conquer the old dolls' house. Determination also manifests itself when the mouse father defines their new status: "'We aren't toys any more,' said the father. 'Toys are to be played with, and we aren't...'" (146).

The son is glad to reduce his responsibility after his father's spirits have revived: "Having worked out with his father the strategy to be followed in the coming hours, he was now content to be a drummer boy until the battle should be won" (159). Contrary to Freudian theory, it is possible for the mouse child to return to his inferior position and stay there. Even though the material link no longer exists, father and son do not give up each other's company because they share the same aim, that is living with the family at

"The Last Visible Dog". The son's dreams have come true, and since he does not seem to have any new ones, the development of the pair of eponymous heroes comes to a close.

But such a solution is too cheap to be satisfactory. Did the two clockwork mice need to become independent and experience so many adventures only to end up pacing forever around the platform of their house instead of dancing below other people's Christmas trees? It is obvious that Hoban tried to establish a surface message that propagated the society of family and friends as the ultimate reason of existence. But below the surface, there is a second message contradicting the first, one that had to be kept from finding an outlet at the time *The Mouse and his Child* was written. It is an affirmation of that "radical spirit of life", of "our outlaw strength that is brother to our lawful vigour", as Hoban defined it in "Thoughts on a Shirtless Cyclist..." (13). In other words, the novel indirectly touches upon the conflicts that may arise if an individual's happiness depends on other things than a family – on freedom, for instance. The characters who are most reluctant to join the family or society, who acknowledge their changing needs and act accordingly, represent that vital spirit. They are outsiders, yet move things. But for the tramp, Frog and Manny Rat the clockwork idyll at the end of the novel would be impossible. If the mouse child had not broken clockwork laws crying under the Christmas tree (23), the mice's journey would never have taken place.

Manny Rat clearly shines out among these characters. His needs often clash to such an extent that he suffers more than his "victims" from the resulting conflicts. Although the novel's ending tries to make us believe that even a Manny Rat can be pacified by fully integrating him into a family, it is clear from an earlier passage that Manny will never be happy subduing the greater part of his nature. A sympathetic undertone accompanies the description of the moment before he fails to blow up the dolls' house; Hoban cannot condemn the rat's relapse into his ratty self:

> As Manny Rat climbed the pole up to the power lines beside the tracks he was a happier rat than he had been for a long time. Dusk had become night, the darkness caressed him lovingly, and he wished he could prolong this moment of delicious anticipation. But he dared not risk failure if he was ever to know peace of mind again. (188)

Manny is certainly no "Dickensian villain", as A. Joan Bowers calls him in her study (90). The novel offers, but at the same time rejects, the comparison in the scene where Manny is temporarily forced into the role of "Banker Ratsneak" (who may be a parody of Uriah Heep). For, unlike such an invariably villainous character, Manny often questions his motives and sometimes reacts in surprising ways that contradict the stereotype, for example, at his first encounter with Frog and the mice after their escape from the dump:

> Manny Rat hesitated. The frog was utterly helpless against him, yet the rat became uneasy. He had always feared the fortune-teller a little; he felt him to be not only a prophet of good and bad luck, but its active agent as well. He drew nearer, and staring past the frog, he saw the mouse child staring back at him, the night sky mirrored in his glass-bead eyes. Manny Rat felt himself by some strange magnetism drawn to the father and the son, felt that something was wanted of him, forgot almost that he was there to smash them. He shook his head and picked up a rock. 'Step aside, Frog,' he said; 'I'm going to smash your friends.' (54)

He does not pursue his victims out of selfishness but because he cannot help being an instrument of an inexplicable obsession:

> He grew morose, and felt himself half overcome by funk. Why must he go on pursuing clockwork mice, he asked himself. ... And what would his reward be in the end? By the time he smashed these trumpery windups his name would be forgotten at the dump, his enterprises taken over by younger, upward-moving rats. ...
>
> But Manny Rat had no choice left; some force beyond himself was pulling him whichever way his quarry turned. He wound the elephant, cursed forlornly at the now empty provision bags she carried, and shuffled on as if at the end of an invisible chain by which his prey would drag him to his doom. (105)

Although they threaten his existence, Manny feels attached to the mice. When they are hurled into the Beaver dam, "He felt a sudden pang, and knew that somehow he was going to miss them" (113).

The rat's character is so complex that another literary model must be used by way of comparison: Hoban has in fact equipped Manny Rat with many traits of Nostromo, the eponymous hero of what Hoban calls "Conrad's best" (Hoban and Haffenden 124). Joseph Conrad's "particular approach to the moral aspect of action and its consequences" (Hoban and Bodmer 9) has always fascinated the author. Manny's conflict after making the windups self-winding resembles that of Nostromo before he decides to reward his efforts with the concealed and forgotten San Tomé silver:[3]

> He had crowned the victory of those who ruined him, and the strain upon his moral fibre was too great; however black his sins had been, such high atonement was a heavy burden on him, and his mind almost gave way beneath it. Manny Rat clutched desperately at sanity, and with a sigh he gave himself again to evil. (186)

3 See especially part three, chapters 10 and 12 of *Nostromo*.

The same obsessive attachment to something threatening the integrity of the mind and the feeling of wasting extraordinary skills in the service of undeserving others make Manny and Nostromo break moral rules. Both of them fall, Nostromo for the first time in his life, Manny again, because they cannot possibly subdue their nature and their superiority for good. The preservation of their selves makes them decide against society.

The latent second message of the novel, which justifies living up to one's individual needs, seems to be wiped out by Manny's conversion into a servile Uncle Manny at the end. But apart from Hoban's sympathetic treatment of Manny's fits of ratty behaviour, there is another hint that the writer was not convinced of the truth of this conclusion. He actually planned to write a sequel to *The Mouse and his Child*, *The Return of Manny Rat*, in which he would have undone the rat's reformation, as an excerpt from his draft, published in "Thoughts on a Shirtless Cyclist...", shows:

> ... a student revolt at The Last Visible Dog, where Manny Rat teaches 'Tinkering 1' and 'Salvage and Repair (Advanced)' forces him to reassess his life. It is borne in upon him that his apparent reformation and dedication to good may have had no better motivation than his toothlessness.... He leaves The Last Visible Dog and strikes out on his own again... (CY 16)

Incidentally, Hoban never managed to finish the sequel because he took the appropriate steps to which the subtle second message of *The Mouse and his Child* had led him: taking his needs seriously, he gave up his established position and broke with his family in order to feel alive again. He allowed himself to act in a way that Manny Rat had had to be prevented from.

2.5. Certain Ideas

To finish the chapter on *The Mouse and his Child* I should like to point to a few basic ideas that will recur or be expanded in Hoban's later works. The world is presented as a battlefield where good and evil are often two sides of the same coin. Life means change and exchange, and survival usually has to be paid for by mutilation. The two mice, for instance, lose all their fur and their clothes on the journey from the toyshop to the dump, the elephant ends up with one eye, and Manny Rat becomes toothless. Victories turn out to be defeats and *vice versa*: the clockwork toys need to be shattered and crushed in order to develop, and Manny in the end points out to them that they could not be winners it he had not been their enemy: "'... Could you have won vat victory if vere had been no Manny Rat to be defeated?...'" (175).

Complementary characters irresistibly attract each other, not necessarily as lovers but rather as opponents or friends whose involvement with each other sets action cycles in motion (e.g. the mice and Frog: 47; or the mice and Manny Rat: 54). In *The Mouse and his Child* this process could also be described in terms of a Hegelian dialectic: thesis (the mice) and antithesis (Manny) are eventually resolved in a synthesis (the extended family circle). But there are already numerous signs of scepticism about the permanence of resolutions (e.g. Manny's relapses into bad behaviour). This scepticism will turn into the conviction that people often cannot maintain a relationship except to accomplish one action cycle together and then part (e.g. William and Neaera in *Turtle Diary* or Pilgermann and Sophia). Having been transformed rather than destroyed by its outcome, they are ready for another action cycle (Jachin-Boaz is even involved in two new cycles: i.e. the fight against the lion and his life with Gretel): those who fail to respond to its vortex because they stubbornly hold on to the past are discarded by life (e.g. the alter egos of Kleinzeit, or Goodparley and Lissener in *Riddley Walker*).

In *The Mouse and his Child* those characters live best who act as if they were free agents in an absurd existentialistic universe, responding to their vital needs and desires and accepting the consequences (guilt and punishment if they have caused harm to others, or rebirth as altered beings). But these impulses are the means by which life, as a superior agent disregarding human subjectivity, enables people to respond to the action cycles it offers them. Ultimately Hoban's characters lack absolute autonomy. As far as the two toy mice are concerned, the tramp personifies the life force although the mice are altogether unaware of his interventions. He mends the windups in such a way that they can walk straight and orders them, first, to be tramps and then to be happy (25, 200). Manny Rat, or Frog's life force, on the other hand, defies personification: they are not only ruled by their instincts but also feel subject to a fate they cannot escape (41, 105). Moving from clockwork mice to human characters, Hoban will considerably refine those ideas. The tensions between life and death drives will be examined more closely: Hoban's protagonists will learn to accept their mortality without thereby turning suicidal. From Jachin-Boaz to Fremder all protagonists reach a point at which they are seduced into giving themselves up like the mouse father at the bottom of the pond. Unlike the mouse father, however, who must be saved by his son because his vision of the elephant is insufficient to stimulate his will to survive (124), most of them will find in themselves the resources to resist resignation. The idea that life is a superior agent will gradually evolve into a mystical awareness that all phenomena are connected despite their differences: when the characters offer themselves to apparently contingent opportunities, insights, dreams, and visions, they will come closer to this unity than by any conscious and intentional effort. The closest *The Mouse and his Child* gets to Hoban's later mysticism is the scene in which Frog, the quack and professional fortune teller, unexpectedly finds himself able to predict the two mice's future from the pattern formed by sunflower seeds: "All else beyond the pattern in the snow departed from his vision; his ears hummed, and other sounds all vanished, leaving him alone with the voice of his mind and the dark seeds dancing in the stillness of their mystic changes" (41). Just as fate manifests itself in a pattern in order to reveal itself, there are other things capable of communication, for example, clocks: "It was the clock that spoke next, startling them with his flat brass voice. 'I might remind you of the rules of clockwork,' he said. 'No talking before midnight and after dawn, and no crying on the job.'" (20). Hoban's world is full of such anthropomorphized objects and abstract entities even though this will become more evident in the novels written after *The Mouse and his Child*, for speaking mirrors and walls, a speaking Apple II computer or God are no doubt more unusual than speaking clocks, toys and animals, whose communicative ability follows the convention of fairy tales and fables. Whatever speaks to the characters may also threaten them. But Hoban's protagonists are never completely helpless. Most of them have, or develop, a strong sense of humour to master difficult situations and to overcome their fear of the possible. The two clockwork mice do not differ from their successors in this respect; they laugh after their narrow escape from the jaws of the "Meadow Mutual Hoard and Trust Company's" badger guard (46), and they also laugh on the eve of the battle for the dolls' house (151).

A sense of humour is not the only requirement to deal with a problematic situation, however; self-knowledge is yet more important. It is by assessing their past that the characters can define their position in the present and react appropriately to a given situation. Thus, the elephant knows after reflecting on her past career that she need not be too scared of Manny Rat: "... here was a rat to be encountered, and he should be confronted firmly, as she had met all adversity thus far" (43). The realm of the past is often represented by ponds or oceans, as A. Joan Bowers, who has analyzed several of Hoban's books for children, points out. She goes on:

> Hoban, like Tolkien, seeks 'the satisfaction of certain primordial human desires,' not in fairy tales but in the mythic symbol of a sinking back into and an acceptance of the past – symbolized by mankind's evolutionary origins in the ocean – in order to live fully here and now. (Bowers 86)

It is therefore not astonishing that the mouse child should see himself for the first time at the bottom of a pond and recognize himself because of his immediate ancestor: "... he had never seen himself before, but he recognized his father, and therefore knew himself" (126). In Hoban's later novels and short stories, the characters will also assess their past, not only by symbolically returning to their evolutionary origins in the ocean but also by searching their legends and myths and their language for witnesses of lost days. Herman Orff in *The Medusa Frequency* will expose his mind to an EEC shock treatment. The self-knowledge thus gained never fails to intensify the characters' defiance of adversity. Yet, the aim of their efforts undergoes gradual changes, to describe which will be one of the tasks of subsequent chapters. "Happiness" of the kind the mouse child aspires to and achieves is an illusion. Nevertheless, this insight has not led Hoban to write tragedies. His characters always succeed in making some sense out of their existence even if the losses they experience grow more and more serious.

3. The Lion of Boaz-Jachin and Jachin-Boaz (1973)

3.1. Exploring the Realm of Consciousness

Readers who know *The Mouse and his Child*, with its abundance of characters and settings, will feel cast into an almost empty space when they read the opening chapter of Hoban's first novel for adults. Characters who remain schematic hardly contrast with the poor, monotonous, dry background. The novel's first sentence states what there is not rather than what there is: "There were no lions any more" (9). It takes some time to understand that the sense of loss and monotony which pervades the landscape at the beginning of the novel is not an objective feature of the place but the projection of a character's, Jachin-Boaz's, anxiety. Though a sentence like "The temperature was controlled by a thermostat" (9) cannot be directly assigned to Jachin-Boaz's perception, it represents the kind of stasis he would be aware of, as a later, unambiguous example shows: "Behind his closed eyes he saw the map of his town in which the square, the town pump, the stone laundry sinks, the street of the merchants and he himself were fixed and permanent" (11).

Throughout the novel, countries, cities, rivers and the sea remain nameless. Although the novel's settings do bear resemblance to certain areas of the world, i.e. to the Near East, the Continent and England, and though the city across the channel is endowed with all the attributes of London, they are not to be identified with any factual locations. In their vagueness, they can be exclusively related to the characters' maps of the mind. Every detail mirrors an aspect of their consciousness instead of being at the service of realistic description; landscapes are inner landscapes. Hence, two different characters may perceive different places in a nearly identical way:

> The street lamps seemed luminous fruits, bursting with knowledge. Boaz-Jachin tasted their light in his mouth and wondered who he was. (28)

> To Jachin-Boaz the street lamps seemed luminous fruits bursting with knowledge. He tasted their light in his mouth and marvelled that this was he, Jachin-Boaz, tasting the night and the love he had found in the great city. (32)

On the other hand, the same place may of course evoke varying associations in different characters. The desert, for example, is the lion's domain for Boaz-Jachin (174). But his mother can only think of it as an area of failure since her father wasted his money on the attempt to cultivate his place in the desert, while her husband ostentatiously stayed in the little town near the desert instead of pursuing an academic career (37).

Words, too, are subject to the characters' projections. Thus, the dying farmer's last word "Forgive" triggers four different reactions, which reflect the intentions, needs and disappointments of those standing around the death bed:

> 'Always the humorist,' said the mother.
> 'Benjamin he forgives,' said the son. 'Always.'
> 'Maybe he meant you,' said the doctor.
> 'Maybe he's asking,' said Boaz-Jachin. 'For himself.' (85)

The disparate associations entailed by the word "home" are even more interesting. In the novel, it is only a positive term when it means a place that is "printed on the map" of a character's mind (47), hence a *familiar* place. Boaz-Jachin's second journey to the lion-palace illustrates what is meant, especially when he is comparing his first impressions of the palace (cf. 19) with his present feelings:

> ... In the moonlight he went to the building where the lion-hunt reliefs were. As before, the door was unlocked.
> Boaz-Jachin opened the door, and the lion-hunt hall with the moonlight coming through the skylight was now a place where he had been. It was a place of his time, a home-place. (42)

The traditional referent of "home", however, the place of one's *family* has become problematic for most characters. Bad memories and frustrations mar the aspect of familiarity. Jachin-Boaz, for instance, is haunted by thoughts of "lifelong despair" (10) at home and indulges in thoughts of an early death. But he cannot make up his mind to leave his family until looking for a lion lends his escape a purpose and a direction.

Especially on Sundays, the vitriolic essence of "home" at its worst is laid bare: illusions are destroyed and children traumatized for ever. Jachin-Boaz still suffers from childhood Sundays (170), and so do his wife and Lila (37, 29). But for the "tightly furled man" of the mental hospital Sundays have become a proper obsession:

> '... Man is a product of his Sundays. Don't talk to me about heredity. Darwin went to the Galapagos to get away from the Sunday drive with his parents. Mendel pea'd. Everybody tells a boy about sex but nobody tells him the facts of Sunday. Home is where the heart is, that's why pubs stay in business. Forgive us our Sundays as we forgive those who Sunday against us. Parent or child, no difference. Lend me a Monday, for Christ's sake.' (176)

The decision between staying at home and leaving is very difficult to make since comforts and frustrations often balance each other. If none outweighs the other, the mind turns into a battlefield and risks being destroyed by conflicting inclinations, unless some new impetus settles the matter. Jachin-Boaz is luckier than the tightly furled man, who prefers being insane to going home:

> 'Lovely wife, children, home, weather, central heating, career, garden, shoelaces, buttons and dentistry. All modern conveniences, or nearest offer, lovely bank lessons, music account, lovely miles to the gallon. Lovely 'O' Levels, 'A' Levels, eye levels, level eyes. Lovely level eyes she has and sees through everything but.'
>
> 'But what?' said Jachin-Boaz.
>
> 'That's what I mean,' said the tightly furled man. 'The butness of everything. I don't go home any more...' (159)

Whether or not people turn and stay insane depends not only on their prospects for the future but also on their readiness and ability to control and be responsible for the actions that are produced by their urges. The "letter writer", another patient in the hospital, enjoys regularly having his brain switched off to escape his frightening visions:

> 'Electro-convulsion therapy. Shock treatment. It's lovely. From time to time when the faces get too many for me I act up and they let me have it. Ever so soothing. (...) One forgets a good deal. ... Everyone ought to have a portable E.C.T. box, like a transistor radio. It isn't fair to leave a chap all alone and unprotected at the mercy of a brain. ...' (175-176)

However, the letter writer is not always as helpless. Certain manifestations of the brain are so attractive that "'... Victims become proprietors'" (158). As long as these manifestations do not overwhelm their victims, they remain *extensions of reality*, products of the imagination, "possibilities" (158) rather than dangerous obsessions. Only "straight people", who do not wish to incur even the slightest risk inherent in possibilities, "'... agree that some things are not allowed to be possible, and they govern their perceptions accordingly. Very strong, the straight people'" (158).

Hoban in fact subverts the simplistic distinction between sane and insane in two ways: with characters like Jachin-Boaz, Boaz-Jachin, Gretel and, last but not least, the constable at the end of the novel, who all see the lion and act accordingly, he insists on a category of people who are perceptive enough to recognize even those things which could pose a serious threat to them, but who still dare to tackle their problematic visions. Such characters stand for people who do not shy away from insights which might require them, for example, to overthrow social conventions or to alter their lives completely. Unlike "straight people", they strive to liberate themselves from frustrations. Thus, they may become capable of living a fuller life. I will come back to this point in the next chapter.

Secondly, by maintaining that "straight people" are only more censorious about their perceptions than those in the mental hospital, Hoban humorously challenges conventional definitions of reality like, for instance, the one given by the *Collins Dictionary of the English Language*: "that which exists, independent of human awareness" (1216). This definition may of course imply that there are more things than we are able to perceive, but it does not answer the question how many of the things we do perceive are real. Hoban's definition could be summarized in the formula that reality is everything that has an effect on us, be it a concrete object or "merely" an idea, dream or memory (cf. Hoban and Haffenden 135; Hoban and Myers 9; or CY 13). What can be touched, "objectively" measured and rationally explained may no longer be thought more real than what we feel.[1] When Jachin-Boaz tells the psychiatrist about the lion, this equivalence is established: "'Right,' said the doctor. "So let's not split hairs about whether he's real. He can do real damage. He's a real problem that has to be coped with one way or another.'" (64).

Like certain Romantic and Surrealist writers, Hoban boosts his readers' confidence in non-rational sources of information while challenging, though

1 Christine Wilkie writes, "Hoban has begun a line of thinking in which he seeks to confound the consensus of reality and unreality" (30). But I think that the connotations of the verb "confound" are too negative to describe Hoban's deliberate effort to change the consensus.

not completely denying, the value of all that is "too neat, too calculated, too little cognizant of unknown places" (121) – like Jachin-Boaz's master-map. Step by step, this symbol of scientific precision and craftsmanship will lose the mystique that its first description inspires:

> Jachin-Boaz had for a number of years been working on a map for his son. From the many different maps that passed through his hands, from the reports of his information-gatherers and surveyors, from the books and journals that he read, from his own records and observations, he compiled a great body of detailed knowledge, and that knowledge was incorporated in the map for his son. He added to it constantly, revising and making the necessary corrections to keep it always current.
>
> ... It was to be nothing less than a master map that would show him where to find whatever he might wish to look for, and so would assure him of a proper start in life as a man. (11-12)

Boaz-Jachin immediately detects some weaknesses in his father's ambitious map. First of all, there are no lions to be found with its help, which shows that the range of wishes is limited to those things that are "allowed to be possible". Moreover, *if* the map were complete one day, it would deprive its users of the pleasure of gathering knowledge. The son feels that the finding is more important than the find: "'If everything that is found is never lost again, there will be an end to finding some day,' said Boaz-Jachin. 'Some day there will be nothing left to find'" (12).

Jachin-Boaz cleverly silences his son's doubts, "'... would you prefer that all knowledge be thrown away so that you might be ignorant and the world new? ...'" (12), but a little later, one of the surveyors confirms the son's playful, maybe also slightly mischievous scepticism by questioning the very nature of knowledge:

> 'For years I have sighted and measured and located this point and that point on the face of the earth,' said the surveyor, 'and I have gone back to the same places to find my stakes pulled out as boundaries waver and lose accuracy. I sight and I measure and I plant the stakes again, knowing they will be pulled out again. It is not only stakes and boundaries that are lost – this is what there is to know about maps, and I tell you what I have paid years to learn: everything that is found is always lost again, and nothing that is found is ever lost again. Can you understand that? ...' (17)

Knowledge, however scientifically gathered and skilfully preserved, will never be able to replace personal experience since it is subject to constant changes.

The map-maker's wife has always objected to the "pornographic" function that maps have for her husband: "How strange that all these years he had been busy with maps, with paper ghosts of finding, with finding masturbation, and all the finding in him dead!" (110). But Jachin-Boaz begins to harbour doubts about it only after the first appearance of the lion: "What is a map? There is only one place, and that place is time. I am in the time where a lion has been found" (51). Eventually, he will even burn the master-map. While burning the physical map, he gets access to the map of his mind, which contains the sum of his experience: "He remembered Boaz-Jachin as a baby, laughing in his bath in the sink..." (188).

When Boaz-Jachin understands all the implications of the surveyor's words, on the other hand, he does not destroy the map he has drawn to fix the stations of his pursuit of the father. Having never attached undue importance to his father's map or to his own, he now need not destroy it to let go of the values associated with it. He is in an aggressive mood but feels that the map is not the right object to vent his feelings on: "'I'll keep it the way people keep diaries, but I don't need maps for finding anything.' He ground his teeth, wanted to roar, wanted to do violence to something" (154). Whereas maps prove to be useless for finding things, intuition leads Boaz-Jachin to his aim, the big city, where he finds both his father and the lion. Yet, even the perceptive son sometimes disbelieves the voices in himself: "'Every fucking thing talks to me.... Leave me alone for a while. I'll talk to you some other time. I can't be rushed all the time. ... I don't even know if he's there! ... I don't even know if I'm looking for him in the right place.'" (163). Only in the end does he fully acknowledge that he must take his perceptions seriously because they convey reliable information, not fantasies:

> He must have known it always, from the time he had first seen the frowning face of the dying lion biting the wheel. He had made his feeble attempt at maintaining the fiction of ordinary reality, had placed the advertisement in the trade weekly. But it was towards the lion that he had been moving the emptiness in him these many miles. And it was the lion's call that he had waited for here in this city. (184)

A last example for Hoban's enhancing the status of non-rational sources of information is his treatment of dreams and other manifestations of the unconscious within the novel. Jachin-Boaz's despair, his impotence with his wife and his unfair neglect of his son are the result of problems rooted in his adolescence. A conflict with his father and mother has been repressed and is now fought out in his unconscious since he is neither able nor ready to sort it out consciously. Yet, what is unconscious does not disappear; Jachin-Boaz pays for the repression of his past with a troubled emotional life. Nightmares haunt his sleep, and occasionally, the truth comes to light by way of slips of the tongue: "If only he could have the comfort of his mife, his wife, rather, without his wife! Whother, whether he could get along without her he doubted" (131). His wife never really attracted him sexually. When they got married, Jachin-Boaz wanted a second mother, not a partner.

His dreams are equally revealing, and not at all "boring and irrelevant" or screwing up "a reader's concentration, his suspension of disbelief and everything else", as Auberon Waugh writes in his review of the novel, launching a general attack on dreams in fiction (302). Representing most of Jachin-Boaz's long dreams scenically, Hoban did not need to interpose an artificial authorial narrator between his readers and the map-maker in order to explain what is going on in him. The narrative simply shifts from the point of view of conscious Jachin-Boaz to the "point of view" of his unconscious, the "other" within him, which is as strange as another person. We are shown rather than told that as long as his two sides are separated by an impermeable barrier of repression, Jachin-Boaz won't be able to improve his situation.[2] We can then witness, how more and more bridges are being built from both sides as Jachin-Boaz learns to overcome his resistance to looking at the problems of his early years. Although he is convinced that he cannot remember his dreams at all, certain dream elements, e.g. the idea that his university failure was an intellecual suicide (133), become important arguments in his conversations with the lion (135). On the other hand, his conscious examinations of his situation and the actions resulting from them make his dreams move towards the moment at which he can not only remember, but also let go of, the past and so become able to affirm the present (11, 15, 39, 75, 90f. 118f., 132, 170). After a final crisis in the mental hospital (171), he is able to say yes to life as it presents itself: "A wave of terror flooded his being. No, no, no. Yes. No way back" (181).

The dreams appear in a fairly authentic form since Hoban abided by the rules Freud had discovered to be in action in the transformation of a latent content of the unconscious into dreams, i.e. operations of dream-work (*Traumarbeit*) such as condensation (*Verdichtung*), displacement (*Verschiebung*), or considerations of representability (*Rücksicht auf Darstellbarkeit*).[3] In the first long dream (15), Jachin-Boaz's arms and legs are to be cut off by a "scissorman" because he has "done something terribly bad", which might refer to his failed university exams. He is promised "great relief", but after the left arm has been severed, Jachin-Boaz opposes further punishment. This implies that he is aware of some guilt but does not accept being made completely

2 Wilkie has used the opposition between showing and telling, too, discussing the effect of the novel's style: "Hoban does not *tell*, he *shows* by means of hints and glimpses and strange prophecies, and he achieves this by use of language that is ruthlessly pared down, assonantal and elliptic" (30).

3 See Freud, chapter VI of *Die Traumdeutung;* or for a more concise presentation, chapter VI of *Der Witz und seine Beziehung zum Unbewussten*, 129ff.

disabled and dependent as a punishment. Unfortunately, he only reacts when he has already been partly dis-armed, which is a hint about his sexual impotence with his wife. The details about the scissorman, "huge, dressed all in black, with great hunched shoulders, a long red nose and a beard like that of his father" point to his dead father's threatening personal and sexual superiority, which is also apparent in the scissorman's disbelief in Jachin-Boaz's ability to carry his own members.

His mother figures in his dream as well. She first told him of the scissorman: "The scissorman punished boys who wet their beds by cutting off their noses. Had she said noses?" (15). Apart from the obvious sexual connotations, the word "wet" may also be interpreted in the figurative sense of "inexperienced" or "weak" while "noses" corresponds with the dream element that will reappear in a later dream as "noes" (118). Hence, the mother's threat takes on a larger dimension; a son who is too weak to fulfil his parents' ambitions (university) has no right to say "no" and follow his own "nose". She will punish him for his father's death, which his academic failure seems to have brought on, by preventing his plans to travel around the world, as Jachin-Boaz's second dream shows. In this dream, she and the wife deny Jachin-Boaz the map that symbolizes the world: "'You're too little to have one...'" (39).

The second dream interestingly occurs to Jachin-Boaz *after* he has left his wife. It becomes quite obvious that he still feels bound to his mother's and his wife's demands. It will take many more steps until Jachin-Boaz can accept his new life without feeling any remorse. The notion of guilt loses its abstractness since the processes within the unconscious, which absorb a good deal of a subject's vital energy, have been made visible.

3.2. The Precarious Relationship Between Fathers and Sons

Not only the dreams but also the relationships represented in the novel exemplify Freudian theory – perhaps a little too ostentatiously. Families are split because parents feel sexually attracted to their children, fathers always project unfulfilled wishes onto their sons, and *vice versa*. With his two protagonists Hoban tries to solve the problem – father and son overthrow the oedipal pattern of mutual hostility when they recognize how pointlessly they envy each other's fate since time will put an end to both their lives at last. If the novel still intrigues, it is through its imagery and the way in which Hoban brings about the reunion of father and son.

First of all, I would like to have a look at the lion, whose function can be deduced from Hoban's description of his notion of relationships: "... what happens between individuals is often a triangular arrangement. ... Here's person A and person B, and element C is the way they want things to be. That's the bonding element between them" (Hoban and Myers 9). By means of following the lion, element C, through the book, it will be possible to recognize all the subtle changes in the protagonists' mutual feelings which are necessary to accomplish their reconciliation. Although it is Boaz-Jachin who conjures up the lion who will play a role in the novel, the lion's very first appearances in the title and the motto of the novel indicate that he needs to be related to both protagonists and seen as an aspect of something supreme. However, within the novel, the first lion to appear after the elegiac beginning is a prosaic iron door-stop. Boaz-Jachin accidentally looks at it and takes the lion as an example of something that cannot be found with his father's map. The son's choice triggers an unexpected reaction in Jachin-Boaz:

> As he spoke there opened in his mind great mystical amber eyes, luminous and infinite. There blossomed great taloned paws, heavy and powerful. There was a silent roar, round, endless, an orb of reflection imaging a pink rasping tongue, white teeth of death. Jachin-Boaz shook his head. There were no lions any more. (14)

While the lion reminds Jachin-Boaz of death and of the necessity to change his life before it is too late, his family think that his search for the lion is no more than a cynical excuse for running away (16). Soon, though, Boaz-Jachin starts vibrating with lion sounds himself (18) and goes out to look for "'A place of lions. A lion-place. A lion-palace'" (18) in order to find his father and the map. Having seen the lion of an ancient relief, Boaz-Jachin feels in himself the lion's impotent rage against his armed hunters and the king:

> ... being with the lion he tasted in him, raging, the memory of the trap and the fall, the blue oblong of sky above him, the dark faces looking down into the pit.... The lion could kill them with a blow of his paw if they would stand before him, but they were too cunning. The lion was a child to them. (22)

Identifying with the lion, Boaz-Jachin at the same time assigns the role of the king whose spear kills the lion to his father and is shocked at the insight that it is the wheel of the king's chariot, which more and more turns out to be the symbol of time, "that pulled him up on to the spears" (20). "'The king is nothing. Nothing, nothing, nothing,' said Boaz-Jachin. He began to cry" (21).

The rage against his father undergoes a first change; it is transcended into a vital force that makes Boaz-Jachin strive for equality with the run-away man:

> He, son of the map-seller, map-maker, map-lover, had no talent for maps, could not make one that was not stupid and ugly and disfigured, and this was his father's way of punishing him – to leave him mapless and alone with his deserted mother, stuck in a dark shop like an old man... (24)

Experience and competence need to be acquired before the son is able to pursue his father. Whenever he takes the appropriate steps, the "being-with-the-lion" feeling elates him affirming his ambition. It occurs on the day he loses his virginity (30) and when he succeeds in making a neat full-size copy of the lion on a piece of paper (31). Each loss of ignorance and weakness is symbolized by the removal of one arrow or spear from the drawn lion-body (36, 42f.). Offering his drawings in front of the relief (43), he obviously conjures up the lion, for it is in the subsequent chapter that his father is haunted by the beast for the first time. But yet another insight has been gained by Boaz-Jachin although he dislikes accepting it at the beginning: the wheel in the relief is guilty not only of the lion's death but also of his father's escape, and it will not be stopped by the lion's rage: "Boaz-Jachin shook his head. 'Biting the wheel is not enough,' he said" (36).

With the rage gone out of him, Boaz-Jachin feels empty. The "being-with-the-lion" feeling urges him to leave home and keep moving:

> Sometimes Boaz-Jachin saw his face reflected in the wheelhouse windows, recalled the blank face of the king, the frowning face of the lion-king. The being-with-the-lion came back for a moment and was gone again. Again the emptiness, the urge ahead towards something gone out from him. (101)

In fact, the lion-feeling leads him to the reunion with his father, which is necessary for his peace of mind; for finding the father and the lion without the master-map will be proof of Boaz-Jachin's independence. The father will have to acknowledge the son even though he failed as a map-maker. Thus, after having been a rather puerile challenge to the father, the expression of Boaz-Jachin's rage, a symbol of strength and masculinity, and an indefinite urge towards an unknown city, the lion at last stands for Boaz-Jachin's right to recognition: "'... He held up a suit of clothes for me to jump into: the wanderer. Here's your map. Then he ran away with the map. I jumped into the wandering clothes. Is he happy now?'" (155).

Since Boaz-Jachin is convinced in the end that "The father must live so that the father can die" (184), he prevents his father from being devoured by the lion. Jachin-Boaz's long refusal to recognize his son need not be redeemed by his death: "Boaz-Jachin leaped from the other side on to the lion's back, his face against the coarse mane and hot tawny skin, his arms embracing, fingers clutching raging death" (190).

With regard to Jachin-Boaz, the lion also changes his meaning in the course of the novel. At first, the image of death impending but not at all welcome, the lion turns into a romantic mark of distinction after Jachin-Boaz's first encounter with the phantom: "Thinking about the lion he felt himself walking differently, set apart from other men, marked out for a danger, possibly a death, that was unique. He carried himself with melancholy pride, like an exiled king" (50). But when his initial surprise is over and Jachin-Boaz goes to meet the lion a second time, his cowardice is revealed in his attempt at domesticating the animal with beefsteak and in his undignified leap into the river to escape the lion's attack (52). Having failed the test of his prowess, he cannot make up his mind whether or not to encounter the lion again because the sense of his virtual death remains hidden to him. Only after seeing a psychiatrist does he associate the lion with punishment from his family (66-67). The psychiatrist's interpretation enables Jachin-Boaz to reflect upon his situation and to begin to understand why he left home. On his own initiative, he wonders whether the lion is "simply a punishment" (71). His doubt is confirmed when he sees a picture of the lion-hunt relief in a book bought by one of his customers, for he recognizes that his lion's rage ought not to be directed against himself but against the wheel of time: "The wheel on the cage-wagon that brought the lion to the place of his death was the chariot wheel that hurried the king to his own death farther on its track" (75).

Thus the lion no longer represents a punishment but turns out to be a fellow-sufferer, "We are countrymen" (76), a supreme force of life fighting against time and death, "'My lord Lion,' said Jachin-Boaz. 'I trust in being. I trust in you...'" (78), and an embodiment of the rage of every son opposing the plans his father has made for him: "'Lion,' he said, 'Brother Lion! Boaz-Jachin's lion, blessed anger of my son and golden rage! But you are more than that. You are of me and my lost son both, and of my father and me lost to each other for ever. You are of all of us, Lion!'" (79). Although the lion knocks him down at the end of this encounter, Jachin-Boaz goes to see him again. He is getting reconciled to the idea of death, "'Comrade Lion, you will kill me or you will not kill me...'" (93), and many of the frustrations of his life are on the way to be cured, "'Doctor Lion,' said Jachin-Boaz..." (93). However, a last obstacle is brought to light. Jachin-Boaz suddenly discovers his responsibility for the course of his life, which implies that he can no longer blame his father for everything that went wrong; at a decisive moment he was too weak to oppose his father's wishes: "I wanted the black-and-silver leather, the sombrero, the shining pistols. I chose the microscope and the test tubes. Are you looking at your watch, Doctor Lion?..." (94).

The lion at first punishes him for this insincerity by turning his back on him, a punishment far worse than death because he deprives the supposed coward of the chance to refute his reputation in a fight (94). But in fact, Jachin-Boaz punished himself long before the lion was conjured up. When he failed his university exams many years after his fateful lie, as an act of belated opposition, he could not help interpreting his father's death as a direct consequence of his failure. As the analysis of his dreams has shown (cf. ch. 3.1), though, the price he paid for his guilt was high enough. The members of his family actually owe him more than he owes them, but this is as yet hidden from him. Jachin-Boaz has so far only reached the core of his problems. Chapter 17, in which his crisis takes place, is placed at the centre of the novel; it closes the first half and is followed by three chapters on the initiations of other characters into a new life.

Chapter 18 ends with Boaz-Jachin naming a group of rocks which sank the boat on which he travelled the "Rising Son Rocks" (106) – after the boat-owner who instantly decided to open a restaurant rather than to expose himself to the vagaries of the sea again. The beginning of the wife's second life is described in chapter 19, and Gretel's decision to share her life, happy or unhappy, with Jachin-Boaz in chapter 20. The interpolation of chapters on Jachin-Boaz's wife and Gretel, and of one about the lion (ch. 23) agreeably disrupts the strict symmetry of alternating chapters about Boaz-Jachin and Jachin-Boaz.

To prove his right to a life of his own, Jachin-Boaz must now go on to defend his belated opposition and to have the argument with his father that the father's early death prevented. The lion therefore returns as soon as Jachin-Boaz is ready:

> 'Always the frown, like my father,' said Jachin-Boaz. 'How was I to be a scientist, father Lion?...' (...)
>
> 'One of my teachers said it was an intellectual suicide when I failed my examinations. But science is knowing, and how could I know anything, how make a profession of knowing? Little things, yes. Places on a map.
>
> 'When you kill yourself you kill the world, but it doesn't die. He'd had a bad heart for some time, so it couldn't have been my fault altogether. Why did he never talk to *me* ? Why did he seem always to be talking to a space that I hadn't moved into? Why was he always holding up an empty suit of clothes I never did put on. A sleeve with no arm in it struck him down. An empty shoulder turned away from him. He closed his mouth and lay down, but he is more alive in me than I am. ...' (134-135)

The lion is an opponent that Jachin-Boaz has to defeat not only for his own sake but also for Boaz-Jachin's: "'... if you kill me I shall then be more alive than ever, strong as the brazen tyre on the wheel. My son will feel me heavy and unfinished on his back, big in his mind.'" (135-136). Yet, the intervention of Gretel and a constable interrupts Jachin-Boaz's long repressed struggle for truth and peace (136f.), he is not allowed to experience the "sunlit violence with calm joy at the centre of it" (130), the threat and the promise that the lion offers.

In the mental hospital he is taken to Jachin-Boaz nearly gives himself up. Although the lion accompanies him there, he does not continue the struggle. When he attacks the lion out of sheer jealousy of the other patients, the lion disappears (171, 175). Jachin-Boaz is shocked enough to develop a strategy to get out of hospital: "He would have to be good, be quiet, muffle his terror and wait for his rage until he was out of here" (177).

His endeavours are rewarded. No sooner has he left the hospital than the lion appears to him once more, representing all the aspects of existence: "No magic. Reality unbearable, inescapable. Violent death. Violent life. Being beyond all reasonable bounds. Being unbounded, terrifying, violent medium of death and life, indifferent to both, contemptuous of mortal distinctions" (188). It is in the face of supreme being that mortal concerns such as guilt, fear and anger become petty and insignificant. Confronting the lion without reservation, Jachin-Boaz is reborn at last, and so is his son:

> Jachin-Boaz, Boaz-Jachin screamed in blinding fires of pain, raw nerves and ripped flesh flaming, muscles torn, ribs cracking, lion-entered, lion-killed, lion-born, howling in millennia of pain, impossibly absorbing infinities of lion. Blackness. Light. Silence. (191)

The physical and mental distance between father and son is abolished through the lion's catalytic influence on both. This would be less evident if Hoban had not arranged the two protagonists' journeys in two parallel narrative strands which allow the reader to discover correspondences between the various stages of their development. Contrary to another comment by Auberon Waugh, i.e. that "their adventures have nothing to do with each other except that Boaz has apparently sent the lion to torment his father" (Waugh 302), there exists a very close relationship between the protagonists' seemingly independent steps towards each other.

Chapters 2 and 3 describe their first reactions to the reversal of roles; while Boaz-Jachin resigns, Jachin-Boaz indulges himself in his defiance toward the traditional fairy-tale pattern: "Now he, Jachin-Boaz was the old man out in the wide world seeking his fortune, the old man who wanted a new story and would not agree to be dead. The young man was left at home to be a shopkeeper and the companion of his deserted mother" (26). Chapters 5 and 6 juxtapose different motives for the relationship between males and females,

Jachin-Boaz's need for superiority – which he believes to be "Love without purpose" (34) – Gretel's longing for a fatherly friend, the wife's wish to escape from the house of her parents and make her dreams come true, and Boaz-Jachin's feeling of duty towards his mother. Chapters 6 and 7 point to Jachin-Boaz's dreams of adventures that could never be fulfilled because, as chapters 7 and 8 show, his mother and his wife effectively prevented him from taking the necessary steps. Just so, Boaz-Jachin now risks being trapped by *his* mother and by his girlfriend Lila:

> There's no knowing what she might do now, he thought. She might well turn into some kind of invalid and I'll have to take care of her. ... He's run away and left me to clean up after him. Boaz-Jachin stayed home from school for the two days that his mother spent in bed, and Lila came to the house in the evening and cooked for them. (41)

And so on. The list of analogous experiences of father and son could be completed with examples from nearly every couple of successive chapters, but I would like to add only one more example. While the father has to keep quiet in order to be released from the mental hospital (ch. 32), Boaz-Jachin falls into a passive, meditative state (ch. 31): "He had no sexual appetite, wanted no one to talk to, read nothing. Often in the evenings he sat quietly in his room doing nothing. ... The feeling of emptiness rushing towards something became waiting stillness" (173-174). He only moves again (ch. 33) after his father has been released (ch. 32); the lion's roar leads him to the place where he will be reunited with his father. The two narrative strands converge in the novel's final chapter, where an immense primal scream abolishes the last differences between Jachin-Boaz, Boaz-Jachin and supreme being. Equivalence, gained by the father's making up for what he missed in his youth and the son's loss of cruel innocence and ignorance, provides the basis for their future relationship.

Yet, what will this relationship be like? How will Boaz-Jachin react to Gretel and to the baby she will give birth to? As its predecessor, *The Lion of Boaz-Jachin and Jachin-Boaz* stops at a moment of happiness. But there has been a noticeable development since *The Mouse and his Child*, to bring out which will be the task of a last short chapter.

3.3. Bigger Animals, Sharper Teeth

Anthony Thwaite's comparison of the two novels describes the main difference between *Lion* and *Mouse* quite well:

> Innocence, simple Innocence, is the heart of *The Mouse and his Child*, for all the rude shocks of such tyrants as Manny Rat; in the new book, Mr Hoban confronts Experience, and that is a harder theme to encompass, because it is distracting in the number of its masks and subterfuges. (Thwaite, "Fathers and sons", 37)

A fruit of experience the novel repeatedly spells out is the paradoxical truth, "everything that is found is always lost again, and nothing that is found is ever lost again" (17, 50, 120; etc.). The characters no longer appreciate what is "fixed and permanent" (11, 21), especially with regard to human relationships. The old family idyll does not work once in the entire novel: couples who stay together like Mina's and the young farmer's parents or the doctor and his wife hate each other (cf. chs. 16, 22, 25, and 32). Some people get separated before hatred makes a split inevitable, like Boaz-Jachin and Lila (ch. 10), others stay single or avail themselves of mistresses and lovers in order to assure a certain degree of change and excitement, like the lorry driver, the divorced woman or Jachin-Boaz's father (cf. chs. 12, 29, and 30).

The lorry driver and his parents certainly form the most surreal of all distortions of the innocent Mouse family in the previous novel:

> '... My mother was a whore.'
> 'What was your father?' said Boaz-Jachin.
> 'A pimp,' said the driver, 'and a homosexual as well. Classical profession, classical principles. Sometimes he made love with my mother as a special favour, but he never intended to have children. I represent the triumph of whoring over pimping....' (58)

Yet, not even Jachin-Boaz's and Gretel's relationship seems any firmer than that of the lorry driver's parents:

> 'It'll be all right, whatever happens,' said Gretel. ...
> 'What do you mean, whatever happens?'
> 'If you leave me. Or if the lion...'
> 'Do you think I'll leave you?'
> 'I never know. But it does not matter. I'll love you anyhow, and so will the baby...' (180)

Although sexuality is almost omnipresent in *The Lion of Boaz-Jachin and Jachin-Boaz*, and though the characters are meant to be of flesh and blood, they remain abstract and represent types rather than individuals.[1] They are figures in Hoban's formula of existence, born from the Assyrian stone relief like the lion, the king and the wheel. Hoban does not refute this: "I think it [*The Lion of Boaz-Jachin and Jachin-Boaz*] was weighted in favour of ontology

1 See ch. 8.4 for a detailed discussion of sex and gender stereotypes in the novel.

versus character" (Hoban and Haffenden 131). Thus, Lila, the wife and the divorced woman can be seen as a cluster of characters who stand for various (st)ages of the same type of woman whereas Boaz-Jachin, his father Jachin-Boaz and his grandfather, also called Boaz-Jachin (64) belong together like printing plate and print – even if Jachin-Boaz denies any such relation between himself and his son: "'My son,' said Jachin-Boaz. 'He's not me turned around. I don't know who he is. I don't know him very well'" (181). But, as has been shown, each of them left undeniable traces on the other's character, strong enough to influence the course of their lives. Their first names are derived from "the pillars that stood in front of Solomon's temple," as Hoban writes in "Thoughts on Being and Writing" (70). Thus, grandfather, father and son stand for seekers of wisdom who do not differ but in their ways to reach one and the same aim.

Whereas the characters of *The Lion of Boaz-Jachin and Jachin-Boaz* resemble their predecessors in their need to recognize the vital force in themselves and the inevitability of death, they differ from them in so far as the terror, pain and loneliness they have to accept in exchange for wisdom are no longer restricted to moments as they were in *The Mouse and his Child*. When the mouse father accepted sinking into the mud, his anxiety was soothed (MC 124). But Jachin-Boaz's making friends with death is accompanied by the insight that anxiety lasts as long as existence and cannot simply be soothed by accepting it, nor can it be dissolved by love: "Here, anchorless and lost in this time with Gretel he was alone with the terror but no more alone than the person-to-be in her womb. Sunrise, caught. Night again. Hello, night. No darker than ever. No darker than before I was" (186-187). If anything in *The Lion* is restricted to moments, on the other hand, it is happiness, since "Now is the only time there is" (188). The awareness of everlasting mystical moments, i.e. of moments which are "always now", as we will find them in *Pilgermann*, is only implied in the promise that "nothing that is found is ever lost again". Wilkie therefore concludes her analysis by stressing the novel's pessimism:

> *The Lion of Boaz-Jachin and Jachin-Boaz* is a fundamentally pessimistic novel, and although it has wit, it is relatively lacking in humor, which probably reflects the fact that Hoban was not smiling when he was writing it. It was from this position and in this frame of mind that Hoban moved into his next book, *Kleinzeit*, to which he brought a dimension of what has since become the familiar Hoban wit and wry humor, which first appeared in *The Mouse and his Child*. It suggests a development in his thinking and a degree of ironic detachment from the events and aspects of life and living which were so oppressive in *Lion*. It also suggests a development in his attitude towards

> and insight into human behavior and the position of humankind in the universe. (35)

One might emphasize the humorous twists more than Wilkie does, e.g. by pointing to scenes such as that at the end of the novel, when the pathos of the reunion of father and son is balanced against the comedy of the constable's resigning his post (191f.), or by pointing to Hoban's satire of psychiatric "cures" and methods of testing the patients' sanity (160, 177f.). But compared to Hoban's subsequent novel, *The Lion of Boaz-Jachin and Jachin-Boaz* is indeed a serious book.

4. Kleinzeit (1974)

4.1. The Hidden Soul of Harmony

The Lion of Boaz-Jachin and Jachin-Boaz could be interpreted as an adult readoption of themes first developed in *The Mouse and his Child*, with special emphasis on the relationship between fathers and sons. But also *Kleinzeit* and each of its successors take up and enlarge upon one or several of the concerns of Hoban's first book: *Kleinzeit* is mainly concerned with a middle-aged man's coming to terms with death, *Turtle Diary* with the nature of relationships in general, *Riddley Walker* with the situation of the skilled outsider, *Pilgermann* with an individual's continual attempt to define his or her place in the universe. *The Medusa Frequency*, returning to a more modest subject, adresses losses, especially the loss of love, while *Fremder* deals with the idea of the leap necessary to escape from trouble. As Hoban's focus shifts, certain elements do not reappear (e.g. the son in *Kleinzeit*), others are added (e.g. the Orpheus-and-Eurydice theme), a third group of elements preserve their function even though their appearance becomes slightly changed (e.g. the muddy pond turns into the mental hospital, the latter into Hospital, or Gretel turns into Sister). The narrative situation of *Kleinzeit* is the same as in the previous novel: it is a narratorless third-person narrative, basically a personal narrative situation with many dialogic scenes. The point of view occasionally shifts from Kleinzeit to Sister, but the text can also take recourse to an exterior impersonal perspective from which we can witness surreal conversations such as the one between the yellow paper and Word (160ff.) or that between the inscriptions on the walls, the film posters and the ads in the empty corridors of the Underground at night (24-25). In the first chapter, "A to B", we are alerted to the advantage we have over the characters in an ironical metafictional scene. Kleinzeit tells an imaginary audience:

> All right, said Kleinzeit, let me put it this way: you read a book, and in the book there's this man sitting in his room all alone. Right?
> The audience nodded.
> Right, said Kleinzeit. But he isn't really alone, you see. The writer is there to tell about it, you're there to read about it. He's not alone the way I'm alone. You're not alone when there's somebody there to see it and tell about it. Me, I'm alone. (8)

Actually, he assumes the role of a first-person narrator in this "interior dialogue" with his bored narratees, but this does not affect the narrative situation of the novel. The writer is only implied in the text, as are we, the readers. Even though the text and we may know more than most characters, we are not omniscient. Both author and readers belong to the extralinguistic realm whereas the characters (including potential narrators and narratees) are textual elements. Unless there arises in the latter a "transcendental" (metafictional) awareness that they are part of a greater whole, i.e. of a text produced by a writer and read by a reader, their point of view remains limited, as is Kleinzeit's in this scene. Kleinzeit eventually succeeds in recognizing that he has been the object of Word's manipulations. Word, though, is not the narrator of Kleinzeit's story but only another character whose point of view regarding its status in the text is as limited as Kleinzeit's. Word's pretension to omnipotence – cf. "I employ gods" (162) – is foiled by its extreme forgetfulness.

After *Kleinzeit*, Hoban gradually reduced the reader's advantage over the characters. In *Turtle Diary* the privilege is not entirely suspended yet. Although the first-person point of view of diary entries excludes passages which describe events from an external perspective, we are allowed to read the diaries of two protagonists and therefore know more than they do individually. *Riddley Walker*, finally, opens a series of genuine first-person narratives, unbroken except in the short stories "Dark Oliver" and "The Ghost Horse of Genghis Khan".

In *The Lion of Boaz-Jachin and Jachin-Boaz* surreal and subjective elements such as the lion, Jachin-Boaz's dreams, or subjective descriptions of landscapes served to illustrate the kind of insights that were necessary for the two protagonists to bring their conflict to a close; in *Kleinzeit*, however, such elements are only secondary to, or in the service of, the gallows humour that pervades the novel. Certain critics rejected *Kleinzeit* on these grounds, for instance, Anthony Thwaite:

> To adopt the nomenclature of his Dr Pink, his whimsies are in danger of becoming over-stimulated and too often he appears to have a bad dose of the charming inconsequentials ... nothing seems to matter but puns and wise-cracks. (Thwaite, "Chapters of accidents", 39)

Anticipating this kind of criticism, Hoban made his protagonist say:

> 'Of course it's no laughing matter,' said Kleinzeit. 'You mustn't get me wrong. Sometimes one's got to laugh, you know, or go mad.'
>
> 'And,' said Schwarzgang.
>
> 'Laugh *and* go mad,' said Kleinzeit. 'Right again.' (51-52)

Since it is death Kleinzeit has to cope with, all the gaiety gets as thin as a film. Yet, it is the only possible way for a man whose name does not mean "hero" to prove anything near heroism when he succeeds in making his death easier to bear for others and himself. Laughing, Kleinzeit refuses to be scared of his death and so, heroically, surpasses the conventional standard of behaviour. When Haffenden quoted Bergson's remark, "The comic expresses, above all else, a special lack of adaptability to society", Hoban agreed with this view: "Well, society has to do with consensus. Everybody agrees on the lowest common denominator of reality that they can deal with, and the comic or the visionary or the ecstatic may choose not to abide by that consensus. I don't" (Hoban and Haffenden 135). The novel allusively places Kleinzeit in the tradition of Cervantes' mock-epic *Don Quixote* (13, 71). But there are also affinities with the more specific tradition of Jewish humour although, by contrast to Jachin-Boaz, Pilgermann or Fremder, Kleinzeit's Jewishness is not explicit. As Sarah Blacher Cohen writes in her introduction to *Jewish Wry. Essays on Jewish Humor*:

> The fact that ... *shtetl* Jews could so cleverly ridicule themselves and their God prompted Freud to claim that their self-mockery was the most distinguishing feature of Jewish humor. ... Freud attributed the Jews' excessive ridicule of themselves to the excessive aggression they had to conceal to survive in such an inimical society. Their self-directed mirth was a camouflaged form of their masochism. ...
>
> Jewish humor, however, is not only based on the masochistic characteristics of the Jews expressed in their self-critical jokes. It has also been a principal source of salvation. By laughing at their dire circumstances, Jews have been able to liberate themselves from them. Their humor has been a balance to counter external adversity and internal sadness. (Cohen 4)

Kleinzeit's weapon is language, as Gillian McMahon-Hill has recognized, too: "Language plays the games on Kleinzeit that it did on Jachin-Boaz. (...) Even if he is, and not through choice, a part of the game, Kleinzeit learns to play these jokes himself as well as experiencing them" (McMahon-Hill 52). Thus, it is no surprise that Word should be "personified" in Hoban's second adult novel: "Kleinzeit was between sleeping and waking when he became aware of Word for the first time. There was a continual unfolding in his mind, and the unfolding, continually unfolding, allowed itself to be known as Word" (71). Together with Hospital, God, Death, Underground, the mirror and other talking objects and ideas it is engaged in leading men with a "straight life" astray (118). Kleinzeit, Redbeard and other patients of ward "A4" are victims of an insidious conspiracy, at the centre of which is the yellow paper. It menaces potential writers who are tired of making an effort to fill it with words: "Write it or I'll kill you, said the yellow paper. And the story of you will come to an end this morning" (73). Redbeard is punished because he refuses to obey the yellow paper; first he loses his shelter (91) and in the end his health (116).

Kleinzeit, who slowly but steadily turns into a detective,[1] tries to find out more about the case: "If, as we suspect, yellow paper occurs in all cases, it might be interesting to learn the histories of those who recover" (125).[2] When he learns from Sister that nobody has survived and been discharged from Hospital so far, he realizes that nothing but his "Athenian" spirit of defiance is responsible for his still being alive (106-108, 126), and he doubts whether he

1 According to Tzvetan Todorov's "The Typology of Detective Fiction" (1966), *Kleinzeit* is a suspense novel, combining the revelation of a mystery, which characterizes the so-called "whodunit", with the interest in the detective's exposure to danger during investigation, which normally characterizes the "thriller": "the suspense novel ... keeps the mystery of the whodunit and also the two stories, that of the past and that of the present; but it refuses to reduce the second to a simple detection of the truth. As in the thriller, it is this second story which here occupies the central place. The reader is interested not only by what has happened but also by what will happen next; he wonders as much about the future as about the past. The two types of interest are thus united here – there is the curiosity to learn how past events are to be explained; and there is also the suspense: what will happen to the main characters? These characters enjoyed an immunity, it will be recalled, in the whodunit; here they constantly risk their lives. Mystery has a function different from the one it had in the whodunit: it is actually a point of departure, the main interest deriving from the second story, the one taking place in the present" (50-51).

2 The correspondences between medical anamnesis, detective work and the process of reading have been discussed extensively in semiotic studies of the detective genre; see e.g. Thomas A. Sebeok and Jean Umiker-Sebeok, "'Sie kennen ja meine Methode.' Ein Vergleich von Charles S. Peirce und Sherlock Holmes" (1979), esp. pp. 51ff. Arthur Conan Doyle himself was a doctor (54). He based his most famous invention, Sherlock Holmes on his teacher, Professor Bell, whom he had admired for the logic with which he sought to discover the causes of his patients' diseases (54). In the Holmes stories, the social gaps left by murder victims are like open wounds; because of his ability to read all signs properly, it usually does not take Holmes long to discover a culprit and thus "heal" society from the "disease", i.e. crime, which has befallen it (75).

Kleinzeit deviates from the classical detective novel, in so far as the protagonist's discoveries do not heal him or society: the pain from A to B cannot be cured but must be accepted. But, in Sister's words, Kleinzeit learns to make "the right use of his sickness" rather than to allow the doctors to cut off what distinguishes him from other people (19). Also see Herkommer's discussion of Kleinzeit's disease as an utterance of the mind speaking through the body (Herkommer 93-98). Christine Wilkie has discussed Kleinzeit's illness in relation to gender concepts (Wilkie 39); since this approach requires an altogether different theoretical framework, I have postponed my response to her interpretation to ch. 8.4.

will not soon be beaten by the yellow paper. For although the three lists he makes to analyze his and his friends' situation help him to write three pages of his first novel (123-125), the yellow paper is never easy to please. It only accepts him after fights, for instance, with Death:

> Kleinzeit grabbed the frying-pan from the kitchen, slammed the hairy black fingers with all his strength.
> I'LL GET YOU LATER, said Death, SEE IF I DON'T.
> Right, said Kleinzeit. He went back to the plain deal table to start the second paragraph.
> You're so brave, said the yellow paper. So strong, so virile. Take me. (122)

He feels inclined to give up his struggle when he begins to suspect that the Athenians lost their war in spite of their fighting spirit (126); but Word, distracted and erroneous as it may be, personally encourages him to continue:

> Yes, said Word, in the immortal words of William Wandsworth: 'hoof after hoof...' Keep that in mind, my boy. (...)
> Wordsworth, said Kleinzeit. What are you going on about?
> What I said, said Word: the caterpillar tractor concept. 'My horse moved on,' he said, 'hoof after hoof'. It's perfectly obvious, I should think, that he had in mind an endless revolving tread shod with horses' hooves, thus prefiguring today's machines of war and peace. ...
> Kleinzeit had stopped listening. I'll start running again in the mornings, he said. Buy a tracksuit tomorrow. (126-127)

Kleinzeit's sensitivity to messages and his reflections on the production of literature (8) obviously qualify him to be singled out by Word, who has a certain influence on the yellow paper. It is Word who decides which of the potential victims may survive the conspiracy: "Let them die in their hundreds and their thousands, from time to time one of them must wiggle through. I see to that" (160). This information, though, as well as the entire dialogue between the yellow paper and Word in "The Machine from the God" (160-162) is not accessible to Kleinzeit.

The "blackmailing" of Kleinzeit starts with a pain he feels in his "hypotenuse", and his "diapason" is hard and swollen (7). On his way to work, he finds "a sheet of yellow paper, A4 size, on the floor, unstepped-on" (8). Of course, Dr Pink, a deep one, can only "explain" Kleinzeit's pains within the limits of his understanding:

> 'The hypotenuse of course is the AB connection that keeps your angle right. Subtention. Well and good I say, for as long as you can keep it up. ... You may experience flashes from A to B as hypotenuse, while maintaining right angle, begins to skew. That's when I say, you know, Time, gentlemen. Time for hypotenuse to go. Some of my colleagues have pointed out that obtuseness or

> acuteness invariably follows its removal. My answer is So what. You can jolly well keep your angle right while everything else collapses around it and then where are you.' (77)

However, Kleinzeit, who is scared of possible complications and frightened by a misprint on the form he is to sign, "I the undesigned..." (79), prefers to leave Hospital and live with his inadequacies because they are a part of his life : "'I'd like to think about this for a bit before I sign it,' he said. (...) Hospital said nothing, had no quips and cranks and wanton wiles" (80).

His intuition saves him from destruction. Redbeard, another victim of the yellow paper about whom he first dreams before he meets him (33, 55ff.), will give him the decisive hint. His account of his experience with the demanding yellow paper (91) enables Kleinzeit to discover the link between the patients' diseases and their finding sheets of yellow paper:

> 'As long as I kept doing what the yellow paper wanted I could unlock that door. I had a place to lay my head, make a cup of tea. No more yellow paper, no more door.'
>
> 'Where did you get the key?' said Kleinzeit.
>
> 'From the last yellow-paper man.'
>
> 'What do you mean, "the last yellow-paper man"?'
>
> 'Thin bloke, looked as if he might go up in flames at any moment. Don't know what his name was. Used to go busking with a zither. Yellow paper got to be too much for him, same as it did for me. Don't know what's happened to him since.' (91)

Kleinzeit and we in fact do know what has happened. Redbeard's description of his predecessor's looks allows us to identify "Flashpoint", i.e. the first patient Kleinzeit spoke to in Hospital (16), who little later died saying quietly, "'Arrow in a box'" (23).

So as not to die prematurely, Kleinzeit must find out what it is the yellow paper wants him to write. His first chapter "Hero" (108), however, violates the paper and is thrown off later like dandruff:

> He shook the paper, brushed it off. Nothing there. Black marks, oh yes. *Ink* on the paper right enough. Nothing else.
>
> What's happening? he said.
>
> Nothing's happening, said the yellow paper. Why don't you make something happen. Hero. (167)

Since Nothing (with a capital N) is special about him, Action cannot be of use to him for good because it exhausts Kleinzeit, who is no Prong Studman after all (172). So Hospital advises him to remember who he is in the first place, "Be I-Don't-Know" (173). Re-membering himself like Orpheus in Thrace (147) instead of making up far-fetched stories, Kleinzeit will turn into a writer.

Looking back at moments of harmony, describing what efforts were necessary to achieve them, his vain attempts at retaining them, and his involuntary exposure to unpleasant memories, to forgetfulness, and to further dismemberment is what will stay on the yellow paper.

With this insight, the "blackmail case" is solved. Herkommer thinks that Hoban disrupts the pattern of the detective novel before a satisfactory solution has been found and questions have been answered (Herkommer 111f.). To corroborate evidence she quotes the following passage:

> How had he come to this with the yellow paper, like some dreadful marriage to a frog princess who would always be a frog.
>
> For a time there had been mystery, complexities, excitement, riddles full of promise: the yellow-paper, foolscap, and Rizla men, the permutations of barrow full of rocks, the posibilities of STAFF ONLY and its key. None of it had been explained, none of it mattered, he had no questions. (184)

But I think that there are two remarks to be added. Firstly, the quotation from p. 184 must be seen in the context in which it belongs. After the climactic moment in which Kleinzeit had a vision of a "circle, fat and black on yellow paper" (180), he craves for more like an addict. Hospital accommodates him by recalling three other moments of harmony, beside the one he has just experienced, from "Hall of Records" (181f.). But these memories cannot prevail against a question he knows to be more urgent, and of course it is the one which makes explicit what surface successes such as love stories and recoveries of health and harmony make people forget, i.e. the backside of the human condition:

> Place of dismemberment? said Kleinzeit.
> Everywhere, all the time, said Hall of Records. (182)

This head-on confrontation with the death drive is aggravated by the fact that he suffers from withdrawal symptoms when Dr Pink decides to take him off all drugs (183). He is too weak to apply his imagination and irony to his perception of reality; mortal terror therefore nearly overwhelms him: "All at once the streets outside seemed one vast desolation, Underground the very abyss, the thought of sitting on that freezing floor with his glockenspiel was appalling. Fleets of Morton Taylor lorries thundered past, changing gears contemptuously" (183). When the yellow paper is "inert and lifeless in his hands" (184), too, he at first seeks to shirk responsibility by dismissing all the answers he has found. Denying that anything has mattered or been explained, he above all tries to get rid of his insight into the backside of the human condition: this is what the excerpt from p. 184 shows. After five days without any drugs, however, the bleakness of existence is already more tolerable than at the beginning. His sarcasm returns: "We have laboured diligently and we are back where we started from" (185). And eventually, he finds sufficient strength to live according to the results of his investigation. He makes friends with Death and manages to write a "Couple of pages a day" (190).

Secondly, Herkommer argues as if the novel had followed the pattern of a classical detective plot: at one point she compares Kleinzeit with Dupin, Holmes, Poirot and Wimsey (Herkommer 109), i.e. with "immune" detectives who, by solving a case, fully recuperate the damages done to society by a criminal; they re-establish law and order, which have only been temporarily suspended by the crime. As we have already seen, however, Kleinzeit is not immune but exposed to danger like the detective in a thriller or a suspense novel. The yellow paper challenges him very much like the "femme fatale" in a Chandler novel. Slavoj Zizek writes in *Looking Awry*:

> In this case, then, it is the detective himself ... who undergoes a kind of 'loss of reality,' who finds himself in a dreamlike world where it is never quite clear who is playing what game. And the person who embodies this deceitful character of the universe, its fundamental corruption, the person who lures the detective and 'plays him for a sucker,' is as a rule the femme fatale, which is why the final 'settlement of accounts' usually consists in the detective's confrontation with her. This confrontation results in a range of reactions, from desperate resignation or escape into cynicism in Hammett and Chandler to loose slaughter in Mickey Spillane.... (63)

In the excerpt from p. 184, the inert yellow paper is rejected as a "frog princess". Kleinzeit tries to blame "her" for his depression in order to regain what Zizek calls "his imaginary, narcissistic identity" (66), i.e. the fiction that wholeness and immunity exist if disturbances are removed. But in fact he is aware that nothing is gained by that gesture: the "disease" which has befallen him and his fellow patients, i.e. mortality, cannot be cured by simply rejecting one of its potential instruments. He will therefore expose himself to the yellow paper again, accepting his fate, and this gesture will be rewarded by Death, who lets him draw "in one smooth sweep a fat black circle, sweet and round" (191). In a genuine suspense novel, the detective's acceptance of fate is "a suicidal gesture" (Zizek 66); it is no less so in the comic suspense novel *Kleinzeit*: although Kleinzeit is rewarded at the very end of the novel, we have already seen him collapse trying to grasp what the yellow paper wanted him to express (168). In *The Medusa Frequency*, Herman Orff's fits of angina (e.g. MF 123) and his sterile periods of writer's block (MF 13) will underline the element of danger even more.

Readers of *Kleinzeit* cannot help feeling drawn into the process of discovering connections between the individual parts of the novel. Like the protagonist they want to find out what is going on, in what ways his suffering and his writing talent are related. Words and images send them in various directions so that what seemed to be mere nonsense suddenly does make sense. But the keys have to be picked up. Whereas Kleinzeit's insights are the result of his discovery of *correspondences* between his, Orpheus's and his fellow patients' fate, the readers' way is additionally signalled out by *incongruities* such as misused words, telling names, surreal events, in short, by humorous effects. It should perhaps be stressed that many of these effects are humorous and extraordinary for us, but not for the characters. In their fictional realm it seems to be natural that Death is a monkey-like creature or Hospital a jealous and sometimes destructive lover of its patients and nurses. We, however, are invited to interpret the distortions. Like the narrative situation they give us an advantage over the characters.

One example of a key that has often been neglected by reviewers are Kleinzeit's diseased organs, with names that are borrowed from geometry and music. Some critics contented themselves with the observation that such organs are "bizarre" (Thwaite, "Chapters of accidents", 39), and that the "misuse of words" contributes to the production of fun (Anonymous, "In jugular vein", 345). McMahon-Hill at least recognized that the parody of medical language is only an aspect of a more general attack: "All the terrifying mumbo-jumbo of modern medicine – its jargon, its drugs, its technical complexity, its appalling paraphernalia – is put sharply into a new and sardonic perspective" (50). But if the production of fun and the satire of the medical industry had been Hoban's only objectives, he might as well have used witty neologisms or numbers to name Kleinzeit's organs. Yet, just as Kleinzeit's sensitivity to details and his distrust of Dr Pink's authority protect him from becoming Hospital's victim, readers who inquire into the meaning of the patients' unusual diseases, organs, names and pastimes will begin to understand the principles according to which all the seemingly disparate elements of the novel have been arranged.

I would like to illustrate my point by following the associations triggered by Kleinzeit's "hypotenuse" and his "diapason". In its abstract geometrical sense, the hypotenuse is that side of a triangle opposite the right angle. It is also the diameter of the circle that is formed by all the possible right-angled triangles over the hypotenuse. If the line, which traditionally goes from A to B, is shortened or lengthened, the angle opposite the line (at point C) will no longer be 90°. As Dr Pink's words have shown (cf. above), the hypotenuse influences Kleinzeit's perceptive abilities, for its removal could cause obtuseness or acuteness (77) – Hoban makes use of the slipping of meaning in these words. Even if the right angle is preserved, there is a danger that its balance might be lost. Instead of being situated at its highest pitch above the middle of a horizontal hypotenuse, the right angle might wander to the right or left, up and down, and the hypotenuse might become skewed, which is what happens to Kleinzeit (75). Asymmetric triangles and triangles about to topple over are the result. This apparently affects Kleinzeit's mood, as one of the many meanings of "pitch" suggests: "'... We don't want him to lose axis but at the same time we've got to watch his pitch. We'll run a Bach-Euclid Series on him, see how he tests'" (30).

"Pitch" and the letters A, B and C extend the field of associations to a musical context, and so does Kleinzeit's "diapason". For a diapason is either a tuning-fork that vibrates at a certain pitch (usually at the note A), or, as the definition of the *Collins Dictionary* shows, "either of two stops ... usually found throughout the compass of a pipe organ that give it its characteristic tone colour" (409). Related to Kleinzeit, his swollen diapason indicates the painful formation of a new characteristic voice. As soon as he tries it out for the first time, writing a television commercial for Bonzo toothpaste on the yellow paper he has found on his way to work, he loses his job as a copywriter:

> 'We open on a man pushing a barrow full of rocks. No music, just the sound of his breathing and the creaking of the barrow and the sound of the rocks bumping along. Then we move in for a close-up. Big smile as he takes a tube of Bonzo out of his pocket, holds it up, doesn't say a word. ...' (11)

The relation between a modern Sisyphus's pushing a barrow full of rocks and brushing one's teeth is not clear enough, too "literary", maybe, for the "Creative" Director (11).

Discordant sounds and incongruent triangles will reappear in various of Kleinzeit's activities. He first learns to play a glockenspiel in a "truncated-triangle-shaped black case" (27). Then he tries to remember his past, retrieving the points C ("see") opposite his hypotenuse; he is afraid of arriving at B ("be", or rather "not to be"?), his death, "too soon", while A, his birth, is "Too far ever to get back to" (51). At the beginning, he can only approach the time twenty years ago, when he killed a tomcat (63f.). Some time later he remembers his father's funeral (67) and Folger Bashan, an enemy he had at school (75).[3] The negative memories prevail until making love with Sister

3 Folger Bashan will actually cross the threshold between memory and reality. He will enter Kleinzeit's adult life as Dr. Pink's locum (138). Although he does not remember Kleinzeit, he

provides a first positive point to be put on record, unchaining a whole series of other – good and bad – memories (87f.). Their sum, the circle or, if incomplete, the polygon that they form, will ultimately make up Kleinzeit's life and influence his judgment on himself. The more points he can remember, the fuller will his life appear to have been. The vision of a perfect circle towards the end of the novel will therefore signal a short moment of perfect harmony (180).

When he goes busking with his glockenspiel, he plays as badly as his hypotenuse is skewed. In return, the money he gets is for Sister (the third element procuring the "bond" between Kleinzeit and his "listeners") rather than for his music (82). It is no wonder that Underground and another busker call him "Ponce" (100). So Kleinzeit decides to enrich his music with poetry. Since A and B are letters of the alphabet as well as musical notes, the step from music to poetry is not very far. Kleinzeit's first poor little poem, written on a piece of yellow paper, consists of three lines, the first series of poems of three items (103). His fourth poem, however, marks a turning point:[4] "Walk in danger, walk in error, / Walk ahead in Morton Taylor" (111). The poem is as incongruous as his inner triangle. But for the first time, incongruity serves a purpose and is not only a matter of incompetence: "Esoteric, thought Kleinzeit. Keep them guessing" (111). He has written a poem that baffles his readers' anticipations because it does not end in the regular rhyme that the phrase "mortal terror" would supply. By means of preventing formal harmony, Kleinzeit literally takes the edge off the potential disharmony of contents, which, however, cannot be entirely excluded from a reading of the poem. The two lines are in fact a scaled down illustration of the way in which the novel works: unexpected events, humorous turns, misused words, puns and all kinds of seeming nonsense turn Kleinzeit's making friends with death into a comic suspense story. Because of the incongruity between form and contents, it is a pleasure to read the novel although the theme of death, normally suppressed by people who do not suffer from a disease (also see Nox's remark "It's the sort of thing one tends to put off", 141), is literally breathing in its every page up to the end:

> I'll turn off here, said Death when they came to the third bridge. See you.
> See you, said Kleinzeit. (191)

---

still poses a threat: it is from him that Kleinzeit will eventually learn that the Athenians indeed lost the war against the Spartans (155).

4 Four is a Hermetic number (cf. MUM, WP 200). Whether or not this symbolism plays a role here, it is at any rate a mental leap which separates this poem from the sentimentality of Kleinzeit's first one.

After writing the "Morton Taylor" poem Kleinzeit has many more intermediate steps to take to achieve roundness. He must, for instance, suffer a collapse which removes the last traces of regularity and shape within him:

> He packed up, went to a telephone, rang up Sister as the pain arrived. No longer a simple A to B, C to D, E to F affair, it was a complex solid polyphonic geometry of contrapuntal many-coloured lightnings and thunderous volume, bigger than any Morton Taylor lorry, so big that it was no longer inside him, he was inside it. (114-115)

Compared to Pilgermann's illuminations, this vision seems rudimentary, but in terms of the novel itself it is definitely a mystical, or transcendental, moment when Kleinzeit perceives himself as we have been perceiving him, i.e. as a character within the intricate labyrinth of sound, colour and space that the novel represents. His mind loses control, but afterwards his investigations proceed steadily.

Is it not astonishing how far the pursuit of two elements, "hypotenuse" and "diapason", has already taken us? The associative chain has not come to an end here, however. It leads onward to Milton's poem "L'Allegro", not accidentally a poem with a musical title (179). Although only the first lines of Milton's text and its ending are quoted in *Kleinzeit*, "L'Allegro" turns out to be another micro-representation of the novel within the novel. The poet, like Kleinzeit, must find a way to harmony. Melancholy blocks the way, so he invokes the voice of Mirth, just as Kleinzeit takes recourse to laughter and to Thucydides to lose his fear of death. The voice of Mirth, in the role of a new and better Orpheus, sets the "hidden soul of harmony" free. So does Kleinzeit, by remembering himself and thus taking on the Orphic role. Once this parallel has been established, it is possible to explain why, earlier on, Hospital was described as having "no quips and cranks and wanton wiles" to hold Kleinzeit (80). These qualities accompany Mirth in Milton's poem. Hospital's function is not to restore harmony but to withhold it from the seeker for so long that he is raging with desire, if strong enough, to retrieve it himself; like Orpheus, whose head had to swim against the tide to get away from the beach at Lesbos (142-143), he must work hard for his release. Hospital corresponds with the "mazes" that have to be run through in the Miltonic poem, and with the "chains" that "ty" harmony. It is a touchstone to separate those capable of renewal from those incapable.

The conclusion Kleinzeit reaches after listening to the poem, "'What is harmony,' said Kleinzeit, 'but a fitting together.'" (180), is not only reminiscent of Hospital's comment on Orpheus's remembering himself (144), but it could also be seen as a metafictional comment on the way we are to read

Kleinzeit. "Fitting together" is the essence of the novel's harmony, a process, not a pre-established fixed pattern or quality of the text. In this respect, Kleinzeit sharply differs from *The Mouse and his Child* and *The Lion of Boaz-Jachin and Jachin-Boaz*, where the reappearance of certain motifs, e.g. of Bonzo cans or the lion, established a clear surface coherence. The harmony we experience in *Kleinzeit* is commensurate with the number of links we are able to establish between the individual parts of the text and with our ability to remember what belongs together. As Herkommer writes:

> E. M. Forsters Unterscheidung zwischen 'story' und 'plot' ist bei diesem Roman von Nutzen. Die 'story' als 'the chopped-off length of the tape-worm of time' ist in *Kleinzeit* in der Tat nicht sehr vielversprechend, aber 'the plot' gestaltet sich als verwickelt und vielschichtig und zwingt den Leser, die 'narrative of events' zu ordnen und in einen kausalen Zusammenhang zu bringen. Neugier, was als nächstes geschehen könnte, genügt als Lesemotiv nicht... (86)

Depending on the starting points of our connections, the quality of our memories and our willingness to recognize correspondences, harmony may be perceived or remain hidden. In whatever shape it has been found, it will be lost again and must newly be looked for. The more we agree to play the game of the text, the more worthwhile an activity will our reading have been in the end.

4.2. Dislocutions

Fritz Senn's term "dislocution", which he defined in the eponymous essay "Dislocution" (1983) in order to describe a characteristic feature of James Joyce's novels *Ulysses* and *Finnegans Wake*, may also be applied to the subliminal processes at work in *Kleinzeit*.

> Dislocution ... suggests a spatial metaphor for all manner of metamorphoses, switches, transfers, displacements, but also acknowledges the overall significance of speech and writing, and insinuates that the use of language can be less than orthodox. The prefix should alert us to a persistent principle of *Ulysses*, evinced in a certain waywardness, in deviations, in heretical turns, but also in multiple errors and miscommunications. ...
>
> Some methodical typology of *dislocution* would be a natural next step, but even if it were feasible, the gains of systematic neatness would not make up for the intrinsic falsification. For dislocutions are not so much isolable qualities as they are entangled processes. (Senn 202)

He goes on to list diverse manifestations of dislocution in *Ulysses*, for each of which there can be found corresponding examples in *Kleinzeit*: Kleinzeit, for instance, experiences "transformations in space" (Senn 202) when he finds his flat bared of all his belongings just as he wished it to be earlier on (9, 101). This would not be of interest, however, if the loss of his belongings did not encourage Kleinzeit to write his first poems, which again leads to other associations. The more a text dislocutes from any starting point to another, the longer will it entertain its readers.

Senn continues, "*Ulysses* reshuffles its elements, and with a difference" (Senn 203). Hoban's reshuffling a certain amount of themes within the canon of his novels is a feature I tried to illustrate at the beginning of the previous chapter. But also within *Kleinzeit*, the phenomenon can be observed. The list Kleinzeit makes to sort out his situation resembles a first draft of the novel (123). Many things are still missing (e.g. hints about the Orpheus and Eurydice myth) and the order of items does not correspond with the chapter sequence at all. But of course Kleinzeit has not completed his story yet. Here, as elsewhere, the differences invite interpretation.

Another kind of dislocution is the "anachronistic hybrid" (Senn 204). We find it in the name Kleinzeit gives himself at the end of the story: "Orpheus on the National Health" (185). It is not only this nickname, however, but the whole "idiosyncratic assimilation" (Senn 206) of the myth of Orpheus and Eurydice which falls under the heading of dislocution. Hospital radically reshapes the myth, turning it from a linear sequence of events into a cycle: its trick is to add a new episode, Orpheus's "re-membering" himself, which closes the gap between the head of Orpheus lying stranded on the beach at Lesbos and Orpheus's next journey to the Underworld:

> Day and night the head of Orpheus rages on the beach at Lesbos. (...) After a certain number of days the head was kicked into the sea. (...) The head bobbed in the water like a coconut, then moved out to sea. ... It was one of those grey days, ... the water was lapping quietly at the beach as the tide came in.
>
> In? said Kleinzeit. Not out?
>
> In, said Hospital. The head swam out against the tide. (...) Think of it with the moonlight on it, swimming towards Thrace. Think of it reaching the coast, the estuary, the mouth of the Hebrus. ...
>
> To the place of his dismemberment? said Kleinzeit.
>
> To that place, said Hospital. Think of the head of Orpheus snuffling in the reeds by the river at night, sniffing out his parts. ... There is a sighing perhaps, you can't be sure. Someone unseen walks away slowly.
>
> He's found his members, said Kleinzeit. He's remembered himself. (143-144)

The dislocutionary process is continued when Kleinzeit and Sister identify with and later distance themselves from the mythic couple. In fact, as we shall see in ch. 8.4, their dislocution of Hospital's version of the myth is absolutely vital for them.

Senn goes on, "The so-called stream of consciousness is also a dislocutionary sequence. There is always some latent continuity, but tracks are switched all the time. From any one point reached, all possible directions are open" (Senn 206). Kleinzeit's problem at the beginning of the novel is the very blockage of his "stream" of consciousness:

> In his mind Kleinzeit saw a corridor in the Underground.
> Why? he said.
> I'm just showing you, said his mind.
> What? said Kleinzeit. No answer from his mind. (17)

Unlike Stephen Dedalus, Riddley Walker or Pilgermann, he is not overwhelmed by a wave of chaotic associations that tear him hither and thither. His ideas lead him nowhere at first, not even back to his way to work, which at least the readers might remember to be associated with the Underground corridor (7).

Quoting is another means of dislocution, "... especially when the original wording is modified" (Senn 206). Word itself carries this principle to extremes when it makes "Barrow full of rocks" a mnemonic for "The hidden soul of harmony", a line from Milton's "L'Allegro". He explains to the shocked yellow paper: "If you have a nice thing to think about you don't want to keep it out in plain view all the time, you know, with the virtue getting rubbed off it. Keep it dark is what I say" (161). The yellow paper reproaches Word for frustrating many human minds, but Word does not care about them; its main concern is to keep readers busy for it despises literature that is only "spelling" (cf. Kleinzeit's first conversation with Word in "Firkin? Pipkin?", 71f.):

> For a flash through your mind, for an odd tune come and gone like lightning, men suffer and die riddling where there is no riddle, digging where there is no treasure.
> Why not, said Word. That's what men are for. (161-162)

A dislocutionary category I could not find to be at work in *Kleinzeit* are "a variety of temporal disruptions: in the experience of reading, in the narrative action, and in the book's language viewed historically" (Senn 208). There is rather a surplus of continuity when Hospital locks Orpheus and Eurydice into an endless mythical loop. But in *Riddley Walker* disruption will be of decisive impact. The futuristic form of English in which this novel has been written constantly clashes with today's Standard English, which has survived only in a manuscript of the legend of St. Eustace. The difficulty of translation that ensues for us in trying to understand the language of Riddley and his contemporaries is equivalent with theirs in deciphering the "old" manuscript. Translation is of course another synonym for dislocution: "... in translating every thing is displaced into another culture and speech" (Senn 210).

Fritz Senn concludes his essay assuming that dislocution "... might even stand for all those effects that make us respond, spontaneously, with laughter. Humor may be a matter, yet to be determined, of dislocution" (Senn 211).[1] In regard to *Kleinzeit*, this assumption is true, as has been shown in the previous chapter: a straight story about a divorced man who loses his job, falls ill and does not know whether his artistic vocation will ever pay would definitely not be funny. The dislocutionary shifts make these existential problems (seem to) shrink to a manageable size; as a result psychic energy can be used for the solution of the problems rather than to be wasted on inhibition and anxiety. Readers are in an even more privileged position: not having to solve Kleinzeit's problems themselves, they can discharge all their aroused excitation as laughter.

4.3. Smalltime Heroism

Kleinzeit ends almost as it started. The "almost" matters considerably although he is not aware of changes at first, as his sarcastic answer to Hospital shows:

> The distant horn sounded as in the Beethoven ouverture, then a mild flash, A to B. Oh yes, said Kleinzeit. Everything is in good order now. We have laboured diligently and we are back where we started from.
>
> Like Orpheus, said Hospital.
>
> Yes indeed, said Kleinzeit. Orpheus on the National Health. (185)

For his dissatisfactory job as a copywriter he has found a new one as a novelist (hitherto unpublished, of course), the loss of time has been repaid by the gain of Sister. There is no telling, though, how long Kleinzeit will be supported by Word. At any rate he will encounter Death again, but the prospect cannot frighten him any more. For even if Death threatened and teased him at the

---

1 In fact, the relationship between dislocution and humour need not be determined any more; Freud provided a link in his study *Der Witz und seine Beziehung zum Unbewussten* (1905): for what else but dislocutions are the operations of the unconscious which "Witzarbeit" has in common with "Traumarbeit", i.e. condensation, displacement and considerations of representability (Freud, *Der Witz*, 71-72, 129ff; also see above, ch. 3.1)? They are the stylistic means by which the unconscious disfigures preconscious ideas which would not be tolerable otherwise.

beginning of the novel, it is the simian creature which finally endows Kleinzeit with a most valuable gift: the ability to reproduce the circle of harmony on a piece of yellow paper. This is as close as Kleinzeit can possibly get to the "thingness" of harmony as he has experienced it (191).

In what respect do the other characters fail where he succeeds? In contrast to Dr Krishna, Dr Bashan, Maximus Jock, or Prong Studman, Kleinzeit is middle-aged, imperfect, weak and unsuccessful, seemingly the born loser. Yet, this contrast is relative, for as soon as he is compared with Redbeard and his other fellow patients, those who could have been Orpheus but failed, it becomes obvious that he does indeed have the qualities of a genuine hero of romances such as exceptional courage, patience, liberty, talent, perseverance, modesty and luck.

Flashpoint dies because he is too brilliant; knowing too many things he cannot concentrate on a single topic and, as a consequence, his "spectrum" bursts (23). Cyril Piggle, on the other hand, is too impatient to wait for things to happen; he cannot even wait for his health. Keen on crime fiction – his favourite is Joseph Conrad's *The Secret Agent* (120) – he does not survive surgery of "imbricated noumena", or overlapping speculations, as his disease could be paraphrased (176).

The most important alternative character, however, is Redbeard, Kleinzeit's "*alter ego*" (MacKillop 63). A foreigner in London and at first mistaking the term "foolscap" for the description of a certain paper quality (59), he even has traits of the author (cf. Hoban and Jenkins 1). He is an unlucky character, Red-Beard, mouldy like the things in Kleinzeit's fridge which are "growing quietly bearded ... and no one to open the door and make the light go on" (94). Redbeard is also a potential Orpheus, but he is never conscientious enough to take his chance (42) or to do his job on his own (65). He ends up with a "slipped fulcrum" (116) and is too depressed and fed up to pull himself up again to continue his life. There is no Eurydice for him to rouse his ambitions after Sister has declined his invitation to go busking with him (65). Giving way to his parasitic disposition, he also takes advantage of Kleinzeit's charity: selling most of his host's belongings he provides himself with money for "'... Drink, women, etcetera...'" (117). Only once does he do something in return for his personal profit. Apart from selling valuable objects, he also clears Kleinzeit's flat of all the superfluous rubbish that usually obstructs the space necessary for new and better things (101), that is, of relics of an identity that belongs to the past and should be forgotten. Redbeard takes pains to give a bare room to the future writer who needs losses to write about:

> Believe me it was a lot of trouble but I did it for you.
>
> RED (101)

Just *because* Kleinzeit experiences losses of health and property, he gets a chance to give proof of his heroic qualities. Sister can watch him make "the right use of his sickness" (19) and thus find out that he is the man she has been waiting for, whereas the Krishnas and Bashans are barred from entering the competition because they have no obstacles to surmount.

In "Thoughts on a Shirtless Cyclist..." (1971), Hoban wrote three years before the publication of *Kleinzeit*:

> Heroes who can do something well are still considered necessary for children. And if many of today's books for grownups offer us a selection of the infirm and the awkward, the losers who lap up defeat like chicken soup ladled out by a Jewish-mother kind of fate, we need those too: the composite hero of the collective, cumulative, juvenile-adult imagination has got to have some anti-heroism about him in order to the [sic] complete. Certainly anything that closes the gap between the real and the ideal makes the hero more useful for everyday reference ... A hero no better than the reader, however, will scarcely last a lifetime. And I think that heroes who excel and win all kinds of good things are the best kind. Myself, I can't use a mythology in which there is nothing to win and consequently nothing to lose. I have to have something to try for, and the more excellence I can manage the better I feel. In that respect Robin Hood has been a great help to me all my life. (CY 8)

In many ways Kleinzeit is such a "composite hero" closing the gap between the real and the ideal. But he is not so close to the figure of Robin Hood as Riddley Walker will be: "asexual and pure, mercurial, airy almost, Ariel-like – a natural innocent, murderous but sweet-natured, light and quick" (CY 9). Since Kleinzeit is a comic character, his smalltime heroism comes closer to another figure who is indirectly conjured up in the novel. When he prepares himself for Hospital, he packs José Ortega y Gasset's *Meditations on Quixote* (13). Don Quixote's spirit of defiance to the ultimate futility of things, which resembles the spirit of Thucydides's Athenians without being restricted to a martial context, is necessary to perform the "action cycle" of Orpheus and Eurydice in which Kleinzeit is involved – no more and no less.

In his introduction to a Picador edition of the *Household Tales* by the Brothers Grimm, written in 1976 and republished in *The Moment under the Moment*, Hoban explains the idea of an action cycle referring to the cyclic version of the myth of Orpheus and Eurydice:

> No system is static; it is always in the process of becoming what it is not. Any putting-together charges whatever is put together with the energy that will tear it apart. The winding-down of one system is the winding-up of another. The condition is circular: it doesn't matter where you apparently

> enter the cycle. Be Eurydice lost, and the energy of that system will put together the Orpheus who has lost you and the music with which he will gain entrance to the nether world. Be Orpheus, and the energy of that system will be scattered when the Thracian women tear you apart. Be the Thracian women, and your tearing-apart of Orpheus will release the energy that puts him together again with Eurydice unlost. Eurydice and Orpheus and the Thracian women are only the costumes: the actors are the being lost, the losing and the finding, the gathering and the scattering. The actors are the action cycles continually moving in us and in all things.
>
> If we are being lived by action cycles at the same time in us and beyond us, what is there for us to do? Everything. The action is abstractly *plus* or *minus*, *yang* or *yin*, *in* or *out*, *towards* or *away from*. It is we who clothe the action with ourselves. It is we who decide the character of the action, whether it be, in human terms, vital or deadly. (MUM, HT 148)

The Orpheus and Eurydice myth is not just an arbitrary example, but it is of particular significance in Hoban's texts. In "Thoughts on Being and Writing" (1975), he explicitly links the figure of Eurydice to the Freudian notion of the death instinct, or death drive:[1]

> George Steiner speaks of 'the image we carry of a lost coherence, of a centre that held.' He also says:
>
> > Because it carries the past within it, language, unlike mathematics, draws backward. This is the meaning of Eurydice. Because the realness of his inward being lies at his back, the man of words, the singer, will turn back, to the place of necessary, beloved shadows. For the scientist, time and light lie before.
>
> It seems to me that that 'lost coherence', the image of which we do indeed carry, is not the order of an earlier and better time but the original order of inanimate matter. And our constant longing for it is what Freud has described as the death instinct ... (66)[2]

Kleinzeit has to make the choice between the vital way of remembering himself by writing, and the deadly way of remaining dismembered and blocked in Hospital. The "logic" of the myth clearly makes giving in to the death drive the more attractive choice. But although the outcome seems hopeless to begin with – for what Orpheus could resist Eurydice and who could overcome death? – he swims against the stream as Don Quixote once attacked the windmills. The hero, according to Ortega y Gasset, is a character who does not simply put up with things as they are but who seeks to change the course of events.[3] Although he may suffer or fail, he cannot help trying to create new forms of

1 My preference for "death drive" to "death instinct" as translation of Freud's term "Todestrieb" into English will be explained in ch. 8.3.

2 Hoban's quotations are from George Steiner, *In Bluebeard's Castle* (New Haven: Yale University Press, 1971), pp. 8 and 135.

3 See *Meditationen über "Don Quijote"*, p.166f.

behaviour rather than to give up prematurely. Hence, there eventually also arises a need for Kleinzeit and Sister to abandon the fatal mythical cycle once it has come full circle. The steps of this process, especially what it entails for the relationship between Kleinzeit and Sister, will be discussed in ch. 8.4.

However, Kleinzeit's regeneration depends not only on heroic qualities but also on the banal amount of time he is biologically entitled to. Kleinzeit – whose name may also be translated as "little time" – does have the time, however limited it may be. Nox, by contrast, is aware of his lack of time, which counteracts all his good intentions and ideas: "'... I should have liked to finish the story, the idea of getting into that pretty blue picture absolutely fascinated me, especially with the teapot, which struck me as more mystical than the other pieces. But I haven't the talent. Nor, it seems now, the time.'" (130-131). There will come a time when Kleinzeit won't be able to remember himself anymore, however. Rather than to be repressed, the awareness of mortality forms a permanent counterpoint to the heroic theme. Whereas Ortega's modernist definition of heroism draws the picture of a hero who will always be able to escape the materiality of his origins and to ignore his weaknesses, Kleinzeit is a postmodern protagonist who must and can face up to his limitations. Barbara Herkommer therefore repeatedly stresses the dialectic process to which he is exposed; her reading implies that Kleinzeit's story is in fact an altogether typical postmodern narrative:

> Die Zerstörung der Harmonie, die Zerstückelung und die Wiederherstellung, das 're-membering', gehen in einem dialektischen Zusammen- und Widerspiel vor sich.
>
> Wolfgang Welsch zeigt in seinem Werk *Unsere postmoderne Moderne*, dass Postmodernismus zwei konträre Strömungen umfasst: eine holistische Tendenz mit einem postromantischen Einheitsdenken auf der einen Seite, auf der anderen Seite eine Auffassung, die auf die 'Pluralität des Heterogenen', die 'Divergenz unterschiedlicher Lebensentwürfe und Handlungsformen' setzt. Also steht 'Ganzheits- versus Differenzierungsheil'. Eine dritte Sehweise des Verhältnisses von Vielheit und Ganzheit bezieht beide Pole aufeinander (...).
>
> In diesem Sinne lässt sich meines Erachtens Kleinzeits Krankheitsweg über das Erinnern verstehen. Die Gesundung ist kein festes 'Resultat', das Gefühl momentaner Ganzheit ist eine stets 'offene Ganzheit', und die Suche nach Harmonie, nach Heilsein stellt sich in einem fortwährenden Prozess als Lebensaufgabe. (113)

To finish with, I would like to broach one more point whose discussion will also be postponed to ch. 8.4. In *Kleinzeit* the hero, smalltime or failed, is always a sick "man of words" while women are associated with health, or else with inanimate matter. Neither of the victims of Word and the yellow paper is a woman. Hoban apparently follows tradition when making the active part of the action cycle a man and the passive one a woman. Active equals masculine and male, and passive, feminine and female. But the dislocution of the Orpheus and Eurydice myth by Kleinzeit and Sister themselves will actually call this dichotomy into question. At one stage Sister says: "'In the story Orpheus looked back and lost Eurydice, but I don't think that's how it was. I think Eurydice looked ahead and lost Orpheus...'" (164). She thereby opens up the perspective on a virtual reversal of the myth, that is on the story of Orpheus's being lost or sent away ("get lost!") by Eurydice. Her interpretation prefigures later characters such as Melanie Falsepercy from *The Medusa Frequency* and certain women scientists from *Fremder*. Kleinzeit and Sister's own solution, however, indeed tends towards a change of the sex-gender system rather than towards a mere reversal of its terms.

5. Turtle Diary (1975)

5.1. Incredibly Real

Turtle Diary is the most realistic of Hoban's novels, the only one without any supernatural[1] or science-fiction[2] elements, and hence "the most accessible of all Hoban's novels" (Butts 24). A divorced man and an unmarried woman find out that they both aim to liberate the turtles of London Zoo. William G. and Neaera H. devise and carry out a plan despite their anxieties and reservations about each other and about doing something as reckless and incompatible with their self-image as abducting turtles. This plot is embedded in alternating diary entries which give us an idea of many other, and no less important, aspects of their lives, e.g. William's problematic attachment to the past or Neaera's dissatisfaction with her career as a writer of children's books. William has a brief affair with Harriet, a colleague from the bookshop in which he works, while Neaera in the end falls in love with George Fairbairn, the Head Keeper at the aquarium who supports their undertaking. In 1985, the novel was turned into a film by John Irvin and lost many of its virtues in the process.[3] Hoban had self-consciously tried to preserve the story from being simply "charming and warmly human" as "in a film with Peter Ustinov and Maggie Smith" (55);

1 For a distinction between "natural" and "supernatural", see ch. 11.1.
2 See chs. 6.4 and 10.1.
3 See Christine Wilkie's extensive discussion of the screen adaptation (53-55).

William criticizes "that sort of film" for being "only charming because they leave out so many details, and real life is all the details they leave out" (55). Irvin's film with Ben Kingsley and Glenda Jackson, or more precisely Harold Pinter's screenplay, on the other hand, completely ignored such metafictional hints and eliminated all those details again which Hoban had added to make his novel come closer to real life.

Whereas Gillian McMahon-Hill finds *Turtle Diary* "Hoban's finest writing yet" (53), i.e. up to 1976, Dennis Butts writes in 1982, i.e. after the publication of *Riddley Walker*, that *Turtle Diary*

> ... deals with problems of loneliness and alienation ... in a somewhat schematic way ... (...) ... there is a certain sense of slightness and self-consciousness about it all. The comedy of William's neighbours works well enough, but the nature of the protagonists' dilemma is perhaps too familiar by now and the symbolism of the turtles too predictable to be as effective as the use of the lion earlier. (23-24)

I do not agree that the novel should be criticized because of the familiarity of certain themes or because the symbolism of the turtles is too predictable. Neither would I subscribe to Butts's view that there is a sense of slightness; I would rather emphasize the book's apparent *lightness* and consider it one of its virtues, a trait which distinguishes it from both the seriousness of *The Lion of Boaz-Jachin and Jachin-Boaz* and the gallows humour of *Kleinzeit*. Despite a very small number of dramatic incidents, e.g. Neaera's nightmare of a shark or William's fights with his untidy neighbour Mr Sandor, the book achieves an overall quality Hoban described as "laminar flow" in his 1972 essay "Time Slip, Uphill Lean, Laminar Flow, Place-to-place Talking and Hearing the Silence":

> Laminar flow is the way the water moves past a swimming dolphin. ... There is almost zero turbulence, the flow of the water is laminar, and there is optimal swimming efficiency. Sometimes we can feel something like that – swimming freely in our own element, moving beautifully and smoothly in the medium of our own life, going forward and making good time. If you've ever known it you want to feel that way as much as you can, and you don't want to take that feeling away from anyone else. (TS 45)

The drawback of so much apparent ease is of course that the novel risks being underrated, as both Herkommer (134) and Wilkie have pointed out, too:

> *Turtle Diary* has all the promise of being a popular novel: familiar, easy reading, conforming to generic conventions.
>
> But the illusion [of familiar expectation and readerly security] is short-lived and herein lies the achievement of this novel. In it Hoban is dealing with constructed reality in the most intense way possible. He brings to it all

> the themes of previous works: living is still a very grim business; people for the most part continue to be some sort of blight upon the world and continue to be variously in or out of tune with either the knowledge or the rhythm of Creation, or both. Here, however, Hoban builds the themes into the minutiae of unheeded daily actions and activity. He does this against a stark juxtaposition of the fact of mortal reality which is the ever-present specter of death. In so doing, he casts a horrifying and threatening shadow upon the otherwise uncomplicated and ordinary business of everyday living. (Wilkie 47)

Butts is right to say that *Turtle Diary* is rather self-conscious, however; the two diarists do not leave many interpretations to the readers, as William's summary of what the turtles meant to him illustrates:

> The turtles would be swimming, swimming and it occurred to me for the first time that for me they'd always be swimming. I'd never know whether they'd got to where they were going. At first I'd been obsessed with setting them free. Then it had become a heavy task I was committed to. Then we did it and afterwards it seemed a blank and empty thing. Now it felt a good thing again. The turtles were swimming to where they wanted to be. But that was *their* swimming, they couldn't do mine. (179)

While everything that regards the turtles is too outspoken, *Turtle Diary* can also be seen as an interesting refinement of a theme prepared in its two predecessors, that is the nature of reality. The novel explores the implications of the quotation from Ortega y Gasset's *Meditations on Quixote* that Kleinzeit reads in Hospital:

> If we examine more closely our ordinary notion of reality, perhaps we should find that we do not consider real what actually happens but a certain manner of happening that is familiar to us. In this vague sense, then, the real is not so much what is seen as foreseen; not so much what we see as what we know. When a series of events takes an unforeseen turn, we say that is seems incredible. (KL 69)

Hoban's most realistic novel is preoccupied with examples of "incredible" reality, or as Wilkie has called it, with "constructed reality" (47): what is foreseen does not happen; on the other hand, whatever happens is hard to believe for the characters: "I drove home, parked the van, unloaded it. Not a dent or a scratch on the great bulgy thing, I couldn't believe it" (149). William has just discovered that he has been capable of preserving the immaculate whiteness of the hired van, which lends a touch of heroic perfection to the turtle adventure and proves that his fears were unjustified. Neaera's expectations are baffled in a similar way. Rushing through her dinner one evening because she thinks that William and Harriet are sitting unaware of her presence at a table next to her own, she finds out that her embarrassment was completely unfounded: "I passed the booth, they both looked up at me. It wasn't William G. and the girl from the bookshop. It was two people I'd never seen before" (120). Minor as such episodes seem to be compared with the liberation of the turtles, they nevertheless teach the characters to take themselves seriously and to acknowledge their right to be where they are.

On the other hand, unexpected events prevent the protagonists from becoming too self-important. Thus, the suicide of his neighbour Miss Neap thoroughly shakes William after he has just begun to feel easy on his own on a Sunday:

> A frightening thought had been growing in me. I'd always assumed that I was the central character in my own story but now it occurred to me that I might in fact be only a minor character in someone else's. Miss Neap's perhaps. And I didn't even know the story. (186)

The novel's narrative structure supports such explicit refutations of centrality: in a double diary the "centre" must be located in the space between the two protagonists. Herkommer repeatedly addresses the possibilities of identification first-person narratives normally offer to their readers; she rightly underlines how in this novel, self-ironical commentaries of the diarists create distance rather than to invite identification (115, 119-121). But here, it is also the presence of two diarists rather than just one which obstructs any naive identification. In fact all characters are minor characters, perhaps not in someone else's story but in the dynamic network of reality which links everyone to everyone else, i.e. in the diverse chain reactions triggered by open action cycles (see ch. 4.3).

Although the characters are part of a larger whole, or more precisely, of an open and pulsating structure, they often disregard or fearfully repress possibilities inherent in contacts with other people. William, for instance, is not enthusiastic at all when he meets Neaera for the first time. Her interest in turtles shocks rather than intrigues him, and there is no instant solidarity between them; their meeting is not only incredible but as uncanny as an encounter with a double:[4]

> ... eerie that she was reading about sea turtles. Obviously I can't be the only one thinking about them but I had the shocking feeling that there was another one of me locked up alone in a brain with the same thoughts. Me, what's that after all? An arbitrary limitation of being bounded by the people before and after and on either side. Where they leave off I begin, and vice versa. (45)

4 See Freud, "Das Unheimliche" (1919), on the effect of doubles, esp. p. 257.

Or Neaera is deeply surprised to find that George Fairbairn's fate should be linked with hers to form a "pattern of coincidence unrecognizable in the single dot" (156):

> George Fairbairn had been a background person until now. Now he was the dot before my face, the face before my face. Knowing that I should never see the whole picture I didn't bother to ask myself what it was.
>
> He had seemed so medium, so unspecially placed between the top and the bottom of life that I hadn't really given him full human recognition until that evening when he brought out the champagne. I'd assumed that he was married, part of a closed circle, no lines moving on his map. (164)

Coincidences are just as important as contacts between characters. Incredible though they may be, they are real enough to harbour changes, action, fulfilment, not only defeats. Often they encourage the characters to believe in life, as an episode quoted by many reviewers illustrates:

> Sermons in stones. The other day coming home from work I noticed for the first time a manhole cover near my corner. Square plate in the pavement, K257 on it. ... When I got home I looked up K257 in the Köchel listing in my *Mozart Companion.* It was the Credo Mass in C. *Credo.* I believe. (114)

To acknowledge rather than ignore coincidences and other people's existence is essential for characters paralyzed or exhausted either by painful memories – cf. the effect of William's dreams of his ex-wife Dora and their girls (93) – or by pessimistic and frightening pictures of the future such as Neaera's vision of the outcome of the turtle adventure; like the Eurydice envisaged by Sister in the previous novel, Neaera risks being barred from a better future by looking ahead too much:

> The whole thing is quite likely to end in disaster with the van and the turtles and us overturned in a ditch somewhere in the middle of the night, all blood and splintered glass, groans and whimpers. Maybe we'll be killed outright, and all for some stupid notion long since gone out of my head. Oh shit. (124)

But the catalytic effect coincidental finds have on the finder or complementary individuals exert on each other manifests itself precisely when those pictures of the past and the future lose their strength and the pressure to act becomes more compelling than all inhibitive forces.[5] Thus, George Fairbairn's phone call revitalizes William's self-confidence: "He was talking to me in a matter-of-fact way as if I really existed and was a real grown-up person who could drive vans,

5 Neaera uses the image of colliery horses and miners to describe the catalytic effect: "A large strong animal and a man together add up to more than a man and an animal. They aren't afraid of the same things, and where the senses of one leave off, those of the other go on" (118).

be at a certain place at a certain time and do what I'd undertaken to do. Incredible" (122). And William's phone call to Neaera similarly forces her to give up her ambivalent position:

> Perhaps I could still back out of it. But there was his voice coming out of the telephone and I said yes, Thursday would be all right. ...
> I looked at the telephone after I'd put it down. Sly thing, getting words out of me I'd no intention of saying. (123)

Although her fearful vision follows William's phone call, the awareness that it is no longer possible to retract helps her to overcome her fear by concentrating on the preparations: "Blankets. We'll want a bit of a rest before the drive back. Pillows. Surely he won't book hotel rooms, it isn't that kind of thing. No, no, just let it be done and out of the way as quickly as possible" (124).

The readers' expectations are no less baffled in this novel than the characters' since the novel "behaves" in a totally non-fictional way. Hoban purposely abstained from turning the story into an action thriller by leaving out possible moments of tension that the turtle snatch might have offered: the Head Keeper supports the enterprise, nobody else interferes, there is no accident to hold up William and Neaera, and not even the sea compels the two protagonists to give proof of extraordinary skills or more than usual solidarity. Neither is the novel a romance: against all romantic expectations, which become the stronger when William and Neaera think that they have "too much in common ... to be comfortable in each other's presence for very long" (59; or 126), they do *not* fall in love as they might do in a film. Everything is so incredibly real that the expected stories just do not happen.

The contrast between conventional narratives and this novel is often brought out by William's reflections on films he has seen; apart from dismissing "charming and warmly human" films (55), William is also aware of unrealistic performances of heroism and virility:

> I rang up a van-hire place. £2.75 per day, 2 1/2 p per mile, £10 deposit. God, how I hate the thought of driving the thing. In films people like Paul Newman and Burt Lancaster leap into vehicles they've never seen before, cars, lorries, buses, locomotives, anything at all, and away they go at speed. Sometimes they have to fight with someone first, knock him out before they can drive away. Well of course that's how it is in films. How can reality be so different? (121)

The quotations underline the discouraging effects of certain, usually trivial, thrillers and romances on their consumers: while the identification with heroes and heroines may cause a pleasant sensation for as long as the film (or a novel) lasts, the recipients' own shortcomings and their lack of rewards and love emerge more painfully afterwards. As William writes: "Cinemas are cosy until you have to go home, TV feels like self-abuse" (93). Neaera is quite astonished when reality for a change treats her as if she were in an old film: "Someone got out of a taxi and I got in. Just like a film I thought. People never have to wait for taxis in films. Old films, that is" (82). Generally, her approach to films is more detached and less resentful than William's. She indeed "reads" films with an artist's eye and is surprised that they sometimes succeed in comforting her even though she would never expect such an effect.[6]

William's neighbour Miss Neap, on the other hand, a woman interested in everything "cultural" (116, 178) and working at a theatre-ticket agency (29), is perhaps a victim of too high expectations nourished by art. The plays, operas and novels she came in contact with at work or in her free time presumably did not sensitize her to the thin line between the unreality of romantic achievement and the extremity of death. It is a middle line difficult to cling to, but it ensures life, if nothing else. Since only little is known about her, my interpretation of her suicide is speculative. Did she mean to rouse other people's interest? She might have enjoyed the sense of authorship and superiority over those who did not know what she was up to. Or did she simply resign herself to her social insignificance, i.e. to the fact that nobody offered her an interesting "role" on the stage of life? Whereas in art, suicides are usually the culminating points of tragic narratives, their reasons being e.g. disappointed love (Madama Butterfly), the discovery of incest (Iocaste) or something as mundane as unpaid debts (Madame Bovary), Miss Neap's suicide is inexplicable, an instance of unforeseen, incredible reality. What is clear is that she planned and executed her suicide with due consideration for her neighbours and her mother (181f.). Even her funeral arrangements, that is her refusal of a service, of viewing and flowers aim at a lasting effect, as William recognizes:

> Well, funerals are for the living. For good or ill one sees the dead removed from the scene and the departure is final. Miss Neap having been cheated of companionship while living wished to remain an undeparted presence when dead. Fair enough. (188)

The reason why she did it, though, is unfathomable. Unlike William and Neaera, Miss Neap was apparently unable to feel challenged by the fact that "the end of all things need not be difficult" (152). She could only become active to stage her suicide and consummate her desire for death but not to make her life worth living.

---

6 In ch. 8.4, I will provide a detailed analysis of her reception of the 1933 version of *King Kong*.

What the novel tries to do is to give an impetus to survival. Constantly baffling expectations, *Turtle Diary* encourages the readers to abandon the idea of glamorous climaxes. Unlike sarcastic Kleinzeit (cf. KL 185), William notices a minor improvement in his situation at the end of the novel: "Nothing was different or better and I didn't think I was either but I didn't mind being alive at the moment" (190). Indeed, there was a time when he enjoyed his slow decay, too, like the mouse father from *The Mouse and his Child* sinking into the mud: "What a weird thing smoking is and I can't stop it. I feel cosy, have a sense of well-being when I'm smoking, poisoning myself, killing myself slowly" (28). So the end, even though it is matter-of-fact, neither happy nor unhappy, represents a small progress. Taking risks for other people or other creatures is shown to be an ethical alternative to circling selfishly around one's own unfulfilled desires or to Miss Neap's act of self-destruction. But it does not solve all problems once and for all; as William writes: "You can't do it with turtles, that's all. You have to fight Mr Sandor and everything else. Every day, every inch of the way" (162). As in *Kleinzeit*, achievement is not a matter of great deeds, fights with monsters and the like but with everyday obstacles. Neaera draws a similar conclusion from the turtle adventure:

> Thinking about the turtles I could feel the action of their swimming.... All they had was themselves but they would keep going until they found what was in them to find. In them was the place they were swimming to, and at the end of their swimming it would loom up out of the sea, real, solid, no illusion. They could be stopped of course, they might be killed by sharks or fishermen but they would die on the way to where they wanted to be. ...
>
> I was in my ocean, this was the only ocean there was for me, the dry streets of London and my square without a fountain. No one could make me freer by putting me somewhere else. I had as much as the turtles: myself. At least I too could die on the way to where I wanted to be. Gillian Vole! Not enough, not nearly enough. (170)

No doubt, though, "swimming" is easier for someone who does not mind being alive. Paul Gray's comment characterizes the authorial stance underlying this kind of outcome quite precisely: "A romantic would emphasize the heroic, a realist would squint at the mundane. Hoban tries something harder: to see both, and the hairline truth that lies somewhere in between" (72).

The text again and again disagrees with the fictional models it recalls, inviting the readers to be not only surprised but also feel satisfied within the scope of their own abilities. Perhaps this disagreement might be classified as a dislocutionary device as well and be added to the list begun in chapter 4.2. Since Hoban restricted the number of dislocutionary starting points in *Turtle Diary* to natural elements, the novel may be less intriguing for readers who enjoyed the overtly incongruous and riddling qualities of *Kleinzeit*. On the other hand, it would be unfair to say that *Turtle Diary* does not do enough to keep its readers active. For, besides making them discover "incredible" turns, the novel, i.e. especially its double-diary form, induces them to concentrate on the parallels and divergences in William's and Neaera's thinking. The comparison is worthwhile, as the next chapter will show.

5.2. The Arithmetic of Action

Gillian McMahon-Hill's enthusiasm for the skill manifest in the organization of the narrative strands of the novel is justified but a bit vague:

> What is new in this novel is the detailed organization and structuring of the protagonists' thoughts. They are skillfully ordered so that the novel progresses in certain ways, considers specific themes, while the two people seem just to be thinking aloud, responding to a situation as it develops. Because so much of their narrative is just a statement of aspects of their inner selves, the task is much more complex than the mere telling of a story from two points of view. The thought patterns have to be developed concurrently, and the external 'story' that is happening to both characters is only one of several stimuli working on them. Thus, always although they reach similar or coordinated conclusions, it is from different directions, and in different ways. There is ample opportunity within this structure for things to become boring, repetitive or muddled, and this never happens. (Mc Mahon-Hill 54)

Several of the characters' motives for doing certain things as well as their opinions about each other, about the turtles and about their experiences shall now be compared. The aim is to find out in what ways the novel progresses and in what sense the characters reach their conclusions from different directions and in different ways. Taking my cue from the novel's title, I will begin by following the turtle strand as if it were the "main story". In a second step, I will relate this approach to Roland Barthes's suggestions about a structural analysis of narratives and go on to discuss those aspects of the novel's narrative organization which risk being underrated in this type of analysis.

The first disparities between William and Neaera manifest themselves in their reasons for going to the Zoo. While William suddenly feels the urge to see an octopus after dreaming of one which has inpired him with fear of "being looked at by an octopus no matter how small and harmless it might be" (7), Neaera goes to the Zoo to see an oyster-catcher (23). She saw excerpts from a film on oyster-catchers on a TV screen while buying an aquarium for her water-beetle. The birds' lonely aloofness, which reminded her of herself, instantly attracted her (9f.). Craving a challenge is opposed to finding kindred beings even though both motives are related to a concern for one's self-image.

Both protagonists are disappointed, however; this is the first parallel in their experience. Since there are no octopuses in the Aquarium, William discovers the turtles and is impressed and surprised at their ease, which would be complete but for their small tank, "a glass box of second-hand ocean" (8). The turtles' perfect movements cannot tempt him to go to the Zoo again at once: his visit has depressed rather than cheered him, and the novel therefore opens with a negative statement, i.e. "I don't want to go to the Zoo any more" (TD 7) – an initial sentence which faintly recalls the first sentence of *The Lion of Boaz-Jachin and Jachin-Boaz*. After a while, though, William changes his mind (18). He indulges in turtle fantasies (see 12f., or 20f.) which become a substitute for "living life" (55).

Neaera is disappointed, too. Although she does find a few oyster-catchers, they are unattractive from near, "so accessible as to be unobservable" (24). When she turns to the Aquarium in search of "illumination" (25), having "avoided the lions, the rhinoceroses and the elephants" (25), i.e. dangerous and heavy animals, she senses that the turtles have been less spoiled by life in the Zoo than other animals; there is a certain awe in her approach to them: "I'd been aware of the turtles for some time before I went to look at them. I knew I'd have to do it but I kept putting it off. When I did go to see them I didn't know how to cope with it" (26). Like William she admires their underwater flying, but at the same time, she feels superior to these inmates of a "prison for animals" (23) and is sad about their helplessness (27). While William identifies with the turtles' imprisonment (20), and in his fantasies, with their swimming, Neaera imagines setting them free: "I imagined a sledge-hammer smashing the thick glass, letting out the turtles and their little bit of ocean, but then they'd only be flopping about on the wet floor" (27). She is keenly aware that her feeling of superiority would vanish in other circumstances: "I'm always afraid of being lost, the secret navigational art of the turtles seems a sacred thing to me" (27; also see 42f.). In both cases, then, the protagonists' interest in the turtles, i.e. the trigger for the "main" story, is ironically a by-product of their foiled intentions.

William's problem is his inability to make the best use of the present because his thoughts are often melancholically turned backwards (see e.g. 46): his prison is the past. Neaera, on the other hand, cannot make out any positive changes in the future. As in the fantasy of smashing the turtle aquarium, her determination is again and again dampened by her pessimism. In regard to finding a partner she seems to have resigned completely, as her reaction to getting a female water-beetle shows: "No males available ... That's life" (15).

Their opinions about each other reveal a tendency in both to project their own qualities and weaknesses on the other. Hopeless Neaera finds William a "hopeless-looking man with an attentive face and an air of fragile precision like a folding rule made of ivory" (49). Troubled William, on the other hand, notices Neaera's "troubled face" (45) and speculates that she is "a woman who's accumulated the sort of things in her head that I have in mine" (46). Moreover, he thinks that she is "shy" and "vulnerable" (56) and her basic look "doubtful" (126). But in many respects they are indeed cast in the same mould. For example, they are both sensitive to the cynical reference to turtle soup on a sign at the Aquarium (12, 27). Or the diffidence and the vulnerability they have in common nearly prevent them from making each other's acquaintance. At their first encounter in the shop, Neaera seems to be bent on escaping as soon as William turns out to know more on turtles than an average shop assistant might be expected to know (46) – this is a first delay to their common undertaking. When they later meet at the Zoo neither of them can say more than hello (56), both are astonished and angry that the other does not take the initiative (56, 64). But William's pity for her and Neaera's urge to help the turtles finally provide the required impact for them to tackle the problem. They become, in Neaera's terms, "the mother" and "the father" of an action (79).[1]

Neaera is the more active partner at first, hence the "father". After all, it is she who goes to see William in the bookshop again, cursing him "for not being man enough to speak up and broach the subject" (64) when they met at the Zoo. William is assigned the role of the "mother" because he has the required physical and practical abilities to make Neaera's impulse become a reality: he can drive a van, build crates, is strong enough to carry the turtles, etc. They do not complement each other as partners in a love affair; William prefers "young and pretty" women (46) while Neaera objects to William's "incompleteness" (58). Hoban once said, and this is what the protagonists know, too (59, 126), that "they would not be able to get together beyond the one action they accomplish" (Hoban and Haffenden 136). They only fill up each other's gaps with regard to everything that concerns the turtle enterprise, backing up each other like animals making love, "Male and female face the same way, seeing what's about them" (108) or like the toy clowns William has noticed:

> There's a cheap little toy one sees at various shops, a little flat wooden clown hanging from strings between two sticks. You squeeze the sticks and the clown somersaults. His body and face are in profile and he's made so

---

1 The use of the parental metaphor will be the starting point for a re-reading of the novel in terms of gender theory in ch. 8.4.

> economically that one cut shapes the back of him and the front of the next clown to come from the same piece of wood. (127)

It is also in this position that they fall asleep after launching the turtles: "First we lay on our backs then we rolled over on our sides. The space rolled over with us, stayed quietly between us all night, shaped of the front of me and the back of her" (142).

The roles of "father and mother" are not fixed throughout the action, and the terms "active" and "passive" may be interchanged in everything that happens. Taken on its own, William's driving the van could be seen as an active contribution, but Neaera feels annoyed because she thinks that he is not active enough: "I kept saying 'Too close' and being irritated at the sound of my voice and his having to be told" (133). Complementarity is merely understood as the precondition for an action, not at all as the romantic glue and guarantee of a permanent relationship. Although William and Neaera have been conceived as "two aspects of one entity" (Hoban and Haffenden 137), the binding element of their relationship disappears at the moment when the turtles are launched and the action cycle "Turtle Liberation" has been completed.

Barbara Herkommer emphasizes the occurrences of the verb "happen" in both protagonists' accounts of the launching (TD 141, 142; see quotations below); she stresses the similarity of their perceptions of the event, discussing the variations in their diary entries as a stylistic means to prevent tiring repetition (Herkommer 118). I think, though, that Hoban aims at a more complex effect: although there are moments which bring out similar interests again, e.g. when both are laughing about Neaera's allusion to a scene in *King Kong* while the turtles are being lowered into the sea (141), it is above all William and Neaera's disparity which becomes obvious in their descriptions of the launching. Variations are not only stylistic variations but they indicate in what respects the two diarists differ. For Neaera, launching the turtles is a moment at which she can enjoy companionship even though she was convinced earlier on that this would forever be impossible for her; in her diary entry, the first-person plural form of pronouns is used very frequently and the launching appears as an example of excellent team-work:

> *We*'d neither of us bothered to find out about the tide in advance. Whether it was in or out *we*'d launch the turtles. ... I stopped caring about signs and omens and whether it would go well or badly. *Our* part in the rhythm of things was to put the turtles in the sea and however it went would be the way it went. ... I stopped caring about people waking up, I felt relaxed and invulnerable.

> *We* rounded the corner, went down the street. ... 'It's in,' *we* both said at the same time. The wind hit *us* in the face, *we* heard the crashing of the waves as *we* half ran round the next corner and up the incline to the outer harbour. ...
>
> Back to the van *we* went without a word. ... At the breakwater *we* wrestled the crate off the trolley, laid it on the steps as on a slipway and lowered it with the rope through the ringbolts. 'Don't be alarmed, ladies and gentlemen,' I said, 'those chains are made of chrome steel.' William must have seen the film, he was laughing whilst standing on the steps with the tide breaking over his feet.
>
> I gave him slack as he up-ended the crate on the edge of a step, he tilted it forward and with a great splash the turtle hit the water and dived. *We* hugged and kissed each other, ran back for the next turtle, launched it, then the next. Each one dived under the wild water and was gone. It was done, it had actually happened. Three empty crates and the turtles safely off. (140-141; emphasis added)

The excerpt also illustrates her habitual fear of the future: launching the turtles allows her to suspend her dread of "signs and omens" temporarily. In William's account, on the other hand, first-person singular and impersonal sentences prevail; Neaera does not exist in his perception until after the event:

> When I felt the wind on my face and saw that the tide was in it seemed all at once that I didn't need any answers to anything. The tide and the moon, the beacon on the headland and the wind were so *here*, so *this*, so *now* that nothing else was required. I felt free of myself, unlumbered. Where the moon ended and I began and which was which was of no consequence. Everything was what it was and the awareness of it was part of it.
>
> The crates came out of the van and onto the trolley easily, went up the incline smoothly, there was no separation between crate and trolley and me and motion. It happened, turtles happened into the ocean, champagne happened in the moonlight.
>
> On the way back to the big car-park we stopped at the public lavatory. (142)

For him, the launching is a moment at which his past identity is wiped out. He integrates into the present as if he were reborn, without any sad memories to mar the action.

After both have been given what they wanted to give to the turtles, William need not feel responsible for Neaera any more, and she need no longer urge him to do something for her. Their main differences, Neaera's hopelessness with regard to the future and William's doubts about his ability to master a present situation emerge in all their diary entries even where they seem to agree most unanimously. The last two chapters may illustrate my point once more. Neaera typically defines the new quality of her life in terms of a diminished fear of the future: "It used to be that I stayed up till all hours and still felt time-starved, none of the day seemed to be metabolized into living.

Now the minutes make me strong" (189). William, on the other hand, is glad that the present is for once no worse than the past, as has already been pointed out (190; cf. ch. 5.1). There is more to be said about the protagonists, of course. But since this chapter is mainly concerned with the organization of the narrative, a closer examination of William and Neaera's mental constitutions will have to be postponed to ch. 8.4.

Since hopelessness and melancholy are so closely related, they are hardly ever complementary. Only if one results in active though rather helpless determination (Neaera) and the other in patient though not particularly determined assistance (William), positive action will be the outcome. When Neaera as a writer of unconventional children's books was read by the father William G., the outcome were delighted children (68f.); when they joined to set the turtles free, the result was an action in the service of life; and when Neaera's future poems for adults are sold by the shop-assistant William G. (80, 170), art instead of more best-sellers will be circulated. The novel's progress is commensurate with the two protagonists' willingness and ability to move something and be moved in response to observations and experiences they make, and to opinions and characteristic features they have. But even the two most complementary characters would be unable to achieve anything at all if their ways did not cross or their insights happened too late or too early. Coincidence and simultaneity are two crucial factors for a successful action, as the alternating chapters on William and Neaera show. That is, unforeseen and unforeseeable elements are indispensable ingredients of the arithmetic of action. If William had not worked at the bookshop where Neaera went to look for books on turtles, she would have had no way to find him later. If his thoughts had not been filled with turtles at the time she came to the shop, he might not have noticed her at all later at the Zoo. In each of the initial chapters at least one of the conditions that will bring William and Neaera together is fulfilled.

Once this principle has been recognized, it is no longer difficult to follow the turtle strand. The additional details about the characters and their lives, however, usually form the major part of a chapter and during a first reading of the novel it is impossible to tell these pieces of information from the ones which belong to the turtle snatch. We have to wait until chapter 6 to recognize that the theme of the turtles, which is emphasized by the novel's title, concerns not only William but also Neaera. One could dissect the novel to remove the "details" and lay bare the "relevant" bits of information – this is no doubt what happened when the novel was turned into a film script. In the first chapter, all but the short fourth paragraph, where William's first impressions of the turtles are described, would have to be cut. Neither the octopus nor the birds, neither the children and the real gorilla he also notices nor the boy with the little rubber gorilla will have a direct influence on William's adventure with Neaera; they are simply part of his going to the Zoo. But these details are by no means less important than the parts which lead to the "main" action. After all, it is they which ensure the literariness and, at the same time, the critical realism of the novel; they give us hints about the protagonists' dispositions, their everyday life and their worries; they are parts of other stories which may in the long run turn out to be more important than the turtle adventure; last but not least they make the readers wonder what is going on. As in life, the "main" action must at first remain "enmazed as the reader proceeds with the writer" (Hoban and Haffenden 124). Or in William's terms, we get a taste of the details of "real life" other narratives often simply leave out (55).

The distinction between "main" story and "details" which I have enforced so far could be described, according to Roland Barthes's "Introduction to the Structural Analysis of Narratives" (1977), as a distinction between different units of content, that is, in particular, between "nuclei" and "expansions" (i.e. "catalyzers", "indices", and "informants"): "expansions can be deleted, nuclei cannot" (269). The units are defined as follows:

> ... units [of the class of functions] are not all of the same 'importance': some constitute real hinge points of the narrative ...; others merely 'fill in' the narrative space separating the hinge functions. Let us call the former *cardinal functions* (or *nuclei*) and the latter, having regard to their complementary nature, *catalyzers*. For a function to be cardinal, it is enough that the action to which it refers open (or continue, or close) an alternative that is of direct consequence for the subsequent development of the story, in short that it inaugurate or conclude an uncertainty. ... Between two cardinal functions however, it is always possible to set out subsidiary notations which cluster around one or other nucleus without modifying its alternative nature.... These catalyzers are still functional, insofar as they enter into correlation with a nucleus, but their functionality is attenuated, unilateral, parasitic; it is a question of a purely chronological functionality..., whereas the tie between two cardinal functions is invested with a double functionality, at once chronological and logical. (265-266)
>
> As for the other main class of units, the indices, an integrational class, its units have in common that they can only be saturated (completed) on the level of characters or on the level of narration. ... A distinction can be made ... between *indices* proper, referring to the character of a narrative agent, a feeling, an atmosphere ... or a philosophy, and *informants*, serving to identify, to locate in time and space. Indices always have implicit signifieds. Informants, however, do not, at least on the level of the story: they are pure data with immediate signification. (267)

But it is precisely the hierarchies underlying these classes of units, and structural analysis in general, that are, if not subverted, then at least called into question in *Turtle Diary* and Hoban's other novels. Even though Hoban actually appears to agree with the structural definition of characters as "participants" or "actants" in a "sphere of actions, these spheres being few in number, typical, and classifiable" (Barthes, "Introduction...", 278),[2] the characters' individual acts, the more extensive actions in which they participate, and other elements of their experience, e.g. their psychic disposition, are equivalent in his novels. The idea of narrative as a dynamic network in which the nuclei of one strand can be catalyzers in another one, and vice versa, is more appropriate for Hoban's fiction than the structuralist notion of a linear chain of nuclei which are hierarchically organized while they follow a one-dimensional logic.[3] For what indeed is "the" story of *Turtle Diary*? There would be something deeply dissatisfactory about a plot summary reducing the novel to the turtle abduction; most discussions of the novel actually address this point, see the inverted commas and the adjective "only" in McMahon-Hill's characterization of the novel, "the external 'story' that is happening to both characters is only one of several stimuli working on them" (54).

Let me simply list the other stories which would have to be regarded as subordinate in a rigid structural analysis: William is a divorced man who must find a way of overcoming not only the loss of his family but also the suicide of his father when he was still a baby; he lives in a rented room and there are different episodes resulting from his contacts with his neighbours; moreover, he works at a bookshop, enjoys watching customers and has a brief affair with his colleague Harriet; in the course of the novel, William tries out various esoteric therapies until he finds a book on shamanism which indeed helps him

2 See Neaera's awareness of patterns, i.e. "Only a certain number of things can happen and whatever can happen *will* happen. The differences in scale and costume do not alter the event. Oedipus went to Thebes, Peter Rabbit into Mr McGregor's garden, but the story is essentially the same..." (TD 50-51). This thought illustrates Hoban's idea of action cycles (MUM, HT 148, cf. ch. 4.3) and prefigures Lorna Elswint's mystical intimations of our being subject to a cosmic mind (RW 6-7, cf. ch. 6.4).

3 Although Barthes describes the "fugued" structure of narrative, he merely refers to the imbrications of various sequences of *nuclei* of the same story in one another (275). He does address episodic structures, e.g. that of an epic as a "narrative broken at the functional level but unitary at the actantial level" (275). Since episodes are closed sequences forming themselves a sequence on a higher level of organization, they do not deviate from the structural model, however. But what the model cannot account for is a narrative in which characters are engaged in several *simultaneous* stories which are independent of each other except that they use the same characters as their medium (but are the characters really the "same" in this case?). This is a consequence of a discourse being different from a sentence, despite their analogies, upon which structural discourse analysis is founded (cf. Barthes 255). While a syntactic subject cannot be at the same time the syntactic object *of the same clause*, the subject of a narrative can indeed be the object of a simultaneous other narrative produced by the same discourse. And this is not only a matter of different perspectives of the same story, e.g. of "two adversaries in conflict over some stake", a possibility Barthes briefly addresses in ch. III.2 (279), but it is a problem of different independent stories taking place at the same time.

to get a better grasp on his life. Certain characteristics of William would have to be classified as mere indices in a structural analysis, i.e. as "static" units decorating rather than constituting the story; but his ability to turn his observations into comical or philosophical texts, see his parody of a quarrel between the oyster-catchers he has seen at the Zoo (18f.) or his reflections on a visit to Port Liberty (37-40), might be the origin of a future story of his turning into a writer. Neaera's "other" stories are no less interesting: A successful writer of children's books, she has reached a point at which she feels the need to develop and eventually begins to write poems; her emotional life is troubled because of the death of her fiancé many years earlier: it is therefore a crucial step forward for her when she can open herself to a relationship with George Fairbairn; visits to Polperro and the Zoo trigger reflections about the exploitation of animals and the landscape: Neaera must learn to come to terms with these sad aspects of existence without wearing herself out. The sheer abundance of "details" must alert the readers to their importance: in a stylistic rather than a structural perspective, they have to be regarded as foregrounded, i.e. they call for interpretation.[4] Most of them will therefore be looked at in detail in ch. 8.4.

Another aspect which would have to be neglected in a structural analysis is the novel's metafictional problematizing of the referential function of films, literature and other kinds of art. Barthes writes in "Introduction...":

> ... the ultimate form of the narrative, as narrative, transcends its contents and its strictly narrative forms (functions and actions). This explains why the narrational code should be the final level attainable by our analysis, other than by going outside of the narrative object, other, that is, than by transgressing the rule of immanence on which the analysis is based. Narration can only receive its meaning from the world which makes use of it: beyond the narrational level begins the world, other systems (social, economic, ideological) whose terms are no longer simply narratives but elements of a different substance (historical facts, determinations, behaviors, etc.). Just as linguistics stops at the sentence, so narrative analysis stops at discourse – from there it is necessary to shift to another semiotics. (286-287)

Linguistics has developed considerably since this statement was made; it has, for example, recognized that language itself contains coded elements which establish semantic links from one level to another. The combination of units (e.g. turning sentences into paragraphs, etc.) is not simply an aspect of language use (parole) but one of the system itself (langue). There are *immanent* elements which transcend not only the boundaries of the sentence

4 For a definition of foregrounding, a term coined by the linguist M. A. K. Halliday, see the beginning of ch. 6.2.

(e.g. discourse markers such as "firstly, finally", etc.) but also those between the sentence and the extralinguistic world (e.g. deictics such as "this, here, now", etc. which refer to the communicative situation). Analogically it might be said that nothing is gained by banishing aspects of reference from a systematic study of narratives – particularly if a narrative self-referentially points to the problem of the codes determining its own reception and "use" in the world. The "rule of immanence" need not be transgressed by including such elements in a systematic discussion; what rather happens is that the systematic discussion will be freed from certain blind spots.

Barthes's dismissal of the referential function of narratives as an object of study actually prevents reflections about the interactions of "art" and "real life". Rather than to ask questions about the mimetic as a possible form of a referential relationship (whether problematized, as in *Turtle Diary*, or merely implicit, as in more traditional examples of realistic literature), he categorically rejects it, mystifying the spectacle instead:

> Claims concerning the 'realism' of narrative are ... to be discounted. ... In all narrative imitation remains contingent. The function of narrative is not to 'represent,' it is to constitute a spectacle still very enigmatic for us but in any case not of a mimetic order. The 'reality' of a sequence lies not in the 'natural' succession of the actions composing it but in the logic there exposed, risked, and satisfied. ("Introduction...", 294)

This was perhaps originally a defence against the implications of "bourgeois" realism, see Barthes's polemic against the "reluctance to declare its codes" which "characterizes bourgeois society and the mass culture issuing from it" (287). But the question must be permitted whether the rigid separation of "art" and "life", which is effected by banishing referential aspects from a systematic study, and the stress on an abstract logic which does not tolerate its opposite, i.e. contingency, are not themselves relics of the positivism underlying realism.

In Hoban's novel, as we have seen, the coincidental and the unforeseen, as aspects of represented reality, are as important as the logic of action cycles (which are meant to be representations of reality, too). The representation of reality is not naive but based on the recognition that the referent, i.e. "real reality" rather than the reality consensus which a naive realism confuses with it, will forever be ungraspable. The critical realism of *Turtle Diary* always alerts the readers to the constructed "reality" of the novel: its aim is to alter the reality consensus by encouraging the readers to believe more in things they have been taught to regard as "unrealistic" or "impossible" and to act accordingly. In Hoban's nonrealistic fiction the reality consensus may be challenged more ostensibly (see chs. 3.1 and 11.3). In this novel, however, in which it is interrogated in terms of the credibility of experience and the possibilities of change (rather than in terms of the borderline between the natural and the supernatural or the psychic and the physical), the intention to alter the consensus is no less serious than in the other works. For ultimately, and despite the gap which always separates the social and the literary constructs of reality from their ungraspable referent, the way we define the consensus will have an influence on us and therefore on reality itself.

Part II:

Through a Garden of Forking Paths to the Brink of the Abyss

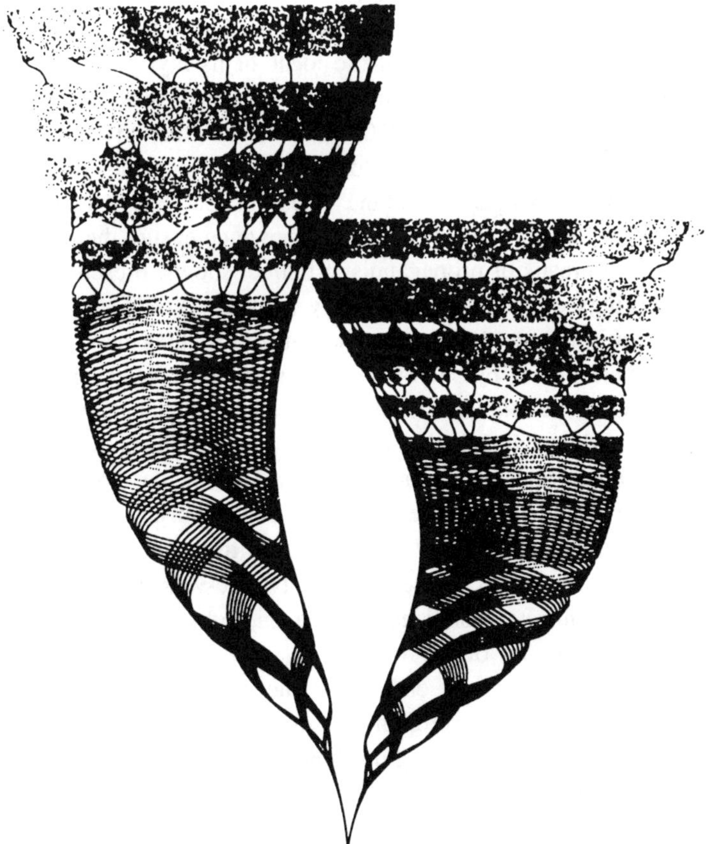

6. Riddley Walker (1980)

Riddley Walker's language is seductive in its riddle-like quality; it arouses the curiosity of any reader, urging her to follow Riddley's track right to the end of the novel. How does this language work? What does it all mean? Why has the story been written in a special language? While pursuing these questions, the reader may feel uneasy, like Riddley. For is it not this curiosity that leads scientists and scholars to probe the secrets of matter and mind? We love to solve riddles and to name our discoveries even though the knowledge we gain may destroy us. We cannot leave alone what we fail to understand. Riddley leaves his village to find out "what the idear of us myt be" (RW 7).[1] His journey takes him around the remains of Kent, which was devastated by a nuclear catastrophe approximately 2500 years earlier. "Inland" is inhabited by farmers and hunters who must work for the farmers so as not to starve. The "Pry Mincer", Abel Goodparley, and the "Wes Mincer", Erny Orfing, head the government. The "Big 2" and regular Eusa showmen ensure the obedience of the Inlanders by means of propagandistic puppet shows, presented on tours, and ritual killings of an "Ardship" every twelve years. The "Ardship" is vicariously punished for the catastrophe caused, as they believe and keep affirming in their shows, by one of his ancestors, Eusa. Wild dogs haunt the forests, preventing the Inlanders from leaving their settlements unless there is urgent reason to do so. Riddley's escape from How Fents is prompted by an intolerable accumulation of meaningful events. The few days of his travelling bring on more changes than the millennia since the catastrophe. Having refused to be the "connexion man" of How Fents, the shaman whose duty it is to interpret the Eusa shows of the "Big 2", twelve-year-old Riddley in fact connects, and disconnects, more ideas, people, and substances than anyone else since the time of Eusa, our time. An old and blackened Punch figure determines the further course of his life: he eventually chooses to be a travelling puppeteer. Neither religion nor science and politics can tempt him after his adventures. It is by making up shows that he will seek answers to the questions which continue to haunt him.

There is a potential for both progress and destruction in every kind of knowledge, an uncanny duplicity, as the novel impressively demonstrates. Knowledge entails responsibility. There is potential guilt even in the readiness to learn names because putting names to things and learning them means making them usable, and the *use* of knowledge never excludes its *abuse*; often

1 All page references refer to the 1982 Picador-Pan edition of the novel.

the difference sets in only gradually. Two human needs must always be balanced against each other: on the one hand, the need to preserve life, and on the other, the longing for an intensification of experience, which sometimes involves higher risks (think of mountain climbers, parachutists or bungee jumpers) and/or must be paid for by faster consumption (as smokers know). Imbalance is caused by privileging one need over the other; it is also the consequence of an abuse of knowledge, for in order to privilege one need over the other, it is necessary to suspend, i.e. abuse in the widest sense, at least one's knowledge of the existence of the other need. In terms of attitudes towards literature one can recognize the two needs in the extreme demands, that literary texts either help us to cope with life, or that they be wholly self-referential aesthetic artefacts – the risk we take in both cases is that a work which does not satisfy our aesthetic or practical expectations will not only fail to intensify our experience respectively fail to help us but also prevent us from doing anything more useful or pleasurable in the time it takes to read it.[2] Ideally, of course, works of art minister to both needs. But the means by which they attempt to reach this aim varies considerably.

In *Riddley Walker*, the medium itself, the novel's invented language lends itself to the readers's oscillating between use and abuse. It allows an uncritical reader to ignore the novel's cautionary content, when she is immersing herself in the formal aspects of the language without interrogating their motivation. One reviewer, for instance, has seen only the "touching – often hilarious – homage to the gift of naming that made us human and somehow survives Doomsday" (DeMott 1), missing the fact that the book shows the naming and counting of people and things to be the origin of destruction, a sign for the loss of innocence and intuitive knowledge, "1st knowing". Goodparley explicitly warns Riddley of the power inherent in words: "'... Words! Theywl move things you know theywl do things. Theywl fetch. Put a name to some thing and youre beckoning. Iwl write a message if I have to but I wunt word nothing moren that on paper...'" (118). He here suggests that language is a magical instrument: especially written words are spells whose signifieds will inevitably affect the world by calling up referents in external reality. As the novel will show, Goodparley is too pragmatic to believe in magic himself; but he is a master of rhetoric: he knows very well how to manipulate his listeners, how to make his words "fetch" them. One of Riddley's discoveries on his journey is that language can create imaginary worlds, virtual realities. In other

2 Linda Hutcheon writes in *Narcissistic Narratives*: "The act of reading partakes of man's lived life; what he reads competes, during that act, with the empirical world he inhabits. If this is seen as desirable, then one speaks of the freedom, the liberation of the mind through art; if it is not, then one talks of literature as 'escape' in derogatory terms" (77).

words, he discovers the gap between word and world. Language can, and usually does, but need not refer to a concrete reality – his Punch show is the direct result of this insight. Whether or not ideas are put into practice depends on those who develop and disseminate them; whether or not warnings are heeded, on those who perceive them. Without a subject to mediate it, a potential meaning cannot be actualized.

While Goodparley is interpreting the *Legend of St Eustace*, Riddley willy-nilly reaches the outer limits of the philosophy of language, too: he must learn that a second gap, one between signifier and signified structures the sign itself. Because of this gap, language can be seen as a pure play of signifiers, one signifier relating to many others and therefore conveying no fixed meaning at all. For Riddley, who has set out believing in *one* meaning, the learning process is painful: "... I wisht every thing wud mean jus only 1 thing and keap on meaning it" (140). The readers have been facing the ambiguities of Riddley's narrative from the novel's beginning. Since most of his words refer to several words in contemporary Standard English, meanings and connotations have never been unequivocal. The invented language of *Riddley Walker* thus works like the tile pattern of Hoban's subsequent novel *Pilgermann*: "... the next time you look there's something different about it" (PG 128). It is on the basis of the gap between signifier and signified that the readers can draw pleasure from Hoban's dislocutionary language, indulging in associations which vary from one reader to the other. Dislocutions or puns could not come into being if there were a one-to-one relationship between signifiers and signifieds. As Jeffrey Porter writes:

> Following Freud, recent theory has shown that puns are by nature disruptive. As Jonathan Culler notes, the pun is a good example of the instability of linguistic systems, for its power to produce meaning in violation of codified relations calls attention to the arbitrary nature of signs.... In this way, word-play always reminds us of the inherent duplicity of language, which, by undermining the explicit, complicates the whole process of signification. (463)

This amounts to two readings, i.e. that of the "original" narratee,[3] who reads for "the meaning(s)" of Riddley's story, the signified he intended for it, and that of contemporary narratees, who find joy in adding further layers of signifiers to the network of the text, multiplying its meanings further. A strategy of oscillation between both positions, in analogy to any critical approach, appears advisable for contemporary readers. It will then be possible to enjoy the novelty and playfulness of the language while keeping in mind

3 Actually, Riddley is his own original narratee: after all he writes down his story in order to keep track of his thinking.

the cautionary aspect, the "Orfing qwickness" (187), the melancholy or regressive but also life-prolonging tendency of the content. Moreover, I will attempt to oscillate between my own reading and that of other critics, for of all novels by Hoban, *Riddley Walker* is the one which has stimulated the greatest number of reviews, critical essays, and mentions in histories of postmodern literature or studies of nuclear fiction.

All contemporary readers have not enjoyed the wordplay. For the novel's language has also been interpreted as an unmistakable symptom of destruction and decay: "English, too, is in ruins" (DeMott 1), "There just don't seem enough words to describe exactly what has happened" (Butts 25), "It's presented in a degenerate kind of English" (Hoban and Haffenden 138), "a sort of Dark Age dialect, a rural punk pidgin speech of primitive people" (Thwaite, "Bad time and after", 28). But in fact it should astonish us how much Riddley can express, how many fine differentiations are possible, on how many registers from the philosophical down to the earthy he can actually draw. The English "in ruins" turns out to be still fairly complete at second glance, which is why I prefer to call it "Inland dialect". Have these critics simply mixed up the properties of signifier and signified? Did the post-apocalyptic setting of the novel shock them to such an extent that they automatically concluded Riddley's expressive powers to have become as impoverished as his surroundings? Matters might be more complicated.

What I have so far presented as a clear-cut dichotomy between intriguing language and cautionary content, in order to illustrate possible traps, must now be replaced by a more dialectical approach: in fact, language and content colour each other. On the one hand, there are stylistic features which clearly document the nuclear disaster and its consequences. We are, for instance, constantly made aware that Riddley cannot simply rely on a stock of well-defined concepts but must develop them while thinking about his situation. In my analysis of the language of *Riddley Walker* in chapter 6.1, I will try to combine linguistic description with evaluative interpretation in order to do justice to these intricacies.[4] The most substantial essay on the language of *Riddley Walker* to date is Jeffrey Porter's "'Three Quarks for Muster Mark': Quantum Wordplay and Nuclear Discourse in Russell Hoban's *Riddley Walker*" (1990). Porter focuses on the lexicon – certainly the most interesting linguistic level – interpreting alterations as a means of expressing criticism of high technology. But phonology, orthography, syntax and the ways in which Riddley uses his

4 Geoffrey N. Leech and Michael H. Short's "Checklist of Linguistic and Stylistic Categories" from *Style in Fiction* (1981) has been a useful tool for my analysis of Inland dialect.

language, i.e. the pragmatic aspect, lend themselves to interpretation, too.[5] A comparison with three other novels in which language is more than a medium in chapter 6.2 will, as I hope, shed further light on the special achievements of Inland dialect. On the other hand, sparks of innovation, hope and humour, which inform the dislocutionary language, illuminate the novel's content, too; aspects of plot and narrative structure will be examined in chapter 6.3, aspects of genre, setting, and character, in chapter 6.4.

6.1. "Words! Theywl move things..."

> "All of us here, however, definitely realize that a linguist deaf to the poetic function of language and a literary scholar indifferent to linguistic problems and unconversant with linguistic methods are equally flagrant anachronisms."
> (R. Jakobson, "Linguistics and Poetics", p. 377)

Riddley Walker is not the only text in which Russell Hoban has creatively remodelled language but the one in which the remodelling is most extensive. The use of dislocution as the structuring principle of *Kleinzeit* has already been discussed. Unconventional forms, however, from words to entire conversations, are also to be found in *The Mouse and his Child*, *The Lion of Boaz-Jachin and Jachin-Boaz*, *Turtle Diary*, *The Medusa Frequency*, *The Moment under the Moment*, and *Fremder*. They often serve to caricature characters,[1] but fulfil other functions as well. There is on the one hand a pure pleasure in the quality of sounds,[2] on the other, the desire to give expression to ideas for which there exist no words in Standard English.[3] Even in *Pilgermann* there is an example, when Pilgermann twists the religious invocation "Jesus Christ our Saviour" into the parodic exclamation "Jesus Christ how savoury", wondering "how eager those words [i.e. the invocation] are to be said" (PG 68); but otherwise this novel differs from the others since the intricacies of the

5 Examples of essays which examine aspects of orthography, syntax and of language use are Natalie Maynor and Richard F. Patteson's "Language as Protagonist in Russell Hoban's *Riddley Walker*" (1984), David Dowling's "Russell Hoban's *Riddley Walker*: Doing the Connections" (1988), and Marie Maclean's "The Signifier as Token: the Textual Riddles of Russell Hoban" (1988).

1 See for instance the psychiatrist's "tick-tock" language in *Lion* (177) and the oystercatchers' quarrel in *Turtle Diary* (18-19).

2 Cf. MUM, BB 184, where Hoban discusses the formulae for calling up dangerous beings that he has found in a Lovecraft novel. In *Fremder*, Caroline impresses Fremder by quoting a sentence in H. P. Lovecraft's invented language "Cthulhu-speak" (FR 39).

3 See the "footplacers", "London Transport owls" and "wincer-boise" in MUM, FP 214ff. Gösta Kraken's "Krakenspeak" (MF 107-108) combines all these functions; moreover it might be seen as a parody of the language of *Riddley Walker*.

religious texts explored here already cause plenty of interpretative problems. Further functions emerge in *Riddley Walker*.

Spelling and pronunciation have been brought closer together, which makes the reading of *Riddley Walker* awkward and slow at first. As experienced readers we are used to reading entire words; since many of them do not appear in their familiar shapes in *Riddley Walker*, we have to return to reading letter by letter like pupils learning the alphabet – an uncanny experience, as is everything that forces us to repeat patterns of behaviour or fall back on beliefs we regarded as overcome.[4] Uncanniness will soon make way for the joy of discovery when we realize that we are still able to develop adequate strategies. Often it is sufficient to read out loud what one cannot immediately understand. For example, one result of a process involving metathesis and syncope, "parbly" (1) becomes perfectly recognizable aurally as "probably". But this is not the only reminder of childhood. Maynor and Patteson point out that certain phonological differences between Standard English and Inland dialect imitate differences between the languages of adults and children in the early stages of language acquisition:

> Jill and Peter de Villiers list seven phonological processes common in young children. Six of these processes are recurrent in the language in *Riddley Walker*: (1) reduction of consonant clusters (*dint* for *didn't*, *hisper* for *whisper*), (2) deletion of final consonants (*leas* for *least*, *trubba* for *trouble*), (3) devoicing of final consonants (*behynt* for *behind*, *ternt* for *turned*), (4) substitution of stops for fricatives (*diffrents* for *difference*), (5) fronting of consonants (*teef* for *teeth*), (6) phonological assimilation (*minim* for *minute*). (Maynor and Patteson 21)

In many cases the new orthography would represent a step forward in spelling reform, since it does away with letters utterly superfluous (i.e. silent) in the old spelling, e.g. "cud", "tho", "littl", "tords" (*passim*). Apostrophes have disappeared, too, which, again, makes a difference for the eye but not the ear, e.g. in "aint" or "youve" (*passim*). But like certain forms which are already in current use, e.g. "nite" (*passim*), words spelt in these nonstandard short forms will inevitably be associated with the writing of children and uneducated people or the eye-catching slogans of advertisements. Numbers are not spelt out but appear as figures, even if they are parts of derivations: e.g. "14nt" for "fortnight" (196). It is due to such changes, I think, that Inland dialect tends to be described as an English "in ruins": rather than reflect an awareness of genuine losses, such descriptions reflect current attitudes towards deviations from the standard and, more generally, feelings of anxiety about changes.

4 See Sigmund Freud, "Das Unheimliche" (1919), p. 271.

Certain forms used by Riddley are archaic rather than simply ungrammatical by contemporary standards. The word "and", for instance, has been replaced by the ampersand, "&", wherever teams of two cooperate: e.g. in "Goodparley & Orfing" (27); "&" is used more frequently in the *Eusa Story* (28-34), which signals, in conjunction with other orthographic variations, an older stage of Inland dialect. Maynor and Patteson, too, think that the language contains "echoes of earlier stages of English: *childer* (children), *lorn* (forlorn), *afeart* (afraid)" (21). This can be seen, on the one hand, as a regression to a more "primitive" stage of the English language (see above, Thwaite's description); on the other, though, it shows that language often preserves the memory of a past its speakers can no longer remember.

The changes concerning phonology and orthography sketch out tendencies we will also encounter at other levels: changes bring on disorientation, helplessness, a sense of loss of what was familiar and appreciated, but they also revitalize our senses, challenge our creative abilities, and make us rethink evaluations.

Examining the lexicon, the inventory of words, hence of ideas and things known in Inland, allows us to specify further what has been lost or gained. At this level, dislocution is most effective. It is not only orthography but also morphology that has been subject to change, and cohesion is often involved as well: for instance, when the new spelling turns a simple word from Standard English into a group of words, e.g. "comping station" (11) for "compensation", or into a compound, e.g. "idear" (7), combining "dear" and "idea". Porter has coined the terms "fission" (456) and "contamination" (457) for these two processes. Maybe one could also call the second process "fusion": being a term from nuclear physics like "contamination", "fusion" nevertheless does not denote a negative process.[5] The changes bring to bear new connotations and associations which both reflect upon the original expression and create cross-references to the context. An example that is as significant as cynical is "spare the mending" (124) for "experimenting"; it suggests that too much experimenting with dangerous ingredients does not leave anything to mend, so one can spare oneself the trouble entirely. The new term is a proper dislocutionary starting point, for its associations also reflect on the setting of the novel: a world devastated by excess experimentation. Another term that combines a whole series of significant associations is "dyergam" (120) for "diagram". Goodparley uses it to refer to the wall painting, which he takes to *be*, not to represent, *The Legend of St Eustace*.[6] In "dyergam" the words "dye", "die" and

5 Connotations are a different matter, of course, but they affect fission and fusion alike.
6 There is a reproduction of the wall painting in *Riddley Walker*. Expanded Edition, p. 222.

"game" can be discerned. Thus it reaches out to the children's game *Fools Circel 9wys* (5) with its fatal consequences for the real Ardship of Cambry but it also recalls some other aspects of the novel, for example that it contains dyers and dy(e)ing (in all senses of the homophone) and that it is, for us, an intellectual game at deciphering or "dislocuting". Goodparley is quite right to say, "theres mor connexions nor wewl ever fynd reveals of" (123).

Folk-etymologizing like Riddley and Goodparley in chapter 14, we are as prone to error as they are since the only difference between the characters and us consists in their doing it backwards in time while we are trying to tune in to a fictive future. We may well laugh about *their* translation errors. After all, as Dennis Butts has recognized, "... this muddling confusion, this attempt to explain a historical event by using erroneous evidence, is one of Hoban's greatest jokes in the novel" (26). But at the same time it should be kept in mind that their errors and mistakes *tragically* lead to the rediscovery of gunpowder that was forgotten for years. This is a broad hint that interpretations are not necessarily reliable but nevertheless dangerous. We must more often call into question what we seem to know for sure. Or as Porter writes, "Clearly language knows things its users do not, as though it had a mind of its own" (461). Not even trying to explain incomprehensible expressions and phrases by means of considering the contexts in which they appear will exclude misinterpretations altogether. The word "Eusa", for instance, never clearly refers to one person or thing in our language. Goodparley connects Eusa with St Eustace (122), but we might as well connect the name with the USA or the former USSR, considering their global superiority at the time the novel was written: "Eusa wuz a noing man vere qwik he cud tern his han tu enne thing" (28). Also "you" and "us" can be heard in the name, and the notion that "EUSAS HEAD IS DREAMING" Riddley and his friends (58) points to us as the readers of fiction in whose heads pictures of the story unfold like dreams. Like Orph-*EUS*, Eusa was decapitated by an angry crowd (117). Eusa may also be connected with Jesus as in the exclamations "O Eusa" and "Eusas sake" (187). Moreover, Eusa's "circel of the towns" (205), imitated in the game *Fools Circel 9wys*, resembles the *Via Dolorosa*. But there are further associations offered by the text: If Eusa's head was a computer (91), Eusa could have been its user. Eusa is whoever connects things, (mis)understands them, is able to see relationships; there could be "you see" or "you say" in the word (206), for Eusa is also the one who passes his knowledge on to others. Eusa bears the responsibility for whatever happens, and the multiple choice of associations makes it impossible for us not to be addressed in one way or another.

Through "conversion between word classes" (Lake, "Riddley...", 97) the use of certain lexical items of our language has been broadened. So with regard to prepositions which are used as verbs: "... I over the fents and off with the dogs" (71). It is far from true that there are not enough words in this language to represent what happened before and after the catastrophe. Words we may miss in Inland dialect have often been replaced by telling and lively new coinages. "Arga warga" (72), the popular expression for "trouble" (besides the official term "Trubba", which is used in the ritual to welcome Eusa showmen, cf. 35) recalls the growling of dogs as well as the German word "Ärger"; it onomatopoeically represents what is meant. And from Lissener's simply phrased sentences, "Who run the Power Ring who ben too close to Power who gone Badstock crookit and seed of the crookit? Us the same the Eusa folk" (77), it becomes perfectly clear that he is speaking of genetic mutations among the offspring of computer specialists, the "Eusa folk", in consequence of radioactive contamination – people who have not enjoyed the benefits of a higher education may find my paraphrase, with its many Latinate terms, more difficult to understand than the Ardship's words. The critique thus implied is that there are too many – unintelligible or euphemistic – terms in our own time, rather than an insufficient number in Riddley's, which serve to hide such truths as the dangers inherent in the use of radioactive substances – our loss, their gain.

Certain items of the lexicon of Inland dialect cannot fail to have a strong emotional impact on the readers. It contains many expressions which are considered rude and informal in our time but not by Riddley's contemporaries, for instance, the expressions "pissing down rain" for "pouring with rain" (35) or "arse over head" for "head over heels" (102). All the same, there actually *are* slang expressions in Riddley's post-apocalypse dialect since there sometimes exist several expressions referring to the same thing: "mouth", for example, can be "mouf" (72) or "meat hoal" (62).

An even greater emotional appeal of the lexicon is founded in the drawing backwards of language, an idea we have come across earlier on (cf. ch. 4.3, the excerpt from George Steiner's *In Bluebeard's Castle*). Penelope Lively, too, has recognized this: "The ghostly presence of organized society and technology survives in the ... speech of these inhabitants of Inland" (Lively 58). The ghostly presence of our own time forces us to look into a mirror and see what we constantly risk losing. Riddley's language is an urgent warning to our address, or, as Benjamin DeMott writes:

> Riddley Walker is in part a book about voids and absences ...

> 'People crave to be kinder,' said Brecht correctly. But the consequence of craving for a kinder world can be blindness to – or contempt for – our existing moral and intellectual capital. Quietly and tellingly *Riddley Walker* chides such contempt... (25)

Like Orpheus, we start mourning for what is lost, although our having to look ahead like Eurydice (another association for "Eusa"?) will invariably bring on new losses. Such verbal ruins of our civilization can be found in words like "blipful" for "meaningful, symbolical" (13), or "pirntowt" for "sum" (93). The semantic shifts of all these terms have become possible because their original referents (e.g. printouts) have ceased to exist. There are no more mathematical formulas or computers to associate them with.

Many shifts add critical connotations to words, especially when technology and science are involved. See, for instance, my discussion of "spare the mending" earlier on. Porter has noticed that "a positive term from science or technology acquires an ethically negative sense by mutation. Through punning a neutral word is transformed into a dyslogistic one" (460). He borrows Kenneth Burke's term "perspective by incongruity" (from *Permanence and Change* and *Attitudes toward History*) to describe the effect of such shifts. Like Fritz Senn's term "dislocution", "'perspective by incongruity' [is] a mode of understanding wherein meanings usually pertaining to one context are transferred to another" (Porter 460). But whereas dislocution neutrally refers to incongruous textual cohesion, leaving the evaluation of its function to the reader's judgment, Burke is obviously interested in the moral dimension of the mode:

> As Burke explains, perspective by incongruity is a method for understanding matters by verbal 'atom cracking.' By splitting meanings from their customary usage, one frees them for application elsewhere. Because such a method is likely to bare semantic relationships our rational vocabulary necessarily ignores, ... it has the potential to reorder our customary categories. In this way, Burke concludes, perspective by incongruity can 'remoralize' a problem by 'accurately naming a situation already demoralized by inaccuracy' ... (Porter 460)

In the example "where theres Power theres foller" (101), the process of remoralizing can be observed at work: in the context in which the last word is used by Lissener, it means "followers"; but the saying might as well mean that where there is power, there is "folly". There are also cases of lexical dislocution which fulfil other than ethical functions, however. The semantic shift effected by the word "mynd" (7), for example, suggests that the ability to think about one's thinking, of saying "my mind", constitutes subjectivity: in a sense we find here a condensed form of the Cartesian "Cogito ergo sum".

However, this implication is meant ironically. For the sentence in which "mynd" has been placed, and its position within the narrative – Lorna has just told Riddley, that she feels inhabited by something larger than herself (6) – dispels illusions of ownership and control even where we think that we are most intimately at home, in the world of our "idears", that is in "our" minds:[7]

> Wel I cant say for cern no mor if I had any of them things in my mynd befor she tol me but ever since then it seams like they all ways ben there. Seams like I ben all ways thinking on that thing in us what thinks us but it dont think like us. Our woal life is a idear we dint think of nor we dont know what it is. What a way to live. (7)

The shift from "mind" to "mynd" therefore acts as a red herring, calling into question notions of epistemic autonomy, rather than as a means of remoralizing a term. Only thinking about the consequences of this lack of autonomy will bring on the issue of ethics, but not the semantic shift itself.

In summing up the results of his comparison of *Riddley Walker* and Walter M. Miller's *A Canticle for Leibowitz* David Dowling writes that the "worlds of both Miller and Hoban are worlds of fission not fusion" (*Fictions of Nuclear Disaster*, 208). Goodparley, on the other hand, strives for nothing but unity, fusion, synthesis: the recuperation of all that has been shattered, lost and injured: "... what evers in 2wl be come 1" (136) – even though he does not hide the fact that overcoming duality often implies killing one half of a pair: "'... The 2 of Granser and me be come jus only the 1 dinnit. You know how I partit from him? (...) I kilt him.'" (136). Examining the language of *Riddley Walker*, however, so far suggests an oscillation between fission and fusion as the governing principle of both Inland dialect and, by analogy, of Riddley's world. The reading process is a permanent zigzagging between the attempt to make sense and finding that sense undermined again, between taking notice of losses and inventorying additions and replacements.

With regard to syntax, deviations from Standard English are few and far between. Double, or even multiple negation, for example, has become common usage in Inland dialect: "Not to lern no body nothing I cant even lern my oan self..." (199). We may be shocked at such a development, but we must also acknowledge that the multiplication of negation markers reinforces the lack expressed, the absence of intention, the "No". Relative clauses have been replaced by other constructions. Otherwise, the duplicity of change is less

7 In Lacanian psychoanalysis, Riddley's insight would amount to a recognition of castration, the inscription of the Other in the subject: "The Other is the locus in which is situated the chain of the signifier that governs whatever may be made present of the subject – it is the field of that living being in which the subject has to appear" (Lacan, *The Four Fundamental Concepts of Psycho-Analysis*, 203).

obvious in the syntactic features of Riddley's language. Verbless sentences[8] (1), a tendency towards coordination (2) and parataxis (3) in more complex constructions are characteristic of his style, even though subordination (4) can be found as well:

> (1) Him on 1 end of the spear kicking his life out and me on the other end watching him dy. (1; in this example, the predicate is clearly lacking)
> (2 a) On my naming day when I come 12 I gone front spear *and kilt a wyld boar* he parbly ben the las wyld pig on the Bundel Downs any how there hadnt ben none for a long time befor him *nor I aint looking to see none agen.* (1; emphasis added; this example, the novel's first sentence, also illustrates Riddley's preference for parenthetical insertions, "he parbly ... Downs", instead of relative clauses, also see below, 4 c; the clause introduced by "when" is an example of subordination)
> (2 b) He done the reqwyrt he ternt and stood and clattert his teef and made his rush and there we wer then. (1; parataxis links the first clause to the following series of coordinated clauses; the absence of the colon is felt)
> (2 c) Its all 1 girt thing bigger nor the worl *and lorn and loan and oansome.* (6; emphasis added; coordination also links phrases, especially in appended structures such as the one in this example)
> (3 a) Coming back with the boar on a poal we come a long by the rivver *it wer hevvyer woodit in there.* (1; emphasis added to the clause which has the function of an adverbial clause but is juxtaposed with the main clause instead of being introduced by the adverb where)
> (3 b) There is the Hart of the Wud in the *Eusa Story* that wer a stag every 1 knows that. (2)
> (4 a) Wel I cant say for cern no mor *if I had any of them things in my mynd...* (7; emphasis added)
> (4 b) Ther leader he wer a big black and red spottit dog he come forit a littl *like he ben going to make a speach or some thing* til 1 or 2 bloaks uppit bow then he slumpt back agen and kep his farness follering us back. (1; emphasis added; the preposition "like" is used as a subordinating conjunction as it often is in informal English)
> (4 c) ... a danger thing *as cudnt be trappt* offers its self. (13; emphasis added; here we have one of the rare examples of a subordinating modal clause substituting for a relative clause)

These are mainly features of (informal) spoken language,[9] reminding us that Riddley lives in a culture where most people are illiterate. Moreover, Maynor and Patteson interpret certain syntactic features as imitations of child language:

> ... the syntax in *Riddley Walker* suggests that of a child going through the necessary experimentation in mastering sentence construction: case errors ('Dad and me we jus come off forage rota and back on jobbing that day,' 8), double negatives ('That dont mean nothing tho,' 8), tense errors ('When Dad

8 By "sentence" I mean the sequence of words between two periods (or equivalent punctuation marks, i.e. question mark or exclamation mark).

9 See for instance chapter 3 of John Stephens and Ruth Waterhouse's *Literature, Language and Change* (1990) for features of a speech-based syntax.

> ben a live I all ways ben there when he done the wotcher,' 38), grammatical conversions ('Arnge flames upping in the dark and liting all the faces roun,' 22). (21)

Considering that the sub-culture of children has always been oral, as Marie Maclean points out in her article "The Signifier as Token: The Textual Riddles of Russell Hoban" (213-215), and that Riddley is a twelve-year-old boy, there is no contradiction in Maynor and Patteson's and my own classification of certain features as children's respectively as speech-based language.

The length of sentences is the last syntactic feature I would like to focus on before concluding this chapter by a brief examination of the pragmatic level. For instead of an unpunctuated stream of words, or many simple sentences, we find a great number of clause clusters forming complex and compound sentences, or periodic sentences, which contain all types. Sentences (2 a), (3 b) and (4 b) above, for example, might be subdivided in at least three simple or complex sentences each, that is, main clauses with or without subordinated clauses. Is there a reason why Riddley has linked clauses in this way? It appears that themes organize the chains of clauses, which present individual aspects of one theme: in (2 a), for instance, the theme is the killing of the boar, and its clauses contain information about who did it, when, and why this was a special event. Sentence (4 b) circles around the leader of the dogs. The two sentences following (4 b) illustrate how Riddley begins a new sentence whenever a piece of information is sufficiently important to act as a new theme: "I took noatis of that leader tho" – Riddley continues to be aware of the leader while the other members of the group lose interest once they know that the dogs are at a safe distance; "He wernt close a nuff for me to see his eyes but I thot his eye ben on me" – here is another new theme: Riddley feels that he has been singled out by the leader, too. Incomplete sentences, on the other hand, can be interpreted as afterthoughts added to provide explanations for what is obvious only for Riddley or his friends, that is, he is prefiguring readers who might not share his presuppositions: "They give us ful days meat at Widders Dump and Reckman Bessup he wer ther connexion man he brung the comping station. *What we callit dead mans iron and he carrit on his back*" (11; emphasis added). Although these features create the impression of spontaneity, of an account that was written down as it came to Riddley's mind, the grouping of themes into what one might call "micro-paragraphs" within normal paragraphs facilitates the reading considerably. Given the fact that commas occur only after formulas introducing direct speech, and that semicolons are absent, Riddley's portioning of information qualifies him as a good narrator who knows where to place pauses and emphases.[10]

I would now like to turn to Riddley's use of the language. One of the things he is able to recognize and express is the dialectic tension between opposing forces that may bring on change. The principle occurs to him while he is kneeling in the old crypt of Canterbury Cathedral. Like mystic writers and philosophers before him, Riddley is about to find words for metaphysical concepts. The fact *that* he finds them at all is comforting, but centuries had to pass before this could take place:

> ... It come to me what it wer as made them peopl time back way back bettern us. It wer knowing how to put ther selfs with the Power of the wood be come stoan. The wood in the stoan and the stoan in the wood. The idear in the hart of every thing.
> ... If you cud even jus only put your self right with 1 stoan youwd be moving with the girt dants of the every thing the 1 Big 1 the Master Chaynjis. Then you myt have the res of it or not. The boats in the air or what ever. What ever you done wud be right.
> Them as made Canterbury musve put ther selfs right. Only it dint stay right did it. Somers in be twean them stoan trees and the Power Ring they musve put ther selfs wrong. Now we dint have the 1 nor the other. (...)
> ... From now on when I write down about the tree in the stoan Iwl write *wud* not wood. You see what Im saying its the hart of the wud its the hart of the wanting to be. (156-160)

Here, he defines the "would", the potential for good and evil that is to be found in everybody, every action, everything. "Putting oneself wrong" is choosing the more destructive possibility offered, that is *abusing* technological, personal, religious or political power. It is the choice which manifests somebody's death wish. Although the alternative, "putting oneself right", cannot stop the detrimental effect of time – after all, we are "living on burrow time" (110) – it at least provides conditions that make life easier, more enjoyable and as long as biologically possible.

Inland dialect is not only capable of expressing such insights but its prose is often poetical. At the beginning of chapter 2, for example, the first sentence

10 The comparison with Brian Aldiss's *Barefoot in the Head,* where the syntax gets altogether loose in the end, will bring this out very clearly. However, there were interpreters who nevertheless complained about the punctuation of *Riddley Walker*, e.g. David Lake: "In Riddley's convention, commas are used only before direct speech, colons only before lengthy quotations, and semicolons do not exist. The justification for these conventions must be that they mirror Present substandard usages; but since commas are used before speeches, could they not have been used elsewhere? Commas between sentences are an extremely familiar feature of substandard writing, as any teacher of freshman composition can attest every week. A comma, if not a period, between all sentences would have made *Riddley Walker* vastly easier to read" ("Making the Two One: Language and Mysticism in *Riddley Walker*", 163). Lake's analysis of the role of mysticism is definitely more illuminating than his comments on language and will be duly appreciated in ch. 6.4.

contains an interior rhyme, and the third is rhythmically structured in dactyls: "Walker is my name and I am the same. Riddley Walker. Walking my riddels where ever theyve took me and walking them now on this paper the same" (8) – using metric feet to describe someone called Walker is an ingenious little detail. Riddley's language is equal to the simple poetry of children's rhymes, folk tales and ballads (cf. chs. 1 and 2) as well as to the more advanced demands of the prose lyric that is used in the description of Bernt Arse, the dead town where Riddley finds Lissener:

> There we wer then in amongst the broakin stoans the grean rot and the number creaper with the rain all drenching down and peltering on them dead stoans stumps and stannings. Spattering on crumbelt conkreat and bustit birk and durdling in the puddls gurgling down the runnels of the dead town. (74)

Assonance and alliteration combined with an image of destruction add up to a vignette of expressionistic power.

Finally, I want to take a look at the forms of humour Riddley is able to convey. First of all, the Punch and Pooty shows must be mentioned (128-135, 209-213). Their humour is mostly crude and worlds apart from the sad and subtle humour of *Turtle Diary* and *The Lion of Boaz-Jachin and Jachin-Boaz* or even from what I called gallows humour in *Kleinzeit*. Greed, sexuality and cruelty are freely displayed by Punch, who is only weaker than the devil, not necessarily better:

> Punch says, '*What if you dont get your swossage back?*'
> Mr On the Levvil says, 'Iwl have my sumfing out of you then it dont make no odds to me.' (...)
> Mr On the Levvil hes wynding his self up for it he says, 'Ready for it and ramping for it and here I come.'
> '*And here it comes,*' says Punch. Which that iron sossage comes zizzing out of him and in to Mr On the Levvil. BANG! Flattens him dead. (...)
> 'Hooo,' says some 1 coming up then. Its a goast its got a skul face and all in wite. That skul has horns and a littl poynty beard. 'Hooo,' says the goast agen.
> '*Whos that*?' says Punch. He dont look easy at all. (...)
> The goast says, '... When you done for Mr On the Levvil you put me on to you. ...' (133-134)

At one moment during the performance, a pregnant woman superstitiously leaves the room to protect the baby in her womb from being "contaminated" by Punch's crookedness (209). Since everybody is not ready to accept or understand that there is a difference between reality and fiction, and that Punch's amorality is licensed by the figure's very artificiality, Riddley even experiences aggressive opposition from a member of the audience of his first Punch show before he can bring it to a purging close:

> No sooner does Punch get his hans on that babby nor in comes a big hairy han which it grabs Punch and my han inside Punch.
>
> Its Easyer he yels, 'You littl crookit barset I tol you not to try nothing here!' (213)

As the strain on Easyer's morals was too strong, he would not wait for the relief and laughter at Punch's punishment. In fact, his aggression must have been the direct result of his fear that the greedy wooden figure would never find a superior. Subtler forms of humour, which reveal the weaknesses of heroes and villains earlier, would prevent such misunderstandings right away. Yet, again, Riddley is only just rediscovering the subtleties of our own literature. His way is not at all harmless, for the dangers he incurs because everybody does not understand his intentions, may one day lead to a violent death.[11]

There actually is a subtler form of humour in the first Punch show, though, that is, a passage in which the Ardship of Cambry's title is parodied, which of course undermines the authority of the title-bearer: "Mr Clevver says, 'I myt be the Pry Mincer of Binland and I myt be the Hard Bitchup of Cantser Belly only I aint...'" (133). Outside the Punch shows, the forms of humour are less crude, too. Genuine gallows humour is apparent in Riddley's remark about stealing a watchman's weapons at Bernt Arse: "He bint too big a man I cud use his bow wel a nuff. I took his knife as wel I emtit his pockits too I thot I myt as wel hang for a ram as a lam" (73).

Considering all the achievements and important functions of Inland dialect, it is a splendid understatement of Hoban to say, "I had no idea that the language was going to be such a big thing ... for the readers" (Hoban and Myers 14). At any rate, about fourteen drafts were necessary until Hoban, who had never had any philological training or consulted linguists, found the form that satisfied the requirements of his material:

> ... the first version began in straight English and went on to page 500. I didn't theorize about it, but as I worked it obstinately insisted on moving out of straight English into a corrupted English. Now that I think of it, I don't see how it could have been conceived otherwise. Language is an archaeological vehicle, full of the remnants of dead and living pasts, lost and buried civilizations and technologies. The language we speak is a whole palimpsest

---

11 A danger even contemporary writers are exposed to: since the publication of his *Satanic Verses* in 1988, Salman Rushdie has had to face being killed by Iranian fanatics. Although the Iranian president revoked the official death sentence in September 1998, Rushdie will have to continue being cautious. The tragic irony of his situation is all the more pungent because Rushdie is quite aware of an author's responsibility for the effects of his art, as the analysis of his earlier novel *Midnight's Children* in chs. 8.4 and 11.2 will show.

> of human effort and history. The language of the debased and degraded future that Riddley lives in is bound to be full of uncomprehended remnants of what we have today; to have written that novel in received English would have been ridiculous. One thing I thought it would do would be to slow the reader down to Riddley's pace of intake; the reader would have to plod through word by word and take things in along with Riddley. (Hoban and Haffenden 138)

It indeed does slow the reading down, but, as Riddley's last words go, "Stil I wunt have no other track" (214).

6.2. Foregrounded Language: A Comparative Analysis

It will now be useful to have a look at three other novels in which language is, in Halliday's term, "foregrounded": "Foregrounding, as I understand it, is prominence that is motivated ... ; a feature that is brought into prominence will be 'foregrounded' only if it relates to the meaning of the text as a whole" (334). Geoffrey N. Leech and Michael H. Short have complemented this definition by pointing out that texts with foregrounded linguistic features are usually "opaque": Such "prose is opaque in the sense that the medium attracts attention in its own right; and indeed, the interpretation of sense may be frustrated and obstructed by abnormalities in the use of the lexical and grammatical features of the medium" (29). But this is no drawback since, as we have seen, the readers' fascination with texts of this kind grows with the degree to which they have to participate in discovering and interpreting meanings conveyed by foregrounded elements. Earlier on, cf. chs. 4.1 and 4.2, dislocution was shown to have the same effect. This is by no means coincidental for dislocution, as might now be said, is also a manner of foregrounding aspects of a text, more precisely, of foregrounding textual cohesion by the very incongruity of cross-references, and intertextuality by the differences between an text and its "distant echoes".

The use of foregrounded elements in literary texts may be restricted to a few unusual lexical items: they may have been borrowed from another language than English, e.g. from Russian in Burgess's *A Clockwork Orange* (1962), see below; Kurt Vonnegut, Jr., on the other hand, uses words from a mock-Caribbean dialect in *Cat's Cradle* (1963). Various motivations inform the use of such terms. Vonnegut, for instance, tries to get away from preconceived moral notions. Thus, "foma", a central term in the pseudo-religion "Bokononism", stands for the "harmless untruths" that can "make you brave and kind and healthy and happy" (6). This word is not burdened with the negative connotations of "lie", which is usually associated with moral corruption rather than humane traits. Once Vonnegut's readers have understood the value of things that may be subsumed by "foma", e.g. life-affirming fiction, or religion that abstains from dogmatizing, he can go on to caricature the dangerous positivism of truth-seeking scientists whose lack of imagination, the source of "foma", on the one hand forces them to play around with real substances instead of ideas and, on the other, prevents them from foreseeing the havoc that may be wrought by their inventions. In certain science fiction novels, e.g. Samuel R. Delany's *Babel-17* (1966) or Ursula Le Guin's *The Left Hand of Darkness* (1969), words from invented "extraterrestrial" languages, or the absence in these languages of words which we would consider indispensable ("I" and "you" in *Babel-17*, or "male" and "female" in *The Left Hand of Darkness*), depict unfamiliar forms of being and thinking. The protagonists must take pains to familiarize themselves with the idioms of the extraterrestrials they meet because they are unable to cope with problems arising from such encounters as long as they do not understand the ideas that have been shaped by their opponents' languages.

ANTHONY BURGESS: *A CLOCKWORK ORANGE*

The foregrounded terms in Burgess's *A Clockwork Orange* serve to distance readers from what is familiar rather than to present new ideas or ways of being; in this respect they resemble the foregrounded elements in *Cat's Cradle, Kleinzeit* and *Riddley Walker*. Unlike the languages of Vonnegut's and Hoban's novels, however, language in *A Clockwork Orange* does not lend itself to aesthetic play so much as it seeks to illuminate its functions in society and in the groups constituting society.

Alex's "nadsat-talk" (87) is only one type of jargon that we encounter in the novel. In its own self-referential way the novel keeps reminding us that wherever there is a group of people who define themselves as a group, they will share a language; in *A Clockwork Orange,* this merely implies a specific vocabulary: an old cell-mate of Alex's speaks "all this very old-time real criminal's slang" (68), and the girls whom Alex seduces use "'Swoony' and 'Hilly' and other weird slovos that were the heighth of fashion in that youth group" (38), as Alex lets us know, seemingly unaware of the weirdness of expressions of his own such as "heighth" or "slovos".

Because the Prison Chaplain is aware that he may not be understood by Alex, he asks: "'Do I make myself clear?' He didn't, brothers, but I nodded that he did" (76). In this example, we are alerted to another function of language: while it unites members of a group, it also fences off outsiders. Alex falls back upon a lie when answering because he is wary of setting up a barrier between himself and the man whose trust he was so eager to win. But by failing to ask for an explanation he also precludes himself from fully understanding his situation and from overcoming the limitations of his thinking. Thus, he is unlikely to grasp the importance of the question that the Chaplain goes on to ask him: "'... Is a man who chooses the bad perhaps in some way better than a man who has the good imposed upon him? ...'" (76).

Language may be used as a weapon, for propagandistic purposes as by the government and members of the opposition, or as a means of creating distance and establishing one's personal superiority. Alex, lusting after the nurse when he comes to in hospital, cannot help noticing her defensive use of language:

> But this nurse like jumped and dropped her book on the floor and said:
> 'Oh, you've recovered consciousness.'
> That was like a big rotful for a malenky ptitsa like her... (133)

Opponents are defeated once they have been silenced. Thus, the prisoners are silenced by the Prison Chaplain and the warders (63), Dr Branom by Dr Bronsky (91), the Prison Chaplain by the Governor (100), and F. Alexander by his political friends (128) as well as by the "Intinfmin" (138). Alex is prevented from speaking up by all of them up to the penultimate chapter, when it is the Minister who has to ingratiate himself with *him* in order to save his skin. Because the Minister needs him, Alex may even insult him with impunity in his own vernacular: "'Yarbles,' I said, like snarling like a doggie. 'Bolshy great yarblockos to thee and thine.'" (138).

The ingredients of "nadsat" are analyzed by clever Dr Branom: "'Odd bits of old rhyming slang.... A bit of gipsy talk, too. But most of the roots are Slav. Propaganda. Subliminal penetration" (91). A modern sociolinguist would agree with his analysis but not his interpretation. Speakers are not merely passive victims of propaganda. Whether or not they speak the standard language as defined by the mainstream culture in a society or one of the nonstandard varieties depends on their social ambition:

> Labov first introduced the notion of covert prestige by pointing out that while even speakers who use high proportions of stigmatised linguistic forms ... will tell you (and believe) that such forms are 'bad' and 'inferior', we have to suppose that at some level they *want* to use them. ... This, then, is prestige in the sense of being favourably regarded by one's peers, and of signalling one's identity as a member of a group. (Chambers and Trudgill 99)

If we recall Alex's avowed allegiance to "the other shop" (34) and remember that the novel was written in the early 1960s, at the peak of the Cold War, we may be tempted to seek an ideological answer to the question why most loan words in "nadsat" are of Russian origin. David Cowart interprets this fact as a "vague suggestion ... that communist influence will wax strong on the British working class" (77). Burgess's own explanation, however, quoted in Coale, shows that his protagonist had better be regarded as the representative of a broader phenomenon:

> I went to Leningrad and discovered that they had these *stiljagi* there, they had teenage riots and gangs, cult of violence, so it struck me that if I could combine East and West in a single persona, teenage person, it should be appropriate to use a composite dialect that is Russian and English.... (88-89)

By using Russian expressions as well as English (pseudo-)archaisms such as "betokeneth" (13) and rhyming slang, "appy polly loggies to thee or thine" (10), Alex signals his unwillingness to conform to mainstream culture and its language.

Like Riddley Walker's vernacular, Alex's is set against a small number of passages of Standard English. Unlike Hoban, however, Burgess is not primarily interested in exploring the consequences of misunderstandings between the speakers of different varieties but, above all, in exposing the hollowness and hypocrisy of certain expressions, mostly of high affective value, in either tongue. Thus, when he is arrested, Alex recognizes how little his "droogs" are worth (53f.). A "friend" is no better, though, if this is the proper word for addressing somebody one is going to drive into suicide in the name of "Liberty", the "Future", and a "Cause" (128f.), as F. Alexander's political friends do: "We have you, friend, and we keep you" (129). Being "sane" and "healthy" (86) becomes a questionable aim too if it can only be achieved through brainwashing, here "Deep hypnopaedia" (137). Most of Alex's "helpers" clothe their selfish aims in euphemisms of this kind, whether Deltoid offers to save him from himself (33), the Prison Chaplain explains to him why he cannot protest on his behalf (76), or the Government prides itself on having "cured" Alex of his "criminal instincts in a fortnight only" (104). Though their language and their ways of life may be more sophisticated than Alex's, they resemble him and his "droogs" in one point: "Power, power, everybody like wants power" (143). As a matter of fact, Alex would be able to use Standard English if he wanted to, as his conversation with Deltoid early in the novel illustrates. He is capable of such sentences as "'To what do I owe the extreme pleasure? Is anything wrong, sir?'" (32). But they are so extremely stilted that Deltoid cannot overlook their implied sarcasm; he grows "very weary" when "nadsat" seems to sneak into Alex's utterances as if of its own: "'I've been doing nothing I shouldn't, sir,' I said. 'The millicents have nothing on me, brother, sir I mean.'" (33). It is quite obvious that Alex *prefers* to cling to his own brand of badness and to the language associated with it.

Alex's continued preference for "nadsat" up until the end of the novel might give us a clue for the interpretation of what looks, at first glance, like the onset of a genuine reform: he is probably the only one who believes that, with the last chapter of the novel, "a new like chapter" is beginning (148). Burgess even agreed to an omission of this chapter in the Norton edition of *A Clockwork Orange* though he admitted in an interview with Charles T. Bunning that Alex "turned out in the American edition to be a mere clockwork figure, I suppose, who's just impelled towards evil by some deterministic force, which is not what I intended at all" (quoted in Coale 98). In the last chapter, we are once more invited, however implicitly, to locate the source of evil in our Humble Narrator as we are witnessing Alex's last act of washing himself free from guilt and responsibility for the atrocious deeds he committed in his former life:

> But youth is only being in a way like it might be an animal. No, it is not just like being an animal so much as being like one of these malenky toys you viddy being sold in the streets, like little chellovecks made out of tin and with a spring inside and then a winding handle on the outside and you wind it up grrrr grrrr grrr and off it itties, like walking, O my brothers. But it itties in a straight line and bangs straight into things bang bang and it cannot help what it is doing. Being young is like being like one of these malenky machines. (148)

He rightly recognizes that what he believed to be his own way of asserting individuality was just another clockwork aping of conventions, those of an underground culture with its own set of adamant rules regarding fashion and language. But he is completely mistaken if not altogether insincere to present this way of life including its violence as an indispensable ingredient of youth, as something that cannot be helped but must be suffered just like a children's disease. "Nadsat" helps him to deceive us, his "brothers," for there appears to be no word for personal responsibiliy; he need not worry about blaming himself for what "happened" to him. In Standard English, there would be no way to dodge responsibility; but early in the novel, he derided those writers of articles on "Modern Youth" who would lay the blame on teachers, parents, or "THE DEVIL THAT WAS ABROAD" (35) and thus made it plain that he was aware of his own role. Moreover, unlike Riddley Walker, Alex hardly ever demonstrates that, like every language, his vernacular has a creative potential; one of the exceptions is the scene when he disrespectfully and step by step deflates the "Minister of the Interior or Inferior" to the "Min" (138). But for the greater part of the novel readers are exposed to an almost endless repetition of the same few dozen terms: "droog, veck, ptitsa, tolchock, slooshy, viddy, and all that cal..." (*passim*). And, as Coale points out: "Nadsat ... is a language of objects: its vocabulary, like that of most slang, consists of words for concrete and physical things or actions, rather than abstract ideas or thoughts" (89).

By making no real effort to expand his limited vocabulary and, hence, his view of the world, Alex *chooses* to imprison himself and remain a "clockwork orange" for good: "And so it would itty on to like the end of the world, round and round and round, like some bolshy gigantic like chelloveck, like old Bog Himself ... turning and turning and turning a vonny grahzny orange in his gigantic rookers" (148). This view of the human condition is by no means valid, nor is it his own: Alex has borrowed it from the naive writer F. Alexander, who is, as we know, just "another Alex" (124).

While containing Alex's report of his increased boredom with violence, the last chapter ironically undermines our belief that there will be a change for the better. When he once corrects one of his stereotype "nadsat" phrases, it is only to substitute a Standard English stereotype for it: "At eighteen old Wolfgang Amadeus had written concertos and symphonies and operas and oratorios and all that cal, no, not cal, heavenly music" (147). He fails to see that what is special about the juvenile geniuses to whom he is comparing himself here and in subsequent sentences, Mozart, Rimbaud, and Mendelssohn, is not their early accomplishment but their successful search for an idiosyncratic form of expression. It is indeed no deterministic force which impels Alex first towards evil, later towards the bland conventionality of his parents and Pete, but his own stubborn refusal, or maybe simply his being too lazy, to find a voice and make choices of his own.

WILLIAM GOLDING: *THE INHERITORS*

Whereas the foregrounding of lexical items can be found fairly frequently, other levels of language such as orthography, morphology, syntax or textual cohesion are less often affected. This may be one of the reasons why works such as Joyce's novels *Ulysses* and *Finnegans Wake,* Faulkner's *The Sound and the Fury,* or Pynchon's *Gravity's Rainbow,* to name just a few, are so disturbing yet unforgettable. In *Riddley Walker,* as we have seen, it is foregrounded orthography and a lexicon of high dislocutionary potential besides a few examples of non-standard syntax which most effectively bring out the underlying theme of the comfort and loss inherent in change. Since here, as in the examples of lexical foregrounding discussed above, foregrounding is mainly achieved by means of *deviation* from the norm of Standard English, it is comparatively easy to point to.

In the case of William Golding's *The Inheritors* (1955), however, language is not deviant and yet opaque; we are alerted to its importance by references to the status of communication and silence with the Neanderthals:

> One of the deep silences fell on them, that seemed so much more natural than speech, a timeless silence in which there were at first many minds in the overhang; and then perhaps no mind at all. (34)

> Now the thing was settled the people became restless. They knew in their bodies that something was wrong, yet the word had been said. When the word had been said it was as though the action was already alive in performance and they worried. (37)

Three different points of view can be distinguished in *The Inheritors*: Lok's, Tuami's and that of the implied author in the passage of narration at the end of chapter 11.[1] A juxtaposition of terms referring to members of the Neanderthal tribe will show this: in section 1 (11-216) , they are always referred to by their first names, personal pronouns or "the people"; in section 2 (216-222), "the red creature" and the *neuter* pronoun "it" make us painfully aware that our connexion with Lok, through whose mind most of the previous events were filtered, has been broken; in section 3 (223-233), finally, they are referred to by personal pronouns such as "they" or "he", or by the epithets "the forest devils" (224), "the little devil" (229), or "the devil brat" (231). The term "people" no longer refers to the Neanderthals but to the inheritors (223). Textual ruptures thus manifest themselves which might be interpreted in the light of the novel's outcome: continuity is no longer possible for the Neanderthals after the invasion of Homo sapiens. The incision is so momentous that there cannot be continuity in the text either: a new style is required to convey the outlook of the winners in the evolutionary struggle.

Yet, looking merely at the lexicon provides insufficient explanation for the peculiar emotional impact of section 1. The two linguists M. A. K. Halliday (systemic grammar) and David A. Lee (transformational generative grammar) therefore applied the tools of their respective disciplines to syntax and thus came to a number of interesting conclusions.[2] Halliday prepared the ground by dissociating foregrounding from deviation: "... syntax need not be deviant in order to serve a vision of things; a foregrounded selection of

1 Strictly speaking, the latter section contains *nobody's* point of view; features of subjectivity are not to be found in the text. Howard S. Babb therefore speaks of the "cultivated impersonality of Golding's account" (54) at this stage.

2 N.B. Halliday restricted his analysis to a corpus consisting of three excerpts: A, pp. 106-107, from "The bushes..." to "'I am coming!'"; B, pp. 215-217, (i) from "Lok staggered..." to "dropped over the fall", and (ii) from "The red creature..." to "under its chinless mouth"; C, pp. 228-229, from "The sail..." to "over water". Lee's sample sentences have been selected from the entire novel.

everyday syntactic options may be just as visionary, and perhaps more effective" (340). Analysing the passage in chapter 5 when Lok is watching the new people Halliday writes:

> It is particularly the lack of transitive clauses of action with human subjects ... that creates an atmosphere of ineffectual activity: the scene is one of constant movement, but movement which is as much inanimate as human and in which only the mover is affected, nothing else changes. (344-345)

This observation is significant for, as he explains further down:

> Transitivity is really the cornerstone of the semantic organization of experience; and it is at one level what *The Inheritors* is about. ... man's interpretation of his experience of the world, his understanding of its processes and of his own participation in them. (354)

Lee supplements a set of syntactic features that equally contribute to the shaping of the Neanderthals' vision of the world (cf. Lee 91): (i) natural objects are used as subjects of verbs of movement and volition, e.g. in the sentence "The cliff leaned out as if looking for its own feet" (Golding 25); (ii) parts of the body are subjects of verbs which normally require animate subjects, e.g. in the sentence "Lok's ears spoke to Lok" (104); (iii) pronominalization is used less frequently than in the final section, e.g. in sequences such as "*The man* had white bone things above his eyes ... *The man* turned ..." (106; emphasis added); (iv) deletion also occurs less often, e.g. in the sequence "Then suddenly Lok reappeared. *He* shot forward, head down. *He* flashed across the log with a tremendous shout. *He* leapt ..." (20; emphasis added) instead of "He shot forward..., flashed across the log..., and leapt."; (v) the average sentence is simple; (vi) repetition is frequent; (vii) there is a "curious use of progressive aspect in certain contexts" (Lee 91);[3] (viii) if conjunction occurs, there often seems to be no obvious logic at work, e.g. in the sentence "A stick rose upright *and* there was a lump of bone in the middle" (Golding 106; emphasis added); (ix) stative verbs are used to describe events, e.g. "was gone" instead of "disappeared" in "Then suddenly she was writhing

3 Lee examines the scene of the inheritors' escape on p. 216 and comments: "The effect of a series of simple pasts ... is that of a smoothly running film where each event leads into the next one without any unexplained gaps. The impression is one of an ordered universe where everything fits together. I suggest, however, that when we have a series of progressives [as on p. 216] the effect is rather that of a badly edited piece of film where we flick from one event that 'is happening' to another, then to another, without any information about the connection between them" (88).

herself round the corner and was gone" (99). According to Lee, features (i), (vii), (viii) and (ix) account for "a certain disjointedness or dislocation of experience" and consequently confirm Halliday's earlier analysis (91). Moreover, Lee provides an interesting interpretation of features (iii), (iv), (v), and (vi): these reveal a language close to deep structure, which ultimately implies that

> ... [Golding] has adopted a language whose syntactic character evokes, in the reader's subconscious mind, the world of the child. (...) If, then, the hypothesis developed here has any validity whatsoever, I suggest that it provides at least a partial explanation for the powerful impact of the work. (93)

When discussing passage B, pages 215-217, Halliday does not take into account the threefold change of perspective upon which my segmentation of the novel has been based. His choice of excerpts is founded on the assumption that the book consists of two distinct parts with distinct languages and a transitional area between them. My sections therefore do not correspond exactly with his excerpts: A is part of section 1, B (i) forms the end of this section; B (ii) is the beginning of section 2; and C is part of section 3. I think it is important to notice the two ruptures the text presents when Lok's perspective (section 1) is replaced by an impersonal perspective (section 2) and the latter eventually makes way for the perspective of the inheritors (section 3). It is not difficult to find reasons why Golding might have interposed an impersonal perspective, located both outside Lok and the inheritors, between sections 1 and 3: to avoid a direct confrontation of Lok's and Tuami's perspectives; to eschew the sentimentality that might have resulted from representing the last thoughts and impressions of the desperate and lonely Lok; maybe to by-pass representing the last moments of a dying being because that was to be the theme of *Pincher Martin*, Golding's subsequent novel; certainly to enforce the fact that we have no choice but to identify with the inheritors in section 3: the pitiless impersonal point of view of section 2 is stranger than Lok's ever was and harder to bear, in the long run, than the "familiar" point of view of the inheritors. Rather than to examine the ruptures, though, Halliday underlines the mediating function of the languages of B: "the first paragraph [B (i)] is basically in Language A and the second [B (ii)] in Language C" (349). While it is no surprise that B (i) and A share the same language, the information that B(i) "does provide some hints of the change to come" (349) indicates what must be interpreted as an increase in Lok's perceptive abilities:

> There are a few instances ... of a human 'agent' (actor in a transitive clause); not many, but one of them is Lok, in *Lok ... picked up Tanakil*. Here is Lok acting on his environment, and the object 'affected' is a human being, and one of the tribe! There are some non-spatial adjuncts, such as *with an agonized squealing*.... There are abstract nominal [sic]: *demoniac activity, its weight of branches*. And there are perhaps more modifiers and complex verb forms than usual. None of these features is occurring for the first time; we have had forward-looking flashes throughout ... But there is a greater concentration of them in B(i), a linguistic complexity that is also in harmony with the increased complexity of the events, which has been being built up ever since the tribe first impinged on the people with the mysterious disappearance of Ha.... (349-350)

Glimpses at passages outside Halliday's samples show that this development is not continuous and linear but subject to phases of progression as well as regression. Usually, new responsibilities increase Lok's understanding of the world; he discovers the inheritors' ambivalent attractiveness after Fa has disappeared. At that moment he shows greater sensibility and does them more justice than they will ever be able to do him:

> 'Now I am Mal.'
>
> All at once it seemed to him that his head was new, as though a sheaf of pictures lay there to be sorted when he would. ... They showed the solitary string of life that bound him to Liku and the new one; they showed the new people towards whom both outside- and inside-Lok yearned with a terrified love, as creatures who would kill him if they could. (191)

Intoxication and fear as well as Fa's reappearance, on the other hand, limit his understanding; Mal goes "out of his head" again (206).

Differences between individual characters – a specific literary concern – are only occasionally hinted at in the articles of the two linguists, e.g. when Halliday points out that Fa is more intelligent than Lok (Halliday 350), or when Lee quotes a few examples of the direct speech of other characters to underline features he has previously found in passages whose center of consciousness is Lok (cf. Lee 90, 93, 95). This, no doubt, deliberate "neglect" is due to their method of choosing samples which mainly contain representations of Lok's consciousness, with hardly any examples of direct speech. I will therefore try to supplement their analyses by presenting a couple of observations I made while examining and comparing examples of direct speech.

The first of these concerns the amount of direct speech granted to the characters: more than 330 utterances (exclamations such as "Ai!" have been counted individually) are produced by Lok, over 240 by Fa, around 70 by Nil and Mal, 30 by Liku and 26 by Ha. The inheritors' utterances are far more restricted. For when they are described in section 1, the perspective is Lok's, to whom their dialogues make no sense, and section 3, which represents their perspective, is very brief: whereas Vivani speaks but once, Vakiti (Tuft), Tuami, Marlan, Tanakil and Twal are to be heard up to nine times. Their utterances are hardly any more complex than those of the people, which contradicts expectations and shows how close they still are to the Neanderthal group despite the obvious differences between them. Significantly, Liku's and Tanakil's last quoted words are each other's names: up to the end each of them is desperately trying to establish communication with the other (157, 232). Liku's utterances are of course quite simple because she is a little girl. Most of them are related to food or pleasure. One sentence, however, shows her aware of her ability to act and achieve certain things. When they have returned from foraging, she proudly lets Mal know: "I have frightened the beaks away, Mal" (58). The combination of a transitive verb of action with a human subject is, as Halliday has shown, uncommon for one of the people. This could be another hint that, given the time and the proper stimuli to learn, the Neanderthals might well have acquired the ability to cope with the inheritors if their number had not been so small from the outset.

Yet, some of the inheritors' utterances would be inconceivable with the people. The one time Vivani speaks, for example, she says: "My breasts are paining me" (228). For the people there is no need to *talk* about pain since their sympathy for each other is so deep that they are, in the literal sense of "sympathy", able to share pain. See e.g. the episode when they follow Mal, imitating the movements caused by his weakness (22f.). There are also words peculiar to the life of the inheritors which do not occur in any of the people's utterances: "hunting" (228), because they cannot kill any living creatures; "master" (229), because the relations within the Neanderthal group are based on affection and "natural" filial respect rather than on abstract forms of power and pressure; "devils" (229), finally, because the people do not know malice, hence feel no need to project their own shadow onto a supernatural being.

Like the inheritors, on the other hand, the people *are* able to build if-clauses, which contradicts Lee's absolute claim that "Ifs ... are lacking in Lok's world" (90).[4] The Neanderthals are just discovering the usefulness of

4 It is interesting to notice that there is not one occurrence of "if", or of "because", in section 2, though: reasoning and making hypotheses would be inappropriate in a context where we are bound to the *impersonal* perspective of the implied author, or of nobody but indifferent nature. There is in fact only one coordinating causal conjunction in the following sentence: "There was no noise at all now except for the fall, *for* there was no wind and the green sky was clear" (216-217, emphasis added). In nature, there are no reasons for noises greater than those of the fall except meteorological ones. A water rat's perspective for a brief paragraph replaces the impersonal perspective: "The water rat concluded from the creature's stillness that it was

hypotheses though they often have difficulty in expressing what is not yet real. Conditional clauses can be found both for Lok (49) and Fa (49, 69, 133); for the latter, as is no surprise, in a greater number. Moreover, there are a few examples of conditional verb-forms in their utterances, e.g. in Mal's penultimate order: "Do not open my head and my bones. You would only taste weakness" (87).

With regard to the ways in which the Neanderthal people refer to themselves and their interlocutors, Lee's analysis calls for some modification and differentiation, too. Lee only considers a small number of self-references in the third person to corroborate further evidence for his thesis that the language of the people resembles child language (95). I think, however, that it is indispensable to distinguish between those instances in which they appear to be unable to apply the "proper words", i.e. "I" and "you", to refer to themselves and their interlocutors, and those in which they use third-person forms to patronize their interlocutors. Thus, in direct opposition to Lee's thesis, the child Liku always – except once – correctly refers to herself as "I"; talking to the insolent "beaks", however, she uses her own name: "Go away, beaks! This is *Liku's* meat!" (55; emphasis added). It is mostly when talking about the past or the (virtual) future, for which they have no particular tenses, that the people refer to themselves by their proper names. In order to mark the temporal distance they "disconnect" themselves from their present being; see e.g. Mal recalling a childhood memory (15), or Lok's fantasy of finding food for his hungry family: "'*I* have a picture of *Lok* finding a tree with ears that grow thickly –'" (24; emphasis added). Fa, on the other hand, takes recourse to her and Lok's proper names whenever she wants to establish her superiority over Lok; she talks to Lok as if *he* were a child:

> She came back and looked down at him. He got up carefully.
> 'Fa says "Do this!"'
> He waited obediently. Mal had gone out of his head.
> 'Here is a picture. Lok goes up the path by the cliff where the people cannot see him. Fa goes round and climbs to the mountain above the people. ...' (206-207)

Lok is the main character in the novel, as is apparent from the predominance of his perspective and the number of his utterances in direct speech. Yet Fa's greater intelligence emerges from her actions and the quality of her utterances. She uses the causal interrogative "Why?" (27) and wants to know

---

not dangerous. It came with a quick rush from under the bush and began to cross the open space, it forgot the silent figure and searched busily for something to eat" (220).

the reason for things long before Lok does: "Must Liku come with us because Mal said so?", she says as early as p. 46. Lok's only "Why?" in direct speech is to be found on p. 99, when he is asking Fa why she is shivering. She is generally more sceptical than he is; as they find some honey, Lok rejoices but analytical Fa counters his optimism: "This is old honey from the time when we went down to the sea..." (51). Lok apparently learns to think about certain ideas from Fa, thus his question "How will you feed him [Nil's baby]?" (163), takes up a question asked by her earlier on: "How will they [the inheritors] feed the new one without milk?" (131). The same is true for Lok's usage of the preposition "like": he first echoes Fa's sentence from p. 46, "To-day is like yesterday and to-morrow" (47), then uses the word several times without being aware of it (49, 95, 97, 120) before he consciously "discovers" it as an analytical tool: "Now, in a convulsion of the understanding, Lok found himself using likeness as a tool as surely as ever he had used a stone to hack at sticks or meat" (194). The most interesting detail about this passage is no doubt the comparison of language to tools for hacking: language cuts the world and its phenomenons apart (there may be an allusion to the etymology of "analysis", i.e. a "dissolving", cf. *Collins Dictionary*) – this brings to mind Goodparley's well-meant warning about the danger inherent in words (cf. RW 118). We can often listen to Fa groping for words to say "new things" (62-63, 49), but as with Lok, confusion impairs her command of language and cohesion gets lost: "When you went down the rock. I am climbing the rocks because I am frightened. Men came to the overhang" (112).

A devaluation of the word goes along with a greater range of expressive ability. Whereas for Mal and the old woman words are sacred and must by all means be obeyed since they are as good as reality, both Fa and Lok know that they have an existence independent of reality, that is, they allow a speaker to make assumptions: "Perhaps Ha is not in the river. Perhaps he is on the island with the other. Ha was a mighty jumper" (96). When Lok becomes too chatty, however, the old woman aggressively stops him: "The old woman would not interrupt him. She seized a great bough instead and hurled it into the fire. Lok sprang to his feet with a cry, and then was silent" (96). Fa is aware that it may be of use to withhold certain information: "Do not tell the old woman that you have seen the ice women" (97). Yet, unfortunately, it is her very concealing the truth of Liku's death from Lok so as to spare him that will bring on their disaster in the end. Had he been told, he would not have spoilt her clever plan for rescuing the baby, and they might have escaped after all (206ff.). As in *Riddley Walker,* new skills and inventions, in this case the calculated, or "diplomatic", use of language and silence turn out to have a useful as well as a harmful sides.

Mal and the old woman as the oldest couple of the Neanderthal tribe are not only aware of the sacredness of words, they also tend to a rigid differentiation of language use between the sexes. It is remarkable, for instance, that the old woman has no proper name while the other females do have one, and she never but once refers to herself by a first-person pronoun; this is after Ha has disappeared: "... There is no hope in Mal. Therefore let *me* speak." (70; emphasis mine). She only asserts her self and begins to give orders when Mal is dying and Lok appears to be unable to lead the group. Fa's suggestions, on the other hand, are repeatedly discounted by her:

> Fa began to talk eagerly. Nil was sniffing noisily and listening.
> 'If there is another then Ha has gone with him. Let Lok and Fa go –'
> The old woman made a gesture that stopped her.
> 'Mal is very sick and Ha has gone.' She looked at each of them in turn. 'Now there is only Lok.' (69-70)

The law she cites twice is "A man for pictures. A woman for Oa..." (95). The old woman is usually addressed with due respect. While they are crossing the river, even Mal uses a third-person pronoun for her while Liku is addressed by a "you":

> Mal walked to the old woman and spoke gently.
> 'Will she carry it across now?' (...)
> Mal bent down to Liku.
> 'Will you cross?' (19)

Only when her corpse is floating in the water do we learn that she was Lok's mother; even though she may have been Nil's, Ha's and Fa's mother as well, her closeness to the mother goddess Oa was of greater importance to the people than her physical motherhood (109).

Mal speaks more often than the old woman does. One might even say that it is his main function to speak for the people since he possesses authority as the oldest male in the group, and his experience enables him to coordinate their activities. One third of his utterances are orders, i.e. language is his basic tool for imposing his will on the group. While the old woman is responsible for the fire and for the worshipping of Oa, which requires silence,[5] he preserves and passes on Neanderthal lore. His memories of crucial events in the history of the people serve them as guidelines to the solution of practical problems. Although his attitude towards language differs from that of the

5 Cf. Fa and Lok's visit to the sanctuary with its echo effect; loud voices would cause the icicles to fall and bury all intruders (81ff.). Golding of course also uses the Neanderthals to affirm sexual stereotypes about the "natural" behaviour of men and women in an unfallen society.

younger generation, his language in itself is neither more nor less complex than theirs. However, being the speaker is by no means a position superior to that of the priestess; their harmonious coexistence ensures the stability of the group. As Kinkead-Weekes and Gregor phrase it: "The group is directed both by the Old Man and by the Old Woman. (...) The matriarchal religion and the patriarchal government and tradition direct their whole attitude to life and death" (76-77). Among the inheritors, the leader's authority is no given. Even before we are able to understand what they are saying, we can observe with Lok how one of them, supposedly Marlan, must shout to establish his superiority (110). He cannot take it for granted that his companions listen to him.

Speaking without necessity or purpose is a sign of lesser intelligence. Being wise (not only according to Neanderthal standards) means having ideas prior to the ability to verbalize them. It is no accident that Ha, who would have succeeded Mal had he not been killed early on, "has many pictures and few words" while "Lok has a mouthful of words and no pictures", as Fa rightly characterizes them at the beginning of the novel (38). Ha is a proper man of action like the heroes of ancient myths. The question that arises is why Golding did not make Ha the protagonist of his novel, or Fa, but Lok. Kinkead-Weekes and Gregor offer the following explanation for the preference of Lok over Fa:

> It is significant that Lok rather than Fa should be the medium of our vision. Given the incomprehension of the People as a whole, faced with Otherness, to employ the simplest and most loving of them is to forestall our tendency to judge, and to force us for as long as possible to 'look without seeing', as Lok does. The basic mode of perception is affectionate and trusting long after it should have changed; and long after it has changed in Fa because of her greater intelligence. (85)

What applies to Fa is true for Ha, too. Ha would have seen sooner than Lok that the inheritors represent a danger and would probably have acted accordingly by taking the people to a safer place. Since he is one of the people I do not think that he would have taken revenge if Lok had been killed in his stead. Albeit Ha has proven capable of teasing Lok with his "cynical ears" (38), he would have stopped short of physical violence. One might argue that Fa after all becomes capable of hurling stones at the inheritors, too, when she and Lok are trying to abduct the baby for the last time (210). Nevertheless, she does not intend to hit anyone but to capture the inheritors' attention so that Lok can snatch the baby from Vivani. Because Ha is the first to encounter one of the new people and follow him, however, taking a risk as is his wont to do but "glad" as well as "frightened" according to Nil (66), he is bound to lose his life.

There may be yet another reason why Golding chose Lok as the principal character. Rather than merely less intelligent he seems to be, above all, *younger* than Ha and Fa; in his sudden vision of the fire catastrophe of his early childhood, "a greater Fa fled ahead of him" (198). In my opinion he stands at the brink of adulthood like Huck Finn or Riddley Walker or Alex in Burgess's novel, still childlike enough to enjoy playing with Liku but already old enough to make love to Fa and Nil. Everything might become of him. By contrast, Ha and Fa have already taken certain decisions; while Ha tends to the conservatism of Mal and the old woman, whose decisions he does not question even if he feels that they are wrong (36f.), Fa's line is more progressive, i.e. unlike Nil, she utters criticism and makes suggestions even though she is not supposed to do so as a woman (46). The chances thus are that Lok might become like the inheritors who so fascinate him, but as we watch him in his and Fa's penultimate confrontation with them, the impossibility of such a step becomes obvious – he remains completely unaware of his own power and of the terror he can inspire in his opponents (210). Unlike Alex or the inheritors, Lok cannot *choose* to be vicious and violent, not even at the moment when danger is greatest for him; he remains innocent. Or as Kinkead-Weekes and Gregor write: "Without the willingness to impose the will at any cost; without the world-view that recognizes no more essential value than the preservation of the self and its imposition on the universe, if need be by destroying whatever is in the way, there can be no Fall" (107).

Right until the end, Lok does not even learn when and how it is proper to impose his will. Although his perceptive abilities, and at the same time his grasp of language have increased in the course of the novel, he does not have sufficient presence of mind to order Fa, who has been hit by one of Marlan's missiles, to jump to the shore before it is too late; nor can he react as quickly as Ha did when he saved Mal from drowning in the first chapter. Lok talks to the tree instead: "The tree swung into the current with Fa sitting limply among the branches. Lok began to gibber again. He ran up and down on the terrace. The tree would not be cajoled or persuaded" (216).

BRIAN ALDISS: *BAREFOOT IN THE HEAD*

The third novel to be analysed is Brian Aldiss's *Barefoot in the Head. A European Fantasia* (1969). It features an adolescent protagonist, too, and its language conveys more than the basic facts of his story. While Jeffrey Porter assumes that with "the exception of *Finnegans Wake*, no work has gone so far as *Riddley Walker* toward shaping an idea of quantum language as originally glimpsed by Heisenberg" (450-451), I will argue that Aldiss's novel actually goes further than Hoban's. The result, however, is less attractive than *Riddley Walker*. *Barefoot in the Head* not only undermines its protagonist, but it also sabotages the aesthetic appeal of its dislocutionary language by means of exaggeration. Otherwise Aldiss' novel resembles *Riddley Walker* more than any of the novels presented so far, in essentials as well as details (many quotations have been chosen because they anticipate elements that will return in *Riddley Walker*): The setting is Europe after a third world war in which the Kuwaitis have dropped a PCA bomb, short for "Psycho-Chemical Aerosols", on Europe. The bomb was filled with drugs, with the result that most of the surviving population either indulges in psychedelic dreams or else in suicidal motor races on a dense network of motorways. This network is being expanded at the loss of arable land despite a widespread famine – one of many symptoms of an age of unreason in which all structures have become unsettled. While some people nostalgically wish to reinstate the values of pre-psychedelic life, others try to use the situation and the (anti-)hero of the age, nineteen-year-old Colin Charteris, to build up new power structures. Colin, however, refuses to play their game and slips away; his non-philosophy is one of constant movement for "if there is no trip there is nothing" (187). He will not be turned into a saviour figure and scape-goat, defying all those intent on making new myths in the old style: "I refuse to hit the worn-out Creased or anti-creased way. For me new tracks and stuff the old ding-dong the belfrey-belt" (249).

Language mirrors Colin's development from the clichéd hero of pulp fiction, who arrives at Metz making "towards the shabby hotel, walking like a warrior across desert, a pilot over a runway after mission ninety-nine, a cowboy down silent Main Street" (14-15) to the elusive non-type of psychedelic man:

> The words stoned him. Since he had reached England, the psychedelic effect had gained on him daily in gusts. ... Every thought multiplied into a thousand. Words, roads, all fossil tracks of thinking. He pursued them into the amonight, struggling with them as they propagated in their deep burrows away from the surface. Another poem: On the Spontaneous Generation of Ideas During Conversation. Spontagions Ideal Convertagion. The Conflation of Spongation in Idations. Agenbite of Auschwitz. (93)

The last group of words, in which the Joycean "Agenbite of inwit" (Joyce 22) has been dislocuted into "Auschwitz", points to the literary model characterizing the new era: In a world in which there "has been a war, a dislocation" (51) and earlier in the century, an Auschwitz, language must be dislocutionary to convey "the profusion of [Colin's] confusion to listeners" (55). The aim is a language in which the new age of change and absolute freedom, or of complete madness, is reflected in verbal viscosity, a language in which lexical, syntactical, and textual boundaries and rules need no longer be slavishly respected. The analytical either-or is dismissed, and so, eventually, is punctuation:

> So he Friends think fuzzed in diseither-organisated for midpaths neither for nor anti what he said its Those whore not for me are agrainst me just a bit more punchy phallacy in westrun style there's a newtrality to cultivate to be more receptive look for shades patterns where this goodevil stuff cant rise... (259)

In contrast to *Riddley Walker* or *Finnegans Wake*,[6] the disintegration, or adaptation, of language to the new reality, proceeds in steps. In the first chapter, "Just Passing Through", language generally abides by the rules of Standard English, with a few exceptions: on entering the Hôtel des Invalides, where he is going to rent a room, Colin is haunted by a vision: "As he walked forward, eyes adjusting, the hall took on existence – and another existence patterned with patterned tiles where other people *jurassickly* thickened the air and a shadowed saint stood upstairs in dim – and dusty detail" (15; emphasis added). "Sick" and "Jurassic" have been combined to form a portemanteau word of the kind we encountered in *Riddley Walker*. It is a proper dislocutionary starting point which may be related both to the epigraph ("Stone Age") and the end of the novel, when people are no longer capable of *living* but only of dumbly admiring Colin's philosophy of movement. During the Jurassic period, dinosaurs and ammonites flourished, but it was their fate to become extinct and petrified. If people "jurassickly" thicken the air, their own extinction and petrification seems inevitable. At this stage, the saint enters the vision – providing a flash forward to Colin's future role but also a reference to his favourite literature, Leslie Charteris's "Saint" novels about Simon Templar (19, 40, 135) – yet Colin wakes up to the reality of the entrance hall before anything more tangible can manifest itself. His second vision in this chapter, when he hallucinates being God (22f.), is free from non-standard expressions or constructions; Colin realizes, however, that he has picked up the contagion as well (24).

Poems and pop songs are irregularly interpolated between the chapters, fulfilling a similar function as the legends and tales in *Riddley Walker*. From the fourth chapter, "Multi-Value Motorway," songs even intrude into the text (e.g. 97f., 106, 189f.). On the other hand, there are neither poems nor songs

6 Both Scholes and Rabkin in *SF* (91) and William Atheling, Jr. (alias James Blish), in *More Issues at Hand* (138ff.) have compared the language of *Barefoot in the Head* to that of Joyce's last novel.

to be found between chapters five and six, "Still Trajectories" and "Auto-Ancestral Fracture". The poems and songs comment on the experiences and feelings of various characters (e.g. 30, 33, 268). They may also anticipate events which will take place later in the novel (e.g. 32). Their form and quality varies considerably: they run the whole gamut from the banality of certain popular hits (e.g. 54) to the typographical experiments of concrete poetry (e.g. 78f., 82f.). Most poems are more than purely ornamental additions. They reinforce central issues of the novel. Thus "*The First and Future Paradise*" (75f.) brings up the theme of the Fall and underscores the growing awareness of entropy and imminent catastrophe that was haunting the sixties and early seventies.[7] The first poem with dislocutionary word games is to be found on p. 121, "*Trying to Love*": while it echoes Colin's puns on Angeline's name in the preceding chapter (cf. 96), its shape typographically imitates her pregnant body. Otherwise the language of the poems and songs remains remarkably conventional up to p. 265, long after the language of the prose passages has turned non-standard. The poems "DEATH OF A PHILOSOPHER" (280) and "CHARTERIS" (281), which end the novel, prevent the readers from suspending disbelief altogether and from identifying with the protagonist; his ideas should be viewed with caution, as the ending of "CHARTERIS" underlines: "The bombs were only / In his head / On a memorial tree / A joker wrote / KEEP VIOLENCE IN THE MIND / WHERE IT BELONGS" (281).[8]

In the second chapter, "The Serpent of Kundalini", ruptures occur mainly at the textual level. Colin seems to arrive more than once at Dover but in two of the three times his ship is said to have arrived there (34, 39), this will gradually turn out to have been an illusion. The borderline between truth and illusion is never altogether clear; Colin asks himself: "To what extent was a vision an illusion, to what extent a clearer sort of truth?" (40). The third arrival of the ferry therefore seems as illusionary as the previous ones: "Over the sea, the ship came. Up the hill, motors sounded. In the head, barefoot, a new age" (51). We cannot even be sure if Colin's conquest of England and the continent will really take place; the last stanza of "CHARTERIS" after all begins: "The bombs were only / In his head..." (281).

Examples of dislocution appear twice in this chapter: reflecting on the meaning of England, Colin characterizes it as "the million *manarchies* of ruined minds oerthrown" (35; emphasis added). The mon-archy has turned into

7 Vonnegut's *Cat's Cradle* (1963) and especially Pynchon's novels *V.* (1961) and *Gravity's Rainbow* (1973) offer further illustration of this awareness.
8 A motto which prefigures Riddley's first mystical insight: "EUSAS HEAD IS DREAMING US" (58).

a country of mad-men, individuals who do whatever they like and, abiding by no law, live in anarchy. Blake's phrase of the "mind-forg'd manacles" of course rattles somewhere in the background, too, indicating not only that Colin's perception of England is literary through and through but also that a totally unbridled country is no better than one that is "charter'd", i.e. constricted, as in Blake's poem "London": opposites meet. The second example is "LOVE BURROW" (38), an expression that occurs in another of Colin's visions of the future. Since it will "not resolve into GLASGOW" (38) when he tries to interpret the vision, Colin dismisses it as "some sort of Freudian nonsense" (38-39); but in view of subsequent chapters we can relate it to "Loughborough" (65), where Colin will take the self-made prophet Brasher; it is also at Loughborough that his desire for love will eventually be gratified: Angeline, Brasher's wife, consents to follow Colin after her husband's death (88).

In the third chapter, "Drake-Man Route", dislocutionary examples become too numerous to count. Among the most original ones is "that Arabian nightmoil" (67), in which the Arabian Nights turn into turmoil and nightmare; Colin uses this expression to refer to Europe stricken by the Arabian PCA bomb. Though Sindbad the Sailor does not appear,[9] there are substitutes for him, e.g. Sir Francis Drake, as the title of the chapter shows (and cf. 60) and Captain Kidd (60); Coleridge's Ancient Mariner is conjured up when Colin defines his new status: "*Zbogom,* what am I now if not more than man, mariner of my seven seizures" (69) – "seizures" refers to the seas, Colin's conquests, and maybe his fits of madness. Syntax shows first signs of "decay" or imbalance; elliptical and deviant sentences alternate with endless lists (see e.g. 55f., or 70f.).

The vocabulary which conveys Colin's perceptions is rich in anthropomorphic images. Many nouns have been converted into verbs, e.g. "dominoed" (56), some intransitive verbs are used with direct objects, e.g. in "Charteris muscled his Banshee past the van" (56). Since change and movement are regarded more highly than "things" – cf. "[The true human spirit] could only be seen in and by movement" (36) – it does indeed make sense that a great number of verbs should have been added to the lexicon or that their usage has been expanded. Punctuation, especially commas more and more frequently fail to structure Colin's streams of consciousness or his and Banjo Burton's utterances. Nevertheless, there still *are* periods, question marks as well as quotation marks (see e.g. 58f.).

9 Joyce's exhaustive variations on the theme of Sindbad in *Ulysses*, cf. the penultimate "answer" in "Ithaca", might have deterred Aldiss.

The contrast between Colin's present state of mind and language and that of earlier times emerges clearly if we look at the beginning of his memory of his father's funeral (62). Sentences are mostly simple, clear and straightforward, facts told one after the other. The transition could be no brisker than at the moment when we are forced to return to the muddy present of the narrative:

> 'Daddy!' he cried.
> And past the greeneyes swinging right past Stones with headlights and Leeds Permanent all bordered up a glimpsed group of girls running down a dark turn legs and ankles what the blackbirds on the bloody field... (63)

In Phil Brasher, Colin finds a competitor for the rank of spiritual leader. But Brasher's description and his utterances foreshadow his death:

> *Ashen* he mounts back his anger on an unsound rampant saying, 'I'll not ride anywhere with you or where the *lorries* sweep. Isn't there a limit a *limbo* a limit somewhere isn't there? ...' (...)
> 'Tell me nothing you parisher this is my *perish* ...' (66f.; emphasis added)

Colin is not superior at all, however; thoughts, first of two women (64), later of a "white-thighed woman" (68), i.e. of Angeline, keep intruding into his mind.

Chapter four, "Multi-Value Motorway", opens with a representation of Angeline's thoughts. We immediately perceive that she has not been affected by the psychedelic drugs for her train of thought is logical; moreover she cannot understand Colin's "message" but only "his power" (84). Her presence stabilizes his thinking to a certain degree. Whenever he indulges in an effusion of dislocutionary associations, she stops him: "'... Don't go daft. Talk proper.'" (93). His sentences become simpler and more intelligible than in the previous chapter; here is, for instance, the first version of his later "advice" to the masses (259): "'... Think in fuzzy sets. There is no either-or black-white dichotomy any more. Only a spectrum of partiallys. Live by this, as I do – you will win. We have to think new. Find more directions make them. ...'" (86). There is a tendency to verbless structures and long lists of objects when his perceptions are represented (93f., 103). We also get a glimpse of the book he is writing; his last sentences still display the abbreviations typical of a draft in which conjugated verbs and articles are missing:

> ... Fiction to be mental photographs, motion to be supplied purely by reader. Music as harpoon to sleeping entrails, drown out the howls of smaller dogs. Action a blemish as already in existence. Truth thus like a pile of photos, self-cancelling for self-fulfilment, multi-valued. Indecision multi-incisive and non-automatic ... (102)

Beside the inclusion of pop songs, chapter four introduces another new element, that is the change of narrative perspective. Until now, Colin's perspective has been predominant in the prose parts of the text. We are on the Inner Relief Road in Loughborough, where Brasher's accident is going to take place and move from Angeline's point of view (84) to Brasher's (85), then to Colin's (85-88); double spacing precedes the next change of perspective and setting: we are now with the Burton brothers and their friends in a shabby and dark room somewhere in Loughborough (88-91). However, no sooner have we become accustomed to these clearly marked shifts than we have to face an ambiguous transition back to Colin's view. In the middle of a conversation between Banjo Burton and Robbins, we suddenly find ourselves with Charteris and Angeline, who cannot have arrived at the Burtons' room yet because they are still looking for the Banshee after the accident (91). Thus, we are once more alerted to the possibility that the whole novel might be nothing but one of Colin's hallucinatory dreams. Incidentally, Lewis Carroll, Aldiss's Victorian predecessor in regard to dream visions in an experimental style, is explicitly mentioned in this chapter (95).

Colin and Angeline's encounter with their alter egos Jan and Marta Koninkrijk gives direction to the next chapter, "Still Trajectories", in which the motorcade is travelling southwards. While the progagonists may be said to live up to their dreams, the Koninkrijks are at first completely stuck in the mud of stagnation and repressed love for other partners. Marta is suffering from schizophrenia; she spends all her lonely days trying to arrest time and revert to her childhood in order to retrieve the lost love of her father. Jan's repressed desire for life and love, on the other hand, finds an outlet in his obscene craving for the carnage of car crashes, orgasmic catastrophes, or "catagasms" (132), on the motorway he is supposed to supervise. As long as they see each other, both make sure that they hide their obsessions. On their own, however, they may be overwhelmed by the repressed contents of their unconscious. Only at the peak of crisis do their languages completely defy control; Jan's gives away his necrophilia by its suggestive vocabulary, his impatience by its elliptical syntax:

> The speedometer his thermometer, creeping up and familiar dirty excitement creaming in him. For someone the moment of truth had come big grind the necessary whiteout the shuttling metal death 3-Ding fast before the windscreen and still many marvellous microseconds safety before impact and the rictus of smiling fracture as the latent forces of acceleration actualised. (141)

Marta's language takes on the outer appearance of an ancient verse drama. Although her "confrontation" with her father is not written in verse, each line begins with a capital letter (145f.). When her drama has been acted out, on the other hand, the typographical setting reverts to normal (cf. 148f.).

It is Colin who effects the liberation of the couple. He makes Jan aware of his repressions (145), and acts the part of Marta's father to free her from her spell (147). We recognize that it is he who is addressed by her as her father from the descriptive terms which characterize the figure in her "drama": "... He *half-leaned, half-stood, half-understanding* / The scent of trauma in the scene..." (147; emphasis added). For it is by means of modifications like "half-" that Colin evades clarity in this chapter (143) besides taking recourse to his habitual dislocutionary word games such as "question marks the antidope for auto-motion" (137; cf. 137f. for entire sequences).[10] But while helping other people to escape the treadmills of their former lives, Colin becomes more and more entangled in the role of a saviour; in view of his "message", it is a sign of failure that he is now compared, and compares himself, to well-known figures such as Christ (134f.) and Simon Templar (135). Hence, irony clearly informs such descriptions as "The hero half-coughs in answer" (135). Even though he preaches to his disciples "Don't get automatic!" (144), he has become automatic and repetitive himself in the meantime.

The crisis of Colin and his "movement" reaches a climax at Brussels, in chapter six, "Auto-Ancestral Fracture", he and his followers are bribed to stay either by means of drugs or excessive flattering. The Mafia finance a film by Nicholas Boreas which is supposed to celebrate Colin's survival of the car crash of the previous chapter. The artistic repetition of this event serves various purposes: director Boreas may indulge in his narcissism (179) and his voyeuristic greed for other people's death (161, 173), Colin's new manager Cass and the Mafia enjoy the massive profits they can make with the motorcaders (156). Colin, finally, gets sufficient time to give in to his sexual desire (152f., 159f.) and his violent megalomania: "'I am the grate I am where fools burn for greater light and from me shall come a new order...'" (155). Only Angeline objects to the state of affairs but she does not succeed in influencing either Colin or Boreas to use their talents in a constructive way (160, 175, 178); moreover the remains of the PCA bombs have begun to

10 Three variant dislocutionary transformations of "acceleration" are to be found: "catceleration rides splinternity" (134-135), "godding it across the skidways in creasingack selleration" (137), and "creasing axle aeration" (138). In *Riddley Walker*, we find another variant as Lissener says to Riddley: "If we go to Fork Stoan weare keaping the circel which thatwl be axel rating the Inner G you know" (86).

affect her, too (175). Repetition permeates everything to underline the degree of decadence the motorcade has reached. This does not only mean that words and phrases are repeated (e.g. "line", 182), but it may also take the form of alliteration in sentences such as "'... There'll be a group-grope tonight – any grotesque grot they grapple...'" (174). Repetition also occurs at the morphological level; Aldiss satirizes the contemporary beatniks and their countless happenings in coining such terms as "musicniks" (152), "grotnik" (153), "artnik" (175), "smash-in" and "sing-in" (168), "starve-in" (174), "carve-in" (187), "stunt-in" and "death-in" (171), etc.

Dislocutionary word games are embedded in the semantic fields of certain metaphors or of characteristics of the situation, that is, they occur within clusters of words referring to seafaring, animals, flowers, eating and starving, or violence. When Colin and Angeline are quarrelling, they nearly upset all the seven seas:

> '... Be pacific!'
> 'Sea my Azov! ... Caspian kid! ...'
> 'I'll baltic where my thighs thew my honey, I the upandcoming!'
> 'You subserbiant Dalmatian! From now on you go adriantic up some mother tree – just don't profligainst me!...' (153-154)

Jealousy and lust deprive Angeline, Colin and Marta of their humanity; the "carnality" of their relationship and the "animal" nature of their passions are underlined by terms for animals, meats, spices and other kinds of food (174; also see 154, 158f.). Once Brussels is burning, allusions to Nero's Rome (196) and to death and the apocalypse become predominant (200).

Yet, there are also passages in which language may be metaphoric but otherwise quite regular – with exceptional intrusions of dislocution which underline as well as undermine the regularity of their contexts (e.g. 160-165, 191-194). Tension between the regularity of form and the irregularity of content is created when the absurdity of life after the bomb is described:

> The parliament still took its conclave but all the ceremony these last two months had brought were these laws passed: a law to stop the drinking of the good earth; a law to prohabit [sic; dislocutionary intrusion] hats from becoming unseen when the sun set; a law to make Belgian hounds sing the night away like nightingales... (157)

The disgust Nicholas Boreas evokes is due to a similar contrast. On the one hand, he is no more dazzled from the drugs than Angeline. At least he thinks that he is sane and superior to the "acidheads" (194). On the other hand, he hails the destruction of Western civilization (179) and cultivates an eccentric appearance and life-style:

> A mighty figure he was, bare without a hair, though with a poet's eye he had schillered his breasts and pate by dint of a bronze lacquer to lend a sort of piebald distinction. (...)
> Whitewhale-like he rose, brushing black ramshorns from his knotted sheepshanks ... In his veined eye gleamed the real madness... (161)

He is as dangerous though not as unfathomable as Moby-Dick, as the allusion to Melville's classic implies; after all, contact with him will bring out the capacity for homicidal violence in Colin (cf. 198f.). The language describing the film project is regular as well (162-165), and so is most of the description of the shooting (168ff.), but whenever the dummies in the crashbound cars are mentioned, dislocutions occur more frequently: female figures have "amenorrhoea" (169); immediately before the crash scene is shot, they are on the "vergin of extinction" (171). This might imply that they have a mind confused by the bombs, too. Boreas calls them "dimmies" to belittle them (172) albeit the man in charge of the props, Ranceville, insists – in a dialogue of ironical ambiguity – that they are as "human" as he and Boreas are themselves (171). The dummies are "More terrible than humans" (183) when they die, though. Angeline is one of the first who can watch unedited bits of film at Boreas's house; they are described with linguistic ruptures and a great many examples of dislocution:

> Expressions blank of dismay the dummies had their heads cracked and chipped and knocked and shattered and ground and mashed and eggshelled and blown away with new miracle Crump aiming their last ricochetting nanocheek towards the impactpoint of speedeath the ipaccint of speeeth ipint seeth inteeth ih i i i . (183-184)

The director named after the god of the north wind and associated with Neptune (161) appears to be the calm eye of all vortices, reponsible for the generation of an ever increasing number of tumults which will eventually destroy Brussels. Ironically, Colin associates him with fire; to him he is the "artifacer [who] could help blow blazes from his parky wavering nature with the bellows of his conterfaking craft" (199). But vile Boreas is as helpless as the panic-stricken masses when Brussels turns into an inferno; he holds on to treacherous Cass, who will stab him in his own swimming pool after being attacked by him (196f.). Angeline saves Colin even though he tries to murder her, taking himself for a Cro-Magnon, her for one of the hateful Neanderthals of an earlier vision (198; also see 187).[11]

---

11 Even though *Barefoot in the Head* is a "post-bomb" novel, these allusions link it with *The Inheritors*. The PCA bombs invert the process described in Golding's novel: this time the reasonable, analytical "predelics" are extinguished by the unreasonable "psychedelics".

If the Brussels chapter is a journey to hell, the last chapter of the novel leads Colin and Angeline *per aspera*, or through Polizeikommandant Laundrei's purgatory, to "Ouspenski's Astrabahn". Its opening is characterized by the drivers' exhaustion: wheels are – as it first seems, superfluously – called "tired" because the pun affords a metonymical reference to the drivers (219). Repetition, dislocution and syntactical incongruity prevail (219). Colin appears to be the centre of consciousness of the first paragraphs; his tired thoughts and impressions are alternatingly reproduced or represented, but apart from scanty references in the first or third person, and a small number of conjugated verbs in the present or past tenses respectively, the style gives no hint as to where one mode begins and the other ends. Throughout the chapter, the narrative structure will raise questions. While "Ouspenski's Astrabahn" sets out in the manner of the novel's previous chapters, that is as third-person narration without a personal narrator, we suddenly have to face intrusions by a first-person narrator: "Many things that *I* said at *that* time must have surprised *my* companions in this strange adventure very much. *I* was surprised by much *myself*" (225; emphasis added). Colin here appears to remember and tell the events from some vantage point in the future, maybe at the time he entertains his last disciples with stories of his youth (263f.). A few lines further down he is again referred to by his pseudonymous family name Charteris; that is, if the narrative instance has really switched to first person, it does not persist in this. Other intrusions of this kind are to be found on pp. 227 and 252. Another borderline that is blurred in this chapter is the one between speech and narrative; very often direct speech turns into narrative without any end-of-quotation marks (e.g. 224, 229, etc.).

The use of periods is foregrounded too. When the motorcaders give in to sleep after their escape from Brussels, periods disappear for the first time (220f.); thoughts are not developed to the end, associations follow each other freely as "Aged amokanisms of comprension guttering" (221). Colin and his new mistress Elsbeth's love making is described without any periods, too, until a dash signals the tactless intrusion of German policemen who arrest the travellers and impose, not law and order, but a more rigid syntax on the loose streams of consciousness of their prisoners: "Breaking in the harsh cries of uniform throats and yells of drivniks together with some rumpling and footmaching where the pace is fractured" (221). A little later, when Colin is

---

Dislocution might in this case be interpreted as the opposite of differentiation, a return of language to some primeval muddle. Apart from these allusions, I could find no evidence that *Barefoot* is indeed a response to *Inheritors*. However, Aldiss is more than likely to have known this novel; in his history of science fiction, *Billion Year Spree* (1973), he calls it a "masterpiece" (117).

falling asleep in prison, periods disappear again and so do capital letters, which used to mark the beginnings of new paragraphs (236).

Laundrei personifies the opposite of the motorcaders' flexibility. He is the archetype of all satirists' caricatures of the ugly German fascist: his whiter than white uniform hides a man who is fixated on authority, law, order, cleanliness, science and pedantic correctness but subject to an excessive sexuality; as with Koninkrijk, his language gives away his repressed desire (232). Of course, he is affected by the chemical bombs like anyone else but in addition obsessed by the wish to save the world from disorder and madness, that is, to destroy it, by means of Hydrogen 12, a substance he hopes to be able to produce after mastering his sexual problem (233). Since he presses Colin to help him (233), Colin concocts a cunning plan to prevent him for good from synthesizing the dangerous substance: he seeks to block Laundrei's creativity by prescribing altogether mechanical sexual drills (234f.).

Laundrei heeds his "worms of advice", as Colin notices before falling asleep, overhearing the obscene drill which is supposed to "tranceform" the whole police squad (235). Laundrei's obsessions blind him to the realities of life after the bomb. At the very beginning, Colin "snuffed that the Schwabe fell apart uniform-wise many without belts or buttons or boots or Klimpenflashengewurstklumpen to their name and even the jackets hung upon a bygone hook elsewhere" (222). In prison, the differences between hippies and policemen disappear altogether (243). It is above all thanks to Laundrei's proneness to delusion that Colin survives the "last little testicle" (235) of his sainthood: he is to walk over water. He is prepared to drown when Laundrei suddenly screams as if the miracle had indeed happened (240). He has mistaken "a figure striding on the far bank" for "Charteris in a black mack sly and dry and spectral!" (240). Colin himself believes in a schizophrenic hallucination: "... the horrors still my damned slavonik addled acid head of schizogod!" (240). But as we will see after Colin's release, the "sly and dry" figure (246) was nobody but Colin's Uriah-Heepish "humble serpent" (247) Cass.

Angeline is afraid of his power to tempt Colin to play Christ once more, but this time, Colin does not succumb to Cass's flatterings: "'Leading is out makes blindness and the old swingdom of heaven is just a slopporific. Opium of the pupil.'" (250). Colin disposes of the "paracide", as Angeline calls him (251), by sending him to Berlin with Laundrei (253). After they have left, dislocutionary passages for a while adhere to standard punctuation. From p. 259, though, "Living barefate in sheughs...", punctuation is dropped almost altogether while capital letters continue to mark the beginnings of new paragraphs up until the end. Dislocution is less frequent towards the end when "Driver man" becomes "pedestrian" (260). The principle underlying these transformations seems to be that there is no principle; readers have to deal with ceaseless changes and find their way through the jungle of language very much like the protagonists. For Colin there begins "a new age the postpsychotomimetic age free from anshirt shittoleths and the grey grimmages stripped off" (252). He does his best to give his unwelcome followers "holy law okay but spiced with heresy" (264). Ultimately, though, he fails to have it both ways: the heretic is forgotten but the saint exploited by the tourist industry (264).

In Burgess's *A Clockwork Orange*, Alex's continued preference for his non-standard juvenile slang serves as an indicator of his unwillingness to conform to the norms of society. Just as he chooses to use bland "nadsat", he is a criminal of his own free will. However, insincere or naive and gullible speakers of Standard English are the butt of Burgess's satire, too, because they do their culture a disservice by making it look inferior and unable to cope with Alex and his likes. For the protagonists of the other novels discussed, the use of nonstandard English is not a matter of their choice. While the Neanderthals Lok and Fa are challenged to make new distinctions and find words for new experiences only when stronger competitors drive them out of blissful ignorance and verbal restriction, Colin Charteris shakes himself free of old distinctions and attempts to retrieve paradise under the influence of drugs. *The Inheritors* and *Barefoot in the Head* are complements: both novels locate evil in civilization, with Standard English as the symbol of, and chief means of conveying, its values and its shortcomings. Moreover, in both novels the evil of civilization is rooted in the deficiency of "human nature". Golding's novel expresses the pessimism with which the author returned from World War II.[12] The "inheritors'" language gives away the full measure of their corruption. Aldiss's novel, on the other hand, presents an imaginative ironical reversal of General Curtis Lemay's threat to the address of the Vietnamese, which precedes the novel as its epigraph: "Tell the Vietnamese they've got to draw in their horns and stop aggression or we're going to bomb them back into the Stone Age" (9). The question Aldiss asks is, what if Europe were bombed back into the Stone Age? Would we have a chance to return to an anti-authoritarian idyll and to a multivalent language free from stereotypes? There is only the faintest kind of optimism implied by the outcome of the novel, as far as Colin Charteris is concerned, but ultimately, the prospect is bleak. In *Riddley Walker*, finally, the consistent use of Inland dialect on the one hand

12 See Golding's essay "Fable" in the collection *The Hot Gates*, especially pp. 86-87, or the interview with John Haffenden (Golding and Haffenden 112-113).

reminds us of what we constantly risk losing; that is, civilization and Standard English are not presented as altogether condemnable. On the other hand, we begin to see that the new variety also has its comforts: dislocutionary Inland dialect is often better suited to explain the complexities and ambiguities of a situation than Standard English with its tendency to simplify and disambiguate.

I have already pointed out that Porter links the linguistic experiments of Carroll, Joyce, Pynchon, Barth, DeLillo and Hoban to the discoveries of quantum theory:

> Not surprisingly, postmodern thought has seen in wordplay an alternative to the instrumentalist concept of language, arriving at a position anticipated by Heisenberg thirty years ago. Following the lead of Derrida, ... critics wonder what would happen to our view of language should we come to see wordplay not as a minor prank or anomaly but as a central fact of meaning. (...) ... the answer seems to be that we would be faced with a nonlinear notion of language that reversed orthodox priorities, favoring equivocation over predictability and nonidentity over identity, dedicated less to cause than to effect – a notion, in other words, which was nonrepresentational and rested on the assumption that language itself is intelligent. Existing well outside the normal rules of discourse, the result would be something on the order of quantum rhetoric, a 'pluri-dimensional' language, in Derrida's words (*Grammatology* 86), where the free play of double meaning would be favored in conformity with the emerging ontology of the new physics. In the indeterminate universe of quantum theory, where an electron can behave like both a particle and a wave, ambiguity, as Heisenberg noted, is a perfectly valid form for thought to take. (464-465)

As we have seen, *Barefoot in the Head* takes ambiguity to extremes. Readers must take pains to get the gist of a text characterized by disruptions at all levels of language. Aldiss's way of putting "quantum rhetoric" into practice acts as a deterrent: the multivalent language used in the novel is no valid alternative to current Standard English. *Riddley Walker*, on the other hand, wants to encourage its readers to be open to moderate innovation. Hoban has therefore wisely restricted the number of foregrounded elements. Fission and fusion mainly affect the lexicon, whereas punctuation and syntax still form structures that are known from (children's or informal) spoken English, if they do not altogether agree with the stylistic conventions and the grammatical norms of written Standard English. In addition, the novel's constant first-person point of view allows the readers to familiarize themselves with Riddley's idiom. Thus it is relatively easy for them to follow Riddley's tale while surprising lexical dislocutions nevertheless keep them on the alert for additional insights.

6.3. The Plot: Breaking the "Fools Circel"

I will now turn to the question in what respect the plot of *Riddley Walker* relates to the message conveyed by the formal and semantic qualities of Inland dialect. *The Mouse and his Child, The Lion of Boaz-Jachin and Jachin-Boaz* and *Turtle Diary* employ fairly regular pairs of parallel narrative strands to show how constant antagonistic or complementary forces and characters react with each other. Kleinzeit's development, on the other hand, can be described as the completion of three interrelated action-cycles, that is lack, gain and first signs of the loss of work, of love, and of health. Riddley's way is less regular, hence more difficult to describe. His route consists of a series of circles and progressive movements; it is a chain-reaction with different people and circumstances leading to various results such as the rediscovery of gunpowder, of spirituality and of art for the sake of entertainment and enlightenment.

The fourteen drafts did not only serve to perfect the language of the novel but also to prevent the story from drifting in too many directions:

> It got simpler ... there was a time when *Riddley Walker* had a girlfriend, a woman-friend, and ... there were many more characters. There was much more of the folklore of his people – many of their stories of various kinds. And what happened was – yes, it did get more fabulous in its approach, tighter and simpler and more boiled-down. (Hoban and Myers 13)

However, as the few left-over characters constantly change sides and hence "tend to be uncertain figures ... never wholeheartedly for or against Progress so that there are no very definite parties, no Goodies-and-Baddies" (Lake, "Riddley Walker. Pilgermann.", 98), the text seems to pulsate with a kind of unstable, unpredictable energy; it might stop at any moment, with one of the episodes forcing Riddley to meet his death. Hoban was confronted with many problems. He told John McEntee in 1977, three years before the novel was published:

> All my past novels were pretty simple technically. They were set in the present. They required no great amount of research. The characters in the situation might be taxing emotionally, but they were well within my grasp technically. (...) [About *Riddley Walker* he said:] It's a slow hard struggle to get the thing done. (Hoban and McEntee, no page ref.)

To begin with, I want to have a look at the "Chaynjis" (34) Riddley is exposed to. The events that bring on change for Riddley do not happen at random. The structure is therefore not as loosely episodic or plotless as it may appear at first glance. Patterns manifest themselves. There are six major movements to be distinguished in the novel, or six stages in Riddley's development:[1] The first movement is a short episode, described in chapter 1, in which Riddley kills a boar, "the las wyld pig on the Bundel Downs" (1). It is important to notice that it was the *last* boar because the existence of Riddley's tribe, their life as hunters cannot go on as before if they have nothing else to hunt for; a new form of life is impending. The movement of the episode is therefore unidirectional and linear like the way from the Bundel Downs to How Fents: there is no way back. The only choice left for How Fents seems to be to join one of the farms and give up their traditional way of life. But Riddley does not see this as yet. The events of his naming day only raise questions in him that Lorna Elswint, the "tel woman" refuses to answer: "She said, 'Riddley Riddley theres mor to life nor asking and telling. ...'" (5). However, she earthily draws his attention to the basic question present in all of Hoban's novels, the question about the sense of life: "'... May be weare jus only sickness and a feaver to it or boyls on the arse of it I dont know...'" (6-7). The question instigates Riddley's thinking; it is the first impulse that has ever made him look for answers, and it has also led him to write down his experiences:

> Our woal life is a idear we dint think of nor we dont know what it is. What a way to live.
>
> Thats why I finely come to writing all this down. Thinking on what the idear of us myt be. Thinking on that thing whats in us lorn and loan and oansome. (7)

The next stage in his development is described in chapters 2 to 10. Riddley, who commutes to Widders Dump for work every day, loses his father three days after his naming day. On the same day, a baby is born dead at Widders Dump, and Riddley kills the leader of a pack of dogs who seems to sacrifice his life for Riddley and his dead father. Outwardly a simple series of repetitive linear movements from How Fents to Widders Dump and back, the second stage challenges Riddley by confronting him insistently with death. In terms of his mental development, then, these chapters mean anything but stagnation or repetition: they prepare him for his independence. For Riddley again asks questions about the sense of the events he has witnessed, and the answer is refused him a second time, but he at least gets instructions from an old "connexion" man as to the method to interpret such experiences himself. Riddley indeed succeeds in finding an answer: "'The far come close took by the littl come big.'" (13). His sudden maturity brings on many obligations and also an estrangement from his surroundings: "This day tho every thing begun to look different. Like I never seen it befor." (14). Moreover, it is an essential

1 See the map on p. 140.

aspect of the second stage that Riddley finds out that different interpreters differ in their opinions about the same basic events. Lorna's story *Why the Dog Wont Show Its Eyes* (16-19) and her interpretation of Brooder Walker's and the baby's deaths (23) characterize her as somebody afraid of a return to the technological knowledge of Bad Time, i.e. our present, with its destructive "clevverness" that can already be found in the life of farmers. The only form of knowledge she is not averse to is "1st knowing", a kind of intuition that allows people to live in harmony with nature, that is with the Mother Goddess who manifests herself as "Nite" or "Death" (17).[2] Lorna's opponents are Abel Goodparley and Erny Orfing, the two leaders of Inland who initiate Riddley into his vocation as a "connexion" man. Before they perform the "Eusa Show", the puppet "mystery play" used for propagandist besides religious purposes, Riddley witnesses a quarrel between the "Big 2":

> Goodparley said, 'Erny youre such a downer youre going to down your self right in to the groun 1 day. You can say what you like Im saying wewl get it put to gether weve got it all in front of us and going to make it happen. Youre looking sideways but Im looking frontways and going to get every body moving that way form and fents boath. I dint come Big 2 to stan in the mud and sing for boats in the air...' (39)

Having come across the nostalgic, the ambitious (or uncritically progressive) and the moderate points of view, Riddley at first refuses to take anybody's part: "I dint realy want to get mixt in with it. I jus kep shut" (39). But then he adapts, takes his scar and firmly intends to adopt Lorna's nostalgic point of view in the interpretation of the Eusa Show that the Big 2 presented the night before. He even defines a style for his connections:

> I had in mynd to take it slow and make it solid. Put 1 thot to a nother like ring poals in poal hoals and holders to ring poals and rafters to holders and the reveal on top of it all like thatch. So you cud all ways go back from the reveal and get a good look at how the woal thing ben bilt and that wer going to be the Riddley Walker styl. (57)

Yet, it is not for Riddley to make any decisions; he is and will further be subjected to the thoughts, people, objects and events that "come" to him, like his first connection: "The thot come to me: EUSAS HEAD IS DREAMING US" (58). As his seemingly useless message frustrates the villagers, they mock and threaten Riddley the day after. He does not have sufficient authority to remain their spiritual leader. At the end of the second movement, a re-definition of his

2 The gendering of characters, views and types of behaviour will be discussed in ch. 8.4.

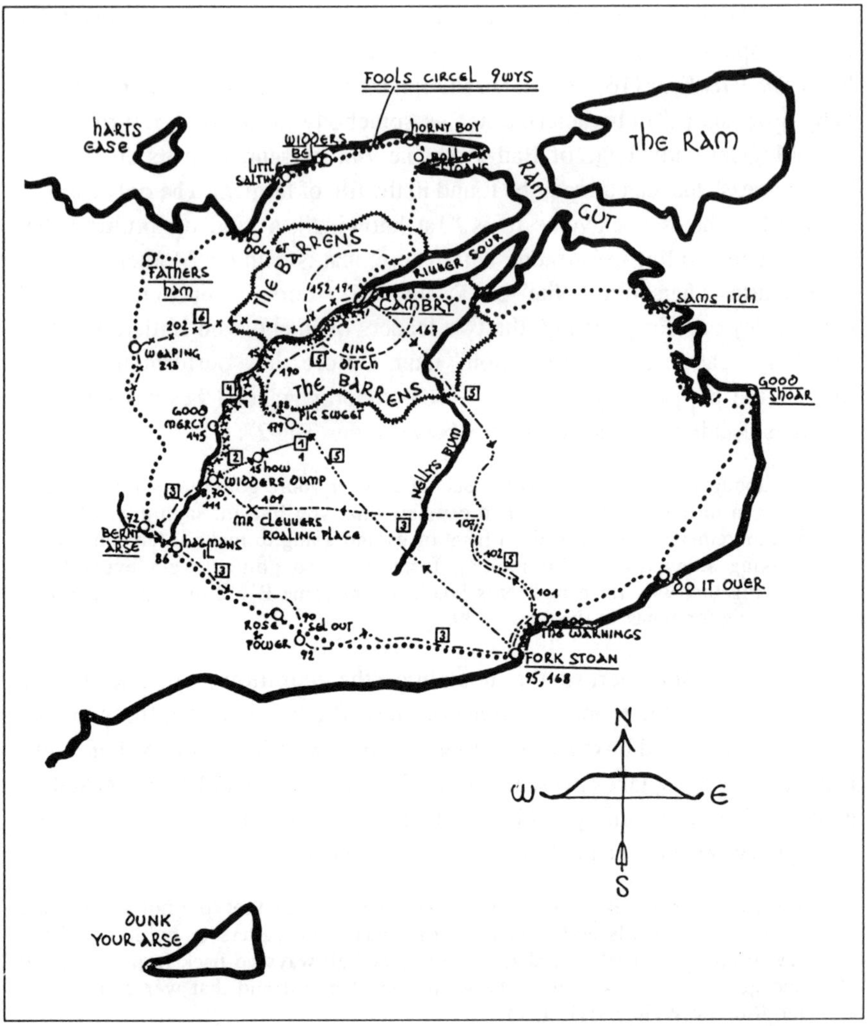

Riddley's Journey

Map based on Russell Hoban's map of Inland. Drawing by Daniel Studer, 1998.

Legend:

------	movement 1	xxxxxxx	movement 4
....	movement 2	– ··· – ···	movement 5
– · – · –	movement 3	x – x – x	movement 6
••••••••	Fools Circel 9wys		
CAMBRY	The dead towns along the Fools Circel 9wys.		
152	Figures are page references to the Picador-Pan edition of *Riddley Walker*; thus "152" refers to Riddley's arrival at Cambry at the end of movement 4, described on p. 152.		

role is urgently needed since Riddley loses not only his authority but also his security. His particular relationship with the dogs has provoked envy and superstitious fears among the other villagers. After a row, Durster Potter even attempts to shoot Riddley but is killed by the new leader of the dogs in turn. Since no one has witnessed the incident, Riddley is suspected of murder (64f.).

What the first movement only suggested and the second made necessary becomes inevitable at the beginning of the third movement in chapter 11: Riddley must leave and cannot return to How Fents because he knocks down his superior at Widders Dump, the Ram official Belnot Phist. Riddley has found an old Punch figure which he does not want to give to Belnot. It all takes place without much reflection; Riddley escapes head over heels: "It wer my feet done it by ther selfs I never give it no thot at all" (70). While the second movement was outwardly represented by several journeys between How Fents and Widders Dump, the third movement, which ends with Riddley's return to the dump in chapter 13, describes a first circle. The dogs initially determine the direction of the circle. They take Riddley from Widders Dump to Bernt Arse (70), where he sets free his "moon brother" Lissener (72), the current "Ardship of Cambry" who is awaiting interrogation by Goodparley. At Bernt Arse, Riddley discovers his ability to follow his own intuitions when he and Lissener are wondering where to go next:

> I pirntowt we bes not go the straites way. Keap off the main tracks where we cud. I wer jus going to say les Eas roun by Monkeys Whoar Town and Norf up a long the Nellys Bum when I had like a mynd flash of colourt lites with clicking and bleaping it wernt like nothing I ever acturely seen nor heard only in dreams. I cud like feal the woal circel of the dead towns in me and see a line of grean lite sweaping roun that circel from the senter. (...) I said, 'Dont break the circel yet.' The words jus come out of me by ther selfs I bint thinking them at all. (85)

Riddley's travelling in a circle does not imply that he returns to Widders Dump unchanged. On the contrary. At Fork Stoan, he experiences the fascination of technology when he sees the nearly intact machinery of an ancient power plant: "... I begun to get some idear of the shyning of the Littl Man. Tears begun streaming down my face and my froat akit. (...) 'O what we ben! And what we come to!'" (96). Riddley begins to sympathize with Goodparley's belief in technological progress:

> Up to then I ben agenst Goodparley and I ben agenst what ever he wer for. ... Now all on a suddn Eusa and Eusas head and the Littl Shyning Man be come some thing woaly diffrent in my mynd to what they ben befor. How cud any 1 not want to get that shyning Power back from time back way back? (96-97)

Apart from feeling a desire for this kind of knowledge, Riddley and Lissener also find one of the ingredients to realize power, sulphur. Even though Riddley is anxious about the effect their find has on him, he cannot help contributing to its preservation by means of eliminating evidence that could rouse potential pursuers to follow him and Lissener to Cambry: "I had that bag in my han I begun to feal like it wer liting up the dark like a torch and bleaping follerme all over Inland. Suddn I wantit the nite to get darker I wantit dark a nuff to smuvver it qwyet. ... That Powers working me all ready..." (101). Lissener, planning to challenge the Ram's leadership together with his people, the Eusa Folk, sends Riddley back to Widders Dump after they have left The Warnings. Since Lissener is convinced that Belnot Phist will be their ally against Goodparley, Riddley reluctantly agrees to leave him. His own determination, which brought them to Fork Stoan, has waned by the time he arrives at Widders Dump. Travelling in various directions, his mind only holds on to a vision of the barren Zero Ground of Cambry:

> ... the woal time I wer thinking them thots part of me wer heading for Cambry with Lissener wylst a nother part wer wunnering when some thing wud come up to stop me. (...) With my mynd going all diffrent ways stil my feet gone jus that 1 way. ... Far far back behynt my eyes some other place some other time the dry dus rising and the hotness wivvering on the air. No me. Jus barrens and the dry dus blowing. (108-109)

Riddley notices the danger he is in only when the trap snaps shut behind him; Goodparley has been waiting for him at Widders Dump ever since he grew aware of Lissener's and Riddley's escape (112).

The fourth movement, which will take Riddley from Widders Dump to Cambry (chs. 14 and 15), starts with a longer break for Riddley (112). Goodparley turns out to be the indirect "director" of what has been going on so far and also of the events that ensue:

> '... Realy I wunt have to do nothing only tern you luce and let you run and youwd persoon get every thing all happent out and moving ... Yes thats all itwd take to get us moving frontwards agen is you and me working to gether. Abel Goodparley and Riddley Runner. Riddley Orfing. Why cant I have you for Shadder Mincer in stead of that dretful littl Orfing on my back and dragging his feet all the time.' (113-114)

Riddley has been Goodparley's fool, a puppet on his string, running his own private *Fools Circel 9wys*:[3]

---

3 See p. 5: "Horny Boy rung Widders Bel / Stoal his Fathers Ham as wel / Bernt his Arse and Forkt a Stoan / Done It Over broak a boan / Out of Good Shoar vackt his wayt / Scratcht Sams Itch for No. 8 / Gone to senter nex to see / Cambry coming 3 times 3 / Shama pax and get

> He said, 'O yes I beleave you parbly you dont even know your self what levvils youre working. *Horny Boy* which is what you are the same as any yung man. *Rung Widders Bel* Ive heard about you and Lorna Elswint shes out livet moren 1 husbin and manys the time youve rung her bel. *Stoal his Fathers Ham as wel....*' (115)

According to Goodparley's interpretation, he has only reached the stage "'... *Done It Over*. You gone over this here fents in the morning and back you come doing it over agen at nite...'" (116). But also his experiences in and after Widders Dump are part of the fool's circle which will only end when he arrives at Cambry. Widders Dump will in fact turn into a "Good Shoar" as soon as Goodparley has discovered Riddley's Punch figure (125) and taken a liking to the boy. They even find out that they are "moon brothers" too (136). Yet, Riddley also feels obliged to Belnot Phist, who is being tortured while Goodparley entertains Riddley with *The Legend of St Eustace* (118ff.), the story of his life (125ff.), a Punch and Pooty show (128ff.) and more details about Eusa's experiments (138ff.). Scratching "Sams Itch" might be Riddley's patting Goodparley's back (125), but also his relieving Belnot Phist from his torture (142). Moreover, it might be referred to his encounter with Granser on his way to Cambry; he feels a strong urge ("Itch") to stay with the charcoal-burner:

> What I wer lissening wer Power. ... The 1 Big 1 or the Spirit of God or the Littl Shyning Man or what ever. I cud feal that yellerboy stoan scrabbling to get out of its bag I cud feal how it wantit to get to that old man and I cud feal as he knowit what to do with it. (147)

His fear and the dogs, which still accompany him, make him move on to Cambry thus "scratching", i.e. relieving his urge (148). However, just as the boar prefigured Riddley's leaving his fence, Granser fills him with a new expectation regarding Punch and the 1 Big 1: "That old man sung his littl song and he put that waiting inside me" (149).

Cambry brings on a whole series of changes for Riddley, he loses as much as he gains. First, he becomes aware that the bond with Lissener no longer exists, but as if to comfort him – as if this *could* be a comfort! –, Big Old Father Power rapes him: "Fealt the Power in me I fealt strong with it and weak with it boath" (153). Then he tries to become one with the Mother Goddess but fails (155). His frustration stirs up a new longing in him; he now wants to know how his ancestors "put ther selfs with the Power of the wood be come stoan" (156). He feels the need for spirituality. His orientation is

---

the poal / When the Ardship of Cambry comes out of the hoal". On the map, the nine stations form a centripetal helix ending at Cambry.

troubled as it was at the end of the previous movements: "Too many things coming in at 1ce. Like all ways. Mixt up I wer like all ways" (161). But the contemplation of a picture that resembles Goodparley, the very picture responsible for his change of opinion about power – "I wernt looking for no Hy Power no mor I dint want no Power at all" (161-162) – provides him with a new destination: "The picter of Goodparley wer big and sprawly and the words wer wrote littl and close kep. Tite face. Orfing. Hoap of a tree. Tree in the stoan. Fork in the tree. Fork Stoan" (165).

In chapters 15 and 16, Riddley accomplishes a second circle, his fifth movement and one in which all his former longings for Punch, Power and Spirituality become gratified. When he saves Goodparley's life at Fork Stoan, the former Pry Mincer immediately takes the chance to ask Orfing, who is the new Pry Mincer, for his permission to perform Punch and Pooty shows with Riddley. Since Orfing is not naive about the political effectiveness of art, nor about his former partner's undiminished powers,[4] Goodparley must use all his rhetorical skill to persuade him. But eventually they get "letshow" (174f.). Leading blind Goodparley to Granser, Riddley becomes witness of the "1 Littl 1". The important thing about this episode is that Riddley's complete lack of ambition both makes him acquainted with the secret of the mixture and saves his life, for he first obeys Goodparley, who tells him to go and watch Granser, then Granser, who sends him out of the hut before he lights the gunpowder (188). Absent-minded once more, he returns to Cambry a second time after the two old men have been blown up: "My feet begun to walk me down rivver tords Cambry" (190). At the Ring Ditch, he finally defines a relationship to Power that is viable and will neither overwhelm nor frustrate him; he finds out what being *with* the Power is: "Its the not sturgling for Power thats where the Power is" (191). He has found a principle of hope that enables him to enter "the woom of her what has her woom in Cambry" (191) in a totally unspectacular way which does not disturb the dark of the night or exhaust him (191f.). Having experienced the ideal way to be, he is even able to cheer up Erny Orfing, who has grown totally disillusioned: "'Riddley dyou think theres hoap of anything?' – I said, 'Theres new earf on the barrens all the time.'" (192-193).

A fairly long break then allows Riddley to meditate on his past and the future. It is at Cambry that he starts writing down the story of his life we have been reading. The gap between experiencing and narrating "I", or Riddley the character and the narrator, which was clearly visible, for example, at the

4 Goodparley may be old and blind but certainly not "broakin", as he tries to present himself (174): he strongly resembles toothless Manny Rat before the latter tries to blow up the dolls' house (MC 183f.), and Orfing knows him well enough to see through his pretence.

beginning of the novel when Riddley referred to his writing by means of a footnote (2), has been closed for the first time. The present time adverb "now" corresponds with the present tenses of his verbs: "Right now there aint even no Pry Mincer..." (197). But the fact that his story does not continue in the present tense, "I *liket* the idear of making up shows..." (197; emphasis added), indicates that the rest of the novel is told from a new period of rest, a new vantage point about which we will not learn anything. The narrator's here and now at the end of the novel can no longer be located because his account ends before it has reached the present a second time. Thus, we are in some ways "lef hanging" (59), like the puzzled villagers after Riddley's first connection, and his voice prefigures that of Hoban's next narrator, Pilgermann. Riddley also defines a new style which resembles Hoban's own way of writing (cf. above, ch. 1, pp. 12-13): "Ready to cry ready to dy ready for any thing is how I come to it now. In fear and tremmering only not running a way. In emtyness and ready to be fult" (199). His style allows him to be with all the characters he writes about, open-minded and unprejudiced, just as he is able to represent every figure of his Punch show. All his experiences provide a stock of usable material: "That boar kicking on the end of my spear hewl be in my shows I dont know how but hewl be there..." (201).

The sixth movement, from Cambry to Weaping[5] and onwards, starts in the middle of chapter 17. The definition of Riddley's new style is already part of it since the preceding change of narrative perspective clearly marks the beginning of the last stage in Riddley's development:

> Walker & Orfing. I *liket* the idear of making up shows only with things how they *are* now I *wernt* all that kean to road no show I ratherwd live qwyet and ly low til we *seen* who come out on top. It *wer* Orfing as wantit to start showing. (197-198; emphasis added)

The temporal distance between character and narrator is visible in this passage. There is a new gap between the present tense form "are" (reinforced by the adverb "now"), which refers to Riddley the narrator's new vantage point, and the past tense of "wernt", which of course corresponds with the pastness of Riddley the character. As the passage further shows, Erny Orfing is at first the driving force deciding on the strategy they are to adopt, for Riddley's consciousness is once more reduced to an intuitive level of intake: "I wer seeing it mor with my stummick nor my eyes" (202).

5 Nancy Dew Taylor's observation that Weaping is "*not* a part of the Fools Circel 9wys" is worth pointing out. Riddley and Erny's journey to that place is indeed "an indication of the fracturing of the cycle" (36). If people are free to define new destinations, history need not repeat itself. Caution nevertheless must not be abandoned: the place name Weaping suggests both "weapons" and "weeping".

Only when they are stuck in front of the gate at Weaping Form and Riddley starts questioning the situation they are in, "Whynt we stay hoalt up? Whynt we go somers far a way?" (205), his own answers fetch his mind back into the present: "Becaws you cant stay hoalt up. Becaws there aint no far a way. Becaws where you happen is where you happen" (205). He takes the initiative: since their punishment for Goodparley's death is required by the "Big Man" of Weaping (204ff.), Riddley makes Punch "punish" him:

> I ternt my back to the gate and Mr Punch come up looking at them over my sholder. He wer waving his stick he made his cock fessin noys. Rrrrrrrrrrrr. He said, '*Ah putcha putcha putcha.*' Which he begun to beat me with his stick. Them on the gate begun to larf. I cud feal ther eyes on Punch and I wer hoaping hewd say some thing funny. He dint tho. (206)

Apart from this action, Riddley remains very restrained as regards the terms of his first show. It is up to the members of the audience to set up rules of presentation, and they obviously do not always agree:

> We tol them it wernt no Eusa show nor we dint think we shud do no wotcher only ther connexion man Deaper Flinter he wer Rightways brother he said they wunt let us show without we wotchert 1st. So we got our hash and rizlas only diffrents wer he said if it wernt no Eusa show we shunt get the woal wotcher. (...)
>
> They wer mummering in the front row it wer about the show talk. Deaper Flinter said it wernt right doing the Eusa show talk if it wernt no Eusa show. Which Rightway Flinter said there wernt going to be no show without no show talk not wylst he wer Big Man any how. ... Which Deaper said Rightway cud do what he liket only he wernt going to say the name of Eusa if it wernt no Eusa show. (207)

Without Riddley having to persuade anybody, those who understand the sense of Punch and Pooty shows follow and protect him after the first show has been interrupted by ignorant Easyer. For Riddley's and Erny's way of life provides an answer to the problem what Inlanders, and especially inhabitants of fentses, can do instead of submitting to the life of farmers at a time when there is nothing left to hunt for: they can now become travelling artists if they want to be "on the move" (213) again, "boredom-killers" instead of boar-hunters. It is an alternative way of life that will bring on as much danger, excitement and uncertainty as the life they led before. Hence, even though Riddley's way has not led him back to How Fents as yet, the novel moves back to the initially raised question. The overall metaphorical movement of the novel is no circle but a three-dimensional helix, however, for its beginning and end are separated through Riddley's development. It is a structure that symbolizes moderate progress: the circle is broken by adding another dimension to the otherwise two-dimensional geometrical figure; there is no violent rupture. The helix is thus a synthesis between line and circle. Moreover, it recalls the structure of chromosomes, i.e. the genetic programmes for our lives. David Dowling writes in *Fictions of Nuclear Disaster* (1987):

> Like Miller [i.e. Walter M. Miller, Jr., the author of *A Canticle for Leibowitz*], Hoban sees history as cyclic. His answer to the question of evolution is that sooner or later gunpowder and rockets will be re-invented. Both writers are obviously sympathetic with the quest of their heroes for a password into history, their attempt to get the show on the road again. What concerns them both is the spirit in which that step is taken. Miller's characters are polarised between the claims of God and Mammon, and at the end Miller skilfully balances the claims and blindnesses of both religion and science. Hoban goes a step forward (or is it backwards?), away from the outward institutions of the cathedral and the laboratory, to suggest the need for a personal re-orientation towards what is happening. (207)

The fact that he is wondering if the step towards personal re-orientation is a step forward or backward shows that he does not fully take into account the moral dimension of Riddley's development. If all individuals begin to assume responsibility for their lives in making certain choices while rejecting others, history, too, can leave its fool's circle and move on in a constructive (three-dimensional or centrifugal) helix instead of leading centripetally to general annihilation at Ground Zero. It is not by chance that one of the central tenets of feminism is that the personal is political.[6] And from an altogether different camp, from seventy-year-old Albert Einstein came the following assessment regarding sources of hope:

> There seems to be no doubt that in all countries power lies in the hands of power-hungry men who practice little restraint when it comes to realizing their ambitions. This is true whatever the form of the political machinery, dictatorial or democratic. Power not only relies on coercion but on subtle persuasion and deception which is accomplished through the educational system and through all media of public information.
>
> You ask whether self-restraint in research on the part of creative thinkers and scientists might not prevent the further development of the technological means of mass destruction. I do not believe that salvation can be expected even if the scientist should adopt such a policy.... (...)
>
> One can only hope that there are enough people the world over who possess the intellectual and moral integrity to resist all the nefarious

6 See, for example Chris Weedon, who writes: "The belief that the personal is political is one of the founding assumptions of contemporary feminist theory and practice. The personal encompasses both the nature of the individual, whether this be seen as innate or socially acquired, and individual experience of the world" (74). The quotation has been taken from "Language and Subjectivity", the fourth chapter of her study *Feminist Practice and Poststucturalist Theory* (1987). The chapter is interesting precisely because Weedon affirms the validity of the tenet despite poststructuralist ideas about subjectivity, in relation to which she discusses it. See especially her conclusion (106).

> influences brought to bear on them. While it might possibly be helpful to organize such people, the usefulness of such organization tends to be overestimated. What is important is that individuals have the honesty and courage to stand up for their convictions on every occasion. (Einstein 510-511)[7]

By locating responsibility in individuals, Einstein avoided repeating the fruitless disputes in which responsibility is pointlessly shifted from one group of society to another. Salvation, if it comes at all, comes from individuals who resist, be they scientists, politicians, or members of any other group.

So far, my analysis has only been focussing on the dynamic parts of the novel, but it would be an act of infidelity to the text to disregard all the passages that regularly interrupt the flow of the story: I) *Hart of the Wood* (2-4), II) *Why the Dog Wont Show Its Eyes* (16-19), III) *The Eusa Story* (28-34), IV) the Eusa show interpreted by Riddley (41-50), V) the Eusa show interpreted by Brooder Walker (53-56), VI) *The Lissener and the Other Voyce Owl of the Worl* (82-83) VII) *The Bloak as Got on Top of Aunty* (87-90), VIII) *The Legend of St Eustace* (118-119), IX) Goodparley's Punch and Pooty show (128-135), X) the philosophical text *Stoan* (158-159), XI) a conversation between Punch and Greanvine (166-167), XII) Riddley's Punch and Pooty show (209-213), and various poems, songs (e.g. *Fools Circel 9wys*, 5, 76), and jokes that are not particularly set off from the main body of the text. "Interrupt" may not be the right word, though. For even if it is true that they "interrupt the tempo of the narrative" (Lively 58), they provide us with a background that increases our understanding of the characters' ways of thinking and acting. Their contents link the people of 2347 O.C. with their immediate and remote past, juxtaposing different ways of life and warning the Inlanders of greed and of the abuse of power in all forms. A brief song in the second chapter, for instance, gives an account of what happened to London during Bad Time (although most Inlanders probably do not even know where and what London was, having never set foot outside their fentses and forms): "London Town is drownt this day / Hear me say walk a way / Sling your bundel tern and go / Parments in the mud you know / Greaf and woe dont you know / Pick it up its time to go" (9). Although each of these short pieces could be seen as an independent unit within the novel, they contribute to the coherence of the text in so far as certain excerpts or interpretations are taken up at later stages in order to be developed further or refuted. Eusa 5 and 6, for instance, are quoted again in chapter 12 (97) to describe Riddley's eagerness to make things happen: he here uses the Eusa story as a source for his analogies. But in

---

7 This is the excerpt from a letter Einstein wrote to a worried Australian pathologist and Quaker on 18 February 1949; for the entire letter see *Einstein on Peace* (1960), 510-511.

chapter 15, which opens with Eusa 7, Riddley utters his disbelief in Lorna's story *Why the Dog Wont Show Its Eyes*, dismissing it as overly cautionary:

> That story of why the dog wont show its eyes where it tels of putting the 1 Big 1 in to the Power Ring which the very 1st time they woosht it roun it ternt the nite to day then every thing gone black I dont beleave that. Looking at them stannings I knowit inside me they musve had that 1 Big 1 going round there regler. (150)

As we have seen before, Hoban is interested in a plot that uses both "static" as well as "dynamic" elements without giving preference to either type. The phenomenon also characterizes *Turtle Diary* (cf. ch. 5.2) and its predecessors. The dream sequences in *The Lion of Boaz-Jachin and Jachin-Boaz*, too, have been shown to be more than fanciful extensions of the plot since they contain keys to Jachin-Boaz's behaviour. Finally, the dislocutions in *Kleinzeit* all depart from "static" or fixed elements in the text such as names of diseases or patients. Yet, in *Riddley Walker*, the principle of dislocution, which makes the static interpolations and the language come alive, is much more foregrounded than it was in any of Hoban's previous novels. The graphic prominence of most interpolations and of the novel's language compels the readers to find explanations for Hoban's choices; they achieve more than "literariness" since they convey part of the novel's meaning. The very distinction between "static" and "dynamic" will collapse if what happens in and through the "static" interpolations is compared to the actual absence of action (other than body movements) while Riddley overtly hurries from one place to the other, e.g. during his night run from Cambry to Fork Stoan (167f.). But let's nevertheless maintain the distinction for heuristic reasons.

In "Russell Hoban's *Riddley Walker*: Doing the Connections" (1988), David Dowling presents the following interpretation of the sequence of interpolations (numbers I, II, III, VI, VII, VIII, IX, X, and XII in my list; Dowling does not include the Eusa shows or the dialogue between Punch and Greanvine):

> The sequence is significant. The first three stories are, or claim to be, parables of our fall from grace through the invention of nuclear power. In each story, a parent takes life from a child. The fourth story [VI] is Lissener's and is devoted to the importance, not of making connections or telling, but rather of listening, sustaining the world by careful attention to it instead of acting upon it and threatening it: we must 'lissen everything back'.
>
> The centre story [VII] is offered as an explanation of the name 'Hagmans Il' (Hinxhill) – a man seduced by the inescapable aunty, Death, in disguise. But this story is undercut by the revelation that the name Hagmans Il may be a corruption of 'Hogmans Kil,' whose source is a completely different story about a woman who killed her brutish husband there.

> In the first half of *Riddley Walker*, then, we see a progressive reduction in the power of stories to provide meaningful answers to the people's predicament, until the *aporia* of Hagmans Il opens up a bewildering world of hearsay and etymological obscurity.
>
> The second half of the novel reinstates story, but in a performative context. Goodparley decodes the Eustace story [VIII] for his own ends, seeing secreted in the life of the saint the chemical formula for gunpowder. The Punch and Judy show [sic; IX] is a dramatic performance, which is followed by Riddley's own lyrical outpouring in 'Stoan.' [X] The only non-narrative piece, it is an expression of his feeling of oneness with the universe brought on by his proximity to both the cathedral and the power station at Cambry. Finally we are left with Riddley's own performance of the Punch and Judy show [XII], which does not simply present Punch's violence but engages in dialogue with the audience.
>
> Riddley, then, proceeds from being a listener to being a teller to being a performer, in a steady evolution from a faith in received meaning and encoded connection, to an acceptance of mystery and an extreme epistemological scepticism. (184-185)

This is a convincing interpretation into which the excluded interpolations can be easily integrated: the two Eusa shows [IV, V] illustrate how the secret *Eusa Story* is transformed into a political instrument of the Ram. But the shows' effectiveness is limited: an intelligent connexion man with a different political interest won't find it difficult to subvert their message; a mystic like Riddley, on the other hand, will develop altogether different associations than the ones he is expected to bring up. The Punch and Greanvine dialogue [XI] is Riddley's first performance, even though it takes place without an audience. Playfully dramatizing ideas formulated in *Stoan*, he might just have discovered a way to less violent puppet shows but is not yet aware of the possibility himself.

What I find less convincing is the ending of Dowling's interpretation. Can one really speak of "extreme epistemological scepticism" by the time Riddley has turned into a puppeteer? The ending of Aldiss's *Barefoot in the Head* would be a more suitable candidate for this description. It is true that the last two chapters of *Riddley Walker* are full of questions and formulas by which Riddley expresses his uncertainty. The crucial question "what the idear of us myt be" (7) cannot be answered once and for all but must be asked again and again. But certain answers have been and will be found by Riddley, even though they are rare, provisional and personal, perhaps also conveyed through indirect channels. He writes, "If youre a show man then what ever happens is took in to your figgers and your fit up its took into your show. If you dont know whats happent sooner youwl hear of it later youwl hear your figgers tel of it 1 way or a nother" (201). Moreover, as a performer he will have to answer for what his figures show. The little boy who taunts him singing "Dont go Riddley Walkers track / Drop Johns ryding on his back" (214) knows about Riddley's responsibility; and Riddley knows about it, too, although he would prefer to remain ignorant. In the end, however, he affirms his choice: "Stil I wunt have no other track" (214).

The question I asked at the beginning of this chapter may now be answered: while interpolations fulfil a similar function as the "ruins" of the past did on all linguistic levels, that is showing the characters' indebtedness to but also their need to proceed from their past and directing the readers' attention to their present achievements and errors, the novel's "movements" may bring on comfort and progress but also further mutilation and death: "We livet and we kep our eyes and our cocks and balls that time any how. What the nex time wil bring no 1 cant never say" (207). Hence, the novel's plot clearly reflects the duplicity that could be observed to be at work in its language. Nevertheless, this does not entail that "anything goes". When Dowling writes, "Hoban, and finally Riddley, refuse to enter the fiction of resolution into an answer, a third term. Instead of synthesis, we have, to the last, oscillation. History repeats itself, Riddley's people rediscover gunpowder, and Hoban refuses to say whether this is for good or ill" ("Russell Hoban's *Riddley Walker*...", 186), he insinuates that both author and narrator are moral relativists. But this is not the case. Oscillation suggests a movement with potential turning points at which certain choices about the direction must be made, and these choices entail responsibilities. Both Hoban and Riddley deliberately refuse to *teach* their readers, that is, to persuade them into sharing their values: "Not to lern no body nothing I cant even lern my oan self..." (199). Yet, this does not mean that there are no answers at all, or that all answers are equally fallacious; ultimately, it is a way of referring everybody back to themselves. Personally Hoban does not withhold his view; in February 1986, immediately before the première of the stage version of *Riddley Walker*, he told Robin Thornber:

> 'The Soviet and US governments, with their monstrous phallic displays of missiles, both fail to perceive the bomb for what it is – it is the enemy of all of us and should be dealt with that way. It's a failure of mythopoeic perception. If our myth-making faculty were not shrivelled up and atrophied we could see it. The world has lost the faculty of recognising monsters, demons, and devils.' (...)
>
> That's why Riddley Walker is an optimistic piece, he says. 'Because it's the story of the development of an artist.' (Thornber 10)

6.4. Riddley's World: Science Fiction, Revelation, Nightmare, Accident Risk, Survival Scenario

"We talked our way into our nuclear nightmare, word by word and story by story. As long as we remain ignorant of this conversation, we make ourselves helpless to alter it. But our stories create, as well as reflect, the public conversation we live by. Perhaps we already are telling ourselves stories that contain alternatives to species suicide. If not, we need to begin."
(Martha Bartter, *The Way to Ground Zero*, p. v)

The long title of this last chapter on *Riddley Walker* points to the almost inextricable complexity of a novel which concerns a multitude of disciplines from literature to the sciences and from psychology to theology. Riddley must find a way of dealing with all the aspects of his world, but his attitude varies. He is what he is at a given moment: learning step by step, undergoing change, succumbing to temptation or distancing himself when he can no longer identify with certain positions. Barbara Herkommer stresses his being under way, walking, thereby establishing himself as a character on a journey, one of the oldest plot types (135). Indeed the journey is the perfect figure to represent the human condition; since Riddley is a character undergoing a series of changes, the function of the journey changes with him: it starts out as a picaresque escape from a place in which Riddley can no longer stay, continues as a quest for scientific knowledge until that aim becomes obsolete and is replaced by the quest for spirituality, which turns the journey into a pilgrimage; finally however, Riddley recognizes that travelling is an aim in itself which allows him to ponder the "idear of us" (7): rather than to find a definite answer to this question, he starts writing down what he has found out so far while continuing the journey as a travelling puppeteer.

SCIENCE FICTION?

Owing to its setting in the future, though, the novel can also be discussed in terms of its proximity to the science fiction genre. Hoban is "reluctant to label his novel science fiction" (Maynor and Patteson 18), and David Lake writes in his review for *Foundation: The Review of Science Fiction*, that albeit a "classic of fringe science fiction" ("Riddley Walker. Pilgermann", 97-98), it is "post-Bomb sf" only "on the surface" (96). Without getting too entangled in ongoing debates about what science fiction really is or should be,[1] basing my analysis on Robert Scholes and Eric Rabkin's *Science Fiction:*

1 The topic will be addressed once more in ch. 11.1, where science fiction is discussed in relation to magic realism.

History, Science, Vision (1977) and Barbara Puschmann-Nalenz's *Science Fiction and Postmodern Fiction* (1992), I would like to highlight a few features which might have earned Hoban prizes such as the "John W. Campbell Memorial Award for Best Science Fiction Novel" in 1982[2] or induced compilers of lists of "best science fiction novels" to include *Riddley Walker*.[3] However, since it also figured on best-books lists of "mainstream" literature, together with fiction by Anthony Burgess, Margaret Atwood, Iris Murdoch, John Updike, Raymond Carver or Nadine Gordimer,[4] that is in a context in which a conventional science fiction novel is not likely to be mentioned, it must have qualities which noticeably distinguish it from the average output of both markets. For two of the "nuclear critics" who have discussed Hoban's novel extensively, that is David Dowling and Peter Schwenger, *Riddley Walker* is not just one novel among many but an exemplary nuclear fiction.[5] Its unstable "place", then, appears to be the fruitful dark area between science fiction and contemporary experimental fiction – fruitful and at the same time frightening, since it is concerned with a theme that poses an extreme challenge both to the imagination and to our ethical capacity.

Mary Shelley's *Frankenstein* (1818) is generally given credit for being the first science fiction novel;[6] unlike the utopian fictions and imaginary voyages

---

2 According to the "Biographical Notes" kindly sent me by Hoban's publishing company Jonathan Cape.

3 E.g. David Pringle, *Science Fiction: 100 Best Novels* (London: Xanadu, 1985).

4 See e.g. the (London) *Time Out* list "The Other Best Seller" of February 5 to 11, 1982, p. 21; or Robert H. Harris's list of "The 20 Best Books of 1981" compiled for *The Saturday Review* 8 (December 1981), pp. 75-77.

5 Cf. David Dowling, *Fictions of Nuclear Disaster* (1987), esp. pp. 193 ff.; and Peter Schwenger, "Circling Ground Zero" (1991), p. 254. Also see note 2 and the bibliography of Schwenger's essay for references to further examples of "nuclear criticism" (260-261). A first tentative definition of "nuclear criticism" is to be found in the unsigned introduction to *Diacritics* 14 (Summer 1984), "Proposal for a *Diacritics* Colloquium on Nuclear Criticism": "By Nuclear Criticism is meant something positive and something unavowed, a new topic and an explicitation of what is already everywhere being done. This proposal arises, on the one hand, out of reading a certain amount of recent criticism and critical theory and feeling that without exception it recounts an allegory of nuclear survival; and, on the other, out of the sense that critical theory ought to be making a more important contribution to the public discussion of nuclear issues." (2). Six years later, William J. Scheick added in "Nuclear Criticism: An Introduction", published in *Papers on Language and Literature* 26.1 (Winter 1990): "Whether written with social/political fervor or intellectual abstraction, nuclear criticism aims for a redirection of critiques of cultural artifacts from the remote spatial void of poststructuralism to the apposite inner-spatial realm of human ethos. Just as the meaning of the word 'nucleus' altered from something faraway to something nearby, nuclear criticism aims to transform the poststructuralist distant and abstract emphasis on the indeterminacy of the meaning of any thought or word to an immediate and relevant emphasis on the determinacy of at least one meaning: the utter reality of predictable death, of the total extinction of all life, in terms of the nuclear referent" (5).

6 N.B.: The term "science fiction" was coined about a century later; it developed from "scientifiction", Hugo Gernsback's name for "the Jules Verne, H. G. Wells, and Edgar Allan Poe type of story – a charming romance intermingled with scientific fact and prophetic vision", as he defined the stories which were published in his pulp magazines (quoted in Scholes and

which preceded her novel, *Frankenstein* derived its impact from the shocking awareness that, all at once, fantasies might be precipitated into realities and the future be altogether different from all experience:

> In order to appreciate the nature of the first future shock we must imagine how people of the pre-modern era visualized the future. In ancient times most people saw the future as being simply a continuation of the present – until the end of the world. For many, the myth of a golden age, from which men had fallen and to which they might be restored at the end of time, provided some comfort. But the notion that the world would change regularly is simply not a part of human thought until modern times. Plato, who saw as far as anyone, saw only cycles – as tyranny, oligarchy, democracy, anarchy, and, once again, tyranny succeeded one another in time. (...) ... science fiction could begin to exist as a literary form only when a different future became conceivable by human beings – specifically a future in which new knowledge, new discoveries, new adventures, new mutations, would make life radically different from the familiar patterns of the past and present. ... Mary Shelley changed her reality by simply projecting a scientific advance that *might* be made *some* day upon her own historical time. She introduced a piece of a possible future into her own world... (Scholes and Rabkin 6-7).

Hoban, too, has imagined a possible future; unlike Mary Shelley, though, he did not even have to project a scientific advance to explain the destructions and mutations of 2347 O.C.: nuclear power plants, power rings (e.g. CERN in Geneva), atomic and hydrogen bombs were already part of our reality when *Riddley Walker* was published in 1980. Even though the arms race has subsided since the USA and the USSR agreed to reduce their nuclear weapons in 1987 ("conventional" weapons are another matter),[7] there are still sufficient bombs, atomic or otherwise, available to wreak global havoc; and nuclear power plants continue to produce waste nobody knows how to dispose of for good, although there have been no more spectacular accidents since Chernobyl exploded in 1986. Whereas *Frankenstein* was inspired by the first future shock, *Riddley Walker* responded to a climate whose motto was coined by the punk generation of the late 1970s and early 1980s, i.e. "no future".[8] Significantly,

---

Rabkin 37). The term was coined in 1923 and defined by Gernsback in 1926, but no date is given for the first appearance of "science fiction".

7 See Martha A. Bartter's "Chronology: The Atomic Bomb" in *The Way to Ground Zero* (1988), p. 16. Her study impressively demonstrates the interaction between science fiction literature, science and society, especially where the development of and reactions to the first atomic bombs are concerned; as a matter of fact the bomb triggered a boom of the genre because people all at once felt that they had been catapulted into a veritable "science fiction world" (116). One of those who reported the bombing on 6 August, 1945, said, confusing the monster with its producer in the usual way (but perhaps there is a certain truth in this error): "'For all we know, we have created a Frankenstein! ...'" (Bartter 115-116).

8 Scholes and Rabkin date the "end-of-the-world motif" as a "persistent preoccupation in science fiction" back to Mary Shelley, too (8), i.e. to her novel *The Last Man* (1826). But it definitely took the explosions of the first atomic bombs to turn the idea of global destruction from being a remote possibility into a concrete and ever-present man-made threat.

the 1 Big 1 stops the time count, and with it the awareness of time, for an unknown number of years. The latest date from our time found by the Inlanders on the ruined walls of the Power Ring is 1997 A.D.: whether or not the catastrophe took place right then or later and how much time passed until they started counting the years again, however, is uncertain, as Goodparley tells Riddley (120).

With H. G. Wells, a further leading figure of science fiction literature, who used to call his novels "scientific romances" (Scholes and Rabkin 19), Hoban shares the belief that imagining the future is vital. In *Experiment in Autobiography* (1934), Wells recalled a lecture held in 1902:

> I called this lecture *Discovery of the Future* and I drew a hard distinction between what I called the legal (past-regarding) and the creative (future-regarding) minds. I insisted that we overrated the darkness of the future, that by adequate analysis of contemporary processes its conditions could be brought within the range of our knowledge and its form controlled.... We should be less and less bound by the engagements of the past and more and more ruled by a realization of the creative effects of our acts. We should release ourselves more and more from the stranglehold of past things. (quoted in Scholes and Rabkin 15-16)

Of course Wells was more optimistic and also more naive than Hoban regarding our power to control the form of the future: by 1934 the atomic bomb, whose invention and use in a devastating mid-century war he had imagined in his 1914 novel *The World Set Free*, had not yet exploded. Would he have published his book, had he known the consequences? Leo Szilard, the physicist "whose work on particle physics made the atomic bomb possible" (Bartter 103), felt encouraged to leave Germany for Britain after reading *The World Set Free* in 1932; after emigrating to the USA, he did everything in his power to equip the USA with this weapon rather than wait for his former colleagues in Nazi Germany to develop it first. Both Wells and Szilard no doubt meant well: they sought to prevent the use of the bomb. But the chain-reaction of events in which they took part disregarded their intentions and ultimately led to a renewed arms race. Riddley's development can be taken as an index for the degree to which Wells's and Hoban's prospects for the future agree or disagree. His orientation changes from being mainly concerned with the past, that is with the reconstruction of the 1 Big 1, to the "future-regarding" question of what the "idear of us" might be. But he is aware that the past will continue to exert its influence on the present and loses all illusions about the controllability of the future. Before he and Orfing leave Cambry for Weaping Form, he spells out the problem:

> Orfing and me we know weare living on burrow time but then who aint. The way things are now it aint jus only you dont know whos going to go bang nex you dont even know where the arrer myt come from with your name on it you cant be too sure whos your frend and whos your nemminy life aint qwite as simpl as it use to be. (197)

Hoban's "analysis of contemporary processes" suggests that we mostly underrate, rather than overrate, the darkness of the future, if we imagine it at all, because we underrate the darkness in ourselves. He closes his novel by making Riddley wonder why Punch is "crookit" and will "all ways kil the babby if he can" (214). Where Wells demands that we be "ruled by a realization of the creative effects of our acts", Hoban is aware that every creative and well-meant act has a destructive underside which might only manifest itself in retrospect, and vice versa. Acting rationally does not necessarily prevent catastrophes. Unlike Wells, Hoban does not simply locate evil in "animal appetites" (Scholes and Rabkin 20). There is no recipe for happiness; we can only ask ourselves again and again if the decisions we have consciously taken need to be reconsidered and if our intuitive acts were right or wrong. *Riddley Walker* therefore cannot possibly draw an "utopian" picture of the future (Scholes and Rabkin 27). "Dystopian" though it may be (Scholes and Rabkin 26), however, we are not to become indifferent or hopeless: we determine, and must answer for, the kind of guilt that we accumulate in the course of our lives.

This overall concern with responsibility and guilt, but also the desire for spirituality which is kindled when Riddley learns from Lorna that we are lived by a mysterious "thing in us what thinks us but it dont think like us" (7) and when he visits the ruins of Canterbury cathedral, link the novel to another subgenre of science fiction, religious science fiction. It developed from the religious epics of Dante, More and Milton, and the anti-science fiction and religious fantasy of C. S. Lewis. Since the latter genre also informs *Pilgermann*, I will quote another longer passage from Scholes and Rabkin:

> The worlds of Dante and Milton remain separate from science fiction because they are constructed on a plan derived from religious tradition rather than scientific speculation or imagination based, however loosely, upon science. They populate the cosmos neither with fantastic creatures for their own sake nor with beings of speculative significance, but with angels, devils, and other products of a specifically religious world-view, which guides the fictional creation, sets limits for it, and lends it powers of credibility for the faithful. (...)
>
> After Newton and Milton, who were contemporaries..., science became increasingly materialistic and drew literature with it away from the fantastic space of religious epics and toward a more and more materialistic domain, which culminated in the naturalism of the late nineteenth century. But following these two centuries of increasing materialism and determinism, the

> scientific pendulum began to swing the other way, and literature to move with it. ... As science fiction reached out for more speculative territory it entered the area formerly occupied by the religious epic. ... It should not be surprising that this invasion of religious space by science fiction should provoke a new religious fiction to arise and contest the field with the growing body of science-fictional works. ... Science had shaken the historical and cosmological foundations of the Judeo-Christian religions. But it had not succeeded in providing a set of values for man beyond the experimental ethics of scientific research itself. As the twentieth century (note that this designation of time is itself both specifically Christian – A.D. – and very unscientific) progressed, the need for values beyond those of research and development became more apparent. ... Perhaps it was inevitable that such a development should provoke the sleeping giant of religious fantasy. (42-43)

Whereas Lewis sought to defend a specifically Christian ethic, which he accepted unconditionally, against one constructed by philosophers "upon hypothesis rather than revelation" (Scholes and Rabkin 49), Riddley's world is not simply one which has deliberately rejected the Judeo-Christian tradition, a world twice fallen, but one which has lost the connection to that tradition, i.e. something inconceivable for Lewis. For Goodparley, A.D. means "All Done" (120) – and there is no reincarnation of Merlin as in Lewis's *That Hideous Strength* (Scholes and Rabkin 47), or any other human being of our time to correct his misreading and reinstate the original meaning of the two initials or the religious terms used in the *Legend of St Eustace*. Nevertheless Riddley experiences revelations, and they move him in significant ways (cf. his sudden abandoning the desire for "Hy Power" at Cambry, 153). He is a mystic like Pilgermann, religious in a non-institutionalized way. For Hoban, the quantum physics of our age is no reason to abandon the idea of God or a more general divine principle, as it would have been for Einstein, who preferred to reject quantum physics with the words "God does not play dice" rather than to alter his idea of the divine (Scholes and Rabkin 47). According to Hoban, a religious writer is "a writer who is always examining the position of one's self in the universe. *Riddley Walker* was the first novel that I thought of as being a religious novel, in that it was definitely doing that, that's what it was concerned with" (Hoban and Bodmer 2). What is divine is "the hart uv the stoan hart uv the dans. Evere thing blippin & bleapin & movin in the shiftin uv thay Nos. Sum tyms bytin sum tyms bit" (191); the devil, on the other hand, Mr Clevver or Mr On The Levvil or Drop John, is whatever stops the movement, that which disconnects, but even that might be part of "the girt dants of the every thing" (201). How morality can nevertheless be developed from this all-embracing mystical view of the universe will be discussed later.

The representative of religious science fiction with whom Hoban is most often compared is Walter M. Miller, the author of *A Canticle for Leibowitz*

(1959).[9] In his post-holocaust novel, the future of the survivors is described in three parts set in the twenty-sixth, the thirty-second and the thirty-eighth centuries A.D. In the end, the earth is destroyed by a second nuclear holocaust while a spaceship saves a small community of believers. As in Lewis's novels, there is no room for an individualistic world view in *A Canticle*: the protagonists are monks. All events are subservient to biblical notions of the apocalypse: our planet meets its predestined fate from which only a select few can escape to the heavens. Significantly, the novel is written in third-person narration, adopting at the end of each part the non-human point of view of buzzards and eventually a shark, a technique which is reminiscent of the transitional section of Golding's *Inheritors*. As far as human history on earth is concerned, the plot is closed in the most literal sense possible. Hoban's novel is less pessimistic even though many interpreters claim that they can detect the same kind of circularity in its theme and structure as is to be found in Miller's. As we have already seen, however, the plot does not support such an assumption. Since the question of the role of circularity is crucial for the interpretation of *Riddley Walker*, it will be resumed later on.

Viewed synchronically rather than diachronically and considering formal features beside the contents, it is harder to classify *Riddley Walker* as a science fiction novel proper: it turns out to be a postmodern novel making use of certain science fiction motifs (future setting; nuclear disaster as trigger for plot and action; mutants). Barbara Puschmann-Nalenz has compiled a very useful list of contrasts between science fiction and postmodern texts (108);[10] so as to

---

9 See David Lake, "Making the Two One: Language and Mysticism in *Riddley Walker*" (1984); Thomas J. Morrissey, "Armageddon from Huxley to Hoban" (1984); Peter Schwenger, "Writing the Unthinkable" (1986); or Jeffrey Porter, "'Three Quarks for Muster Mark': Quantum Wordplay and Nuclear Discourse in Russell Hoban's *Riddley Walker*" (1990); David Dowling has dedicated the entire seventh chapter of *Fictions of Nuclear Disaster* (1987), i.e. "Two Exemplary Fictions", to the comparative analysis of RW and *A Canticle*, and he also discovered another interesting source text, Jack London's *The Scarlet Plague* (1910), cf. p. 207. In the interview with Michel Bodmer, Hoban acknowledges having read Miller: "Years ago, and when I came round to re-interpreting the Eusa Story wrongly, I recognised that I was doing a variation on what he did with the electrical diagrams. That's all right, I arrived at it in my own way, it's not as if I was just lifting something" (Hoban and Bodmer 5-6).

10 N.B.: Puschmann is quite aware that SF is an open genre sharing a great number of features with other genres, especially popular ones: adventure stories, western, detective fiction, etc. (6, 109). Its specific component, however, "the dominant, is first of all the relation of fictitious and empirical world. In this point the genre differs from other fiction, serious as well as popular. (...) The question 'What if?' underlying SF not only renders a 'willing suspension of disbelief' possible at some points while generally the ruling principles of the known reality retain their validity; it also makes these principles an indispensable premise. At the same time it applies strategies which make it easier for the reader to yield to the imaginary by encouraging the shaping of illusions.

The presumed suspension of the familiar concept of reality is – and this is a central paradox of the genre – linked to the preservation of a 'realistic' and 'rational' world concept. That means that the SF-reader has to accept the premise that in the world represented there he encounters a universe different from the one he knows, and he has to accept at the same time that this other world has the same status of reality as the empirical one" (109). In Table 1, the

Table 1: Structural Pattern of Genre Conventions
(based on Puschmann-Nalenz, 108)

Postmodern Novel	*component*	*Science Fiction*
emphasizing consciousness non-teleological procedure open-end structure multivalent, deconstructive	*1. predominant structural element*	action-dominated suspense-orientated teleological development *closure*
no clear borderline between fiction and reality; reality is subjective	*2. status of the fictional world*	postulate of reality; no questioning of axiomatic truth of an objective reality
narration is fictionalized auto-reflexive	*3. narrative situation and perspective*	narration is not thematic in the texts
introspective, reflective, dis-interested in public issues (?), anti-hero (?), vague	*4. protagonist and constellation of characters*	active and rational character, knowledge-able, a leader (?) and individualist, possesses integrating abilities
intra-subjective "experienced time"; emphasis on narrative techniques (flashbacks, citation)	*5. use of time and space*	time-travelling motif emphasis on material of the *plot*
metaphors, connotations, parody, self-reflecting techniques or interior monologue, auto-referential	*6. narrative techniques*	"conventional" presen-tation, relatively "straightforward" story, narrative se-quence recognizable
reader is included, reflections on the reader and the audience; disruption of the reader's illusion	*7. conception of the reader and reader-response*	reader not reflected autonomous fiction willing suspension of disbelief
provocation and disorientation of the reader; highly intricate texts; ambiguities form the thematic focus; insecurity of the reader intended	*8. effect of text; objective of narrative process*	no lasting insecurity or disorientation of the reader; degree of sophistication not too high

dominant is the second component. I will come back to the status of the fictional world in SF when discussing magic realism in ch. 11.1.

illustrate my point I have underlined the features which apply to *Riddley Walker* and put question marks where the classification poses problems (see Table 1): Most of my choices will be self-explanatory: my previous analyses of the novel's language and plot will justify the classification as postmodern novel in regard to components 1, 6 (dislocutionary language, parodic misreading of the Eusa Story) and 8 (disorientation, alienation, slowing-down of the reading process, duplicity on all levels). As first-person narration the novel automatically fictionalizes its narrative process; apart from drawing attention to his own writing and telling, Riddley also comments on the stories told by other Inlanders (comp. 3). Flashbacks and citations deepen the vast amount of experience Riddley accumulates within a relatively short objective time span (ca. one month): intra-subjective "experienced time" is given more weight than experience for the sake of promoting a plot (comp. 5). On the other hand, it is due to Riddley's being a reliable and competent narrator that the narrative sequence is nevertheless recognizable without difficulty, a characteristic of popular fiction and science fiction (comp. 6). What mainly turns *Riddley Walker* into a postmodern novel is of course Riddley's unsettling trance revelation: "EUSAS HEAD IS DREAMING US" (58). It not only calls into question the status of Riddley's world (comp. 2) but also affects our, the readers', status: we are implicated in the events even though Riddley does not directly address us or consider the question of who will read his narrative (comp. 7).[11] Finally, the fact that question marks appear above all where the protagonist is concerned (comp. 4), is perhaps symptomatic: he is introspective and reflective, but can one say that he is not interested in public issues or an anti-hero when his private decisions overthrow the entire social system of Inland? Moreover, he is active and knowledgeable but learns to be cautious about the purely rational, i.e. "clevverness". Having the "follerme" (61), he indeed possesses integrating abilities, yet rejects the role of a shaman he has inherited from his father. He does not want to be a leader in the sense of a figure of authority; the decisions he takes, however, turn him into an exemplary figure. His attributes defy classification so plainly that here will be found the most original ideas of the novel. Riddley is a Hobanian hero, the heart of the novel, poised between the self-withdrawal and anti-heroism of postmodernist protagonists and the overt machismo of certain SF heroes (see Puschmann's discussion of her fourth component, 90-102).

11 By contrast, Miller's *A Canticle for Leibowitz* clearly belongs to the science fiction genre: all its components contribute to such a classification.

WHAT HAPPENED?

After these preliminary observations on the novel's generic status, I would like to focus on Riddley's world and the characters who populate it, those components which are primarily responsible for the novel's association with science fiction. The question of what exactly happened will be addressed first. At first glance, everything seems to be clear: an immense nuclear explosion, a consequence of making use of the "1 Big 1", ruined not only England but all of Europe and probably the whole world. To pin down the exact nature of the 1 Big 1, the reasons for the catastrophe, and the historical context in which it occurred, however, is impossible. When one examines the stories which have preserved the memory of the event, its prehistory and its consequences, the "1 Big 1" turns out to be a floating signifier (like a personal pronoun or a deictic), that is an expression whose meaning cannot be fixed once and for all because it depends on the context in which it is used. We have already seen that the catastrophe cannot be dated: there is only a so-called *terminus post quem*, i.e. 1997. It is equally difficult to say what happened. Before we actually reach the *Eusa Story*, the central myth of Inland which is learned by heart by all connexion men, we hear Lorna Elswint's story *Why the Dog Wont Show Its Eyes* (16-19). To Riddley's surprise, Lorna's narrative of the loss of intuitive 1st knowing in exchange for rational thinking mentions two protagonists: a man and a woman build the Power Ring around Cambry because they need electricity to augment their property by night as well as by day. Here the "1 Big 1" is "the No. of the Master Chaynjis" (19), the number or formula, but also the destructive "No" of a nuclear chain reaction, the fission which is to take place within the circle of the Power Ring: "They put in the 1 Big 1 and woosht it roun there come a flash of lite then bigger nor the woal worl and it ternt the nite to day. Then every thing gone black. Nothing only nite for years on end" (19). According to this story, then, the catastrophe is the result of an accident with unprecedented consequences for the whole planet.[12] By contrast, Riddley has learned that a certain Eusa was responsible for the disaster. When he confronts Lorna with the deviation, her answer prepares the readers for complications: "'You hear diffrent things in all them way back storys but it dont make no diffrents. Mosly they aint strait storys any how. What they are is diffrent ways of telling what happent.'" (19). A few pages later, we are told what Riddley had known so far: *The Eusa Story* (28-34). Eusa, its protagonist, is a scientist working for Mr Clevver, the Big Man

12 Perhaps the explosion of Chernobyl in 1986 will forever prevent the development of nuclear power plants as dangerous as the Power Ring around Cambry. But the future is open as regards other civilian projects in which the accident risk will be just as underestimated as it was in the novel's Power Ring.

of Inland, when a war breaks out. Mr Clevver demands that Eusa invent a weapon to defeat all enemies by just one strike, i.e. "1 Big 1" (29). Disregarding warnings by his dogs Folleree & Folleroo, Eusa tracks down the Littl Shynin Man the Addom[13] who is to give him "the No. uv thay Master Chaynjis" (30). But Eusa must pull him apart in order to be able to see the Master Chaynjis: the myth literalizes the meaning of analyis, i.e. "a dissolving", like Golding's *Inheritors* (cf. ch. 6.2). It agrees with Lorna's story in so far as the discovery of the nuclear chain reaction is the decisive moment after which the devastating catastrophe becomes possible. The Power Ring is mentioned, too. This time, though, it serves to make the "1 Big 1", which is put in "barms" by Eusa (31): "... then him & Mr Clevver droppit so much barms thay kilt as menne uv thear oan as thay kilt enemes. Thay wun the Warr but the lan wuz poyzen frum it the ayr & water as wel" (31).[14] According to the *Eusa Story*, then, a nuclear war brought on disaster and the blame is placed on one particular person. Of course this raises the question of Eusa's identity. The answers given by various interpreters are rather telling: Cowart, who investigates the relationship between history and the contemporary novel, thinks that "Eusa's identification with St. Eustace is essentially a red herring" (93) and then goes on to offer only one, the most obvious association triggered by that name:

---

13 Incidentally, parts of the names of the first two atomic bombs can be detected in the name of this Christ-like "third" Adam, the atom, i.e. "Little Boy" and "Fat Man". In general, parallels to the history of the development of the atomic bomb are surely intentional. But the differences nevertheless impose their own dislocutionary laws: the novel must be interpreted in more senses than just as a bleak parody of historical events. In the essay "Pan Lives" (1983), Hoban explores the sadness of childhood, relating growing up to Adam and Eve's fall from grace. Describing his five-year-old son Ben's patience with dangerous tools, he nevertheless cannot exclude that the little boy will one day turn out to be a destroyer; as in *Riddley Walker*, thinking about the potential for good and evil eventually evokes the image of the atomic bomb, but here it is the Japanese name for the bomb dropped over Hiroshima which unfolds its uncanny connotations: "And yet, I can't know what might be in him waiting to rise up towering like a giant mushroom-shaped cloud. The Japanese called the bomb that fell on Hiroshima *Gensu Makkadan*, 'the Original Child Bomb'. Well, it's a chance you take when you decide to have children and keep the human race going. There was a toy sold a few years back, a box with an on-off switch. When you switched it on a little hand came out of the box and switched it off" (MUM, PL 139).

14 According to David Dowling, Einstein's survival scenarios for a nuclear war changed considerably in the years between 1945 and 1950: "In 1945 Einstein argued that although two thirds of the world's population might be destroyed in a war, 'enough men capable of thinking, and enough books, would be left to start again, and civilisation could be restored.' But by 1950 he was writing less sanguinely, 'In the end, there beckons more and more clearly general annihilation.' The Doomsday Clock, an invention of alumni of the Manhattan Project in their *Bulletin of the Atomic Scientists*, concurs with Einstein's grim prediction; at present its hands are at a few minutes to midnight, closer than they have ever been" (*Fictions of Nuclear Disaster*, 83). *Riddley Walker* is obviously modelled on the more "optimistic" scenario – a wise decision. For by showing that instant annihilation would be unlikely and how incredibly hard it would be to belong to the "soar vivers" (116), Hoban effectively counteracts the secret hope for comfort which energizes the death wish of those who time and again aspire to "final" solutions; Gerard Manley Hopkins has coined an apposite term for this kind of suicidal despair, i.e. "carrion comfort".

> The real antitype of Eusa is the country responsible for splitting the atom and thereby giving the division and alienation of modern society a basis in physics itself. Eusa, one realizes, is the eponymous projection of 'USA', the United States of America, the nation that, as the first nuclear power, gave a whole new meaning to the terror of history. (93-94)

Such an interpretation oversimplifies the novel's concern. Cowart not only fails to interpret the spelling of the name (Why is it not "Usa", if only the USA are implied and the association with St. Eustace is merely a red herring?) but also overlooks the point made by the divergence of Lorna's story and the *Eusa Story*, i.e. that it is questionable to name scapegoats in the past if the same or similar mistakes are made again and again in the present. Barbara Herkommer's examination of the difference between St Eustace and Eusa, which results in the description of two opposed patterns of behaviour, therefore opens a wider field of interpretation (155f.): the Christian martyr is opposed to the destructive scientist, one is sanctified, the other punished.[15] However, I think that the split runs right through Eusa, as it does through every possible referent of that name (see ch. 6.1, where I presented a range of associations which can each at one point be fitted into Eusa contexts); Lissener's little poem about Eusa underlines his ambivalence: "He wer crookit he wer Badstock / He wer not boath sides the same / Which the knowing brung the doing / And the doing brung the shame" (77). Everybody can become Eusa; the irresponsible scientist and the saint are only two extreme actualizations of him. The decisions we take and the changes we go through define what kind of Eusa we are, that is, in what ways we contribute to the making of the 1 Big 1 and Riddley's world. In the interview with John Haffenden, Hoban said:

> There's a little piece in the latest issue of *Time* magazine about slips of the tongue, how words and their opposites form a kind of constant partnership in the mind – and not just the opposites but all kinds of peripheral and secondary meanings. I think that that's so, there's no such thing as a simple meaning for anything: things always move in reflective, refractive and diffractive modes. (Hoban and Haffenden 134-135)

It is mainly this recognition and persistent application of multivalency to all the elements of the novel, science fiction motifs, language, and characters alike, which turns *Riddley Walker* into the extraordinary book it is.

As if the fundamental disagreement on the inventors and the use of the 1 Big 1 were not enough, Goodparley offers a third explanation for the state of

---

15 For further interpretations of the *Eusa Story* see Porter (466-468), Dowling (*Fictions...*, 206), Wilkie (58-59), or Lake ("Making the Two One", 165-169).

their world: "May be it wer the barms what done it poysening the lan or when they made a hoal in what they callit the O Zoan. Which that O Zoan you cant see it but its there its holding in the air we breave. You make a hoal in it and Woosh! No mor air" (120-121). Goodparley prefers blaming the ecological catastrophe for poisoning the land for he is interested in a rehabilitation of science. His performance of Eusa in the show Riddley had to interpret, where Mr Clevver was blamed for stealing Eusa's computer and causing a disaster (49), was designed to fulfil the same purpose. But of course a hole in the ozone layer could not immediately account for all the signs of destruction that characterize Inland: Goodparley's idea that air could escape through the hole is naive. On the other hand, if we stick to Lorna's initial commentary that "it dont make no diffrents. Mosly they aint strait storys any how. What they are is diffrent ways of telling what happent" (19), one could also think of a chain reaction in which one thing led to the other: if the environment was more and more polluted and the reduction of the ozone layer led to poor harvests, then famines could have triggered wars, and these could have turned power plants into massive local bombs. The order of events is of no importance; different causalities might be constructed. What happened at any rate is that a disastrous chain reaction was set off when a sufficient number of wrong decisions or non-decisions had prepared the ground for it.

INLAND IN 2347 O.C.

The result is Riddley's world, Inland. Its location is east Kent minus the isle of Thanet, which has become a separate island, the Ram, on which the central government of Inland has its seat. Both Lissener's and Goodparley's sequels to the *Eusa Story* (77-79, 116f.) and a song sung at work (9) mention a flood which drowned large areas of the country when Eusa had been beheaded, that is shortly after the catastrophe. Whether or not the western parts of what used to be England are inhabited, too, is uncertain: the raid on Abel Goodparley's childhood fents could be an affirmative hint (126). Mostly when "Outland" is mentioned in the novel, however, it is by reference to people who approach Inland by boat, i.e. probably from France (53, 100). The ancient street system is still in use but most of the larger towns of our time are no longer inhabited: they are dead towns serving as stationary prisons for the Eusa folk, the forty-five mutant descendants of the "Puter Leat", computer specialists and scientists who were purposely kept alive after the catastrophe (77, 92). The prison holes are guarded by "hevvys", security men or soldiers from the Ram, but otherwise the dead towns are haunted by packs of wild dogs like the woods surrounding the settlements. Most Inlanders either live in permanent settlements, the "forms", growing what they can on the muddy and contaminated ground, breeding sheep and cattle, and melting iron. Or they live as nomads in temporary settlements, the "fentses", hunting and gathering food during "forage rota" or "jobbing", i.e. trading their workforce for meat and other products of the forms (8). The men from the fentses do the dirty work of digging out old machines from our time. Since their nomadic way of life apparently no longer sufficiently feeds them, more and more fentses lose their independence. The forms are quite willing to swallow fentses, and the government does not seem to be averse to this tendency, as the Eusa show Brooder Walker had to interpret a few years earlier demonstrates (53-57), for fents dwellers are regarded as less loyal subjects (197). Certain fentses, among them Riddley's, have so far managed to resist, but with the extinction of the last boar and the forms' insatiable greed for land the situation grows more and more hopeless for the nomads (36f.). Aggression is in the air: Riddley is aware that there has been a loss of trust and goodwill among the Inlanders since the days of his grandfather. In his day, the Pry and the Wes Mincer used to travel with no more than six bodyguards to be protected from the wild dogs; but Abel Goodparley and Erny Orfing, the current Big 2, never travel without bringing fifty additional bodyguards from the Ram (27). The dyers and the charcoal burners hold marginal positions in Inland society: although their products are welcome, they are superstitiously shunned by most people, for their skills are suspect: in stories like *Hart of the Wood* (2-4), the Inlanders learn how the recovery of every kind of technological knowledge during and after Bad Time has had to be paid for by sacrifices. For the secret of making fire and charcoal, for instance, a couple sacrificed their child to a diabolic "clevver looking bloak" (3), "the aulder kincher" (4), and then lost their own lives; perhaps this was originally a reference to accidents which occurred as soon as fire was used again, but as David Cowart remarks, among unsophisticated peoples historical records tend to be quickly modulated into myths (93). For Cowart the setting of *Riddley Walker* creates a world which resembles the Iron Age:

> Riddley lives in a backward age indeed, an age in which human life exemplifies the Hobbesian formula: nasty, poor, brutish, and short. He lives, in two senses, in an Age of Iron. It is an Iron Age in comparison with the golden age of high technology and it is an iron age [sic] in the archeological sense. This imagined Iron Age of the future, of course, mirrors the actual Iron Age of the past – the Iron Age in England, that is, which began about 500 B.C., much later than in the Near East. Hoban dates Riddley's era in such a way as to make its distance from the present – apparently a little less than twenty-five hundred years – approximately equal to the distance from the present of the original Iron Age. (86)

This is a helpful first analogy. But the differences between 2347 O.C. and 500 B.C. must be stressed more emphatically. While our own ancestors could indeed dream of a lost golden age and its recovery through the gradual improvement of their condition, our fictive descendants are constantly reminded not only of the technological superiority but also of the imperfections of the age of high technology: their central myth is not one of a god or hero, as Cowart has noticed, too, but one of a failed scientist: "... in observing a ritual that collapses the time between Eusa and themselves, Hoban's characters return not to a golden age but rather to hell itself, that other locus classicus of timelessness" (90). They are caught in a double bind: on the one hand, the legends which tell them of airplanes and films tease them to retrieve what has been lost; on the other, their stories and myths warn them against the "clevverness" required to invent such things. Cowart points out that "The iron of this Iron Age seems largely to consist of found iron" (86); this shows in his view that "the people of Riddley's day, though backward, have probably managed to avoid the more radical regression to a Stone or Bronze age [sic]" (87). One could also insist, though, that the Inlanders would not even have progressed to the Bronze Age if they had not had the possibility of recycling objects from our own time. Inventors during the Iron Age probably felt elated when they discovered something new. We, excavating remains of their time, can measure the advances made since then. Riddley, however, grows up in a world in which new inventions are stigmatized as much as finds from our time, e.g. the black thing which kills Riddley's father, probably a railway carriage or a locomotive: "... I never did fynd out what it wer. Jus 1 mor thing to make us feal stupid" (26).

Although burning cities, famines, plagues, floods, and acts of cruelty, e.g. the witch hunt for intellectuals and mutants, or cannibalism among the desperate survivors, belong to the past (2-4, 87), the Inlanders still suffer from the aftermath of the catastrophe. The mortality rate is high: accidents and diseases do not let anyone grow old. Riddley's father dies at thirty-three (10); his mother died seven years earlier from "coffing sickness" when Riddley was only five years old (15). Many of his friends have not reached maturity (93). Stillbirths and malformations are still common (23, 25). This has two consequences: maturity is reached early, at the age of twelve (1), and the taboos regarding sexual intercourse do not appear to be severe: nobody objects to Riddley making love to the "tel woman" Lorna Elswint, the oldest woman in the fents who could well be his grandmother and is said to have survived many husbands (5, 115). Since every life is precious, a well-defined system of compensations, "comping stations" (11), seeks to ensure the maintenance of working relations between forms and fentses in cases of accidents; to atone for Brooder Walker's death, for instance, the connexion man of Widders Dump, Reckman Bessup, must carry "5 10wts of iron" (50 pounds) to How Fents and then ask Riddley if he will take it off his back (15): thus the ritual externalizes both the acknowledgement of guilt and delivery from it. To die is to go "with Aunty", or in a more vulgar version, to be raped by the female triple goddess of birth, death and night whose name might be a conflation of aunt, atrophy, entropy and eternity (12, 17; also see *The Bloak as Got on Top of Aunty*, 87-90). The burial rite, on the other hand, celebrates the Inlanders' escape from the materiality of their world: after having been burnt on the "bye bye hump" (21), they hope to rise "Pas the sarvering gallack seas and flaming nebyul eye...", as their funeral song goes (21). Finally, the Eusa cult, as has been said before, is political rather than religious. Intended to prevent a renewal of Bad Time, the institutionalized Eusa shows are used by the Ram to supervise the forms and fentses; the Ram governments define themselves as a moral elite and as guardians over the inhabitants of the mainland as well as over the Eusa folk they breed as scapegoats and deterrents (117). However, Lissener claims that the Ram, greedy for power, have always been after the secret of the 1 Big 1 and that they have been perverting the Eusa shows and also the ritual tortures of Ardships following the path described in the children's song *Fools Circel 9wys* since the beginnings of the cult (78f.). The ritual has therefore lost its effect as deterrent precisely in those inner circles who are in charge of its preservation. The "connexion men" in the forms and fentses, whose task is to interpret the Eusa shows, mediate between the Ram and their communities. It is an inheritable post but before being allowed to take the Eusa scar (40f.), the candidates must take an initiatory exam carried out by the Pry and the Wes Mincer to prove that they have learnt the *Eusa Story* by heart and are able to make connexions (36-40). The interrogation also serves to sound the candidates' political opinions. Riddley, who expresses his dismay at the loss of land for his community to hunt on, is nearly hit by a hevvy and reprimanded by Orfing. But Goodparley spares him, for his own plans are based on the assumption that something new can only come into being if old customs are radically altered (37, 39): as we have seen in ch. 6.3, Riddley will for a short time fulfil all of Goodparley's expectations.

SCIENCE: RIDDLEY'S MOON BROTHERS

In what I called movements three and four in the previous chapter, Riddley's growing fascination with science and his eventual loss of interest are contrasted with the attitudes of his three moon brothers Belnot Phist, Lissener and Abel Goodparley: "Riddley fends off these tempters like Thomas Beckett

[sic] in Eliot's *Murder in the Cathedral*. Indeed, his spiritual agon reaches its climax in the ruins of Beckett's [sic] church" (Cowart 92). Punch could be taken as the main emblem of their ambition and destructivity. Belnot Phist, who appears to aspire to the post of Pry Mincer (106), tries to be faster than Goodparley in collecting the ingredients for gunpowder. It is mainly due to his ambition to find "Eusas head", an intact computer, that the heavy black object found near Widders Dump has to be excavated in one piece (8, 26). But as soon as Riddley finds the Punch figure near the place where his father died, Belnot's downfall begins: they literally exchange places for Riddley drags him down into the mud to climb out of the excavation site and escape with the figure he wants to keep at all cost (69). Belnot is the first moon brother to die, for Goodparley suspects that a plot has been mounted against him. He takes his former "boy" (105) prisoner at Widders Dump when Riddley returns from Fork Stoan with his share of the sulphur found there. Whereas Belnot Phist does not divulge any secrets under torture, he whispers the formula for the 1 Littl 1 to Riddley before dying (142). Riddley, who has been persuaded by Lissener that Belnot Phist might be their ally against Goodparley (106), has relieved him from the hevvy's torture (142). Without struggling for knowledge and power, then, Riddley has got further than Goodparley by the end of the third movement. The situation is altogether ironical, for Goodparley's aim is, after all, to put the Littl Shyning Man together, not to tear him apart once more (38). Herkommer rightly underlines that his materialistic view of the world prevents him from being able to grasp the difference between the material elements of the 1 Big 1, on the one hand, and the Spirit of God and the Littl Shyning Man as transcendent powers, on the other (Herkommer 163). For him science is religion, as his interpretation of the *Legend of St Eustace* illustrates. Riddley will reintroduce the distinction between these two disciplines at the end of the fourth movement (161-165), though, having been given an early hint by Erny Orfing, who has always opposed Goodparley's view (39).

Lissener was the first moon brother set free by Riddley after his escape from Widders Dump. While he, the direct descendant of the mythic Eusa, should know how dangerous the rediscovery of scientific knowledge can be, he turns out to be as greedy as Goodparley. Finding sulphur at Fork Stoan excites him as much as Riddley (100f.). Unlike Riddley, though, whose interest in the sciences abates when the desire for spirituality begins to fill him at his first visit to the cathedral of Canterbury, Lissener's ambitions grow: he seeks to reestablish the Eusa folk in positions of power and to take revenge for the millennia during which they were scapegoats and guinea pigs of the Mincery. His thinking is elitist; he feels a deep contempt for Goodparley: "*He* never ben the Puter Leat he never ben the Power Leat him and his Mincery. Pontsery is what he come out of and shitful servis" (74). As soon as he can get hold of Goodparley, having united with the Eusa folk at Cambry, enlisted Orfing's help and gone back to Fork Stoan, he therefore hangs his former torturer by his hands (169).

Goodparley is tougher than Belnot Phist was, however. When Riddley eventually cuts *him* down, after hurrying from Cambry back to Fork Stoan himself, Goodparley immediately notices how Riddley slips bits of sulphur into his fit up. Not even being blinded can change his mind: he is more determined than ever to pursue his projects, that is to show Punch shows and eventually produce gunpowder (175). A resilient survivor since his childhood fents was raided from Outland (126) and his foster father Granser selfishly induced a group of travelling salesmen to rape the boy on the night before his twelfth naming day, thus trying to keep him dependent (137), Goodparley has always made the most of his most painful defeats. Stabbing Granser and stealing his Punch fit up, he ran away with Mincery men and eventually became the Pry Mincer of Inland. Having deposed him with the help of the Eusa folk, Erny Orfing now cannot reject Abel's wish to travel around Inland with Riddley as Punch showmen, while the Eusa folk feel that the eyeless man is more powerful than ever (175). A little later, however, when Riddley has led him to Granser and the latter turns out to know how to make gunpowder, too, in other words, on the day Abel Goodparley's most cherished plan is realized, he dies. It is due to Granser's solicitude and to Riddley's lack of scientific ambition that Riddley himself survives the explosion (188).

Lissener does not live any longer than Goodparley and Granser. Carried away by memories of the time before the catastrophe, i.e. by inapplicable "vantsit theary" which he conjures up in his "some poasyum" with the Eusa folk (194), he is not interested in the bomb which has meanwhile been made from his share of sulphur. A group of hevvys, impatient with the inability of the Eusa folk to remember the formula of the 1 Littl 1, has wrung it out from a dyer, for the dyers have preserved the secret of gunpowder like the charcoal burners. Ironically, the "simple" and practical knowledge of how to make the 1 Littl 1 proves dangerous enough: a drunken hevvy who is rudely sent away by Lissener lights the fuse of the bomb out of spite and blows up the Ardship and three other Eusa mutants (195). Hoban attacks militarists and scientists alike: the former for making thoughtless use of inventions whose effects they are probably neither competent nor imaginative enough to judge, the latter for withdrawing into ivory towers instead of caring for their own fates as well as that of the rest of the world. Orfing survives like Riddley because he does not interfere with the events any more when they have developed a dynamics of their own. Since he can tell the difference between a necessary and a false struggle, he escapes as soon as he can. At Cambry, for both the centre of a philosophy of caution, whose emblem is Greanvine, they meet again and join to form a new union of artists. But before examining more closely the connection between the spirituality emanating from the ruins of Canterbury cathedral, the hope symbolized by Greanvine, and art, I will take another look at Lissener, the only male figure whom Riddley cannot recognize in Greanvine's face: "What wer it made the Ardship odd 1 out then?" (161).

To answer Riddley's question Lissener's various attributes must be looked at in detail. As the Ardship of Cambry, that is, as Eusa's direct descendant, he has been bred to atone for Eusa's guilt. The reviewer A. Alvarez therefore felt reminded of the ritual killings of sacrificial kings described in Frazer's anthropological study *The Golden Bough* (Alvarez 16). Unlike these kings, however, who mostly stand for the spirit of vegetation and are killed at regular intervals or when they have grown old and weak so that the vegetation can be reborn (see Frazer *passim*), the Ardships, who are killed in their heyday, stand for the spirit of catastrophe. In theory the Ardships are killed to *prevent* a renewal of the 1 Big 1, by deliberately, i.e. ritually, discarding the scientific knowledge the Eusa folk have preserved in their collective memory (a memory which has grown quite patchy, though). Whereas Greanvine can be interpreted as a representation of the spirit of vegetation which belongs to an ancient pre-catastrophe tradition, the Eusa folk and the ritual to which they must submit only came into being through the catastrophe: they are an oddity kept alive only through special breeding, something the regenerative cycle of nature would seek to eliminate or normalize again. The ancient emblem therefore cannot possibly represent them.

There is also a psychoanalytical interpretation of Lissener and the Eusa folk: for as long as only the government (as super-ego) knows of their existence, they resemble a head kept apart from the face (the consciousness, or ego, of the Inlanders) and the body (Inland), i.e. the Eusa folk personify repressed information, the censored memory of a traumatic event. Lissener's face cannot possibly resemble Greanvine's, Eusa's and all the other characters' *faces* because he is the *head* of Eusa, a *no-body* in Inland society. The faces of the Eusa folk are "Faces like bad dreams" (169), faces that must not be seen in broad daylight. The secrecy of the ritual according to which the Eusa mutants are bred and the practice of executing only the Ardship, that is, of destroying information only in tiny instalments, point to a compromise of the government, though: the repressed is obviously not only feared but also desired. The government abstains from eliminating all the traces of the catastrophe not only to preserve a memory of the terror but also because there is hope that the hidden Eusa mutants may one day become useful. Riddley can only acquire "1st knowing", intuition or instinctive knowledge, before the contact with Lissener enables him to learn more about science and technology. What happens when Lissener and Riddley meet is that repression is undone; in other words, Eusa gets his head back. In fact, this is a reversal of the plot of the first Eusa show Riddley had to interpret: "Mr Clevver says [to Eusa], 'Thats it then Ive emtit you out right a nuff. Now Ive got the head with the knowing and youve got the head with the nothing.'" (46-47). Moreover the – so far literally effaced – mutants gain recognition: their nightmarish faces and bodies are no longer hidden from the Inlanders, they become parts of their reality. The question is of course if the mutants can survive when abandoned to their fate and if there is room for both "normal" Inlanders and mutants. Lissener's death is definitely a bad omen for the Eusa folk.

At the beginning of the novel, Lissener is the main complement to Riddley, later his opposite. He is born not only on the same day of the year, the "2nd Ful", like Goodparley and probably Belnot (136, 141), but also in the same year as Riddley (75) – his uncanny double. For the Jungian interpreter Jack Branscomb, Lissener is Riddley's shadow (34).[16] So he certainly is; but in the Freudian perspective, which is based on a dualistic view of the drives, this description can be refined and supplemented: while Lissener embodies self-destructive tendencies and auto-erotic desire (see his description of the "some poasyum", 103), Punch is the shadow of aggression and violent sexuality. While Riddley and Lissener are complements like Eusa and Addom, "2 1/2s uv 1 thing" (34), travelling from Bernt Arse to Fork Stoan, Riddley liberates and guides Lissener and looks after him when he has a fit (91); at the same time he gradually turns into a "lissener" himself (97), sometimes perceiving things Lissener does not, and vice versa: "... some times when we wer boath lissening hy 1 of us wud starve the other like when 1 boat puts a nother in its wind shadder" (97). The more alike they become, however, the more their separation is impending. Lissener once deliberately provokes Riddley to force him back into independence, and Riddley is quite aware that his own existence is at stake – he is about to become the Ardship's shadow: "He put his han on my sholder I fealt like when he took it a way itwd leave a wite shadder behynt" (94). While Riddley dreams of bursting into thousands of separate pieces in the so-called "1/2 dream" (91), Lissener's "gethering dream"

16 "If the repressed tendencies, the shadow as I call them, were obviously evil, there would be no problem whatever. But the shadow is merely somewhat inferior, primitive, unadapted, and awkward; not wholly bad. It even contains childish or primitive qualities which would in a way vitalize and embellish human existence, but convention forbids!" (Jung, *Selected Writings*, 90).

gives expression to his desire to be at one with the universe (90f.). Their dreams, however, stand in direct contrast to what they are by day: Riddley the Inlander is an everyman who feels that he has "every 1 and every thing" on his back (106), whereas Lissener is "no 1", at the same time a nobody or no-face and a number one, the first of the Eusa folk and the first Ardship who has succeeded in coming "out of the hoal" (76). Alone, the mutants feel like "scattert peaces of a broakin pot" (103). It is only after their separation, i.e. the closer Lissener gets to gathering with the other Eusa mutants, that Riddley indulges in the loss of his self and the wish that something stop him (107f.). Even though it looks as if Lissener were the stronger of the two, then, he is the one who will eventually die, while Riddley is the one to survive. Just as it says in the song about Eusa's two boys: "1 to live and 1 to dy..." (104).

In Lissener's own myth, *The Lissener and the Other Voyce Owl of the Worl* (82f.), he represents himself as the saviour-child of the world who undoes the work of destruction of an owl, listening back by day the sounds of the world which the owl is trying to swallow at night. Interestingly, Lissener's is an attribute of the night in Lorna's tale *Why the Dog Wont Show Its Eyes* (17). Since he is a personified nightmare, there is no contradiction, though: nightmares indeed store and work through what has been banished from consciousness and accessible memory, but they must do so without drawing attention: remembered nightmares are accidents; significantly the Lissener in the myth is a child who escapes the owl's attention. By entering the reality of the Inlanders, breaking out of the "Fools Circel" of dark prison holes in dead towns, the symbolic space assigned him by the ritual, Lissener loses his function. Lissener's rebellion signals his awareness that a reversal of the role of the Eusa folk has already taken place anyway. Goodparley has been abusing his position to retrieve the knowledge of the ingredients of the 1 Big 1: the owl has taken notice of the kid. Lissener is therefore no longer willing to die for his ancestor's guilt. He no longer wants to be used but aspires to become a user of knowledge himself like his ancestor. Of course this also entails that he and the Eusa folk might accumulate guilt themselves again. It is consistent that Lissener is compared with "the Other Voyce Owl of the Worl" (170) precisely when he has assumed the role of Goodparley's torturer. There is no trace of a saviour in him now; on the contrary, his euphemistic words echo those of Mr On The Levvil and Punch in Goodparley's Punch and Pooty show when he says, "'May be theres stil a littl some thing we can do them tho.'" (172; also see 133). But he does not want to destroy them; he is satisfied with blinding Goodparley: "'... Onlyes thing wewl do is make him lissen bettern what hes done so far. Hes all ways telling and asking yet he dont never lissen to no 1 nor nothing.'" (173). Riddley, on the other hand, is merely knocked unconscious so that he cannot help Goodparley. There is yet another distinction between Lissener and the mythical Other Voyce Owl: while the owl's inattention merely enables the child to reconstruct the world but not to kill the owl, Lissener's loss of interest in his surroundings once he has joined the Eusa folk costs his and three other lives. For Riddley, Lissener's death is a sign that an era has come to an end: "It looks to me like that Fools Circel is broakin now I dont think therwl be no mor regler hevvys nor Eusa folk in dead towns from now on" (196-197). The time has come for nightmares to be separate from reality again, to happen inside the head or be represented in stories, instead of taking place in real life. *We* are warned not to let them emerge into the bright daylight.[17] What is history for Riddley is, as yet, only a science fiction novel for us; his gospel ought to be our revelation; and the "accident risk" that we accept day by day for the sake of comfort, the "survival scenarios" scientists regularly develop, have turned into Riddley's world.

Withdrawing from science, Riddley is more daring and progressive as a philosopher, theologian, historian and artist. He loads guilt on his shoulders by thinking about and naming things, arousing people's curiosity, inviting them to see old customs in a new light, moving them, but above all, by writing everything down: like Eusa, he thus externalizes the contents of his head, making his knowledge usable for other people. Herkommer points out that the *Eusa Story* is a secret of state never presented in its entirety to the people (149); by writing it down Riddley therefore commits a sacrilege as well as high treason. He is also Eusa in so far as his connexions ultimately contribute to the differentiation of ideas. Rightway Flinter, the Big Man of Weaping, is quite justified in his scepticism when he says to Riddley and Erny Orfing before letting them enter the form:

> 'Theres all ways some kynd of clevverness waiting somers near or far its all ways waiting to happen its all ways waiting for some 1 to pul it some 1 to fetch it some 1 to bring it down on the res of us. And them what fetches it who ever they myt be theyre Eusa....' (206)

Nevertheless, as Rightway and his brother Deaper, the connexion man, will find out, being Eusa as a scholar, theologian or artist is not the same thing as being a scientific Eusa. In the end the two Flinter brothers will join Riddley and Erny.

17 Here the warning is merely implied while Aldiss spelt it out in the last lines of *Barefoot in the Head*, undermining it, however, by attributing it to a joker: "A joker wrote / KEEP VIOLENCE IN THE MIND / WHERE IT BELONGS" (281). Also see ch. 6.2.

THEOLOGY: FROM LORNA TO GREANVINE AND BEYOND

As a theologian, that is as the official shaman or "connexion man" of his community whose task is to interpret Eusa shows, Riddley departs from both the official "Mincery" line, with its commandments and bans that are liable to propagandistic abuse, and Lorna's matriarchal fundamentalism. Though he has inherited his post from his father, passed his exam as connexion man and been initiated into secrets of the "tel women", he becomes a true shaman above all because of his trances, his dreams (e.g. the "1/2 dream", a typical shamanic dream, 91), and the bond various animals establish with him: a boar and an old leader of a pack of dogs deliberately run into his spear so that it seems that they have sacrificed themselves for him (1, 12); later on he will speak with the dogs and understand their signs as if he were their equal (164).[18] Thomas J. Morrissey thinks that he is "Too original a thinker to be a loyal connexion man..." (211). His originality is not only a rational one, however: it is thoroughly mystical, as David J. Lake's inspired reading of *Riddley Walker* in terms of mysticism shows:[19]

> The original/ultimate unity of all being, and the pragmatic disunity of beings – this double theme is at the heart of the philosophy of Inland. This philosophy may be called 'mystical,' but it is not abstruse. It is merely the perennial philosophy of the Upanishads, Lao Tzu, Plotinus, Eckhart, Wordsworthy [sic], William Blake – and the Gnostic Gospel of Thomas, which furnishes the epigraph of the novel. ("Making the Two One: Language and Mysticism in *Riddley Walker*", 164)

In fact Lorna is a mystic, too: it is from her that Riddley first hears about the "thing in us it dont have no name" (6): "'We aint a naturel part of it. We dint begin when it begun we dint begin *where* it begun. It ben here befor us nor I dont know what we are to it. ... It thinks us but it dont think *like* us. It dont think the way we think" (6-7). Her mysticism could be called dualistic, given the way she presents this "thing" as radically other, according to Stace's distinction between monism, dualism and pantheism:

> Dualism is the view that the relation between God and the world, including the relation between God and the individual self when in a state of union, is a relation of pure otherness or difference with no identity. Monism is the view that the relation is pure identity with no difference. Pantheism is the view that it is identity in difference. (Stace 219)

---

18 Cf. Mircea Eliade, *Schamanismus und archaische Ekstasetechnik* (1956), pp. 22-23, 105.

19 Lake has based his analysis on Walter T. Stace's *Mysticism and Philosophy*, which proved to be useful to my own study, too. Lake's essay is particularly instructive when he traces echoes from the Gnostic Gospel of Thomas in *Riddley Walker* (cf. Lake 167f.). Eliade points to the link between shamanism and mysticism (*Schamanismus*, 17).

In this point I disagree with Lake, who does not distinguish between Riddley's and Lorna's mysticism, calling both versions pantheistic, an attribute that is more fitting for Riddley's (165).

Riddley can indeed conceive difference in unity, as Lake's list shows:

> For him the Unity is sometimes conceived abstractly (for example, as the number '1'), sometimes as a Nature goddess with the symbolic aspects of Moon, Night, Death (p. 17), or rain (passim), 'her what has her woom in Cambry' (p. 154); or less commonly as a male God, a more active aspect (p. 153); or Eusa (pp. 43, 58); or, in the Eusa Story, the 'Littl Shyning Man the Addom' (p. 29), who was in origin a figure of Christ crucified. (165)

His pantheism is the moving force which turns him into an innovator. Perhaps it is his curiosity which separates Riddley from Lorna, or else the generation gap between them, which accounts for her greater respect for the numinous.

Quoting G. G. Scholem, Stace writes that dualism was adopted particularly by mystics firmly anchored in monotheistic religions, e.g. by Jewish mystics (229). Lorna is similarly anchored in tradition, and more, she is its guardian. Being the "tel woman", the priestess, her task is to interpret events concerning the Inlanders' life and death, e.g. "getting the tel of the head" of the boar hunted by Riddley on his naming day (5) or interpreting Brooder Walker's death at his funeral (22-24); her task is also to preserve stories (16-19), and above all to maintain the connexion to the Mother Goddess. In her case, mysticism has therefore not brought out rebellious traits but conservative ones: she is nostalgic, seeking the new in the old. Whenever she acts in public, she preaches a return to 1st knowing, but none to the technology of our own time (24, 66).

Riddley at first decides to follow his teacher, lover, and mother substitute. His first shamanic revelation is to be a prophetic warning against scientific progress, i.e. "The man as got the hevvyness took off him wer ready to take on some mor" (58). But he cannot prevent it from being deflected into a "trants reveal" that relativizes the state of affairs. "EUSAS HEAD IS DREAMING US" (58) points to the possibility of waking up so as to change things, without condemning or preferring the dream. The definite twist towards mysticism and against institutionalized forms of religion, however, will take place at his first visit to Cambry. By that time he has escaped from How Fents, separated from Lissener, been turned loose again by Goodparley, and the dogs have prevented him from following his urge to stay with Granser: had they not been with him, he would no doubt have been the first victim of the 1 Littl 1.

At Cambry he experiences the peak of desire to "happen that 1 Big 1" for Goodparley (152). His distance from Lissener is at an extreme for he compares himself to the Other Voyce Owl: "So sad I fealt then. Sad and emty with a crying in me. I fealt like that Other Voyce Owl of the Worl musve lissent the woal worl a way and every thing gone" (153). The gratification of his desire for Power, which he confuses with the Spirit of God at first, biased by Goodparley's interpretation of the *Legend of St Eustace*, takes place as a grotesque fantasy of homosexual rape (153). Since homosexual desire is usually rejected by Hoban's characters,[20] we can gauge by the fact that Riddley indeed wants to be raped by Power how much he has become estranged from himself. Then, however, he suddenly feels "a nother way" (153). Riddley's conversion, the moment when science and religion become two different approaches to the world, is encoded as a sudden surge of sexual desire for the Mother Goddess (153f.). His failure the first time he tries to be with her establishes a hierarchy of values: the connexion to the Mother Goddess is harder to maintain than that to Big Old Father Power: it requires another access than phallic display.

Humiliated, Riddley withdraws into the crypt, the "woom of her what has her woom in Cambry" (155), where he first undergoes a symbolic death and is then prepared for his rebirth (see the imagery and his lack of words):

> I fel down on to my knees then I cudnt stan up I cudnt lif up my head. The 1 Big 1 the Master Chaynjis it wer all roun me. Wood in to stoan and stoan in to wood. Now it showit 1 way now a nother. The stoan stans. The stoan moves. In the stanning and the moving is the tree. Pick the appel off it. Hang the man on it. Out of the holler of it comes the berning chyld. Unner the stoan. See the bird boan. Thin as grass. Be coming grass.
>
> I opent my mouf and mummering only dint have no words to mummer. Jus only letting my froat make a soun. (156)

He grows aware of the duality of everything, the "idear in the hart of every thing" (156). Obviously the Eusa folk were assembled in the crypt, too, before being led to Fork Stoan by Lissener (155); but they remained impervious to the spirituality of the place. Riddley, on the other hand, contemplates the stone trees of the crypt and experiences by way of a mystic vision, captured in *Stoan* (158f.), what was blown into our consciousness when the first atomic bombs exploded – the blurring of the distinction between matter and energy:

> You myt think a stoan is slow thats becaws you wont see it moving. ... That dont mean its slow tho. There are the many cools of Addom which they are the

20 Also see ch. 8.4, n. 34.

> party cools of stoan. Moving in ther millyings which is the girt dants of the every thing its the fastes thing there is it keaps the stilness going. (158)

Dowling quotes from Joseph Wood Krutch to illustrate the change of consciousness effected by the nuclear age:[21] "The matter that disintegrated privately over the American desert and publicly over Japan ceased in those instants to occupy space. At those instants, therefore, the meaning of the term 'materialist' disappeared as completely as the disintegrated atoms themselves" (quoted in Dowling, "Russell Hoban's ...", 181). Eventually the image of Greanvine evolves out of Riddley's musings on the stone men who accompany every man while he is alive:[22]

> Theywl stay unner the groun longs youre on top of it. Comes your time to ly down for ever then the stoan man comes to the top of the groun they think theywl stan up then. They cant do it tho. Onlyes strenth they had ben when you ben a live. Theyre lying on the groun trying to talk only theres no soun theres grean vines and leaves growing out of ther mouf. Them vines getting thicker and pulling the sides of the mouf wide and the leaves getting bigger curling roun the head. Vines growing out of ther mouf. Vines and leaves growing out of the nose hoals and the eyes then breaking the stoan mans face a part. (159)

The sudden awareness of mortality drowns his ambitions. He is filled with a new central idea: "THE ONLYES POWER IS NO POWER" (162). The moment of his rebirth is a festival of music and colours to which he completely abandons himself.[23] When he emerges from the crypt, the dogs, too, dance with him, "moving with the souns and colours" (162). While they first danced the dolly shape of the former cathedral walls (154f.), they now run "the idear of Greanvine" (162). Eventually they take Riddley to the place where a carved wooden figure has been hidden: "It wer Greanvine. Carvit out of wood and paintit it wer may be 1/2 as big as a real face" (163). Since all the dogs are with him now, also that half of the pack which had followed Lissener when they separated earlier on, he concludes that Orfing has taken Lissener prisoner (164). Riddley asks the leader dog to show him the way to the Ardship. He is instantly taken to the outpost of Cambry, where he finds a drawing of

---

21 Krutch is the biologist whose thinking about the mortality of protozoan organisms once frightened Jachin-Boaz into leaving his family (LN 132-133, also see Hoban's bibliographical reference to *The Great Chain of Life* in that novel).

22 Many ideas developed by Riddley while he is at Cambry will return in essays and fragments collected in *The Moment under the Moment*: e.g. "Pan Lives" (MUM, PL 125-140), "Portknockie" (MUM, PK 208-213), "Footplacers, London Transport Owls, Wincer-Boise" (MUM, FP 214-216), "Mnemosyne, Teen Taals, and Tottenham Court Road" (MUM, MT 217-236), or "Thinking about Hermes" (MUM, CO 243-245).

23 A similar rebirth scenario will accompany Fremder's jumps out of the spacecrafts *Clever Daughter* and *Clever Daughter II*: they are possible when his mind speaks to him and his consciousness gives way to more archaic powers (FR 4-5, 16-17, 35, 182).

Goodparley as Greanvine and the inscription "HOAP OF A TREE" (164); although he does not know yet that Goodparley has been deposed by Orfing and Lissener, he intuitively alters the drawing, turning the vines growing out of Goodparley's mouth into the horns of a stag. The transformation makes Goodparley resemble the Littl Shyning Man: is this an expression of Riddley's desire to see him torn apart, or an intuition that every dying person retrieves innocence? Perhaps these options are really inseparable. Playing around with the inscription he eventually finds out where Lissener, Goodparley and Orfing must be (165), but he waits for the night to follow them to Fork Stoan, as a Hermetic wanderer at home on the "muddy track in a black nite with the rain pissing down" (167-168). The fact that he can move so easily at night underlines his newly found state of grace, as Lorna's story *Why the Dog Wont Show Its Eyes* illustrates: "Every day has the shape of the nite what it come out of. The man as knows that shape can go in to the nite in the nite and the nite in the day time" (17). His premonitions turn out to be true: Goodparley, not Lissener is being tortured (169). Asking for an explanation, Riddley learns from Erny Orfing that "HOAP OF A TREE" has been "the go word of the arper sitting in the Mincery year on year it ben past down 1 shadder mincer to the nex" (171).

Peter Schwenger has found out that the inscription "HOAP OF A TREE" and Orfing's subsequent exegesis in fact echo an Old Testament passage, i.e. Job 14:7-9 (*Letter Bomb*, 137):

> '... theres hoap of a tree if its cut down yet itwl sprout agen. And them tinder branches theyre of wil not seaze. Tho the root of it works old in the earf and the stick of it dead on the groun yet even jus only the smel of water and itwl bud and bring forit bowing like the plan. ... Inland may be cut down yet them branches wil keap coming. Peopl may try to kil them branches only itwl be the peopl what fall down and dy them branches wil grow out of ther moufs which thats our blip and syn.' (170-171)

For Schwenger, Orfing's appropriation of both Old-Testament wisdom and the figure of Greanvine is undermined by the novel: "... the multiple interpretations of Greanvine (linked to still more multiplicities in regard to other images) call into question expectations of understanding and mastery" (*Letter Bomb*, 140). Earlier I suggested that Greanvine be interpreted as a representation of the spirit of vegetation; as Frazer shows, this can be reconciled to the fact that the figure is found near the ruins of a Christian cathedral, for Christianity borrowed many of its symbols and images from older traditions.[24] Barbara Herkommer has identified him as a foliate man, a wooden ornament from the roof truss of the Cathedral (167). Schwenger adds: "The face Riddley finds is that of the so-called Green Man, a common motif in medieval architecture, as well as in stained glass, illuminated manuscrips, and paintings. Studies of the Green Man's meaning usually come to no conclusion about that meaning" (*Letter Bomb*, 139). However, certain limitations restrict the field of interpretation. Cowart's view that "Greanvine's, then, is the face of Adam, the universal face of mortality" (141), for example, disregards Riddley's exclusion of Lissener (161) as well as his effort to distinguish between representations of dead women and dead men:

> A woman in this place by the woom of her what has her woom in Cambry wuntve bothert hiding a way this face of a man with vines and leaves growing out of his mouf. This here man dying back in to the earf and the vines growing up thru his arse hoal up thru his gullit and out of his mouf. Not a woman thing. Becaws a woman is a *woom*an aint she. Shes the 1 with the woom shes the 1 with the new life coming out of her. You wunt carve a womans face with vines and leaves growing out of the mouf. (163)

Greanvine's, then, is the face of male mortality, a representation inherited from pre-catastrophe cults of ancient mother goddesses. The fact that Riddley denies that it is "a woman thing" (163) has not escaped Schwenger. His interpretation is cautious, though, for the essentialist thinking which is expressed in a statement of difference derived from the biology of men and women, could arouse a controversy:

> Whether one agrees with Riddley here depends on how one interprets those vines and leaves. Do they remind us of our necessary dying back into the earth, or are they a sign of new life? If the latter, they would seem entirely appropriate to one who has new life coming out of her – or perhaps they are superfluous, redundant. Perhaps it is men who need to be reminded, by the image of a hole at their center, of that ambiguous space from which arise all possible meanings, which we choose to classify with death or life, being or nothingness. (*Letter Bomb*, 141)

---

24 See Frazer, *The Golden Bough*, esp. his description of tree-spirits and his discussion of the myths of Adonis and Attis (chs. 1-2, 9-10, 28-31, and 34-35). In ch. 37, Frazer discusses the relationship between Christian festivals and more ancient traditions: he assumes that Easter has been harmonized with the earlier festival of Attis, celebrated at the time of the spring equinox, a date relevant in the regenerative cycle of the vegetation. In Hoban's thinking, Christ and the year-king belong together, too. He writes in "Portknockie" (1981): "All round Portknockie harbour are great iron rings secured by iron eyes to concrete and to stone.... The iron eye that holds the ring is also like old wood, like a branch thrust up through the concrete and doubling back into it. What does it say, this iron-into-wood? It says what the ribs and columns of the crypt of Canterbury Cathedral say: those stone columns are the trunks, those stone ribs of the vaulting are the branches, they are the living wood of Christ and the year-king become trees of stone. They say what this iron-become-wood says: Now I show it to you this way, now I show it to you that way" (MUM, PK 212-213).

I think that Schwenger is on the right track, however. For even though a true mystic will stress the paradoxical unity of things we represent as oppositional pairs, e.g. male and female, inside and outside, the Mother Goddess and the paternal God, or as distinct entities, e.g. grass, wood and stone,[25] Hoban responded to the historical fact that the late 1970s and early 1980s were saturated with militaristic macho behaviour (cf. the quotation from Thornber at the end of ch. 6.3). In the interview with Paul Shand, he interpreted Riddley's failure with the Mother Goddess as the consequence of an imbalance between masculinity and femininity:

> When Riddley first goes to Cambry he comes to Zero Ground. ... First he wants to be buggered by the Big Old Father and right after that he encounters ... The Mother Goddess – and he feels 'all juicy for her'. So he gets his big erection and tries to dance with her but he can't sustain it – he's not man enough yet. And that's absolutely crucial. The male element of the world is not yet man enough to have its proper relationship with the Great mother [sic] Goddess – the fruitful darkness from which everything came. It keeps trying to prove its masculinity and power by blowing hell out of the world. Which is not the way to do it. (Hoban and Shand 36)

His answer is therefore the expression of sympathy for a matriarchal system in which the castration of man is visible in symbols and rituals. The question is, of course, if Hoban's view of sexual difference has undergone a radical transformation since *Turtle Diary*, where gender and sex were seen as so independent that a female character could turn into the "father" of an action, the male, however, be its "mother". Since I am a woman reader, my own first reading of *Riddley Walker* left me worried that Hoban seemed to propagate a return to matriarchy and the mystification of Woman; taking into consideration the historical context in which the novel was written and respecting the

25 See ch. 2.5. "Extrovertive Mysticism" of W. T. Stace's *Mysticism and Philosophy*, which he opens with a quotation from Meister Eckhart, Riddley's mystical ancestor: "'All that a man has here externally in multiplicity is intrinsically One. Here all blades of grass, wood, and stone, all things are One. This is the deepest depth.'" (63); or ch. 3.6. "The Word 'God'".

Hoban is aware that by naming things they are invariably reduced (cf. "Pan Lives", MUM, PL 130). In "Household Tales by the Brothers Grimm", he explicitly acknowledges the insignificance of naming and assigning sexes to mythical characters (MUM, HT 144). Nevertheless, we cannot do without names and language if we want to interfere with what is going on around us: a mystic who enjoys his ecstatic experiences for their own sake abuses his gift and becomes guilty of "spiritual gluttony" (St. John of the Cross quoted in Stace, 340). So Hoban writes in "The Bear in Max Ernst's Bedroom or the Magic Wallet" (1987): "Dionysus and the other and Hermes account for some of the action that keeps us popping like popcorn in a popper but there's no end to it, really, and no end to the names and words that need to be found to provide handles for it, and all of the names and words are out in the real reality beyond the limited-reality consensus. We haven't got a lot of time, the world is being destroyed by people to whom hairspray is real but the ozone layer is not.... The survival of the human race depends on a realer grasp of reality than we've been capable of so far. The survival of the human race depends on recognizing what lives in the human mind and learning how not to be annihilated by it" (MUM, BB 192).

difference between the author and his narrator, however, I now think that it is the attempt to give an impulse towards balance and away from phallic poses that has prompted his aesthetic choices. Hoban's seeming return to a dated form of essentialism will be looked into once more in ch. 8.4.

Moreover, there is another hint that Greanvine is not to be seen as the definite new role model for Riddley and that his veneration for the Mother Goddess does not lead to a fundamentalist nostalgia for matriarchy: On the one hand, he continues to be fascinated with Punch, on the other, his development does not end with his first visit to Cambry. On the contrary, his new motto "THE ONLYES POWER IS NO POWER" (162) is put to the test during the fifth movement and found wanting: he is knocked unconscious at Fork Stoan and cannot prevent the Eusa folk from blinding Goodparley; but the most dangerous situation is the episode of the 1 Littl 1: he submits totally to Goodparley's and Granser's instructions and survives only because Granser is considerate enough to send him out of the hut before lighting the fuse (188). His commitment to passivity, which exposes him to danger whenever he is with other people, will therefore be corrected when Riddley seeks shelter at Cambry for the second time (191). Schwenger, too, has noticed that it is "the play between Punch and Greanvine" which "seems to sum up what is at stake" (*Letter Bomb*, 140), but he does not pursue the implications of this idea. For him, Riddley has learned his lesson when he has accepted his symbolical castration and let go "of his earlier exhilarated commitment to recapturing the power of the time before Bad Time" (141). Nevertheless, it is only at the end of the fifth movement that Riddley finally achieves a dynamic balance which allows him to oscillate between daring and caution, and between phallic Power and the Mother Goddess: a balance which will enable him to become an artist in whom the political mover and the pantheistic mystic can live in paradoxical unity. The entire description of Riddley's arrival at Cambry shows facets of Riddley's new condition (see 190-192): The self-confidence with which he positions himself on the regenerating Zero Ground of Cambry in the middle of a pitch-dark night is just as meaningful as Riddley's perception of the stillness of the place and the life-giving movement of the wind, his openness to feelings inside him, the leader dog's gesture of friendship, and his laughter at, and invitation to, the ghost of Power which overwhelmed him the first time. Nevertheless he does not triumph, his ecstasy bears no resemblance to the sexual excitement of his earlier visit: instead he corrects, or refines, the motto which he gained then, and this time, ordinary letters rather than capitals, and a quotation from the *Eusa Story* are sufficient to convey the message:

> Its the not sturgling for Power thats where the Power is. Its in jus letting your self be where it is. Its tuning in to the worl its leaving your self behynt and letting your self be where it says in *Eusa* 5:
>
> > ... in tu the hart uv the stoan hart uv the dans. Evere thing blippin & bleapin & movin in the shiftin uv thay Nos. Sum tyms bytin sum tyms bit. (191)

He is both strong and weak: he cries for the dead he has lost but need not undergo a symbolic death himself to enter the crypt of the cathedral, the womb of the goddess. On the other hand, there is no spectacular climax either when he arrives: he only lights a candle and finds that the crypt is empty.

THE PUPPETEERS

Just as this new way of being integrates body, soul, and intellect, the masculine and the feminine, it is also reconcilable with society. Without anyone else he is "No 1". Riddley no longer aspires to Hermetic seclusion but goes to look for the person whose absence he keenly feels. The dogs take him to another orphaned human being in search of company: Orfing, who actually hoped to find both Goodparley and Riddley and who mourns for his former rival and friend when he hears the story of his death (192f.). Like Riddley, Orfing has to find a new function after his task of overturning the Pry Mincer's government has been accomplished. It is he who suggests that they show puppet shows together, insisting, though, that Riddley be the main puppeteer for he is aware of his own limitations as performer (196). They spend a fortnight at the outpost of Cambry, waiting to see how the situation in Inland will develop. The central goverment has been replaced by interim local authorities: "its what they call a care maker Mincery with regenneril guvner men from the Ram at all the forms" (197). Once more it is from the dislocutionary expressions themselves that potential dangers for the future are signalled: what good can be expected from "care makers", "Mincers" or "guvner men" who are "regenneril": regents and generals, generally ill? When Orfing feels that the time for moving on has come, though, and he sets store by his intuitions (198), Riddley trusts Orfing's advice although he would prefer to "live qwyet and ly low" a little longer (197). It must be approximately one month after his twelfth birthday now, as his information on the transformations of the moon ("Ful of the Moon" on his birthday, 4, to "Dark of the Moon", 190) and on the time spent at Cambry ("a 14nt", 196) indicates.

Riddley develops Punch and Pooty shows out of the contemplation of the figures of the two fit-ups he has inherited from Goodparley (199-201). Even though one set serves an educational or religious purpose and the other is for "pure" entertainment, Riddley senses that all figures stand for more than themselves; as puppets they are not figures of speech but speaking figures whose potential is flickering through their humble appearance: "Iwl give odds Pootys mixt up with that Moon Sow" (200). There are invisible connexions between the two sets, and one figure is even identical: "Mr Clevver. Which hes Mr On The Levvil and hes callit Drop John as wel. There he is the name changes but he dont. In all that 2ness there he comes up hes the 1" (200-201). So as not to incur the wrath of "that care making Mincery", however, Riddley and Erny decide to use only the Punch and Pooty figures, for which Goodparley was given "letshow" by Erny (201). The shows will be enriched by Riddley's experience (201), particularly by the deaths he witnessed, but he does not write any scripts in advance. He likes the "chemistery and fizzics" of improvised performances because those moments make him keenly aware of the "very Chaynjis that the Littl Shyning Man tol Eusa of" (199). Although it is impossible to locate the vantage point from which he is telling us about the time when he and Orfing left Cambry, it is clear that he must have had sufficient time to gather experience and improve his skills after the first interrupted performance at Weaping. Otherwise he could not know what every performer knows and enjoys:

> You myt talk about how youre going to show you myt think about it only on the nite there it is if its the 1st time or the 100th it aint never happent befor it aint nothing you know any thing about. ... Theres a prickling all over your skin and you feal like therewl be sparkls coming off you in the dark. (199)[26]

Riddley and Erny's lives are at stake as soon as they leave Cambry. As has already been said earlier, Rightway Flinter the Big Man of Weaping Form wants to see them pay before he lets them enter through the gate, identifying them with Eusa, and Riddley complies with this demand by making Punch beat him (206). There might come a time, though, when mock-punishments cannot calm the inhabitants of the forms and fentses they visit; they might then be decapitated like guilty Eusa or torn apart like the innocent Littl

26 His maturity is quite remarkable throughout the novel, even though not quite realistic for a twelve-year-old: Hoban was fifty years older than Riddley when he praised Ornette Coleman's saxophone improvisations in the essay "The Bear in Max Ernst's Bedroom" (1987), reverting to scientific metaphors like Riddley: "... Ornette Coleman and his colleagues weren't blowing product, product was no part of their blowing. I think they were blowing process.... They were blowing metaphysical rambling shoes and quantum physics midnight specials and the uncertainty principle. Process, not product. No product to lose, no risk" (MUM, BB 188). As a thirty-three-year-old jazz fan, i.e. in 1958, he had only been able to perceive such play as "risk-taking" and was promptly rebuked by Don Cherry, who had been on stage with Coleman: "'Man, we ain't taking no risks – however we're blowing, that's how we're blowing tonight.'

I staggered back, annihilated. It was as if he had taken the Protestant work ethic and broken it across his knee like a cheap fiddle" (MUM, BB 187).

Shyning Man. Easyer's attack during Riddley's first performance hints at such a possibility (213). Art is not harmless. As Hoban told Michel Bodmer:

> We take it for granted that art is creative, we don't always take it for granted that it's destructive. I think that art looks into more and more dark corners, and as art puts names to more and more things, it calls up more and more demons that have to be dealt with, and in this sense I think it can be called destructive. It opens doors to new dangers all the time. (Hoban and Bodmer 14)

The danger need not even be external; when David Brooks asked Hoban if a writer exposing himself could be traumatised by this, he replied: "Killed by it! You can get dead from it literally. You can get yourself into a place from which there is no return" (Hoban and Brooks 78). Riddley himself is worried that he might yet turn out to be the "aulder kincher" from the story *Hart of the Wood*, who taught a man and a woman how to make fire and in return asked them to give him the heart of their child (2-4, 201).

On the other hand, Riddley's new relation to power, not struggling for power, an expression of passive resistance or active tolerance which will henceforth determine his thinking and acting, makes him rather resemble Christ as defined by Oscar Wilde in "De Profundis":[27]

> He realised in the entire sphere of human relations that imaginative sympathy which in the sphere of Art is the sole secret of creation. He understood the leprosy of the leper, the darkness of the blind, the fierce misery of those who live for pleasure, the strange poverty of the rich. ... '*Whatever happens to another happens to oneself,*'... means 'Lord Christ's heart and Shakespeare's brain.' (Wilde 923)

Imaginative sympathy also includes an understanding of the cruel: after all, the protagonist of Riddley's show is Punch, whose cockiness he must understand as well as the cleverness of Mr On The Levvil in order to be able to play them and otherwise prevent himself from adopting their behaviour. What is interesting is that Greanvine, who served as Punch's interlocutor in an improvised dialogue before Riddley left Cambry for the first time (166f.), is not added to the dramatis personae of the Punch and Pooty shows: is he present anyway in so far as the puppets are made from wood, and the wood is made

27 The definition of Riddley's new literary style (199; see ch. 6.3) partly echoes Wilde's description of the way Christ influenced people, too: "Indeed, that is the charm about Christ ... he is just like a work of art himself. He does not really teach one anything, but by being brought into his presence one becomes something and everybody is predestined to his presence. Once at least in his life each man walks with Christ to Emmaus" (Wilde 934). According to Russell Hoban, however, "De Profundis" was no source he had consciously used: "Odd, your mention of Wilde's *De Profundis*. I read it when I was about 20 and haven't looked at it since. It may well have imprinted itself on my mind although I can't remember any of it now" (Letter of 28 May 1989).

from the tree which grows out of Greanvine's mouth? Is he there as the sublimating power which turns real greed and cruelty into artistic representations of both? Riddley, at any rate, oscillates between both poles, Punch and Greanvine. In his art, there is room for both the transgressive and the regenerative principle, or, as Hoban put it in a much earlier essay, i.e. "Thoughts on a Shirtless Cyclist" (1971):

> I think that we need our outlaw strength alive and brother to our lawful vigour. The one is not healthy without the other. I keep calling the elements outlaw self and lawful self, but that is unfair, really, to the essence of the thing. Society defines the terms of lawful and unlawful, because society makes the laws. And society is a retarded child with a loaded gun in its hands; I don't completely accept society's terms. Something in us makes us retell that myth; some drive there is in us to find and name the demon in us that is more real than laws and conventions that tell us what is right and what is wrong. And that demon is, I think, the radical spirit of life: it is the dark and unseen root system of our human tree whose visible branches are so carefully labelled and scientifically pruned by us. (CY 13)

In this essay he also said that the figure who symbolized the "radical spirit of life" best was Robin Hood – a proto-Riddley. Just as Punch will find himself reflected in Greanvine's face (160), Robin Hood carries his death with him:

> After the first reading of the book, the death and the last arrow were always there waiting for Robin Hood and me; he carried that death with him, carried that last arrow in his quiver always. He seems such a year-king! He seems in his green and lightsome strength, always to hasten toward his sacrificial death that will bring forth from the winter earth another spring. And like a year-king, he must be given up, cannot be kept. (CY 13)

In Riddley Walker, Hoban has created his own Robin Hood of the future, one aware that the arrow with his name on it might already be under way (197). But he postponed the moment of death to *Pilgermann*. For in *Riddley Walker*, the question of life, of how to live and how to improve the quality of living in another than a purely materialistic sense, was more urgent.

IS THERE HOPE?

Riddley's world displays the same ambivalence as his language and the plot of the novel. While the characters have perhaps good reason to mourn the loss of "them boats in the air which they callit them space craf and them picters on the wind which that wer viddyo..." (193-194), they may at the same time rejoice in the fact that the worst part of the catastrophe lies behind them and that they do have a chance to avoid their ancestors' mistakes. Their very survival is a chance.[28] There are abundant signs that a change is imminent; Riddley is not the only character who deviates from established ways of being: from Lissener to Rightway Flinter and from the last boar to the new leader dog, both people and animals respond to the feeling that a new leaf is being turned over. The question is, of course, what they will do with their chance: will they let it slip or is there hope?

Most interpreters of the novel are pessimistic. Like Dowling, whose opinion has already been briefly discussed in ch. 6.3 (cf. excerpts from "Russell Hoban's *Riddley Walker*...", 186), they think that the message of *Riddley Walker* is that history will repeat itself, e.g. Schwenger:[29]

> Circularity provides both structure and theme in *Riddley Walker*. ... In the course of the novel gunpowder is rediscovered – the 'One Little One' [sic] as opposed to the 'One Big One' [sic] which resulted in Bad Time. That too, it is implied, will come again, further along the temporal circle. (Schwenger, "Writing the Unthinkable", 45)

If history were indeed to repeat itself, Riddley' s "guilt" as an historian, would be founded on his refusal to be a censor trying to prevent progress. He is often "Mixt up" (161), ready to acknowledge the potential for good and evil in everything and hence an advocate for the right to choices rather than for strict rules. He does not withhold any information even if he knows that it may serve to produce new abuses, e.g. with regard to the scattered but complete formula of the 1 Littl 1 (cf. 4, 123f., 142, 182ff.): A terrorist would be able to produce gunpowder with these instructions.

But if there were indeed nothing to be done to prevent the catastrophe from happening *again*, where would we then have to look for the novel's impulse and encouragement to try and prevent it the first time? After all Schwenger, for instance, demands that a "literature of nuclear holocaust" be no "anodyne" but a genre with the power to awaken its readers rather than plunge them into another version of the numbness with which the world reacted to the shock of the Jewish holocaust and the first droppings of atomic bombs ("Writing the Unthinkable", 38). In his opinion, novels like *Riddley Walker* prevent a numbing effect in so far as they postpone giving an answer to the question of the nature of the catastrophe: "the question of the bomb is bound up with the whole question of man's nature" (46). Moreover, *Riddley Walker*

28 Michael Dorris and Louise Erdrich criticized the novel (along with half a dozen other post-apocalyptic novels) as "irrationally optimistic" (24) because it presupposes that there will be survivors at all.

29 Also see Wilkie (61), Porter (453), or Cowart (87).

> ... gives us the courage to endure the process of questioning. The 'chaynjis' that we go through in coming to terms with the bomb and with ourselves will be many; all are inadequate for understanding the ground zero of our existence. Yet, ... the points on this Fool's Circle may imply its center. (46)

He concludes that most of the works he presents in his essay, among them Maggie Gee's *The Burning Book* (1983) and Walter M. Miller's *A Canticle for Leibowitz* (1959),

> ... do not dictate a response to the nuclear threat so much as they make response possible. Imagining as best we can, what might lie in the future has left us with little more than numbness. But the literature of nuclear holocaust shows that the same imagination which presents to us unendurable possibilities may also help us to endure – not to endure a holocaust but our anticipations of one, our fears and even our hopes. (48)

Convincing though such a reading may sound at first glance, especially where it points to the intimate connection between the catastrophe and human nature, it nevertheless fails to stress sufficiently Riddley's role as narrator and character and also betrays a superficial analysis of the meaning and symbolical implications of the *Fools Circel 9wys*. Riddley is more than a reader or interpreter "whose ultimate revelation is about nonrevelation" (46): if that were the case, he would never stop being an irresponsible fool. However, he is a moral subject who discovers and assumes responsibility for his actions and (mis)interpretations; his book is de- as well as con-structive, deconstructive in the best sense of that term;[30] and finally, his function is to be an example, a *possible* response to the nuclear threat. Moreover, to use the *Fools Circel* as a metaphor for the entire process of Riddley's questioning the human condition ("Writing the Unthinkable", 46; and "Circling Ground Zero", 260) and as one for the structure underlying his journey ("Circling Ground Zero", 256, 260) is to disregard not only his development but also the ostensibly irregular course of his actual journey through Inland.[31]

---

30 See Christopher Norris's Afterword in *Deconstruction*. Revised Edition (1991) for a survey of grossly distorted to more adequate usages of this term (136-138).

31 Derrida explicitly warns those who always stress the repetition of the same in his essay "No Apocalypse, Not Now", which was published in the Nuclear Criticism issue of *Diacritics* 14 (summer 1984): "... the critical zeal that leads us to recognize precedents, continuities, and repetitions at every turn can make us look like suicidal sleepwalkers, blind and deaf *alongside the unheard-of*; it could make us stand blind and deaf alongside that which cuts through the assimilating resemblance of discourses (for example of the apocalyptic or bimillenarist type), through the analogy of techno-military situations, strategic arrangements, with all their wagers, their last-resort calculations, on the 'brink,' their use of chance and risk factors, their mimetic resource to upping the ante, and so on – blind and deaf, then, alongside what would be absolutely unique; and it, this critical zeal, would seek in the stockpile of history (in short, in history itself, which in this case would have this blinding search as its function) the wherewithal to neutralize invention, to translate the unknown into a known, to metaphorize, allegorize, domesticate the terror, to circumvent (with the help of circumlocutions; turns of phrase, tropes and strophes) the inescapable catastrophe, the undeviating precipitation toward a remainderless

As I tried to show in the previous chapter and in this one, Riddley is someone who seeks ways out of treadmills: since he was a boy playing the game *Fools Circel 9wys* he has always enjoyed "busting out", that is breaking circles, but he would also enter them again to continue the game (5). Likewise, he leaves How Fents to travel through the wilderness with the dogs but he will in due course enter other fences, forms and various dead towns, following both straight and circular paths, partly following, then again leaving the *Fools Circel* and establishing contacts with other people rather than to avoid society for good. Oscillating between various concrete and abstract positions, pausing deliberately or being held up by obstacles, he personally learns to be reluctant and cautious with regard to scientific knowledge, political power and "being a man" but is ready to load "guilt" on his back as an artist, historian, philosopher and theologian, and these choices are meaningful, they define him as an individual. Only metaphorically does he complete the circle once, until what I called the fourth movement ending in his first visit to Cambry (150ff.). On the other hand, as Goodparley's "theary" of nuclear fission, developed from *The Legend of St Eustace*, shows (119-124), texts are liable to intentional or unintentional misinterpretation. It makes a difference if you really follow the *Fools Circel* or only do so in a figurative sense, and there is also a difference between following it knowingly or unknowingly. Even though words *can* and *do* "fetch" people, they are not cogent. Other than rational channels may present people with alternatives to the vicious circles depicted in verbal formulas such as *Fools Circel 9wys* or "history repeats itself". At Cambry, it is Riddley's body which turns him into the receptacle for "a nother way" (153). But since mystical moments do not happen to everybody, Riddley must revert to words to communicate what he has experienced. This is not only difficult, but it will perhaps also produce new misreadings, new vicious circles: "Some times theres mor in the emty paper nor there is when you get the writing down on it. You try to word the big things and they tern ther backs on you" (156). Nevertheless he tries to communicate what he has found out, seeking to establish a connection between us and what he has recognized as "the idear in the hart of every thing" (156). Peter Schwenger is uncomfortable with the idea of immanence implied by Riddley's mysticism; he tries to dismiss a pantheistic reading of the novel ("Circling Ground Zero", 257). When Riddley describes the "thing what lives inside us and afeart of being beartht" (156), he thinks that the focus is on the word and on the power of narratives made up by words set in motion (Schwenger 258). He is right,

cataclysm" (21). It is not only the uniqueness of something worse than all precedents that might be overlooked by such blind investigators, however, but also the the uniqueness of something better.

but only partly so, for in Hoban's universe the word *is* God: in "Pan Lives", he writes, "Can God and word and reason be thought of separately? Obviously not" (MUM, PL 127). Calling himself a religious writer, he would not subscribe to the either-or implied in attempts to explain away what does not suit rational interpretations.

MYSTICISM AND ETHICS

The question is of course: can one be at once a mystic who experiences the unity of everything and an ethical subject who makes meaningful choices, and in particular good choices? Walter T. Stace variously addresses this subject in *Mysticism and Philosophy*, for mysticism, and especially pantheism, has often been accused of blurring moral distinctions: "... if, as pantheism alleges, the world with all that exists in it is divine, then the evil in it is divine too" (246). Stace's immediate reply to such a charge is as follows:

> There is a sense in which it must be said that, if this is true of pantheism, it is just as true of dualism, or of any possible theory of the relation of God to the world; ... the problem which evil offers to all philosophies which include the conception of a good or righteous God is substantially the same. (247)

There are mystics who do not seem to be troubled by the problem; others

> ... may take refuge in any or all of the familiar theological evasions – for instance, that evil is a privation of being and therefore does not really exist, or that the appearance of evil is due to our partial and finite vision and would disappear if we could see the universe as a whole, or that evil contributes to the good of the world in the same way that a part of a work of art which would be ugly if it were isolated contributes to the beauty of the whole picture. (249)

Particularly the middle "evasion"[32] will inform *Pilgermann* (see the scene in ch. 3 in which Jesus makes Pilgermann tune in to visions of a cosmic pulse in which opposites are merely aspects of an ongoing movement, 22-23), and to a certain extent it also informs *Riddley Walker*, with its persistent references to the good and evil in everything and everybody. Stace continues:

32 I think, the term "evasion" is too derogatory since it suggests that those who try to provide an explanation are themselves unable to see that it is limited and merely of heuristic value. Hoban, at any rate, is aware of the ineffability of mystical insights; he again and again reflects on limitations imposed not only by the limitations of language but also by the limited understanding of those addressed. Riddley's awareness of difficulty has already been quoted (156). In *Pilgermann*, Hoban will be even more outspoken: "God said a great many things in the time when it was manifesting itself as YHWH; some of them may well have been misunderstood or written down wrong. Or it may be that he put things in a very simple and vivid way so as not to require too much of the general understanding. Space and time have in them no Gan Eden and Gehinnom, no Heaven and Hell as what could be called places, and I cannot believe that anyone can now take seriously the idea of a soul that is simply righteous or wicked" (PG 68). The only other option would be to become silent, but that, of course, would earn the mystic the charge of self-indulgence.

> But we can still ask what the mystic's practical attitude tends to be. ... H. C. stated that the problem of evil finds in mystical experience no intellectual or logical solution but the problem dissolves and ceases to exist. There *is* no intellectual solution. But a point of view is reached by the mystic in which he will achieve some sort of acceptance of evil while yet at the same time continuing to reject and fight against it. This is itself a paradox. (...) Does not Job's famous cry, 'Though he slay me, yet will I trust in him,' breathe somehing of the same spirit? (249-250)

In chapter 8, Stace attempts to formulate a mystical theory of ethics:

> The basis of the mystical theory of ethics is that the separateness of individual selves produces that egoism which is the source of conflict, grasping, aggressiveness, selfishness, hatred, cruelty, malice, and other forms of evil; and that this separateness is abolished in the mystical consciousness in which all distinctions are annulled. The inevitable emotional counterpart of the separateness of selves is the basic hostility which gives rise to Hobbes's war of all against all. The natural emotional counterpart of the mystical awareness that there is, in that reality which the mystic believes himself to perceive, no separateness of I from you, or of you from he, and that we are all one in the Universal Self – the emotional counterpart of this is love. And love, according to the theory, is the sole basis, and also the sole command, of morality. (324)

Even though he must admit that it can only attain the status of a "hypothesis among others" (332), he invokes the authority of mystics themselves:

> That part of the theory which asserts that love and compassion are actually parts of the mystical consciousness must be accepted as true, since it is so stated by those who have that consciousness. ... love can flow from it into the world and be *a* source of ethical action. ... We are left at least with the assurance that the mystical consciousness should be, for those who possess it, a powerful motive and impulsion towards ethical, and therefore social, action. (333)

In the second section, he examines the problem in a historical and sociological perspective, trying to find out whether, in practice, mysticism has indeed been able to promote the good life or whether it has mainly served as an excuse for self-indulgence, as many critics see it: "It may even be suggested, by those who cultivate so-called depth psychology, that what the mystic is 'really' trying to do is to go back into the warmth of his mother's womb" (334).[33]

33 Freud in fact interprets the fantasy of a return to the mother's womb as an expression of castration anxiety and impotence (cf. "Hemmung, Symptom und Angst", 279). The mystical feeling of oneness with the universe, "oceanic feeling" is explained away by him as a regression to infantile narcissism: "die Wiederherstellung des uneingeschränkten Narzissmus" (cf. "Das Unbehagen in der Kultur", 204). At the beginning of the essay Freud admits that he only felt coerced to deal with mysticism in a serious way because an "excellent man", i.e. Romain Rolland, tried to convince him of the existence of "oceanic feelings". (197-198).

For Riddley, as we have seen, this return to the maternal womb indeed takes place when he hides himself in the crypt of Canterbury cathedral, which is to him the womb of the Mother Goddess (156). But he does not want to stay there since the desire for society proves to be stronger than the fear of being reborn. Like any one of the mystics, whose reputation Stace vehemently defends in the lines which follow upon the statement of the criticism levelled against them, "he seeks to show to others the path to salvation which he has found. He is a teacher of what he conceives to be the good life" (Stace 334).

Being an artist rather than a religious leader, Riddley approaches the task of taking social action by indirection. It is by kindling a longing in us to find out for ourselves what to "put oneself right" means rather than to go on finding out what the 1 Big 1 was and how it worked, as the old cautionary stories do, that Riddley tries to "fetch" us away from the deadly circles: "Them as made Canterbury musve put ther selfs right. Only it dint stay right did it. Somers in be twean them stoan trees and the Power Ring they musve put ther selfs wrong" (157). He asks us a riddle for which there is not one but a great number of solutions which prove to be more or less adequate when put to the test. He does not teach dogmatic truths but does what the best teachers do: he gives an impulse and lets his students discover for themselves what they must learn, for what you have found out for yourself is what stays. He remains committed to his office of connexion man in a responsible, self-critical, anti-authoritarian and unorthodox way, inviting us to go our own ways rather than to simply tread in his steps. Goodparley once told him, "What ben makes tracks for what wil be. Words in the air pirnt foot steps on the groun for us to put our feet in to" (116). Nothing compels us to follow those steps, however. If Riddley's ultimate revelation were really about "nonrevelation" and if he really believed that there were no sense in looking for answers since they are "all" equally "inadequate", he would hardly bother to become an artist, putting words on paper or figures on the stage over against all difficulties, epistemic and physical.

A CONSTRUCTIVE IMPULSE

Among those who have worked out this constructive impulse of the novel are Barbara Herkommer, Nancy Dew Taylor in her brief but insightful essay "'... you bes go ballsy': *Riddley Walker*'s Prescription for the Future" (1989), and David Lake, whose essay "Making the Two One..." has already been mentioned. Barbara Herkommer proceeds by pointing out the negative connotations of circles and circular structures in the novel: the children's game *Fools Circel 9wys* turns out to be a cruel ritual for Ardships and a structure breeding lust for power (Herkommer 150f.); the riddle of the 1 Big 1 – here she quotes Northrop Frye's definition of the riddle as "a circle of words" drawn around a subject (150) – is a deadly trap leading to destruction (151); Goodparley is victimized by his repetition compulsion (152);[34] and finally, both Riddley and Goodparley are trapped in the fool's circle of their own language and thinking when trying to interpret *The Legend of St Eustace*, which requires altogether different patterns of thought to become intelligible: Goodparley enforces the relationship between the twentieth-century text and the *Eusa Story* to such an extent, that his exegesis becomes a blatant and parodic example of "misreading" (Herkommer 157f.). She again and again points out that Riddley must break these circles and find other directions to protect his body and preserve his moral integrity – at least as far as this is possible, since fragility and vulnerability ultimately cannot be escaped (153f., 160, 167). When she tries to determine the wider significance of this act, or of this series of acts, however, she underestimates their overall disruptive and creative potential. Quoting from Derrida's "Structure, Sign and Play in the Discourse of the Human Sciences" to contrast an open structure (without a centre or limits) with a closed one,[35] she focuses on the performative freedom Riddley acquires after leaving Cambry – this is in line with her constructive argument.[36] But she also concludes that the ability to move, play and tell freely presupposes Riddley's renunciation of power and his remaining outside the closed circle of a community governed by a central power (154).

Two objections must be raised to this interpretation. First of all, Riddley's story and especially his new life reveal that the so-called closed circle and the absolute necessity to preserve it are myths. There is no "outside" of a "closed" circle any more because the chain-reaction of events triggered by Riddley's escape from How Fents has abolished the institution, i.e. the Ram with its hevvys, the Eusa folk and the Big 2, which saw to the stringent

34 Even though Freud is not mentioned here, Herkommer appears to be familiar with the psychoanalytical implications of the term, for earlier in her study, she mentioned Freud's essay "Erinnern, Wiederholen, Durcharbeiten" (1914), where the term was used for the first time (Herkommer 103, n. 31). It might nevertheless be useful to add that Freud's continued encounter with the phenomenon of repetition compulsion in dealing with neurotic patients eventually led to his tentative definition of the "Todestrieb" (death instinct or death drive) in "Jenseits des Lustprinzips" (1920). His theory of the drives will be examined more closely in ch. 8.3. Also see ch. 4.3: for Hoban, Eurydice embodies the death drive.

35 The excerpt chosen by her is the following: "... structure ... has always been neutralized or reduced, and this by a process of giving it a center or referring it to a point of presence, a fixed origin. The function of this center was not only to orient, balance, and organize the structure – one cannot conceive of an unorganized structure – but above all to make sure that the organizing principle of the structure would limit what we might call the *freeplay* of the structure" (see Herkommer 154; her source was pp. 247-248 of *The Structuralist Controversy*, edited by Richard Macksey and Eugenio Donato, i.e. the first published version of the paper Derrida had delivered at Johns Hopkins University in 1966 [Baltimore and London: Johns Hopkins UP, 1972]).

36 By contrast, Schwenger, who also quotes from Derrida's essay, emphasizes the absence of a centre or a central truth in Riddley's world (cf. "Circling..." 257).

enforcement of the Inlanders' belief in these myths (RW 196f.):[37] by repeating the secret sacrifices of Ardships and watching over the official propagation and interpretation of the *Eusa Story* the Pry and the Wes Mincer would define the Inlanders as a closed society with a common origin and the Ram as its central power. Actually, though, the potential freeplay of the structure has always been part of its organizing principle, as the last lines of the *Fools Circel 9wys* show: "Sharna pax and get the poal / When the Ardship of Cambry comes out of the hoal" (5). As long as the Ardships' tour of Inland took place under the surveillance of various Pry and Wes Mincers, the freeplay of coming out of the hole/whole was limited of course: an Ardship could only come out of his diverse prison holes to be questioned and eventually decapitated; thus the structure could be presented and preserved as, or reduced to, a closed circle with nothing branching away from it but dead-end streets in dead towns. Yet Riddley's intervention reactivates the freeplay of the structure. The figure "9" of the *Fools Circel 9wys* can be taken as its icon, that is, an open circle with a way – out, or leading to wisdom (i.e. "fools circle while to go 9wise is wise..."), or to a wider circle, or merely to a dead end of another sort? I should say that it depends on the individual who chooses this way. In order to move, play and tell freely, then, one must not necessarily give up society but merely discourage it from believing the myth that it is closed and unchangeable. By becoming a puppeteer rather than a solitary eremite hiding away on Ground Zero, in the crypt-womb of Canterbury cathedral, or in the wilderness of the forests, Riddley takes the decision to challenge and change society rather than stay "outside" (and thus indirectly confirm) its imaginary "closed" circle: "Whynt we stay hoalt up? Whynt we go somers far a way? Becaws you cant stay hoalt up. Becaws there aint no far a way" (205).

This takes me to my second objection. As soon as one's actions influence the possible range of actions of other people, power is exercised. Michel Foucault writes in "The Subject and Power":

> Power exists only when it is put into action.... (...) A relationship of violence acts upon a body or upon things; it forces, it bends, it breaks on the wheel, it destroys, or it closes the door on all possibilities. Its opposite pole can only be passivity, and if it comes up against any resistance, it has no other option but to try to minimize it. On the other hand, a power relationship can only be articulated on the basis of two elements which are each indispensable if it is really to be a power relationship: that 'the other' (the one over whom power is exercised) be thoroughly recognized and maintained to the very end as a

37 Perhaps it was also triggered earlier, by his illicitly keeping the Punch figure found in the mud; or earlier still? As early as in chapter 2, Riddley tells us, "I dont think it makes no diffrents where you start the telling of a thing. You never know where it begun realy. No moren you know where you begun your oan self" (8).

> person who acts; and that, faced with a relationship of power, a whole field of responses, reactions, results, and possible inventions may open up. (...) In itself the exercise of power is not violence; nor is it a consent which, implicitly, is renewable. It is a total structure of actions brought to bear upon possible actions; it incites, it induces, it seduces, it makes easier or more difficult; in the extreme it constrains or forbids absolutely; it is nevertheless always a way of acting upon an acting subject or acting subjects by virtue of their acting or being capable of action. (788-789)

Renouncing power, as he does after his first visit to Camby (162), does not make Riddley any freer but it invites violence: as soon as he accompanies Goodparley to Granser's hut, his passivity nearly kills him. Granser's talking head nevertheless does not allow him to dodge responsibility for what happened:

> Lissening him then words come to me: What if its you whats making all this happen? What if every thing you think of happens?
> I said, 'I never thot of my father getting kilt did I.'
> Words come: Dint you?
> Then I wernt sure. I said, 'I wont think no mor.'
> Words come: That dont make no diffrents. If you dont think then some thing else wil think your thots theywl get thunk any how.
> I said, 'What can I do then aswl be my oan doing?'
> Words come: Whats the diffrents whos doing it?
> (189-190)

The last question is not rhetorical. Whoever does or fails to do something thereby determines whether the place in space and time he or she occupies is one at which the freeplay of the structure continues or stops, whether a hole be blown into existing networks, or certain links be strengthened while others remain unused. This affects not only the one who acts but also those who occupy places in space and time within the sphere of influence of the acting subject. Foucault writes, "power relations are rooted deep in the social nexus, not reconstituted 'above' society as a supplementary structure whose radical effacement one could perhaps dream of" (791). The question of who is doing it determines not only how, where and when it will be done but also how influential the action will be. To renounce power wholesale, then, is to give away the possibility of intervention, of defending oneself, of resistance (the struggle against power and violence); it is to support any action an acting subject might envisage and thereby increase his or her sphere of influence. Riddley therefore eventually decides to renounce not *power*, but the *struggle for* power. Although Herkommer has quoted the relevant passage immediately before presenting her conclusion (cf. 153), she fails to consider the subtle difference Riddley introduces when telling us that "It aint that its *no* Power. Its the not sturgling for Power thats where the Power is" (RW 191). His resolve is not to avoid society but immerse himself in "the girt dants of the every thing. Sum tyms bytin sum tyms bit" (201). If his performances exert an influence on the way of life of other Inlanders, he will accept his power and pay for it; but he will do nothing to enforce his views.

Nancy Dew Taylor starts out from Riddley's power to influence his surroundings. Whereas Herkommer rather underrates his influence, Taylor at first tends to overemphasize his function by presenting him as an heroic leader rather than a possibility. Her working assumption is as follows:

> What Hoban offers us in this novel is what heroic art has always offered us: an example of the individual's refusal to knuckle under to Fate without a fight. That fight, that struggle – though it may end in total or partial defeat – allows the individual some sense of worth and of dignity within his own life. Such individuals change the course of history – or die trying. Such individuals are the only hope of any society, Riddley's or ours. As the epigraph states, 'There's no one else.' Through his novel, then, Hoban challenges us to become Riddley Walkers. (31)

She then goes on to examine the learning process which turns Riddley into a figure of hope: Pessimistic stories and cautionary myths that he has always known or hears on his journey make the beginning; they challenge Riddley to find solutions for his life so that history won't repeat itself. Since the narratives fail to say how, he must find his own way (31f.). But Riddley also learns from the people and animals whom he meets on his journey (32-34). His understanding of right and wrong doing deepens in the course of these encounters: he learns what it means "to pay for what one has done wrong" and "to accept and bear one's hump. The hump is sin, guilt, the fall, the 1 Big 1, Bad Time; it is each man's recognition of his individual and his collective guilt" (34). Finally, "Riddley must act; he must make some kind of move by which he will attempt to change his world. He does so by creating stories" (35). For Taylor, Easyer's interference with Riddley's show is already a first promising sign for the future: "this time the baby is 'saved.' (...) ... he prevents the violence from happening; he prevents a repetition of history" (37). Here my reading differs from hers, however. As I argued in chapter 6.1, the result would have been even more promising if it had not nearly cost Riddley's life; Easyer's trying to kill Punch (respectively the puppeteer) is not a very effective or intelligent means of preventing history from repeating itself but an act of foolish violence, a false struggle. If art is indeed to "have a hand in shaping the future" (Taylor 35), the artist must learn and produce subtler shows which will not provoke any more false struggles. But Taylor does not ignore the element of danger altogether; she only fails to recognize it in the realm of art: "Riddley's future, like ours, is uncertain. There are dangers ahead, changes that will have to occur if Riddley and his roaders are to change the world" (38).

To sum up what will encourage Riddley and his newly won group of travelling puppeteers in the future (38), she quotes from the improvised conversation between Punch and Greanvine in chapter 16 (166f.). Her quotation stops where Punch is saying, "The end cud be any part of the way its in every step of the way thats why you bes go ballsy" (167). This is not the novel's only "prescription for the future" (see the title of Taylor's essay), however. While it is certainly important to be able to "go ballsy", it is equivalent to the advice to become like Punch (and Easyer), and I doubt that the novel or Riddley are so assertive. Listening to the end of the conversation and to Riddley's comment will actually cast light on a slightly different and wiser moral:

> Greanvine said, 'Is that how you all ways go?'
> Punch said, 'I am the balls of the worl I am the stoans of the worl. I am the stoans and I have my littl stick.'
> Greanvine said, 'Is that your tree then is that your living wood?'
> Punch said 'Yes thats what it is its that same and very wood what never dys.'
> Greanvine said, 'Wel then is there hoap of a tree?'
> Punch said, 'Theres hoap of the wud in the hart of the stoan.'
> Greanvine said, 'What stoan is that then?'
> Punch said, 'Balls. Which thems the stoans what never dys.'
> Wel of coarse Punch wud say that. Thats how he is hes that way myndit. Me I dint have Punchs balls nor I wernt all that sure them wer the stoans what never dys. (167)

Riddley has learned to recognize his limitations and to derive from this self-knowledge the proper balance between caution and courage. This is the best he can do to work for a future that is better than the past. It is in this sense that we are encouraged to become *like* him. At the same time, though, if we heed this advice, we will distance ourselves from Riddley, we will never *be* him but go our separate ways, for we can then indeed prevent the future from ever plunging into anything as horrible as the world in which a Riddley Walker must learn to get his bearings.

7. Pilgermann (1983)

As is usually the case with the later works of an artist, *Pilgermann* defies "fast" analysis, even more than *Riddley Walker* did. This time, though, it is not the language which slows down the reading but the complexity of theological and ethical concerns and the overwhelming imagery of the novel. Impatience and misunderstanding characterize many responses to it; thus, a reviewer wrote:

> If you embark on this pilgrimage, beware: to make it to the end, you'd better have a strong stomach as well as a high tolerance for Biblical rhetoric and for writing that often clinks along as portentously as the armor-clad soldiers. Moreover, while the book's ambition to confront timeless questions is admirable, some of the mystical profundities that Pilgermann dredges up turn out to be alarmingly old hat. (Lehman 92)

Would he have had second thoughts about his unfavourable evaluation if he had been aware that mystics cannot possibly be original because they all refer to a revelation that imposes its own conditions (see Stace *passim*)?

My contribution to the discussion of *Pilgermann* will often consist of questions rather than answers, e.g. the question where the book starts, which is intimately linked with the way we are to read it. Does it start with Hoban's dedication of the novel to his daughter Esmé; a dedication which is accompanied by a quotation from I Kings 19: 12: "... and after the fire a still small voice" (3)? In this case, as a private communication, it has to be left alone by the critic. Or are the three quotations from the Old and New Testaments and the Quran its "proper" beginning (7)? We would then be invited to take part in a religious fantasy or an intellectual meditation on theological subjects. Russell Hoban's Acknowledgements tell us that a visit to Montfort in Galilee helped him to find a setting for the "further action" that was waiting to be precipitated "into the time and place of its own story" after he had completed *Riddley Walker* (9). The novel is thereby contextualized by its author, which implies that a comparison with its predecessor should be made. But perhaps *Pilgermann* really starts only with the narrator's announcement "Pilgermann here" (11), a summons to take notice of the rather special narrator, and then continues with his tuning himself back in to an unnamed German town in the year 1096, which kindles expectations concerning historical fiction and the postmodern novel. It even contains science fiction motifs (time travel, computer terminology, etc.) despite its medieval setting. I cannot say what *Pilgermann* is: it borrows elements from all these fictional and non-fictional genres, and to identify it as only one of them would entail the exclusion of the others. Only a multiple reading can do justice to its diverse aspects.

Readers who attempt to read the novel in terms of just one category, e.g. as a historical novel, will find fault with it for being too contemplative and intellectual:

> Hoban's religious intellectualism becomes most evident in the four-page appendix wherein he identifies his scriptural quotes and other sources. Like Borges or Pynchon he strikes me as more metaphysical than novelistic, and I gather he is searching for a medium to convey his manifold skills and thoughts. ...
>
> In *Ararat* D. M. Thomas seems content as a clever textual trickster. Hoban wants more from his words and overreaches with them. I hope he hits upon the formula. (Bell-Villada 539-540)

The "formula" has of course already been found; it *is* that of writers like Borges or Pynchon, or of those artists who are mentioned by Pilgermann himself: Vermeer, Schubert, Bosch and others. The question is why it is dismissed by the critic. I do not think that *Pilgermann* causes problems because it is a hybrid book. Most postmodern novels are wild cross-breeds of different genres. It is rather its mystical view of the universe, its self-conscious religiosity, which may challenge the readers' own point of view. I agree with Christine Wilkie who writes at the end of her own brief analysis:

> In *Pilgermann* Hoban is taking his readers into an uncertain territory of time and space; into a territory that will cause them to question things as they appear, and to contemplate instead the actuality behind presented reality. It is a pilgrim journey that they will not undertake lightly. For some it will prove to be unbearable. (Wilkie 75)

Even though the metaphysical foundation of *Pilgermann* is the same as that of *Riddley Walker*, the use of (an often unusually elaborate) Standard English and the discussion of existing religions, that is of Judaism, Christianity and Islam rather than of invented cults diminish the distance between the readers and the subjects presented. Just as the private and the public, the fictional and the non-fictional concerns of the author are mixed in the opening and closing pages of the book, *Pilgermann* fails to respect the boundaries between "art" and "life" behind which readers can normally hide to evade a personal response. It was no doubt easier to accept Riddley's "connexions" because they could be explained (away) as tentative approaches to the world of a twelve-year-old boy growing up in a "primitive" society. Moreover, deciphering Inland dialect was an aesthetic pleasure which probably induced certain readers to focus less on the contents of the novel. In *Pilgermann*, however, we hear the voice of a grown-up narrator. And the mystical insights he gains as well as the journey to his death which he experiences, unfold in the midst of our own cultural heritage.

In an interview, Hoban said that he basically let the book "happen" to him: "Obviously I rewrote many times, I always do that, but I wanted it to be like a Jazz improvisation, in that material comes in and changes, and things drift in and out" (Hoban and Bodmer 3). Everybody does not like improvisations, however. Philip Horne, for instance, criticizes "the novel's inspirational self-importance" in his review (15):

> The torrent of random Zen wonderings ... and of big questions and big answers ... justifies itself by an aesthetic of irresponsibility. The writer does not know what he is doing, and this makes his intuitions more valuable. 'I describe what I do not understand because I am lived by it,' Pilgermann claims at one point. ... The same condition is ascribed to a much greater Author: 'It is my belief that God is of an artistic temperament and has therefore chosen to let his own work be beyond his understanding.' That 'therefore' may well give us pause. The corresponding attitude for the reader is perhaps stated when Pilgermann and his friend discuss the tiled design they have built in Antioch: 'May it not be that the best way of conducting oneself with this pattern is simply to take it in without any thought and to enjoy in it the presence of the Unseen?' Such an invitation to abdicate judgment and plunge into the worldlessness of 'all'-inclusive superstition needs to be declined. (Horne 15)

This criticism invites analysis: First of all, Horne's evaluation of the novel's seeming randomness is not supported by objective criteria. The plot is looser than the helix-shaped one of *Riddley Walker*, but not random; it is oriented towards the death of the protagonist, which gives life both to the narrator, as he self-consciously points out (55), and to the author's meditations. *Pilgermann* could be divided into three parts according to the stages of a rite of passage: 1) transgression, fall, rupture: the Jewish surgeon Pilgermann commits adultery with Sophia, the wife of a Christian tax-collector; he is unmanned in a pogrom; 2) departure, transition, transformation: after seeing Jesus, Pilgermann embarks on a pilgrimage to Jerusalem; at first, he finds the dead body of the tax-collector, who has been killed by relic-gatherers; later, he meets a madman who kills his bear and a group of starving pilgrim children; Death himself ("Bruder Pförtner") begins to keep company with him; at an inn, Pilgermann takes revenge on the peasant who has unmanned him and he also kills his sow; ghosts and a personification of his own young death join him; crossing the Mediterranean, he is abducted by pirates and taken to a slave market in Tripoli; 3) arrival, death: Bembel Rudzuk, a wise Turkish merchant, "buys" and befriends him; they sail to Antioch, build Hidden Lion, a pattern with tiles, and experience the beneficial as well as the uncanny sides of a work of art intended to make the divine visible; finally, they die fighting the intruding Frankish crusaders.

If the success of Pilgermann's journey were measured in terms of his reaching the original aim of his pilgrimage, i.e. Jerusalem, he would have failed. However, as Herkommer has noticed, the concrete journey defined by Pilgermann's geographical way is of secondary importance; it is merely a trigger for a spiritual journey (170). Helix-shaped subplots can be made out within the linear three-part structure, e.g. from Pilgermann's castration to his taking revenge, or from the planning of Hidden Lion to the insight that it was foolish to actualize the project. As in *Riddley Walker*, helixes symbolize moderate progress (cf. ch. 6.3): they do not suggest that a process has reached its definite conclusion. The idea of ongoing processes, of one helix leading on to the next and of one being interwoven with others, is also supported by the fact that certain cohesive elements connect the novel from the beginning to the end, e.g. the dislocutionary appearances of various Sophias, both human and nonhuman; each reappearance adds a new shade to the idea of her.

The story is embedded in a narrative frame and supplemented with long philosophical interludes on such themes as identity, time, or heaven and hell. I suppose that Horne particularly refers to the latter when he dismisses the entire novel as a "torrent of random Zen wonderings". Still, he disqualifies himself rather than the novel, for the interludes are linked with the story: "Like the crows flapping up from the hanged men my thoughts scatter and like the crows they return to what they were feeding on" (55). Horne's expression "'all'-inclusive superstition", which I take to refer to the mysticism of the novel, on the other hand, shows that the reviewer above all feels uncomfortable about the irrationality of religious thinking: this must be accepted as his personal opinion. The charge levelled against the novel's alleged "invitation to abdicate judgment" must be rejected as a further distortion of facts, however. The impossibility of abdicating judgment and shirking responsibility is printed on practically every page of the book. Like Riddley, Pilgermann and Bembel err in certain respects but they learn from experience. Very soon after the last of the passages quoted by Horne (i.e. "May it not be..." from PG 146), they find out that their own decision not to interpret Hidden Lion has no influence on other people: "Hidden Lion had a life of its own ... (...) ... the forward edge of a pattern's visible expansion is attractive, it excites in people and in things a desire to shape themselves to it, to meet it and move with its advance" (148-149). There are certain artists who try to distance themselves from the reactions provoked by their works – like scientists who blame the users of their inventions for the damage caused by them. Hoban is too self-conscious to revert to evasion, however, or to indulge his narrator. After one hundred Christians have been slaughtered on the tiled floor, Bembel instantly silences Pilgermann's attempt to shirk responsibility for effects triggered by the tile pattern they have built; he spells out that their creation is presumtuous:

> 'All things being contiguous,' I said, 'Hidden Lion can as well be an effect as a cause; it cannot be proved to be the beginning of a chain of evil.'
> 'Sophistry cannot help us,' said Bembel Rudzuk; 'every action has its consequences and the consequences of the action of making Hidden Lion cannot be without evil.' (181)

Judgments will be made invited or uninvited, whether the person, text, or object is understood or not, for judgment does not necessarily depend on understanding. Even if God were "of an artistic temperament" (98) and did not understand his creation, Pilgermann later tells us that "the will of God was simply that everything possible would indeed be possible. Within that limitation the choice was ours, the reckoning His" (182).

How can a novel that resembles a jazz improvisation be described if one is not prejudiced against it to begin with? Perhaps, as Hoban does, by taking notice of the material that drifts in and out, and by tracing its changes. I will first look at how this material is presented, borrowing metaphors from an essay Hoban wrote while he was working on *Pilgermann*. Then I will discuss the role of the three monotheistic religions which figure in the novel and show how the protagonists emancipate themselves from orthodoxy. Another brief chapter will place Hoban within a network of artists who can also be understood as pilgrims to the mystery that moves us, that is, writers, sculptors and painters whose works help the narrator Pilgermann to "speak from between the pieces" at all (11). Finally, and this will be my most personal response to the novel, Sophia's role in *Pilgermann* shall be examined, and called into question, by way of a comparison with Fevvers, the winged picaresque heroine of Angela Carter's *Nights at the Circus* (1984).

7.1. Chaos, Sounds and Stillness

Hoban has never neglected his work; his manner of writing springs from certain aesthetic intentions, as is made evident by excerpts from "Mnemosyne, Teen Taals, and Tottenham Court Road", an essay first published in 1982:

> Shiva's drum beats time and creates sound which is the vehicle of speech and the conveyor of revelation, tradition, incantation, magic, and divine truth – all of which rely on or collaborate with memory. With the gyroscope of

> memory we navigate our forward course both mental and physical, whether from bathroom to kitchen, Tchaikovsky to Bach, or ten leagues beyond the wide world's end. Through memory we refer, we connect, we recall, we retain, we bring back, we hold on to. (...)
>
> Memory is the natural and necessary partner of music. ... music ... relies on memory to hold in our minds the passage of sounds through time.
>
> ... When we come to [music] such as Bach's *The Art of Fugue*, however, something else enters into it: we find ourselves not so much retracing a track of note-by-note sound as experiencing a mode of being to which sound is a rite of passage and a way of the spirit to a place beyond music, a place where memory cannot reach, where every time is now. The music that puts us in that place does not depend on memory; it is without greed, makes no demands; it doesn't ask to be remembered. By such music Apasmara Purusha – who is Forgetfulness and Heedlessness, who is life's blindness and man's ignorance – is overwhelmed, defeated, crushed beneath our foot at the very outset because there is no need to remember, nothing to remember: there is only being and the flicker of time/no time, dance and stillness. (...)
>
> What's happened is that I've come to a time when I don't want much emotion in my music; I don't require either to be uplifted or downput by it. ... I don't want much emotion; I want the dance in the stone. That's how I think of it: the dance in the stone; not the foam forever fading in the wake of our forward motion. ... What I'm after more and more is on the other side of heartbreak; it's in the stone of things, with bare, spare music that not only doesn't ask to be remembered, it does not ask for anything at all, makes no attempt to hold on to the beat of Shiva's drum, which is after all nothing especially eastern or exotic: it is only that same everyday drum in the heart of the atom, the same in Hammersmith as in Hyderabad, moving to the beat of the stillness in the dance and the dance in the stillness. (MUM, MT 219-222)

"Sound" and "stillness" are key words in this quotation. Actually they can be applied to all levels of a novel's form and contents, e.g. as literary metaphors to describe Hoban's preference of an economic to an exuberant style, or of still small voices to heroic shouts. The criteria which will help to identify elements as either of the two are their relationship to time and space, and their degree of memorability: Most sounds ask to be remembered; they are the basis of language and move in more or less ordered ways. Stillness, on the other hand, cannot be remembered; there is no movement or transformation of space, no time which passes, no language. Sounds can vary by degrees, approaching stillness; stillness itself, however, is an absolute mode defined precisely by the absence of everything variable. A third term is offered in an excerpt from the beginning of the essay, when Hoban is speaking of his way of listening to All India Radio:

> Sometimes reception is beautifully clear, and the chromatic splendours of the classical Karnatak style build palaces of sound all round me in my Fulham work-room. ... At other times the ionosphere is unfavouring: Shiva as

> Destroyer, Kali with her necklace of skulls, garish polychrome demons dance in my short wave receiver, roaring and crackling and filling the room with chaos which is, after all, to be expected; I accept it without complaint. (217)

Blurred borderlines, irruptions, disorientation, and irregularities characterize "chaos", distinguishing it from well-defined sounds. Like stillness it does not ask to be remembered, but its complex movements or noises, and its creative and destructive dynamics clearly distinguish it from stillness. The fact that it is hard to decide where *Pilgermann* actually starts is an example of chaos in action. This is not meant to be a value judgment. For accepting chaos, as Hoban does, is rewarded with occasional glimpses of far-away regions; there may eventually occur sounds which function as rites of passage to the place desired by him in the essay, that is the "place beyond music ... where memory cannot reach, where every time is now". Chaos, in other words, mediates between sounds and stillness: it prevents sounds from continuing for ever, but it also intrudes into stillness to prepare the ground for new sounds.[1] I would now like to apply the three metaphorical categories to different elements in *Pilgermann* and show how they account for the phenomena that have been praised or criticized by reviewers.

Stillness, sound and chaos usually coexist in the novel, for example in the narrator: he introduces himself by an invented name because he cannot remember his original name and is only "waves and particles" or an owl (11) – in his shapelessness, we have an instance of chaos; his forgotten name, on the other hand, has been swallowed by stillness. It is not easy to accept "him" without complaint, especially if this unusual protean medium is compared to the bright boy Riddley Walker. But then of course, the crimes and atrocities which Pilgermann tells us about, most of them suffered, others committed or witnessed, by him, surpass the cruelties witnessed by his predecessor. Sympathizing with Riddley does not challenge our emotional capacity to the same extent as sympathizing with Pilgermann. He has been dead for centuries, but not to be still and rest in peace. He must assemble his particles and broadcast his waves because there are receivers like the author, eager to listen to the things Pilgermann has to tell. Probably he would not make the effort at all if he had not been compelled by his mystical call to be a pilgrim at the service of something larger than himself (26, 32f.). He is moved by the same question as Riddley, namely what the idea of us might be:

1 Descriptions of chaos tend to be chaotic themselves; not even chaos theorists, whether they are mathematicians, physicists, or scientists from other areas, can agree on one formula, as James Gleick's selection of quotations at the end of his study *Chaos. Making a New Science* (1987) demonstrates (cf. 306f.).

> 'But what's it all about?' I cry.
> 'If I could tell you that it wouldn't be a mystery,' says God. 'Let it be enough that I ask for your help.' (God has of course not actually been speaking here because he is no longer manifesting himself as He; but God as It has put these words into my mind.) (PG 201)

Unlike Riddley, however, Pilgermann asks the question aware, like ourselves, that humankind has failed more than once; there is not just one (for us, virtual) catastrophe to account for but an entire series: "The possibilities of choice were beyond all calculation and the probability of wrong choice so high as to be almost a certainty. Only God could think of such a game, and only humans would bother to play it" (182).

The fact that Pilgermann takes on an identity at all, i.e. a "*poste restante* for whatever addresses itself to the persistence of memory" (69), and that he speaks in a distinctive voice is an instance of sound. However, he resembles a musical archaeologist striving to reconstruct a melody from sound fragments revealed by chance and mixed with fragments from other melodies. His access to personal memories is often as blocked as it was for Kleinzeit: "Not all of my experience is available for recall by my Pilgermann identity, only that in which the energy of the input was above a certain level" (102). On the other hand, he sometimes feels irresistibly drawn to telling about events he did not experience himself: "How there are vortices in the space-time! My mind keeps spinning down to Manzikert where in actuality I as Pilgermann never have been" (100). Hoban obviously seeks to break open the limited frame of one lifetime through Pilgermann's chaotic afterlife memories. Departing from the medieval pogrom experienced by Pilgermann, for instance, he can also address the Holocaust (40), choosing indirection as a way to approach the worst crime of the twentieth century. Personal identity of course dwindles to insignificance beside human catastrophes of such dimensions. Names, dates or places become secondary. Pilgermann can therefore remember no more than a few facts of his biography: He was a Jew born in the year of the battle of Manzikert in 1071 (96). When he was a boy, the sight of an owl flying over the ruins of a burnt house deeply impressed him (11). Later on, he studied medicine at Salerno (103). Nothing else is known about his childhood or his education. By 1096, he lived in an unnamed German town (14).[2] A minimum of coherence sets in

2 *The Atlas of the Crusades*, edited by Jonathan Riley-Smith, gives the following information on the persecution of Jews: "To the Church, the justification for the First Crusade was the Muslim occupation of Jerusalem; but many crusaders, before they had even left for the Holy Land, began a vendetta against the Jews, holding them responsible for the Crucifixion. There were anti-Jewish riots at Rouen in France, in Bavaria and Bohemia. By far the worst outbreaks of anti-semitism occurred in the Rhineland, where the Jewish community at Mainz, one of the largest in Europe, was annihilated. Churchmen tried, with varying degrees of success, to stop

only after this point because his memories are more numerous. Pilgermann remembers how he first saw Sophia, how he was castrated immediately after he had made love to her, and how one thing led to the other until he died in Antioch in the summer of 1098:

> If I had my proper parts I'd not be on this road; that's a simple truth, not to be argued with. ... Climbing that ladder is what I'd be doing as often as I had the chance. But how long could that have continued, my garden of Eden? Even God had to put Adam and Eve on the road before he could get on with the story. Thinking, thinking, and I can't think how I could have gone on living without coming on this pilgrimage, without being as I am being now. When I had my proper parts I must have been blind and deaf, the world had not come alive for me, I had never talked with Christ, had never put my feet into the footsteps of my road away, had never, alone in a dark wood, seen the light of Now. (55)

Despite his transition from a historical character to a form of energy Pilgermann is allowed to preserve one external feature: "I no longer have a mouth with which to smile wryly but I think that the waves and particles of me must be arranged in something like a wry smile" (13). But by endowing his narrator with an ability hitherto reserved for Lewis Carroll's Cheshire-Cat, Hoban mocks rather than accommodates those who expect more details and more "concrete life".

Pilgermann's first twenty-five years, then, have left next to no traces in his memory. All the crucial events of his life, i.e. those which have turned him into a mystical pilgrim with an afterlife, took place in the two years before his death. Being an unstable entity, an action that does not stop, "it only changes", Pilgermann now speaks from where he is, that is "from between the pieces..." (11). Nine hundred years after his death, his mode of expression is necessarily closer to stillness and chaos than to everyday discourse although he tries hard to make himself understood. The paradoxes and abstractions which characterize his style often lull the readers until they are ready to open their minds to the stillness behind the words:

> It is not from the loss of Sophia, the loss of Christ and the loss of God as He that the pain comes, no. It is from the pain that God comes, that Christ with his lion-eyes comes, that Sophia in all her beauty, her splendour, and her passion comes. It is from the cosmic intolerable of the nothing-in-everything alternating with the everything-in-nothing that all things come. This great pain, this ur-pain, swims its monstrous bulk in deeps far down, down, down below that agony of loss in which I grind my teeth remembering the golden bell of Sophia's nakedness and the sharpness of the knife of joy. (87-88)

---

these outbreaks, but every major crusading appeal during the 12th century was to set off fresh attacks on the Jews" (28).

Where the effect fails, though, he plunges us into chaos. Pilgermann is aware that much of what he tells us sounds "odd" because, as he warns us at one point, "... precision with words is impossible" (70). Sometimes he prefers to remain silent. Particularly traumatic events are deliberately censored by him, e.g. the slaughter of one hundred Christians on Hidden Lion:

> The sacred is not to be imaged, there is no image to put to what God is nor is there any reason to want an image of such a thing. The evil that he has created is also in its inexplicable way sacred and not to be described beyond a certain point. Suddenly are these long-legged shore birds, these gleaners of the tideline, netted. Suddenly, with their dark faces, their speechless mouths, their uncircumcised members, their frozenness into such time as there will be until the end of time.
>
> That is as far as I shall go with these words and the images they bring. What happened, happened.
>
> Afterwards the bodies are taken away in wagons. (174-175)

Metaphors (e.g. "shore birds" for the victims), a general verb ("happened") for a more precise one, and a gap between the paragraph ending with "happened" and the subsequent one beginning with "Afterwards" actually cut out the massacre itself. They cut it out in such a way, however, that it is revealed to the imagination rather than hidden. Moreover, all the other massacres and murders which have been mentioned in the course of the novel are implicitly actualized as well. Where Pilgermann chooses a gap, a hole in the narrative, his mode of expression *is* stillness indeed, not merely sound functioning as a rite of passage to stillness.

The distinction between sounds which function as rites of passage to stillness, sounds which are instrumental for our everyday life and unintended detours into chaos affects not only individual sentences and paragraphs, but the narrative as a whole:

> Sometimes I don't know anything at all for large spaces; sometimes I know many things all in the same place. My perceptions are uneven, my understanding patchy but I have action; I go. I can't tell this as a story because it isn't a story; a story is what remains when you leave out most of the action; a story is a coherent sequence of picture cards ... (38)

Tenses shed some light on the function of various parts of the narrative. The gnomic present is by definition a rite of passage to stillness: it characterizes presentations of "action", that is of essential events or "picture cards" within the general narrative which are eternally present in Pilgermann's consciousness. Past tense, on the other hand, is normally used for the story, i.e. for the presentation of historical and logical sequences or for details he need not necessarily remember. By calling one mode "story", the other "action", Hoban makes explicit what could also be seen in the relationship between the interpolated stories and the main story of *Riddley Walker*: since the apparently static engenders the dynamic, their opposition is called into question. The gnomic present is not to be mixed up with the actual present of his narrating and of his philosophical meanderings although their difference is not always recognizable at first glance. The actual present connects each sentence with its own particular "now". Even though "waves and particles" cannot be described in terms of time and place,[3] the narrator becomes subject to time as soon as he speaks, which accounts for the fact that he can appear as a voice or as an owl and change his opinion from one sentence to the next: "Well, which is it then – does he know or doesn't he know? I have no idea. No, I don't believe that he knows. (...) But wait, maybe he dreams of such a thing constantly..." (28). Such changes belong to the (hi)story of his afterlife. The example is characteristic of the beginning of chapter 4, where we see the narrator at work: he is asking himself a multitude of questions in order to reconstruct logical sequences between moments of stillness. Although certain things become clearer to him, e.g. "Now I see why there must be a tree of knowledge in the garden of Eden: it bears that fruit which cannot possibly be resisted" (31), he cannot account for everything. Occasionally, but very rarely, Pilgermann also uses the historical present, which must not be confused with the two other present tenses. Like the past tense, the historical present is anchored in the story of the experiencing I, as adverbs of past time show: "It occurs to me *then* that it might have been my castration as much as anything else that started him [the tax-collector] on his penitential pilgrimage" (52; emphasis mine). Here the historical present lends special emphasis to a moment of insight in the past, making it present without giving up the distinction between this type of experience and that of timeless moments described in the gnomic present tense. Pilgermann underlines the fact that certain insights did not have to wait for his afterlife. The historical present is often said to compete with forms in the epic past, i.e. sentences in the past tense accompanied by adverbs of present time. But Pilgermann does not use these two story modes in the same contexts. Epic past particularly occurs in scenes of high emotional intensity:[4]

---

3 See e.g. Stephen W. Hawking, *Eine kurze Geschichte der Zeit*, esp. "Die Unschärferelation", pp. 75-85, in which he presents paradoxical facts about quantum-mechanical reality; or Douglas R. Hofstadter, *Metamagical Themas*, esp. ch. 20, "Heisenberg's Uncertainty Principle and the Many-Worlds Interpretation of Quantum-Mechanics", pp. 455-477.

4 See Franz K. Stanzel's discussion of the distinction between gnomic, historical and synoptic present tenses in *Theorie des Erzählens* (1985), pp. 41-43, 48, 135-136, 145-146. He

> History! I felt myself impaled on history, my own and the world's. The horror, the horror of cause and effect! The horror of the pitiless and implacable chain of one thing following another from the beginning of the world to the end of it with never a pause, never a year of Jubilee, never a clearing of the record! O God! to come so far and to end with so little. *Now* it *was* like that torture in which the victim, his belly opened up and one end of his entrails tied to a post, is made to walk round and round the post unwinding his guts. (222-223; emphasis added)

Since the major changes between actual present, past tense and gnomic present are used systematically throughout the novel, its narrative structure cannot be described in terms of a simple duality between the story and the frame in which it is told: Pilgermann's two perspectives, as narrator quivering about space and as the castrated Jew whose story he tells, are transcended by a third one whenever he reaches an everlasting moment. The temporal distance between narrating and experiencing "I" is abolished, not because the story catches up with the here and now of the narrating, as it did in *Riddley Walker*: In *Pilgermann*, narrating and experiencing "I" become identical in *timeless*, or eternal, epiphanic moments.

Looking at the beginning of the novel will illustrate Pilgermann's oscillation between frame, story and moments of stillness. At first, he refers to the events of his past using verbs in the past tense; present tense refers to the discourse situation, i.e. to the present time of his narrating:

> I *was* on my way home from the house of the tax-collector. ... I know that he *was* an official of some kind.... (...)
>
> Myself, I think I may have been a tailor or a surgeon or something of that sort. Whatever I *was*, my services *had* so far never *been* required by that man or his household. (13-14; emphasis added)

But the memory of Sophia makes his account lose all its pastness:

> Her name <u>is</u> Sophia: Wisdom. There's allegory for you, the vision of naked Wisdom and the Jew lusting after her. And such nakedness! It <u>continues</u> in my eye, splendouring. It will always be there, an image of such power as to confer

also draws attention to the competition between historical present and epic past, cf. pp. 41-42. The term epic past ("episches Präteritum") was coined by Käte Hamburger (cf. *Die Logik der Dichtung*, 63-78); she claims that historical present and epic past are functional equivalents: "Daher können wir ohne Ausnahme in jedem fiktionalen Kontext, der das historische Präsens aufweist, dieses wieder durch das Präteritum ersetzen und werden keine Veränderung unseres Fiktionserlebnisses bemerken" (98). Hamburger argues only in terms of the *reader's* experience of the fictional text. In *Pilgermann*, however, the formal distinction is used to show the narrator's emotional involvement in, respectively detachment from, the narrative: whereas the historical present signals emotional detachment combined with a sense for the ongoing validity of an insight, the epic past underlines the narrator's sympathy for the feelings of his past self (suffering, excitement, impatience, desire, etc; cf. e.g. 32f. or 118).

> unending Now upon the mind that holds it. Always now the great dark house in the Keinjudenstrasse late at night. Always now I, the solitary late-night Jew walking where he is not wanted. (14; emphasis added)

Although these words must be read as a sequence, they function as the "rite of passage" to a place where every time is now and where sequences no longer exist. I have underlined the verbs in the gnomic present tense; by contrast to the remaining conjugated verbs, the underlined ones do not only refer to the present time of the discourse situation. Both verb forms in the gnomic present and verbless constructions indicate the stillness of this frozen moment.

After a relapse into the past tense in the paragraph beginning with "Jews are known to be clever but I did nothing clever..." (15), Pilgermann returns to present tense narration in the second sentence of the following paragraph: "I hear the hooting of an owl..." (15). His making love with Sophia is as timelessly present as his castration, the subsequent cries to God, and God's silence:

> Still no word from God. The blue sky is perfectly blank, the smoke of the burning synagogue drifts in the still morning air; it's going to be a hot day.
>
> 'God!' I cry, 'Whatever you are and whatever I am, speak to me! O Lord, do it for thy name's sake...' (19)

Nothing moves until – as another change of tense underlines – "the air began to shimmer and Christ appeared to me" (20). A fairly grotesque dialogue ensues between Pilgermann, who did not pray for *that* kind of help, and Jesus, who insists on being responsible for the mutilated man:

> I said, 'I want to talk to your father,' then I held my head and waited for his answer to echo inside me.
>
> He said, 'Humankind is a baby, it always wants a face bending over the cradle.'
>
> I said, 'God's our father, isn't he?'
>
> He said, 'God isn't a he, it's an it.' (21)

Despite terrible pains, Pilgermann is aware of the cruel irony inherent in his situation. After cuckolding a Christian tax-collector, he is castrated by a pack of Christian Jew-hunters. Thanks to the very tax-collector, who seems to be ignorant of the adultery committed by his wife and Pilgermann, Pilgermann's life is spared. On top of it all he gets assistance from the one in whose name pogroms are carried out. But how are we to interpret the fact that this scene is presented in the past tense, i.e. as story rather than as action? If my assumptions about the function of tenses are correct, then past tense signals that the irony of the situation as well as Pilgermann's initial quarrel with

Christ won't matter in the perspective of eternity. Moreover, the appearance of a divine figure obviously does not in itself turn a scene into a moment of stillness. As long as Pilgermann rejects Christ, his experience is simply an insignificant intermezzo which might as well have been otherwise. Ultimately, he cannot refuse his helper (as little as one can "say no" to a lion or to Death, 128, 226), and this is the fact that will last. Briefly before Pilgermann notices the victims of the pogrom and a pattern in the cobbled stones, the tense changes to the present again:[5]

> We are walking, I am leaning on Jesus; with his right arm round me he keeps me from falling. I feel the strength in him rising like a column. ... Suddenly there is so much space between the Jewish quarter and the rest of the town! Suddenly the Christian roofs are sharp and distant, they are looking away. In the great space all round the synagogue the bodies of the dead are vivid, the blood fresh and dark on the cobbles that seem to have put themselves into patterns I have not noticed before: there are twisting serpents, shifting pyramids, I see the face of a lion that comes and goes. (21-22)

The pattern, too, will stay with him and leave its mark on his design of Bembel Rudzuk's tiled floor (123). At first, though, he tries to determine what is and what is not part of it.

Wondering whether the pattern requires that it must always be Jews who are killed by others, Pilgermann asks Christ for an explanation:

> 'Thou Jew,' I say to Jesus, 'tell me about this conversion of the Jews.'
> 'What conversion?' says Jesus.
> 'From life to death,' I say. 'Why does it keep happening? Why is it God's will?' (22)

He is refuted, however – not by words, but by the image and the sensation of a mighty cosmic pulse in which human distinctions such as those made between different religions are altogether insignificant. The question is not wrong; it must remain unanswered precisely because never ceasing to ask it is essential. Both Pilgermann's question and Christ's reaction are therefore rendered in the gnomic present:

> Jesus turns his face to me and opens wide his eyes. There come upon me such a shuddering and a blackness, such an expanding pleroma, such an intolerable fullness that I am filled to bursting with it. I open, open, open but cannot contain it, I explode in all directions to infinity, I contract to a point,

5 The series of progressives at the beginning of the quotation recalls the effect of the scene when the Neanderthals try to escape from the inheritors in Golding's novel (cf. ch. 6.2): "... the effect is ... that of a badly edited piece of film where we flick from one event that 'is happening' to another..." (Lee 88). In Hoban's terms one could speak of the flickering of individual picture cards.

> I explode again from the point, I come back together and return shuddering and full of terror. (22)

It is not up to Pilgermann to know the details. He is not to be omniscient but to represent the pattern as far as it is accessible to him. After a further relapse into doubt (past tense, cf. 24-26), he sums up his assignment in a series of verbless constructions and sentences in the gnomic present which emphasize his endless suffering:

> I, Pilgermann, poor bare tuned fork, humming with the foreverness of the Word that is always Now. Unbearing the unbearable, intolerating the Intolerable, being not enough for the Too-Muchness. I, poor harp of a Jew twanging incessantly in the mouth of Jesus, in the lion-mouth of Christ Pandamator, Christ All-Subduer. There is a point where pattern becomes motion; the pattern has found me and I must move, must be aware of moving, must be a motion, and an action of the Word. (26)

The cosmic pattern is formed by all moments of stillness. As Christ's "harp" and his "bare tuned fork", or as a mystic, Pilgermann will have to move forever between the moments of stillness which delimit his Pilgermann identity, leading a chaotic existence of creative unrest. His mystical vocation is both a more blissful and a more terrifying experience than it was for Riddley: there is love-making with Sophia as *unio mystica*, as Herkommer has pointed out (189); but castration and the suffering of being a medium of the divine are part of it as well. Pilgermann speaks from experience when he says: "I know that the pain waits in the joy as the dragonfly waits in the nymph" (88). In *The Mouse and his Child*, the emotional states associated with nymph and dragonfly are reversed: Miss Mudd suffers while she is a nymph; she only begins to enjoy life when her dragonfly body eventually breaks out of its nymphal encasement (cf. MC 128f.). In the cosmic perspective, though, in which causalities can be reversed like time, it no longer matters if pain waits in the joy or vice versa. What energizes the "action of the Word" is that the one will always turn into the other. The pattern of the tiles which is called the "Willing Virgin" by the brickmaster Tower Gate (128) or "Hidden Lion" by Pilgermann (123) is just one approach to, or a reduction of, the more general pattern: it is an instance of sound while "Word" or "God" or the "Unseen" is both stillness and chaos, infinite and not to be contained in its totality by the human mind.[6] Contemplating Hidden Lion Bembel nevertheless recognizes the paradoxical unity of motion and stillness in the Unseen:

6 Readers interested in the kabbalistic aspects of Pilgermann's mysticism will find an excellent discussion on pp. 184ff. of Barbara Herkommer's study.

> 'This motion that we see is the motion of the Unseen.... This power that we see is the power of the Unseen, and it is both conscious power and the power of consciousness. Here already are two of my questions answered: motion is in the pattern from the very beginning because the motion is there before the pattern, the pattern is only a mode of appearance assumed by the motion; consciousness also is in the pattern from the very beginning because the consciousness is there before the pattern, the pattern is only a kind of window for the consciousness to look out of. ...' (146)

Even though Hidden Lion is marked as a reduction, the validity of the ideas it represents is not restricted to the novel: the images visible in the pattern reappear several times inside *and* outside the narrative. Wherever there is a description of treason or traitors, or of uneven lines and rivers, the "twisting serpents" of the pattern are implicitly or explicitly alluded to (e.g. 21f., 100f., 170f., 197). The "shadowed pyramids" can be recognized in Mount Silpius and Mount Sinai (111f.), in anything that is "strange and surprising" in its actuality (125), or in the "gathered flaunt and power" of the stronghold of Montfort in Galilee (9). Firouz the traitor is particularly sensitive to the implications of David's Wheel:

> He spread out his fingers as if gripping a small wheel, he rotated his outspread, hooked fingers. 'It turns,' he said, 'there is a turning in it: the turning of the sun and the moon and the stars; the turning of the wheels of fate and fortune. Thus do we see that at the centre of the universe there is a turning, there is a turning at the heart of the mystery. ...' (143)

The passing of time and particularly cyclic returns such as the return of migrating animals (7, 236) are subsumed by the image. But David's Wheel also points to falls from grace: "'David's Wheel,' he [Firouz] said. 'David slew Goliath and became a great king. And yet he turned, did he not. He turned from what was right, he turned to the wrong....'" (143). Sinning is a turning away of and from God, hence "'The murderer too sees God ... and perhaps more than others. ...'", as Bembel has recognized (115-116). The "lion" and the "virgin", figures manifesting themselves alternately at the centre of David's Wheel, are actualized in the constellation of stars which fascinated Russell Hoban in Galilee (9). At the beginning of the novel, they encourage Pilgermann to pay a visit to Sophia: "I see three stars burning between the Virgin and the Lion, they are like a gesture, a Jewish gesture, the hand flung up, fingers spread: Well then! What are your intentions, will you block the road for ever?" (15). Finally, they also glimmer at the moment of Pilgermann's death (236).

Virgin and lion usually belong together in Hoban's works. "'... The lion is hidden in the willing virgin...'" (128), as Tower Gate tells Pilgermann after he has explained why "The Willing Virgin" is the official name of the pattern:

"Because the next time you look there's something different about it" (128). Being more obsessed with the lion's presence and absence, i.e. with violence, loss and danger (143, also see 21f.), Pilgermann is unable to perceive the virginal aspect of the pattern until a vision of Jerusalem manifests itself; it is as unstable as the Willing Virgin described by Tower Gate: "I was uncertain of the meaning of this apparition; sometimes I thought one thing, sometimes another" (150). The conjunction of virgin and lion is a complex image that condenses the attraction, the danger, the price and reward of all that is life-affirming and at the same time menacing because it forces a subject to call into question its previous life; it is the Janus-faced emblem of the radical spirit of life, i.e. of desire and mystical experience. Pilgermann pays with his maleness (25f.), with loneliness and exclusion from his community (135), and, at last, with his worldly life (236). But each loss brings with it new insights and further questions. Even though he once believed that "Sophia was the beginning of my Holy Wisdom and Bohemond would be the end of it" (211) – a time-bound error, hence in the past tense – there are still new things to learn: "Is this perhaps God's gift and mystery, that he puts the world in and on each one of us as if there is no one else?" (212).

It is not only the images of Hidden Lion which extend into the world of the characters and the author but also the structural principles underlying its composition (repetition of a basic unit, illusion of contiguity with infinity) and the way in which it is conceived, built, interpreted, called into question, and finally destroyed. The scene in which a mute boy draws two irregular shapes on the stone ground not yet covered by tiles but only marked by the chalk lines of Pilgermann's draft prefigures the inevitable intrusion of chaos into the symmetry of the geometric pattern (125f.). The silent child is father to the man at that moment: Immediately before the boy turned up, Pilgermann had begun to fetishize the project, seeing it as a source of power and as a means of restoring his lost manhood (125). The boy's intervention curbs his narcissistic aspirations. Pilgermann no longer minds, but feels relief that the tiled floor cannot be accomplished at once:

> Then the grey sky opened and down came the rain. As it poured down and drenched me to the skin my heart leapt up to meet it, I didn't know why. That rain, the prospect of which had only a moment before filled me with despair, was now bringing me ease and refreshment. (126)

The pattern also establishes a bond between *Pilgermann* and Hoban's other works. In his review of *The Medusa Frequency*, Eric Korn was the first to ask whether Hobans's books are "variations on certain obsessive themes, or ... parts of a greater whole" (Korn 949). Barbara Herkommer concludes her study *Das Muster in Bewegung* by investigating what had to remain a question in Korn's review. She traces the development of motifs and other structural elements from *The Mouse and his Child* to *The Medusa Frequency* with reference to the features of Hidden Lion (237-249). Focusing not only on analogies but also on the dislocutionary shifts between the pattern and the novels, she manages to capture the dynamic openness of the "cabalistic unity" (Korn 949) rather than to nourish assumptions about a closed totality.

In the face of such a powerful matrix, there arises the question if there is a relationship between Hidden Lion and Jung's notion of a collective unconscious. The collective unconscious consists of universal archetypes, i.e. "typical forms of behaviour which, once they become conscious, naturally present themselves *as ideas and images*, like everything else that becomes a content of consciousness" (Jung, *Selected Writings*, 16). The pattern obviously *works like* archetypes: several people independently spot the same images or give it the same name (123, 143, 151, 157) although, as Bembel underlines, "the pattern is in actuality abstract" (146). Moreover, the pattern *comes from* the unconscious: it could then be one of the images moulded on archetypes, according to Jung. But Hoban does not stop at this point. Although the pattern comes from the unconscious, its idea does not originate there. The ideas embodied by Hidden Lion have permeated the universe before there were people to represent them; the unconscious is merely one channel for them to pass through. Hidden Lion is a necessarily reductive representation of a far more complex cosmic pattern, which is itself a reduction, i.e. "a mode of appearance" of a universal motion, or "a kind of window" for an infinite consciousness to look out of (146).[7] There might be a relation of self-similarity between all channels of motion and consciousness and the overall cosmic pattern of which they are part, but their different scales entail different degrees of differentiation for the ideas which pass through them:

> We assume always too much, we assume what cannot be assumed. We see dots so we connect them with lines and we claim to know what the lines and dots signify. There is a marching, there is a galloping, there is a hissing of arrows, a clashing of swords; or it may be that there is simply a stretching forth of the neck to the sword, there is a wrapping in the Torah scroll, there is a burning alive and we assume (always the assumptions) that these things are happening to different people. We assume that the Frank is distinct from the Jew who is distinct from the Turk but I cannot now think of it as being like that. It seems to me now that that busy line, that motion in the circuitry, did not leap from one dot to another: from the leap of its original impulse its being continued

7 For more details see the discussion of Lorna's and Riddley's mysticism in ch. 6.4; or Hoban's definition of his metaphysical position in the interview with Christine Wilkie, published in the Appendix of her study *Through the Narrow Gate* (101).

> on its way to flash into Christian, Jew, Muslim, fortresses, rivers, dawns, full moons, battles, crows, the wind in the trees, anything you like. (100)

Jung, on the other hand, actually claims that the collective unconscious is not merely one of many windows, i.e. a specific man-sized channel for perceptions, ideas and drives. According to him, archetypes are the *source* of religious ideas as well as of all other ideas humankind has had about itself and the universe:

> All the most powerful ideas in history go back to archetypes. This is particularly true of religious ideas, but the central concepts of science, philosophy and ethics are no exception to this rule. In their present form they are variants of archetypal ideas, created by consciously applying and adapting these ideas to reality. For it is the function of consciousness not only to recognize and assimilate the external world through the gateway of the senses, but to translate into visible reality the world within us. (Jung, *Selected Writings*, 16)

The implications of this view have been expressed by Anthony Storr in his introduction to Jung's *Selected Writings*: "... whereas Nietzsche stated that God was dead, Jung rediscovered God as a guiding principle of unity within the depths of the individual psyche" (Storr 25). Being less respectful one might say, Jung reappointed God after dethroning and shrinking Him to a manageable size – and this, for practical reasons. In "Approaching the Unconscious", the opening essay of *Man and his Symbols*, he defends religious beliefs and other thoughts that cannot be proved because they are "useful" (89); he goes on:

> Man positively needs general ideas and convictions that will give a meaning to his life and enable him to find a place for himself in the universe. He can stand the most incredible hardships when he is convinced that they make sense; he is crushed when, on top of all his misfortunes, he has to admit that he is taking part in a 'tale told by an idiot.' (89)

Yet, must it still be pointed out, at the close of a century of atrocious nationalistic wars and genocides such as the Holocaust, that "general ideas and convictions" which promise to give "a meaning" to people's lives have more often been abused and proved to be disastrous than "useful"? What is true for ideologies applies even more to religions. Those who need and wait for God to make sense of their existence ever so easily fall prey to those who pretend to know what God means and wants. Jung's utilitarian version of God is therefore in many ways more terrible than Nietzsche's dead one.[8]

8 Those who start out from the premise that "Nothing is the ultimate truth", as the mouse child does at the bottom of C. Serpentina's pond (MC 125), at least won't waste any time waiting for divine help.

For Hoban's protagonists God cannot be confined to the psyche. Nor must the idea of a mystical unity be instrumentalized in the way Jung proposes. Bembel Rudzuk tells Pilgermann early on, while they are discussing alchemical processes, that he is interested in thought processes that are continual offerings; anything else is greedy (109). In his view, believing in God is an attitude of trust, not one of expectation or of unconditional obedience to supposedly divine orders; God's will is not of the order of sound: "'... We are in his hand, knowing nothing. When anyone tells me that God wills this or that, whether he be Christian or Muslim I grow uneasy.'" (131). Bembel's words not only prefigure Pilgermann's disgust at the arrogance of the Frankish crusaders whose motto is "*Deus le volt!*" (164, 234) but also his own criticism of stories such as that of Abraham and Isaac, respectively Ibrahim and Isma'il, in the Old Testament and the Quran (178). Neither Pilgermann nor Bembel can derive a total "meaning" of their lives from their mystical quest: they mean different things for each other and for other people, and they can retrospectively try to define the meaning of their experiences in terms of their figurative pilgrimage. But there is no ultimate divine affirmation; nor do they find "their" place in the universe. If they find anything it is a way to be.

One of the things they learn is to give up possessiveness. For mystical visions are far from reassuring: as chaotic intrusions they decenter the protagonists and encourage, or force, them to move on from where they are. The protagonists must again and again assess their position relative to other people – ethical behaviour presupposes this kind of reflection – and relative to the unity to which they offer themselves. But there is no point at which they can lean back complacently and enjoy "wholeness", as defined by Jung, for good.[9] Unity implies a complete dissolution of the subject: "its" proper "place" is everywhere, hence nowhere; when a subject has reached the "goal", it no longer exists as subject.

After saving Pilgermann from destitution, Bembel teaches him most of the things he needs to know to become a mystic. Although Pilgermann is educated and his traumatic experiences have made him receptive for extraordinary insights and visions, Bembel also sensitizes his perception to less spectacular manifestations of the divine (109). It is therefore legitimate to ask why Bembel needs a helper to build the pattern with tiles at all, or why he is so emphatic about their meeting: for him it is the "fourth leg" (108) that completes the "three-legged horse" of the universe, enabling it to accomplish

9 Hoban's ideas about the experience of the divine are closer to Lacan's notion that it involves *jouissance*, i.e. reaching a point at which meaning falters and the subject realizes its split condition (cf. "God and the *Jouissance* of ~~the~~ Woman" and "A Love Letter"). See chapter 8.3.

its "journey to the red heifer" (106),[10] and before long he calls Pilgermann his brother (114). When Pilgermann tries to find out what will be expected of him, Bembel at first reverts to the stereotype that he is a Jew and therefore intelligent: "'A Jew will consider anything,' he said." (106). A little later he gives a more complex reason which, however, is still related to the same stereotype: Pilgermann belongs to the same people as Abraham, who in Bembel's opinion "personifies the elemental complementarity that moves the universe" (108). Only when they know each other better does Bembel reveal that an inexplicable impulse prompted him to approach Pilgermann on the slave market. Sceptical about the way Prodigality advertised the Christian pilgrims – "'... Buy a Jerusalem pilgrim and all this mystical force can be yours!'" (115) – he suddenly found himself addressing Pilgermann (115). The reason why it had to be Pilgermann is as unfathomable as the reason why he had the idea to make him devise a pattern: "'This idea came into my mind. An idea is an eye given by God for the seeing of God.'" (115).

Although he is wise and wealthy now, having been "active and adventurous" in his youth (160), Bembel is a passive and modest character at heart. He does not need to be physically castrated to take notice of Death and God. Unlike Pilgermann the surgeon, who was a womanizer before he was unmanned, passionate and ready to break laws to gratify his desire, Bembel has never been aggressive or ambitious. The story of his naming, which he tells Pilgermann on the night before they die, underlines that he has flourished thanks to the ability to react rather than to act and strive (223-227): When he was an apprentice or "boy" to a Tripoli merchant, he accompanied a caravan which was attacked by robbers. All his companions were killed, so he ended up having to defend his life against four robbers. While he was defeating one after the other, his mind was busy making up little songs. From these he would later derive his new name. Humble despite his youth, he did not triumph over the robbers' death. Like Pilgermann when he killed Konrad and his sow Bodwild (66), or Riddley when he killed the boar on his naming day (RW 1), Bembel became keenly aware of his own frailty: "I recognized that it could just as easily have been the robbers alive and I dead..." (225). Death then appeared to him, promising him a good life provided that he never forgot "whose child" he was: "'... when I say it's time for bed you must come promptly and cheerfully; you might as well do it with a good grace because in any case you'll have to come – no one can say no to me.'" (226).

10 Hoban has added a footnote referring to Numbers 19 in the Pentateuch to help the readers understand the symbolism of the red heifer (238): it is the sacrificial animal whose ashes the Israelites were ordered to use for the preparation of purifying water.

After this fairy-tale beginning, Bembel's life has always been closer to stillness than Pilgermann's. Having been alone all his life, he has never had a woman and children to love nor has he ever failed. But we would probably not live if our lives were meant to be no more than rites of passage to stillness. Chaos therefore intrudes into his daily routine. It seems that Bembel must meet Pilgermann so that the gaps in his experience can be closed.[11] His resistance against attempting a project as daring and immodest as Hidden Lion is eroded by his finding someone ready to devise a pattern. After this, a dream and Tower Gate's willingness to bake the tiles despite his initial reservations (145) suffice to make Bembel drop his original project, i.e. an evanescent pattern made with sun-dried mud tiles (130). Using the metaphors of the novel, which originate in scriptural metaphors, one could say he passes through the fire all sinners feel in their souls when the awareness of his failure gradually dawns upon him (148, 152). Unlike clay passing through fire, however, the awareness of his fallibility turns him into a humane rather than a hard or complacent man: "To me it seems that the best we can hope for in life is honesty of error; more than that is not to be expected. Sometimes we can see what is wrong action but that doesn't make anything other than that right action" (227).

Despite their original temperamental differences, Pilgermann and Bembel eventually react alike. Bembel, too, sees Sophia and her little son in one of his last dreams although he has never met her: "'You have a woman and a child to love,' said Bembel Rudzuk. 'I have only you and I have been eating the scraps from your table'" (227). He does not fall in love with her; this is not the point of the dream. But he begins to understand what unconditional love for another human being is. Pilgermann's renewed devotion to Sophia teaches Bembel to live up to his friendship with Pilgermann. Instead of striving for a smooth passage from life to death, as has always been his aim (227), Bembel dedicates the remainder of his life to Pilgermann's impossible last-minute attempt to escape from Antioch (228) and to the support of his morale when they are intercepted and locked up by Firouz (230-234). He does not mind breaking his contract with Death on behalf of his friend; thus, Death's "child" grows up, substituting responsibility for self-sufficiency. According to Sura 96: 6, 7, quoted by Hoban at the beginning of *Pilgermann*, self-sufficiency is a sin in Islam: "Nay, but man doth / Transgress all bounds, / In that he looketh / Upon

11 My attempt to make sense of Bembel's life must remain speculative precisely because there is no ultimate instance to pass judgment on him. There are only the facts of his life as they present themselves. Without recourse to the metaleptic construction of a meaning-making God, to an ideological aim or to other people, the meaning of life cannot be defined but as a tautology, i.e. the meaning of life is to be as it is.

himself as self-sufficient" (7). However, it would be a simplification to say that Bembel eventually turns into a perfect Muslim, for self-sufficiency and responsibility do not mean the same things in the novel and the Quran. For Muhammad Asad, the translator of *The Message of the Qur'an*, sura 96 implies...

> ... that all moral concepts – that is, all discrimination between good and evil, or right and wrong – are indissolubly linked with the concept of man's responsibility to a Supreme Power: in other words, without such a feeling of responsibility – whether conscious or subconscious – the concept of 'morality' as such loses all its meaning. (*The Message of the Qur'an* 964)

In the novel, on the other hand, the first obligation of human beings is to each other: religion follows from ethics rather than vice versa. By means of his ethical act, Bembel transcends the boundaries of his personal existence; it is a side effect rather than the result of a conscious effort that he now comes closer to the infinite Unity to which he has always aspired than by means of all his earlier alchemistic and artistic offerings of his self.

Immediately before Bembel and Pilgermann die, all their actions are coordinated; they rush to Hidden Lion "as one man" (235). What ultimately makes them alike is above all their readiness to open themselves to both the otherness of someone they love and the otherness of the man who will kill them. When Bembel's body is eventually cut in two by Bohemond's sword, his entire being is perfectly tuned to the paradox of motion and stillness that he has always recognized as the essence of the divine:

> Now I see what I have seen before in the darkness and the brightness in my mind, I see leaping and still like a butterfly transfixed by lightning the elegance of Bembel Rudzuk as he attacks Bohemond; I see the great Frankish sword that has been going up and down like a post-hole digger suddenly leap like a live thing as Bohemond shifts his grip and now a track of brightness horizontally cleaves the darkness, cleaves the purple-blue, cleaves with its savage arc the body of Bembel Rudzuk; now in two pieces falls the body of Bembel Rudzuk to the broken tiles of Hidden Lion. (235-236)

Pilgermann could be called the quintessence of Hoban's novels even if the genuinely "novelistic" passages are rare. As Hoban is trying to perform "on the other side of heartbreak", it is logical that his narrator should prefer thinking to telling, and telling to showing, or, in terms of the visual metaphors used by the novel, that his narrator cannot always present memorable images or scenes. There is a remarkable contrast between this novel and *The Lion of Boaz-Jachin and Jachin-Boaz*, where there was no narrator and the presentation of events was mostly scenic. But there are passages, e.g. the one describing Bembel's death, where it is obvious that Pilgermann has the "willing look" of Vermeer when he painted his *Head of a Young Girl*: "... the look with which Vermeer looked upon her face, that is the look with which everything must be seen; yes, even the severed limbs. Everything that is, everything that happens must be seen with the eye that is in love with seeing" (97). It is precisely Pilgermann's readiness to open himself to the person or thing seen rather than to attempt to master it which distinguishes his willing look from a possessive look. The willing look makes the viewer extremely vulnerable because he does not remain hidden but exposes himself to the unpredictable consequences of the look of the other. In *The Medusa Frequency*, for example, Herman Orff will experience vulnerability as disappointment: his willing look is not always returned in kind. Taking recourse to the painting by Vermeer again, Hoban will show that the viewer "in love with seeing" may suddenly have to look at his own fallibility and mortality and that such a sight can be lethal. In *Pilgermann*, though, there is only a limited awareness of danger: the willing look usually engenders goodwill in return, see e.g. the reaction of the Jewish community when the tax-collector suddenly looks at them "as one looks at other human beings" (34), or Pilgermann's response to Bembel's look on the slave market (106). The only exception is the final scene, when the protagonists encounter the terrifying Frankish warrior prince who brings death no matter how he is looked at: the face of Bohemond, whom Pilgermann calls "Questing", "Elijah", "Messiah", "my world and my Jerusalem" (235-236), remains invisible. His helmet screens his eyes: even if he were touched, impressed or scared by Bembel and Pilgermann's courage, Bohemond the conqueror could not show his humanity. The openness of his victims bounces off his armour, making him seem to be untouchable.[12]

I should like to end this chapter on chaos, sounds and stillness in *Pilgermann* by pointing to some particularly impressive "picture cards", i.e. images *of* chaos, sound and stillness which have left indelible traces in Pilgermann's memory. There is, for instance, the description of a nocturnal Muslim raid on the Frankish camp. It is an image of chaos because the darkness of the night precludes almost all vision, leaving Pilgermann exposed to sounds whose sources he cannot always identify:

---

12 Bohemond must have been moved all the same by what he experienced for he turned into a "public lecturer" after his return. Jonathan Riley-Smith writes in his essay "The State of Mind of Crusaders to the East 1095-1300": "When Bohemond of Taranto toured France in 1106, in a triumph which culminated in his marriage to the king of France's daughter in Chartres cathedral, many French nobles wanted him to be godfather to their children. He lectured about his adventures to large audiences and his experiences as a prisoner of the Muslims became incorporated in the *Miracula* of St Leonard, whose shrine he ostentatiously visited" (71).

> The sound-picture gathered itself into a forward movement, came towards us, passed beneath us, appeared in front of us on the bridge in the dark images of itself, the dark gleamings of iron and leather, the forested lances nodding, the shaking of reins and bridles as the horses tossed their heads. The clop of hooves, the clinking and the jingling passed into the darkness across the river, quickened unseen to a trot, a canter; for the first time then the kettledrums were heard, they pounded out the headlong gallop of the charge as voices whooped in war cries, voices called on Allah. There came then Frankish cries to Jesus, cries to God, cries of 'Saint-Gilles!'
>
> Suddenly the clamour of the drums is heard again – a different beat, the choppy rhythm of unluck and about-turn. Here now the Turks are coming back in thunderous flight across the bridge. 'To the gate!' they cry. 'Back to the gate!' cries Yaghi-Siyan at the head of the rout. '*Deus le volt*!' cry the Franks, 'Saint-Gilles!' 'The gate!' cry the Turks. With these shouts we hear the clash of weapons, the screams of horses and of men, the groans and curses, the grunts and trampling and scuffling of men fighting for their lives, and the splashing of men and horses into the river. 'Saint-Gilles!' goes up the shout, it seems very close, almost beneath us. '*Jesu*!'
>
> Back across the bridge ebb the voices of the Franks. 'There is no god but god!' shouts Yaghi-Siyan, and once more the Turks gallop across the bridge and into the darkness beyond it. (186-187)

The change of tenses marks the place at which the story is passing into action on account of the scene being "a paradigm of the rushing forward, the rushing back, that so much of history is made of" (185); in other words we are here dealing with the *idea* of history. Obscurity, i.e. the difficulty of understanding what is going on, an aspect of chaos according to the definition presented at the beginning of this chapter, is its essential feature (185). The scene has been anticipated in a reflective passage; Pilgermann then spoke of "the systole and diastole of the siege of Antioch" in which he recognized "the reciprocal action of that asymmetry without which there would be only stillness and silence" (167). The scene literally illustrates this abstract thought. Pilgermann does not impose any clarifying visual images on the "sound-picture" of chaos: his willing look accepts that there is next to nothing to see. Earlier I said that the willing look makes the viewer vulnerable because it exposes him to the look of the other; here, however, he is above all disoriented.

Only later, when a wounded man explains what happened, will we learn why the Franks suddenly moved back across the bridge after being almost beneath Bembel and Pilgermann, ready to invade Antioch through the gate: a riderless horse obviously scared them (188). Storytelling and historiography turn raw history into a series of causes and effects; the image of chaos gradually turns into a sound chain: by means of explanations the intrusion of chaos into stillness is ordered, made intelligible, and, to all appearances, mastered. A responsible historiographer or storyteller, however, does not suppress the inexplicable phenomena: Pilgermann is one of this kind whenever he makes an effort to establish links between moments of stillness, or to present simultaneous events and impressions as a sequence of sentences. He draws attention to the chaotic remainder within the ordered sound chain: "The Franks put to rout by a riderless horse! Surely here is a sign for those who know how to read it! Surely here is an action parable!" (188-189).[13]

Early in the novel there is a scene illustrating a rite of passage to stillness. Pilgermann begins his pilgrimage at night, walking towards a dark wood and thereby approaching the origin of space and time, on the other side of which there would be stillness; since he is still on this side, he cannot prevent surges of fear and doubt:

> Inside my head I have stopped talking, I am quiet. I give myself to the old, old night that waits within me, the old, old night in the old, old wood. (...)
>
> I listen for my Bath Kol but I hear only the thumping of my heart and the sound of my footfalls. Why am I on this road through the dark wood? I am afraid. What have I to sustain me? Jesus has appeared to me but what have I to do with Jesus? I think of the tax-collector, perhaps he too has passed through this wood wondering what would sustain him. 'Thou Jew!' whispers the Bath Kol suddenly, whispers the Bath Kol in my ear in the dark wood. 'My Jew!' whispers the Bath Kol.
>
> In fear I go forward. The quietness of the Bath Kol draws itself together in the dark, becomes a point of silence from which a hugeness grows. In the hugeness I perceive this wood, this rising ground to be the Mount of Venus between the opened thighs of the mother-space that is time. The wood is clamorous with the silence of birds and demons and great wordless mouths full of sharp teeth. When I close my eyes I see the colour of the dark: it is a strong purple-blue, very luminous and vibrating like a crystal. (43-44)

It is Death who takes him near the "place where memory cannot reach, where every time is now" (MUM, MT 221) – without claiming him yet. Being still

13 Letters from crusaders document their irrational fears as well as their belief in divine signs, see e.g. Riley-Smith: "One of the most striking features of the letters from crusaders and the eyewitness narratives is the growing feeling of astonishment that prevailed in the army which crossed into Syria in 1097 and proceeded to Antioch and eventually to Jerusalem, with the heavens glittering with coincidental but actual pyrotechnics – comets, auroras, shooting stars – and the nights disturbed by visitations: Christ, the saints, and ghosts of crusading dead who returned to assure the living of the validity of relics or the certainty of heavenly rewards" ("The State of Mind... ", 78-80). Amin Malouf's study *The Crusades through Arab Eyes*, on the other hand, shows that the Muslim exponents mentioned in the novel such as Yaghi-Siyan's son-in-law Rudwan (or Ridwan) of Aleppo were by no means immune to superstition and paranoia: "Ridwan was barely more than twenty in 1097, but his personality was already shrouded in mystery, and the most terrifying legends about him were rife. Small, thin, of severe and sometimes frightening countenance, he is said (by Ibn al-Qalanisi) to have fallen under the influence of a 'physician-astrologer' who belonged to the order of Assassins, a recently formed sect that was to play an important part in political life throughout the Frankish occupation. The king of Aleppo was accused, not without reason, of making use of those fanatics to eliminate his opponents. By means of murder, impiety, and witchcraft Ridwan aroused the distrust of nearly everyone, but it was within his own family that he provoked the most bitter odium" (22-23).

alive Pilgermann can get no closer to that place than by envisaging the dead body of the tax-collector and the light of absolute Now with his eyes closed:

> In those crystalline vibrations I seem to see a pale green phosphorescence in the shape of a man hanging head downward by one leg. He is hung by one ankle, his other leg is bent, the bent leg crossing the straight to make an upside-down figure four. His arms are bent to make a triangle on each side, his hands are behind him. He fades with the purple-blue and I hear the low voice of a bell that nods to the walking of an animal. 'Thou also,' says the rough and broken voice of the bell, so I know it to be the bell hung from the neck of Death's pale horse. (44)

Coming upon the actuality of the putrid corpse a little later, however, Pilgermann is overwhelmed by emotion: sadness mingles with anger, fear, and with a longing for Christ, who seems to have gone away for ever (45). He could not accomplish his pilgrimage if he were not fetched back into the reality of his physical existence, the world of sounds.

The last scene I would like to discuss self-reflectively highlights the revitalizing power of sound. Its context is as follows: Pilgermann dreams of the fall of Jerusalem, which is to take place a year later, in the summer of 1099 (215). After the event, the city is presented in a frightfully clear picture, a still-life painting but for the groans of those who have not yet been released by death and for the stray dogs, the crows, the vultures and the Frankish invaders who are violating the bodies of the victims (215). Although the chaos of war has extinguished almost all sounds, the remaining ones allow Pilgermann to identify the time and place as well as the participants. He spots murdered Sophia among the dead bodies, but there is also something moving near her: a two-year-old boy, their son, "crawls out of this midden-heap of history" (216). Pilgermann is not allowed to follow him any further. His young death summons him back to his own time and place, that is to Antioch in June 1098. His dream, "this waking sleep-travel, this night journey to a day that is coming" (216), was meant to be a rite of passage to Pilgermann's own death, which is to take place on that day. The ghosts of all the dead who accompanied Pilgermann before he embarked at Genoa are gathered around his bed when his young death informs him: "His lips are moving, they shape the word, 'Tonight'" (217). At first he is ready to obey, but the facts which have been presented raise his hope:

> I nod. 'Tonight!' I say. I am ready, even eager. As comradely as I am with Bembel Rudzuk, as close as our friendship is, yet am I closer to these dead. As a pilgrim acquires merit by making the journey to Jerusalem, so have these acquired not only merit but magical power by completing the journey to the end of themselves, to the fullness of their action. In death they are intensified,

> they are more than themselves, they are more than philosophies; they are geographies, histories, they are sciences and guides for a soul sore troubled and perplexed. Where they are, where Sophia is, there would I be.
>
> But Sophia is not standing before me with the other dead. Suddenly I recall that she is not dead. Jerusalem has not yet fallen to the Franks, this is not yet the year 1099, it is still 1098. Sophia is alive! Our little son is not alone among dogs and corpses. ...
>
> 'Tonight' is the word shaped by the lips of my young death. This is the last day of my life! Only a moment ago I was eager to join the dead but now everything is different, I am not a dry tree, I have a son, I am needed by my child and the mother of my child, I must find them. Life is calling me now, not death. (218)

Feeling and logic combine to pull Pilgermann away from death. What is interesting is the hierarchy of values: his friendship with Bembel is not as strong as the desire for death inspired by his dead fellow pilgrims; there is no symmetry between them: Bembel is more attached to Pilgermann than vice versa. Pilgermann's desire for Sophia, on the other hand, for a living Sophia to be precise, overrules the attraction of the dead pilgrims. This scene, then, is a powerful counterpoint not only to the many scenes which describe Pilgermann's growing fascination with stillness but also to the reverence for stillness expressed in the essay "Mnemosyne, Teen Taals, and Tottenham Court Road". With the renewed desire for life there arise feelings of remorse and even hatred for Bembel: "I have spent my time playing with patterns and it has come to this. There leaps up in me hatred for Bembel" (221). The gnomic present indicates that this is not merely a time-bound error: a certain ambivalence about his mystical work and his friend are part of the Pilgermann configuration. It is also part of his pattern, however, that after Bembel's account of his naming and their thwarted attempt to escape from the city (both presented in the past tense), Pilgermann will be able to establish his peace of mind again; Bembel's "silent stillness in the darkness" of the prison cell eventually calms Pilgermann (234).

Pilgermann's willingness to look at ugly scenes as well as at beautiful ones is apparent in disgusting descriptions of Pope "Unguent's" dream of hell (54-55) or Bruder Pförtner's abuse of pilgrim children (61). Although they are counterbalanced by the poetry of scenes like Bembel Rudzuk's earth dance (158-159), the description of his boat's approaching a port (110) or by the humour of Bembel's and Pilgermann's first encounter at Tripoli (105ff.), the horror of the scenes of death and destruction is hardly tolerable. To see more would be as terrifying as Pilgermann's first insights into the mystery of creation (22ff.). Hoban was merciful when he interposed, between us and the scenes of horror, a narrator who cannot fully identify with the role of storyteller and historian: "Not only is storytelling denied me but history also – I may well be reporting nothing more than spiritual images and metaphysical illusions" (205). The reflective passages and his chatty interludes again and again relieve us from a surplus of strain; they impart some of the narrator's afterlife detachment. On the other hand, the left-out parts give life to, and reinforce, the ones presented. Too much horror would blunt our sympathies whereas the spaces left open for our imagination keep us engaged. In fact, Pilgermann's comment on the unfinished tile pattern could also be seen as a description of the way the novel works: "It became evident to me that the forward edge of a pattern's visible expansion is attractive, it excites in people and in things a desire to shape themselves to it, to meet it and move with its advance" (149).

7.2. Spiritual Emancipation

In *Pilgermann* Hoban juxtaposes the three most important monotheistic religions, that is Judaism, Christianity and Islam. Being no theologian, I will restrict my interpretation to the novel's presentation of them, taking recourse to the Bible and the Quran only occasionally to illustrate certain arguments. None of the three religions is praised as the absolute and only doctrine since they can all bring on death and destruction if abused, but also open doors to wisdom if observed by enlightened spirits. Characters who represent a particular religion are often further apart from each other than from characters of another religion. Thus, Christ is opposed to the "Soldiers of Christ" (164), especially to the "un-Christ" Bohemond (198), and to the so-called "vicar of Christ", Pope Urban II, whose dreams predict the evil consequences of the crusades he has instigated himself (36f., 54f.). Bembel Rudzuk stands out from other Muslim characters such as the proud and merciless Yaghi-Siyan (170ff.) and the authoritarian Imam (141). Pilgermann, finally, distances himself from the Jewish community and especially from their representatives, the quarrelsome Rabbi and the worldly Nagid (132ff.).

The Jewish religion is characterized by both repeated suffering and the law of retaliation. At Antioch, Pilgermann describes the implications of being a Jew thus:

> Such an interesting moment, that moment before someone who is not a Jew asks you if you are a Jew! The world being as it is, any live Jew is a survivor in that there will always be other Jews within living memory who are dead only because they were Jews. So whoever asks, 'Are you a Jew?' is saying at the

> same time, 'Are you one of those who has not so far been slaughtered?' To answer yes to this question has at one time and another assured the death of the answerer. At that moment in Antioch Jews were not being slaughtered but nevertheless the question would not be a neutral one, ... No, it would be a question with an under-question: 'Are you a Jew who dies without fighting or a Jew who makes trouble?' (139)

The beginning of the novel is set on a day of mourning, Tisha b'Av: "the destruction of the First and Second Temples" and the Israelites' turning "aside from the land of milk and honey" (13) are commemorated by fasting and prayers. Pilgermann is not mourning at the time: being not particularly devout (19), though aware of the manifold forms of anti-Semitic discrimination (14), he is on the way home from his nightly visit to Sophia, the wife of a tax-collector, rejoicing that *he* did not turn aside from the "land of milk and honey" that was offered him (13). His happiness does not last, however. He is castrated as one of many victims of the anti-Jewish riots which accompanied the crusades (cf. ch. 7.1, n. 2). The mutilation inscribes his ambivalence on his body: on the one hand, he is castrated because he is a Jew; on the other hand, he cannot be a member of a Jewish congregation any more as a eunuch – a fact he will later use to his advantage, i.e. as an excuse for not joining the Jewish congregation at Antioch (132f.). At first, though, he needs help. Jesus appears to pick the bleeding man up and take him home. Herkommer rightly underlines that the encounter with Christ does not convert Pilgermann to Christianity (183): His Jewish heritage continues to determine his actions. But his encounter with Christ initiates a mystical quest which will eventually make him sever all ties to institutionalized forms of religion.

Feeling remorse for committing adultery with Sophia, he begins to think of ways to make amends for his deed. Inspiration comes from "the daughter of a voice, what is called in Hebrew a Bath Kol", which sends him on a pilgrimage to Jerusalem (32). It is not only the place where Solomon built his Temple, "Flesh made word, soul made word, world made word" (32). In the 11th century, Jerusalem was also the place at which widespread fears (and hopes) about the Last Day crystallized themselves:[1]

> There came to me the thought that the world is full of mysterious, unseen, fragile temples; it was in these many temples that God used to dwell among us;

1 Incidentally, the coming of the Messiah, or the return of Jesus, is the signal of the end of the world in all three monotheistic religions. Medieval Muslims were no less affected by apocalyptic fears than Christians and Jews, as Robert Irwin's essay "Islam and the Crusades 1096-1699" emphasizes (217). Pilgermann writes: "True, it was a pope who had first called for this great going of multitudes to Jerusalem but no pope could have moved so many people had not God truly willed it" (33).

> they are easily destroyed, these temples, as I had destroyed the temple of the tax-collector's privacy in his wife. How many of them still remained? How many temples between us and Christ's last day, between us and the eternal faceless action of God as It? Quickly, quickly must something be done before all the temples were gone. (32-33)

It is therefore a city which exerts an enormous "pull" on all contemporary seekers of salvation (as Cambry did in *Riddley Walker*). While Pilgermann is on the way, however, a strange encounter with pilgrim children lays the foundation for an altogether different view of Jerusalem; when Pilgermann worries about the children's ability to reach their destination, the children's leader, endowed with Christ's eyes and his voice, silences him:

> Looking at me out of his eyes I see the lion-eyes of Christ, and I am frightened. I hold my head because I know that when he speaks his voice will be a woodwind voice that comes from inside my head and resonates there. 'Jerusalem will be wherever we are when we come to the end.' (64)

Before he arrives at Genoa, Pilgermann has the opportunity to take revenge on the peasant Konrad and his sow Bodwild, who have castrated him.[2] Retaliative violence strikes back on those who have committed a crime. Jews and Gentiles are equally affected by it, for the aim of retaliation is to re-establish parity between contending parties. Pilgermann significantly accompanies his revenge by drawing the star of David in the air (66). He feels attracted to the martial side of Judaism and does not want to identify with those who die "without fighting". Especially the sound of the shofar, the ram's horn, excites his feelings: "The urgent maleness of that trumpeting always lifted me and quickened my blood: it was so much a call to action, it was so utterly not the murmur of praying, swaying, weaponless victims – was it not itself the weapon of the ram that had borne it?" (161). On the other hand, though, he also appreciates the intellectual challenge of a religion with a spiritual notion of God rather than a cult of materialistic idol worship. In so far, he thinks that the destruction of Solomon's Temple was justified:

> ... He had chosen the Jews for His vessel, He had chosen them to be the ark of the idea of Him and of It, the idea of the Unseen, the Ungraspable, the Unknowable, the idea never to be contained by the mind that is contained by

---

2 Although the pogrom is the expression of a conflict between Christians and Jews, Hoban also relates Pilgermann's castration to the Attis cult, i.e. an ancient cult of the Mother Goddess. When Bodwild accompanies Pilgermann as a ghost, the sow lets him know that she is "descended from the Moon Goddess, from Diana herself" (77). As in *Riddley Walker*, religions are presented as palimpsests of traces from diverse cults which do not simply cancel each other out (cf. interpretations of the figure of Greanvine in ch. 6.4, or Riddley's association of Pooty with the Moon Goddess, RW 200).

> it. He had chosen them to be mind-heroes, to open their minds to the idea that could not be held by any mind, and what did they do? They fouled themselves, they rolled in the dung and the degradation of the seeable, the knowable, the ordinary. They said to stocks and stones, 'Be thou our God.' (94, also see 99)

It is from this position that his mysticism will begin to take root. His reflections, and the children's motto that Jerusalem is wherever they "come to the end" (64), lead him to the conclusion that a pilgrimage to the real Jerusalem is not the right means to save the world: "It is the Jerusalem of the heart that must not be forgotten because in the Jerusalem of the heart is the heart of the mystery where lives the idea of the unknowable that is God" (95). When his adventurous sea-passage on two ships called "*Balena, Whale*" (103) and "*Nineveh*" (105) therefore takes him to the slave market at Tripoli and from there to Antioch, he has no insurmountable difficulty in adapting to the situation – he is no Jonas. Eventually he will dismiss the "idea of attaining Jerusalem before it was too late" altogether, denouncing it "as being made of that kind of mental sugar-candy that melts in the hard sunlight of reality" (185).

At Antioch he declines an invitation to join the Jewish congregation (132-135). The "stocky, muscular, red-haired, quarrelsome-looking" Rabbi who hates scholars (132f.) and the "tall, grand-looking" and pragmatic Nagid, whom he instantly nicknames "Worldly ben Worldly" (134), do not embody those spiritual principles he has begun to embrace. Pilgermann particularly objects to the idea of being united with a community by nothing but external signs and rites that have lost or never had a deeper sense, such as the yellow belt and turban of the Jews of Antioch (135), an arbitrary mark of their ethnic discrimination (Christians have to wear blue turbans, cf. 171). Even though he feels nostalgically attracted to the festivities of the Jewish High Holy Days, e.g. Rosh Hashanah (New Year) and Yom Kippur, when sins are forgiven and the atonement with God is renewed (160f.), he knows that the divine laws have nothing in common with the commandments hewn into Moses's two stone tablets (201). The only Jew who interests him is Bembel's merchant friend Mordechai Salzedo. Twice this man encourages him to define his position: the first time, wondering "Where he is" (162), Pilgermann affirms his individual spiritual quest (163). The second time, Salzedo's question whether he is ready to die kindles Pilgermann's desire to survive: suddenly he is eager to find out whether Sophia is still alive (203).[3] The other Jews of Antioch, however,

3 Salzedo's biographical background foreshadows that of Sophia and her boy: like the toddler in Pilgermann's prophetic dream of the fall of Jerusalem (215-217), seven-year-old Salzedo survived the slaughter of Jews and Muslims at Barbastro in Spain in 1064, while his parents were brutally murdered (202).

repel him with their "stone eyes" (213) and their fanatical belief in the coming of the Messiah; for them, this is not merely a metaphor of their death, but they really expect the rebuilding of the Temple and the restoration of the "glory of Israel" in the near future (212): "... I realized that I was not of their world, I was no longer even of my own world, I was well on my way to where I am now" (213).

Both Wilkie (72) and Herkommer (184) have compared Pilgermann to the Wandering Jew Ahasverus. While Wilkie does not detail the reasons for her comparison, Herkommer refers to Pilgermann's restlessness, which is related to the fate of the Jewish people to live in exile (Herkommer 184). Apart from Pilgermann's calling himself a "child of the night, a child of departures" (43), which she has quoted, there might be added the Nagid's awareness that the "Jews are scattered over the face of the earth" (134), or Salzedo's guess at Pilgermann's thoughts, "That to be a Jew is to find yourself doing all kinds of things in all kinds of places" (202). But I think it is also important to underline the differences between Pilgermann and that figure who is not to be found in the New Testament itself.[4] The legend of Ahasverus is medieval: there is, for instance, an illustration of the Wandering Jew in the 13th-century *Chronica maiora* of Matthew Paris (Corpus Christi College, Cambridge, MS 16, folio 74, verso). It shows a Jew who refuses to carry Christ's cross and is subsequently condemned to immortality. The illustration quite obviously served as anti-Semitic propaganda. In the novel, the challenge Pilgermann must face is not one of relieving Christ of a burden but one of solidarity with the dead Christ whose passion is complete. Christ's "horizontal head" (60), which is visible in the landscape through which Pilgermann is travelling to Genoa, becomes visible only, like the lion hidden in the tiles at Antioch (123), if the head of the viewer is tilted and no longer vertical; this is, of course, a gesture symbolizing submission, or a sign of an acceptance of mortality. Initially reluctant, Pilgermann will eventually give up his resistance to tilting his head, in other words, there is no offence on his part. Before the fall of Antioch, he is ready to join "the motion of the hidden lion" (163). By that time, though, particular religious affiliations have made way for a more general idea of the divine, so his readiness to die can no longer be classified as a solidarity with Christ only but with all those "impaled on history" like himself (222).

The Jewish tradition into which he was born is absorbed into his individual spiritual quest, too. One figure, though, continues to hold an important

4 Christ is mocked by soldiers but there is no mention in any of the four Gospels of a Jew who mocks him on the way to his crucifixion or who refuses to carry his cross.

position in his thinking, i.e. the Old Testament prophet Elijah.[5] Pilgermann regards "Bohemond as Elijah, Elijah as enemy, enemy as messenger of God ... as teacher" (211); the name Elijah here stands for the bringer of the fall of Antioch and of Pilgermann's own death: "... for me the taking of Antioch will be the Messiah and Jerusalem both" (214). At other times he meant other things to Pilgermann:

> ... Elijah for whom a chair is placed at circumcisions, Elijah for whom a place is set at the Seder, for whom a glass of wine is poured, for whom the door is left open ... feeling himself alone the covenant-keeper, Elijah with a silence all around him and a still small voice inside him. Elijah who bows himself to the earth and puts his face between his knees and waits for the rain, Elijah who runs away and throws himself aside until the angel of God calls him to action. Elijah fed by angels, fed by ravens, Elijah the magical, the one of us. (213)

In prison, impatient Pilgermann craves to see "Elijah running ahead of Ahab's chariot" (233). But these other aspects fade before the one which predominates in *Pilgermann*. The epigraphs of the novel, i.e. quotations from the Bible and the Quran dealing with the difficulty of recognizing divine summons for what they are and the need to see oneself as part of a larger whole (5-7), provide the framework for this aspect: "His guises are many, one doesn't always know who he is, one doesn't always recognize him. One must make connexions, must find the combination that he is a part of. By learning to recognize Elijah one learns to recognize Messiah" (213-214). He is the sign for the beginning of the end. The prophet continued to fascinate Hoban: he called him "the quintessential, the engodded stranger" in the appendix to *Pilgermann* (240). But before he could go back to the manifold aspects of Elijah in *Fremder*, there was the head of Orpheus to be dealt with in *The Medusa Frequency* .

The representation of Islam is as balanced as the representation of the two older monotheistic religions. But if particular characteristics are to be emphasized one might point to two aspects which emerge from the novel: the discrimination of unbelievers (132, 134, 171) and a draconic penal system (171-175, 191). Islam must be adopted by all those who do not wish to be discriminated against. The discrimination is not only of religious but also of political, worldly nature – non-Muslims, as the novel shows, "were required to register and to pay the djizya or poll-tax" (132). Islam turned into a basically active, even aggressive religion after the battle of Badr in 624. Muhammad Asad, the translator of *The Message of the Qur'an*, writes in the introduction to Sura 8:

5 See I Kings 17, 1- II Kings 2,12.

> The spirit of passive sacrifice, so characteristic of their [the Muslims'] earlier days, received its complement in the idea of sacrifice through *action*. The doctrine of action as the most fundamental, creative element of life was, perhaps for the first time in the history of man, consciously realized not only by a few select individuals but by a whole community.... (*The Message of the Qur'an* 237)

In *Pilgermann*, Yaghi-Siyan's decision to massacre one hundred innocent Christians on Hidden Lion because of the betrayal that a few among them are suspected of also illustrates my point (171-175).[6]

In his Introduction to the Penguin Classics edition of *The Koran*, the translator N. J. Dawood draws the following picture of Islam:

> Mohammed, who disclaimed power to perform miracles, firmly believed that he was the messenger of God, sent forth to confirm previous scriptures. God had revealed His will to the Jews and the Christians through chosen apostles, but they disobeyed God's commandments and divided themselves into schismatic sects. The Koran accuses the Jews of corrupting the Scriptures and the Christians of worshipping Jesus as the son of God, although He had expressly commanded them to worship none but Him. Having thus gone astray, they must be brought back to the right path, to the true religion preached by Abraham. This was Islam – absolute submission or resignation to the will of Allah.
>
> The Koran preaches the oneness of God and emphasizes divine mercy and forgiveness. God is almighty and all-knowing, and though compassionate towards His creatures He is stern in retribution. He enjoins justice and fair dealing, kindness to orphans and widows, and charity to the poor. The most important duties of the Muslim are faith in Allah and His apostle, prayer, almsgiving, fasting, and (if possible) pilgrimage to the Sacred House at Mecca, built by Abraham for the worship of the One God. (Dawood 10)

What is immediately striking is the authoritarian tone of this doctrine, and the claim to be able to set right the errors committed by both Jews and Christians. Moreover, the observance of religious duties is often of a very practical nature. The novel shows how Christian orphans are indeed taken care of after the massacre (193); or the purchase of Pilgermann is an instance of fair dealing at its very best (105-107). But Islam also has a spiritual aspect, which is conveyed above all through Bembel Rudzuk: "Bembel Rudzuk, while a perfectly respectable member of the Muslim community, was known to be a strongly individual thinker" (141).

Like Pilgermann, Bembel examines the deeper sense of religious

6 To forestall all suspicion of partiality, let me add right here that in the novel, the Christian crusaders behave no more commendably when they aggressively defend "their" Holy City instead of observing the Christian command to love their enemies and passively resist attacks (cf. Matt. 5, 38-42). The crusaders' motives will be examined more closely below.

prescriptions. He confesses that he is "not devout in the usual sense of the word" (135). Although he observes the rule of fasting on the Tenth of Muharram, the Muslim equivalent to the Jews' Yom Kippur, it is mainly for the reason of refreshing his mind. In contrast to the stupid Thamud, a people destroyed because they failed to honour the "she-camel" of God, he thus hopes to be always able to recognize a divine gift in whatever form it should be presented (135f.). Sometimes he shows devotion where there are no written laws to oblige him. Since he unconsciously feels that the design of Hidden Lion manifests God, he considers himself a pilgrim even though he does not go to Mecca: "'What I said was: "At Thy service, O Lord, at Thy service." These words are to be spoken only on pilgrimage to Mecca but I could not refrain from saying them'" (120). Moreover, Bembel acts on impulse, interpreting spontaneous ideas as eyes "given by God for the seeing of God" (cf. his decision to build Hidden Lion with Pilgermann's help, 115), and he is susceptible to revelations of all kinds, particularly to dreams which come to him on the "twenty-seventh of Ramadhan, the Lailat al-Qadr, the Night of Power on which Muhammad received his first revelation" (158). Certain instructions of the Quran are not heeded by him, however, e.g. his friendship with the Jew Pilgermann would not be acceptable to an orthodox Muslim (cf. Sura 3: 116-119). He also distances himself from the Quran in a central question: like his friend (see 173), he believes "that the Last Day is every day" (179), not a remote terminal point in the future. Personal responsibility must be derived from an ongoing individual recognition of failure rather than from an external code delaying punishment to a mystified Day of Judgment (cf. Sura 1). Bembel's religious convictions have become internalized like Pilgermann's. The two friends' agreement in essential questions underlines that mysticism obviously tends to cancel out differences exaggerated by the institutionalized religions.

Unlike the Quran, the New Testament forbids the Christian community to spread aggressively. Salvation depends on each individual, and mercy, i.e. not only *divine* mercy but also mercy shown between people, is one of its central tenets. Even though Christ's authority explicitly extends no further than to the spiritual domain (cf. Matt. 22, 15-22), his influence on everyday life was inevitable. Pilgermann is aware of this: "... the Jesus I saw was not a soft mover, and Caiaphas's concern indicates that Jesus's following was such as could well have moved Rome to take away both place and nation from the Jews" (73). Nevertheless, the aggressive practice of fighting wars against non-Christians is not established in the New Testament itself. When crusades began to be conducted, it took decades of rhetorical effort to pervert Christian doctrine sufficiently and establish "theological" justifications for the "holy wars" of the so-called "soldiers of Christ". Before Urban II succeeded in launching the First Crusade, other popes "had tried but had not been able to set these thousands moving towards Jerusalem" (98), as Pilgermann points out. Perhaps the most popular argument was the one provided by Guibert of Nogent (1053-1124), one of the chroniclers of the First Crusade, who wrote in his "Gesta dei per francos":

> God has instituted in our time holy wars, so that the order of knights and the crowd running in its wake ... might find a new way of gaining salvation. And so they are not forced to abandon secular affairs completely by choosing the monastic life or any religious profession, as used to be the custom, but can attain in some measure God's grace while pursuing their own careers, with the liberty and in the dress to which they are accustomed. (quoted in Riley-Smith, "The State of Mind ...", 78)

The "new way" was in fact a relapse into the ways of Old Testament warrior princes like Saul or David, as Pilgermann recognizes, comparing Bohemond to those two kings (213). Especially when the Second Crusade was being prepared, the propagandistic efforts were intensified: Bernard of Clairvaux wrote a controversial apology for the Templars, "De laude novae militiae" (before 1136), to legitimate "Christian" aggression.[7] Of course, contradictions between doctrine and religious practice manifest themselves in all three religions. But since the New Testament does not keep track of more than a century of Christian history during which the apostles and their followers basically had to defend themselves against their persecution, it does not show many fallible or aggressive Christians. Later martial, missionary or racist excesses therefore cannot appear to be anything but capital offences against the precepts of Christianity.

The range of Christian characters presented in the novel is wider than that of characters from other religions. What many of them have in common is that they are not sure of their allegiances: Sophia commits adultery (16); her husband, the tax-collector, first brings Jew-killers to the town, then apologizes to the survivors of the pogrom (33f.), and eventually, he dies on a penitential pilgrimage to Jerusalem (45); he has fallen into the hands of a couple of

7 Another fifty years later Pope Innocent III even offered the crusaders who were being recruited for the Fourth Crusade "... a *guarantee* of the act of grace, mercy, and love by which God consented to treat a penance as though it was satisfactory. It may not be going too far to suggest that the indulgence really came into its own in the thirteenth century, when it was formulated in a way people could understand, although there was still some confusion about it and St Thomas Aquinas had to answer worries about exactly when it became operative" (Riley-Smith, "The State...", 82; emphasis added).

murderers, Udo and his wife Sophia (48-50), who kill their victims to turn them into relics they sell to Christian churches; there is a pope tormented by nightmares of hell (36f., 54f.) as well as Antiochian Christians caught in the nightmare of history, "compelled by forces beyond them to keep moving in all directions and to be incessantly busy in many ways" (168). The apostate Firouz, a former Christian who converted to Islam and became commander of three of the four hundred towers of Antioch (138, 170), will eventually betray the Muslims to the crusaders (235). Single-mindedness characterizes only the naive and the dumb, i.e. the pilgrim children, who cling so steadfastly to their belief in Jesus and their salvation that no hardship can make them deviate from their path (59-64); or the peasant Konrad, who sticks to his narrow-minded anti-Semitic prejudices even when he is a ghost (79-83). Bohemond, on the other hand, is altogether inscrutable: Pilgermann repeatedly points out that he has "no chance of understanding him" (197). Although many of the Christians mentioned here have made Pilgermann suffer, he abstains from simply condemning them: there are again and again remarks which undo his differentiations, moments at which he *is with* those who were his opponents, e.g. when he suddenly remembers "the weight of the mail shirt that rusted the skin and chafed the body bloody" as if he had been one of the Franks moving towards Antioch (101).[8] His feeling of guilt for committing adultery with Sophia arises not only from an awareness that he has transgressed religious laws but above all from his intense thinking about the tax-collector (28-31); he realizes what pain he has caused: "I made that tax-collector poorer when I enjoyed his wife" (31).

The fact that Christ appears among the characters does not imply that he is human. Pilgermann is more and more convinced of his divine and unfathomable nature. The first time Christ appears to him, Pilgermann is unrespectful and addresses him as a fellow Jew responsible for the pogroms carried out in several European cities at the time: "In your name they kill the seed that gave you life" (27). Christ's answer, "From me came the seed that gave me life" (27), however, makes him reconsider his view; gradually, Pilgermann's thinking about the mysterious figure turns more abstract:

8 To "be with" an other is not the same as to identify with him or her. The other does not become part of the subject but remains other; this is a form of empathy Hoban has described since his first novel. To be with a lion requires the same readiness to open oneself to the other as to be with turtles, with power, or with a woman or a man one loves. The willing look (cf. ch. 7.1) is another example. Isn't "being with" as close as one can get to the precept to love one's enemy which is stated in the Sermon on the Mount (cf. Matt. 5, 44)? No doubt, "being with" presupposes maturity, for the subject must resist its narcissistic desire to identify with, or to appropriate and destroy, the other.

> I had begun my pilgrimage wanting to save the many mysterious, unseen, fragile temples of the world so that Christ would not leave us as God had done when he ceased to be He. Now as I thought about it I found that Christ as a limited identity had already departed from my perception and been absorbed into the manifold idea of himself. (163)

Christ is often identified with light effects: during his first appearance, the air begins to "shimmer" (20); later he illuminates the corpse of the headless tax-collector with "a light like a candle in a tabernacle" (45); or on the boat trip from Tripoli to Suwaydiyya Pilgermann feels "such a Nowness in the light of the day" that Christ leaps into his mind (109). Although Pilgermann at first distinguishes the light of Christ from the "brillance of total Now", "that epiphany of light immanent in our being and experienced in certain heightened states as the light-as-bright-as-day within the night" (47), it will become clear that the light of Christ and the light of total Now emerge from the same source of energy, i.e. "the intolerable bursting of the beginning of all things ... that unimaginable violence which is God as It" (164).

There is one meditation on the idea of Christ I would like to look at more closely because it will make visible a number of parallels and differences between *Pilgermann* and *Riddley Walker*:

> ... the idea of sorting comes into my mind. ... I pick up a bit of broken stone and as I hold it in my hand I feel the sorting that goes on continually inside it: this way, that way, this way, that way, Christ in every stone with arms outspread, not raging as he judges between the elect on his right hand and the damned on his left ...: he himself abandoning all self, is the rule and the scale, the pointer that wavers on the beam. He is entranced, he makes no judgments although he is the judge: he is a necessary, an essential instrument in the sorting process and it is the process that has brought the instrument into being. ...
>
> I have understood so little in my lifetime! Now in the centuries of my deathtime I am just beginning to understand a little more but my consciousness is not continuous ... Perhaps there will never be the possibility for me to understand what Christ is. I understand that he was born from the idea of him.... That he is essentially a sorter I also understand; the sorting of course follows on that disparity without which the universe could not maintain spin; I think that I knew that even before I read Plato's *Timaeus*....
>
> That good and evil should be sorted along with right and left, up and down, light and darkness and all other complementarities is clearly in the nature of things, and that Christ should be a medium of this sorting is also clearly in the nature of things; but the rest of what he is continually moves on ahead of my comprehension like a great whale cleaving cosmic seas; I try to grasp the essence of him but I grasp only the fading wake of his passage. (206-207)

Like Riddley in *Stoan* (RW 158f.), Pilgermann often begins his meditations starting out from everyday objects or phenomena: stones inspire him most (also see his remarks on "the freemasonry of the stones" which "know that they are all one thing", 94), but water (the sea, a river, or rain) and light effects can be equally stimulating. As the references to Plato and to the whale at the end of the quotation show, a whale which might be the one which swallowed Jonas, or Melville's *Moby-Dick*, he can also complement his thinking with metaphors borrowed from a cultural context ranging over several hundred years. There is not only one central myth at his disposal, but the Bible and the Quran as well as literary and philosophical texts, paintings, reliefs, and buildings. Despite this advantage, however, there are certain ideas which become the more ungraspable the longer he thinks about them: in his mystical meditations, Christ is a floating signifier like Eusa, the "1 Big 1", or the "It" which Riddley set out to think about in Hoban's previous novel. Whereas Riddley had no choice but to think about things himself, Pilgermann self-confidently asserts his independence in spiritual matters: "I have questions", Pilgermann says at one point, "for which neither the Gospels nor the Holy Scriptures offer answers. Theologians and fathers of the Church cannot confound me, they have no firmer ground on which to stand than I" (73-74).

Under Bembel's guidance Pilgermann gradually turns into a pantheistic mystic, that is, he is able to recognize "identity in difference" like Riddley (Stace 219). Violently reminded of his Jewish roots at the beginning of the novel, when he is victimized in a pogrom, he starts out as a dualist, addressing God as a powerful Other (21). It takes some time for him to overcome his background, those "centuries of moral reckoning" which also feed his surges of nostalgia in regard to the Jewish congregation (160). But in the end, he locates the divine in himself: "... He was in us, one couldn't get away from Him, that was the Fire of it, that was the Garden of it, at the centre of every soul and contiguous with infinity" (182).

Even though Pilgermann and Bembel are more truly religious in their mystical quests than their "brothers in faith", they are not surrounded by a hypocritical aura of saintliness. Bembel's criticism of demonstrations of obedience to God's alleged will has already been addressed (cf. ch. 7.1). Occasionally, Pilgermann's remarks are cynical and more than verge on blasphemy, for instance, when he mocks the Jewish custom of having a chair and a meal ready for Elijah on Passover by saying that there is a "bucket ... for Elijah" in the prison cell (233). He finds the temporal coincidence of Christ's crucifixion (Easter) and the Jews' salvation from their Egyptian yoke (Passover) a good joke (137). Herkommer warns against underrating such statements, especially against interpreting them as mere aesthetic language games: in her view Pilgermann is trying out several ways of approaching the divine, and the irony or humour in many of his commentaries is nonetheless the expression of an ethical attitude (Herkommer 185f.) – the humorous to cynical undertones, then, must be related to the serious implications of the contents like the dislocutionary language of *Riddley Walker*.

As has already been shown in ch. 7.1, when Bembel's fallibility was discussed, however, Pilgermann's disrespect is not only a form of critical or ethical involvement with the divine but it also fulfils a function in his personal process of maturation; since Adam and Eve the awareness of individual responsibility and the ability to tell good from evil has always presupposed a transgressive act: "Life has no value, means nothing until we have paid for it with the sin of disobedience; only after that original sin does one's proper life begin. ... And yet, and yet! I have done wrong, O God, I know it" (31). In the Bible and the Quran, the divine punishment which follows upon transgression usually triggers a process of purification leading to a more advanced state. In the novel, on the other hand, recognition of guilt in the form of an empathic act of solidarity with the victim (e.g. Pilgermann's recognition of what he did to the tax-collector) replaces divine strokes of lightning or dramatic scenes such as Adam and Eve's expulsion from Paradise. Spiritual development still presupposes a passing through fire, "still there are covenants to be made between the pieces, between one fire and another" (12), but in the novel this process has been internalized like all other kinds of religious experience. Degrees of spiritual maturity can be derived from the processes undergone by Jonas, Abraham and Christ:

> 'Jonas was half-baked,' said Tower Gate; 'he was still unfinished and without wisdom when the whale vomited him up. No, as a metaphor Jonas is not in a class with bricks. ... Neither is bread, ... bread is baked and eaten and becomes excrement. Brick, which is bread of earth, bread of our origins, is also baked – like Abraham it is put into the fire and like him it emerges hard and enduring, ready to shelter the humble and the mighty both. ... It is eaten by time but only slowly ... No excrement.' (127-128)

Jonas was useful only once, like bread, while Abraham's wisdom lasted longer, like bricks. The last transformation, actualized in Christ's death, on the other hand, frees the soul from the confinement of a body subjected to the mutilations of time. Thus, it is not simply hardened but turned into indestructible energy which can enter the dance of the cosmos as in the strange and fascinating vision Pilgermann has at the very beginning of the novel:

> Jesus is the great dead Lion of the World and in his mouth is the live black body of Christ Radiant. The great dead lion is walking the rocks and desert, walking the mountains and the high ground, looking down on deep gorges where rivers serpentine, and in his mouth the live black body of him the one radiant, him the Christ flickering his black-body spectrum, flames all dancing on the live black body of him in the mouth of the great dead lion of himself. (23)

The ending of *Pilgermann* evidently hinges on the symbolism of excrement, bricks, and energy, too: the "fallen" Christian Bohemond, "foul and stinking with excrement that stains his scarlet cross as he stands on Hidden Lion lifting his sword vertically with both hands and plunging it down again and again" (235), is diametrically opposed to Pilgermann and Bembel. Ready to sacrifice their lives instead of escaping from Antioch after Firouz has played "Judas", they prove to be more truly "Christian" than the giant warrior. The cross that will be formed by their corpses and Bohemond's vertical body indicates that another pair of the "fragile temples in which God used to dwell" (63) has been shattered. Bohemond has lost his innocence, his soul is fouled like the Christian attributes on his clothes, but Pilgermann's and Bembel's souls, to all appearances, become pure energy.[9] Killing them, Bohemond's sword strikes horizontally, making rainbows that signal Pilgermann's and Bembel's reunion with the divine, as God, as Christ, or as It (236).

7.3. Speaking from Between the Pieces

One of Pilgermann's reflections on himself can be interpreted as a sign of his (and Hoban's) awareness that the things he has to say place him in a long tradition of artists "after" (respectively before) him: "I am only a mode of perception irregularly used by strangers" (206).[1] He explicitly mentions the painters Bosch (29, 44, 46, 55), and Vermeer (97), the unknown sculptor of a relief at Naumburg Cathedral (70) and the Austrian composer Schubert (55); all of them succeeded in representing parts of the mystery of existence in small details such as particular representations of faces and gestures, sounds that convey an essential mood or perfect approaches to the light of absolute Now.

9 The "purity" of this transformation, though, will be examined more closely in ch. 7.4.

1 This play with temporal succession makes light of what Harold Bloom has called the "anxiety of influence" in his eponymous study; it also recalls T. S. Eliot's 1919 essay "Tradition and the Individual Talent", which Hoban has imaginatively explored in "Thoughts on Being and Writing" (1975), see esp. pp. 67ff. Affirmation of influence is the positive aspect of a subjectivity otherwise defined in terms of a loss of self and identity; it is the opposite of the narcissistic striving for wholeness, authorship and control.

But there are also literary allusions to be found in the novel, motifs and techniques of writers whom Pilgermann does not mention but Hoban might have had in mind, if only as "idea pheromones" (240) when he was composing the novel. A decisive impulse was given by Herman Melville's *Moby-Dick*. *Pilgermann* certainly swims in its wake in Hoban's imitating such formal devices as adding quotations, a kind of preface and an epilogue to the text. More important still is the slow pace of both narratives, caused by the philosophical meanderings of their narrators at the cost of a straight story line. In the interview with Michel Bodmer, Hoban mockingly defended his "right" to write like Melville:

> I haven't got the kind of reviews I was hoping for at all, and I knew that I was running that risk, because I allowed myself to ramble on with my thoughts the way Herman Melville does in *Moby-Dick*, and if people don't think I'm as good as Melville, they don't think that I deserve to ramble on about my thoughts. (Hoban and Bodmer 3)

Shakespeare, and especially his *King Lear*, is another absent presence in *Pilgermann*. Although Bembel Rudzuk's sentence, "Striving too hard for wisdom has made me a fool" (148), is *no* quotation from the tragedy, it resembles the Duke of Albany's insight "Striving to better, oft we mar what's well" (I.iv., l. 345); and its content crystallizes the self-knowledge Lear gains in the course of the play, above all, through his fool's wisecracks (see e.g. I.iv., ll. 93ff.). Can it moreover be that Pilgermann's self-pitying remark about being a "poor bare tuned fork" (26) is an echo of Lear's sympathetic words to Edgar, "... thou art the thing itself; un- / accommodated man is no more but such a poor, / bare, forked animal as thou art" (III.iv., ll. 104-106)?

It is essential to notice, though, that Hoban does not simply quote these works. His dislocutionary modifications usually signal that he went on thinking about the ideas developed in them. The same is true for Pilgermann's exclamation "The horror, the horror of cause and effect!" (222), which cannot but recall the last words of Joseph Conrad's notorious Kurtz in *Heart of Darkness* (111). Pilgermann's modification, "of cause and effect" condemns the cold logic by which linear history enchains us without a chance of our going back in time to alter the past, while Kurtz's utterance is altogether elusive. The first-person narrator Marlow thinks that Kurtz has "pronounced a judgement upon the adventures of his soul on this earth" (112), but this might simply be an interpretation coloured by desire: Marlow is quite obsessive about Kurtz's "moral victory" (113), admitting that his imagination "wanted soothing" after his return from the heart of darkness (114). Pilgermann's exclamation is definitely no moral victory in a bland conventional sense, for he curses the fact that he was not bolder when he sinned:

> I would sin again but I would be fierce and strong in my sin, I would go armed and wary in my sin, I would kill for it, would claim Sophia against all odds, I would die fighting if necessary but I would die complete, not a eunuch. What a fool I had been, neither a sheep nor a goat, suffering the loss of goodness without the rewards of badness, Aiyee! (223)

As an opposition to Death, though, his entire reaction to the dream of Sophia's death at Jerusalem establishes him as an ethical subject, as I will show in the next chapter. Kurtz dies immediately after his exclamation, whereas Pilgermann is allowed to recover at least partly from the passage through hell to which his night journey to the fall of Jerusalem has condemned him. He does not turn insane or lose all control over himself like the tragic characters Kurtz, Lear or Ahab. When he dies, he is ready with every fibre of his being, although this poses a problem of another kind (cf. ch. 7.4).

Anthony Thwaite compared *Pilgermann* to John Bunyan's *The Pilgrim's Progress*: "The eponymous figure is of course a pilgrim, or, at least, that is the name he calls himself; and there are ways in which Hoban's book is a sort of cabbalistic, gnostic parody of Bunyan, a series of dark sayings" ("Pilgrim's Progress", 33). There is indeed good reason to point to parallels between the two books, which manifest themselves, for instance, in Pilgermann's encounters with bearers of allegorical names such as the various Sophias (cf. chs. 2 and 6), Prodigality (106) or Tower Gate – once called Efficiency (127). But as Herkommer points out, there are significant differences between the two texts in terms of their plot: the plot of *The Pilgrim's Progress* is linear and closed; moreover, Christian indeed reaches the Celestial City whereas Pilgermann abandons his pilgrimage to Jerusalem for an internalized quest of the divine (Herkommer 187). What must also be added is that *Pilgermann* was not conceived as a parody of Bunyan's dream vision, for Hoban has never read *The Pilgrim's Progress*, as Wilkie writes (72).

Hoban presumably let himself be inspired not only by English but also by German literature, more precisely by Goethe's *Faust*. Like Goethe's protagonist, Pilgermann imagines himself to be the object of a bet between God and Satan (35f.). And in the following passage, he equates woman, wisdom, spirituality and beauty as the Chorus Mysticus does in the terminal lines of *Faust II* :

> I know that the dome and the woman both are manifestations of something elemental that is both beauty and wisdom and it is for ever in danger, for ever being lost, torn out of our hands, violated. (89)

> CHORUS MYSTICUS: Alles Vergängliche / Ist nur ein Gleichnis; / Das Unzulängliche, / Hier wirds Ereignis; / Das Unbeschreibliche, / Hier ist es getan; / Das Ewig-Weibliche / Zieht uns hinan. (Goethe 383-384)

Pilgermann's more pessimistic view springs from the fact that he is the one who must lose what is dear to him before moving on while Goethe's Chorus Mysticus describes these dynamisms from a detached, i.e. supernatural or nonhuman, position, ignorant of the suffering of both the violated woman and the man who has lost her. Maybe if Faust could speak at this moment, he would use Pilgermann's words. Pilgermann indeed speaks "from between the pieces" (11), supplying the lines that have remained unsaid in other texts. There is yet another difference which must be mentioned. For many women readers at the end of the twentieth century references to the Eternal Feminine, however implicit and indirect, have become rather suspect. I will therefore go on to discuss Angela Carter's novel *Nights at the Circus* (1984) as a critical response to the tradition of mystifying woman and also as a response to Hoban's novel. But Pilgermann's thinking about Sophia does not stop at the point which I have just quoted. The next chapter will therefore examine to what degree Carter's criticism is applicable to *Pilgermann*; on the other hand, I will try to work out how much of what is to be said on the subject has actually been integrated into the novel as a scrupulous self-criticism which Pilgermann imposes on himself.

7.4. Sophia or / and / with Fevvers

> "*One*: Samson in the vineyards of Timnah; *Two*: the lion comes roaring at Samson; *Three*: Samson tears the lion apart. That's a story but actually the main part of the action may have been that there was a butterfly in Samson's field of vision the whole time. The picture cards don't show the butterfly because if they did they would have to explain it. But you can't explain the butterfly."
> (Hoban, *Pilgermann*, p. 38)

In *Nights at the Circus*, a novel published in 1984, one year after *Pilgermann*, Angela Carter appears to answer the gloomy battle scenario and the mysticism of Hoban's novel with carnivalesque exuberance and a picaresque heroine bursting with vitality and Cockney wit. Whether or not she actually read *Pilgermann* and other novels by Hoban is unimportant; parallels are so numerous, though, as will be shown below, that their being accidental would verge on, well, a miracle. Carter considers a narrative "an argument stated in fictional terms" (quoted in Sage, *Angela Carter*, 50). Whenever she discusses themes which can also be found in Hoban's works, the latter are therefore addressed at least implicitly.

ANGELA CARTER: *NIGHTS AT THE CIRCUS*

Fevvers, half woman, half swan, a celebrated trapeze artist at the close of the nineteenth century, and Pilgermann, who occasionally assembles his particles to manifest himself as an owl, are not exactly birds of a feather but antagonists in certain respects. Whereas he uses his afterlife to reconstruct his tuning in to the moment of death, she escapes from various "gilded cages" and assaults upon her life to welcome the arrival of the twentieth century with blissfully inventive love-making and cosmic laughter. An angel of this world and without the slightest interest in the divine, she is only a feather's-breadth away from the hard-boiled Marxist materialism of her foster mother and manager Lizzie; nevertheless, a mere feather's breadth can make a world of difference between a rigidly closed and a more tolerant and open system in which even owls of Pilgermann's kind would find room. Lizzie is a tough little woman with a moustache, a London-born Italian versed in the arts of household magic and political analysis. Initially she was a whore and at first pretends to have been an ardent Roman Catholic who converted too many of her clients in the brothel (27, 292) – but actually she had the "habit of lecturing the clients" on fairly controversial topics such as "the white slave trade" or "the rights and wrongs of women" (292). So the madame, Ma Nelson, set her to work as a housekeeper. Lizzie has preserved her habit of preaching. Occasionally this leads to quarrels between her and Fevvers, who is not only more tolerant but also increasingly dedicated to the journalist Jack Walser, more so than to the class struggle and the war between the sexes (60, 279). Otherwise, however, they are an excellent team who have no trouble making Walser listen avidly to their joint stories for a whole night, "two Scheherazades, both intent on impacting a thousand stories into the single night" (40). The picaresque account of the story of Fevvers's life from her birth to her present life as an international star forms the first part of the novel and is entitled "London".

Lizzie found baby Fevvers on the stairs at Wapping, without a navel like Eve and supposedly hatched from an egg like Helen of Troy, the beautiful daughter of Leda (or Nemesis) and the Swan. Lizzie and her colleagues named her Fevvers, because there was down growing on top of her shoulderblades, but when she was to be christened, the vicar insisted on the more conventional name Sophie (13) – a name weighted with significance, as is clear from *Pilgermann*. Women are shown to have other problems with naming than men: Pilgermann has forgotten his original name but can freely choose a new one (as can Bembel Rudzuk) and, like Riddley, he must often take pains to find words for mystical insights; the women in this novel, on the other hand, are inventive enough, they are mostly concerned with reality, but they nevertheless have difficulty in establishing their own terms in a system in which the prerogative of naming seems to have always been Adam's. As regards the connotations of her legal name, Fevvers prefers not to be called Sophie, least of all by strangers (88, 187), and her behaviour – she loves to wink and launch "quips, mostly on the lewd side" (8) – is diametrically opposed to the behaviour recommended to the seeker of wisdom in the biblical Proverbs of Solomon (Prov. 10: 10, 23). In terms of *Pilgermann*, Fevvers (Sophie) combines the seductiveness of the first Sophia, i.e. of Pilgermann's beloved, with the physical punch of the second Sophia, i.e. the murderess he will encounter on his pilgrimage, undoing the cliché that a woman cannot be *both* attractive *and* powerful (also see below, where the steps of Pilgermann's mystification of Sophia and his sudden demystifying awareness of what he has done to her will be looked at in detail).

Until Ma Nelson's death, Fevvers first poses as Cupid in the entrance of the brothel (23), and later, when puberty makes her wings grow, as Winged Victory armed with a sword (25). Soon acquiring a reputation as the "Virgin Whore" (55), she spends years of passive waiting and being looked at in a realm where a clock in the form of Father Time permanently chimes midnight or noon. The clock is a duplicitous object – like everything else in this brothel, including the prostitutes who only play at being "objects" of sexual desire while pursuing other aims (45): on the one hand, it creates the impression that time has been set at nought, contributing to the illusion that a brothel is a space in which every kind of desire will be gratified (29); on the other, the figure of Father Time paradoxically also holds symbols of mortality in his hands, i.e. a scythe and a skull which undermine the illusion. Fevvers, at any rate, relies on the passing of time – earning her money as a living statue, she does not desire stillness. Although she cannot say what she is waiting for, least of all a Prince Charming to kiss her awake (39), she knows that she is developing: she resembles Hoban's Miss Mudd, the nymph who awaits her transformation into a dragonfly in *The Mouse and his Child*.

Fevvers uses her free time to practise flying although at her premiere, when she jumps from a mantelpiece, it feels to her as if she jumped into an abyss. She badly hurts her nose, having hovered only for a split second and then fallen "like Lucifer" (30). The novel plays with the figurative connotations of falling: as in *Pilgermann*, falling is a necessary step towards development. But while Hoban's novel mostly treats falls in terms of transgression and unethical behaviour, Carter often presents what would normally be considered a fall, as the preliminary to an act of liberation which may be dangerous but also profitable.[1] For Fevvers the ability to fly will later help her to assert herself and more than once saves her life: the "impossible" or "unnatural" feature is what defines her; her fall, on the other hand, causes harm to nobody but herself: the simile which compares her to the arch-seducer is therefore comically inappropriate. Figurative falls receive a similar treatment. The prostitutes scoff at the idea that they are regarded as "*damned souls*" by Baudelaire (38) or as "fallen girls" by the bigoted brother of Nelson who inherits the establishment after the madame's death (44): prostituting themselves they merely sell simulacra of pleasure to men who crave it: real pleasure would be given freely; at the same time they succeed in improving their financial standing: "No woman would turn her belly to the trade unless pricked by economic necessity, sir", as Fevvers underlines (39). Of course she exaggerates the aspect of necessity because acknowledging her love for money might be too shocking – after all, she is a picara considerate of her public image (also see 56). It is quite clear, though, that for a long time prostitution was the only "trade" in which women could not only earn money but become wealthy. There is another aspect of falls. In the last part of the novel, Carter will establish a clear difference between legal guilt and moral responsibility.

1 The question of what constitutes a fall is often addressed only indirectly by Hoban. While revenge receives attention when Pilgermann kills Konrad and Bodwild, or when Yaghi-Siyan slaughters one hundred Christians, self-defence is only implicitly branded as a form of a fall, e.g. in the scene when Pilgermann kills the relic-gatherer Udo (PG 48-49): He jumps from self-congratulation ("When I had balls I didn't have this much balls", 48) to the thought that the world is full of domes, i.e. model heavens which represent the highest ideals and aspirations of mankind; these domes are placed in the foreground of the "vast picture" of which "one is part" (49), an idea familiar from *Turtle Diary*, while the dark wood in which he has just killed a man is a "background detail" (49): that the glittering domes and the dark wood are nevertheless parts of the same picture insinuates potential links and dependency – after all relics are gathered in the name of the veneration of saints, i.e. on behalf of the glory of the domes. But he conveys more than just a criticism of the connection between foreground and background, or of the public face of the Church and its dark underside: the next statement is, as I believe, an implicit metonymic reference to the dark underside of his own act of self-defence: "Now, however, in my little wood in this little night part of the background, I see nothing of domes, I see only the darkness, hear only the owl, listen for Death, listen for my Bath Kol. I hear nothing for a long time...." (49).

Olga Alexandrowna, a battered woman who murdered her drunken husband when he beat her up once too often, comes to the conclusion that her act was justified: she finds herself guilty but not responsible (213). She has spent three years of incarceration exposed to the permanent gaze of a murderous countess. The Countess P. has perversely assumed the position of penal agent to make amends for the murder of her husband she committed for boredom and avarice (211). Sitting on a swivelling chair at the centre of a prison built by her in the form of a wheel, with windows allowing her to stare into every cell, she wants to see other murderesses acknowledge their responsibility because she is unable to repent her own deed: "by their salvation ... they would have procured hers" (212). Although those who repent will be set at large, no inmate has so far declared herself responsible for her crime. No sooner has Olga enumerated a sufficient number of "extenuating circumstances to the lenient and merciful judge in her mind" than she devises a plan for breaking out of prison (213). After the prisoners have assured themselves of the solidarity of the wardresses, for these are "trapped" like themselves (214), they leave behind the obsessive Countess, who remains locked up in her self-made hell (218).

When the brothel passes into the hands of Ma Nelson's brother, the whores set fire to the house. Fevvers and Lizzie go to live with the family of Lizzie's sister at Battersea, in very modest conditions although they can still go to the theatre and the opera (54), until Madame Schreck, who used to tour the country as a "Living Skeleton" (59), offers Fevvers a new job in her "museum of woman monsters" (55). Fevvers enjoys underlining the difference between her two work places – it is a mock-Gothic tale that ensues, full of Sadean allusions:

> Nelson's Academy accommodated those who were perturbed in their bodies and wished to verify that, however equivocal, however much they cost, the pleasures of the flesh were, at bottom, splendid. But, as for Madame Schreck, she catered for those who were troubled in their ... souls. (57)

The women exhibiting themselves there, are "monsters" because they embody, i.e. literalize, metaphors of femininity like Fevvers: she meets, among others, the Sleeping Beauty who never wakes up and is tormented by nightmares of the twentieth century (86), a midget who calls herself the Wiltshire Wonder (64), and the androgynous Albert/Albertina (59). They and Madame Schreck's servant Toussaint, a "black man ... born without a mouth" (55), are all cheated out of their salaries by Madame Schreck. Fevvers is the only one who makes trouble, because she is almost as greedy as her employer, so the old procuress sells her to a fetishistic client who calls himself Christian Rosencreutz.

The pervert is obsessed with phallic symbols (74, 78). The female sex, on the other hand, frightens him: he makes it quite clear to Fevvers that women are entrances to "the vortex that sucks everything dreadfully down, down, down where Terror rules" (77). His scheme is simple, "after much hemming and hawing and mystical circumlocution, at last he gives it to me" (79): being afraid of growing old, he wants to become immortal by "uniting his body with that of Azrael, the Angel of Death, on the threshold of the spring, he would cheat death itself and live forever while Flora herself will be forever free of winter's chill" (79). As soon as Fevvers realizes that she is to be turned into a May sacrifice, she draws Ma Nelson's sword, laughs in the ridiculous old man's face and flies out through an open window (83) to return to Battersea. "The rest is history", she concludes the first part of the novel (87): Fevvers joins a circus and becomes a trapeze star known as the "Cockney Venus" (7).

While Fevvers is telling this episode, echoes of Cixous's "The Laugh of the Medusa" (1976), with its critique of (Lacanian/Freudian) phallocentrism and its deconstruction of the myth of Medusa, can be perceived (see ch. 8.3). Moreover there is a reference to the myth of Orpheus: Fevvers's hair, escaping from its domestication by means of hairpins, gives her "a wild and maenad air" so that "Walser wilted in the blast of her full attention" (78). But Walser need not fear for his life, for the powerful woman whose story he has been patiently listening to is kind to him. Walser is man enough to bear repeated assignments to places traditionally occupied by women (see e.g. his identifications with Lewis Carroll's Alice when thinking "Curiouser and curiouser", 28, 90). To see and learn more about Fevvers, he eventually even applies for a job at Colonel Kearney's circus. Their tour of Russia will form parts two, "Petersburg", and three, "Siberia", of *Nights at the Circus*. Two things are interesting in the light of Hoban's novels: both Hoban and Carter appear to agree that men incapable of facing up to their mortality usually cause the most serious damages. *Pilgermann* could actually be seen as Hoban's most intense and serious effort to correct that tendency from the male perspective. Secondly, the protagonist of his next novel will also be spared by a Medusa because he knows of, and accepts, his vulnerability while other artists die in the attempt to master her. But in other respects the two writers disagree. Since Walser becomes a participant in the "Ludic Game" (103) in parts two and three, exchanging the role of a narratee for that of a protagonist, the narrative strands which are concerned with him and Fevvers respectively can be seen as Carter's attempt to contrast the different dangers and traps in a woman's and a man's experience of the world. Jack Walser's adventures often seem to be modelled directly or parodically on those of Hoban's male protagonists, especially Riddley Walker and Pilgermann. Fevvers's adventures as well as those of other female characters continue to shed light on representations of women in myths and in the arts (including Hobạn's novels). When Fevvers's and Walser's strands converge, on the other hand, there open up possibilities of love and mutuality despite the continued existence and affirmation of irreconcilable differences.

But Carter does not only focus on sexual difference; her criticism of myths undermines all claims about their universal and eternal validity. The Orpheus myth, for instance, will be alluded to once more in the third part: Mignon's performance of the last song of Schubert's *Winterreise* is so powerful that "the fauna and flora of the Siberian forest responded as those of the Thracian forest once did to the music of Orpheus" (268). However, to contest assumptions about the "universality" of both myths and means of seduction she adds, throwing overboard all comparative studies of mythology (and in their wake the psychoanalytic theories presupposing that myths are indeed universal):

> ... the human forest-dwellers were deaf to the mythic resonances, since these awoke no echoes in their own mythology. This music had no charms for them, nor did it soothe their savage breasts at all, at all ... As far as singing was concerned, they preferred an edge like sandpaper on a voice; the honeyed tones of the girl soprano did not strike *their* palates like honey. The magic of her song was alien magic and did not enchant them. (268)

At Petersburg, when Walser and Fevvers are colleagues, they are more distant at first than they were in London. The star resides in the most expensive hotel in town, dining with counts and dukes, while Walser, who is an apprentice to a group of clowns, stays with an old Russian woman and her grandson Ivan. They are the mother and the son of the murderess Olga. Unlike Lorna Elswint in *Riddley Walker*, the baboushka is too exhausted to tell her grandson stories. She merely teases him with a beginning: "There was a pig went to Petersburg to pray" (97). Of course, the boy wants to hear more, but the old woman disappoints him: "Wolf eat him" (97). Earlier than many other males who persist in their pre-oedipal narcissism, little Ivan must learn that women are not there to gratify his every desire; there is no jealous castrating father to instil the knowledge in him, his mother took care of that years ago, but neither is there a need for one. The chances therefore are (and this means hope) that he will not turn into a copy of his father: when the circus departs for Siberia, Ivan will make his first attempt to run away from home. But Walser, who ran away himself as a boy, solicitously sees to it that the too "young gazooney ain't gonna run away with the circus, not for a few years yet" (192).

Walser did not choose to become a clown. A pig, Colonel Kearney's Sybil, in fact sealed his fate as Konrad's Bodwild (this descendant of Diana) sealed Pilgermann's; even though Sybil did not castrate him, she spelled out the terms of his humiliation by means of pointing to alphabet cards:

> Sybil studied the cards for a moment, squinnied again at Walser, appeared for a few moments sunk in thought, then, with her questing snout, she nudged out:
>
> C-L-O-W-N.
>
> And sat back on her haunches, gratified. (...)
>
> 'So, young man,' he [Kearney] said, 'now you are a first-of-May [sic]. Don't ask me how the cognomen arose – it's what we allus calls the neophytes, the virgins in the ring, the green beginners in the art of playing. (102)

The role reversal is explicit: now Walser is the virgin – which is no advantage anywhere except in romantic fantasies. Although he thought he could accompany Fevvers as a kind of holiday from his usual chores as a war correspondent, e.g. by feeding the elephants (90), it will soon become clear that Kearney's promise to land him "safe and sound home in the good old U.S. of A." is due to be broken more effectively than either of them could have anticipated (103). Remembering Fevvers's adventure with Rosencreutz, we can guess what lies in store for a First-of-May. But the meaning of Greanvine from *Riddley Walker* comes to mind as well: Walser obviously risks being sacrificed as a year-king in the "feminine" O of the circus ring, which is perhaps a vestige of the altar of the Moon Goddess (as only Sybil will know).

At first, Walser thrills, "as always, to the shop-soiled yet polyvalent romance of the image" of the circus ring (107):

> What a cheap, convenient, expressionist device, this sawdust ring, this little O! Round like an eye, with a still vortex in the centre; but give it a little rub as if it were Aladdin's wishing lamp and, instantly, the circus ring turns into that durably metaphoric, uroboric snake with its tail in its mouth, wheel that turns full circle, the wheel whose end is its beginning, the wheel of fortune, the potter's wheel on which our clay is formed, the wheel of life on which we all are broken. O! of wonder; O! of grief. (107)

The circus ring is structurally related to Pilgermann's tiled pattern: a duplicitous central symbol of metonymic and metaphoric significance. But whereas Hoban's Hidden Lion is a dynamic image including its own creation, distortion and destruction, with David's Wheel as one of several images to be seen in it, Carter's circle is a polyvalent but unchangeable unit which suggests endless repetition without a way out. The circle also occurs in other novels by Hoban: in *Kleinzeit*, the action cycle of Orpheus and Eurydice comes full circle; T. S. Eliot's line "In the end is my beginning" is used in *Turtle Diary* (160); the wheel of fortune is conjured up by Frog in *The Mouse and his Child* (41); and the wheel on which we are broken is both the wheel in Jachin-Boaz's dreams (LN 81) and the Fools Circel from *Riddley Walker*. Hoban usually makes his protagonists break the circles in his novels when they have passed through all the stages of such an action unit. By contrast, Carter instantly brands the circle of the circus ring as a confining and dangerous structure: "O! of grief". The death drive obviously energizes the spectacles staged in the sawdust: Lamarck's chimps perform "their frolics with an air of grave melancholy" (109), and the Princess of Abyssinia's tigers regularly turn the ring into a "perfect death trap" (112).

Walser at any rate soon loses his sense of wonder and is lucky to survive the series of outbursts of violence which will afflict him. When he spontaneously tries to save Lamarck's wife Mignon from a loose tiger after she has been deserted by the "Strong Man" Samson (111), i.e. her lover, he is nearly killed; irony rather than admiration characterizes the description of his "heroics":

> Walser recovered the use of his limbs. Before he was aware he had made a decision, he hurled himself down the amphitheatre towards the amber-eyed brute just as it was about to spring. Involuntary as his heroics, Walser let rip a tremendous, wordless war-cry: here comes the Clown to kill the Tiger!
>
> Kill it, how? Strangle it with his bare hands, perhaps? (112)

The scene recalls both Jachin-Boaz's encounters with the lion and Riddley's escape from Widders Dump: while Hoban boosts his readers' trust in intuitive reactions, Carter contrasts Walser's ineffectual intervention with the Princess's competent recovery of the beast directly after Walser has been knocked unconscious (113). She suggests that more control, competence and reason rather than none are required in this realm in which desire is less repressed than elsewhere. For the circus only seems to be able to "absorb madness and slaughter into itself with the enthusiasm of a boa constrictor and so, continue" (180), but the suffering must in fact be endured by the artists themselves. This is not a general attack on intuition, however. Actually, Carter criticizes it here, above all, because it is inappropriate to its context; she does not fail to point out that it is sometimes altogether impossible to be reasonable when desire succeeds in breaking through all barriers of repression. Fevvers herself will snub reason when Lizzie tries to talk her out of her desire for Walser at the end of the book, calling her Sophie for the first time (279).

The clowns are more jeopardized than artists with more ostensibly dangerous numbers. While the latter can take precaution against the external dangers to which they expose themselves, the clowns are threatened by mental insanity. Abjecting themselves,[2] they perform their wild spectacles on the very barrier which is to confine, and prevent eruptions of, madness straight from the centre of the death drive. Carter's satire is harsh: the clowns are shown to be suicidal failures who proudly provoke their own collapse (119). She means twentieth-century intellectuals and writers when she describes clowns, and there are sufficient allusions to modernist and post-structuralist notions, e.g. when the Master Clown, Buffo the Great (his real name is George Buffins, 118), is described as "the centre that does not hold" (117): the allusion to Yeats's "The Second Coming" brings out the main point of the clowns' antics throughout the novel (also see 243). George Steiner's essay "Silence and the Poet" (1965) seems to have been parodied as well; he writes "Where the word of the poet ceases, a great light begins" (59). In Carter's novel, the lights dim when the clowns have become silent: the summary of the clowns' most popular show pokes fun at theories and literary texts which aspire to the place of religion, the work of "masters" who are utterly ineffectual in bringing about change (also see 152) because they do not know the least thing about living ("This giant is the victim of material objects. Things are against him", 116); moreover, the clowns are mainly experts at staging their dying and resurrection:

> They do a favourite 'Clowns' Christmas Dinner', in which Buffo takes up his Christ's place at the table, carving knife in one hand, fork in the other, and some hapless august or other is borne on, with a cockscomb on his head, as the bird. ... But *this* roast, such is the way of Buffo's world, gets up and tries to run away... (...) He adores the old jokes, the collapsing chairs, the exploding puddings; he says, 'The beauty of clowning is, nothing ever changes.'
>
> At the climax of his turn, everything having collapsed about him as if a grenade exploded it, he starts to deconstruct himself. His face becomes contorted by the most hideous grimaces, as if he were trying to shake off the very wet white with which it is coated: shake! shake! shake out his teeth, shake off his nose, shake away his eyeballs, let all go flying off in a convulsive self-dismemberment.
>
> He begins to spin round and round where he stands.
>
> Then, when you think, this time, Buffo the Great *must* whirl apart into his constituents, as if he had turned into his own centrifuge, the terrific drum roll which accompanies this extraordinary display concludes and Buffo leaps, shaking, into the air, to fall flat on his back.
>
> Silence.
>
> The lights dim. (117)

2 See Julia Kristeva, *Powers of Horror*, esp. pp. 12-18 and 26-29.

Since Carter's criticism concerns every "pilgrim towards death" (Steiner, "Silence and the Poet", 61), and also the more obscene facets of the dance of death, which will be presented to Walser when the clowns initiate him in the kitchen of their landlady later on (124), *Pilgermann* is of course criticized more seriously than elsewhere. Walser, at any rate (and I cannot help silently inserting Walker each time his name is mentioned), has "no great taste" for the dionysiac orgy and slips out of the kitchen "through one of the fissures of the revelry" as soon as possible (125). This recalls the scene when Riddley avoids Granser and Goodparley before they are blown up. It won't come as a surprise that Buffo later assigns Walser the role of the sacrificial Human Chicken (152), nor that he nearly kills him on the closing night at Petersburg when his reason snaps. Unlike Pilgermann at the end of the novel, Walser wants to stay alive: "Walser, his reflexes exquisitely refined by fear," takes "a gigantic leap into the air" to escape Buffo's carving knife (177). Carter also uses the clown episodes for a dismissal of a reverence for Christian passion. But there will be an opportunity to come back to this subject later on.

Walser's changes so far are considerable: He started out as a twenty-five-year-old careless picaro without any "*personal* touches to his personality":

> ... Walser survived the plague in Setzuan, the assegai in Africa, a sharp dose of buggery in a bedouin tent beside the Damascus road and much more, yet none of this had altered to any great degree the invisible child inside the man.... If he was afraid of nothing, it was not because he was brave; like the boy in the fairy story who does not know how to shiver, Walser did not know *how* to be afraid. (10)

By the time the circus departs for Siberia, he has not only fallen in love and experienced jealousy for the first time in his life (145, 156, 179-181), but, having been attacked by a tiger, Mignon's jealous ex-lover Samson (165), and finally Buffo the Great, he has learned how to be afraid. The journalist he once was, who could always maintain the pose of a detached observer, has been exchanged for the humiliated clown and lover (145, 181). The circus ring seems to be a trap specifically designed to make Walser grow up.

Fevvers must learn to be wary of other traps. All her years of experience in the brothel, a Gothic museum and the circus ring have left her altogether unchanged: she is such an expert confidence trickster that hardly anyone has ever had proof of the authenticity of her wings. She takes pride in fooling everyone by stirring their curiosity without divulging her secret; at the same time she translates her knowledge that there *are* indeed wings to protect her into coolness: an act of sabotage on her trapeze by a family of high-wire dancers therefore cannot harm her reputation at all (159); she reacts as if she were a "normal" human being. Only Walser begins to ask himself whether she is a "freak" rather than the humbug he believed her to be despite her autobiographical account:

> And though he was altogether unwilling to believe this might be so, still he was enchanted by the paradox: if she were indeed a *lusus naturae*, a prodigy, then – she was no longer a wonder.
>
> She would no longer be an extraordinary woman, no more the Greatest *Aerialiste* in the world but – a freak. Marvellous, indeed, but a marvellous monster, an exemplary being denied the human privilege of flesh and blood, always the object of the observer, never the subject of sympathy, an alien creature forever estranged.
>
> She owes it to herself to remain a woman, he thought. It is her human duty. As a symbolic woman, she has meaning, as an anomaly, none.
>
> As an anomaly, she would become again, as she once had been, an exhibit in a museum of curiosities. But what would she become, if she continued to be a woman? (161)

What indeed? What is the difference between being Fevvers and being Sophie, or, to put the question more precisely, what is the difference between her self-representation, her legal representation and the real referent of these names? Is the anomaly really meaningless, no more than a transcendent fiction metaleptically construed from the representations? Walser's reflections are a parody of semiotic arguments often put forward to counter essentialist definitions of femininity which insist on there being an essential, irreconcilable difference between the sexes. It is not only the relation between sex and gender that is concerned here, however; the episode raises a more general question about the lack of a one-to-one correspondence between one's hypothetical, because ineffable "core" of identity and the ways in which this identity can never be inserted into reality in any other way than by means of representations: Fevvers's marvellous wings are a cipher for the ineffable, alien "element" which will always establish a difference between what she really is and what the reality consensus allows her to be. She is both a woman and a freak, Fevvers and Sophie, and in addition something neither she nor anyone else can put into words, a stranger to herself. Dangers arise again and again from the fact that there is not only a mismatch between her self-representation and representations of her by other people but also a gap between the ungraspable "essence" of her being and her self-image.[3]

---

3 These insights will also manifest themselves more and more clearly in Hoban's subsequent novels and short stories. Especially the stories collected in *The Moment under the Moment* are instructive, see e.g. "The Man with the Dagger" (1989), when Noir sings her little song of difference (MUM, MD 9). For a discussion of the tensions between reality and the Real, see ch. 11.

After the catastrophes experienced by her colleagues on the closing night (Buffo is not the only one who snaps), she contemptuously but triumphantly saves the performance (180). The circus ring is her safe haven. It is outside the ring, in a reality coloured by elements it has borrowed from the arts (e.g. expectations nourished by fairy tales, films, etc.), that she is vulnerable. While she is ignorant of her weaknesses, vanity and greed nearly eat her up after the last performance, enthralling her more than anything else: she must experience a defeat to lose her megalomania (182). A dinner with an immensely rich Grand Duke teaches the picara the lesson she has not learned so far (184-192). He is not only physically stronger than she but at least her equal as a confidence trickster: he nearly succeeds in convincing her that he is "not as other men" (187). The Grand Duke is a collector of mechanical toys, dolls and eggs made from jewels. He seems to know a good deal about her, for many of the scenes displayed by the interior of the eggs depict scenes from her life. She cannot resist his invitation since he has already showered her with valuable presents. He is aware that diamonds are her "best friend" (179), as she teases Walser before departing like Cinderella in the Grand Duke's "glamorous droshky" (182). The anachronistic reference to the Monroe song "Diamonds Are a Girl's Best Friend" at this point underlines the permanence of certain kinds of wish-fulfilment fantasy. But Fevvers' desire for wealth is called into question the moment she enters the Grand Duke's cold and sterile palace: the essence of materialism, which she is given a chance to experience, revolts her, although her naive belief in a more "social" way of displaying one's riches is satirized, too, and would no doubt be shredded by Lizzie:

> Always the same! thought Fevvers censoriously. Money is wasted on the rich. For herself, if she'd been as Croesus-wealthy as her host, she'd have fancied something like the Brighton Pavilion to call home, something to make each passer-by smile, a reciprocal gift to those from whom the wealth had come. (184-185)

Fortunately the Grand Duke is neither omniscient nor omnipotent but vulnerable as a man. When she realizes that he is going to shrink her to the size of a miniature and lock her up in the gilded cage in one of his delicate eggs, having broken Ma Nelson's sword to disarm her and demonstrated in different ways that he is out to appropriate her every feather – a potential Bluebeard rather than Prince Charming –, her "instinct of self-preservation" and her "wits" (191) turn out to be better friends than her jewels. She can escape by taking advantage of his lapse of consciousness during orgasm to run away – ironically, it is the very symbol of virile power which thwarts his desire for omnipotent control. When the Trans-Siberian Express departs from Petersburg,

Fevvers, too, is no longer the woman she was when the tour started: the experience of her vulnerability has opened her eyes to other than material values. I therefore do not quite agree with Lorna Sage who claims that Walser undergoes a more profound change than Fevvers: "... Fevvers, though she runs out of peroxide and breaks a wing, stays her own woman throughout, and keeps her mystery, the picaresque heroine whose experience rolls off her like water off a duck's back, or almost..." (Sage, *Angela Carter*, 47).

Having been cured of her greed, Fevvers begins to consider Walser: he is the first man who has ever succeeded in making her fall in love (204). But a bomb outrage by which the train is stopped in the middle of a snow-covered Siberian nowhere land, separates them (205). It is as if a fairy had granted an implicit wish of hers, for immediately before the explosion she theorized:

> We have no right to be here, in all this *gemütlich* comfort, stuck on our fat bums down this straight track from which we never deviate, like tightrope walkers in a dream traversing an unacknowledged abyss in five-star comfort, through the deep core of winter and this inimical terrain. (199)

Now she is indeed exposed to the harshness of this "pre-Adamite world" (199) (at least she thinks so, actually it will turn out to be populated by a whole range of Adams of a very familiar kind), with a broken wing and without the option of a fast escape to a safely anchored circus ring. The circus has turned into a heap of fragments and broken shards of mirror, and all except Sybil and the Colonel, who seems to be "made of india-rubber" (205), have suffered minor or major losses. Most of the Princess's dancing tigers have "gone into the mirrors" (205). Fevvers cannot find Walser although the other clowns "bubble up from the smithereens of the hard class" (206) as if the outrage had been an ordinary evening performance. Lizzie, on the other hand, has lost her magic handbag with the clock and everything else needed to dye Fevvers's hair and her feathers (226).

The artists are abducted by a band of outlaws, the heavily armed "brotherhood of free men" (229) who look like "comic-opera" bandits (230). Their leader tells Fevvers that they were banished to Siberia because they had taken "vengeance ... upon those minor officials, army officers, landlords and such like petty tyrants, who forcibly dishonoured the sisters, wives, and sweethearts of flesh and blood we all once had" (230). Fevvers reacts cynically since she cannot stand men who turn women into the cause of their hostilities (also see her earlier remark about "a woman's place – that of the cause of discord between men", 150):

> So that's where women come into the libretto! Absent friends!
> 'What do you mean, "dishonour"?' I says ...

> 'Wherein does a woman's honour reside, old chap? In her vagina or in her spirit?'
>
> Which pithy quibble wouldn't sound badly set to music ... Nevertheless, it troubled him, although it might have been I spoke a dirty word that momentarily stemmed his flow. He sucked in his moustache braids and chewed them vehemently, unused to having his opinions questioned.
>
> 'I do think, myself,' I added, 'that a girl should shoot her own rapists.' (230-231)

In *Pilgermann*, it will be remembered, the tax-collector's anti-Semitism is eventually traced back to his jealousy of his unfaithful wife Sophia. And the protagonist's first thought of responsibility arises from the sudden insight into the wrong he has done to the cuckold, long before he finally begins to think about the woman left behind without a thought both by her husband and himself. But since Hoban exposes his narrator's weakness, the novel abstains from naively asserting old stereotypes.

The leader does not want to listen to Fevvers but falls on his knees before her to implore her help. The outlaws blew up the train because they believed the rumour (spread by Kearney) that Fevvers was the fiancée of the Prince of Wales and could move Queen Victoria to "to ask the Tsar to forgive" them so that they might return free men to their villages (231f.) – this is yet another version of male communication through women. Fevvers feels at once moved to tears and to laughter but then she takes pains to unravel the misunderstanding, plunging the ferocious-looking but naive leader into a deep crisis when she enlightens him on the indifference of the mighty: "What idle folly is this, that you fancy these great ones care a single jot about the injustice you suffer?" (232). A transformed and softened Samson, who will later declare his intention to be a brother and servant to Mignon and the Princess rather than to persist in misogyny (276), now uses his strength to stop the outlaw leader's "fury of disappointment", unleashed on the objects in his tent (233).

An anarchist Escapee finds the camp of the outlaws, immediately beginning an argument with Lizzie over the measures required to change the world: he speculates on the improvement of human nature through a soul striving for harmony and perfection; she, on the other hand, soberly denies the existence of a soul, referring instead to historical conditions which have created institutions such as the monarchy, in which a Grand Duke can collect toys while "wretched peasants ... pay for his extravagances" (239-240). Fevvers interrupts and is given news of Walser (241): the Escapee has been told of him by the women who escaped from the Countess's prison; they found Walser in the debris of the train but left him behind when a search party approached the place. For they did not want to be stopped on their way "to found a female Utopia in the taiga", a "little republic of free women" (240). Carter points to the internal contradictions of their separatism: not only is the survival of their republic heavily dependent on donations of sperm, but the women's moves and decisions are always determined by those they flee. No one can be "free" under such circumstances.

Fevvers, having just been so artificially cool as to demand that "a girl should shoot her own rapists" (231), is now waiting for Walser to save her and Lizzie. Her foster mother instantly takes her to task for her sentimentality, however (241). The mood in the camp is so low that Lizzie eventually asks the clowns to cheer up the outlaws, for if there should really be a search party under way, they will have to persuade the outlaws to let them go and run away rather than shoot them. The clowns comply: "They danced the night into the clearing, ... they danced the dance of Old Adam who destroys the world because *we* believe he lives forever" (243; emphasis added), and the outlaws "indeed broke out in laughter ... It was the bitter laugh one gives when one sees there is no triumph over fate" (243). A blizzard finally swipes both the clowns and the outlaws from the face of the earth, while the other artists and the Escapee place "their faiths in reason" (243), waiting in a hut for the storm to pass. If the clowns failed to inspire Fevvers and Lizzie with a belief in their lost master, they nevertheless kindled something resembling superstition: "... all that Liz and I know is, the clowns made an invocation to chaos and chaos, always immanent in human affairs, came in on cue" (244). Fevvers refuses to take a position in the question of whether what has happened has been real or not. She tells the Escapee:

> 'Look, love,' I says to him, eventually, because I'm not in the mood for literary criticism. 'If I hadn't bust a wing in the train-wreck, I could *fly* us all to Vladivostok in two shakes, so I'm not the right one to ask questions of when it comes to what is real and what is not ...' (244)

Being rid of their captors, the little group trudge through the snow until they reach a house near a stream, i.e. the "Conservatoire of Transbaikalia" (245), inhabited by a very old teacher of music who has run wild in the years of his lonely exile (247). Mignon and the Princess, who have become lovers, will stay there with Samson (275f.), planning to compose new music for the new century which is fast approaching. Kearney and the Escapee decide to return to civilization and business as usual, while Fevvers insists on going to look for Walser (280). For when Mignon began to sing a song, no longer merely "a kind of fleshy phonograph, made to transmit music of which she had no consciousness" (247) but a woman inspired (i.e. literally endowed with a soul) by her love for the Princess, she charmed not only animals of the taiga but also attracted a group of native Siberians, among them Walser riding on a reindeer, looking like "a wild, wild woman" though he has also grown a long beard like Santa Claus (250).

Fevvers's yearning for Walser makes her indulge in plans about modelling the "New Man" (281), a companion fit for the "New Woman" she herself proposes to be: she is satirized because there is nothing new about her project except that the old patriarchal roles are reversed. Meanwhile Lizzie demands that Fevvers think about earning money again, not for her sake, but for "the struggle":

> '... perhaps it is a sign of moral growth in you, my girl (...) that you pursue this fellow only for his body, not for what he'll pay you. Inconvenient as your acute attack of morality might prove in the long term should it become chronic, as far as the financing of the struggle is concerned.' (282)

Quarrelling they find a native woman who has just given birth altogether on her own, owing to superstitious fears that helpers might endanger the life of the baby. Again Lizzie tries to dissuade Fevvers from giving in to her desire for Walser, presenting the opposition between freak and woman as alternatives between which one must choose although Fevvers, as has already been said, will always be both:

> '... this tableau of a woman in bondage to her reproductive system, a woman tied hand and foot to that Nature which your physiology denies, Sophie, has been set here on purpose to make you think twice about turning from a freak into a woman.' (283)

But while they slowly move on towards a village, united only by their practical solidarity for the two foundlings (Lizzie's maternal solicitousness obviously belies her theoretical reservations about motherhood), Fevvers obsessively goes on to try and convince Lizzie of Walser's usefulness as an "amanuensis" specialising in women's history (285), painting an utopian picture of the future full of allusions to Ibsen, Blake and Cixous. Lizzie, though, sees "storms ahead ... When I look to the future, I see through a glass, darkly. You improve your analysis, girl, and *then* we'll discuss it" (286). At last they enter a hut, unknowingly interrupting a bear sacrifice to initiate Walser into shamanism (287).

Walser is already a "new" man, but not at all in Fevvers's sense. He lost his memory when their train was sabotaged, undergoing a symbolic death, and, having been buried in the snow under cloths and napkins (209), is "reborn" when Olga wakes him up with a kiss on his contused forehead (222). While

Vera, Olga's lover, regards the scene in terms of a role reversal, "'The old tales diagnose a kiss as the cure for sleeping beauties,' said Vera, with some irony" (222), Walser experiences it as the fulfilment of a regressive fantasy: "'Mama,' he said. That universal word" (222). After feeding him, the women leave him behind to escape from the search party. Walser crows like the Human Chicken he played at the circus: the egg which he has been given to suck triggers fragments from his buried memory. When he realizes that the "kind ladies" have left him, he tries to follow them "but soon forgot his quest in his enchantment at the sight of dappled starlight on the snow" (224). A fool not unlike Wolfram von Eschenbach's Parzival, though abandoned by his potential foster mothers rather than abandoning them himself, he is found by a shaman:

> The Shaman was not in the least surprised to see Walser, for he had drummed himself into that state of transcendental ecstasy demanded by his profession and his spirit was now disporting itself with a company of horned ancestors, of birds with fins and fish on stilts and many other physiologically anomalous apparitions, amongst which Walser cut rather an everyday figure. (237)

The imagery is borrowed from Bosch, one of the painters admired by Pilgermann, and when Walser is given a drink of urine, his mind somersaults and he quotes Shakespeare while being carried to the Shaman's village upside-down (like Pilgermann, though here, the quote is not from *Lear* but from *Hamlet*, II, ii): "'Oh! he declaimed to the oncoming Siberian dawn. 'What a piece of work is man!'" (238). The demystification of shamanism which will follow raises questions not only about the metaphysics of *Pilgermann*, but also about the nostalgia for shamanism expressed in *Turtle Diary* and the resumption of the theme in *Riddley Walker*.

The description of Walser's apprenticeship with the Shaman in chapter eight of part three is used for an analysis of the limitations of shamanic cosmogony while a shaman's obsessive professionalism is being underlined:

> There was nothing vague about his system of belief. His type of mystification necessitated bare, if illusory, fact, and his mind was stocked with concrete specifics. With what passionate academicism he devoted himself to assigning phenomena their rightful places in his subtle and intricate theology! ...
>
> ... They shared a common dream, which was their world, and it should rather be called an 'idea' than a 'dream', since it constituted their entire sense of lived reality, which impinged on *real* reality only inadvertently.
>
> This world, dream, dreamed idea or settled conviction extended upwards, to the heavens, and downwards, into the bowels of the earth and the depths of the lakes and rivers, with all whose tenants they lived on intimate terms. But it did not extend laterally. It did not, could not, take into account any other interpretation of the world, or dream, which was not their own one. Their dream was foolproof. ... A closed system. ... The Shaman's cosmogony, for

> all its complexity of forms, impulses and states of being perpetually in flux, was finite just because it was a human invention and possessed none of the implausibility of authentic history. And 'history' was a concept with which they were perfectly unfamiliar, as, indeed, they were with any kind of geography except the mystically four-dimensional one they invented for themselves. (252-253)

Mortality, in this view, is merely a stage in a "perpetually recurring cycle of return", hence "death was not precisely mortal" (258), as in Buddhism; nevertheless, the Shaman cannot help mourning for the bear cubs which "must" be sacrificed for the spirits: death is painful in every system. Although there is no first-person pronoun referring to a narrator proper, the seemingly "objective" third-person narration is so saturated with evaluations and other marks of subjectivity, e.g. the exclamation mark after "theology", that the ominous "omniscient" narrator of realistic fiction can be identified. Again and again this artificial instance accentuates the passing of time (see e.g. 237, 254) despite the Siberians' belief in the timelessness of the space they occupy: their "cultivated indifference" to historical change, which "masked fear" (254), is presented as a dangerous delusion because it does not prevent intrusions into their allegedly "closed" system. Fur-traders have infected them with gonorrhoea, railroad tracks run across their territory, and there is an increasing number of foreign "devils" popping up everywhere as the settlement of R. grows (253f.): "... how much longer would this community of dreamers be able to maintain the primitive integrity of its collective unconsciousness against the brutal technological actuality of the Age of Steam?" (254). Rather than to pursue the questions raised by unfamiliar elements, the tribe incorporates them in their dream world, and this is seen to be the reason for their cultural ruin. The narrator does not accuse the Shaman of consciously misleading the tribe, but the "extenuating" circumstances offered to his defence rather incriminate him more: "The Shaman most certainly was *not* a humbug. His was the supreme form of the confidence trick – others had confidence in him because of his own utter confidence in his own integrity" (263).

Yet, doesn't this patronizing description highlight the problem of communication between different kinds of reality consensus rather than to offer valid criticism? I think that there are numerous hints that the "objective" narration is at least as much in need of interrogation as the object of its criticism. What basis is there, for instance, for the certainty with which the hidden "omniscient" narrator dismisses the dream world of the tribe as "only inadvertently" impinging on "*real* reality"? Doesn't the rather scathing dismissal of the Siberians' dream world show that realism is perhaps more incapable of taking "into account any other interpretation of the world" which is not its "own one" than the "magic realism" of the native Siberians (260), who do not exclude and destroy what is other but assign it a place in their system? Clearly crazy Walser stands a better chance of regaining his wits in their system than he would in ours, for here he would be locked up in an asylum. On the other hand, there is also the danger that he will find himself "condemned to a permanent state of sanctified delirium" (254) should he return to his former identity but be anxious not to lose his status in the native community: to achieve social acceptance of development and difference is problematic in any system, though definitely not as dramatic as the "omniscient" narrator thinks when using the verb "condemned". It is hard work to assert one's identity, as women know, too (cf. the discussion of Fevvers's being a freak or a woman), but it is possible and also necessary. The arrival of Fevvers and Lizzie, at any rate, will provide Walser with the required "theory of his difference" (260) so that his memories will again become different from his dreams. On the other hand, isn't the value of historical awareness in general, and of memories in particular, relativized if they fail to modify personalities (and thereby people's actions), as in Walser's case?: "If those experiences had never, heretofore, modified his personality to any degree, now they lost all potential they might have had for re-establishing Walser's existential credibility..." (252). The blind spot most obviously manifesting itself is the "omniscient" narrator's confusion of realism with reality and of realistic historiography with "authentic" history. Since Carter's preferred mode is magic realism, it is clear that the "voice" heard in this chapter is not hers. She attacks the certainties of the "omniscient" narrator as well as she caricatures those of the Shaman in scenes in which his interpretive "skills" are shown (255f., 261).

In this indirect sense, then, Carter obviously agrees with Hoban's view that we had rather be open and take the information presented, for instance, in dreams more seriously. Other information continues to be valid, too, of course. There is nowhere in Hoban's fiction a suggestion that we should limit ourselves to dreams in the manner of Carter's natives. He is not a primitivist, as I will also argue in ch. 8.4, but rather tries to encourage us to use all our mental abilities better. Riddley significantly distances himself from Lorna Elswint's exclusive trust to "1st knowing" but remains open to ideas which come to him this way. The same is true for Bembel Rudzuk and Pilgermann. The rationality defended by Carter's "omniscient" narrator, on the other hand, is just as subject to blindness as the epistemology of her natives: the satirical display of Goodparley's exegesis of the *Legend of St Eustace* could have served as the more explicit model for the implicit ironical criticism Carter presents in her novel.

The professionalism of shamans and the potential abuse of their position, and of metaphysics in general, for political purposes are addressed in both *Riddley Walker* and *Pilgermann.* Riddley prefers to go his own way and become an artist rather than a shaman, because his mystical visions prevent him from being the confidence trickster he is expected to be; he withdraws from his post rather than to impose his view on others with a shaman's authority. Pilgermann's view of the religious communities involved in the First Crusade, on the other hand, is critical enough to call into question the "truths" propagated by them. What both protagonists experience as mystical unity is abstract, ineffable, and not to be used as a source of instruction the way the spirits and dreams of Carter's Shaman are. Rather than to freeze them in absurd rituals, mysticism liberates Riddley and Pilgermann from material and traditional fetters. Moreover, although Pilgermann has an afterlife, it does not cancel the fact of his mortality: the pattern of his life has been made and is not to be improved in reincarnations.[4]

In one aspect, though, Carter and Hoban's differences are irreconcilable: whereas the shaman (or mystic) and the woman can meet, the imitator of Christ's passion is and remains a clown who will find no mercy in the eye of the feminist beholder. For Christianity invites a craving for salvation through death and glorifies suffering, which are both categorically rejected in her novel. The clowns are therefore dismissed as a good riddance by Lizzie and not sadly missed by Fevvers, when their dance of death in honour of their absent leader ends in their being carried away in a blizzard (244). Since Pilgermann and Bembel in the end give up trying to preserve their lives, preferring to seek out Bohemond when they are released from prison, they actually choose the sacrifical position which Carter makes her protagonists fight.

Fevvers is the model for this fight. In the Siberian taiga, she is no longer a star versed in the art of making money by manipulating the desire of admirers but a simple stranger exposed to hostile gazes, or as she puts it herself, "only a poor freak down on her luck" (290), seemingly predisposed to become a scapegoat. Her desire for Walser will prompt her to assert herself, however. For it is particularly painful for her that the "object" of her desire, Walser, first treats her as an inimical bear-spirit:

4 In the afterword to Levinas's *Die Zeit und der Andere*, Ludwig Wenzler presents aspects of Levinas's ethics which could be related to the mysticism presented in Hoban's novels; rather than to lead to an indifference to mortality and temporality, mysticism makes his protagonists more aware of them, and it also creates an awareness for the responsibilities they entail according to the philosopher: "Der Tod *nimmt* die Zeit, zugleich aber *lässt* er sie. Und durch dieses 'Paradox der Zeit' gibt er dem Menschen die Möglichkeit, *seine* Zeit zum Tode – zur *Zeit des Anderen* zu machen" (Wenzler 79)

> She felt herself turning, willy-nilly, from a woman into an idea. The Shaman redoubled the vigour of his drumming and began to sing a song with strange yippings and yowlings in it. From an unseen censer, a purple, disorienting incense filled the god-hut, so the Shaman seemed to multiply himself until there were dozens of him, banging dozens of drums in the same appeal to this thing that was and was not Fevvers. In Walser's eyes, she saw herself, at last, swimming into definition, like the image on photographic paper; but, instead of Fevvers, she saw two perfect miniatures of a dream.
>
> She felt her outlines waver; she felt herself trapped forever in the reflection in Walser's eyes. For one moment, just one moment, Fevvers suffered the worst crisis of her life: 'Am I fact? Or am I fiction? Am I what I know I am? Or am I what he thinks I am? (289-290)

Fevvers's anxiety about being turned into an "idea" is perfectly comprehensible. I have already discussed the problem of representation in relation to Walser's question whether she is a woman or a freak and then analysed the danger resulting from the clash between what she really is and what she thinks she is. This time, however, it is the disagreement between her self-image and the "idea" the two shamans have of her which is at stake. I shall relate her anxiety to the mystification of Sophia in *Pilgermann,* in other words, propose to read Sophia keeping Fevvers's anxiety in mind.

THE MYSTIFICATION OF SOPHIA

The mystification of Sophia in *Pilgermann* begins straightaway. Her character has ironically been modelled on the adulteress whom the seeker of wisdom in the Old Testament Proverbs is advised to shun (cf. Prov. 7). Pilgermann self-consciously draws attention to his awareness of the allegorical, and also racist, cliché which is confirmed when he, "the Jew", lusts after "naked Wisdom": he longs to render a "service ... upon the body of that incomparable ... woman" (PG 14). Sexual desire and pleasure may have joined their bodies, but Pilgermann's representation of the act in terms of a cliché, a transgression of laws, a devotional act and a conscious provocation of the anti-Semitic husband has already turned Sophia from a living woman into a cipher for abstract notions: she becomes an allegorical figure, a temptation, an altar, and, as Fevvers would say, "the cause of discord between men" (*Nights* 150). Desire and the sexual act are mystified, too, when Pilgermann writes on the following pages, "I came as one who seeks a miracle; caution seemed sacrilegious ... This is perhaps the centre of time for me, this waiting ... in a state of transcendental desire, in a state of sin made holy by its purity" (PG 15); and then, "The centre of time is, as I have said, the waiting. This is now off the centre, this is the motion of the everything, the action of the universe, the destined world-line of the soul, the living heart of the mystery" (16). And yet, there is also, almost imperceptible, a tiny detail in this series of distancing descriptions which shows us a little bit of Sophia herself. When Pilgermann first sees her through the window of the house in Keinjudenstrasse, "The man moves away and there stands revealed, farther back within the room, the woman naked with her back to the window. Her shoulders are shaking, she has her hands up to her face" (14). Is she crying? Has she been beaten by her husband? We won't be told any more about her domestic drama, except when the ghost of her jealous husband tells Pilgermann about her other lovers, but this might be a hallucination produced by his paranoia. The spiritual aspect is the one which will be deepened at first. Sophia's voice will turn into the Bath Kol, i.e. "the daughter of a voice" through which God will express his intention that Pilgermann embark on a pilgrimage to Jerusalem (32). Later, he tells us that "the Church of the Holy Wisdom, Hagia Sophia ... incorporated itself with Sophia in my mind" because "of its name and the mystery of itself" (49). She is no longer merely an altar now, but a church, an institution.

This spiritualization of course calls forth a violent backlash, the antithesis: no sooner has Pilgermann talked about the Hagia Sophia, which he fails to see after murdering the relic-gatherer Udo, than Udo's down-to-earth "phallic" widow assaults him from the dark (49). As is common in our culture, the split in the idea of "woman" has taken place by which the dangerous woman is opposed to the redeeming one, woman-as-body to woman-as-soul, the murderess to the mother, the demon from the dark background corner of the Bosch painting to the bright dome in the foreground, etc. Both extremes seem to have in common, though, that they must be deserted, defeated or destroyed: Pilgermann gives us the details of his fight with the strong woman: "I land heavily on my back but I bring her down with me and in the struggle that follows I end up sitting on top of her" (49) – like the "Bloak as Got on Top of Aunty" in *Riddley Walker*. The triumph of the "bloak", though, was undermined by irony: when he began to brag about his victory, Aunty's sister Arga Warga instantly killed him (RW 89). Pilgermann, on the other hand, is already castrated. Fevvers, of course, is equipped "only for the 'woman on top' position" (*Nights* 292). After the fight, Udo's widow invites Pilgermann to make love to her, but since he is a eunuch, he cannot do so, and when she asks him to take her with him, he declines once more, for his pilgrimage is a man's business: "I want her to come with me but it would be a kind of holding on; my pilgrimage requires to be a solitary journey; it is a private matter between Jesus and me and the tax-collector" (51). The only wish he does not decline is when she asks for the wedding ring on his finger: it is the tax-collector's, which he has found under the maggoty corpse. In return he gets her knife and eventually learns her name, which is Sophia, too. By giving her the same name, Hoban draws attention to the correspondence between the two women who just seemed to be presented as irreconcilable extremes – here is a first hint that the stereotypes have not been used naively but with the intention of ultimately abolishing the "or" which separates the first from the second Sophia.

When the tax-collector begins to accompany Pilgermann as a ghost, he conjures up the image of a Sophia who is a nymphomaniac with an enormous "lust and ... appetite for the other, for the circumcised, for the lurking Jew" (86): Pilgermann allegedly was not her first lover but one among many. She is thus demystified, appears as a being of flesh and blood, although her husband's description of her sexuality turns her into the equivalent of an animal, a "bitch" or a "wild ass". Pilgermann does not object to the tax-collector's similes and metaphors since he, too, smelled a scent "of lions" and compared her naked body to a "glimmering fish" when he was with her (15); Sophia becomes "freshly real in my mind, the desert animalness of her in the hidden flesh, the covered nakedness" (86). In *Nights at the Circus*, it is particularly in the scene in which Fevvers tricks out the Grand Duke that sexuality is described by means of animal metaphors (*Nights* 191), and references to Fevvers as a "bird" to be trapped in a gilded cage abound – animal metaphors are therefore a sign of danger, or of rhetorical violence, as Isobel Armstrong points out; she writes in "Woolf by the Lake, Woolf at the Circus":

> The novel asks: if a woman *was* a bird, what would she be? ... To be the representation of a fantasy which is itself a representation is to be enslaved indeed, a violence confused by a further violence, as animals – pigs, monkeys – represent women, too, and are treated as women. Yet, the novel, aware of violence and at the same time exuberant, uses fantasy to unmask fantasy, and thus liberates Fevvers into her *own* world of fantasy and play. (271-272)

As for Pilgermann, the memories of Sophia plunge him into a deep crisis. He mourns the loss of her:

> Gone from me for ever, I knew that I was never to see her again. For a moment the loss of her closed in upon me so crushingly that I thought I might kill myself on the spot; it seemed all at once that there was no space, no time for me to live in. Yet here before me was her husband: he too had lost her and death had given him no rest; the memory of her was a wheel on which he was broken again and again. (86-87)

What is interesting is how his mourning is phrased, though: If it weren't clear that both her husband and her lover had left her, one might think that Sophia had run away from them, intending to destroy them. The blame becomes hers. But his thinking about her opens to a new fantasy: suddenly he considers the possibility that "in her womb is growing new life from our sin, our adultery, our triumph! I laughed aloud as this thought leapt up in me. I looked sidewise at the tax-collector, my brother in Sophia" (88). His gloating plainly jars with the word "brother". There is no more blame on her, now, for motherhood purifies the sensual "animal". Her mystification as Hagia Sophia, on the other hand, is modified inversely:

> I know that the dome and the woman both are manifestations of something elemental that is both beauty and wisdom and it is for ever in danger, for ever being lost, torn out of our hands, violated. It is impossible to keep it safe. That ... God-mother and Mother Goddess, that Wisdom of stone and gold, how should it not be violated, ... how should the altar not be smashed? (89)

The information suppressed by this kind of representation is that unlike a dome, a woman can act. Fevvers, for instance, prefers to use Ma Nelson's sword and her wings, and if both fail, there remain her instinct of self-preservation and her wits, as we have seen. The Sophia in Pilgermann's mind, on the other hand, "Wisdom, golden Wisdom itself, is the mother of both the altar and the thing that smashes the altar" (90) – that is, ultimately she destroys herself! There will be one more Sophia, before the name disappears for around fifty pages: appositely it is a vessel, i.e. Bembel Rudzuk's boat (111), a fact which self-consciously underlines the manner in which Sophia has been used so far: as a means of transport of male desire and anxiety.

But Hoban does not simply repeat sexist stereotypes. Or he would not have placed a crying naked woman with her back to the window at the beginning of the novel – like the imagined butterfly in Samson's field of vision when he was tearing the lion apart, a detail which may have been "the main part of the action" (38). His aim is to show protagonists who realize in the course of a redefinition of themselves that their notions of femininity have caused harm to the women they venerate. In Antioch, Pilgermann's distancing from Sophia takes a futher step, at first. He does not mystify her but is about to forget her when he writes: "More and more it was not the face of Sophia and her naked body that my mind offered me in its picures: it was the obscure face of my young death; it was the shadowy form of actuality to come" (165). This seems to take up the words of Wisdom herself in the Proverbs: "... whoever finds me finds life and wins favour with the Lord, but whoever fails to find me deprives himself, and all who hate me, are in love with death" (Prov. 8, 35-36). He indeed begins to think about his own mortality, which he does *not* define over her dead body.[5] When Salzedo directly asks him whether he is ready to die, though, he begins to worry about Sophia's safety:

> I think suddenly of Sophia (she is always in my mind like a continuo above which rise each day's new thoughts of her) and for the first time there comes to me the question: is she alive or dead? Why should she be dead? She is not a Jewess, no one will rape her and kill her on the cobblestones of our town; she is safe there. But is she there? Until now I have never thought of her as being anywhere else, she has been in my mind a world that continues inviolate while I disappear into chaos; in my mind she has been as static as that other Sophia in Constantinople. Now the curtain of my sight sways before me, the earth seems to move sickeningly beneath me, and in a suddenly clear sky the stars wheel as if the world is spinning like a top. (203)

Considering her a participant in the dance of life rather than a stationary safe haven triggers nausea, i.e. a symptom of abjection which shows that he has been shaken in his psychic foundations. So as not to lose his prey to life again immediately before the fall of Antioch, Bruder Pförtner, i.e. Death, lets Pilgermann embark on a prophetic night journey to the fall of Jerusalem (see ch. 7.1 for a summary and quotations): he shows him a murdered Sophia to rekindle his desire for death and their surviving son to appease his narcissistic desire for immortality through the birth of a child (216). As I have already shown, though, Pilgermann is not to be fooled for long. Death displays the "naked ivory goddess" (216) and mother[6] according to all the rules of the art. The scene is a questionable masterpiece of rhetorical violence designed to comfort a male addressee (cf. Bronfen, *Over...*, 378f.). Yet, Pilgermann's reason eventually proves stronger than Death's tempting mirage. Being flattered, "ready, even eager" only for a little while (218), he realises that Sophia is still alive in his own space and time, so he tries to change history despite Death's complaint: "'... I am like a diligent housewife who cleans the house and cooks the meal and lays the table, all is readiness but the expected guest suddenly can't be bothered to come. ...'" (219). In opposing the law, he becomes an ethical subject. His frustration at having failed Sophia is like a passage through hell: he feels impaled on history and exposed to torture (222f.; see ch. 7.1). He imagines how he would act if he had the chance to start again, sinning more boldly, claiming Sophia "against all odds", or dying rather than to be castrated again (223; see ch. 7.3). This is his redeeming feature, as is his

5 See Elisabeth Bronfen's study *Over Her Dead Body* (1992), in which she illuminates, from various angles, the cultural topos that "because the feminine body is culturally constructed as the superlative site of alterity, culture uses art to dream the deaths of beautiful women. Over representations of the dead feminine body, culture can repress and articulate its unconscious knowledge of death which it fails to foreclose even as it cannot express it directly" (xi).

6 I.e. a woman who has fulfilled "her" biological function and can be discarded according to the oedipal formula, cf. ch. 8.3.

resolution to go and seek her with Bembel, after his old friend has succeeded in calming him (228). On the other hand, though, his crisis also manifests a deep-seated distrust of her, for he asks himself, "But what if Sophia hadn't wanted to be claimed by me? What if she wanted her Jew for one night only?" (223). His greatest cowardice was that he did not go to ask her, preferring to adore and mystify her from a distance rather than to risk being rejected by her. Actually, he will betray the woman he saw crying in the window twice more: Shortly before Bembel and he are locked up by Firouz, on their way out of Antioch, he feels irritated that Sophia and his little son have "come thus at the eleventh hour to interfere with the smooth and orderly winding-up of my affairs", selfishly displacing his anger at his own "too-late good intention" onto them (229). And finally, he will betray her when, released from prison, he wastes no more thought on her but at once hurries towards Hidden Lion to die there with Bembel. Although the two men act alike, their striving for death is not equivalent. In my opinion, Bembel has reached the peak of maturity. He proved to be loyal to Pilgermann, ready to break his contract with Death when his friend needed him (cf. ch. 7.1). He is therefore "entitled" to the fight with Bohemond. Pilgermann, however, is disloyal to Sophia at that moment, which casts a shadow on his achievement of the state of "pure energy" through death (cf. ch. 7.2). His only excuse is that he does not consciously choose to abandon her: responsibility stops where desire imperceptibly deprives subjects of the control over their actions. Hoban shows that there is a conflict between the demands of life and those of death which could be resolved only if life were always automatically given its due first; but the duality of drives to which we are exposed (also see ch. 8.3) often foils one's best intentions. The fact that he exposes Pilgermann's failure with regard to Sophia is a sign of self-critical honesty. Pilgermann's eternal suffering is his punishment. Nevertheless, the novel also justifies female anxiety; it explains the butterfly, the crying of Sophia at the novel's beginning, as best it can.

SOPHIA WITH FEVVERS

As for Fevvers, whom I have left suspended at an anxious moment, Lizzie advises her confused foster daughter to spread her feathers and create for herself the place which the two men will not allow her "in their view of things" (290). And indeed, the miracle takes place:

> She was hesitant, uncertain, at first; but then her plumage – yes! it did! – her plumage rippled in the wind of wonder, their expelled breaths. Oooooooh!
>
> As ever, that wind refreshed her spirits. It blew and blew through the god-hut, blowing away the drugged perfumes and smells of old blood.

> She cocked her head to relish the shine of the lamps, like footlights, and, beyond them, the eyes that told her who she was. (*Nights* 291)

Fevvers succeeds in transforming the Siberian god-hut into an arena for herself; she asserts herself like Pilgermann, when he defends the legitimacy of his mystical questions against the authority of the Church fathers (PG 73f.). Walser begins to perceive her and address her rather than go on treating her as a third person, as the horrid idea of her, whose definition is entirely up to him: "'What is your name? Have you a soul? Can you love?'" (291). A dialogue is to replace both her (not altogether reliable) autobiography and his (hardly objective) description of her.

Walser gradually recovers his memory. Moreover, the former picaro and jealous lover has grown a soul, which is ethically defined as the offspring of care and anxiety for an other rather than as a link between the physical and the metaphysical:

> He was as much himself again as he ever would be, and yet that 'self' would never be the same again for now he knew the meaning of fear as it defines itself in its most violent form, that is, fear of the death of the beloved, of the loss of the beloved, of the loss of love. It was the beginning of an anxiety that would never end, except with the deaths of either or both; and anxiety is the beginning of conscience, which is the parent of the soul but is not compatible with innocence. (292-293)

In *Pilgermann*, as we have seen, the one need not exclude the other: the ability to care for and be with an other is what characterizes the soul's most developed stage of maturity, and it is also the closest a subject can get to an experience of mystical unity in life. Yet, *Pilgermann* also sensitizes the readers to the involuntary occasions for stumbling, the interferences of the death drive with the intentions of the living. In Carter's novel, this excuse would be dismissed: for her, exposure to the effects of the death drive is either a deliberate obsession (cf. the clowns) or else due to a foolish lack of caution (cf. Walser's "heroic" but clumsy attempt to save Mignon); her heroine Fevvers, by contrast, foils all attempts to victimize her: instead of conforming to the desire of those who try to turn her into the vehicle for their anxieties about death, she asserts herself as a living subject. The only desire she indulges is sexual desire.

The endings of the two novels therefore point to different programmes: The last scene of *Pilgermann* describes the pinning of Bembel at the moment immediately preceding his death, "leaping and still like a butterfly transfixed by lightning" (PG 235-236); a good death is located at the body of a man who has given life its due and whose self-negation is not the result of weakness but of choice – the autonomous final act in a good life. It is contrasted with

Pilgermann's death, similar in execution but all the same tainted by his neglect of his beloved Sophia. The last scene of *Nights at the Circus*, on the other hand, is concerned with good love. The metaphor of pinning is used, too, but in an erotic sense. It refers to Fevvers's determined directing the "object" of her desire to the bed after Walser has ushered the "object" of his desire into the Shaman's hut: "Walser, whose head was clearing minute by minute, seized her hand and ran her to the Shaman's house but lost the initiative immediately as she pinned him cheerfully to the bed and told him to wait while she freshened up" (293). Right from the beginning, an exchange of subject and object positions emphasizes a dynamics of sexuality: whoever is pinned, will not stay so for good; movement and renewal become possible rather than stillness.

But Carter's utopia does not pretend that it is possible to leave behind all cultural traces and clichés. Freshening up, Fevvers sings "what else but the 'Habanera' from *Carmen*" (293). With Walser's memory there also return the conventional fantasies of the Old Adam, e.g. when he imagines introducing Fevvers as his "wife, Mrs Sophie Walser" (293-294). But she smothers such ideas by her embrace; arguments are not necessary if pleasure compels its own wordless truth: "Precipitated in ignorance and bliss into the next century, there, after it was over, Walser took himself apart and put himself together again" (294). He must once more redefine himself: "... now, hatched out of the shell of unknowing by a combination of a blow on the head and a sharp spasm of erotic ecstasy, I shall have to start all over again" (294). Significantly the last chapter is entitled "Envoi", which means a closure or postscript; but at the same time it is also a word whose etymology points to the continuation of the journey, for an envoi is a message from under way.

Time obviously, literally *matters* in those two "historiographic metafictions" (Hutcheon, *A Poetics of Postmodernism*, 113-115). Mortality always introduces a caesura into the passing of time, whether it is conceived as linear or as cyclical, or, according to a contemporary pluralistic view, which can be identified in both Carter and Hoban, as fractured and multiple.[7] It is therefore from this event, which always causes some-body's suffering, that there must be derived ethical principles which are to ensure the life of the other and prevent the pain and the anxiety connected to its loss.

Pilgermann also considers eternity, demonstrating on various occasions that causalities become meaningless in the eternal perspective, in which time is no longer unidirectional. Suffering and pleasure, however, leave their indelible imprints on the infinite texture of eternity, which is composed of the

7 See Linda Anderson's essay "The Re-Imagining of History in Contemporary Women's Fiction." (1990).

sum of all moments since the universe burst into being; as "moments of stillness" they define the pattern within which Pilgermann must move on his restless post-mortal course. They stick out from the representations of time-bound reality, the "sounds" produced by various attempts at ordering the chaos of experience, establishing links to the Real of a mystical unity just as dreams, as Herkommer is right to point out, establish links to the Real of desire: "Unter der Oberfläche der mit leiblichen Sinnen wahrgenommenen Welt liegt das eigentlich Wirkliche verborgen.... Diese vertiefte Realität wird auch auf der Ebene des Traums offenbar" (178).

Rather than to devalue our "tiny history of tiny days" (PG 201), then, Pilgermann's atemporal, or perhaps pantemporal, perspective draws attention to the urgency of the question "How to live ... in this little space in which we have a self and a name" (201). The pattern to a certain extent "lives us", but our living adds on to it and modifies it. If everything is connected to everything else, we cannot really afford gratifications of narcissistic desire: if a subject unawares gives in to it, an other will have to pay for the subject's selfishness. Pilgermann's desire in the end is for stillness rather than for a retrieval of Sophia: no longer remembering her, he (unconsciously) seeks an exit from the chaos of experience and the network of responsibilities in which history permanently involves us. But perhaps it is his punishment that his new existence as waves and particles has increased rather than diminished his exposure to the effects of chaos and that the moments of stillness between which he must commute resemble a four-dimensional painting by Bosch rather than one by the Douanier Rousseau. It is his punishment that he must eternally suffer from the idea that Sophia cannot but be violated and murdered because of the way he has lived.

Nights at the Circus prefers to argue from this side of the barrier of mortality when addressing atemporality. Several times Carter highlights the dangers of the desire to escape time and history: The clients of Ma Nelson's brothel pay dearly for the illusion of timelessness staged for them there. The escapees from the Countess P.'s penitential panopticon, who snub Lizzie's lost clock with its figure of Father Time, delude themselves. Thinking that they can indeed live their utopia in a realm outside "paternal" history, they will always have to be on the run. For history will again and again close in on them. Finally, in cyclic notions of time which underline rebirth after death and returns of what has been lost, people may find a certain comfort. There is a promise of continuity despite the visible transitoriness of everything. On the other hand, as the Shaman's mourning for the sacrificial bear cub shows, the "comfort" of a return in another incarnation can only theoretically remove the sadness about the loss of an other. Its uniqueness is anchored precisely in its being linked to a specific time and place. Moreover, the belief in an eternal return of the same eradicates every impetus to initiate change when customs have become absurd.

Lizzie is the one who most passionately defends the claims and laws of history against atemporal metaphysical notions of the human condition. Because of her own keen awareness of the passing of time, she can manipulate others through their desire for timelessness, at least as long as she is in possession of her clock. She is open enough to admit that there are different ways of measuring time and defining history, for she tells Fevvers, "Father Time has many children and I think it was his bastard offspring inherited this region for, by the length of Mr Walser's beard ..., time has passed – or else is passing – marvellously swiftly for these woodland folk" (272). But while Lizzie sternly opposes all philosophical and religious ideas which could impair her sense of control by denying the value of time, she is not immune to the temptations which come from her own atemporal unconscious: her affection for Fevvers turns her into "the slave" of Fevvers' freedom, as she sourly complains (279), and her maternal feelings for foundlings belie her theoretical reservations against maternity.

Unlike Lizzie, Fevvers knows that she can also derive strength from the ability of gratified desire to overrule consciousness and the awareness of time: this knowledge saves her life during her adventure with the Grand Duke and it is confirmed by the paradise of bliss and ignorance she experiences while she is making love with Walser. The mistake she does not make, though, is to believe that such moments could last, nor that they could abolish time. The twentieth century starts all the same, but definitely more cheerfully than Pilgermann's life ended. With Fevvers, Sophia could survive on the way to where she wanted to be and would not be condemned to die miserably in the nightmare of an owl.

8. The Medusa Frequency (1987)

8.1. Troubled Artists: The Alter Egos of Orpheus

It is a dangerous look Herman Orff, the narrator of *The Medusa Frequency* risks at the end of the novel; for the young woman he is looking at is no less than one of the three monstrous Gorgon sisters, whose power to turn onlookers into stone is notorious. When Perseus killed her, he avoided any direct look at her by using his silver shield as a mirror. But Herman seems to be neither as heroic nor as bloodthirsty as the "cheating adventurer" (Meaney 28) of classic myth. Being a truly Hobanian character, he does not approach the petrifying monster greedily, so she shows him her friendliest face: "... when I looked up at the Vermeer girl it was Medusa I saw, flickering and friendly, trusting me with the idea of her" (143). In Vermeer's original painting, the snakes that are visible in Frances Broomfield's painting on the dust jacket of the novel do not show. However, an uncanny detail prefigures Hoban's and Broomfield's interpretation: a coiled shape is apparent under the blue scarf, resembling a snake just about to protrude its head. Tuning in to the Medusa frequency is a challenge to Herman. So far he has been caught up in the action cycle of Orpheus and Eurydice like most of the other characters, i.e. the cycle which structures the love stories of a great number of (male) artists in Western society.[1] Medusa, however, will take him to the borderline between life and death.

Medusa's smile certainly does not stop Herman's turning to stone, but it seems to slow down the process. Thus, he can take the head of Orpheus's advice, "'You must do the best you can with what you've got,' said the brain" (120), and write down his story. He does not care that one of his *alter egos* in the novel, Gom Yawncher, finds him "eccentric ... pathetic" and "cowardly" (116) for doing so. After all, Herman manages to get farther than, and to survive, those artists who adopted other approaches to life, love, and art, or to Medusa and Eurydice. Gom Yawncher, an old failed actor, eventually dies, still mourning for his lost Louisa – the Romance spelling of her name might be a hint why their relationship could not but end in a tragic way for him (124) – while the ambitious film director Gösta Kraken dies of a *heart* attack in his greed to overcome "*art* trouble" as soon as possible after having had himself treated by Istvan Fallok's Fairlight computer (141; emphasis mine). The novel opens with Herman's getting the news of Gösta's death: "I was shocked but I can't honestly say I was surprised when Istvan Fallok told me about Gösta Kraken. It could have been any one of us; art is a tough business." (7).

After this rather (he)artless and not unambiguous introductory paragraph, which could be an ironic wink of the author why his narrator has only been able to publish two unsuccessful novels so far, *Slope of Hell* and *World of Shadows* (12), Herman takes us back to the events of last November and early December when he, too, needed to subject himself to Istvan's EEC treatment,

1 See Klaus Theweleit, *Buch der Könige. Band 1: Orpheus und Eurydike* (Basel: Stroemfeld / Roter Stern, 1988).

because he suffered from writer's block (ch. 3). After having been sent to places in his head he has never been to on his own, he begins to see the head of Orpheus who makes him listen to his story, punishing him with fits of angina pectoris for being impatient and incredulous (ch. 5). Occasionally, the head stops talking for a while, but Herman learns to be patient and wait for his return. He and Istvan's mistress Melanie Falsepercy, a reader at the Avernus press who gradually turns into a writer, fall in love with each other (ch. 10), but their affair is short-lived: Melanie will soon leave him again. On a short trip to The Hague, where he fails to see Vermeer's *Head of a Young Girl*, Medusa trusts Herman with the idea of her (ch. 13). He also meets Gösta Kraken for the first time, immediately picking a quarrel with him. Like Istvan, and perhaps even Gom, Gösta has been one of the lovers of Luise, the "Eurydice" Herman lost by being unfaithful to her. Meeting Luise in The Hague allows Herman to let go of the memory of her. Back to London, he feels no longer inclined to work on versions of the Orpheus and Eurydice myth despite the money it would earn him (ch. 14). His conversations with the head of Orpheus continue, however, until Herman absent-mindedly eats up the grapefruit-half in whose form Orpheus has made his appearance (ch. 17). Herman has to pay for his infidelity by a stay in hospital, where he overhears how Gom Yawncher dies (ch. 18). The Kraken, a figure who rises from the depths of his personal computer and who initially did not take Herman very far into his third novel (ch. 2), now begins to do more than simply share Herman's terror: he becomes Herman's new adviser, telling him all he knows about Medusa (ch. 17). He will reappear as the protagonist of Herman's new story *The Seeker from Nexo Vollma* (ch. 25). Gösta Kraken, though, who seems to have started his career talking to the Kraken (cf. the "Krakenspeak" subtitles of his films in ch. 16) but then moved backward in his orientation, towards Orpheus, does not even survive his first discussion with the rotting head of the ancient singer. Istvan Fallok, to whom the head of Orpheus always returns, tells Herman that Gösta insisted on being connected to the Fairlight computer, too, but was too weak to stand the consequences (141).

The question that immediately arises, of course, is why Herman is the privileged character: what is it that distinguishes him from the other artists and would-be artists that populate this metafictional novel about the difficulty of artistic production? I will now examine his *alter egos* to see whether there might be a pattern.

Gösta Kraken is an interesting figure because he represents the kind of artist Hoban has always avoided to become: a totally self-conscious "intellectual", thoroughly familiar with the vocabulary of art critics and eager to make his work match their requirements. Do Herman's and his author's voice coincide when Herman attacks the vain genius?: "'Faltering cadence of my stare' I'm not taking that from you, nor 'self-consuming antistrophe' either. Don't come the deconstructionist with me, you ponce..." (86-87). Or when he confesses, "'I like my ideas to come to me out of ignorance'" (114)? The splitting into two characters rather signals Hoban's distance to both positions: while abhorring and satirizing an extremely abstract jargon, which will frighten off every reader unfamiliar with Greek, Latin, and poststructuralism, Hoban nevertheless shares the themes of those whose language he attacks: Kraken's expression "self-consuming antistrophe of ... silence" (86) corresponds to "the dance in the stone" (MUM, MT 221) and the "bare, spare music" that "is on the other side of heartbreak" (MUM, MT 222), which he has discussed in his essay "Mnemosyne, Teen Taals, and Tottenham Court Road" (1982). Well-read as Hoban is, an obsessive collector of maps and a book lover, the "ignorance" Herman values does not really hold good for him. Unlike Herman, Hoban could turn into the "star" Gösta Kraken if he felt the need to display his knowledge ostentatiously. The complexity of his novels has been increasing over the years and they could indeed be interpreted, like Gösta Kraken's films *Bogs*, *Quicksand* and *Codename Orpheus*, in terms of the poststructuralist philosophy which informs a good deal of postmodernist aesthetics.[2] Besides, it is one of the deconstructionists Herman reviles who has convincingly argued against the possibility of constructing anything "out of nothing"; Jacques Derrida writes in "Structure, Sign and Play in the Discourse of the Human Sciences" (1978):

> If one calls *bricolage* the necessity of borrowing one's concepts from the text of a heritage which is more or less coherent or ruined, it must be said that every discourse is *bricoleur*. The engineer, whom Lévi-Strauss opposes to the *bricoleur*, should be the one to construct the totality of his language, syntax, and lexicon. In this sense the engineer is a myth. A subject who supposedly would construct it 'out of nothing', 'out of whole cloth', would be the creator of the verb, the verb itself. The notion of the engineer who supposedly breaks with all forms of *bricolage* is therefore a theological idea; and since Lévi-Strauss tells us elsewhere that *bricolage* is mythopoetic, the odds are that the engineer is a myth produced by the *bricoleur*. (157)

What the excerpt also shows, though, is that a new myth can be constructed out of the pre-existent parts; bound though we may be by language,[3] language

---

2 It is no coincidence that *Riddley Walker*, *Pilgermann* and *The Medusa Frequency* figure as examples for various facets of postmodern literature in Brian McHale's *Constructing Postmodernism* (1992). Also see Barbara Herkommer's study for a discussion of Hoban's gradual turning into a postmodern writer.

3 See Jacques Lacan, "The Agency of the Letter in the Unconscious" in *Écrits. A Selection* (1977): "... language and its structure exist prior to the moment at which each subject at a certain point in his mental development makes his entry into it" (148).

is an infinitely creative open system which favours the production of an unending number of new combinations of familiar elements.[4] And indeed, the figure who will give Herman's life a new direction is not "new" at all: Medusa has always been waiting for her reappearance, even though the myths which have been dominating our culture for the past millennia have preferred to leave her in the dark, or else, to disfigure her.

Besides signalling the distance between the author and his characters, the split between Gösta Kraken, Herman Orff and the other troubled artists who represent aspects of Orpheus, also underlines, on the one hand, the variety of expressions at the artist's disposal, and on the other, the implications of privileging one form of expression over others. Every choice entails responsibilities. Unmasking Gösta Kraken's intellectual vanity, which goes along with a total absence of conscience – "My behaviour was impeccable..." (88) – Hoban criticizes those who commit themselves to a life-style in which publicity and greed have replaced patience and a genuine interest in communication. By contrast, Herman knows of his responsibilities: "... in each plane of stillness is the moment of clarity that makes you responsible for what you do" (80). Unlike Gösta, but like Hoban, Herman can wait for the right moment: he spends hours meditating on paintings and listening to radio programmes in unknown languages which trigger chains of associations. It is thus the workings of the unconscious which are brought to the fore. While recovering from angina, Herman finally acknowledges the source of his creativity: "'This thing of darkness is where my writing comes from.'" (127). In surreal scenes, Herman fights, kills and walks over the dead body of his "current account" when he feels that he will be prostituting his talents if he accepts work with Sol Mazzaroth, the editor of the X-rated magazine *Classique*, or with Gösta Kraken (93f., 104, 129). He prefers to earn his money by writing comics (132). However, there are worse figures in the novel than Gösta Kraken: Ferdy Phyvemill's ambition, for instance, is stirred only by the acquisition of money and prizes (114) – and that appears to be the only art he knows. The "new myths" of such characters are oriented toward fashions; but usually they are also as ephemeral as these.

Istvan Fallok, the composer obsessed with the themes of Orpheus and Hermes (17), does not mind working with Gösta: unlike Herman, he likes the films of the director even though he finds him "a pretty boring guy" (142). He can tell a good director from a merely commercial one such as Ferdy Phyvemill (114), that is, his taste is more refined than Herman's, who admits

4 John Lyons writes in *Chomsky* (1977): "One of the most striking facts about language is its 'creativity' – the fact that by the age of five or six children are able to produce and understand an indefinitely large number of utterances that they have not previously encountered..." (108).

having taped one of Phyvemill's films and watched it four times (113). But Istvan cannot free himself from the head of Orpheus. Whenever the head has told his story to other artists, he returns to Istvan (141). Whereas Herman learns to let go both of Luise and of the theme of Orpheus and Eurydice, Istvan seems to be condemned to repeat the same story over and over.[5] Instead of moving on to somewhere else, he moves others with his computer: undergoing the EEC treatment once only obviously took him to such a scary place in his head that he preferred abstention ever after (24). Herman cannot help noticing Istvan's haunted look: "He was forty-three, tall and thin, with lank red hair and a long white face and pale hard blue eyes with dark circles under them and he looked awful. He'd never been a very robust or healthy type but now he looked haunted" (22).

In chapter 17, "Where Do We Go from Here?", the clash between pretentious Gösta, reticent Istvan, Herman, who escapes from Hilary Forthryte's business lunch, and a further *alter ego* figure, Gom Yawncher becomes most obvious. Gom Yawncher is a protean character who has appeared in various roles: as a passenger of the underground whose visions have been destroyed by psychiatry (28f.), a waiter at the Cheshire Cheese "speaking with an accent so regional that it used up all his articulation and left nothing over for words" (56), and a quick-witted greengrocer whose rhetorical talents are used for nothing but selling cabbages (60). In chapter 17 he turns into a busker who scorns ambition: "Here I am for all to see and hear, doing my pitiful little dance and playing my Pan-pipes badly. Poor sod. Give him a bob or two. I am what I am and being it in plain sight, not hiding behind a book or dressing up in clever words" (116). The last time Herman meets him, he is an unemployed actor dying in St. Stephen's hospital, where Herman is recovering from angina (ch. 18). That Gom Yawncher should die in a hospital called after the first Christian martyr, who was *stoned* to death, is one of the details that makes all of Hoban's novels worth reading more than once. Does this mean that, despite his desperate call for Louisa, Gom is one of the victims of Medusa? His tattoo at any rate shows "a snake twined around a dagger" (28); and the brief chapter which follows his death suggests that Medusa is present at the hospital, this time manifesting herself through the night sister: "... her white cap flickers, becomes a writhing and a hissing silence. ... her shadowy gaze is on me. ...

5 His first name "Istvan" recalls the German word for *status quo*, i.e. *der Ist-Zustand*. Further significant associations have been suggested by Henri Petter: The second syllable of Istvan's name echoes German *Wahn*, i.e. delusion. Moreover, the fact that "Istvan" is the Hungarian equivalent of "Stephen" establishes an indirect connection between the composer and Medusa, as will be shown in the next paragraph.

her mouth is moving as it moved above the pinky dawn water between the beach and the Island Tamaraca" (126).

Being a completely failed artist, Gom *Yawncher* resembles the resigned Redbeard in *Kleinzeit*. But what is new is the fact that even such an outsider forms part of the action cycle of Orpheus, the "brute artist" (68); it is one of the possible enactments of the ancient singer's dissolution, as the head of Orpheus tells Herman:

> '... I ended up singing for coins in taverns as I had done before I became the Orpheus of the stories.'
> 'How did you die?'
> 'In a drunken brawl.' (120)

Dissolution is not to be mixed up with depersonalization. While the former term refers to the end of an artist's career, the latter describes the artist's self-imposed sacrifice to posterity as defined by T. S. Eliot and quoted by Hoban in his 1975 essay "Thoughts on Being and Writing" (67). Gom Yawncher's criticism of Herman points to the effect that too much depersonalization, the (modernist) substitution of art for life, can have: "'... You're not really living your life – you're pulling the arms and legs and the wings off it one by one. Why don't you take up vagrancy or crime, it's more manly.'" (116). Making up stories of every experience, Herman has neglected his physical condition altogether. Ironically, it is Gom Yawncher's death, not his words, which makes him think of Orpheus's and his own body for the first time (125). In order to be capable of depersonalization Herman must learn to take care of himself or else he will be united with Medusa too soon to communicate his approaches to her. In other words, dissolution must be prevented for as long as possible for the sake of depersonalization, and the troubled artist should aim at a middle way between exhaustion and resignation. Herman may be no Hoban, but provided that he keeps to his middle way, he probably will one day be able to produce a text that does not lead his muse "into insolvency" (12).

There is one more character in the series of troubled artists who remains to be discussed: Melanie Falsepercy. She sticks out like the snakes in Broomfield's version of Vermeer's painting of the *Head of a Young Girl*. For on the one hand, she is female, and on the other, her trouble does not consist in her having lost a Louisa or Luise. On the surface, it is she who seems to be privileged, not Herman: she is young, at the beginning of her career, and Herman admires her for her perfect body (21). For her it is no problem to accept the money offered by Sol Mazzaroth for an adaptation of the Orpheus and Eurydice myth; it is her way of "buying time" so that she can write her own novels. She relativizes Herman's childlike and perhaps also hypocritical, or at least self-deceptive, preference for comics: "'I'm no more commercial than you are,' she said. 'I'm just doing what you've been doing with your comic-writing all these years...'" (111). Eventually she leaves Herman because he sneaks out of every challenging project (111f., 128): unlike the phallic Hilary Forthryte, whose ludicrous and meek partner Ivor Dreft brings out her own strength (113), Melanie seeks a partner who is her equal (110).

Melanie at first also seems to be cast in terms of the Vermeer girl/Eurydice conjunction: Herman discovers a "Melanie Falsepercy look" in the eyes of the Vermeer girl (23); moreover, she is the mistress of Istvan, of Herman, perhaps also of Gösta, that is of three men who think of themselves as Orpheus. Despite this, I think that she is rather another *alter ego* of Orpheus than an embodiment of Eurydice. A comparison with Luise, who "had none of the desperation that produces art" (17), will make this plain – and here we are at the root of her particular trouble: as long as she cannot overcome the role of Orpheus, as Herman eventually does, Melanie creates no better system but simply perpetuates the old one with reversed roles, leaving her lovers before they leave her. But there is something deeply dissatisfactory in this way of life: although acting like Orpheus liberates her from the object position of Eurydice, with which she cannot identify as an artist, it does not sustain the illusion that she can run away from her mortality, her "large death" (138). As I shall show in ch. 8.2, she is aware of this and working hard to make the creative leap from the fool's circle of a mythical system that separates subjects from objects in order to displace mortality from the subject (coded as masculine) to "his" object (coded as feminine). Her task will be to define a feminine subjectivity which can deal with its own mortality in a creative rather than self-destructive way. Having so far examined the situation from the point of view of artists, I will now survey a wider selection from the network of characters, both real and mythical.

8.2. Names on Potsherds

At a first reading it is nearly impossible to grasp all the implications of Herman's fizzy story, in what ways the characters are related to each other, to Orpheus and Eurydice, Hermes and Aristaeus, and what the role of the Kraken and Medusa is. A kaleidoscopic multitude of names and images flashes up all too briefly, since the novel is so short that it ends before shapes and patterns can be clearly distinguished. But even in a kaleidoscope the symmetrical axes which structure the projected images become visible after a while. Repetitions and reflections manifest themselves although it is still impossible to account for the position of every piece of coloured glass.

There are structuring elements in Hoban's novels which equally assist the readers' orientation. Epiphanic moments and places of magic attraction, descriptions of fences, walls, mountains, mirrors, the sea, or of abstract borderlines between day and night or life and death mark significant liminal stages in the characters' quests. They allow the readers to subdivide the plots into moments before and after the episodes thus distinguished.

In *The Medusa Frequency*, The Hague serves as a point of reference of this kind. The eponymous chapter 13, situated near the middle of the novel, presents a climactic stage in Herman's development. Not only does "The Hague" mean "fence", but its literally outstanding position is marked by the fact that Herman has to cross the sea to get there, as if he crossed the Styx to find the Underworld. Moreover, it is the place where Vermeer's *Head of a Young Girl* can normally be found and where the International Court of Justice has its seat – the reference to Eurydice, whose name means "Wide Justice" (46) and the function of whose loss is "the judgment, the reckoning, and the punishment" of Orpheus (118), is evident. It is the Vermeer girl who inspires him to go to The Hague, but when he arrives there, the painting is on loan in the USA: his journey seems to be a failure. However, Medusa speaks to him for the first time, with a face that evolves out of a hallucinatory image of Luise's body rising out of the "dawn water" around Frans Post's Island Tamaraca (89f.). He has seen her earlier on, during the delirious vision which was induced by Istvan's Fairlight computer. But he did not recognize her then, although she came closest to the traditional representations that are known of her: "Closer and closer came the face of Eurydice, her mouth open and grinning, her tongue hanging out" (28). Finally, Herman meets the real Luise at The Hague, which releases him from years of mental bondage to her.

In The Hague, two metamorphoses take place at the same time, so the novel may be divided into what happened before and after Herman went there. On the one hand, he stops being Luise's Orpheus, for when they do meet, a sort of dissolution of Herman's former being takes place: "Time ceased to be an automatic progression: the present moment exploded into millions of sharp-edged fragments and nothing followed. (...) ... all of a sudden it was some other time.... (...) ... she was gone out of my life for ever" (91-92). On the other hand, he is re-born as the vessel of the idea of Medusa: "I came out of myself quite clean, like a snake out of an egg" (90), and feels that the new era will confront him with new demands: "... I could feel the Hermes of it, could feel myself on a night road to somewhere else" (92).

Before The Hague, the head of Orpheus, this self-appointed expert on relationships between men and women, helped Herman to understand what went wrong between him and Luise. He tells his story in a way that leaves no doubt that he and Eurydice were equally responsible for what happened:

> 'Loss!' it said. 'That's what she was to me, you know: she was the loss of her even when she was apparently the finding of her, the having of her. And I was the same to her, I was to her the loss of me. We were the two parts of a complementarity of loss, and that being so the loss was already an actuality in our finding of each other....' (68)

According to him, the loss of Eurydice was not to be prevented by any means:

> 'Yes,' said the brain. 'Eurydice is all that one wants to be faithful to and cannot, and the loss of her is the punishment.'
> 'How did you lose her?'
> 'I lost her when I stopped perceiving her.'
> 'I meant how did you lose her physically?'
> 'She went off to live with Aristaeus.'
> 'She wasn't bitten by a snake, she didn't go to underworld?'
> 'Not in this telling of the story; she simply left me and moved in with Aristaeus.' (118)

When Herman asks him if she left him because of his infidelities, the head is conspicuously evasive: "'I think it was the story that finally did it. When there was love and happiness there was no story....'" (118). Herman's question is grounded in his own biography, for Luise left him nine years earlier because she had found an incriminating letter in his writing folder (26). Being neither an intellecual nor an artist, the only condition she ever asked Herman to fulfil was to be faithful. He, however, proved unworthy of her trust. The dialogue is also interesting because of another detail. In this version of the myth, Eurydice does not die: she is "merely" lost. But her loss still founds Orpheus's art. Before leaving him, Eurydice says: "'... Now that I'm lost you will perceive me fully and you will find me in your song; now that underworld is closed to you the memory of the good dark will be with you always in your song....'" (119). The head of Orpheus is tired of telling this, his story, even in this more harmless version, but the only thing he can do is wait for it to "come out differently one day" (101).

What would be the implications of a different story: would art no longer be a celebration of the loss or death of Eurydice, of Orpheus's other? Would there be another way of finding the "good dark"? For this is obviously Eurydice's function: she grants Orpheus access to the underworld. When Medusa trusts Herman with the idea of her, she actually clears a path to a new way of being an artist. Significantly, Orpheus can no longer be Herman's adviser after The Hague since Medusa never trusted *him* with the idea of her (96).

Although Medusa behaves like a new Eurydice tempting Herman to dedicate himself to her and figuring beside Eurydice in Herman's list of aspects of the Mother Goddess, whose other representatives are the Vermeer girl, Persephone, Luise von Himmelbett and Melanie Falsepercy (47), there is an essential difference between the two mythological women. While Eurydice is associated with temporary "SWEETNESS", "LOVE" and "BEAUTY" that can be lost and betrayed, Medusa, who never reveals more than her face, is beyond loss and betrayal:[1] "THIS IS THE FACE OF WHAT CANNOT BE BETRAYED. ... THIS IS THE ONE TO WHOM YOU CAN BE FAITHFUL" (122). It is the Kraken who provides Herman with this information about Medusa, for Orpheus only knows what lies beyond the Gorgon, not how to approach her: "Behind Medusa lie wisdom and the dark womb hidden like a secret cave behind a waterfall. Behind Medusa lies Eurydice unlost" (121). The Kraken appears to be the one Perseus killed with Medusa's head to save Andromeda. But does this qualify him as Medusa's complement?[2] In the DRAMATIS PERSONAE, Herman lists the following features of his genealogy:

> *The Kraken*, the underhead: by its own account it came into existence when the human mind needed another mind to hold the original terror but it may well be of earlier origin. Eurycide claims to be its mother by a giant squid.
> *Eurydice*, mother? of the Kraken; the vast and ivory nakedness of her rising from the deeps. Luise von Himmelbett and Melanie Falsepercy are the Eurydice of this story, the lost one, the gone one, the one who cannot stay. (...)
> *The Giant Squid*, an aspect of Orpheus, also (in a non-gigantic way) of Orff. Lusting after fishergirls. (46-47)

While his mother and his father, and the human characters associated with them, are complements, there is no hint of his conjunction with Medusa, unless, of course, her idea, or one of the ideas of her, is that of the "original terror" which it is his function to hold. The Kraken says of himself, always in *capital* letters: "I AM THE KRAKEN, ANCIENT OF THE DEEPS, MONSTROUS CEPHALOPOD, GREAT HEAD AT THE CENTRE OF MY MILES OF WRITHING

---

1 At least, she cannot be betrayed without a magic mirror. But it remains to be discussed what, or who, exactly *is* betrayed when Perseus makes use of that medium.

2 According to Jacques Lacan, the sexual relation, i.e. the economy of pleasure, is based on the fantasy of complementarity, which presupposes that there is a totality, a unity which both complements can attain together (cf. "The Meaning of the Phallus", 81; and "God and the *Jouissance* of ~~The~~ Woman", 144); but sexuality causes so much trouble precisely because the other will never gratify one's desire fully (cf. ch. 8.3). What is beyond the pleasure principle, however, is supplementary *jouissance* ("God and the *Jouissance* of ~~The~~ Woman", 144). Lacan here continues to think about the idea of drives Freud developed in "Jenseits des Lustprinzips", 250ff.

TENTACLES IN THE BLACKNESS OF THE ULTIMATE DEEP..." (10-11). Again, there is no hint about the way in which he relates to Medusa, unless she is the blackness which engulfs him, which would make him a part of her. The Eurydice who gave birth to him and his terror (10), could be the one behind Medusa. But in Herman's DRAMATIS PERSONAE, a question mark underlines Eurydice's ambiguity. The description of Eurydice parallels Herman's vision of Luise's body rising from the sea in Frans Post's painting *Gezicht op het Eiland Tamaraca*. Her naked body will turn into the face of Medusa, "a face loosely grinning, with hissing snakes writhing round it in the shining dawn" (90). Still, this does not imply that the figure of the Kraken is her complement – he is rather the mirror image of her head, her double.

In Herman's story *The Seeker from Nexo Vollma*, finally, the Kraken NNVSNU THE TSRUNGH saves the universe from extinction; and it is here that he finds a complement, that is, NABILCA, THING OF DARKNESS: "She was scuba diving when she lost consciousness and woke up in the secret undersea headquarters of the Nexo Foundation" (131). Nabilca is not Medusa, rather a Persephone who can move through various realms: as the Kraken can rise from the ultimate deep to the surface, she can dive down to him; she can move from consciousness to the unconscious, and back. While Medusa is reserved when called up by Herman (129), Nabilca immediately volunteers to help Nnvsnu transmit the "mothercode", which "holds the universe together": "SPINNING HIS MIND LIKE A PRAYER WHEEL HE REVOLVES CONTINUALLY THE NUMINOSITIES AND NEXIALITIES THAT COMMUNICATE THE UNIVERSE TO ITSELF" (132). The use of capitals in his utterances may be a sign that the mothercode will inevitably affect language; and no doubt there is an analogy between the mothercode and the Medusa frequency which alters Herman's writing.[3]

3 The expression "mothercode" recalls the theories of Julia Kristeva: in "Revolution in Poetic Language" (1974), she defines the semiotic *chora* as a "feminine", "maternal" modality which underlies and undermines the symbolic "masculine" system of language; it is basically the semiotic which distinguishes poetic language: "No pure signifier can effect the *Aufhebung* (in the Hegelian sense) of the semiotic without leaving a remainder, and anyone who would believe this myth need only question his fascination or boredom with a given poem, painting or piece of music. As a traversable boundary, the thetic is completely different from an imaginary castration that must be evaded in order to return to the maternal *chora*. It is clearly distinct as well from a castration imposed once and for all, perpetuating the well-ordered signifier and positing it as sacred and unalterable within the enclosure of the Other" (104-105). In chapter 9, the parallels between Kristeva's theory and Hoban's fiction will be further explored: for *The Moment under the Moment* embraces the semiotic more than any other text by Hoban. Kristeva's notion of the semiotic points to a fundamental instability of subjects: they are subjects in process (91), constituted by the dialectic between the symbolic and the semiotic as modalities of one and the same signifying process (92f.). The gendering of the two modalities of language is not unproblematic, though. While it removes subjectivity from biology since both modalities are open to all individuals, it stabilizes associations between femininity and irrationality, on the one hand, and between masculinity and rationality, on the other. More recent discussions of subjectivity such as Chris Weedon's "Language and Subjectivity" (1987), however, stress the

What my insistence on complementarity of course aims at is to show that Medusa's position is beyond the economy of gains and losses. The Kraken says: "THIS IS THE FACE OF MEDUSA WHO CANNOT BE IGNORED, CANNOT BE INTRUDED UPON, CANNOT BE POSSESSED. YOU HAVE NEVER GIVEN YOURSELF TO THIS ONE WHO WILL NOT GIVE HERSELF TO YOU, ..." (121). She is not subject to the system of complementary otherness which structures the relationships of the other characters (action cycles which produce unstable "units") and their exchanges of functions. She may trust Herman with the *idea* of her and show him her *face*, but she does not give *herself* to anyone. Although she does not take *part* in the system, she seeks mediation through its elements: this is the reason why she asks Herman to hold the idea of her in him. She adds her difference to elements of the system, Luise's body, Eurydice's face, the painting of the Vermeer girl, the night sister. Her subjectivity is always preserved in so far as she is the author of her appearances and cannot be possessed. Even though the head of Orpheus asserts that there is "'Only one femaleness, whether it's called Eurydice or Medusa or Persephone or Luise'" (99), it is uncertain whether Orpheus's words can always be taken at face value: "*The Head of Orpheus*, the overhead. It isn't to be trusted, I know that: music with Fallok and a story with me, and the one likely to end up as badly as the other" (47). Orpheus is unable to deal with the difference of Medusa: She requires another perceiver. Tuning in to her frequency, Herman exposes himself to his own mortality. If Medusa is whatever stops all movements and communications, then being trusted with the idea of her, or assisted by something she sends from the darkness into the light, "the mothercode", the "Medusa frequency", is an affirmation of life that comes from the realm of death itself.

The gradual, elusive difference between the other female characters corresponds with an analogous difference between the males. The feature all of them have in common is that they will always be "her man", dedicated to their female complements, whether they have just lost or not yet found them, and whether they have just been lost or not yet been found by them. The distribution of active and passive roles does not depend on the characters'

need to historicize and deconstruct binary oppositions (e.g. femininity/masculinity, conscious/unconscious, or symbolic/semiotic, etc.) while welcoming in principle the Kristevan concept of the subject in process: "The Kristevan concept of the subject in process – of unitary subjectivity as an inherently unstable effect of language – is important. Yet we need to extend the analysis to include a recognition of different types of historically specific conscious subjectivity and the different unconscious formations which underpin them. These types of subjectivity, implicit in different discourses, are always located discursively in social institutions and practices which constitute and govern subjects. For the power of all forms of subjectivity relies on the marginalization and repression of historically specific alternatives" (91).

sexes: complementary roles rather resemble mathematical figures with opposite algebraic signs.

When Herman is left by Melanie, she can either be seen as another Eurydice "who cannot stay" (119), or as a female Orpheus, as I argued in ch. 8.1. The fact that she writes about Eurydice and Orpheus shows this (111). This algebra does not work any more, though, when Medusa enters the picture. Melanie's family name (which is actually her father's name) could be referred to Perseus; incidentally, this is the only occurrence of a reference, however indirect, to the enemy of Medusa. Yet, Melanie Falsepercy is a false Perseus, not one who would kill Medusa to appropriate her power, but one who would become like her. It is culture rather than logic which has led to a situation in which the woman novelist who seeks access to her mortality is not simply the reverse of the male novelist. As Bronfen writes in *Over Her Dead Body*:

> ... the impulse of writing always also presupposes the life of the author, a signature and a position in culture. It is, however, also true that writing, as the act of translating a cultural representation into a performance which exceeds the given text, does for women often mean a writing out of social death, a writing inhabited at its centre by the uncanny resonance of 'death' as silence, effacement, self-denial. This writing can never entirely deposit the topos that links feminine self-articulation with death beyond its system of representation; it can never securely turn feminine death into a canny trope outside, so as to disavow this cultural heritage and be done with its curtailment. ... Seeking to substantiate the feminine self as author, the woman writer also embraces death. The gesture of her writing repeats *and* resists the discursive formation from which it emerges and against which it performs. (404)

Melanie must abandon her *pseudonym*, her paternal "false name", to define her identity in different terms rather than merely in terms of a sex/gender role reversal – the figure she therefore eventually identifies with is Persephone, the goddess of death, as her taped apology shows:

> 'Death is longer than life,' she said, 'and the death of each moment is longer than the moment. The goneness is what we're left with, maybe some of us more than others. It's very hard to *have* anything, isn't it? ... I've always been a sort of phoney percy, you see – Persephone more than Eurydice, with my own little dark realm. Or I'm like Rilke's Eurydike, so full of my large death that I understand nothing ...' (137-138)

Embracing the identity of Persephone will liberate Melanie from the artistic dilemma I have described at the end of ch. 8.1. Whereas Eurydice is condemned to die, so that Orpheus's art can flourish, Persephone has the power to oscillate between the realm of the dead and that of the living. Resuming the

Perseus identity (i.e. that of the "subject of representation", cf. Meaney 32)[4] to describe the experience of Persephone would not require of her the paradoxical task of feeding off her own death. A "false" Perseus's reflection may turn Persephone into an object, too, but since she would not be a dead object but part of Perseus's self, she could find ways of inscribing her subjectivity into the representation, like Medusa.

Herman's role in their relationship is always that of a male Eurydice. At the beginning of the novel, he follows her (Persephone) through the corridors of the London underground to Istvan Fallok's studio, "Hermes Soundways" (19ff.). He stays there to have his head tuned to an olive tree that symbolizes "an entrance to the underworld, a Persephone door" (26). Later on, she (now as Orpheus) finds him at All Hallows church (64), but just when Herman has got used to the idea of staying with her, she leaves him to live with Sol Mazzaroth: "... I was with Sol that weekend. (...) So at least you don't have to feel guilty about me, I did it to you before you did it to me. Goodbye, Herman..." (138). Being a female Orpheus,[5] Melanie seems to avenge Herman's infidelity to Luise (26, 70). By victimizing him, Melanie evens out the guilt that has so long been pulling him down and tying him to the memory of his great love. Thus, she justifies the metamorphosis Herman experiences at The Hague, his liberation from that painful obsession. Because of Melanie it is possible for Herman to make a new start with Medusa, and be the innocent world-child again.

Is it not a broad hint, however, that the egg he comes out of is that of a snake (90)? Two interpretations suggest themselves: on the one hand, he is reborn as a part of Medusa, one of the snakes on her head; on the other, the snake may also prefigure future attempts at infidelity. New sin is lurking around the corner, so that it is probable that instead of peacefully turning to stone and being devoted to nothing but the idea of Medusa, Herman will indeed try to find ways to move on to somewhere else. The very fact that he has written down his story and passed on to us his fictional *reflections* about Medusa, which seemingly ban her like Perseus's shield, is the sign of his attempt to share the burden of this figure. But if he tries to move to somewhere else, he will not get very far: as a snake on her head he ultimately cannot betray her without betraying himself. Albeit Herman has turned into a

4 The quotation will be embedded in its context in ch. 8.3.

5 What is interesting is that her farewell is formulated in such a way that she can be seen *by him* as Orpheus, "I did it to you before you did it to me"; but her identification with Persephone is a hint that she has already accomplished the shift to the paradigm I have sketched out above. *To her*, Herman might be Hades whom she leaves to return to the sunlit world of the living (Sol). Significantly, Eurydice never succeeds in seeing the sunlight again (see Graves, *The Greek Myths*, ch. 28).

kind of Perseus and his text works like Istvan Fallok's Fairlight computer (cf. ch. 6), he treats her with due respect, as the Kraken does whenever he speaks about her: while passing the idea of Medusa on to us, he never spreads the illusion that he could control her appearances and appropriate her power. Still, now it is our task to come to terms with her. In the next two chapters, I will therefore return to Medusa.

But before doing so, I want to look at two figures who seem marginal because they fail to appear in person but who are nevertheless indispensable for the stories of the head of Orpheus and Herman to take place, that is Hermes and Aristaeus. Hermes, "the thief-god, the god of roadways and night journeys ... a shift in the relativities of the moment, a new disposition of energies" (44) is a principle diametrically opposed to the idea of Aristaeus, the bee-*keeper* who gathers "broken bits of fired clay" which "want to come together" and "contain something" (118). They influence Orpheus and Eurydice like a catalyst and a stabilizer, one starting the reaction between the willing couple, the other bringing it to a close. Introducing the two principles, Hoban varies his own idiosyncratic use of the myth of Orpheus and Eurydice as we know it from *Kleinzeit* (cf. chs. 4.2, 4.3, and 8.4), by two further elements. The "myth" that is told by the rotting head (36ff., 61f., 68ff., 98ff., 117ff.) has moved quite a distance away from the one that Robert Graves presents in *The Greek Myths*, for there, Hermes does not appear, least of all as Orpheus's father,[6] and Aristaeus is the one who is to blame for Eurydice's death: "One day, near Tempe, in the valley of the river Peneius, Eurydice met Aristaeus, who tried to force her. She trod on a serpent as she fled, and died of its bite" (Graves 112). Incidentally, this version is mentioned in Herman's discussion with Sol Mazzaroth about the projected adaptation of the myth for Sol's X-rated magazine *Classique* (50); but by that time we have already heard the first part of the story told by the head of Orpheus, where Aristaeus appears as a warner with qualities we have met in Lissener or Jesus, and are tempted to take the head's story for the "authentic" version. It is by juxtaposing various versions, however, that Hoban deconstructs notions such as "authenticity" and even that of the "myth" itself. The *bricoleur* does not try to pass off as an engineer.[7] What if the rotting head were really Aristaeus's and his story an

6 According to Graves, Orpheus is the "son of the Thracian King Oeagrus and the Muse Calliope.... Apollo presented him with a lyre, and the Muses taught him its use..." (111).

7 Barbara Herkommer is right to point out that the myth of Orpheus and Eurydice is being deconstructed rather than just varied as early as in *Kleinzeit*: "Wie Hoban die mythologische Geschichte von Orpheus und Eurydice in *Kleinzeit* gestaltet, kann schwerlich noch als 'Variation des Themas' aufgefasst werden, bei der nach Eliade 'Vorbildlichkeit und Allgemeingültigkeit' als 'wesentliche Dimensionen des Mythos' durchscheinen. Der Mythos wird eher umgekehrt und dekonstruiert" (107). One might also say, though, that notions of myth such as Eliade's betray the mentality of the engineer. In Graves's *The Greek Myths*, on the

attempt to clear his own name from guilt while bringing Orpheus's into disrepute? Would it matter? What remains unchanged in all the possible versions of the story are the splitting and the gathering, active and passive behaviour – the workings of complementary and antagonistic forces.[8] What changes is the names of those who carry out possible actions, but the action cycles must be completed at any rate by whomsoever once they have started to involve participants. The only way of changing matters is by switching to another paradigm.

This takes me to three further characters who have only been mentioned in passing, Istvan Fallok, Lars Nilsen and Sol Mazzaroth. At the time Herman gets the flyer from Istvan Fallok, the latter holds the part of Hermes, moving Herman Orff, who is paralyzed and resignedly waiting for page one of his third novel, to do something for his head. The name of his studio, "Hermes Soundways", is an unmistakeable hint. But his action inevitably causes a reaction – Melanie Falsepercy gets to know Herman and leaves Istvan, who thus turns into a male Eurydice, just as Herman will do when Melanie leaves him. Lars Nilsen, the computer engineer Luise von Himmelbett has married, seems to be her last man and the only exception in a series of lovers who were all unfaithful to her (88). He is no more than a name, that is, he does not appear in person. Thus, there is something of the "mysterious stranger" about him that also characterizes Aristaeus (47). For the time being, he is the man Luise moved in with, their daughter Ursel is almost one year old (92), but maybe, at the end of their second year, he will suddenly turn into another unfaithful Orpheus, provided that the story finds him and Luise as it found her and her lovers before. Sol Mazzaroth is the most difficult character of the trio. The fact that Melanie leaves Herman for Sol's sake might qualify him as a second personification of Aristaeus. But since Melanie is a negative Eurydice,

---

other hand, the ambiguity, instability and even contradictory nature of myths is clearly brought to the fore: although they reflect the desire for stability, performative alterations have always been part of their history (12).

8 Hélène Cixous sees in such oppositional pairs the source of the discontent of our culture: "In fact, every theory of culture, every theory of society, the whole conglomeration of symbolic systems – everything, that is, that's spoken ... – it is all ordered around hierarchical oppositions that come back to the man/woman opposition, an opposition that can only be sustained by means of a difference posed by cultural discourse as 'natural,' the difference between activity and passivity. ... A couple posed in opposition, in tension, in conflict ... a couple engaged in a kind of war in which death is always at work ... it's on the couple that we have to work if we are to deconstruct and transform culture. The couple as terrain, as space of cultural struggle, but also as terrain, as space demanding, insisting on, a complete transformation in the relation of one to the other. And so work still has to be done on the couple ... on the question, for example, of what a completely different couple relationship would be like, what a love that was more than merely a cover for, a veil of, war would be like" ("Castration or Decapitation", 44). What becomes clear in the novel, however, is that the problem is not the couple *per se* but the way in which they deal individually with the reality of death. Herman's (and probably also Melanie's) leaving the story of Orpheus and Eurydice behind shows that he no longer needs to locate mortality in the other; he learns to live with it.

he must be a negative Aristaeus, or another Hermes. The Orphic myth actually offers another option: he is *Helius* (Apollo), whose priest Orpheus became when he returned from Hades (Graves 112f.; see ch. 8.3). His attempt at moving Herman must fail, however, because Herman is not ready to play "OTHER PEOPLE'S ORPHEUS" any more (104). Having found his balance and a new direction at The Hague, Herman is no longer susceptible to Sol's impulses. Sol is therefore Melanie's not Herman's Hermes. But as I suggested earlier on, Sol, "the sun", might also signal Melanie's (hysterical) break with lovers whom she finds in basement studios (21) or crypts (63) and who remind her of her mortality.

Thus, everybody can indeed be everything; when the potsherds are connected, the names inscribed on them will become negligible because the only thing that counts is the vessel they form together to hold the juice of life. If it is broken or one potsherd missing the whole vessel will be affected, no matter which of the potsherds broke, or was lost, first. Hermes and Aristaeus organize the potsherds' horizontal movements and stases, toward and away from each other, whereas the Kraken and Persephone draw attention to the vertical dimension which distinguishes the upper side of each potsherd from its underside. Medusa – mortality, the Real – is the force which will ultimately swallow all of them, making the vessel implode into itself. But as long as she is speaking, she enriches all of them with a sense of the precariousness of their common undertaking. The vase they construct out of their fragmented identities is the world, after all.

8.3. Mythopsychomatics

In this chapter I will examine the links which can be established between the unhappy couple Orpheus and Eurydice and two other mythical figures which have given shape to Russell Hoban's literary texts: Medusa and Oedipus. It is not a coincidence that the same figures also populate psychoanalytic and feminist theories: these myths are, after all, paradigms of a patriarchal society's dealings with sexuality and mortality. The ways in which women and men are defined in them, for example, and then made to correlate with (the loss of) subjectivity and death are not open to free variation; the fate of those who do not conform to the pattern embraced by their society is usually very severe.

The existence of normative myths is a sign, however, that such patterns are by no means "natural". External and internal forces make people deviate from norms and conventions, however often these may have been advertised as paths to happiness. Desires which people striving to fit into society have been taught to repress find outlets from the imprisonment of the unconscious time and again: in dreams or when the body hysterically shows what must not be spoken. Moreover, the norms are subject both to historical change and to geographical variation: claims to the universality of certain patterns of psychic development and behaviour have always been controversial.[1] Although mass culture generally works to perpetuate certain patterns,[2] many writers actively contribute to bringing about change by contesting their validity in literary and/or theoretical texts. They work with and against these patterns, as does Russell Hoban. His dislocution of the myth of Orpheus and Eurydice has already been briefly addressed (see ch. 4.2); his use of the Medusa and the Oedipus myths is no less unorthodox. So as to be able to make differences visible in ch. 8.4, I shall here present a reading of the "traditional versions" of these two myths which points to their shared underlying assumptions.[3]

In a first step, I shall introduce certain psychoanalytic terms which are relevant for Hoban's work. They will form a conceptual framework both for the reading of the myths of Medusa and Oedipus and for the next chapter, in which the development of Hoban's ideas about men, women, and mortality will be traced and compared to the works of other writers. Since Freud's theories about the psyche were often moulded on and illustrated by Greek myths, most of the assumptions underlying the myths also underlie Freudian psychoanalytic terms, first and foremost of course those naming the processes and forces presumably at work in the Oedipus complex.[4] Rewritten myths,

---

1 See for example Gilles Deleuze and Félix Guattari's discussion of the debates over the universality of the Oedipus complex in *L'Anti-Œdipe* (1972): "C'est [Roheim] qui disait sans humour qu'on ne trouvait pas le complexe d'Œdipe si on ne le cherchait pas. Et qu'on ne le cherchait pas si l'on ne s'était pas fait soi-même analyser" (202).

2 See Teresa de Lauretis's study *Technologies of Gender* (1987).

3 My comparison of the two myths is mainly based on Robert Graves' *The Greek Myths. Combined Edition* (1992) and Karl Kerényi's *Die Mythologie der Griechen, Bd. 2: Die Heroen-Geschichten* (1966). Occasionally, I will take recourse to the classical sources themselves. My use of inverted commas while referring to "traditional versions" serves to acknowledge the fact that *the* one and only traditional version of a myth does not exist and never has, as Graves' and Kerényi's presentations indicate: the variants they discuss are often incompatible in regard to major issues and not only in minor details. Still, one of these versions, not necessarily the earliest one, has usually been given preference in being retold century after century; as far as possible I will base my discussion on this version.

4 Freud, though, always read the myths selectively. What he left out is quite interesting. In the essay "From Omphalos to Phallus" (1992), Elisabeth Bronfen points to a significant omission in Freud's reading of Sophocles's *Oedipus the King*: "... he [Freud] elides a significant moment – the death of Jocasta. (...) there is a dream articulated by Sophocles' play other than the one about our incestual desires for the mother and our patricidal hatred and murderous wishes directed against the father – namely a dream of matricide. For directly before Oedipus becomes appalled by his unwitting crimes, indeed just after he has found out he is the murderer of his father, his response is not attonement [sic] but rather the desire to commit another murder. With sword in hand he rushes into the bedroom of his mother/wife, hoping that by killing her he might discharge the guilt he is suddenly burdened with, and thus assert his potency against the curse of facticity which Jocasta brought upon him..." (147-148).

however, usually imply a critique of untenable assumptions, and for this reason, they often also reflect the post-Freudian development of psychoanalysis. Since this is a literary study, the discussion of psychoanalytic terms must remain limited. Footnotes will be used for long quotations and to refer to alternative interpretations and criticism from within the trade; moreover I shall also use them extensively as an open textual "preconscious" to present my own doubts, associations, heretic questions and speculative answers.[5]

The idea of a comparative reading of the myths of Medusa and of Oedipus sprang from Sigmund Freud's brief essay "Medusa's Head" (1940 [1922]). Freud tries to explain why representations of Medusa's head fill onlookers with terror. He argues that the terror is in fact a renewal of castration anxiety, the symptom of an unfinished or imperfectly repressed Oedipus complex:

> To decapitate = to castrate. The terror of Medusa is thus a terror of castration that is linked to the sight of something. Numerous analyses have made us familiar with the occasion for this: it occurs when a boy, who has hitherto been unwilling to believe the threat of castration, catches sight of the female genitals, probably those of an adult, surrounded by hair, and essentially those of his mother. (272)

Although the reference to the Oedipus complex is only implicit, the scene described here of a boy catching sight of his mother's "castrated" genitals and turning "stiff with terror" (272) is easily recognizable as the turning point in the central myth of Freudian psychoanalysis.[6] In Freud's essay "Femininity" (1932), we find a brief summary of what is meant by the Oedipus complex in the development of boys and girls respectively:

> In a boy the Oedipus complex, in which he desires his mother and would like to get rid of his father as being a rival, develops naturally from the phase of his phallic sexuality. The threat of castration compels him however to give up that attitude. Under the impression of the danger of losing his penis, the Oedipus complex is abandoned, repressed and, in the most normal cases entirely destroyed, and a severe super-ego is set up as its heir. What happens with a girl is almost the opposite. The castration complex prepares for the

5 Look at your feet (footnotes) and you will know more about who you are. Oedipus never wondered about the scars mutilating his feet although his very name ought to have directed his attention to this place; Perseus's feet, on the other hand, in fact his whole body, were made invisible by a trick, i.e. Hades's helmet of invisibility: invisibility protected him not only from the remaining Gorgon sisters' fury but also, and perhaps above all, from seeing himself in Athene's shield while slaying Medusa.

6 Freud writes in "Why War?", his address to Einstein: "It may perhaps seem to you as though our theories are a kind of mythology and, in the present case, not even an agreeable one. But does not every science come in the end to be a kind of mythology like this? Cannot the same be said today of your own Physics?" (quoted in Juliet Mitchell, "The Question of Femininity and the Theory of Psychoanalysis", 297). As Mitchell points out, Freud himself was very much aware of the fact that his theories were "Lines drawn to communicate what we know is only a blurred merging" (297).

> Oedipus complex instead of destroying it; the girl is driven out of her attachment to her mother through the influence of her envy for the penis and she enters the Oedipus situation as though into a haven of refuge. (357)

> The wish with which the girl turns to her father is no doubt originally the wish for the penis which her mother has refused her and which she now expects from her father. The feminine situation is only established, however, if the wish for a penis is replaced by one for a baby, if, that is, a baby takes the place of a penis in accordance with an ancient symbolic equivalence. (356)[7]

This is not the whole story, however, as he made clear in the earlier essays "Some Psychical Consequences of the Anatomical Distinction Between the Sexes" (1925) and "Female Sexuality" (1931):

> The matter is made more difficult to grasp by the complicating circumstance that even in boys the Oedipus complex has a double orientation, active and passive, in accordance with their bisexual constitution; a boy also wants to take his *mother's* place as the love-object of his *father* – a fact which we describe as the feminine attitude. ("Some Psychical Consequences...", 307)

> ... there can be no doubt that the bisexuality, which is present, as we believe, in the innate disposition of human beings, comes to the fore much more clearly in women than in men. A man, after all, has only one leading sexual zone, one sexual organ, whereas a woman has two: the vagina – the female organ proper – and the clitoris, which is analogous to the male organ. ("Female Sexuality", 325)

Despite certain similarities in their early psychic dispositions (bisexuality), the development of male and female subjects will take them onto different paths – paths, however, which are far from safe or stable. For according to Lacan, the construction of psychic sexual difference is more closely related to the precarious and divided condition of human subjectivity and to the acquisition of a cultural code than to physical difference. By pointing this out, Lacan defended

7 For critical discussions of Freud's theory of female sexuality see, for example, Juliet Mitchell, "The Question of Femininity and the Theory of Psychoanalysis" (1984), Michèle Montrelay, "Inquiry into Femininity" (1987 [1976]), or Sarah Kofman, "The Narcissistic Woman" (1987 [1980]). In *(Un)Like Subjects*(1993), Gerardine Meaney calls "Femininity" the key lecture in which Freud theorizes "the feminine in masculine terms": "In mapping feminine sexuality and development on to the Oedipal model Freud denies feminine difference and translates woman into not-man" (18). Jacques Lacan's elaboration of Freud's theory emphasizes that what is at stake in the Oedipus complex is not an anatomical difference; the phallus, around which everything turns, is neither an organ (penis/clitoris) nor another object nor a fantasy, as he writes in 1958: "... the phallus is a signifier" ("The Meaning of the Phallus", 79). Nevertheless, his derivations of subjectivity and sexuality were no less controversial than Freud's theories. Jacqueline Rose provides an introduction both to Lacan's shifting positions and also to the arguments of some of his critics in "Feminine Sexuality: Jacques Lacan and the *école freudienne*" (1986). The Oedipus complex and the structure of the unconscious derived from it has not only been criticized by feminist writers, however. There are also male philosophers and psychoanalysts who disagree with the notion of desire as lack: see for instance Deleuze and Guattari's concept of productive desiring-machines in *L'Anti-Œdipe* (1972).

Freud against those critics who, like Jones, insisted on the primacy of a pre-given natural or biological division to save women from Freud's "phallocentric view" (Rose 50f.).[8] The development includes finding love objects to replace the earliest ones which have to be given up and setting up the critical instance of the super-ego; these processes enable the subject to "find a place in the cultural community" (Freud, "Female Sexuality", 326). The most decisive event, however, though situated at different moments in the development of both sexes, is the experience of castration, the decapitation of Medusa. What subjects undergo during the castration complex is really the "splitting" in which "the subjectivity of the subject disappears ... the loss of oneself into one's own unconscious – into the gap" (Mitchell 307), a horror to both sexes. But since one "cannot experience absence, a gap", one "*uses* deprivation to describe the indescribable" (Mitchell 307). Mitchell continues, "The trauma captured in splitting is that one isn't there; the same trauma that castration comes to symbolize is that one is incomplete" (307).[9] It is precisely the conceptualization of splitting as deprivation which instigates romantic (i.e. complementary) notions of sexuality. But the two sexes do not need to regard

8 Montrelay's essay "Inquiry into Femininity" (based on the clinical research of J. Chasseguet-Smirgel et al. which was published in *Recherches psychanalytiques nouvelles sur la sexualité féminine*, 1964) shows that the two views are not absolutely incompatible; or more precisely, her thesis is that the incompatibility of phallocentrism and concentricity (Jones's notion of a feminine libido based on vaginal drives) is constitutive of the feminine unconscious (231). Lacan's claim can only be maintained if drives are considered wholly psychical, which he does, of course; see below. Yet, I am more inclined to consider the drives as intermediary between the body and the psyche, and since the body is sexed besides being distinguished by a number of other features which turn each body into a unique composite, I cannot uncritically adopt Lacan's point of view. Our bodies are dynamic places of exchange where the material and the symbolic interact, or fight for predominance. A Freudian footnote from "Das Unbehagen in der Kultur" (1930 [1929]) is interesting in this context; he writes: "Die Geschlechlichkeit ist eine biologische Tatsache, die, obwohl von ausserordentlicher Bedeutung für das Seelenleben, psychologisch schwer zu erfassen ist. Wir sind gewohnt zu sagen: jeder Mensch zeige sowohl männliche als weibliche Triebregungen, Bedürfnisse, Eigenschaften, aber den Charakter des Männlichen und Weiblichen kann zwar die Anatomie, aber nicht die Psychologie aufzeigen. Für sie verblasst der geschlechtliche Gegensatz zu dem von Aktivität und Passivität, wobei wir allzu unbedenklich die Aktivität mit der Männnlichkeit, die Passivität mit der Weiblichkeit zusammenfallen lassen, was sich in der Tierreihe keineswegs ausnahmslos bestätigt." (235, n. 2).

9 The complexity of this matter cannot be summarized without long digressions; to give the reader at least an idea of what is, and what is not, at stake, I will quote a further excerpt from Rose's essay: "In Lacan's account, the phallus stands for that moment of rupture. It refers mother and child to the dimension of the symbolic which is figured by the father's place. The mother is taken to desire the phallus not because she contains it (Klein), but precisely because she does not. The phallus therefore belongs somewhere else; it breaks the two-term relation and initiates the order of exchange. (...) But its status is in itself false, and must be recognised by the child as such. Castration means first of all this – that the child's desire for the mother does not refer *to* her but *beyond* her, to an object, the phallus, whose status is first imaginary (the object presumed to satisfy her desire) and then symbolic (recognition that desire cannot be satisfied). (...) When Lacan is reproached with phallocentrism at the level of his theory, what is most often missed is that the subject's entry into the symbolic order is equally an exposure of the value of the phallus itself. The subject has to recognise that there is desire, or lack in the place of the Other, that there is no ultimate certainty or truth, and that the status of the phallus is a fraud (this is, for Lacan, the meaning of castration)" (Rose 61-64).

each other as complementary; the dream of becoming whole again is in any case part of the assumption of sexual identity:

> The castration complex is not about women, nor men, but a danger, a horror to both – a gap that has to be filled in differently by each. In the fictional ideal type this will be for the boy by the illusion that a future regaining of phallic potency will replace his totality; for a girl this will be achieved by something psychically the same: a baby. Phallic potency and maternity – for men and women – come to stand for wholeness. (Mitchell 308)

As has already been suggested, however, sexual identity is precarious: fantasies of "Wholeness Regained" serve to appease, though they cannot satisfy, the desire which arises if something has to be given up. Whatever has been repressed might return to challenge the subject.[10]

Although it is *not* normally femininity that is repressed, ...[11]

> ... femininity *does* come to represent this point where meaning and consciousness vanish. Because this point is chaos, that which has been made to stand in for it – made to indicate the gap – is unbearable and will be repudiated. In the loss of balance, something to fill the gap will be hallucinated, a breast; produced as fetish, envied – a penis. The clinical experience of splitting and of castration is horror – penis-envy, hallucination, fetishism are quick relief. (Mitchell 306)[12]

---

10 "For Lacan, the unconscious undermines the subject from any position of certainty, from any relation of knowledge to his or her psychic processes and history, and *simultaneously* reveals the fictional nature of the sexual category to which every human subject is none the less assigned. In Lacan's account, sexual identity operates as a law – it is something enjoined on the subject. For him, the fact that individuals must line up according to an opposition (having or not having the phallus) makes that clear. But it is the constant difficulty, or even the impossibility, of that process which Lacan emphasised" (Rose 52). See above all Lacan's "A Love Letter (Une Lettre d'Âmour)" [sic] for the implications of this opposition. The idea of instability is already present in Freud's thinking about repression; he writes in the essay "Die Verdrängung" (1915): "Man darf sich den Verdrängungsvorgang nicht wie ein einmaliges Geschehen mit Dauererfolg vorstellen, etwa wie wenn man etwas Lebendes erschlagen hat, was von da an tot ist; sondern die Verdrängung erfordert einen anhaltenden Kraftaufwand, mit dessen Unterlassung ihr Erfolg in Frage gestellt wäre, so dass ein neuerlicher Verdrängungsakt notwendig würde" (112).

11 "Before Freud, many doctors and commentators thought that hysterics were women trying to escape or protest their female role; Freud toyed with the possibility that all that was feminine was repressed, the repressed feminine would thus have been the content of the unconscious itself. We are all familiar with how often women are thought to be more in touch with the unconscious, more intuitive, nearer the roots of nature ... Freud's answer was: no, 'we must keep psychoanalysis separate from biology'; repression must not be sexualised" (Mitchell 306).

12 Writing "repudiated" Mitchell seems to be using a term with clear implications in Lacan's theory, being a synonym of "foreclosed" (German "verworfen"); foreclosure (repudiation) is the term "... denoting a specific mechanism held to lie at the origin of the psychotic phenomenon and to consist in a primordial expulsion of a fundamental 'signifier' (e.g. the phallus as signifier of the castration complex) from the subject's symbolic universe. Foreclosure is deemed to be distinct from repression in two senses:

a. Foreclosed signifiers are not integrated into the subject's unconscious.

b. They do not return 'from the inside' – they re-emerge, rather, in 'the Real', particularly through the phenomenon of hallucination" (Laplanche and Pontalis 166). But Mitchell's examples of subjects hallucinating and producing fetishes, *or* developing penis envy show that she is using the verb "repudiated" in the broader, or more ambiguous, Freudian sense, in which it *can* mean "foreclosed" (in the case of fetishists and hallucinating subjects) but also "repressed" or consciously "condemned". A definition of repression will presently be provided.

A psychotic subject forecloses (ignores, expels the notion of) castration from its symbolic system. A hysteric, on the other hand, is thought to refuse the ordering of normal sexuality (Rose 51) because nothing can make up for castration:

> Hysteria was, and is – whatever the age or generational status of the man or woman who expresses it – the daughter's disease: a child's phantasy about her parents: the 'daughter' in the man or woman has not found a solution in homosexuality, maternity, or a career. To 'her' femininity really seems to equal the gap indicated by castration or, in Joan Rivière's words, it is enacted as 'a masquerade' to cover it. She is good at this but it cannot satisfy. (Mitchell 308)

Orpheus's fate perfectly illustrates the effects of hysteria. He is quite happy with the illusory compensations for his lost totality, that is, art and his wife Eurydice, tokens of his phallic (verbal and sexual) potency, until the encounter with Hades, his own future death, calls into question the whole fantasy structure of displacements and representations. Graves's account of Orpheus' career after his return from Hades suggests that Orpheus now entirely shirks the company of women and prefers Apollo to the gods of the underworld – a hysterical reaction:

> ... When Dionysus invaded Thrace, Orpheus neglected to honour him, but taught other sacred mysteries and preached the evil of sacrificial murder to the men of Thrace, who listened reverently. Every morning he would rise to greet the dawn on the summit of Mount Pangaeum, preaching that Helius, whom he named Apollo, was the greatest of all gods. In vexation, Dionysus set the Maenads upon him at Deium in Macedonia. First waiting until their husbands had entered Apollo's temple, where Orpheus served as priest, they seized the weapons stacked outside, burst in, murdered their husbands, and tore Orpheus limb from limb. (...) It is said that Orpheus had condemned the Maenads' promiscuity and preached homosexual love; Aphrodite was therefore no less angered than Dionysus. (Graves 112-113)

The refusal of both mortality and femininity does not silence Orpheus, for he immediately begins to use language again. Yet it is a hysterical language. He no longer sings to tame everything wild but to warn men against women and death, a reaction formation against the repressed knowledge of his own "femininity" and mortality.[13] Sadly, or ironically, depending on the

---

it *can* mean "foreclosed" (in the case of fetishists and hallucinating subjects) but also "repressed" or consciously "condemned". A definition of repression will presently be provided.

13 Kerényi writes: "Die Tat, die Orpheus allein vollbracht hat, war, dass er alles Wilde, sogar die wilden Mächte der Unterwelt, durch seinen Gesang bezwang und bis zu Persephone gelangte" (2: 220). His description underlines the similarity between Orpheus's singing and Freud's project as defined in "Das Ich und das Es" (1923): "Die Psychoanalyse ist ein Werkzeug, welches dem Ich die fortschreitende Eroberung des Es ermöglichen soll" (322). Lacan, too, noticed this analogy: "To resort to a metaphor, drawn from mythology, we have, in

perspective, both women and death strike back when the Maenads kill him. In Hoban's rewritings of the myth, Orpheus figures usually turn hysterical, too, after losing their Eurydices: they become blocked and dissatisfied with their careers and their love life. Making friends with death, however, usually opens up a new mode of being for them. They no longer use language to tame and conquer, or to warn, but to plumb their own experience.

The term "repression" has been used time and again as if it were clear what it meant. Since it is a highly speculative term, however, I will now specify what it means in my text before attempting a reading of the Medusa and the Oedipus myths. It is a key concept since it is through repression that sexuality and symbolization are organised and stabilised to a certain degree. Repression sets up a (transgressible) borderline between the conscious and the unconscious systems of the psyche: in other words, one might call it a (not altogether reliable) interface between unrestrained bodily drives and internalised cultural codes. Its definition has always been, and must remain, speculative, since the task consists in no less than providing the description of the interior of a black box that cannot be opened but must be watched from the outside; moreover hints about its functioning can only be gleaned from its failures, that is, when unconscious ideas find a way of escaping from the black box by becoming conscious (e.g. in remembered dreams, hallucinations, slips of the tongue, negation, etc.) or by manifesting themselves in bodily symptoms (conversion hysteria). In "Die Verdrängung" (1915), Freud distinguishes between primal repression (*Urverdrängung*) and repression proper (*eigentliche Verdrängung, Nachdrängen*):

> We have reason to assume that there is a *primal repression*, a first phase of repression, which consists in the psychical (ideational) representative of the instinct being denied entrance into the conscious. With this a *fixation* is established; the representative in question persists unaltered from then onwards and the instinct remains attached to it. (quoted in Laplanche and Pontalis 334)[14]

Laplanche and Pontalis admit that the translation of the Freudian *Trieb* by "instinct" is not the happiest choice but the one "generally accepted by English-speaking psycho-analytic authors" (214). In *The Four Fundamental Concepts of Psychoanalysis*, Jacques Lacan warns his students against translating *Trieb* by "instinct": "*Trieb* gives you a kick in the arse, my friends – quite different from so-called *instinct*" (49). His translator Alan Sheridan offers a more rational – or less performative – explanation: "Lacan reinstates a

Eurydice twice lost, the most potent image we can find of the relation between Orpheus the analyst and the unconscious" (*The Four Fundamental Concepts of Psycho-Analysis*, 25).

14 The German original can be found in Freud, "Die Verdrängung", p. 109.

distinction, already clear in Freud, between the wholly psychical *pulsion* (*Trieb*) and *instinct* (*Instinkt*), with its 'biological' connotations" (279). I have so far adopted the term "drive", too, and will persist in doing so to avoid confusion with *Instinkt*, i.e. "a hereditary behaviour pattern peculiar to an animal species" (Laplanche and Pontalis 214). I agree that drives are not hereditary behaviour patterns, in contrast to animal instincts; but where Lacan stresses the *wholly* psychical nature of the drive and underlines that – in contrast to the "instinct" – it has nothing to do with energy but with history and remembering (see *The Ethics of Psychoanalysis*, 209, 211-214), I would like to reinstate Freud's notion of drive as "Grenzbegriff zwischen Seelischem und Somatischem" ("Triebe und Triebschicksale", 85) – drive then means both an energetic link between body and psyche (the psyche being drives translated into desires), and the "beyond" of the speaking subject's symbolic universe.

Freud actually posits two distinct types of drives in "Jenseits des Lustprinzips" (e.g. 262), i.e. sexual and death drives. Is it not due to their dualism, that there is such a "thing" as the psyche, distinguished from the drives, or that human subjects have individual histories rather than to follow hereditary behaviour patterns? Since Lacan is only interested in the psychical end product, not in the interaction of the two types of drives, he replaces Freud's dualistic view by a synthesis; it is no surprise that in his view, a drive has "two sides": at one and the same time, it "makes present sexuality in the unconscious and represents, in its essence, death" (*The Four Fundamental Concepts of Psychoanalysis*, 199). I agree with Malcolm Bowie, however, that this is a simplification of the Freudian notion of the death drive: "Here [i.e. in the essay "Position de l'inconscient"] and in numerous other contexts Lacan simplifies Freud's *Todestrieb* ... by deeming that its action is merely immanent to the signifying chain. The subject comes into being 'barred' by the signifier and thereby injected with a sense of death" (162).

In "Die Verdrängung", Freud fails to explain how the drives find "their" ideational representatives, how they inscribe themselves into the psyche as desires ("Wünsche"); in "Triebe und Triebschicksale" (1915), however, he assumes that the bodily source of a drive will influence its psychical function: "Was die psychischen Leistungen der einzelnen Triebe voneinander unterscheidet, lässt sich auf die Verschiedenheit der Triebquellen zurückführen" (87). A trace of this bodily source is therefore likely to be found on every ideational representative attached to a drive, and it is to be presumed that this trace will also characterise the displaced descendants of the primally repressed, even those which find a way of becoming conscious.[15]

Laplanche and Pontalis go on:

> In this way a first unconscious nucleus is formed which acts as a pole of attraction for the elements due to be repressed.
>
> Repression proper (*eigentliche Verdrängung*) or 'after-pressure' (*Nachdrängen*) is therefore a dual process, in that it adds to this attraction a repulsion (*Abstossung*) operating from the direction of a higher agency. (393)

Since repression does not exist prior to the moment of rupture which splits the psyche into a conscious and an unconscious system ("Die Verdrängung", 108), the moment Freud will later name castration, it is clear that in his theory, the ideational representatives which fixate the drives (unconscious desires) must all be related to, virtually identical with, those properly repressed in the Oedipus complex. Deleuze and Guattari, however, reject this model. In their view, the Oedipus complex is but a reduction and distortion of the whole range of repressed desires. It accommodates a society which seeks to exert control over the manifold and not necessarily incestuous desires of its members:

> Le refoulement est tel que la répression devient désirée, cessant d'être consciente; et il induit un désir de conséquence, une image truquée de ce sur quoi il porte, qui lui donne une apparence d'indépendance. ... L'agent délégué du refoulement, ou plutôt délégué au refoulement, c'est la famille; l'image défigurée du refoulé, ce sont les pulsions incestueuses. Le complexe d'Œdipe, l'œdipianisation, est donc le fruit de la double opération. *C'est dans un même mouvement que la production sociale répressive se fait remplacer par la famille refoulante, et que celle-ci donne de la production désirante une image déplacée*

15 Where bodily drives in general are concerned, it is not difficult to figure out that the trace must be linked to the organ from which the drive springs. But what might be the trace of the death drive? (And I do not mean ideational representations of the desire for death now, but the trace or signature of the death drive left on the representations.) Dying after all affects all organs at once, it has no specific place in the body. Perhaps its trace can be derived from the way in which it affects us, that is, as dissolution, as splitting which continues until the aim of the death drive, the return to an inanimate state has been reached. Is then repression, i.e. the split which primarily separates all drives from their representatives and secondarily, the conscious from the unconscious system, a trace of the death drive? Do we not then, paradoxically, owe to the death drive the prolongation of life? For this must be concluded from the fact that repression filters and partly curbs the abreaction of drives to protect subjects from premature waste and exposure to danger. A similar idea is expressed by Freud in "Jenseits des Lustprinzips": "Wenn wir es als ausnahmslose Erfahrung annehmen dürfen, dass alles Lebende aus *inneren* Gründen stirbt, ins Anorganische zurückkehrt, so können wir nur sagen: *Das Ziel alles Lebens ist der Tod*... (...) ... Selbsterhaltungs-, Macht-, und Geltungstriebe ... sind Partialtriebe, dazu bestimmt, den eigenen Todesweg des Organismus zu sichern und andere Möglichkeiten der Rückkehr zum Anorganischen als die immanenten fernzuhalten... Dabei kommt das Paradoxe zustande, dass der lebende Organismus sich auf das energischeste gegen Einwirkungen (Gefahren) sträubt, die ihm dazu verhelfen könnten, sein Lebensziel auf kurzem Wege (durch Kurzschluss sozusagen) zu erreichen, aber dies Verhalten charakterisiert eben ein rein triebhaftes im Gegensatz zu einem intelligenten Streben" (248-249). (When I first typed this quotation, I made a significant "Freudian" mistake: instead of "Streben", I wrote "Sterben"; but this is what Freud's speculation actually boils down to.)

> *qui représente le refoulé comme pulsions familiales incestueuses.* ... Et l'on voit bien l'intérêt d'une telle opération du point de vue de la production sociale, qui ne pourrait conjurer autrement la puissance de révolte et de révolution du désir. En lui tendant le miroir déformant de l'inceste (hein, c'est ça que tu voulais?), on fait honte au désir, on le stupéfie, on le met dans une situation sans issue, on le persuade aisément de renoncer à 'soi-même' au nom des intérêts supérieurs de la civilisation ... (...) L'ensemble de la production désirante ne prend la figure oedipienne bien connue que dans la traduction familiale de son enregistrement, traduction-trahison. (*L'Anti-Œdipe*, 142-144)

Unlike Deleuze and Guattari, however, I am not primarily interested in a schizoid liberation of desire from the social control exerted through repression proper. What interests me is rather the way in which repression as repression of the Oedipus complex conditions subjects.

Let us now briefly return to the first sentence of the quotation from Freud's "Medusa's Head": "To decapitate = to castrate." Freud uses a very poor visual similarity between female genitals ("essentially those of his [the subject's] mother") and Medusa's head to explain the shortcut he takes by equating decapitation with castration. But it is worth examining more closely what actually happens *under* his equation sign. For his analogy could be called the basic formula of patriarchy, the formula according to which patriarchal subjects are conditioned: under the equation sign, it will now be plain, we will find a repressed conditional sentence, i.e. "if your unconscious is normed by the Oedipus complex". Everything an oedipal patriarchal culture has to say about subjecthood, masculinity, femininity, and mortality can be derived from the formula. If, on the other hand, the basic difference between mortality and sexuality is emphasized, i.e. "to decapitate = to kill ≠ to castrate", the Freudian formula will be recognized for what it is, namely a manoeuvre to scare men away from giving in to their drives, from *jouissance*,[16] especially from the

16 For Lacan, *jouissance* is "feminine" enjoyment of the body beyond the phallic economy of the psyche, a synonym of feminine sexuality and mortality. Where masculine or phallic sexuality turns around the notion of lack and desire inflicted through castration, *jouissance* is based on the excessive presence of the body. He writes in "God and the *Jouissance* of ~~The~~ Woman": "Ever since Rabelais we have known that the phallus, her man as she [woman] calls it, is not a matter of indifference to her. Only, and this is the whole issue, she has various ways of taking it on, this phallus, and of keeping it for herself. Her being not all in the phallic function does not mean that she is not in it at all. She is in it *not* not at all. She is right in it. But there is something more.

This something more, mind, be careful not to sound it out too fast. I can find no better way of putting it, because I am having to cut and go quickly.

There is a *jouissance*, since we are dealing with *jouissance*, a *jouissance* of the body which is, if the expression be allowed, *beyond the phallus*" (145).

While *jouissance* is the abreaction of drives indifferent to social conventions (i.e. outside the phallic function), genital orgasm is merely the socially acceptable temporary appeasement of the sexual drive, something Lacan calls "the *jouissance* of the idiot" in "A Love Letter (Une Lettre d'Âmour)" [sic] (152).

Let me repeat that for Lacan, sexuality, be it "phallic" or "feminine", is defined independent of biology; as Rose writes: "For Lacan, men and women are only ever in

desire for death, by linking it to what many of them have been taught to abhor more than the abstract idea of death, namely incest. It is, after all, the desire for their own death rather than the desire for incest and patricide that all subjects must repress in order to live. Once those different kinds of desire have been collapsed into one through the repression of the Oedipus complex, however, they can only return as one horrific image: Medusa's decapitated head. Freud's interpretation of the terror inflicted by Medusa's head need not be refuted altogether: it can indeed be a terror of castration (the punishment for unrestrained sexuality) but it is also, and perhaps above all, a terror of passivity, of vulnerability to bodily drives in general, and of death. The question must then be, however, why it is apparently so easy to collapse the incestuous desire for the mother and the desire for death.

Julia Kristeva's study *Powers of Horror: An Essay on Abjection* (1980), puts this link down to the twofold manner in which the maternal body is normally implicated in the child's development: as abject, that is the "*'object' of primal repression*" (12) and much later, as we have seen in Freud's notion of the Oedipus complex, as the object of secondary repression. Especially the former function is interesting here. Kristeva writes:

> The abject confronts us ... with our earliest attempts to release the hold of *maternal* entity even before ex-isting outside of her, thanks to the autonomy of language. It is a violent, clumsy breaking away, with the constant risk of falling back under the sway of a power as securing as it is stifling. The difficulty a mother has in acknowledging (or being acknowledged by) the symbolic realm ... is not such as to help the future subject leave the natural mansion. The child can serve its mother as token of her own authentication; there is, however, hardly any reason for her to serve as go-between for it to become autonomous and authentic in its turn. (13)

Without abjection the child cannot be born nor can it develop into a subject; abjection is a "*precondition of narcissism*", i.e. the phase preceding the Oedipus complex (Kristeva 12). In the abject, then, the child fixates its earliest potential source of death, but at the same time a source of bliss; it is therefore a fixation that is "permanently brittle" and stabilized only when "a third party, eventually the father, ... helps the future subject ... in pursuing a reluctant struggle against what, having been the mother, will turn into an abject" (Kristeva 13). Incest prohibition tries to hide the archaic mother completely

language ... All speaking beings must line themselves up on one side or the other of this division, but anyone can cross over and inscribe themselves on the opposite side from that to which they are anatomically destined" (73). But if the drives are, as Lacan claims, wholly psychical, why is their enjoyment feminine? And why persist in calling the central signifier of the Symbolic the phallus if it was only for historical reasons, by reference to patriarchal modes of thinking, that it had to be called this way? A contradiction manifests itself: in fact it is built into every attempt to argue, within a system, against its own terms.

under the "castrated" oedipal one and to eliminate every trace of her (i.e. to decapitate her) by assigning her a representative which signifies a forbidden sexual object. Poetic language, on the other hand, "would be an attempt to symbolize the 'beginning'", to achieve a reconciliation with the abject (Kristeva 61). It requires a liberation of the archaic mother, the representative of primally repressed partial drives, from the clutches of the oedipal one, an affirmation of the body, of the sound material and the visual signs through which language speaks. But this is only a first step towards change. The second step consists in developing a notion of death that is not confined to the unconscious or displaced onto another, a conscious notion, in short, which lifts all responsibility from the mother. Her seeming power to kill will then turn out to have always been the subject's own disfigured desire for death. We are back to what Lacan has called "symbolic castration": accepting it corresponds to an affirmation of life that comes from a recognition of the abyss in oneself;[17] in Kristeva's terms this is equivalent to an "abjection of self":

> There is nothing like the abjection of self to show that all abjection is in fact recognition of the *want* [*manque*] on which any being, meaning, language, or desire is founded. One always passes too quickly over this word, 'want,' and today psychoanalysts are finally taking into account only its more or less fetishized product, the 'object of want.' But if one imagines (and imagine one must, for it is the working of imagination whose foundations are being laid here) the experience of *want* itself as logically preliminary to being and object – to the being of the object – then one understands that abjection, and even more so abjection of self, is its only signified. (Kristeva 5)

Moreover, naming the abject means to sublimate it: "In the symptom, the abject permeates me, I become abject. Through sublimation, I keep it under control" (Kristeva 11). In this kind of sublimation, the death drive is turned against itself by an ego still replete with libidinal energy and unwilling to give itself up.[18]

Russell Hoban's fiction is a continued effort to break free from the oedipal formula. When the protagonist of *Pilgermann* says, "What was I before I was castrated? I was already castrated, was I not, by mortality? All of us are castrated by mortality, we are unmanned, unwomanned, we are made

---

17 We are also back to the idea of Medusa, back to the "mothercode" broadcast on the "Medusa frequency", cf. ch. 8.2.

18 Normally, it is the sexual drive that is held in check by the death drive: sublimation then means that object libido sent out from the id is desexualised and turned into narcissistic libido, energy by which the ego maintains its functions such as thinking or mediating between inside and outside; see Freud's essay "Das Ich und das Es" (1923), esp. pp. 298, 312, and 321-324. An essay concerned with the management of drives and the relation between *jouissance*, pleasure and sublimation is of course "Das Unbehagen in der Kultur" (1930 [1929]).

nothing..." (PG 200), this is not a confirmation of the pattern, although the word castration is reminiscent of it, for Hoban actually posits two different kinds of castration, one literal, the other curbing phantasies of immortality. And when, in *The Medusa Frequency*, Medusa's face is one of the faces of death, her femininity and beauty may entail Herman Orff's desire for her, but she cannot be appropriated and killed, as will be shown in more detail in the next chapter. What is to be observed in Hoban's fiction is above all his characters' attempt to learn to express the knowledge of death without evasions that require the death of an other.

The Greek myths, on the other hand, provide images to flesh out the oedipal formula. The processes at work in the repression and destruction of the Oedipus complex are illustrated by the myth of Perseus and Medusa. In other words, this myth is a success story in regard to the development of the patriarchal subject or hero (the romance of Perseus) whereas the Oedipus myth is a story of failure (the tragedy of Oedipus).[19] The myth of Orpheus and Eurydice holds a position in between: after a first phase of success, there follows a second phase of failure and a third one of hysterical compromise leading to an eruption of violence and death; it then illustrates, as I argued earlier, the instability of repression which Freud discussed in "Die Verdrängung" (112; also see note 10 above). But I will now turn to a closer examination of the two other myths, especially of what they have to say about the conditions of success or failure.

The events that lead up to the murder of Medusa precede those of the Oedipus story; all the same they are close enough "historically" to be described in terms of genealogical links. As Gerardine Meaney points out in *(Un)Like Subjects* (1993): "In relation to the Oedipal tangle, Medusa is great-grandmother of the Sphinx" (31).[20] If Medusa's head had not been cut off, Chrysaor, the warrior and grandfather of the Sphinx had not sprung from her neck; that is, the second part of Oedipus's story, his marriage with Iocaste, could not have taken place, for he becomes king as a reward for saving Thebes from the Sphinx.[21] The two stories are not only causally linked, however,

19 Also see Teresa de Lauretis's illuminating discussion of these two myths in ch. 5 of *Alice Doesn't* (103-157).

20 "Chrysaor sprang from the neck of Medusa. He and Callirrhoe were the parents of Echidna, who was half-nymph and half-snake. Echidna and Orthus gave birth to the Sphinx", thus Meaney, whose source is Hesiod (226, n.14). In Graves's description, the Sphinx's parents cannot be identified unequivocally; Echidne and Orthus belong to different couples: "This monster was a daughter of Typhon and Echidne or, some say, of the dog Orthrus [sic] and the Chimaera, and had flown to Thebes from the uttermost part of Ethiopia" (372). Kerényi, however, adopts Hesiod's version, too (2: 83).

21 Of course one could also interpret the connection otherwise: the Sphinx is Medusa's revenge; Oedipus *must* appropriate the Sphinx's ability to ask questions because this is the only means by which the apparent hero can be made aware of his fallibility. Being told by Teiresias that he is the source of all evil triggers an aggressive reaction since heroes are normally the

their plots also show a remarkable number of similarities on the level of structure and content. It is of course precisely where difference separates them, at significant turning points, that the conditions for the outcome of each development can be located. To bring this out the two myths will be read "synchronously" (as far as syntax and analysis allow).

The birth of both protagonists is a problem for one of their male ancestors: Perseus's grandfather Acrisius, the king of Argos, is told by the Delphic Oracle that he will be murdered by a grandson. In the Oedipus myth, Laius, the king of Thebes, is warned by the Delphic Oracle, too, but he must fear murder by a son. In contrast to Acrisius, Laius is also told to prevent the birth of the future agent of his death: he is to subject his sexuality to the divine law. Both kings therefore take measures: Acrisius imprisons his daughter Danaë in a dungeon – a premature burial by which he transgresses the divine law – while obedient Laius puts "Iocaste away, though without offering any reason for his decision" (Graves 371), thereby offending her femininity.

Danaë is impregnated by Zeus himself, as if the god wanted to curb Acrisius's presumptuous aspiration to immortality. When Perseus is born, Acrisius, "not daring to kill his own daughter" (Graves 238), exiles both Danaë and her son. Locked in a wooden ark, they are washed ashore on the island of Seriphos. The fisherman Dictys immediately takes them to his brother, King Polydectes. Iocaste, on the other hand, is left alone with her problem. So she eventually takes revenge on her husband: having made him drunk, she seduces him, and nine months later gives birth to Oedipus. Laius removes at once what is not, now, a token of his potency, but one of his weakness. After baby Oedipus's feet have been pierced, he is exposed on Mount Cithaeron. Only now does his fortune change, for a shepherd finds him and takes him to the Corinthian court. Oedipus is brought up by the royal couple, Polybus and Periboea.[22]

The next decisive step in both myths takes place when the two protagonists have grown up. Perseus undergoes what might be termed, anachronistically in this case, the Oedipus complex: he tries to protect his

---

ones who hold up mirrors to other people; they are not used to being themselves objects of unfavourable representations. Oedipus must therefore be conned into looking at himself in his own mirror. The first time this happens is when he answers the Sphinx's question: "What being, with only one voice, has sometimes two feet, sometimes three, sometimes four, and is weakest when it has the most?" (Graves 372). He is not aware, of course, how much the answer to the riddle refers to him *personally*.

22 It is crucial to see that this mutilation cannot be interpreted as a displaced premature (threat of) "castration", because the real "punishment" takes place *before* the "crime" (patricidal and incestuous desire); it therefore remains utterly meaningless: meanings can only be generated retroactively. Instead of being the moment of the instalment of the super-ego, or of the inscription of the paternal metaphor, i.e. the moment when the subject enters the symbolic space in which the law, chronology and causality matter, baby Oedipus's experience is a purely contingent trauma. He suffers for "nothing". If anyone is "castrated" at this stage, it is Iocaste.

mother from Polydectes's sexual assaults. When Polydectes pretends to prepare the wedding with another woman, Perseus "rashly" offers to provide whatever gift Polydectes might name, "'Even the Gorgon Medusa's head, if need be.'" (Graves 238). Polydectes of course accepts this proposal, for his main purpose is to get rid of the dangerous young man. Perseus embarks on a journey which externalizes the processes at work in the formation of his unconscious: killing a monstrously disfigured representative of the archaic mother, he will also lose the desire for Danaë, or rather, his sexual desire will become detached from the maternal body and ready to be displaced onto another woman; all his fixated drives (not only the death drive) are now linearised under the oedipal flag. In so far as Perseus fails to attack his rival Polydectes, the representative of the law, he represses his desire for Danaë; in so far as he offers to kill Medusa instead, he commits a displaced matricide. One could conclude then that the pattern of success must involve a displaced matricide to prevent the satisfaction of incestuous desire: that is, to decapitate the archaic mother = to castrate the oedipal mother and oneself.[23] At the same time, of course, this process allows the empirical woman who happened to occupy the mother's place to continue her life, and the son's passive desire for death is converted into the active power to kill. But the main point is that the subject is unaware of all these implications: Perseus must not know that Polydectes means to deceive him or that his journey will effect the separation from his mother which it ought to have prevented.

Oedipus, on the other hand, learns from the Delphic Oracle what the future has in store for him: "'You will kill your father and marry your mother!'" (Graves 371). He has already been in terrible pain for "nothing", as his name Oedipus, that is "swell-foot", underlines (Graves 372).[24] Can it be that a faint memory of that early pain now informs and aggrandises the pain he imagines he would feel if he indeed committed the crimes of which the oracle believes him capable? His horror at this prospect can at any rate be seen as a sign that the prophecy has struck a chord in him: he must have recognized his desire. Ignorant that he is an adopted child, he refers the prophecy to Polybus

23 Bronfen's assumption of a dream of matricide being part of the oedipal trajectory, see above, note 4, is indirectly confirmed by the myth of Medusa.

24 As has already been pointed out, Oedipus never enquires into the origin of his name, nor does he try to find out what happened to his feet – before it is too late. Graves suggests in a commentary that his name might originally have been *Oedipais*, i.e. "son of the swelling sea" and that "the piercing of Oedipus's feet with a nail belongs to the end, not to the beginning, of his story" (375). But it is more in accordance with the logic of the myth that he be blind to the very signs that define him. He learns too much *about* himself, but not, until he has committed the crimes, who "he" is. Actually, the Apollonian principle that one should know oneself (written on a wall of the entrance hall to the Delphic Oracle, see Kerényi 2: 83) isn't easy to apply. Apollo himself only adopted it after he had been disciplined by Zeus for trying to depose him (Graves 79). Since most enquiries are made only when one's self-image has been shattered, self-knowledge is usually bound up with the past and lags behind, in true oedipal fashion.

and Periboea and therefore decides against returning to Corinth. Paradoxically, then, Oedipus tries to run away from the experience of the complex eventually named after him. Yet, as is well-known, striving for innocence is precisely what will make him guilty: on the narrow way to Thebes, he kills Laius, whose car has bruised his foot,[25] solves the riddle of the Sphinx, and ends up marrying Iocaste.

Heretic questions come to mind in regard to Perseus: Would he have returned to Seriphos if anyone had told him that he initially tried to protect Danaë for oedipal reasons, that is, so that no other man could come between her and himself? Would he have left if he had been told that by killing Medusa he really killed a representative of the archaic mother in himself? How would he react to Gerardine Meaney's warning that his quest "is an evasion of the conflict with the mother" (27)? Joseph Campbell even argues that Medusa cannot really be killed; he writes in *The Masks of God: Occidental Mythology* (1974): "The 'Great Mother' 'is there to be dealt with all the time and the more sternly she is cut down, the more frightening will her Gorgoneum be'..." (quoted in Meaney, 27). Nobody tells Perseus the plain truth, though. Instead Athene, the virgin goddess who gets pleasure from "upholding the law by pacific means" (Graves 96), and Hermes, "the masculine source of life", support his project of murdering Medusa.[26]

According to Graves, the goddess Athene is in fact a mutilated or unsexed version of the Triple-goddess:

> Athene had been the Triple-goddess, and when the central person, the Goddess as Nymph, was suppressed and myths relating to her transferred to Aphrodite, Oreithyia ..., or Alcippe ..., there remained the Maiden clad in goat-skins, who specialized in war ..., and the Crone, who inspired oracles and presided over all the arts. (99)

Unlike Ares, Athene does not enjoy war but takes up arms only to pacify contending parties (Graves 96). But she reacts aggressively against sexually

25 This is a detail to be found in both Graves (372) and Kerényi (2: 81); the latter names as his source Euripides's *Phoenissae*. The renewal of pain in this place activates Oedipus's trauma, triggering a reaction called "acting out" in psychoanalysis. Freud writes in "Erinnern, Wiederholen und Durcharbeiten" (1914): "... der Analysierte wiederholt, anstatt zu erinnern, er wiederholt unter den Bedingungen des Widerstandes; wir dürfen jetzt fragen, was wiederholt oder agiert er eigentlich? Die Antwort lautet, er wiederholt alles, was sich aus den Quellen seines Verdrängten bereits in seinem offenkundigen Wesen durchgesetzt hat, seine Hemmungen und unbrauchbaren Einstellungen, seine pathologischen Charakterzüge." (211) Oedipus kills his father because the renewal of pain in his foot makes him repeat the rage he must have felt as a baby when he was crippled and exposed but unable to react effectively.

26 See the subtitle of Kerényi's study: *Hermes: Guide of Souls. The Mythologem of the Masculine Source of Life* (1944). Hermes's function will be explored in greater detail in ch. 11.3. Actually the assistance of Athene and Hermes could be interpreted as an allegory for the way in which repression borrows its strength from law and language, and *vice versa*.

active women. Medusa was made ugly by Athene as a punishment for making love to Poseidon in Athene's temple (Graves 127). The ugliness with which she punished the trespasser is the ugliness of her own suppressed femininity. When she assists Perseus in murdering Medusa, she repeats the elimination of what was once a part of herself. Neither goddesses at the service of patriarchy nor mothers can be allowed to be seductive and (sexually) active since the patriarchal system derives its stability (i.e. the stability of language, mental sanity, and political organization) from the control over femininity, and especially over the maternal body.

Perseus's initiation to the looks and dangers of the Graeae and the Gorgons, the instruction never to look straight at Medusa but only at her distorted reflection in Athene's shield, the complicated preparations that must be made in order to gather the sickle, the magic wallet, Hades's dark helmet of invisibility as well as the winged sandals, and the zigzag journey to the edges of the world as it was known then, are a manoeuvre to divert Perseus's attention from what he is really doing while believing in a rescue action for his mother.[27] The success of a subject's development indeed depends on its degree of delusion, or its lack of awareness of the true implications of its acts. Slavoj Zizek borrows Jon Elster's term "states that are essentially by-products" to explain the paradoxical laws governing success and failure:

> The subject engages in a certain activity with the purpose of achieving a well-defined goal; in this he fails since the final result of his actions is a different totally unintended state of things that, however, would not have been brought about had the subject aimed directly at it. The final result could be brought about only as a by-product of an activity aimed at another goal. (Zizek 77)

Oedipus's story confirms this insight: his conscious escape from the desire for patricide and incest results in the accomplishment of both. Although it is only Iocaste who can be represented in his unconscious (as archaic mother), her representative wields power over him in the form of a doubt about his parentage. The myth suggests that the truth of the split between the abject (Iocaste) and the object of secondary repression (Periboea) can make itself felt,

27 The displacements, condensations and substitutions of the dream-work carried out by the unconscious come to mind, cf. Sigmund Freud, *Die Traumdeutung* (1900), 280ff. Poor Oedipus unfortunately has to listen to the naked truth – the Delphic Oracle, which remains the voice of Mother Earth even after the oracle's usurpation by Apollo (Graves 76ff.), is the unfiltered voice of the Real: is it Medusa's voice? Is her voice immortal while the power of her gaze can be appropriated? For this is Gerardine Meaney's interpretation of the murder of Medusa: killing her means becoming the subject of the gaze and of representation: "The denial and appropriation of Medusa's power are done with mirrors ... Control of her image, her reflection in his shield, allows Perseus to appropriate Medusa's power. The live Medusa killed by ***seeing***: the Medusa's head kills when ***seen***. She loses the power of the gaze: Perseus seizes the power of representation" (32). Also see ch. 8.2.

that it is stronger even than his foster parents' denial of the truth (Kerényi 2: 81). The image used is that Oedipus does not resemble his "supposed parents", for which he is "taunted by a Corinthian youth" (Graves 371). But when Oedipus visits the Delphic Oracle to learn the truth and is merely made aware of his desire, the safety system provided by the unconscious can no longer work. Oedipus's conscious inscription of Periboea and Polybus in the places where Iocaste and Laius should be, overrules every shadow of a doubt. His true mother is foreclosed from his symbolic system. Although her representative cannot disappear, it loses meaning, it can no longer be verbalized or associated with other representatives, e.g. with the law; the drives nevertheless remain attached to it, as they remain attached to the trace of a traumatic event until a similar situation, perceived as a repetition, brings about abreaction. Without a proper repression, his desire for patricide and incest cannot be filtered and displaced by the unconscious: when he therefore meets his parents in reality, there is nothing to prevent him from gratifying it. Oedipus, as must be stressed, is not simply a lawless psychotic; he is, on the contrary, a most law-abiding subject. But it is the wrong law he obeys, a second law which cannot undo the first inscription of the drives in his psyche. One could also say that an uncastrated archaic Oedipus lies dormant in the perfectly submissive second one.

Whereas, according to the myths, the identity of the maternal body as abject and as object of repression proper is sufficient to guarantee stability, the father's contribution to success is different. The father is above all the medium of the divine, patriarchal law: he subjects his wife and his children according to the law to which he is himself subjected. The position of "father" need not always be held by the same man provided that the law is always established over the same maternal body. In the Perseus myth his position is held by four male figures: Acrisius watches over his daughter like a jealous husband who fears that her children might replace him in her favour; Zeus the god-head, however, sires Perseus for the sake of the law of paternity, which must triumph over the possessiveness of fathers and husbands; Polydectes represents the castrating father who pronounces an incest prohibition by claiming Danaë for himself; and Dictys, finally is the respectable companion of Danaë when Perseus returns to Seriphos with Andromeda. Returning with a wife proves more than anything else that Perseus has lost interest in the mother. His paternal opponents therefore need no longer fear him; at the same time, however, they lose part of their power over him since the threat of castration, their only means of keeping him down, has lost its force. He is now their equivalent before the law. At this moment, the "father" dies, even though the man and paternity as a principle (or as god: Zeus) continue to live. In this case one might of course ask why Polydectes and Acrisius have to die. The myth provides answers which show that they do not die as hostile "fathers". By the time Perseus comes back to Seriphos, Dictys has taken over the role of Danaë's protector – they are men on equal terms. Polydectes, however, is killed because he is a corrupt and violent king who continues to treat Perseus as an inferior. Acrisius, finally, once more tries to escape his fate, mortality. But, like Oedipus, he induces his downfall precisely by running away. Perseus inadvertently kills him during funeral games for a neighbouring king in whose realm Acrisius lives in exile. In order to be a perfect subject, the hero Perseus must not remain flawless; significantly it is "by the wind and and the will of the Gods" that his discus is carried out of its path (Graves 241). Perseus accepts responsibility: "Greatly grieved, Perseus buried his grandfather in the temple of Athene ... and then, being ashamed to reign in Argos, went to Tiryns ..." (241).

In the last phase of his myth, Oedipus too finds out the truth about his life. Thebes was haunted by a plague until the murderer of Laius was found. But there are various versions of how the recognition of his deeds affects his life.[28] While Homer briefly hints at a battle in which Oedipus loses his life (*Iliad* xxiii.679-680), Sophocles four centuries later tells the story of Oedipus's going into exile at Colonus after he has blinded himself. Both only agree that Iocaste commits suicide after the truth has been discovered; for Homer, her act demonstrates disloyalty to Oedipus, who is left behind to suffer alone for the crime committed by both of them (*Odyssey* xi.278-280). In the tragedy *Phoenician Women* by Sophocles's contemporary Euripides, however, Iocaste does not commit suicide before her two sons by Oedipus have killed each other on the battlefield; blind Oedipus, who has been incarcerated for many years, leaves Thebes when his sons and Iocaste are dead (Kerényi 2:86-87). Psychoanalytic interpretations prefer the Sophoclean version because its emphasis on the horror caused by the discovery of the crimes and on Oedipus's self-blinding allows interpreters to draw an analogy between Oedipus's self-punishment and castration.[29] Graves, though, rejects this interpretation:

> ... though the blindness of Achilles's tutor Phoenix ... was said by Greek grammarians to be a euphemism for impotence, primitive myth is always downright, and the castration of Uranus and Attis continued to be recorded

---

28 Kerényi rightly points to the multitude of interpretations to which this story is susceptible: "Man versuchte der alten Geschichte immer neue Wendungen zu geben" (2: 86).
29 See especially Freud, *Die Traumdeutung*, 265-268 and 389, n. 1; or Kristeva, *Powers of Horror*, 84.

> unblushingly in Classical textbooks. Oedipus's blinding, therefore, reads like a theatrical invention, rather than original myth. (376)

Although I agree with Graves that Oedipus's self-mutilation should *at first* be read literally, I think that the self-blinding is more than a theatrical invention. It follows the logic of failure we have seen at work so far. It is the last "error" committed by the archaic, drive-ridden Oedipus who must always act out his desire – here, the desire not to face the consequences of his deeds –, and it is an error, because blinding himself he cannot undo what he has already seen. He acts like a naughty child who covers his eyes thinking that he can thus make himself and the damage done invisible. He should have remained blind to the truth while he was at the Corinthian court.

By leaving Thebes and becoming a stranger again he signals his willingness to submit to the law: having failed in regard to his sexuality, he at last finds the right attitude towards his mortality. Now, in exile and in regard to his future, his self-inflicted wound can indeed become a sign of his submission. For he has excluded himself for good from the position of power and knowledge gained by seeing. Eventually, though, he also finds out that "in the law's eye", he was innocent in the past because he did not see enough after he had been shown too much about himself by the Delphic Oracle: "I slew who else would me have slain; / I slew without intent, / A wretch, but innocent / In the law's eye, I stand, without a stain" (*Oedipus at Colonus*, ll. 545-548). His mutilation is the sign by which Theseus recognizes him (ll. 551ff.). Identifying with Oedipus, whose youth was similar to his own, though more "ill-starred" (l. 560), Theseus invites him to become a citizen of Athens: "... no alien in adversity / Shall seek in vain my succour, nor shalt thou; / I know myself a mortal, and my share / In what the morrow brings no more than thine" (ll. 565-568). A symbolic bond replaces hereditary ones – a transformation which also affects a subject's personal liability. Julia Kristeva interprets the ending of *Oedipus at Colonus* as a change in the fate of abjection:

> ... it is no longer defilement to be excluded ritually as the other facet of the sacred (social, cultural, one's own) but *transgression* due to a *misreading* of the Law. (...) Incompleteness and dependency on the Other, far from clearing a desiring and murderous Oedipus, allow him only to make his dramatic splitting transmittable – transmittable to a foreign hero, and hence opening up the undecidable possibility of a few truth-effects. Our eyes can remain open provided we recognize ourselves as always already altered by the symbolic – by language. Provided we hear in language – and not in the other, nor in the other sex – the gouged-out eye, the wound, the basic incompleteness that conditions the indefinite quest of signifying concatenations. (*Powers of Horror*, 88-89)

If I earlier classified the two myths in terms of success and failure, these evaluations now have to be examined again. Does Perseus not deprive himself of a unique experience by failing to look at Medusa directly while she is asleep and therefore harmless (since she cannot see him)? Moreover, is there no other option than to cut off her head? Would there be a way of collaborating with her on behalf of his mother? Perseus does not even consider such alternatives: he lacks curiosity as well as imagination.[30] Heeding nothing but Athene's advice, who has made Medusa ugly in the first place, and finally giving her Medusa's head, Perseus unquestioningly subordinates his feelings to reason, his drives to language. He is taught to believe in the illusion that he can master everything. Under these circumstances the knowledge of the power of drives he could gain (by looking at Medusa) is deflected into the vulgar power to kill others (by his appropriation of Medusa's power), a transformation which will also colour his sexuality: he will kill a sea-monster, a rival, and his inlaws in order to conquer Andromeda; the fact that his sexual drive has previously conquered him – "he caught sight of a naked woman chained to a sea-cliff, and instantly fell in love with her" (Graves 240) – is obliterated by the subsequent excess of "heroic" deeds. Perseus can now conceive of himself as the subject of love because Andromeda embodies the perfect object. There is then another loser, a well-known one, in the scenario of apparent success. In patriarchal mythology, women are adored for their statuesque beauty, the outward sign of their submission to the roles they have been assigned: Zeus himself ravished Danaë while she was imprisoned in a tomblike room. As mothers they are briefly lifted to the rank of an indispensable medium of procreation, but this entitles them to no subjectivity: they cannot choose to be mothers, their bodies are not theirs.

On the other hand, there can be success in failure. Oedipus, for instance, protects those who have saved his life, while he takes revenge on those who tried to harm him: his psychic make-up dictates a logic of its own which fails to respect biological links. Moreover, incestuous though his marriage to his mother might have been, it produced offspring within short time. By contrast Iocaste's marriage to Laius had remained barren for a long time, which raises questions about their relationship. But of course, it is only for the gods to pass an ultimate judgment on the actions of mortals. Human judgment, on the other hand, must not be made prematurely, as the endings of Sophocles's

30 It is Medusa who gives birth to Pegasus, the personification of the imagination, through her neck: Perseus is surprised but does not want to "antagonize" him or his brother Chrysaor (Graves 239).

Oedipus the King and *Oedipus at Colonus* underline: "Therefore wait to see life's ending ere thou count one mortal blest; / Wait till free from pain and sorrow he has gained his final rest" (*Oedipus the King*, ll. 1529-1530). "Wail no more, let sorrow rest, / All is ordered for the best" (*Oedipus at Colonus*, ll. 1778-1779).

Although we try to come to terms with our drives (i.e. the Real of desire) and other intrusions of the Real by means of myths, religious rites and legislation, however, we are nevertheless exposed to the possibility that the Real will seek us out to confront us with new phenomena which have no place in existing orders yet. Language and the unconscious can therefore support and protect us only to a certain degree. The patriarchal myths suggest, of course, that Zeus is always in control: "All is ordered for the best". Those who are obedient to his laws and submit to his judgment will fare best in the long run: the extreme cases of a patriarchal subject's fate are delineated in the myths of Perseus and Oedipus.[31] Nowadays, however, it is not only women who find it

31 The two myths examined leave no doubt about the supremacy of Zeus in matters of life and death. What is interesting, however, is the ambiguity opened up by Graves's account of Zeus's relationship with the three Fates: "Zeus, who weighs the lives of men and informs the Fates of his decisions can, it is said, change his mind and intervene to save whom he pleases, when the thread of life, spun on Clotho's spindle, and measured by the rod of Lachesis, is about to be snipped by Atropos's shears. Indeed, men claim that they themselves can, to some degree, control their own fates by avoiding unnecessary dangers. The younger gods, therefore, laugh at the Fates, ... (...) Others hold, on the contrary, that Zeus himself is subject to the Fates, as the Pythian priestess once confessed in an oracle; because they are not his children, but parthenogenous daughters of the Great Goddess Necessity, against whom not even the gods contend, and who is called 'The Strong Fate'" (48). What is revealed by the struggle over supremacy between matriarchal and patriarchal divinities, is the anxiously repressed knowledge that we might never be given a conclusive answer to the question what our lives and deaths are really for, who we are, and what rules we should follow, while the feeling that a divine energy of some kind inhabits and unites the world despite its variability can nevertheless not simply be abandoned.

Psychoanalysts have displaced this struggle from the metaphysical realm to the psyche, rejecting the metaphysical altogether or else appropriating it: Freud repeatedly demonstrates his atheism when interpreting the myth of Oedipus (cf. *Die Traumdeutung*, 266-268) or calling religion a mass delusion ("Massenwahn") springing from an infantile desire for paternal protection (cf. "Das Unbehagen in der Kultur", 206 and 213). The metaphysical is a dimension which simply does not exist for him. Lacan, on the other hand, coquettishly inserts God when he is discussing feminine *jouissance* (e.g. in "God and the *Jouissance* of ~~The~~ Woman", passim, and "A Love Letter", 153-154).

Lacking scientific evidence I cannot *prove* that they are wrong (but actually they cannot prove that they are right either), which is why my subsequent arguments must remain confined to the playground context of a footnote. First of all, I think that the metaphysical cannot and should not simply be ruled out as a dimension of our being; it is presumptuous to take one's own notion of the world (Freud's atheism) as the only valid view. Remaining open to the possibility that there is more to life than what a materialist would admit, turns reality into an open rather than a closed and anthropocentric system. Lacan's "psychotheology", on the other hand, is at best ironical, but it is also an expression of the limitations of his notion of the drive. Lacan simply equates mystical experience with *jouissance*, i.e. the "enjoyment" of the drive, because the former shares with the latter the contingency of its occurrences and the failure of the linguistic function. But I think that what was once personified and called God, may be contingent in its manifestations but nevertheless different from a mere message from our body. Lacan, of course, cannot make this distinction because in his theory drives have been disembodied and seem to come from nowhere. Literally "every-body" is subject to drives but everyone does not become a mystic. And yet the latter may be an aspect of our humanity we simply haven't

difficult to identify with the ideas conveyed by these myths but also many men, as the analysis of texts by Hoban and other male writers will show. Reading the myths against the grain by focussing on contradictory variants and unexplored possibilities of plot development, however, opens up space for more viable alternatives. The continued experience of the fallibility and fragility of all "safety systems", of language, or of laws and conventions meant to uphold the illusion of safety, should actually make us more cautious, more curious, more flexible, dynamic, and tolerant of difference – both within ourselves and between each other. Myths need not be refuted if they do not suggest that the unexpected can be completely domesticated. But mythical images such as that of Athene with the head of Medusa on her aegis is one of the lies on which our symbolic institutions have been founded: they make us believe that the diverse sources of instability for which Medusa stands can indeed be "killed" and appropriated, as women and femininity have been appropriated by men for a very long time. If the Oedipus myth is valid for anything, however, then to show that the most law-abiding subject can actually be *driven* to committing atrocious crimes.

This chapter must not end on a sombre note and in an accusatory tone, however. For those made to represent chaos, instability, the drives, or death by any given system[32] must never tire of returning to the members of the apparently "privileged" group their share of the burden, if that which is excluded by the system be indeed a burden.[33] Hélène Cixous's "The Laugh of the Medusa" (1976) is an early model text in so far as the liberation of women is concerned: working with and against the representations of the patriarchal

sufficiently explored. Even though much of what was formerly attributed to the supernatural can now be identified as having its origin in the psyche – see ch. 11.1 for Todorov's classification of fantastic themes, which is based on this psychoanalytic assumption –, it is probably wiser to remain open to the possibility that there is a difference between the metaphysical and the psychic until there is waterproof evidence to the contrary. Mysticism, in other words, may be another way of experiencing the Real than the experience of drive. Both have in common, though, that they resist to a certain extent our attempts to master them.

32 The patriarchal system thus marginalises women, and men unwilling to adapt to the subjecthood foreseen for them; but mainstream cultures are usually defined by other distinguishing features as well: race, religion , class, etc. are added to the opposition of sexes. The place of the excluded can therefore also be held by members of discriminated races, religions or classes, or by people who defy classification according to these categories.

33 In "From Omphalos to Phallus", Elisabeth Bronfen has formulated the following feminist programme: "Phallic monism ... translates femininity into an enigma for the masculine subject by devising a two-fold symptom-representation – the castrated and the demonic Woman. This Woman becomes the site on to which the patriarchal self can project the recognition of death he is anxious about, and in the double strategy of the symptom, repress this even as he articulates it, because it has been transferred to a different, i.e. sexually other body. For a feminist hermeneutics to *solve* the riddle of femininity means, then, to deconstruct such strategies of repression and denial, and to give back to the masculine subject those aspects of the self he has projected on to femininity – such as loss, drives, facticity, vulnerability – all of which emerge as transformations of the concept of mortality" (151).

system, she shakes its foundations by laughter, exaggerating the contradictions inherent in embracing its terms while at the same time attempting to loosen the iron collar of representation. Cixous's reading emphasizes "feminine" *jouissance* of the entire body in the realm of sexuality; for her laughing Medusa is a figure which aims at dissociating the feminine both from castration and mortality. Rather than to be simply the opposite of Freud's decapitated head of Medusa, Cixous's Medusa at once recalls and overturns that image: being Medusa is both horrible and beautiful:

> They riveted us between two horrifying myths: between the Medusa and the abyss. That would be enough to set half the world laughing, except that it's still going on ...
>
> Too bad for them if they fall apart upon discovering that women aren't men, or that the mother doesn't have one. But isn't this fear convenient for them? Wouldn't the worst be, isn't the worst, in truth, that women aren't castrated, that they have only to stop listening to the Sirens (for the Sirens were men) for history to change its meaning? You only have to look at the Medusa straight on to see her. And she's not deadly. She's beautiful and she's laughing. (255)

In so far as she is alive and beautiful, Cixous's Medusa resembles Hoban's. The approach to her affects the language of the text, too, which is full of ambiguities, contradictions and playful digressions. But Cixous's figure is far less domesticated, or perhaps more energetic, than Hoban's flickering Vermeer version: her laughter tries to shatter all prior definitions and representations. It won't be satisfied with adding a difference to them, although it can actually achieve no more. Cixous proposes a new aesthetic which would be altogether free from traditional models: "Time and again I, too, have felt so full of luminous torrents that I could burst – burst with forms much more beautiful than those which are put up in frames and sold for a stinking fortune" (246). Her utopia culminates in the demand: "... woman must write woman. And man, man" (247). However, she constantly demonstrates her awareness of the impossibility of getting rid of established "phallocentric" representations: the more original her experience, the more dependent is she on familiar metaphors to communicate it ("luminous torrents"). More than once, she therefore ironically subverts her posture of authority, by acting against her own precepts, e.g. writing about men, too, although she says she will "write woman", and stressing the binary opposition between men and women while insisting that sexual difference would in fact have to be examined:

> ... only an oblique consideration will be found here of man; it's up to him to say where his masculinity and femininity are at: this will concern us once men have opened their eyes and seen themselves clearly. (...)

> ... I mean it when I speak of male writing. I maintain unequivocally that there is such a thing as *marked* writing; that, until now, far more extensively and repressively than is ever suspected or admitted, writing has been run by a libidinal and cultural – hence political, typically masculine – economy; that this is a locus where the repression of women has been perpetuated...; that this locus has grossly exaggerated all the signs of sexual opposition (and not sexual difference), where woman has never *her* turn to speak ... (247-249)

Above all, she does not fail to deconstruct, at the very beginning, the key term upon which her argument is based, that is "woman":

> I write this as a woman, toward women. When I say 'woman,' I'm speaking of woman in her inevitable struggle against conventional man; and of a universal woman subject who must bring women to their senses and to their meaning in history. But first it must be said that in spite of the enormity of repression that has kept them in the 'dark' – that dark which people have been trying to make them accept as their attribute – there is, at this time, no general woman, no one typical woman. What they have *in common* I will say. But what strikes me is the infinite richness of their individual constitutions: you can't talk about *a* female sexuality, uniform, homogeneous, classifiable into codes – any more than you can talk about one unconscious resembling another. (245-246)

Even death has a place in her otherwise affirmative text, but it must be resisted (246), prevented from being associated with femininity (255), and from poisoning relationships:

> Let's get away from the dialectic which has it that the only good father is a dead one, or that the child is the death of his parents. The child is the other, but the other without violence, bypassing loss, struggle. We're fed up with the reuniting of bonds forever to be severed, with the litany of castration that's handed down and genealogized. We won't advance backward anymore; we're not going to repress something as simple as the desire for life. (261)

> *Other love.* – In the beginning are our differences. The new love dares for the other, wants the other, makes dizzying, precipitous flights between knowledge and invention. (...) Beyond the struggle-to-the-death that's been removed to the bed, beyond the love-battle that claims to represent exchange, she [the "New Woman"] scorns at an Eros dynamic that would be fed by hatred. (...) Opposition, hierarchizing exchange, the struggle for mastery which can end only in at least one death (one master – one slave, or two nonmasters ≠ two dead) – all that comes from a period in time governed by phallocentric values. (263-264)

Women are fragile and vulnerable (256); this must no longer entail that we tolerate being silenced and killed, assist in the silencing and killing of other women, children, and men, or that we be driven to silencing and killing ourselves. These ideas make up the text's utopia. Cixous leaves open one issue, however; there is no reference to the fact that women are mortal, that death cannot be resisted or repressed for good. It will return violently like everything else repressed if we do not sublimate it. For Cixous, though, sublimation is a waste of energy (255-257): as far as femininity is concerned, which is vaguely synonymous with "the repressed" in her essay (254),[34] she projects an upheaval: "When the 'repressed' of their culture and their society returns, it's an explosive, *utterly* destructive, staggering return, with a force never yet unleashed and equal to the most forbidding of suppressions" (256). Whether or not death is to be expected in the same way is left open.

Man must write man, he must write his own "other history" (Cixous 254). It is to be assumed, however, that if he indeed writes his story differently, he, too, will have to deal with what has been returned to him. Peter Schwenger has aptly sketched this new self-consciousness in *Phallic Critiques* (1984): "A nineteenth-century man could assume his patriarchy with the ease of one settling into a comfortable armchair. A twentieth-century man may assert the same prerogative, but it is an assertion, not an assumption" (9). Let us now have a look "where his masculinity and femininity are at" and how he copes with his vulnerability and his mortality.

8.4. Vermeer Girl into Medusa: The Repressed Returns

Frances Broomfield's painting on the book jacket of *The Medusa Frequency* turns Vermeer's *Head of a Young Girl* into Medusa's head. In chapter 8.2, I argued that the novel thus probably signals Herman's evasion of the idea of Medusa and that it is at the same time a challenge to the readers. But what has to be looked at in greater detail now is the fact that Hoban's and Broomfield's representations of Medusa leave her "alive": the fact that several representations of her are juxtaposed, destabilizes her image, freeing her from the immobility that one representation would impose on her.[1] Moreover, in the story, Herman

34 "... psychoanalysis was constitued from woman, to repress femininity..." (Cixous 254): as we have seen, this is a simplification and gendering of repression Freud himself refused.

1 It stands to reason whether or not the object of a painting has already been "killed" by the act of fixing it onto a screen: isn't the greatest illusion the belief that one can fully deprive the object of representation of its "life"? In *Over Her Dead Body* (1992), Elisabeth Bronfen writes: "... the 'fixing' which occurs in the act of representation is a captation [sic], in Lacan's sense of the *point de capiton*, by which, at certain privileged points, the mobility of the chain of signifiers comes to be arrested or fixed on to a signified. At the same time it is also a puncturing, in Barthes's sense of the *punctum* or obtuse meaning, as a moment or detail of an image that wounds any obvious meaning, that points beyond semantic fixture, because it is discontinuous, indifferent to the narrative, and has 'at least a distancing effect with regard to the referent, to "reality" as nature'. As such the *punctum* disturbs because it opens up a plurality of meaning and reference" (46).

does not kill her or try to get rid of her, but he accepts her appearances whenever they happen to him. Much as she looks at him from the paintings of Post and Vermeer, he can look at her without instantly turning to stone. Unlike the "cheating adventurer" Perseus (Meaney 28), Herman abstains from fighting against Medusa's appearances. When she appears for the first time, her face is still slightly uncanny because it evolves out of a vision of the body of Herman's former girlfriend, loosely grinning. But in the end, her snaky hair is grafted onto the painting of a "girl". That is, unlike Freud's frightening and ugly head of the dead Medusa, Hoban's Medusa seeks access to Herman via one of the idealising and reassuring representations of femininity: a young woman whose expression is not altogether confident, but whose parted lips signal her willingness to open herself to whatever she will be offered. She is not an unapproachable virgin but, at first glance, an image of tempting, though inoffensive female sexuality. Only in *Fremder*, Hoban's latest novel, will the protagonist overcome his need for being reassured by a beautiful young woman; for he recognizes that it makes him vulnerable to manipulation. He will have to struggle against a mad Medusa who does not respect his limits in return for his lack of aggression. He will not have to decapitate her, however, since she has killed her own body years earlier and consists of no more than a giant brain. The only thing he will have to do is to stop perceiving her. For his conscious withdrawal of attention will effectively separate his reality from hers.

The Vermeer girl makes her first appearance in *Pilgermann*, when the narrator is trying to find out how he should look at the siege of Jerusalem and the cruelty of war:

> And the look with which Vermeer looked upon her face, that is the look with which everything must be seen; yes, even the severed limbs. Everything that is, everything that happens must be seen with the eye that is in love with seeing. All must be seen with a willing look. (PG 97)

He here suggests that representation is a matter of willingness, that, in other words, a kind of contract or exchange can be established between the one who represents and the object represented: "From her eyes the unseen looks out at

---

Actually, there are several details with a distancing effect in Vermeer's original painting, too: the snake-shaped structure in the blue scarf I pointed out in ch. 8.1, the dark pupils and the black background of the painting. Lacan's discussion of anamorphoses in *The Ethics of Psychoanalysis* sheds light on the implications of such disturbing details: "... the interest of anamorphosis is described as a turning point when the artist completely reverses the use of that illusion of space, when he forces it to enter into the original goal, that is to transform it into the support of the hidden reality – it being understood that, to a certain extent, a work of art always involves encircling the Thing" (141).

us, and through our eyes looking back into hers also looks the unseen" (PG 97). But this is the heart of all mystifications which underlie complementary thinking, in regard to sexuality, representation and mortality alike: what one tries to rule out by conjuring up mutuality and complementarity is the shock of being overwhelmed by something unforeseeable and unforeseen. What is indeed scary about the young woman in Vermeer's painting is that her eyes fail to show a reflection of the viewer: the "you" of the questions Pilgermann projects onto her does not exist. The unseen indeed looks out from her eyes, but not "at us"; in fact, *we are the unseen.*

And indeed, in *The Medusa Frequency*, there is a moment of desolation in the chapter before Herman travels to the Hague in search of the original painting, when seeking comfort from the painting, he is unexpectedly referred back to himself: "She wasn't there, the virtue had gone out of my poor copies, they were empty of her. The room filled up with a desolation that drained the virtue out of everything" (MF 77). It seems to be a long way from the simple relationships depicted in *The Mouse and his Child.* Yet, certain insights can be traced back to Hoban's earliest longer book. I will now look at the protagonists in Hoban's novels and short stories, drawing attention to parallels with, and differences from, short stories and novels by Jorge Luis Borges, Ernest Hemingway, Thomas Pynchon, D. M. Thomas, J. M. Coetzee, Vladimir Nabokov, and Salman Rushdie. Special attention will be paid to elements from the oedipal pattern and to transgressive moments in which the protagonists' identities are thoroughly shaken: be it in regard to their sexuality, their vitality, or their language.

THE MOUSE AND HIS CHILD

I would like to begin this survey by quoting an excerpt from the happy ending of *The Mouse and his Child.* While their guests are enjoying a Christmas party inside the renovated dolls' house, the family are pacing around the platform:

> The front door opened ... and the seal came out to them. ... 'The year's almost over,' she said. 'It was the best year I ever had. What will the coming ones be like, I wonder?'
>
> 'Better yet,' said Frog authoritatively, and together they continued around the platform, enjoying one another's company in silence. (197)

Fate once more seems to strike despite Frog's assertion when the father breaks the silence: "... he stopped, astonished, as the reciprocally winding springs inside him, having lost a little energy each day through friction, came at last unwound. 'I'm not wound up any more!' he said" (197-198). If his were a human body, he would of course be dead now, but Frog is there to wind him up again: "'Well,' said Frog, 'I don't suppose anyone ever is completely self-winding. That's what friends are for.'" (198) Frog's authoritative voice proclaims that complementarity (here between friends rather than man and woman) averts harm. As I wrote in chapter 2.4, however, this is a clockwork idyll: the figures have moved from dolls' house to dolls' house. The fact that they are clockwork animals rather than dolls proper or human characters underlines the efficiency of social norms, especially norms of gendered behaviour: even a heterogeneous group which consists of a pair of mice, an elephant and a seal can be turned into the American model family of the 1960s. Moreover, the more independent the toys become, the greater haste they make to conform to a human social model. The contrast is perfectly illustrated by a scene which takes place immediately before the battle for the dolls' house. The mouse father has just been repaired by Frog, making a resolution to fight for a territory. When the seal questions the appropriateness of territories for toys, she is not only contradicted by the mouse father but also invited to join the family:

> 'We aren't toys any more,' said the father. 'Toys are to be played with, and we aren't. We have endured all that Frog foretold – the painful spring, the shattering fall, and more. Now we have come to that place where the scattering is regathered.'
> 'What do you mean?' asked the seal.
> 'Be my daughter,' said the father.
> 'Be my sister,' said the child. 'Will you, so we can have a family?' (146)

Of course she will join them, for exciting though her independent life may have been, "it seemed a long and weary time that she had been alone of her kind in the wide world" (147). The spark of innovation cannot possibly be emitted by a "daughter". Directly after the battle, the process continues. After the loss of Manny's former authority has been sealed by laughter, silence returns to the dump (165). The ensuing power vacuum could be filled with something new – but now the family is "completed": the kingfisher, the bittern and Frog become uncles and the elephant is offered the role of mother by the child (who personifies something one might term "gregarious desire", to signal its difference from sexual desire proper):

> 'Now we'll have our house and a family with *three* uncles!' said the child happily. 'Remember when you said it was impossible, Papa? Remember I said I wanted the elephant for a mama, and you said –'
> 'That will do,' said his father. (167)

The father's proposal is far more reluctant than the son's demand, for he remembers how they were snubbed by the elephant while still in the toyshop. Eventually, however, she sufficiently humbles herself for him to feel encouraged, offering that kind of comfort and reassurance which Herman Orff can no longer expect from the Vermeer girl:

> 'Ah!' said the elephant. 'Though perhaps a little taller, she has never really been above him. Were he to speak, he might find an interested listener, a listener who has seen and learned much, who knows at last the true worth of the brave and gallant gentleman she met so long ago when she was young and foolish and thought the dolls' house was hers.'
> 'It's yours now,' said the father.
> 'Only if you offer it,' said the elephant. 'You fought for it and won it.'
> 'I do offer it,' said the father, 'and myself, if you will have both.'
> 'I will,' said the elephant. (168)

The nuclear family is perfect now even though its formation does not at all follow the Freudian path: instead of breaking up a narcissistic mother/child dyad, the father actually has to be cajoled into assuming his position by both the child and the elephant. There are no oedipal complications to be expected in the future either since the figures are asexual despite being gendered. Their development, then, is mainly the result of their encounters with destructive powers and of the cooperation between friends, especially between father and son (see ch. 2.4): as individuals they lose their bearings. The father had to be encouraged by the child earlier in the story, that is in chapter 6, when he was ready to give himself up at the bottom of C. Serpentina's pond – the enemy then was the father's desire for death.[2] After their return to the surface, however, it is control over Manny Rat, the main source of instability, which guarantees their happiness.

Like the uncanny elements in Vermeer's *Head of a Young Girl* Manny Rat links the fairy-tale surface story to another reality in which pleasant wish-fulfilment has to give way to the violent manifestations of drives. At the same time as he represents a danger to the toys, Manny Rat, taken on his own, also embodies the "radical spirit of life" Hoban discusses in "Thoughts on a Shirtless Cyclist..." (13). He is therefore more than just the negative counterpart of the toys: Manny is the anamorphotic spot of the novel, that is, the element which subverts the novel's overt message. The division between Manny and the clockwork toys splits himself. His mind is a site of conflicting needs and insatiable desires: unlike the toys, he is drawn to living both according to

2 Is it too far-fetched to draw attention to the parallel between Medusa and C. Serpentina, the turtle with the snakelike head? Instead of turning those who approach him to stone, though, he discourages them from seeking a way out of the muddy pond and refuses to help those who cannot bear eternal stagnation.

his desire as well as according to social norms. For him, happiness and its opposite are to be found on both sides of the division. He thus resembles real human beings, torn between the moderate (un)happiness of living life according to social conventions and the hazards of living up to their desire.[3]

THE LION OF BOAZ-JACHIN AND JACHIN-BOAZ

Manny is also the link to the characters in *The Lion of Boaz-Jachin and Jachin-Boaz*. The lion as catalyst personifies various aspects of the Real which unsettle the human characters' balance; there is an affinity with Herman's Medusa, particularly when Jachin-Boaz's psychiatrist compares the supernatural animal to a television programme: "'Suppose,' said the doctor, 'that you were the only person in the world who had a receiver that could pick up this particular broadcast.'" (LN 66-67); there is another link in so far as facing the lion means facing up to a conscious decision for life or death (187). But the function of the lion is wider than that of Hoban's Medusa, who confronts Herman only with mortality while the head of Orpheus is responsible for his notion of sexuality. The lion challenges not only the characters' vitality but also their sexuality, like Freud's head of Medusa. The oedipal drama is invoked: it is mainly because Jachin-Boaz has not properly repressed his Oedipus complex that a puerile challenge by his own son – the demand that Jachin-Boaz's master-map show lions (13) – can induce him to give up his former life. He runs away from his family as a belated act of opposition to the ambitious plans of his own father, for whose premature death he has felt responsible most of his life: "He closed his mouth and lay down, but he is more alive in me than I am" (135). Jachin-Boaz is the victim of an implacable super-ego. His career as a map maker obsessed with facts, his marriage to a woman resembling, and agreeable to, his widowed mother, and his pedantic insistence on paternal authority at the beginning of the novel (12) are attempts to atone for the guilt inspired by that cruel instance.[4] By escaping Jachin-Boaz at first aims at a repetition of the story with himself in the role of the father who "would not agree to be dead" and Boaz-Jachin in the role of Oedipus: "The young man was left at home to be a shopkeeper and the

3 See Freud's essay "Das Unbehagen in der Kultur" (1930 [1929]): "... man möchte sagen, die Absicht, dass der Mensch 'glücklich' sei, ist im Plan der 'Schöpfung' nicht enthalten. Was man im strengsten Sinne Glück heisst, entspringt der eher plötzlichen Befriedigung hoch aufgestauter Bedürfnisse und ist seiner Natur nach nur als episodisches Phänomen möglich. Jede Fortdauer einer vom Lustprinzip ersehnten Situation ergibt nur ein Gefühl von lauem Behagen" (208).

4 In fact, Jachin-Boaz's biography resembles that of the obsessed young man described in Freud's case study "Bemerkungen über einen Fall von Zwangsneurose" (1909), i.e. the patient who became known as the "rat man" ("Rattenmann"). With Manny Rat as Jachin-Boaz's supernatural *alter ego* and fictional ancestor, the connection becomes even more evident.

companion of his deserted mother" (26) – in other words, it is the son who is to bear the burden of Jachin-Boaz's mortality, not his wife or later, Gretel. After Jachin-Boaz has sorted out the conflict with his father by projecting him onto the lion, however, he is ready to defeat the lion rather than expose his own son to a similar fate (135).

He need not have worried about Boaz-Jachin, though, for the son does not waste any time: he sets out on his journey to prove his independence. While it took his father years to leave behind the role of Oedipus, Boaz-Jachin almost immediately turns into Perseus, avoiding the traps his father fell into: that is, feeling obliged to stay at home because of his mother, and to marry Lila. The lion-feeling protects him. Moreover, since father and son quarrelled over authority rather than over the body of Boaz-Jachin's mother, Boaz-Jachin need not present a bride to document his lack of interest in the mother. This is an interesting deviation from both the pattern of the Oedipus complex as well as that of the Perseus and Medusa myth: the two men no longer define their relation in terms of their claim to, respectively responsibility for, the mother.[5] Boaz-Jachin seeks his father's recognition, hence is not interested in his death: "The father must live so that the father can die" (184). When they meet, Jachin-Boaz no longer insists on his paternal authority: he is Dictys rather than Polydectes, that is, the castrating father is indeed "dead". The lion as an instrument of rage and the personification of the problems of a father-and-son relationship can therefore vanish: he is consumed while the reunion of Jachin-Boaz and Boaz-Jachin takes place in a surge of violent *jouissance* which abolishes the hierarchical opposition between them (189-191). They are two men on equal terms rather than father and son now. There is life after parenthood, despite the assessment of the biologist observing sexed cells, which aroused Jachin-Boaz's fear of death in his sixth dream: "It must die because it has had children and is no longer needed" (132). The wheel of time may drag us to our deaths, but it also assigns us a certain time span which does not expire as soon as we have had children. Sexuality and mortality are indeed more independent aspects of our experience than microbiology and the spectre of the Oedipus complex would have us believe.

The discussion of men's "liberation" from their mothers and wives seems to suggest that Hoban's novel tries to blame women for the conflicts between men and for their inferiority complexes. This interpretation must be resisted, though. One of the minor characters, the homosexual lorry driver actually

5 Barbara Herkommer, too, discusses the relative insignificance of mothers (70). She emphasizes that this is not to hoist fathers to the position of patriarchs but on the contrary to point to their weakness, their fallibility and also their absence, which are instrumental in the children's suffering (71).

forwards such a view: "'Always the films are full of men with guns. (...) Because we men feel ourselves to be gunless. (...) They should rather make films about the women who take away our guns,' he said. 'Nobody wants the truth.'" (55). Boaz-Jachin, however, to whom these words are addressed, senses that the lorry driver is close to "disarming" him, by making a pass at him: the driver's accusatory words and his behaviour clash in such an obvious way that it is clear that the novel abstains from linking power and deprivation of power to the characters' sexes. Jachin-Boaz's early dreams, too, accuse his mother and his wife of preventing him from living up to his desire. He gradually realises, however, that he cannot blame anybody else but himself for his failures. Oppositions between people are again and again shown to be projections originating in the characters' own divided and incoherent condition. The bookshop owner uses a particularly apt simile for the human condition: "'Every person is like thousands of books. New, reprinting, in stock, out of stock, fiction, nonfiction, poetry, rubbish. ... Different every day....'" (181).

The female characters in the novel must be judged by the same standard. I shall focus on chapters and excerpts of dialogue in which they represent themselves, or are seen through their own eyes.[6] Most of them cannot serve as new "gender models" since they prefer turning bitter in stifling relationships rather than to leave and stand on their own feet. Jachin-Boaz's wife, for example, needs to be left by her husband before she puts ideas she has had for a long time "into practice" (107). Passive and without initiative of her own, she expected her husband to be a successful scientist (109) or, at least, to make other dreams of hers come true (110): he has always been the object of her ambitions. She got married to him in order to escape from her parents (37) and defined her femininity exclusively in terms of her husband's sexual desire – small wonder that his impotence with her "made her feel less than a woman" (110). She accuses him of murdering her, immediately before she is trying to commit suicide, but it is clear that she has never really been alive (37f.). Her life might have taken a different turn, however, for unlike women from earlier generations or different cultures, she had access to a university education. We are not told why she left university without taking a degree, but the context in which we are given this information suggests that she decided to follow Jachin-Boaz and leave with him when he had failed his exams (109). After writing her farewell letter to Jachin-Boaz, in which she conjures up his death (111) – delegating death as she used to delegate life to him –, she feels "fresh and clear and clean" (112). She smiles and pokes fun at an old voyeur advising

6 Of course I am aware that they are at any rate representations of women by a male author; nevertheless, there is a difference between such representations and descriptions of women filtered by the consciousness of a male character.

him to watch sheep and cows rather than young women undressing (113). She also decides to take up painting again (115), but instead of concentrating on being what is in her to be, we witness her falling in love with the first man who promises to realize the less modest ambitions she feels unable to realize herself (114). In some sense, then, she is a hopeless case, but it is her decision. In 1963, Betty Friedan coined the term "feminine mystique" to describe the problem from which women like Jachin-Boaz's wife suffered: educated middle-class women were "brainwashed" by the media, their families and neighbours – or they brainwashed themselves, because freedom was frightening to them – into being "happy housewife heroines" instead of envisaging other future identities for themselves (44).[7] Friedan was not satisfied with raising her readers' consciousness but tried to make them leave the trap:

> The suburban house is not a German concentration camp, nor are American housewives on their way to the gas chamber. But they are in a trap, and to escape they must ... finally exercise their human freedom, and recapture their sense of self. They must refuse to be nameless, depersonalized, manipulated, and live their own lives again according to a self-chosen purpose. They must begin to grow. (309)

I cannot help thinking, however, that it is paradoxical to *order* people to emancipate themselves; giving orders always infantilizes those addressed. Describing the problem is sufficient help if people are indeed able to grow and be free; if not, the problem cannot be solved by bossing them around. Hoban's novel confirms Friedan's observations without pronouncing any "musts". Abstaining from belittling the wife, it nevertheless dispels the myth that the husbands and children of women stubbornly holding on to the feminine mystique are any happier than the wives and mothers themselves. Clearly, this is a lesson the clockwork animals in *The Mouse and his Child* would not have understood.

Gretel, though Jachin-Boaz's new woman, cannot be called a "new woman" according to Friedan either; she desires an object position, aware that this might be difficult: "She wanted to belong wholly to a man, and this

7 See Betty Friedan's best-seller *The Feminine Mystique* (1963). Her study describes an important phenomenon that affected above all American women born in the 1920s and later. Liberating though her book might have been for a great number of unhappy educated housewife-mothers at the time it was first published, it rested on assumptions that are not unquestionable: women who have chosen this life have failed "to grow to complete identity" (77). But what exactly is a *complete* identity? Chapter 13, "The Forfeited Self", unfortunately tries to answer this question. Friedan thereby makes the mistake to replace an old image of femininity she feels dissatisfied with by another one, that of the "new woman", assuming that hers is desirable for all women and engendering futile disputes over the "right way" to be a woman.

man's quiet face was claiming her and she was afraid" (117). In contrast to Jachin-Boaz's wife, she does not expect Jachin-Boaz to realize any ambitions on her behalf. In chapter 5, the fantasy of complementarity upon which their love is founded is explored. Forty-seven-year-old Jachin-Boaz enjoys his superiority over the "girl" who is eighteen years younger than he and exceptionally gentle: "This tall fair girl, the daughter of warriors, naked under him, looking up at him in fear and joy, delight and proud submission!" (34) – a feeling he has never had with his wife, who kept humbling him, e.g. by telling him of his father's mistress (170). Gretel restores his sexual potency, at least until habit and his fights with the lion interfere with their initial bliss (27, 186). Gretel, on the other hand, demands: "'Make me old,' said Gretel. 'Use me up. Wear me out.'" (35). This constellation, polarized even more by the fact that Gretel is a German and Jachin-Boaz a Jew (33), illustrates what Cixous rejects as a form of love that is "merely a cover for, a veil of war" ("Castration or Decapitation?", 44). Yet, Jachin-Boaz never attempts to burden her with his death: he is aware of the vulnerability of his own body (169). And Gretel does not feel pressed into a role in order to meet his expectations; she appreciates that her "essential self" is unconditionally accepted (34).[8]

8 The term "essence", suggesting an unchangeable core of being, has come under attack in poststructuralist discussions of subjectivity: e.g. in Judith Butler's *Gender Trouble* (1990). Especially where the relation between sex, gender, sexual desire and sexual practice is concerned, Butler proposes a performative reformulation to take the place of an inherited "metaphysics of substance": "... *gender* is always a doing, though not a doing by a subject who might be said to preexist the deed" (25). In her view, it is equally impossible to "be" a sex or a gender (19), and therefore, as essentialists do, to derive gender from biological facticity.

Hoban's novels are not free from notions of essential femininity or masculinity. In fact, essentialism is common in popular discourses on gender identity: "The unproblematic claim to 'be' a woman and 'be' heterosexual would be symptomatic of that metaphysics of gender substances. In the case of both 'men' and 'women,' this claim tends to subordinate the notion of gender under that of identity and to lead to the conclusion that a person *is* a gender and *is* one in virtue of his or her sex, psychic sense of self, and various expressions of that psychic self, the most salient being that of sexual desire. In such a prefeminist context, gender, naively (rather than critically) confused with sex, serves as a unifying principle of the embodied self and maintains that unity over and against an 'opposite sex' whose structure is presumed to maintain a parallel but oppositional internal coherence among sex, gender, and desire" (Butler 21-22).

As we will see in this and in later novels, however, it is not at all "unproblematic" for Hoban's characters to be men and women. His essentialism is not a naive one. At first Hoban is definitely more sensitive to incoherences between maleness and masculinity, but in *Turtle Diary*, he will also show a female character who must come to terms with the fact that her life did not allow her to correspond to the traditional stereotype of femininity (wife and mother) she wanted to become.

The binary opposition between the sexes, which Hoban initially uses as a self-evident fact, is replaced more and more by the notion that subjects are subjects in progress. Men who find out that they barely know themselves can no longer judge women by their standards; they learn to put up with a difference that eludes their grasp. *Lion* starts the destabilizing process in so far as it abstains from explicitly gendering contributions to a relationship. Gretel's submissiveness, for instance, is neither presented as an aspect of a femininity derived from her sex – she is not submissive as a woman with every man – nor is it the only feature of her "essential self". Her "essence" is variable enough to encompass both submissiveness and its opposite, resistance. What her "essential self" is, then, depends on who she is with: it is a dynamic, interactive, performative concept opposed both to the notion of a permanent essence and to that of

Moreover, she is also shown in situations in which she is far from submissive: she attacks the lion as courageously (136) as she will later on rebuke the doctor for suspecting her and Jachin-Boaz, the couple of "foreigners", of sexual perversion (149).

Boaz-Jachin's rape of the divorced woman after she has violently attacked him cannot even be called a *veiled* form of war any more (166f.): the pent-up rage of a disappointed wife and mother clashes with the rage of a disappointed son. When John Haffenden addressed the violence of the rape scene in his 1981 interview, that is, eight years after the publication of *Lion*, Hoban's answer showed that he considered aggression to be part of sexuality: "The urge to tear one another apart is always latent even when the intent is to make love" (130).[9] Freud, who has repeatedly pointed out that the sexual and the death drives hardly ever manifest themselves in their pure form, would of course support this view.[10] But why, then, is Boaz-Jachin's love-making with Lila so tender (29f.)? Obviously, because she gives herself to him and he, making love for the first time, cannot do anything else but give himself, too. They demonstrate Cixous's utopia of "other love":

> They observe, they approach, they try to see the other woman, the child, the lover – not to strengthen their own narcissism or verify the solidity or weakness of the master, but to make love better, to invent.
> *Other love.* – In the beginning are our differences. The new love dares for the other, wants the other, makes dizzying, precipitous flights between knowledge and invention. The woman arriving over and over again does not stand still; she's everywhere, she exchanges, she is the desire-that-gives. (Not enclosed in the paradox of the gift that takes nor under the illusion of unitary fusion. We're past that.) ("The Laugh of the Medusa", 263)

Even though this excerpt from Cixous's essay seems to suggest that women only are capable of such love,[11] there are men who do not feel an urge to tear an other apart, who, in other words, try to protect the other from their

---

conscious regulation. Gretel feels that her essential self is valued precisely because, being with Jachin-Boaz, she need not consciously subject herself to any regulations. I want to come back to an idea put forward in the preceding chapter and suggest that her "essential self" is nothing else but the manner in which her desire is structured, the way in which her drives "live her" and make her respond to Jachin-Boaz and other people.

9 Christine Wilkie first drew attention to Hoban's commentary on this scene (cf. Wilkie 34).

10 Cf. e.g. "Jenseits des Lustprinzips": "... im oralen Organisationsstadium der Libido fällt die Liebesbemächtigung noch mit der Vernichtung des Objekts zusammen, später trennt sich der sadistische Trieb ab, und endlich übernimmt er auf der Stufe des Genitalprimats zum Zwecke der Fortpflanzung die Funktion, das Sexualobjekt so weit zu bewältigen, als es die Ausführung des Geschlechtsaktes erfordert. Ja, man könnte sagen, der aus dem Ich herausgedrängte Sadismus habe den libidinösen Komponenten des Sexualtriebs den Weg gezeigt; späterhin drängen diese zum Objekt nach. Wo der ursprüngliche Sadismus keine Ermässigung und Verschmelzung erfährt, ist die bekannte Liebe-Hass-Ambivalenz des Liebeslebens hergestellt" (263). See de Lauretis's discussion of this way of thinking in *Alice Doesn't* (132f.).

11 Of course the deconstruction of the term "woman" throughout her essay prevents such a simplification: I am holding on to it only for heuristic reasons.

aggression, in extreme cases even at the cost of turning their aggression against themselves. While Hoban's view of sexuality (as expressed in the interview but actually contradicted by Lila and Boaz-Jachin's love-making and many other couples from later novels) is too absolute and negative, the one which seems to emerge from Cixous's excerpt mystifies woman: perhaps we should all fare better if we acknowledged the existence of constructive and destructive drives in all of us, whose stimulation is more or less beyond our control, while their abreaction can most of the time be checked – even though, as I argued in chapter 8.3, all safety systems, psychic or social, may collapse. Violent sex scenes and illusions of the unitary fusion of characters who are really caught in a hierarchized, asymmetrical opposition may therefore not be politically correct but they are perhaps more common than ideal situations of love-without-aggression. I do not think that we will ever be altogether "past that". Cixous's utopia can nevertheless show us the direction we must go if we suffer from (without masochistically enjoying!) the *status quo*: It is up to us "to watch-think-seek the other in the other, to despecularize, to unhoard" (264). The more an attachment imitates the constellation of the Oedipus complex, the more likely it is for violence to break out because of an inherent tension: "parents" and "children" always both want to hold on to, as well as get rid of, each other. This assumption would explain both the violence of the rape scene in the novel as well as Gretel's anxiety: after all the divorced woman resembles Boaz-Jachin's mother (164) while Jachin-Boaz and Gretel fell in love when she was talking about her unknown father (33, 117). The option that parity might be established one day is not excluded. Hoban does not pretend that relationships are, or should be, permanent or unchangeable, but he also abstains from mystifying them: loneliness and the terror of being accompany us even at the peak of happiness (see chapter 3.3).

JORGE LUIS BORGES: "ULRIKE"

Jorge Luis Borges's short story "Ulrike" from the collection *The Book of Sand* (1975), his only love story according to the Afterword (92), will be the first text to compare *Lion* with. With its four pages, it is not only the briefest story I know which addresses both the uncanny conjunction of sexuality and violence in relationships and its transformation into something affirmative, but it is also a very subtle example of a text which invokes, at the same time as it calls into question, ideals, stereotypes, and prejudices. Javier, a Colombian professor, meets the Norwegian Ulrike in the lounge of an inn outside the city walls of York. He begins to notice her voice when she declines the offer of a drink with reference to her being a feminist "not out to ape men", hence not feeling obliged to smoke or drink (11). He does not look at her, however, until she comments on the Vikings' conquest of England: "'England was once ours and we lost it – if one can have anything or if anything can be lost.'" (12). There is no doubt an elective affinity between the protagonists. The sentence is also remarkably close – albeit not identical, and difference matters – to the variable motto underlying the development of the characters of *Lion*: "'... everything that is found is always lost again, and nothing that is found is ever lost again....'" (17; also see 12, 21, 37, 50, 64, 108, 110, 120, 185). Javier gradually extends his discovery of Ulrike (12), seemingly adopting the "typical" male behaviour of conquering a woman by looking at her; but it is we who will fall into a trap if we overlook the details which emphasize, on the one hand, her subjectivity, on the other, his rather diffident steps towards her: subjectivity playfully oscillates between them and the "typical" is dismissed:

> A line in Blake speaks of girls of mild silver or of furious gold, but in Ulrike were both gold and mildness. She was tall and slender, with sharp features and grey eyes. Less than by her face, I was impressed by her air of calm mystery. She smiled easily, and the smile seemed to withdraw her from the company. She was dressed in black, which is strange for northern lands, which try to liven the drab surroundings with vivid colours. She spoke a crisp, precise English, rolling her r's slightly. I am not much of an observer; these things I discovered bit by bit. (12)

They go for a walk to Thorgate the next morning, talking about literary figures. She places herself in a long tradition of muses when she identifies with Ann, the woman lost by De Quincey "amid the crowds of London" (13). He thinks that it "is not forbidden" him to kiss her on the mouth and eyes (13). Orpheus and Eurydice come to mind, especially when Ulrike promises to be his once they have reached their destination, on condition that he do not touch her again before they are there. Javier, "a bachelor well along in years", does not consider it beneath him to accept her condition (13). He is free from the possessiveness of Orpheus which made him transgress Persephone's law and lose Eurydice by looking back at her: "I did not make the mistake of asking Ulrike whether she loved me. I realized that this was not her first time nor would it be her last. The adventure, perhaps my last, should be one of many for that splendid, determined follower of Ibsen" (13). He is astonished when she tells him that she considers herself about to die (13). And indeed, his emphasis on his age and the way in which she rejects his wish that the moment should last forever (14),[12] actually place *him* rather than her in the vicinity of transitoriness and death. This impression is confirmed when she

12 It was the one wish Faust had to renounce if he did not want to forfeit his soul, but it is also a wish recalling the desire for death Hoban's protagonists must resist again and again.

proposes to call him Sigurd, pretending to be unable to pronounce his Spanish first name. Javier instantly identifies her with the Valkyrie Brynhild: a norse death goddess who turned human and eventually killed Sigurd in order to be reunited with him in death since their union was impossible in life. Since Javier can hardly keep up with Ulrike's step, he asks her to slow down: "'Brynhild, you're walking as if you wished a sword lay between us in bed.'" (14). Having been lured into expecting a Wagnerian love battle with a triumphal climax and at least one dead body, we are now surprised by the story's actual outcome: no one dies at the inn at Thorgate with its paradisiac wallpaper "in the style of William Morris" (14):

> The awaited bed was duplicated in a dim mirror, and the polished mahogany reminded me of the looking glass of Scriptures. Ulrike had already undressed. She called me by my real name – Javier. I felt that the snow was falling faster. Now there were no longer any mirrors or furniture. There was no sword between us. Time passed like the sands. In the darkness, centuries old, love flowed, and for the first and last time I possessed Ulrike's image. (14)

The lovers apparently leave behind the cultural space in which they are nothing but mirror images of older literary couples – the return to Eden, signalled by the wallpaper of the inn, is the last traditional fantasy they encounter. Their love flows and all mirrors disappear after Ulrike has called Javier by his real name: it is "other love" because returning to their real names, the two lovers invent their own unique experience. "I am for you what you want me to be at the moment you look at me in a way you've never seen me before: at every instant" – this sentence from Cixous's "The Laugh of the Medusa" could as well be Ulrike's or Javier's (264). There is no loser and no winner. Javier's narrative, as a symbolic representation, can of course only commemorate Ulrike's absence owing to the drawing backward of language. Understatement and renunciation of sentimentality nevertheless prevent the lovers' experience from being readable as a Romantic story of loss and artistic recuperation. In the introductory paragraph, Javier announces a "personal memory" of his "meeting with Ulrike" (11), while his last clause spells out that all he ever "possessed", all there ever was to possess and therefore to lose, was her image.

Ulrike at first seems to be a relative of Gretel's. The two women are both tall, fair, energetic and yet mild: representations of women who are desirable because they do not scare the male characters despite their physical beauty. In both cases it is something they say rather than the way they look which arouses their future lovers' interest. At second glance, however, certain differences emerge. While Gretel has been modelled on Russell Hoban's second wife Gundula Ahl (cf. Hoban and Haffenden 130), Ulrike is an ideal woman construed from and against famous literary models and feminist positions. She is so unlike every model conjured up and then rejected, that one eventually begins to suspect that Javier never really met her, despite his affirmations to the contrary at the beginning of the story: "My story will be true to reality or, in any case, to my personal memory of reality, which amounts to the same thing" (11).[13] If their love indeed took place, though, his numerous hints at the historical uniqueness of the event underlines that "other love" is different for every couple of lovers. It does not aspire to exemplarity, universality, or eternal validity. Javier's exclusive love for the Ulrike he met then and there is expressed in the sentence: "I could never have wanted any other person by my side" (12).

Borges's reference to feminism is important: he creates a female character who is a feminist above all by virtue of being whatever she wants to be, free in her choices and not indebted to any *particular* mode of behaviour. Ulrike can impersonate certain figures but also be whatever she is at a particular moment. Throughout the story it is Javier who accommodates to her identifications and eventually to her return to "being Ulrike". It is indeed only an image, *one* image of her, Javier can "possess". Should they ever meet again, both will have changed and there is no guarantee that the chemistry between them, the miracle of desires tuned to each other, will work once more. At this point Borges's "theory" and Hoban's "practical experience" correspond again. A character apparently modelled on a real person is really modelled on a historically specific perception or image, too: this image may be "new" at first, but time can turn it into a cage if the character (and the original model) is prevented from becoming someone else. At the beginning of the novel, Jachin-Boaz is definitely less tolerant of changes than Javier, Gretel, or Boaz-Jachin. For him there is no playful oscillation between the subject and the object positions in a relationship but only a struggle for the subject position. He therefore reacts aggressively to situations in which he feels weak, inferior, compelled to jump into "an empty suit of clothes" held up to him by someone else (see e.g. 135), or mortal; in short, he abhors all challenges to his subjectivity. His encounters with the lion gradually free him from both his fear of death and his castration anxiety: it is the basis on which parity between him and Boaz-Jachin can eventually be established. Before the final showdown, however, Jachin-Boaz's condition is precarious. Gretel knows that his love might not be sufficiently strong to endure imminent challenges and changes

---

13 In ch. 11.2, Borges's approach to the relationship between reality and fiction and their difference from the Real will be examined in greater detail.

(her pregnancy, or the lion) although she believes her own love to be so resistant as to survive even a separation (180). Everyone cannot read such testimonies of devotion without wincing: they smack of feminine mystique, again. However, Gretel's clear perception of Jachin-Boaz shows that she is no deluded victim in need of help. Although another beast might one day come between them, as a challenge to their asymmetry, Gretel is the character who can run that risk. In fact, it has already been diminished by Jachin-Boaz's eventual transformation.

"THE DEVIL'S KITCHEN"

The conflict between the nameless first-person narrator and his wife Gisela in the short story "The Devil's Kitchen" could actually be seen as the continuation of Jachin-Boaz and Gretel's story. Published nineteen years after the novel in *Granta* 42 (Winter 1992), the short story shows a wife who can no longer keep her eyes closed and be silent when her husband engages in an activity which could be harmful for him, as Gretel did before Jachin-Boaz went out to meet the lion for the last time (LN 187). A maternal rather than a girlish figure, Gisela does not hide her reservations about a dolls' kitchen her husband wants to buy in Germany: she doubts that there is room for it in her husband's study (DK 164), notices a suspicious shape in the Polaroid picture he has taken of it (166), and finally criticizes him for sacrificing his sleep while waiting for a story about it; but she is eventually silenced by her husband – an unmistakable token of asymmetry (167).

Though Gisela seems to be the weaker party, the outcome of the story will prove that her husband would have been wiser to leave the dolls' kitchen alone. Their power struggle is in fact a projection of a division within himself: art and life are fighting over his body. Whereas Jachin-Boaz was "man enough" to face a hungry lion, the narrator of "The Devil's Kitchen" is bound to lose in the end because he must make too many concessions to get a story out of the kitchen. He will eventually feel more effeminate than if he had listened to his wife's reservations. For a bunch of Nazi rats who suddenly manifest themselves in the dolls' kitchen shrink him to the size of a doll in order to rape him.[14] Having agreed to be their "little daughter", uncritically cooking for them whatever they wanted him to, sealed his defeat as a man and artist (168). After the event he can only acknowledge an absolute lack of control: "I don't know what to think about what happened; maybe it says more about me than I

14 Here is another link to Freud's case study "Bemerkungen über einen Fall von Zwangsneurose" (1909). While Jachin-Boaz's biography resembled that of the "rat man", the rape of the protagonist of "The Devil's Kitchen" recalls the "rat man's" phantasies, see esp. 43-45.

want to know" (170). In his subsequent remarks, he is quite frank about his responsibility: having muffled his initial dread (164), silenced his wife's doubts and agreed to every perverse condition of the rats (170), he could not help eventually being in a devil of a mess, which is exactly what the German idiom "in Teufels Küche" (in the devil's kitchen) means. He had a devil in him when striving for authorship at any cost. Yet, opening himself to the recognition of his defeat and helplessness is only his first reaction after the traumatic experience, not the beginning of a different – less ambitious – way of life. Having written down the story, his last sentences tell us that he is not going to show it to Gisela (170): he still needs to maintain the pretence of superiority with her, although he is so self-conscious about it that he actually resembles a little boy trying to hide something shameful from his mother. For him, authorship and masculinity are closely related: failures won't deter him from aspiring to both again. A tragicomic figure, he is more determined to regain his sense of control than most of Hoban's male protagonists. His self-consciousness undermines his masculine/authorial assertions, however. He has been in too extreme a situation ever to recuperate a naive attitude again. Unlike the mouse father in *The Mouse and his Child,* who demands respect and a place where a lost unity can be restored (MC 146), the protagonist of "The Devil's Kitchen" knows that his wound cannot be healed. The narrator's ambivalent perception of masculinity in fact resembles that of writers examined by Peter Schwenger in *Phallic Critiques*, e.g. Ernest Hemingway:

> Beneath the blatant *machismo* one finds considerable ambivalence towards the traditional masculine role. These writers recognize not only the role's power and its sense of archetypal fulfilment, but also its limitations, its self-deceptions, its destructiveness. (Schwenger 14).

Russell Hoban's perception of the traditional masculine role is not only ambivalent but critical: after all he published "The Devil's Kitchen" and did not confine it to the private recesses of his conscience like his narrator. Despite the assertions of the male protagonists in his earliest and latest novels and short stories, Hoban has never advertised *machismo* or a masculine standard of behaviour for all characters, either. In the early eighties, he was so critical of the traditional masculine role as to accuse men of womb envy and to express sympathies with matriarchal myths (see Wilkie 110f.).

ERNEST HEMINGWAY: *A FAREWELL TO ARMS*

Looking at the novel *A Farewell to Arms* (1929) by Ernest Hemingway, the American father of the "new Virility School" (Shulamith Firestone, quoted in Schwenger 13), will serve to work out what the difference between an ambivalent and a critical view of the traditional masculine role entails for the representation of relationships between male and female protagonists. *A Farewell to Arms* has been selected for several reasons: it portrays the love between a man battered by life and his notion of an ideal woman,[15] very much like *The Lion of Boaz-Jachin and Jachin-Boaz* or Hoban's subsequent novel *Kleinzeit*; moreover, *A Farewell to Arms* has also been an object of feminist controversy.

In *The Resisting Reader* (1978), Judith Fetterley criticizes the novel for obscuring hostile power relations between men and women by using the mythology of romantic love (xv-xvi); in her view, Catherine Barkley fulfils no other function than that of a scapegoat sacrificed to save Frederic from responsibility and commitment (47, 59-62, 67). Fetterley's attack ends in a bitter accusation:

> If we weep reading the book at the death of soldiers, we are weeping for the tragic and senseless waste of their lives; we are weeping for them. If we weep at the end of the book, however, it is not for Catherine but for Frederic Henry. All our tears are ultimately for men, because in the world of *A Farewell to Arms* male life is what counts. And the message to women reading this classic love story and experiencing its image of the female ideal is clear and simple: the only good woman is a dead one, and even then there are questions. (71)

Joyce Wexler, on the other hand, comes to the book's defense in "E.R.A. for Hemingway: A Feminist Defense of *A Farewell to Arms*" (1981). Arguing that the knowledge of Hemingway's personal *machismo* has too often warped readings of his major novels, she seeks to focus on moments in the novel and details in its narrative structure which underline the similarity rather than the opposition between Catherine and Frederic; she particularly objects to a fundamental inaccuracy detected in Fetterley's reading:

> To counteract the bias of critics whose focus on Frederic tends to blur Catherine's development, a feminist interpretation must concentrate on her. The angriest feminist attack on Hemingway I have seen fails to do this. In *The Resisting Reader* Judith Fetterley is unable to regard Catherine as a distinct character: 'In fact, Catherine's contradictions are *not* resolvable, because her character is determined by forces outside her; it is a reflection of male psychology and male fantasy life and is understandable only when seen as a series of responses to the needs of the male world that surrounds her.' [*The*

15 Catherine Barkley is diametrically opposed to Luz, the female protagonist of "A Very Short Story" from the collection *In Our Time* (1925). Luz is a nurse in Italy like Catherine. The wounded male protagonist falls in love with her; they are determined to get married. As soon as he has returned to America to look for a job, however, she chooses another lover. Her infidelity makes him adopt a wild love life, which leads to his contracting gonorrhea. The story enacts the ambiguity of her first name: Luz can be associated with "lux", i.e. light, or the adjective "loose". Luz thus embodies what Judith Fetterley has called "one of the most persistent of literary stereotypes", i.e. the "castrating bitch" (*The Resisting Reader*, xx).

> *Resisting Reader*, 66] While these statements reflect Fetterley's analysis of women in patriarchal literature, they do not, unfortunately, describe Hemingway's novel accurately. (112)

For Wexler, the criticism leveled at Frederic (and Hemingway) by critics like Fetterley has actually been built into the novel in so far as the mature first-person narrator indicts his own younger self for his "egotism, self-pity, and evasion of responsibility" (112). Wexler will therefore go on to show that neither "demeaned nor idealized by Hemingway, Catherine is clearly presented as a forerunner of the kind of person Frederic has become by the time he narrates the story of his wartime experiences. They are members of the same species, Hemingway heroes" (112-113). At the beginning of the novel, Catherine is not only more experienced in regard to the reality of war but also more versed in the game of love (113-115). Even though Wexler's arguments are convincing so far, she then plays down the degree to which Catherine accommodates herself to Frederic's needs once she has really fallen in love with him: her "geisha-like desire to please Frederic ... is characteristic of Catherine only at the beginning of her love cure" (115). But there are plenty of examples to show that her desire to please Frederic will continue until she dies. Whereas Wexler reads the scene when Catherine informs Frederic of her pregnancy in chapter 21 as a "period of instruction" for Frederic, in which he learns to appreciate *her* "ethic of resolution and reticence" (117), I will try to demonstrate presently that it could also be read as a scene in which she is taught a lesson in masculine reserve. Finally, Wexler's interpretation of Catherine's death fails to reach beyond the perspective of the protagonists: "Catherine's death is as gratuitous as steaming the ants. The mature narrator's judgement confirms Catherine's explanation: 'It's just a dirty trick'.... No one can be blamed" (121). Since we are not reading a true story, but a novel planned and executed by an author, however, it is legitimate to ask why *he* played this "dirty trick" on Catherine. Significantly, Wexler does not feel obliged to concentrate on Catherine any more by now: "Catherine and Frederic discover together the great deficiency of romantic love when she is dying: the spiritual renewal love brings does not outlive the beloved" (122). But did Catherine not know this right from the beginning? Weren't her romantic notions dispelled by her fiancé's death? It is actually only Frederic who discovers something new. Wexler continues: "Frederic walks from the hospital aware only of his loss, but Catherine has anticipated his recovery" (122). Did she then need to die merely for Frederic to learn these lessons? In this case, the price she pays for his education is extravagant, to say the least.

Wexler's effort to stress the similarity of the two protagonists, both to rescue Catherine "from the stereotyped role of the hero's mistress" and the novel from being "unfairly diminished" by angry feminists (122f.), prevents her from asking such questions. Moreover, she also evades the question whether or not sex and gender have their share in determining the protagonists' fates. By leaving these questions unasked and unanswered, however, Wexler herself contributes to diminishing the meaning of Catherine's death. Amends can only be made by bringing out the connection between Catherine's being at once a Hemingway hero, a woman, and the person whose death will move Frederic more than anyone else's. I will begin my discussion of the novel by examining the way in which a Hemingway hero learns the lessons of life and then try to examine how femaleness, femininity and mortality tie in with his system of values.[16]

A point repeatedly made in the novel, especially in the dialogues between Frederic and the priest (cf. chs. 3 and 11), or between Frederic and Catherine (cf. chs. 34 and 38), is that there is a difference between knowing and understanding:

> I tried to tell about the night and the difference between the night and the day and how the night was better unless the day was very clean and cold and I could not tell it; as I cannot tell it now. But if you have had it you know. He had not had it but he understood that I had really wanted to go to the Abruzzi but had not gone and we were still friends, with many tastes alike, but with the difference between us. He had always known what I did not know and what, when I learned it, I was always able to forget. (14)

Frederic (like Catherine) always wants to know, that is to "have had it", to appropriate. He cannot be satisfied with an understanding gained by listening to another person's words, because the one who merely understands is inferior in a hierarchy determined by experience: fools "don't know", they are "stupid from inexperience" (53), boys are the ones who try to understand and learn (27, 57), but it is knowledge synonymous with experience and expertise that people (Hemingway heroes) must aspire to. Experience counts more than formal authority. Among the inexperienced, those who choose not to gain experience which would conflict with their ideals are more respectable than those who are too cowardly or physically unable to do so. Difference seems to be more or less tolerable between men. They can still be friends: Frederic is not nettled by the knowledge that the priest "had always known what [he] did not know"; and

16 A distinction between sex and gender is indispensable to the analysis of the relations between men and women in this novel. Fetterley's charge of an overall hostility towards women will prove to be just as unprecise as Wexler's insistence on the equivalence of the two protagonists.

the priest merely laughs when Frederic calls him a boy because he does not know anything about women and the night (57): he could find it all out if he set his mind to it. The same kind of friendly rivalry links Frederic to his "war brother" Rinaldi (cf. ch. 10).

With most women, however, Frederic apparently tolerates difference only when he can feel superior. Fetterley's analysis of Frederic's contempt for women in positions of authority sufficiently underlines this point (53-55). There is one exception, which she has failed to consider, however: Helen Ferguson. Tough but "nice" Fergy, not "noticed" by Frederic at first (20), is briefly allowed to rise to the status of an elder sister who may resolutely ask Frederic to be more considerate of Catherine without losing his respect (80f.). If she cautions Frederic against getting Catherine "into trouble", it is not from selfish motives such as jealousy or a wish to humiliate him, but because she has seen many women end up having "these war babies" (81). Her superiority derives from her experience, not from her position as a nurse. Having brothers in the army, moreover, she "knows" men and therefore also knows how to bring about an improvement of their behaviour – by linking the promise of respect to a challenge to their ambition:

> 'It would be better if you let her stay off nights a little while.'
> 'I want her to.'
> 'You do not. But if you would make her I'd respect you for it.'
> 'I'll make her.'
> 'I don't believe it.' She took the note and went out. (81)[17]

Unlike Miss Gage, who cannot hide her jealousy of Catherine, Helen Ferguson does not crave his attention: she does not wish to be perceived by him as a potential sexual object. She crossly rejects gestures or remarks on his part which she must interpret as concessions to a feminine sensibility, e.g. his compliment that she is "a fine girl": "'I'm not. Don't try to flatter me....'" (81). By and large she succeeds: her femaleness remains hidden – note, for instance, how often Frederic refers to her family name without using a title, as

17 In *Männerphantasien, Bd. 1: Frauen, Fluten, Körper, Geschichte* (1977), Klaus Theweleit opposes the fantasy scenario of wounded soldiers falling in love with sexually attractive nurses (he explicitly mentions *A Farewell to Arms* as an example) to the reality of these men's needs (I:163-165). For the average World War I soldier a sexual affair with a white nurse would have been equivalent to the breach of the incest taboo; he therefore preferred nurses who did not tempt him (see Theweleit I:161ff.). But Hemingway took measures to "neutralize" the situation. Being a volunteer, Frederic is not a typical soldier. In fact, the phantasy of an erotic attachment to a nurse can become "true" for him and Catherine because he is just as idealized and "special" as she is. Catherine thinks it important to establish that she is not a trained nurse like Helen Ferguson but a V.A.D. (i.e. a member of the Voluntary Aid Detachment) (22f.). And indeed, while he is at best indifferent to maternal or sexually unattractive nurses, at worst hostile (cf. chs. 13-14, and 17), there is never any danger of his falling in love with Ferguson, who is neither unattractive nor maternal, but too professional, perhaps also too disillusioned, to offer herself as a love object (80f.).

if he referred to one of the male characters. Her superiority will come to an infamous end at Stresa, however, when she realizes that she is going to lose her friend Catherine to Frederic (ch. 35). She now appears as Frederic's rival, no longer as a disinterested adviser. He is "sick of Fergy" when she breaks down and lets herself be comforted by Catherine (177), probably because he now assumes that she may feel more for Catherine than friendship. But eventually Catherine assures him that her main feeling for Helen Ferguson is pity, not love; he must not fear that she will try to persuade him to agree to a *ménage à trois*:[18] "'She won't stay afterwards, will she?' – 'No. I'll get rid of her.'"(183).

Wexler indirectly provides more evidence for the hypothesis that Frederic finds it hard to tolerate difference, and especially superiority, in women by showing how, as Catherine and Frederic's "love increases, the differences between them almost disappear" (118). The adverb "almost" is telling: actually, "their" love has two sides. It is mainly due to Catherine's efforts that their differences seem to disappear in the course of their relationship, or rather, difference gives way to complementarity. Catherine does her best to satisfy Frederic's needs, even while she is dying. Where her experience surpasses his, she never abuses her superiority to boss Frederic around but waits until he "has had it" too. Her love can therefore serve as an example of "transcendence of self by serving another", as Wexler writes (120), that is love actualizing the ideal defined by the priest; but since the "other" is in this case a Hemingway hero

---

18 The short story "Mr. and Mrs. Elliot" caricatures a sexually frustrated couple whose childless marriage will eventually turn into such an arrangement: Cornelia Elliot's girl friend moves in with them – not only to type Hubert Elliot's poems but to cry and sleep with Cornelia. Hemingway's joke is above all on Hubert, who set great store by remaining "pure" before he married Cornelia. For his high ideals merely mask the fact that he is a miserable lover. Unlike Frederic, he is not "man enough" to keep his wife for himself. His exaggerated concern for the vulnerability of his body makes him "feminine" without necessity, and that is of course inacceptable for a true Hemingway hero. Those who can, do, and if the price is venereal disease, the *macho* as well as the Hemingway hero will fight it with chemicals and endure the pain rather than to live the abstinent life of a priest. There is an important difference between the *macho* and the Hemingway hero: the former is altogether unable to establish permanent relationships with women, owing to his distorted image of them (see below, where I will discuss further differences), whereas the latter can be faithful once he has found a suitable partner. I do not think that the novel seriously sets up the priest's celibacy as the standard for attitudes toward sexuality, as Fetterley does: "The priest alone is able to carry out the full implications of his culture's attitude toward sex" (52). She deliberately disambiguates one of the most ambiguous sentences in the novel, "He had always known what I did not know and what, when I learned it, I was always able to forget" (14), by giving it the meaning "that sex is a dangerous and wasteful commodity and the best world is one of men without women" (52). Fetterley overlooks Frederic's admiration for Catherine later on in the novel, which relates to his conversation with the priest about the differences between day and night: "... with Catherine there was almost no difference in the night except that it was an even better time" (178). A "clean and cold" day in the Abruzzi might be preferable to lonely nights or to nights with less perfect women than Catherine (14), but she is the exception which justifies a Hemingway hero's fundamental affirmation of sexuality.

with clear-cut notions of how to deserve his interest and respect, Catherine's love is also an example of the "*immasculation* of women by men":

> Though one of the most persistent of literary stereotypes is the castrating bitch, the cultural reality is not the emasculation of men by women but the *immasculation* of women by men. As readers and teachers and scholars, women are taught to think as men, to identify with a male point of view, and to accept as normal and legitimate a male system of values, one of whose central principles is misogyny. (Fetterley xx)

Frederic's need for "sameness" or superiority, on the other hand, is narcissistic. The child must in his eyes be a most unwelcome addition to their "perfect" complementary dyad, but not because of a potential oedipal rivalry. Catherine's motherhood will provide her with a knowledge Frederic will never be able to "have": the child will be a permanent reminder that sexual difference is insurmountable, unlike other differences of experience, or the differences of feminine and masculine behaviour and appearance which are negotiable. The way Frederic reacts to the news of Catherine's pregnancy underlines that difference and danger are linked in his thinking – they are "apart" now, and biology is a "trap":

> We were apart as when someone comes into a room and people are self-conscious. She put out her hand and took mine.
> 'You aren't angry are you, darling?'
> 'No.'
> 'And you don't feel trapped?'
> 'Maybe a little. But not by you.'
> 'I didn't mean by me. You mustn't be stupid. I meant trapped at all.'
> 'You always feel trapped biologically.'
> She went away a long way without stirring or removing her hand. (102)

Catherine cannot immediately react to his difficulty in accepting all the implications of sexual difference (which was desirable enough during the nights they had spent together): she withdraws from him. The way she will comfort him afterwards, however, shows that she trusts in the effectiveness of gendered behaviour to conjure up the phantasy of complementary unity again – as if the "embarrassment" of her sex could be got rid off by giving birth. At first, though, she tests his ability to "serve another", that is to love and accept her the way she cannot help being:

> '"Always" isn't a pretty word.'
> 'I'm sorry.'
> 'It's all right. But you see I've never had a baby and I've never even loved anyone. And I've tried to be the way you wanted and then you talk about "always".'
> 'I could cut off my tongue,' I offered.

> 'Oh, darling!' she came back from wherever she had been. 'You mustn't mind me.' We were both together again and the self-consciousness was gone. 'We really are the same one and we mustn't misunderstand on purpose.' (102)

Her initial explanations invite him to understand her alterity (the woman who is going to be a mother and who must make a conscious effort to be feminine *according to his standard*), but they merely provoke his sarcasm;[19] her subsequent self-denial ("you mustn't mind me") and her assertions that they "really are the same one", on the other hand, bring her back to him. By treating language as a potential source of misunderstandings, she signals that she has accepted his code and is further willing to become the figure he wants her to be rather than to insist on difference. This code will accomplish her transformation into a female version of the Hemingway hero modelled on, though not altogether identical with, a *macho*. Here is Peter Schwenger's summary of Paz's description of this extreme masculine figure:

> The *macho* ... is 'a hermetic being, closed up in himself.' He is invulnerable to the assaults of the outside world and his manliness is measured by that invulnerability. He must always resist the temptation, under adversity or stress, to open up emotionally. Whatever else the outside world may do to him, the *macho* cannot allow it to penetrate his privacy. 'Women,' in this view, 'are inferior beings because, in submitting, they open themselves up.' (*Phallic Critiques*, 43)

The difference between a *macho* and a Hemingway hero must not be disregarded. The Hemingway hero sooner or later loses the belief in his invulnerability; unlike the *macho*, he cannot foreclose it, that is, choose to ignore it. Like Frederic Henry, he only starts out as a *macho*: "Well, I knew I would not be killed. Not in this war. It did not have anything to do with me. It seemed no more dangerous to me myself than war in the movies" (31) – evidently, Frederic is only slightly maturer than the Nick Adams we leave at the end of "Indian Camp". But the plot will stamp his belief as a boy's inexperienced presumption. The Hemingway hero is forced to acknowledge being caught in a trap – his body, at once the source of powerful drives which may impede his thinking, and the vulnerable flesh of which every doctor can dispossess him if he does not watch out (see ch. 32). He grudgingly accepts his symbolic castration by "the world": "The world breaks everyone and

19 N.B. Frederic Henry's standard of femininity ostensibly differs from the feminine mystique of the postwar generation: although he admires personal beauty and youth, he abhors passivity, weakness, and dependence in a woman. A woman's potential for motherhood is an unwanted side-effect of her biology, nothing Frederic would admire or even envy her for. From a feminist perspective it is nevertheless inacceptable that Catherine must model her self-image on Frederic's preferences, or else feel rejected. Gretel, by contrast, does not feel any pressure to conform; she is more autonomous than Catherine.

afterwards many are strong at the broken places. But those that will not break it kills" (178). Even though his code of reserve does not allow him to lament his condition, a restrained release of emotion is possible: the story can be told as long as the narrator adheres to a literary "iceberg technique". Finally, unlike the *macho* the Hemingway hero does not despise all women as inferior beings, as long as they conform to his sexual needs and share his masculine values. Rinaldi is a typical *macho*: unable to make any finer distinctions, he regards women either as more or less despicable whores who can be bought for money or seduced by the (false) promise of marriage (13f.), or else as useless goddesses (52f.). But for Frederic, women need not be dead to be good, as Fetterley suspects.

The female version of the Hemingway hero starts out as the "woman" reviled by the *macho*. Her development involves adopting the code of reserve as well as a certain contempt for her sex, which is an inconvenience added to the fact that she is caught in her bodily trap like her male counterpart. Despite this contempt for her female body, she must not become too masculine in her looks or tough in her behaviour, however. The ability to lead a double life is indispensable. Female Hemingway heroes[20] should be feminine "by night", that is yield their female body to their male lover and heed his preferences regarding her behaviour towards him, but "by day", that is at work or in dealing with other people, they should abstain from deriving any privileges from their sex and be as "masculine" in character (resolute, competent, reticent, practical, brave, etc.) as possible. Catherine nearly overshoots the mark, probably as a consequence of Frederic's earlier reaction to her pregnancy; she is extremely self-conscious when her pregnant body makes it impossible for her to "hide" her sex by day (208, 216, 219) even though Frederic now tries to make her understand that he finds her beautiful. He also – cautiously – tries to prevent Catherine from cutting her hair (212ff.). But since he is no longer the kind of person who would pick a fight over such trifles, he eventually swallows his objections and pretends that a new haircut would be "exciting" (216). One could see this as a sign of Frederic's reformation: for the first time he tries to serve her. But there is still a decisive difference between his

---

20 I won't call them "heroines" since the constructional principle informing their character is that there be "almost no difference". They are designed to conjure up the illusion of sameness and unity which they will eventually crave as much as the male heroes. In this respect, the unhappy young American wife in "Cat in the Rain" is the antithesis of Catherine. Frustrated with her looks, with a life in hotel rooms and with a husband spending his days in bed reading, her wish for a change crystallizes in the childish demand for a kitten. The way she is characterized in the story underlines that she is no female Hemingway hero but an immature girl. Her selfish and indifferent husband can no more aspire to the title of hero than his wife, however. It is only the *padrone* who behaves in an exemplary way; he knows that service and dignity are not mutually exclusive.

sacrificing an aesthetic preference and the kind of sacrifices Catherine has made to accommodate him. A female Hemingway hero may dissent in trivial matters such as the length of her hair, but where certain values are at stake, she must make sure that there is no disagreement between her and her partner. By the time Catherine and Frederic are walking through a snowy Swiss landscape, a hundred pages after she has informed him of her pregnancy, a remark of hers shows that she has by now assimilated the view that a child would be an intruder: "'She won't come between us, will she? The little brat.'" (215). Interestingly, Catherine thinks that her baby is going to be a girl: does this assumption not give away her awareness that for her, the enemy in their relationship is not the child *per se*, but her own uncanny sexual difference, which is a danger to her "Hemingway-hero-self"? By displacing it onto the child, she has placed it away from her alienated self. This overt hostility both to the child and to her sex will have gone by the time she has given birth, though. She asks Frederic about the baby (a boy) when coming to after the Caesarean (231). What is nevertheless strange is that she never asks to see him. She will obviously die without having learned the truth of his death. Could her mourning have caused unwanted noises in the last part of the novel? Is it not conspicuous that her last words express no concern at all for the baby but only for Frederic's future love life, and for a perception of her dying which will leave him free from worries or guilt?: "'Don't worry, darling,' Catherine said. 'I'm not a bit afraid. It's just a dirty trick.'" (235).[21]

The only conclusion I can draw from these omissions is that she was to be seen dying as a perfect Hemingway hero, not as a mourning mother: sharable experience, that is her body's mortality, not its sex was to be the centre of attention. By means of this trick, Hemingway could turn her into a genuine forerunner of Frederic. It is notably the process of her dying which serves his sentimental education, for "You did not know what it was about. You never had time to learn" (232). The dead body itself, fetishized in many Gothic tales and novels, is of no interest to Frederic, as his last visit to Catherine's deathbed shows: "... it wasn't any good. It was like saying

21 A comparison with one of the stories from *In Our Time* will prove useful again. The scene of Catherine's dying sharply contrasts with "Indian Camp". The Indian woman's screams of pain during a Caesarean executed with a jack-knife and without an anaesthetic upset her husband so much that he commits suicide by cutting his throat. According to Schwenger, the story establishes "the fundamental ambiguity of masculine reserve. Not talking is a demonstration of masculine control over emotion; but it is also and ultimately self-destructive" (*Phallic Critiques*, 45). By letting a surplus of emotion "penetrate and possess him", as Schwenger writes (43), the Indian gets trapped in a double bind. The suicidal wound womanizes him (42); had he "screamed unabashedly", however, the "release of emotion might have saved his life, though it would have left him no less womanized in his own eyes and society's" (43). By contrast, Catherine does everything in her power to prevent an outburst of emotion; she calms Frederic as Dr. Adams calmed his son Nick, enabling Frederic to contain his feelings.

goodbye to a statue" (236). Unlike Wexler, though, I do not think that he is primarily taught a lesson on the limitations death imposes on romantic love, or a lesson on the hope of recovery from loss. Nor can I agree with Fetterley, who thinks that Catherine's death is just the culmination of a pervasive hostility towards women, and that it basically serves to restore Frederic's freedom. On the contrary. Her dying in fact "mothers" his own mortality. Even though Catherine's femaleness is suppressed, her dying body is multiply stigmatized as feminine, by the incision of the Caesarean and the knowledge that she is going to die. Whereas Frederic and other men used to "father" her immasculation in life, she now takes the lead in the experience of dying, which is the "end of the trap" for everyone (227).

Dying ultimately lends femininity even to the most masculine of men since having to yield *to* the body is considered as feminine as yielding the body to another. Yielding too early would mean defeat. Rinaldi therefore plays down his syphilis; it is "a simple industrial accident" that can be cured with mercury (127). Everything seems to be under control. He need not yield to his body yet; he can still do as he pleases, even ruin his health by heavy drinking, which he cynically calls "Self-destruction day by day" (124). But Catherine need not consider her dying a defeat either because she lays down her arms to make a separate peace with her mortal body literally only at the last possible moment. Her heroism consists both in yielding no sooner than when it can no longer be helped – unlike the Italian officers during the retreat, who resign themselves to their execution while Frederic still finds a way to escape (ch. 30) – and in accepting her fate once she knows that she is going to die – despite the doctor's attempt to deny her that knowledge: "You are not going to die. You must not be silly" (235). Frederic learns from her the right time to yield to a femininity not derived from the female sex but synonymous here with a yielding to the body's mortality.

Unlike Perseus, who murdered Medusa to assert the masculine control over his bodily drives, killing the personification of his desire for incest and death, Frederic learns when it is time to give up the position of mastery. Hemingway shows through Frederic that he obviously does not share Freud's need to evade and repress the desire for death at all cost, by linking it to the oedipal idea of incest. But Hemingway is nevertheless anchored in the Freudian framework insofar as he, too, links the body – seen as the ambivalent vehicle of sexual difference, but above all as a lethal trap – to femininity. This "femininity" can be appropriated visually, but it has to be kept at bay by a masculine mind as long as possible – deliberately "unremembered" rather than repressed. Only at the last possible moment is Hemingway's Perseus allowed to set the appropriated Medusa free to let her do her work. The novel presents us with the moment when Frederic appropriates his femininity, watching Catherine die, the victim of a helpless or incompetent gynaecologist and of an author wary of approaching the subject of mortality in a more direct way. The "Medusa" he sees dying is beautiful, not a monster, the archaic mother unencumbered by oedipal ballast. Still, he cannot as yet bear the thought of his mortality without displacing it onto the image of another: he needs a dying Medusa to acquaint him with his own hitherto unacknowledged desire for death. The novel briefly lays bare the connection between her death and his desire. For a split second only, as if by a slip of the pen and prompted by feelings of guilt, Frederic acknowledges his desire by identifying with the baby strangled in Catherine's womb.[22] But this subversive idea is repressed straight away by negating it, and finally, death is displaced onto Catherine according to the pattern governing the majority of our culture's artistic creations (also see ch. 8.3): "Poor little kid. I wished the hell I'd been choked like that. No I didn't. Still there would not be all this dying to go through. Now Catherine would die" (232). Catherine will die because Hemingway heroes are not satisfied with reading about the ways of the world, nor with being ignorantly exposed to them; they want to know. But the closest Frederic can safely get to knowing what it will be like to die, that is to yield to his body, is by watching Catherine, mirroring himself in the woman who strove to mirror him. While male characters teach him values such as professional competence (Rinaldi), service (the priest), or maintaining one's dignity at an old age (the Count Greffi), Catherine "excels" in her dying, smiling at Frederic, worrying about his future, cracking jokes when it is "very hard for her to talk" (235), and using even her last words for a sarcastic comment on her situation. Hemingway had to play a "dirty trick" on her, because only a woman doubly

22 The image of the baby boy strangled by his umbilical cord could be called the ***punctum*** of this novel. Instead of turning the womb (as a place where new life is generated) into the opposite of the battlefield, Hemingway shows that death inhabits both of them, and by implication, the whole world. The subject can only choose between two options: he either fights all forces out to kill him, be it the archaic mother or enemies on the battlefield, or else gives in to his desire for death. Fetterley interprets this image as a symptom of Frederic's fear of Catherine, from which results his supposed hostility towards her: "... her death, however much it may be shaped as biological accident, is in fact the fulfillment of his own unconscious wish, his need to kill her lest she kill him" (53). In her view, Frederic is more exposed to danger in the war of the sexes than in the world of war: "In an ironic reversal of expectations, the real danger to Frederic Henry turns out to be not the world of war, the outer world that is so obviously threatening, but the world of love, the inner world that seems overtly so secure" (65). But in fact, the "world of love" is still an outer world compared to the unconscious, the other world inside everyone of us. I think Hemingway's message is more unsettling than Fetterley's interpretation would make us believe. The real enemy is no external "other", the beloved no more than an enemy soldier, but everyone's desire for death, here coded as "feminine". The fact that the strangled baby is male adds a further twist to this interpretation: the image reveals that Hemingway knew that the desire for death ultimately has no gender. At this moment, he subverts the equation between mortality and femininity which otherwise "justifies" Catherine's death. He shows that the equation is a masculine defence to hide the most impalpable truth about the human condition: the knowledge that mortality is inscribed in us even before we are born.

"handicapped" by her sex and by the irrepressible mortality/femininity of her body could set the absolute standard of deathbed etiquette to be imitated by Frederic in the future. Though none of the male characters who die has so many "natural obstacles" to brave (Aymo dies so fast that there is of course no time to give proof of his bravery), they all give themselves up earlier, forfeiting their masculine dignity, for example by deserting from the army while there is no immediate danger to their lives (the two sergeants) or by screaming in pain (Passini). Catherine, however, endures until she loses consciousness.

Earlier on, I raised the question what an ambivalent view of the traditional masculine role (*machismo*) entailed for the representation of relationships between male and female characters. An answer can now be attempted: "femininity" (not women), defined as the body's vulnerability and mortality and the subject's desire for death, is the main enemy threatening the heroic "masculine" postures of both men and women. This "femininity" can be acknowledged and appropriated by Hemingway heroes though it must carefully be kept at bay by subduing signs of weakness and observing a strict code of reserve to oppose emotional outbursts. Ideal couples help each other to maintain their heroic postures: they do not seek to expose or exploit each other's "femininity" but to even it out in an idyll of complementary unity in which the loneliness and the terror of being no longer exist; see Frederic's assertion: "... we were never lonely and never afraid when we were together" (178). Sexuality complicates the picture, especially for female characters; for an ambivalent view of masculinity entails a splitting of the concept of femininity into a "universal" bodily "femininity" and a sexually specific, "essential" femininity. Women who are shown to be able to abide by a masculine standard of behaviour, sharing "masculine" values, suppressing their bodily "femininity" (mortality, vulnerability) and making no allowances for their sex, have to affirm both their sex and their "essential" femininity (the kind of behaviour women have been taught to regard as their own, turning them into sexual objects) in relationships with male characters. Men do not have to "switch": they usually impose conditions on women as they do on their own bodies. The women's task, on the other hand, is not only next to impossible but also unrewarding. For once a female character has managed to oscillate miraculously between masculine everyday and feminine sexual behaviour, she is turned into an exemplary spectacle to teach her male partner and the readers how to face the ultimate truth. Her masterly management of her "essential" femininity turns her into an expert for the handling of that other "femininity". Although Judith Fetterley's anger was grounded in too unsubtle an analysis of the novel, it is justifiable if seen as a reaction to the covert terror informing the role model of an overtly attractive female character like Catherine Barkley; it cannot simply be dismissed as the expression of an evil-minded misreading of the novel. Wexler's rehabilitation of Catherine and the novel, on the other hand, shows that she has fallen into the trap set up by the author. Her reading cannot expose the novel as a gift-that-takes for both men and women. Wexler emphasises Catherine's status as a Hemingway hero but fails to ask whether this kind of heroism is desirable and viable at all. For examining its implications reveals that both men and women are made prisoners of an extremely exacting code. Snubbing conventional morality (e.g. regarding marriage and the status of motherhood), it nevertheless does not increase the liberty of those who observe it. It is a code that enslaves the body. Femininity is deliberately used as the image of dangerous difference and mortality. The code's central term is experience synonymous with appropriation; loss is therefore the absolute evil, and different experience, an enemy to be overcome. Hence, love cannot flow here; it is crippled by the high ideal it must by all means fulfil (sameness and unity against terror and loneliness), and its protagonists are indebted to so many restrictions on their behaviour that it is very unlikely that their limited and ritualized "game of love" will ever last long enough for them to be surprised by genuine feelings. A comparison between Hemingway's novel and Borges's "Ulrike" reveals the impossibility of Catherine and Frederic's love: where Borges simply underlines that love is unique for every couple of lovers, Hemingway's novel suggests that there is only one kind of love worth its name, that is a genuine "farewell to arms": the union of a man and a woman who are united in their fight against the "femininity" of their bodies and their observation of an exacting masculine code of behaviour, a narcissistic relationship between two similar individuals who reassure and confirm each other in most respects. Such love is no sooner found (against all odds) than destroyed again by the multiple dangers of material change. A comparison between *A Farewell to Arms* and *The Lion of Boaz-Jachin and Jachin-Boaz*, on the other hand, emphasizes the claustrophobic aspect of Catherine and Frederic's love. I cannot help asking myself just how "happily" they would have lived in their Swiss chalet above Montreux and how long the "ever after" would really have been if Catherine had not been pregnant and doomed to die. Whereas Hemingway's couple experiences the peak of their love in self-sufficient seclusion, Gretel and Jachin-Boaz remain immersed in their lives, open to changes and aware that their love is important, but neither the only content of their lives nor an experience which can free them from anxiety for good. Where a writer wishes to convey a critical view of the traditional masculine role, male characters cannot solve their problems by finding an ideal woman to confirm the superiority of a specific masculine code and embody those experiences the male character would perceive as threats to his masculinity, i.e. weakness, vulnerability or mortality. As in "The Devil's Kitchen", the male protagonists must suffer themselves if a disrespect for their body, their female partner or their limitations strands them on the brink of an abyss.

KLEINZEIT

In *Kleinzeit*, Hoban's love story between a nurse and a sick man who will turn into a writer, the dangers both of making one's beloved into the source of peaceful rest and of exploiting her for art are addressed in the dislocutions of the Orpheus and Eurydice myth. Kleinzeit's patchy linear summary emphasizes Orpheus's weakness: "Orpheus with his lute made trees and all that, said Kleinzeit. And then Eurydice in the Underworld, he nearly got her out with his music but he looked back and lost her. He wasn't meant to look back" (142). On the surface, Orpheus is too impatient to wait for a signal from Eurydice. Unconsciously, though, he might also wish for her loss because his art had never been as powerful as when he sang to charm Hades and Persephone into releasing her (and indirectly himself). Moreover, in "accidentally" losing her a second time, Orpheus perhaps tries to remove a powerful reminder of his own mortality: since he has been to the Underworld on her behalf, his love for Eurydice will never again be able to sustain the illusion of his potency and immortality but will remind him of his own future death. His unconscious "scheme" does not work, however, because nothing can wipe out the memory of what he has experienced, not even shunning the company of women. Caught in the dilemma between refusing his fate and being unable to forget about it, Orpheus turns hysterical. Hoban has used the myth aware of psychoanalytical implications. His essay "Thoughts on Being and Writing" (published one year after *Kleinzeit*, i.e. in 1975; see chapter 4.3) shows that for him, Orpheus's longing for Eurydice after he has lost her corresponds to the desire for death. An artist must be able to sublimate this desire, i.e. confront the abject and verbalize it rather than give way to hysterical symptoms.

Hospital's cyclic version, though, serves no other purpose than to seduce Kleinzeit and other potential Orpheuses into satisfying their desire for death rather than to repress or sublimate it. The sphinx-like crouching monster is interested in devouring its patients rather than in healing them (39f.):[23]

---

23 Hospital is described as having a huge feline body (39), which establishes links both to the supernatural lion of Hoban's previous novel as well as to the sphinx Léonie in his short story "My Night with Léonie". The "Shackleton-Planck" test, where Kleinzeit is asked to swallow tubes writhing like snakes (68), on the other hand, links Hospital to Medusa. The comparison

maternal and attractive nurses like Sister are its lures. When it adds the episode of Orpheus's remembering himself to the linear version of the myth (cf. ch. 4.2), inviting Kleinzeit and Sister to identify with the mythic couple (48f., 142ff., 146ff., 149f.), it is not being friendly. Hospital seeks to perpetuate an endless action cycle of loss and gain without any escape for those involved. If they succumb to the temptation, they will always be in its clutches. For Eurydice is confined to the Underworld anyway while all Orpheus can do, should he be strong enough to remember himself at all, is oscillate between different realms of death forever:

> Orpheus cannot be content at the inside of things, at the place under the places, said Hospital. His harmony has brought him to the stillness and the calm at the centre and he cannot abide it. Nirvana is not his cup of tea. He wants to get back outside, ... wants to be seen with Eurydice at posh restaurants and all that. Naturally he loses her. She can't go outside any more than he can stay inside. (148)

The difference between the Underworld, or Underground, which is related to Hospital (48), and the beach at Lesbos, Orpheus' "hospital" (143), is negligible: with or without Eurydice, Orpheus will always miss something and be unable to accept his lack. Hospital's interpretation of sexual difference matches its hostility towards life: as in patriarchal myths, women are associated with death and inanimate matter, men with action and life. Only the evaluation of these associations is diametrically opposed to that of the old myths since death is desirable while life is not:

> ... all men are sick. Life is their sickness. Life is the original sickness of inanimate matter. All was well until matter messed itself about and came alive. Men are rotten clear through with being animate. Women on the other hand have not quite lost the health of the inanimate, the health of the deep stillness. They're not quite so sick with life as men are. (150)

While patriarchal myths instrumentalize sexual desire in such a way that males can literally forget about their desire for death, Hospital seeks to strengthen the desire for death through sexual desire. Hospital, too, promises wholeness when the male and the female "complements" unite, although Orpheus's ongoing dissatisfaction in both versions of the myth actually points to an inconsistency in the system. Hospital's dislocution, which merely reverses the patriarchal myth, of course cannot remove the inconsistency.

---

with a "man-eating vine" (171) leads to the image of Greanvine from *Riddley Walker*. Finally, one could also see a connection between Hospital as a huge spider waiting in its web for prey (171) and Pythia's enormous brain-spaceship-cocoon, in which Fremder, the protagonist of Hoban's eponymous science fiction novel, eventually finds himself trapped.

At their first meeting, the danger inherent in Kleinzeit and Sister's relationship is conjured up by an allusion to vampirism: Kleinzeit enjoys rather than objects to being brought closer to the "health" of inanimate matter by the penetration of Sister's syringe; in the realm of death, femininity and masculinity are reversed: "'I want some blood,' said Sister, and sank her hypodermic into his arm. Kleinzeit abandoned himself to sensuality and let it flow" (15). The "Bach-Euclid" test series, carried out by another beautiful nurse and "agent" of Hospital, on the other hand, evokes no pleasure any more though it is still described by way of sexual innuendo; Kleinzeit disguises his sense of humiliation at the Sadean setting in sarcastic comments:

> 'Down your throat and up your bum,' said the comely handmaiden of the see-through machine. 'Drink this, all of it. Cheers.'
> Kleinzeit drank, shuddered.
> 'Now lie here on the table on your side and spread your cheeks.'
> Kleinzeit shrank, spread his cheeks, was buggered by a syringe and pumped full of something. Role-reversal, he thought. Kinky. (32)

If he were Orpheus, he would now have to leave Hospital, abandoning Sister and her colleagues. If Sister were Eurydice, she would not understand his desire for change and life. But both actually want to survive and to preserve their love. They must therefore find ways of distancing themselves from the destructive role model Hospital tries to impose on them, dislocuting both the traditional Orpheus and Eurydice myth and Hospital's version in a way which cuts through the system's inconsistency.[24]

What is this inconsistency? Is it not the difficulty of finding a constructive way of dealing with one's desire for death and with the fact that certain situations require feminine surrender rather than masculine assertion and

---

24 Christine Wilkie speaks of a "contemporary parody of the Orphic myth" (39). However, it seems to me that "parody" fails to describe the variety of functions Hoban has assigned to the myth in the novel: of course, there is a certain degree of burlesque (particularly for the readers), but the classical story and its dislocuted cyclic version also offer relief and elevation; moreover, they pose a threat to Kleinzeit and Sister.

Barbara Herkommer, basing her analysis on Ihab Hassan's discussion of postmodernism, takes recourse to deconstruction and to the Bakhtinian term carnivalization ("Karnevalisierung", 101) to describe the way various source materials have been used in *Kleinzeit* (107). Carnivalization and deconstruction are preferable to parody in so far as these terms underline the calling into question of "authentic" and "whole" master narratives. Both violence and fun are included in the idea of a carnival, the mixing of ingredients of most diverse origins, while deconstruction implies a reading of a text, here of the Orphic myth, that is sensitive to the text's basic assumptions, its rhetorical blind spots and internal contradictions. By placing Eurydice at the inside of things, the dead centre, for instance, Hoban's Hospital spells out what is only implied in the patriarchal myth. But the term deconstruction also implies a very systematic procedure carried out by readers who are not only aware of the text's rhetorical complexities, but also of the limitations of their own interpretation, the generation of meaning, or meanings, being tied to certain conditions. Since this philosophical rigour is absent in the novel's treatment of the myth, I prefer to stick to Fritz Senn's term dislocution. *Riddley Walker*, of course, is an altogether different case (see ch. 6.4).

vice versa? Cutting through the inconsistency does not mean that it disappears. On the contrary, it is doubled: the need to balance life against death drives and femininity against masculinity is not only Orpheus's problem but Eurydice's as well. Christine Wilkie's discussion of *Kleinzeit* merely points to the inconsistency of the Orphic paradigm: "... the central motif is one of Orphic conflict in paradoxical relationship with Orphic harmony in which Kleinzeit seeks to reconcile his highly developed ego-consciousness with his lost, alienated, ancient, and feminine self" (Wilkie 39). Not only does she fail to notice that the paradox implicates both lovers but she also overlooks that the moment Kleinzeit and Sister succeed in becoming aware of the split in themselves, they can no longer be complements in the sense of the myth:

> Kleinzeit ... has arrived at a place that transcends mystery, where he has made friends with Death. And, with Sister as the yin/yang, male/female complement, he has reconciled himself to the incomprehensibility of life. The Orphic cycle is complete, and Kleinzeit has become part of the mythological pattern. (Wilkie 42)

In fact, they turn their backs on the pattern as soon as they realize how harmful it is for the other, and I shall presently highlight the steps of their developments. By contrast, hysterical Orpheus goes on to project mortality and femininity onto the female body although he has recognized them in himself. Frederic Henry, on the other hand, displaces the problem by projecting a gender boundary onto the distinction between body and mind, living according to the principle that his "masculine" mind must control his "feminine" (i.e. vulnerable and mortal) body as long as possible; this solution is more or less "comfortable" for himself but it requires great sacrifices from Catherine Barkley, as we have seen.

Kleinzeit recognizes in a gradual learning process that mortality is the destiny of all his bodily functions just as the death drive is part of his mental equipment and that "feminine" surrender to the symptoms of mortality and the death drive is sometimes a less dangerous, or more vital, response than "masculine" resistance. Being able to oscillate between both ways of being, according to the requirements of a situation, will prolong his life. When his body is unduly effeminated by the treatment in Hospital, Kleinzeit must take up the fight against the doctors and the medicaments by re-membering himself. Nevertheless his body continues to dictate the limits within which he can act. Refusing surgery and going home lie within them whereas exaggerated ambitions are punished by crises (e.g. 136, 168). The Athenians, those embodiments of unflinching masculine resistance, who again and again encourage Kleinzeit to defeat Hospital, after all lost the war against the

Spartans because they were overambitious and continued the struggle rather than to accept the Spartans' offer of peace at an intermediate stage (126). He must therefore develop a feeling for what Herkommer has called the ongoing dialectic between being a suffering patient and an active, resistant fighter (Herkommer 98). By making Kleinzeit first imitate, then distance himself from the Athenians, Hoban quietly but effectually disrupts the traditional links between masculinity and vitality, and between femininity and mortality.

At his first visit to Sister's place, Kleinzeit notices an old clock with a stopped pendulum. He sighs because her belongings, e.g. a poster by the German Romantic painter Caspar David Friedrich and a Sacred Heart (a representation of Jesus's bleeding heart), seem to make time expand (85) – this is intriguing for a man who feels that he has only little time left. While they are making love, he first invents himself "as theme, as subject". The scene is humorous, mixing, as Herkommer points out, "triviale Details wie die Zentralheizung mit phantastischen Bildern des sagenhaften Ortes Atlantis" (106). The scene is also remarkable, however, because it plays with images of losing and restoring the other and oneself without taking recourse to violent clichés. It is, in other words, another example of love that flows because the lovers contain their death drive. But then Kleinzeit is ever so ready to identify with Orpheus (86). The first thing he does on waking up the next morning is to repair Sister's clock (87). Life must go on even if the future will bring on his dismemberment. But it did so before Kleinzeit met Sister, and it will also take place in the future whether or not they will stay together. While Hospital thinks it can withhold the information (150), God lets Kleinzeit know early on that he is not an Orpheus who will be killed by Maenads, mourning for a lost Eurydice, but one who keeps falling apart like everybody else: "Entropy and all that. Nobody lives forever, you know, not even Me" (95). This information is important in so far as it explicitly dissociates Kleinzeit's dismemberment from his love for, and potential future loss of, Sister. There is then no need to remain confined to the action cycle of the mythical lovers: their story has come full circle and can be exchanged for another pattern. So Kleinzeit's own personal Death begins to accompany him like an ugly pet whether he is busking, at home, running, or in hospital (113f., 122ff., 134ff., 146; etc.). The death and dismemberment of a smalltime hero about whom nothing is special as well as moments of harmony are not reducible to relationships between male and female characters. The "broadcast" from Hall of Records at the end of the novel will confirm this insight too; three out of four seasons offered him other sources of harmony than love making:

> Moment, said Hall of Records: Winter, age something. In hospital. Feeling of circle inside self, sweet rhythm. Harmony took place.
> Kleinzeit waited. Will there be anything else? said Hall of Records.
> Place of dismemberment? said Kleinzeit.
> Everywhere, all the time, said Hall of Records. (182)

The pun on Kleinzeit/Orpheus's dismemberment and his remembering himself is possible on the basis that losses and diseases are perceived as kinds of castration. In so far as male characters are concerned, Hoban's thinking moves within the Freudian framework. The female characters receive special treatment, however. They may become instrumental to the "dismemberment" of males, or contribute to their recovery of sexual potency, they may even adopt masculine traits when equipped with "phallic" tools as the nurses in the quotations above, but they are nevertheless not perceived as castrated males who must feel inferior and therefore work hard to deserve recognition like the female characters in Hemingway's novel. At first glance, women seem to have nothing to lose in *Kleinzeit* except the sick "prince" they have been waiting for (10). Female bodies are mystified: there is not one sick woman in the novel. The characters challenged to become artists are always male. Sister, too, thinks that women are healthier than men, that is, literally, not in Hospital's perverted sense. She therefore expects men to make the right use of their sickness, that is to fight for their recovery instead of letting themselves go (19). This is a comically distorted variant of a typical fairy-tale or romance plot, with sickness as the monster which the "prince" must defeat in order to win the heart of the "princess". In *Turtle Diary*, on the other hand, the situation will be more complex: one of the protagonists is a woman writer and there is also a female suicide.

At second glance it will become plain that women have of course other things to lose than merely their male partners. Although they are not "dismembered", they will fall apart, too, not being immune to history. In addition, they must constantly make sure that they are not being sacrificed for art and business, deprived of their dignity, their integrity, and their lives for men afraid of losing their own selves in the stream of being.[25] Hoban writes:

25 Edgar Allan Poe's tale "The Oval Portrait" criticizes a painter who is too obsessed with painting his beautiful bride to notice that his model is dying while he is applying the last strokes of his brush to the canvas. All the blame is placed on the irresponsible painter. The artist acts as vampire, infusing his art with the real woman's life whereas she is too accommodating and humble to oppose her victimization. But Poe's sympathy with her is ambivalent; it is he who has failed to endow her with a sufficient amount of vitality to begin with. Like the mythical Eurydice, the young woman has always already been "dead" because she is altogether unable to exert any influence on the outcome of the story. In Hoban's novels and short stories, on the other hand, potential victims are at least partly responsible for their fates. Sister's refusal of the role of Eurydice is as important as Kleinzeit's refusal to be the victim of Hospital. As the

> ... if we don't go to the edge and over it as explorers, we go over it as hapless victims, because when we stand passive and still, time moves towards us and brings the edge with it. Man's lot is not, I think, to be comfortable except in the active encounter with discomfort. (TB 72)

Woman's lot is to resist identification with an immobilizing comforter, with the uncomfortable edge to be explored by man, or with the passive victim to be thrown over the edge as a scapegoat or a guinea pig. Those who cannot resist, will be exploited not only in art and advertising (24f.) but also in other areas. Attractive nurses boost Hospital's business: the male patients are again and again exposed for their voyeurism and the ludicrous gap between their sexual fantasies and the reality of their situation (10, 69); many are tempted to stay. Kleinzeit is no better than the other patients at first: whenever he sees Sister, he mentally undresses her (14, 29). Once Kleinzeit has turned out to be the desired sick man with the right ambition, however, Sister herself assists him so as not to lose him. In supporting Kleinzeit's resolution to fight for his recovery, she subverts the function Hospital explicitly assigns her:

> I'll tell *you* something, said Sister. You're a dreadful bore. I don't care about Orpheus and Eurydice and all that. I just want Kleinzeit to get well.
>
> He'll get well all right, said Hospital. He'll recover from life. As I said, I keep you. He doesn't get you.
>
> Rubbish, said Sister, put her head on the desk, cried quietly in the lamplight. (150)

Sister exchanges her passive waiting for a more active contribution to their relationship. Although she initially feels as if she were Eurydice, i.e. "entirely inside the world" and unable to get out (29), she does not object to the intrusion of time into her hitherto seemingly "timeless" sphere; she welcomes change in the ward as well as at home, which becomes obvious when she lets Kleinzeit repair the clock in her flat (87). Unlike the inanimate Eurydice imagined by Hospital, she is also able to give up her flat and move in with Kleinzeit. Convinced that "Eurydice looked ahead and lost Orpheus" (164), she once more distances herself from her when she decides not to look ahead and worry about the future (188). Nevertheless, she is aware of the transitoriness of relationships and of her own mortality (187f.). The ticking of the clock she brings with her makes every moment a precious gift. Significantly, Kleinzeit will tack the round black circle he can draw as a last present from Death "to the wall near the clock" (191). In ceasing to hold on to

---

narrator of "The Devil's Kitchen" recognizes after he has been raped, "Dracula is traditionally powerless to cross the threshold unless invited" (DK 170).

one identity, they have both turned into channels for life, as Hoban defined the most important function human beings could aspire to in "Thoughts on Being and Writing": "... the strongest, most passionate affirmation of the self is necessarily the losing of the self in that continuous stream of being in which we change the past and the past changes us" (TB 70). Having nevertheless *been* Orpheus and Eurydice for a short time, in touch with the mythic past, they have experienced their love story in a way that will distinguish it from the mundane experience whose telling "of itself is not art" (TB 71).

The ability to oscillate between "masculine" and "feminine" ways of behaviour not only preserves their love and prolongs Kleinzeit's life, it is also the precondition for his art. Before he can become a good artist, he must learn to respect Sister's integrity. As long as he does not discourage her from accompanying him to the corridors of the Underground where he is busking (81ff.), he confines her to the role of Eurydice. He, on the other hand, is given to understand that he is not really an artist but a pimp (100), not much better than Harry Solvent with his violent *macho* fantasies:

> ODEON, said a film poster. NOW SHOWING: 'KILL COMES AGAIN'. *They were all dying to come with him!* On the poster a man in tight-fitting clothes aimed a double-barrelled shotgun from between his legs. Behind him naked girls lay stacked like cordwood. Around him ships at sea exploded, trains strafed by helicopters ran off rails, castles blew up, motorcyclists rode off cliffs, there was underwater gunplay between frogmen. Starring PRONG STUDMAN, MAXIMUS JOCK, IMMENSA PUDENDA, MONICA BEDWARD. Also starring GLORIA FRONTAL as 'Jiggles'. Directed by DIMITRI ITHYPHALLIC. Screenplay by Ariadne Bullish based on the novel *Kill for a Living* by Harry Solvent. Additional dialogue by Gertrude Anal. (24-25)

The exploitation of women is shown to be but one of many different phenomena resulting from the fact that our culture is not only extremely aggressive, that is dominated by the death drive, repressed and abreacted by turning it against weaker others – "BE KILL. LIVE KILL. KILL LIVES" (24) – but also stupid enough to define aggression as the essence of masculinity: racial hatred and wars have the same source as cheap fiction and films about *macho* heroes and women reduced to the function of sexual objects and murder victims. There is an enormous industrial complex which profits from, and therefore supports, this fatal consensus; and certain women do not consider it beneath them to contribute to the brutalizing of society and the exploitation of their own sex. But Kleinzeit will learn to differentiate his masculinity from the aggressive virility myth spread by Harry Solvent and his kind. An alternative male biography must start as a criticism of popular representations which are daunting rather than inspiring. Sister teaches him that all women are not "wild" about film heroes like Prong Studman or Maximus Jock (26). As an artist, he must learn to respect the Glockenspiel (82f.) or the yellow paper. Writers like Norman Mailer are satirized in the scene when Kleinzeit decides to "throw himself upon it [the yellow paper] like a tiger. Rape. The yellow paper would love it" (106). Peter Schwenger writes in *Phallic Critiques* that for Mailer, the novel was a Great Bitch; "and the proudest boast of any writer who takes on that form is 'Man, I made her moan.' The muse must be subdued and mastered by the male, like any other woman. If not, she is likely to cost him the mastery of his own manhood" (18). Kleinzeit finds out very quickly that the trash produced in this way (108, 122-124) cannot support his narcissistic illusion of mastery for long (167).

Fed up with his virile pretensions, the yellow paper eventually teaches Kleinzeit to write things that will last. Since Word is "male" in this novel and the yellow paper "female", Kleinzeit has to acquire the ability to switch from a "feminine" perceptive mode to a "masculine" productive one and back – his passivity is part of the activity:[26]

> HOW – CAN – I – MAKE – WORDS – STAY – ON – THE – PAPER? said Kleinzeit very slowly, as if talking to a foreigner.
> They'll stay if you don't put them there, said the yellow paper. (...)
> You simply have to find what's there and let it be.... (168)

But he has no opportunity to try this method out at once, for he collapses being too eager to listen to Death's reading the words he cannot see himself on the yellow paper (168). The next moment of crisis, which has been discussed in ch. 4.1, when he feels contempt for the inert and lifeless yellow paper ("frog princess") and nothing but anxiety about his imminent release from Hospital

---

26 Schwenger writes: "I distrust all attempts to assign a gender to language. Inevitably these tell us less about language than about the state of mind of those who are assigning a gender to it" (*Phallic Critiques*, 19). In principle I agree with him, but as his introduction, based to a great extent on feminist research, shows too, it is a fact that linguistic forms and styles have been assigned genders for centuries. The practice is founded as much on convention (or historically variable stereotypes which are regularly contradicted by empirical analyses of the actual writing styles of male and female writers) as the definition of genders itself. Schwenger therefore wisely exchanges his personal opinion for the working hypothesis that "ideas need not be true in order truly to affect us" (2). Hoban moves in illustrious society when making Word male and masculine: Lacan's metaphor of the phallus ("The Meaning of the Phallus") as well as Cixous' propagating a "feminine writing" (*écriture féminine*) ("Castration or Decapitation?", 51-52) to oppose "the phallocentric tradition" ("The Laugh of the Medusa", 251) come to mind. Kristeva's gendering of the semiotic "feminine" and the symbolic "masculine" strata of language ("Revolution in Poetic Language") locates the gender boundary inside every speaker/writer rather than between them. There is no longer a distinction between "feminine" perception and "masculine" production, but production and perception themselves are split. Though the strata are inseparable, a speaker/writer's particular concern with the acoustic or graphic quality of language or with the logical arguments devloped in his or her text makes it possible to distinguish between a "feminine" poetic code and a "masculine" rational code. This is the position Hoban will have adopted by the time he writes *The Medusa Frequency*. His sympathies, as has been said before, are for the semiotic rather than the symbolic.

(183f.), corresponds to Orpheus's attack of hysteria: "Orpheus mourns, mopes about, won't go to parties any more, won't make love with the local women, they say he's queer, one thing leads to another, they tear him apart, and there's the head going down the river again, heading for Lesbos" (148), as Hospital earlier described that phase. The crisis is an attempt to deny in the area of language what he has already learned in relation to his body: i.e. that the death drive, as a component of his psychic make up, must be accepted, and that blocks as well as a passive dependence on inspiration, which foil his aspirations to virile mastery, must be surrendered to. Eventually, though, he succeeds in accepting his femininity. Unlike Orpheus he can exchange the fixed masculine position for an oscillation between masculinity and femininity.

In *Turtle Diary*, Neaera H., the writer of successful children's books, will have to undergo a similar process to turn into a poet. Although it will be less recognizable than in *Kleinzeit*, with its sexed supernatural "characters", that a creative writer will profit from the ability to cross interior gender boundaries, Neaera's development aims at such flexibility. For the difference between struggle and surrender that is explored in *Turtle Diary* corresponds to that between the masculinity and the femininity presented in *Kleinzeit*. Neaera will learn to surrender more often and thus get access to thoughts which her cheerful children's books sought to drive away. Before discussing Hoban's next novel, however, I would like to glance at a few characters barred from this kind of salvation.

THOMAS PYNCHON: *THE CRYING OF LOT 49*, AND *V*.

Thomas Pynchon's protagonist Oedipa Maas from *The Crying of Lot 49* (1966) cannot take a step forward into a creative new existence; she eventually submits to her exploitation like a sacrificial lamb. Her fatal entanglement starts when she accepts the post of executor "or she supposed executrix, of the estate" of her former lover Pierce Inverarity after his death (5). Having got married to a hypersensitive disc jockey five years earlier in order to escape from the California real estate mogul Pierce (13), she now leaves her husband to accommodate the dead man. As she inventories the legacy, especially Pierce's stamp collection, she hits upon the trace of an oppositional postal system, the "Tristero System" (29). At first the discovery seems to lend her existence meaning beyond that of being the dead man's instrument and a prisoner of her own subjectivity. But all traces of the Tristero System lead back to the Inverarity estate (117): the dead "founding father" Pierce (16) and the "brute Other" Tristero (108) may have been cooperating. Antagonistic or complementary, the two unfathomable organisations are given life by Oedipa's obsessive curiosity, by the enjoyment she draws from executing Pierce's will and discovering more and more clues about the Tristero System. Like Kafka's universe, discussed by Zizek in *Looking Awry*, the universe of Pynchon's short novel is one of the super-ego:

> The superego presents ... the paradox of a law that, according to Jacques-Alain Miller, 'proceeds from the time when the Other was not yet dead, evidenced by the superego, a surviving remainder of that time.' The superego imperative 'Enjoy!', the inversion of the dead law into the obscene figure of the superego, implies a disquieting experience: suddenly we become aware that what a minute ago appeared to us a dead letter is really alive, breathing, pulsating. (...)
>
> We must, then, reverse the usual metaphor of 'alienation' whereby the dead, formal letter, a kind of parasite or vampire, sucks out the living, present force. Living subjects can no longer be considered prisoners of a dead cobweb. The dead, formal character of the law becomes now the *sine qua non* of our freedom, and the real totalitarian danger arises only when the law no longer wants to stay dead. (Zizek 150)

After an ethical moment of insight, when Oedipa realizes that she functions as a catalyst, that is as a subject through whom totalitarian structures acquire life, her body begins to produce hysterical symptoms: "Waves of nausea, lasting five or ten minutes, would strike her at random, cause her deep misery, then vanish as if they had never been. There were headaches, nightmares, menstrual pains" (118). Responsibility weighs so heavily on her that she even grows suicidal (122). But after she has survived a crazy nocturnal joyride on the freeway with her lights out (122), she reverts to a hysterical attitude again. Instead of simply resigning her post like her co-executor Metzger (102), she seeks a confrontation with the Tristero, taking the risk of being literally executed herself. The ending is open, but the description of the auction which Oedipa attends suggests doom:

> An assistant closed the heavy door on the lobby windows and the sun. She heard a lock snap shut; the sound echoed a moment. Passerine spread his arms in a gesture that seemed to belong to the priesthood of some remote culture; perhaps to a descending angel. The auctioneer cleared his throat. Oedipa settled back, to await the crying of lot 49. (127)

Although Pynchon has placed his female protagonist in positions traditionally occupied by women (that of the amoral "executrix" of the law, the servant who places her own enjoyment above all other concerns; or later, that of the hysteric, the self-conscious object), his novel is not misogynous. He explains why Oedipa is left with no other option: Her imagination and her self-confidence have been crippled by her education. Educated "at a time of nerves, blandness and retreat among not only her fellow students but also most of the visible structure around and ahead of them, this having been a national reflex to certain pathologies in high places only death had had the power to cure" (71) – these vague sentences refer of course to Senator Joseph McCarthy's notorious anti-Communist investigations in the first half of the 1950s –, the "Young Republican" (51) Oedipa feels unable to change America by creatively making use of Inverarity's legacy (126); she is "just a whiz at pursuing strange words in Jacobean texts" (72), but afraid of "those autonomous culture media where the most beloved of folklores may be brought into doubt, cataclysmic of dissents voiced, suicidal of commitments chosen – the sort that bring governments down" (71). She is aware that her pursuit of clues is really a variation on the consummation of the death wish, "some kind of compensation. To make up for her having lost the direct, epileptic Word, the cry that might abolish the night" (81). Nevertheless, she would find it harder to face an existential void and live in isolation (122) than to be used by her fatherly ex-lover Pierce, or by the enigmatic Tristero System: "Though she could never again call back any image of the dead man to dress up, pose, talk to and make answer, neither would she lose a new compassion for the cul-de-sac he'd tried to find a way out of, for the enigma his efforts had created" (123). Like Oedipus she *must* find a solution to the riddle of the Sphinx. Before she finally decides to await the crying of lot 49, the sale of Pierce's collection of forged Tristero stamps to a mysterious stranger who could be a member of the secret organisation, she sums up her position:

> Either Oedipa in the orbiting ecstasy of a true paranoia, or a real Tristero. For there either was some Tristero beyond the appearance of the legacy America, or there was just America and if there was just America then it seemed the only way she could continue, and manage to be at all relevant to it, was an alien, unfurrowed, assumed full circle into some paranoia. (126).

Cleverer than the average suburban housewife and tougher than her husband Mucho, Oedipa does not allow her psychotherapist Dr Hilarius (a Nazi psychiatrist who experimented on Jews at Buchenwald to make them catatonic) to sedate her with drugs and Medusan faces so that she can no longer perceive the power structures which subject her (10f., 95). Unlike Sister and Kleinzeit, however, and unlike the inventors, artists and musicians of the Pynchon universe, Oedipa cannot maintain an oscillation between different positions. Her imagination is too frail to show her a way out of the claustrophobic plot which rivets her to an alternative between two equally uncanny options: paranoia or hysteria; she cannot be a nobody about whom nothing is special and who can invent herself, that is "getting something for nothing, causing perpetual motion" (59); it is not for to her to make up for entropy by imaginatively confronting mortality itself.

Obsessive Herbert Stencil from Pynchon's earlier novel *V.* (1963) receives much less sympathy than Oedipa. Orphaned and free from any obligation, "the [twentieth] century's child" (52), he nevertheless chases a mysterious woman around the world as his father did before he "died under unknown circumstances" (52). He could actually enjoy a carefree life after surviving military service during World War II, since no one has named him executor of anyone's legacy, but he chooses to hunt V. instead "for no other reason than that V. was there to track down" (55). He does not even give up when he can no longer evade the question whether it is "really his own extermination he is after" (451). The Maltese poet Fausto Maijstral won't provide an answer. He has been conditioned to hunt "the" Woman, too, like all "western men" (451). But he points out to Stencil that he himself has changed: "... Don't try appealing to someone you've only known in a written confession. We do not walk ganged, Stencil, all our separate selves, like Siamese quintuplets or more" (451). Stencil is also contrasted with Benny Profane, the "schlemihl Redeemer" (453) who enjoys life from moment to moment. Like Kleinzeit and Oedipa, Profane knows dissolution: he is haunted by nightmares in which he is walking alone on a street at night and falling apart (39f.). But the awareness of his mortality neither turns him into an artist nor an obsessive seeker of compensation. He is free from possessiveness yet always finds company to divert him while awake; especially women happen to him "like accidents" (134). At the end of the novel we therefore see him not only walk but run down a pitch-dark street, hand in hand with the adventurous young woman poet Brenda, cheerful and not caring a jot whether the street might end in an abyss (455): he is a happy fool who does not think that he has learned anything from his experience (454). Stencil might learn from him, however, for Profane stoutly opposes anyone who expects him to act like the average possessive and/or possessed western man, e.g. Mafia Winsome (288). Of course Profane is too irresponsible and lazy to be a good male role model or a teacher. Artists like the jazz musician McClintic Sphere or Fausto Maijstral are the only male characters who can claim that position.

The females in this novel (except Mafia) are shown to be less prone to support the system anyway. Paola Maijstral, Fausto's daughter, is the subversive antithesis to Oedipa Maas: playing with other children in times of war, neglected by her busy parents, she learned early on to "escape subjugation" (331). Oedipa never enjoyed so much freedom: although her own parents are not mentioned, we learn that she had felt imprisoned in a tower like Rapunzel before her fatherly first lover Pierce cheated his way into it (*Crying*, 12f.), and before him, "Secretaries James and Foster and Senator Joseph" were the "dear daft numina who'd mothered over Oedipa's so temperate youth" (71).

On a trip with Paola, McClintic suddenly knows what could indeed slow down the decay of the world although there is no definite cure:

> 'Paola, did you know I have been blowing a silly line all this time. Mister Flab the original, is me. Lazy and taking for granted some wonder drug someplace to cure that town, to cure me. Now there isn't and never will be. Nobody is going to step down from heaven and square away Roony and his woman [i.e. Mafia], or Alabama, or South Africa or us and Russia. There's no magic words. Not even I love you is magic enough.... Keep cool but care'... (*V.*, 365-366)

Unfortunately the Stencils of this world won't listen to the artists or to women like Paola, who only interest them if they contribute to their crazy quests (52). And the Oedipas have been trapped for so long, first as women, then as educated women, that they can often no longer bear freedom.

TURTLE DIARY

Whereas Pynchon eventually strands Oedipa at an auction instead of making her go into action, the protagonists of Hoban's next novel *Turtle Diary* find that their minimal complementarity indeed forces them to become, in Neaera's view, the "father" and the "mother" of an action (79). There is not much they can do about it: "It seemed to want to happen" (129). As I showed in chapter 5.2, the "parental" roles contrast with the characters' sexes: William, for instance, feels as if the plan to liberate the turtles "were thrusting itself upon" him (48), and Neaera at one stage feels like a penitent rapist: "I ought not to have forced myself into that man's turtle thoughts" (73); but the terms "active" and "passive" become exchangeable and blurred in the course of the action. At the beginning, Neaera finds the inversion of gender hard to accept: in the same diary entry in which she describes her own ability to "trust to luck and plunge into the dark" when a venture is "crucial", like the Caister men her father told her about (63), she curses William "for not being man enough to speak up and broach the subject" (64). It is due to such differences, however, that they *will* eventually liberate the turtles and that they will *have to* liberate them together. Although the title of her new book project about a female water-beetle suggests that she will not go on perpetuating old gender clichés, that is "*Victoria Beetle, Secret Agent.* A woman of action" (15), *Turtle Diary* will demonstrate time and again that she is only beginning to get rid of conservative ideas about gender difference. Actually, she would have preferred to write a book about a male water-beetle had one been available. Initially her attitude to emancipation is as ambivalent as her attitude to the first name given her by a doting father who dominates her memories while her mother is never mentioned: "I don't mind so much being named after a nymph but I really don't care to be associated with the pastoral tradition" (57). If life had not forced her into early independence, she would now be a wife and mother wearing Laura Ashley dresses like her friends (10). She uses a push-chair for shopping and will probably go on using it for as long as she is still young enough to be thought of as a mother rather than a homeless old woman (42). Neaera is forty-three when we meet her (41, 64). She lost her fiancé Geoffrey twenty-three years earlier (50, 57). The shock seems to have turned her into a female Orpheus, for she began to associate mortality with maleness and hysterically avoided any new relationships with men so as not to experience loss again. Between the lines, though, she signals that she remained single for another reason that she dare not put into words; perhaps she was afraid to lose her independence again once she had managed to earn a living by writing children's books: "My generation was somewhat in between things.... More of us were capable of being brought to a halt by something of that sort than young people now would be. Rubbish. Even in the privacy of my own mind I can't be entirely honest with myself" (58). She must eventually have found it more convenient to revive Geoffrey by means of her art than to confront the reality of his absence and her loneliness, or that of another fiancé: writing fiction for children about cuddly animal characters named Geoffrey Mouse, Delia Swallow or Gillian Vole she could sublimate her desire for marriage and motherhood without having to experience the material drawbacks of a life as wife and mother (11, 42, 68). Planning a book on a water-beetle, a predator, however, is the first sign that her fantasies of family life no longer fulfil their compensatory function. By the end of the novel it is altogether clear to her that there is no longer a place for her in the cosy world of Delia Swallow and her likes (169f.).

Another detail which illustrates her transformation is that she initially expects men to deal with all challenges while women are to support them: "Even in matriarchal societies I doubt that there were ever female Beowulfs. Women lie with gods and demons but they don't go looking for monsters to fight with. Ariadne gave Theseus a clew but the Minotaur was his business" (74). But monsters and other horrors will manifest themselves and have to be dealt with whether they are sought out or left alone. Albeit evasive, a woman is just as exposed to them as a man. Moreover, there may not always be a man around to be entrusted with the "business" of slaying the minotaur, or he might require a partner rather than a dependent who can merely give him clues. Hoban may abstain from burdening the female characters with the existential problems of the males, but he does not spare them the confrontation with their own dark side.[27] The trick is to make Neaera have to collaborate, on behalf of the turtles, with a man who is too wrapped up in himself and unheroic to care much for anybody else. William does not perceive setting the turtles free as a symbolic act of procreation or a service to Neaera. For him it has nothing to do with sexuality but is rather a challenge to his inertia, a question of life and death, and Neaera is no more than a supplementary burden, as can be gleaned from his diary entry: "Whatever this awful thing is that I've got myself into, it's my thing and I've got to do it alone with that weird lady" (87). The monster they both have to face is the "blank terror" (79), or in William's words "the intolerable" (75), waiting to crush a reality perceived as fantasmatic and hard to believe in. Neaera suffers a fundamental crisis when the terror manages to emerge despite all her attempts to repress it: having dreamt of a white shark (77) and been forced by William to acknowledge it as her own (78; 86-90), she wakes up one morning feeling alienated from her former self; she has reached a point at which she finds it nonsensical to go on persuading children of the value of life:

> I felt a stranger in my own head, as if the consciousness looking out through my eyes were some monstrous changeling. Here was the implacable morning light on all the books and litter that were always there but nothing was recognizable as having significance. What in the world was it all about, I found myself wondering.
>
> People write books for children and other people write about the books written for children but I don't think it's for the children at all. I think that all the people who worry so much about the children are really worrying about themselves, about keeping their world together and getting the children to help them do it.... Maybe our constant fear is that a generation of children will come along and say: 'This is not a world, this is nothing, there's no way to live at all.' (99-100)

Neaera does not give way to her hopelessness, however. She regains her balance watching the 1933 version of *King Kong*.

Before going to the cinema she feels overwhelmed by various things happening around her: an offer of £1,000 for a book on children's literature weighs as heavily upon her as the decimation of oyster-catchers (109f.). Her

---

27 Miss Neap's suicide is a good example to illustrate this point. Since her story is untold (186), nobody else can reap a benefit from her death. Its meaning remains unknown, there is no lesson to be learnt. William, who is one of the witnesses invited to testify at the Coroner's Court, is keenly aware that the gap she left cannot be closed by the compilation of facts about her last days: "Mrs Inchcliff, Mr Sandor and I swore in turn that we would speak the truth, the whole truth, and nothing but the truth... Not the whole truth. But it was all we knew and all we could say. It stood there like a blind dumb thing and grew tall until its head touched the ceiling" (186). Her suicide does not relieve William of the decisions he must make for himself every day: "To go on working at the bookshop or somewhere else? To live alone or with someone? To stop smoking or not? To go on getting up in the morning or perhaps not?" (179-180).

first observations on the film seek to establish distinctions between herself and the characters of the film. She admires the ease with which Anne Darrow can surrender to the filmmaker Carl Denham both when he finds her stealing apples and later, during a rehearsal, when she does not know what plans he has with her (110f.); Anne simply trusts in the effect of her beauty and her abilities as an actress, doing in other words what is in her to do:

> It's a reversal of the *Schöne Müllerin* theme of the unattainable beauty: the voyeur, the picture-maker, must put his attainable beauty within easy reach of the colossal beast. I watched her scream at the unknown horror she was heading for. That was a good touch, it was absolutely right. She screamed with complete acceptance of her place in life. (111)

Barbara Herkommer thinks that there is a cynical undertone to be heard in these words (122). But Neaera's slightly mocking remarks need not imply anything else than her awareness that a contemporary woman can no longer solve her problems in similar fashion because the world has grown more complex and corrupt. As Neaera notes, her world is overshadowed by the knowledge of the atomic bomb, has lost its innocence and is not "only" suffering from the effects of the Great Depression as it was in 1933, the year in which the film was released (110). When she begins to describe Kong, however, the sense of distance fades: the idea of him proves stronger than her knowledge of the tricks which helped to create the illusion of a giant ape. At first, she half-seriously associates him with various aspects of maleness, as conventional interpreters of the film do (see e.g. Carlos Clarens, *An Illustrated History of the Horror Film*, 94f.). But Kong's loneliness soon directs her thinking towards madness, that which disturbs the reality consensus:

> Kong had no visible male member even when presumably excited but then he was *all* male member in a manner of speaking so that doesn't matter either. On the other hand maybe that's why he only wanted tiny women to play with instead of looking for a fifty-foot-tall she-ape with whom to have sexual kongress. The psychological ripples are ever-widening. Now that I think of it why *weren't* there any other fifty-foot-high gorillas about? What had happened to Kong's mother and father? That too must be part of the pathos of the thing: Kong is an orphan and alone of his kind. Not just an orphan but a giant orphan, a monstrous Tom o'Bedlam. (111)

The image of Anne exposed to Kong brings about Neaera's identification with the woman on the screen, an effect that was inconceivable in the opening sequence:

> It was at the same time laughable and ineffably real. Yes that's a big fake ape,

> ha ha. But the fake ape is only the cipher for the real thing before which we stand with outstretched arms, hands tied, head drooping, and we scream or are silent. (112)

The decisive moment in her reading of the film takes place, though, when she also identifies with Kong, realizing that the threatening Real need not be external; it may originate in the same person who has just been afraid of it: "Marvellous how one's afraid of the thing that's going to break its chains and then so quickly one *is* the thing that's broken its chains and climbed the heavenward spire to be shot down" (113). Now her eyes are open to the ubiquity of madness. 1933 is no longer simply the year of the Great Depression but also that of Nazi book burnings in Germany. Compared to such horrors and to the ones shown in *King Kong*, her everyday reality suddenly appears to be manageable again:

> ... more and more I think that madness is the world's natural condition and to expect anything else is madness compounded. In the train derailment scene in *King Kong* the engine-driver could not believe his eyes when he saw Kong's face rising through the gap where he'd torn away the tracks but that was just another day in 1933. That trains mostly stay on rails, that the streets are mostly peaceful, that the square continues green and quiet below my window is more than I have any right to expect, and it happens every day. (113)

Kong's dying scene also leads to another insight: Neaera notices a bond between Anne and the dying giant gorilla.[28] When his attempt to prevent the aeroplanes from shooting at him fails, Kong does not drag Anne into the abyss

---

28 Although Neaera is, quite literally, a "man's woman" (41), "her" reading of *King Kong* displays feminist sensibility at the moment when she lays bare the film's covert sympathy for Anne and Kong as well as its implied criticism of Denham's voyeurism and greed. Normally, horror films continue the patriarchal tradition of classical myths: sympathy is directed towards a male hero who kills a monster in order to save society and/or marry a woman. The functions of the woman and the monster are similar: both are objects of the hero's gaze, subservient to his desire to appropriate trophies; they are obstacle and prize within the narrative of his way to maturity (see de Lauretis, *Alice Doesn't*, 103-157). What is interesting about *King Kong*, though, is that the hero's role has actually been undermined by being split into three parts: technology, Denham, and Jack Driscoll. Technology (bombs and aeroplanes) has replaced the hero's superhuman skills and is shown as an actor in its own right, so efficient and implacable that no one will be tempted to waste any sympathy on it. Denham, on the other hand, is a ruthless voyeur and businessman who seeks to control our gaze at both Anne and Kong and to earn money with their exhibition. By taking Anne to the jungle and Kong to New York, making them cross boundaries that the hero must normally cross alone, he causes tragedies instead of preventing them. Driscoll, finally, is Anne's insignificant fiancé: being a simple sailor without any special endowments, he contributes no more than the male body of the traditional hero, but he never actually fights against Kong. Anne can simply be "picked up" by him when the tyrannosaurus, Denham, or the aeroplanes force Kong to abandon her. The effect of this splitting is that what will be remembered is neither the "victory" of the aeroplanes, nor the "happy ending" of Jack and Anne's romance, nor Denham's silly final comment that Beauty killed the Beast; the most memorable moment indeed takes place when Kong lifts Anne up and gently puts her down again on the roof of the Empire State Building before his strength fades. Significantly, Neaera, who used to sublimate her desire for marriage in her children's books, does not lose one word on the love story between Jack and Anne.

to die with him: his ego is not constituted in such a way that his defeat could result in self-destruction and/or the sadistic destruction of scapegoats.[29] Being no human male, neither Oedipus nor Perseus, he can relinquish his claim both to Anne and to power without developing any aggressive feelings:

> Weak and swaying, his grip on the spire loosening, he touches her gently, then lets go and falls. The year 1933 was full of many things. Showing with *King Kong* was a documentary film on Hitler's rise to power. In 1933 there was Goebbels officiating at a book burning. 'You do well at this midnight hour,' he said, 'to exorcise the past in these flames.' Exorcise the past. Surely that thought alone was sufficient evidence of madness. (113)

Neaera's thinking about the film in terms of its historical context clearly brings out the difference between the animal "innocence" of the powerful primordial monster and human irrationality and sadism. Her reading foregrounds what might be called a heroism of surrender while it treats Denham's overt praises of civilization and his silly attempt to mystify the power of Beauty – "'Oh no, it wasn't the aeroplanes, ... it was Beauty killed the Beast" (113) – with due disrespect.

The overall effect of the film is cathartic. Instead of wearing herself out by feeling responsible for the salvation of children, oyster-catchers, and the rest of the world, Neaera appreciates the small comforts of her everyday existence again and the scope within which she can still move, take action or make decisions. If she has been "seduced into femininity" by the film, as Teresa de Lauretis would describe the effect of Neaera's identification with Anne (*Alice*

29 A conventional interpretation of the film such as that put forward by Carlos Clarens in *An Illustrated History of the Horror Film* (1967) displays a blatant lack of susceptibility to such differences. Clarence writes: "The makers of *King Kong* went so far they carried the Beauty-and-the-Beast premise to absurdity – the acute disparity of size between Ann [sic] and Kong puts any erotic rapport completely out of the question. And so, the film jumps to a substitute gratification in some spectacular sadism and whopping mayhem: Kong vents his frustration by razing the native village and, when really put out, he turns Manhattan into a shambles " (94). He completely suppresses the fact, noticed by Neaera (112), that Kong respects his chains until the flashlights of the photographers seem to threaten Anne. He breaks loose to protect her. And his acts of destruction by no means substitute for the impossible gratification of sexual desire: he derails a train which does not respect his (i.e. *King* Kong's) right of way as he would clear away an obstacle or a troublesome smaller animal in the jungle – sadism, that is (sexual) pleasure gained from torturing another, is a human perversion that cannot be applied to Kong's actions; it is more applicable to the spectacles staged by Denham.

Doesn't, 155), the identification with Kong relativizes the first one.[30] It is a femininity with a clearly marked entrance for drive energies required in emergencies when the subject must act. The fact that Hoban makes Neaera pay no attention at all to the romance between Anne and Jack underlines that the femininity he seeks to propagate differs from the mythical and the Freudian notions I sketched out in the previous chapter. Being feminine here does not imply being the castrated and inferior other of the masculine subject, its object of desire, incapable of independent action. It implies developing an ego which does not need to enter, overwhelm, possess and control because it knows that it can trust the navigational abilities of the id. Especially the management of sexuality and aggression is no longer entrusted to an ego which might be overambitious under the sway of a severe super-ego, but it is returned to the self-regulatory pleasure principle governing the id. This return of power is possible on the basis of a belief that excessive actions, eruptions of madness or violence, and libidinal aberrations, only happen if there have been previous excesses of repression. Neaera, for instance, considers the Nazi attempt to "exorcise the past" as such an excess. In a sense, then, the novel is radically opposed to the project of psychoanalysis as Freud defined it in "Das Ich und das Es" (1923), when he wrote: "Die Psychoanalyse ist ein Werkzeug, welches dem Ich die fortschreitende Eroberung des Es ermöglichen soll" (322). *Turtle Diary* advocates the release of the conquered id from the repressive influence of an ego corrupted by oedipal identifications.

The film also inspires Neaera to watch animals with new respect: "Madame Beetle swims in her green world expecting neither continuation nor

30 Blonde, helpless and crucified in the scene on Skull Island, Anne Darrow (played by Fay Wray) could be called the cinematic prototype of Woman, the idealised object of masculine desire cinema has again and again invited real women to model themselves on: "Woman is the origin and the aim of desire, the object and the locus of sexuality as defined by man, from his point of view, through his look, his cinema, his institutions" (de Lauretis, *Technologies of Gender*, 104). It must be pointed out, however, that *King Kong*, as a self-referential, and self-critical, film about the making of a film of high box-office appeal, alerts the audience not only to the process through which the unemployed actress Anne Darrow is turned into Woman (or "Beauty", in Denham's language), but it also warns them against the uncanny swiftness with which roles become real. On Skull Island, Anne no longer *represents* Woman: the image that was to be fixed merely within the frames of a strip of celluloid has inscribed itself on her body – now she *is* Woman, the mythical sacrificial bride. Of course, audiences in the 1930s (who did not differ substantially from contemporary audiences of horror films) did not heed the moral or cautionary message of the film at all; *King Kong* on the contrary whetted their appetite for further sacrifices and orgies of destruction: "Through an extravagant and quite mad process of identification, the audiences of 1933 were plainly gratified by these scenes of urban destruction and *King Kong* triumphantly launched a fleet of catastrophe pictures such as *Deluge*, *The Last Days of Pompeii* (also by Cooper, Shoedsack, and O'Brien) and *San Francisco*" (Clarens 95). The process of identification through which they could be gratified by such scenes is of course no madder than the one which allows them to enjoy the "eroticism" (Clarens 94) of stories in which sacrifical virgins are exposed to monsters. But a film critic who would accuse Kong of sadism (see previous footnote) cannot be expected to be anything but blind to the regularity with which cinema in general and a great number of narratives gratify sadistic desire.

sanity, I don't think expectation is a part of her" (113). Although she is not so naive as to believe that animals will not be changed by the contact with human beings (see e.g. her speculations that animals, too, might become decadent in captivity, 25), their way of life demonstrates that by not anticipating any eruptions of madness, by foregoing both resistance and struggle while doing what is in her to do, the drives will work for rather than against her, like animal instincts (97, 113, 134).[31] It is by not resisting her desire to set the turtles free that she will eventually re-discover her own navigational abilities, i.e. what she first believed to be a lost "magical reality" (50):

> I was in my ocean, this was the only ocean there was for me, the dry streets of London and my square without a fountain. No one could make me freer by putting me somewhere else. I had as much as the turtles: myself. At least I too could die on the way to where I wanted to be. (170)

Trust in these abilities will save her from accepting the contract for the book project *From Oedipus to Peter Rabbit: The Tragic Heritage in Children's Literature*, which would overstrain her powers (151). As she found out earlier, "no amount of training will get that book out of me" (123). Unlike Oedipus she need not test her cleverness and meet her doom although she also knows that there is no way back to the Delia Swallow and the Gillian Vole books.

As a further benefit of her new image of herself and without reverting to the role of a mere object of desire, she overcomes the libidinal anxiety which has haunted her since the death of her fiancé. Her relationship with George Fairbairn is therefore free from the gender clichés which dominated her expectations regarding the abduction of the turtles: although his name recalls the dragon-killer and patron saint of England, he is not expected to do anything on Neaera's behalf. She is able to live life on the border of the abyss now, taking risks herself (184). George is someone to swim along with, somebody else who does not mind being alive (183). As Hoban says in the interview with Haffenden, Neaera begins to find "Not so much a new life with George as a new life in which George has been the catalyst" (136). He disagrees with Haffenden's interpretation that George offers Neaera a passive acceptance of life close to surrender or indifference which seems to indicate that she has resigned her struggle: "Neaera isn't resigning her struggle, she's advancing to the point where she needn't make a false struggle" (137). According to its minor status in Neaera's development, their love story has been marginalized more than those between Jachin-Boaz and Gretel or between Kleinzeit and Sister in the two previous novels. It is an effect rather than the cause of Neaera's transfor-

31 Barbara Herkommer has dedicated an excellent chapter to the relationship between animals and human beings: "4.2 Die 'conditio humana' gegenüber der Tierexistenz".

mation. Should they ever split up, Neaera would not feel like the abandoned part of a complementary unit, unable to live a full life: "George had given me so much that even if there came a time without George I could bear it now and not step carefully nor build my broken eggshell with mad patience" (183).

Finally, her relationship to language has changed too. The poetry she will write in the end acknowledges the transformation she has undergone; it is a confrontation with absences and the terror rather than a further attempt to cover them up with "books and papers and plants in the window" (88): "The fountain in the square / Isn't there" (184). Her reorientation could in a sense be said to represent Hoban's own. What is involved is not only a change of genre, but a different way of using language: it is no longer merely a means of communication, or an instrument to consensify children, but a medium to access moods and emotions like music. Neaera's "poetic turn" is the seed for the word games in Hoban's novels, the language of *Riddley Walker* as well as the fragmented pieces of *The Moment under the Moment.*

When we leave Neaera, all problems have not been resolved. The novel is open-ended as its predecessors. It is, for instance, very unlikely that Neaera will be able to earn a living by writing poetry. Will she take the risk of becoming a starving old woman poet rather than to write any further children's books beside poetry?[32] Moreover, empowering though the identification with Kong might be, he climbs the Empire State Building "to be shot down" (113); or Neaera says in the end "At least I too could *die* on the way to where I wanted to be" (170; emphasis added) – gloomy perspectives both. Is there no way in which Anne and Kong, the feminine subject and the id could cooperate and trick out those out to profit from them? Is there no way for the feminine subject to affirm rationality as a part of existence? There is certainly a danger of surrendering too often otherwise and of dismissing challenges too readily. While we cannot accompany Neaera any further, the protagonists of Hoban's subsequent novels will come closer to a dynamic balance by oscillating between various ways of being until conscious as well as unconscious elements of their psyche contribute equally to their personality. Melanie Falsepercy from *The Medusa Frequency*, the second woman writer among Hoban's characters, will definitely be better suited to *live* on the way to where she wants to be, and so will Caroline Lovecraft in *Fremder*. William's function, on the other hand, is precisely to show how to overcome imbalance when surrender has indeed become synonymous with resignation, in other

32 Russell Hoban himself chose the latter way, without having to make too many compromises: the children's books he wrote after moving to London, e.g. *How Tom Beat Captain Najork and his Hired Sportsmen* (1974), were poetical and encouraged children to resist the grown-ups' attempts to consensify them without preaching violence.

words, when there is a tendency to avoid not only a false struggle but all struggle.

William is inclined to surrender too soon. In terms of experience he is "ahead" of Neaera but this is no advantage: he starts from a place on the very edge of the abyss. As a divorced man and father of two daughters (38, 68-71), he has already had the family life she could only enjoy vicariously in her children's books. He can no longer be duped by the oedipal trajectory which promises fulfilment to a man who has succeeded in steering himself and a woman into the haven of marriage. Having been promised more by tradition, he feels all the more cheated by reality. Marriage did not cure him of castration anxiety; it promoted it on the contrary to such a degree (62) that he now feels sexually attracted to young women and girls only (38, 46). He is perfectly aware, though, that even making love to them cannot shut the terror out but for short moments (108). His affair with his colleague Harriet therefore does not last very long; as soon as she begins to make demands on him (121, 125), he loses all interest: "I didn't want to be expected anywhere as a regular thing" (171). At the beginning he thinks that there is "more human solidity in women than in men" (101): a hint that the so-called "negative" form of the Oedipus complex has been actualized in him, that is "love for the parent of the same sex, and jealous hatred for the parent of the oposite sex" (Laplanche and Pontalis 283).[33] Just as Sister thought that women are "healthier" than men,

33 While Laplanche and Pontalis's definition describes the extreme case, William's neurosis is more moderate: there is no jealous *hatred* for his mother but a certain envy. Neither is William's love for his father strong enough to turn him into a homosexual, but his tendency to compare himself to film stars and other male characters indicates his desire for a male figure to identify with (55, 70-71, 75, 121).

Hoban's treatment of homosexuality is not altogether free from anxiety. William, for instance, at one stage compares it to smoking: "With smoking one has a life while dying. How did the Greeks ever run a whole culture without it? Maybe that's why there was so much homosexuality" (71). Neaera, on the other hand, suspects that commercial interests have prompted the many publicized coming-outs (80). But this is before she has suffered her own identitiy crisis. I think the anxiety that both characters are made to express betrays an unacknowledged awareness that their own heterosexuality is not always supported by a sufficiently strong identification with the genders "normally", i.e. normatively, attributed to their sexes. What William will tell Neaera, i.e. "Some people won't look at what's in them, they sweep everything under the carpet" (89), not only applies to mortality but also to sexuality.

By presenting the story through the eyes of a male and a female diarist and identifying with both in his interview with John Haffenden (137), Hoban demonstrated that divergent facets of one's personality can be made to cooperate rather than to sabotage each other. There is no need for a permanent repression of facets which would make the subject disagree with a norm. Since Neacra and William are "mixed" themselves, however, a woman with more masculine traits than feminine ones and a man with a surplus of feminine ones, they cannot simply be read as signifiers of femininity and masculinity respectively, as Christine Wilkie does in her Jungian interpretation: " Neaera H. a type of the noumenal archetypal Feminine and William G. as male ego-consciousness struggling for expression. In these terms their ultimate ambivalence towards each other and their contrary synthesis of the turtle experience is an acceptable contradiction. There is a need for harmony and balance between the male/female, positive/negative elements of their personal, historical, and universal consciousnesses, but there is no need for a synthesis of these binary opposites" (51). William and Neaera are no binary opposites at all; in fact they find each other uncanny because they are too close, psychic doubles almost, despite their sexual

William's mother, his ex-wife Dora and Ruby the wrestler and original therapist all apparently confirm this view. The trip to his birthplace Polperro, however, triggers so many memories of his mother's life, her futile attempts to escape from places where men (her father, her brothers and finally her husband) seemed to seek their deaths (136f.), that he can eventually imagine that she lived no less in dread than he does (178). If he had not already gained this insight, Miss Neap's fate would have converted him. Earlier on, immediately before he begins to lament on the losses he has experienced in his life, contrasting his unhappy life with shamanic ecstasy, he still makes jokes about her apparent imperviousness to mortality:

> Miss Neap baths daily and when she's been before me the bathroom smells very blonde and militantly fragrant, as if mortality could be kept at bay by lavender in the same way that garlic repels vampires. If Dracula and Miss Neap were to have a go I think he'd be the one to come away with teeth marks in his throat. (69)

But then it is she who is found hanging from a hook (hidden behind the pelmet of her flowered drapes – a detail which sums up her drama), while he is still alive (181).

Taking notice of the suffering of others, especially of the women around him and not only of little boys checked by their mothers for fooling around (8), is a sign that neurotic William is on the path to recovery. Initially he is only aware of being critically looked at himself: he dreads the gaze of an octopus and finds an owl's eyes implacable (7). Miss Neap's blue eyes remind him of ice (29). Looking at his face in the mirror to shave is a daily challenge because at such moments, "nothing helps and the great heavy boot of the past is planted squarely in your back and shoving you forward" (28). One memory of his mother is particularly interesting; it is not impossible that his feminine

---

difference and their different histories (45, 58f.). In contrast to Wilkie, Barbara Herkommer overemphasizes William and Neaera's similarity: "Die 'Tagebuch'-Eintragungen lassen sich als Selbstkundgabe zweier Einzelgänger verstehen, die keine geschlechtsspezifischen Merkmale oder prägnanten Unterschiede aufweisen und die sich in dieser Selbstkundgabe so ähnlich sind, dass sie stellenweise nahezu einstimmig, fast 'wie aus einem Munde', verlautbar werden" (119). But this assessment, albeit closer to the text than Wilkie's, is still too unsubtle. Of course they speak as if with one voice – because they are expressions of the same author's consciousness, *representations* of a man and a woman. Minimal though the difference between the two self-portraits of the artist may be, however, it is nevertheless constitutive for the novel itself; and it *is* a gender-specific difference in this case. As I argued earlier on, I think that Neaera's masculine and William's feminine traits put their turtle fantasies into practice; their "normal" feminine respectively masculine traits, on the other hand, fail to make them sexually attractive to each other.

In Hoban's later novels, action cycles will become more complex. Not only will they involve more than two main characters, but they will also be modelled on chemical reactions rather than on procreation. Incidentally, George Fairbairn as catalyst and coordinator of their action already points in this direction.

sensitivity to being looked at is part of her heritage: for she too was aware of birds' eyes, and he has no trouble identifying with her view:

> When I think of her seeing the jackdaws walking on the quay I seem to see them with her eyes and I can see the rest of the scene as well, the grey sky over the sea and the headlands, the white-and-black-and-grey gulls with yellow beaks and yellow staring eyes, the fishermen solid and heavy in the grey light with scales and barrows... (137)

He hates being naked, especially with himself (71), and keeps his feet hidden in shoes because they "don't look as if they will ever walk in happy ways" (92). There might be a certain envy in the way he looks at the "good-looking feet" of the participants of Ruby's Original Therapy session (101). But his hyperbolic description of Mr Sandor's feet is definitely coloured by horror: "His feet turned out as if there were no limit to the amount of space they could take up" (153) – it is as if Sandor turned into the octopus William did not find at the Zoo in the first chapter, a monstrous challenge and a belated substitute for the castrating father he has never had to face. I will presently come back to this subject. William knows from observing his customers (53), reflecting on his shortcomings as a man (61, 115), or comparing himself, like Kleinzeit, to male filmstars such as Burt Lancaster or Paul Newman (70, 121), that sex and gender do not necessarily match according to social norms. Moreover, he is too intelligent to believe that fetishistic objects like telephoto lenses, cars or power tools are efficient (rather than merely ridiculous or dangerous) ways of making up for missing virility. A completely disillusioned prisoner of his imperfect body and his diffident self (71), then, William is in danger of becoming so feminine *in the traditional way*, powerless and immobile like Danaë, Andromeda or Anne Darrow in *King Kong*, without anyone or anything to save him, that he gets dangerously close to giving himself up:

> I had sort of a bursting feeling as if my self were a wall round me that I couldn't knock down or climb over. ... Out of it, away and in the clear. ... Out of it was at the same time into it. There's a wall inside the self as well. Can't get through any more. Can't live is what it amounts to. No place to live. (19-20).

Trying to "exorcise" his feminine traits by imitating a macho did not cure him: leaving his wife and his daughters and then sleeping with a great number of "girls" whom he treated as mere commodities to be used and discarded (this seems to be the contemporary form of dealing with Medusa) did not prevent him from turning to stone: his mind remained attached to the past, unable to be moved by the present or to become interested in the future (46). The mere show of phallic potency also failed to back up his self-consciousness with a sufficient amount of self-confidence and aggression. As a consequence he lost all interest in sex (46).[34] Once more, Hoban presents a male character who must correct the view that vitality can be derived from sexuality; it is based on the same simplification of the links between sexuality and mortality as the claim that death follows upon procreation, which worried Jachin-Boaz in Hoban's first novel. In order to overcome his special Oedipus complex William needs a confrontation with a living father figure (an octopus instead of Medusa), for this is the only process by which the root of his problem can be touched: he must learn to disconnect the idea of death from the signifier of the aged male body.

His own father, who had retired to Polperro to paint before he met William's mother (62), apparently committed suicide by steering his car from the cliffs near Polperro when William was only one year old (86, 137). Choosing the Sphinx's way of ending his life, he did William a bad turn for he deprived his son of a direct encounter with him and thereby of occasions on which William could have tested his masculinity and experienced its limits. As Jachin-Boaz and Boaz-Jachin knew too: "The father must live so that the father can die" (LN 184). The Freudian term "castration complex" with which William himself describes his problem (115), obscures the fact that it is the right *to live as a man who is no longer young* rather than masculine sexuality that is at stake for him. Whereas the desire for death is usually linked to the maternal body by the paternal incest prohibition (i.e. during repression proper), it was linked, in William's case, to the aged body of his father. When his mother showed William the newspaper cutting reporting on his father's "accident" (186), his absent father became not only the cipher for an extremely severe super-ego (untouchable because its dead representative could not be tricked into revealing any of his imperfections having observed his "law" to the letter) but also the unconscious signifier for the abject (the "object" of primal repression, see ch. 8.3), hence William's difficulty with his own middle-aged body and his own sense of being abject. His father as Sphinx and Laius in one person left behind an unsolvable riddle about the reasons for his suicide: "Who knows what might have appeared in the road coming towards him. The rest of his life maybe" (86). William's "solution" lays bare the constitution of his unconscious; he here obviously projects onto his dead father the motive he himself had for leaving his wife (70). His projection shows how close he really is to following him despite his contradictory denials at the beginning of chapter 21, when he is thinking about Neaera's visit. Like

34 His affair with Harriet is precipitated by Ruby's therapy session rather than due to a desire that would also have overcome repression under normal circumstances. After his return from Polperro, he openly shows her that he resents the sexual advances she has been making to him since he began to withdraw from her (162)

the Delphic Oracle she has confronted Oedipus-William with the Real of his desire when telling him of the shark in her nightmare. The only thing he can do to tone down the shock is to negate the desire, negate the negation, and finally displace it onto his father by means of a projection, as we have already seen (cf. above, the quote from page 86):

> It was absolutely uncanny, gave me the creeps. That woman actually thought I'd been thinking of suicide.
>
> I *had* been thinking of it right enough, I often do, always have the idea of it huddled like a sick ape in a corner of my mind. But I'd never do it. At least I don't think I'd do it, can't imagine a state of mind in which I'd do it. Well, that's not true either. I *can* imagine the state of mind, I've been in it often enough. No place for the self to sit down and catch its breath. Just being hurried, hurried out of existence. (85)

Although William at least does not feel guilty of his father's death, it is almost as hard for him to retrieve an affirmative attitude towards life as it was for Jachin-Boaz.

This time, the process does not involve consulting a psychoanalyst. William's visit to the Zoo, where he notices for the first time the turtles' "underwater flying" (71) and their unchallenging eyes (8), and a book on shamanism by Mircea Eliade (61, 71f.) feed his mind with positive ideas: he grows aware that certain caged animals as well as "people prone to terrors and depression" (61) obviously do or did have means of switching off their present situation. Sceptical all the same, he reminds himself that "Port Liberty doesn't exist and Pangaea having separated will never again come together" (61): he is neither a turtle nor an archaic shaman nor a sheepish disciple of the New Age but a contemporary Londoner immersed in a high-tech world without the option of a return to nature or a timeless paradise. Despite such reminders Hoban could not pre-empt criticism such as that by Edmund White, reviewer for the *New York Times Book Review*: "This nostalgia for the mud was gripping (if dangerous) when D. H. Lawrence first explored it; ... But in Hoban's book primitivism has petrified into a received idea, automatically virtuous – and therefore insipid" (6). However, the point is not to advocate primitivism (in *Riddley Walker* Hoban's position has been made altogether clear), but to make the protagonists find ways of accommodating themselves to the world as it is, not by dismissing the rational altogether but by letting them rediscover additional energies lying dormant in their unconscious. The idea that it might sometimes be wiser to seek distraction than to persist stubbornly in a difficult project seems to have struck a chord in William. So as not to break down under the strain of making preparations for the abduction of the turtles, he begins to watch out for "quiet places" in his head and is pleased that the alpha-wave detector indeed furnishes proof that they exist in *his* brain (95). The Original Therapy session, on the other hand, in which people are led to a point at which they must respond to an "original YES or NO?" (102), highlights his ambivalence towards life so inclemently that his ego punishes him with a surge of anxiety: "It was as if the evening had reversed a giant devil-mirror with its picture of a world and I was silvered at the back of things, lost atoms speeding to infinity. Terror was all there was, nothing else" (107). Harriet's company comforts him that night. Afterwards there is no time left to worry: crates have to be built, a van must be reserved, and George's phone call fixes the date for the turtle snatch. One action smoothly follows upon another so that William feels no longer lost: "Atoms speeding to infinity aren't necessarily lost, are they. They're just going where they're going" (127-128). As he and Neaera eventually set out with the turtles, he describes the experience by imitating the language of *Moby Dick*: "Blindly plunged like fate into the lone M4" (131) – the controlling gaze, main instrument of the conscious mind, is as useless now as it was for Melville's sailors on the "lone Atlantic". Without being aware of it, then, William has begun to trust his id, and this trust will weaken the cruelty of the super-ego. Freud wrote in "Das Ich und das Es": "Leben ist ... für das Ich gleichbedeutend mit Geliebtwerden, vom Über-Ich geliebt werden...." (324). By letting go of himself, committing a symbolical suicide, he has paradoxically found a perfect way of being obedient to the law of the super-ego without doing any harm to his body. The launching of the turtles will form the first climax to his striving for dissolution: "I felt free of myself, unlumbered" (142). As I tried to show in ch. 5.2, the actual launching is described in a paragraph of impersonal sentences to underline his sense of freedom from the normal burdens of the ego: the awareness of the passing of time, of lost beloveds, or of danger. But the effect of ecstasy lasts only for a short time: the day after is characterized by a hangover – as usual. William's diary entries show more insistently than Neaera's that the rebirth of the ego is an exhausting process that cannot be accomplished once and for all but must be repeated over and over again.

The success of the turtle adventure is not obvious to William at first, but he is readier to act on impulse now, keen on new challenges like the mythical male hero described by Neaera earlier on, "looking for monsters to fight with" (74). Instead of swallowing his anger when he finds the bathroom and the cooker filthy on the morning after his return from Polperro he immediately goes to look up Sandor at his room (152). Though William's eyes register the imbalance of power between himself and his Hungarian neighbour, a massive man with a big moustache and the body of a wrestler (not unlike Kafka's dreadful father figures), his hands grab him by the lapels of his dressing gown.

He is not anxious but surprised at his own action (153): curious like a little boy during the phallic phase, challenging for the first time a figure of authority to test how far he can go, noticing inequality but being unable to translate it into danger for himself. In Sandor's scissors grip William is reborn for the second time. While Ruby's matronly shape lent credibility to the rebirth scenario, Sandor's pronounced masculinity makes William laugh at the grotesqueness of the situation. But it is nevertheless between his smelly legs that he can let go of himself again although this time the ego is one connected to the past: "I was joined umbilically to all pasts..." (154). When he cannot find a conscious solution to his ambivalence about life even though he adds one argument to another, he eventually drops the question, trusting to his physical response:

> It bloody isn't for me.
>
> Not for me at all. On the other hand what was. For anybody. Nothing really. Not for her when she came out and not for him. Nor would my coming-out be for anyone whatever they might think. In that case why hold on to me. A futile gesture. Life went on, one couldn't stop half way. I was getting angry. There was a redness silently exploding in my mind. Violence. Lovely. Bumpitty bump. (154)

Lucky the first time though feeling half crippled from the fight, William attacks Sandor again when the cooker is still filthy. His ego now starts being less permissive, however, since William's second rebirth is not only exhausting but painful, too. Questions arise during the fight, warnings are given, and there is no instinctive outburst of violence any more to protect William. Before he can act according to his intentions, he finds himself flying against a wall and losing consciousness (161). Sandor has to stay in bed for a couple of days after the fight, for his nose has been broken, but William is nevertheless aware of what the powerful man could have done to him had he really wanted to harm him: Sandor as castrating father has thus taught him to contain his aggression and give in to his symbolical castration, or in plain words, he has shown William the limits of his masculinity. Nevertheless William has for the first time made the acquaintance of his own buried powers. His experience corresponds to the moment when Neaera is identifying with Kong; the sense of imprisonment is gone. The verbal argument, that is a sublimated form of the struggle, now takes the place of physical action. Paying Sandor a visit, William cooks breakfast for him: a gesture of surrender. While chatting they clear cross-cultural misunderstandings: Sandor, who knows five languages, actually expects to be talked to and looked at like a "regular human person" (167); he interpreted William's making a fuss about the cooker as a sign of xenophobia hidden under a "fake smile" (167). William, on the other hand, assures him that he does not hate foreigners. Without imitating Sandor's broken English or giving brisk orders now, he tells him that a filthy cooker provokes him as much as Sandor felt provoked by his polite English reserve (168). Three days later William is surprised to find the bath "almost clean" and the cooker, "just a tiny bit mucky but without the usual smell" (171). Communication obviously worked, at least almost, where physical violence would have failed in the long run: "I could fight Sandor every day and maybe win now and again by foul means if not fair but I had no way of forcing him to clean the bath and cooker" (171). Like Neaera, William has acquired the ability to distinguish between a necessary and a false struggle.

His contact with George Fairbairn, the Head Keeper,[35] finally, consolidates William's newly found balance. Right from the beginning he seems to be "a right sort of man" (48). Although he is middle-aged like William, George becomes his second father substitute – a protective father, this time: "He was talking to me in a matter-of-fact way as if I really existed and was a real grown-up person..." (122). His way of being establishes a standard which serves William as a new guideline for evaluating his own actions: he alters William's super-ego as Sandor did. William feels deeply ashamed, for example, when George treats Neaera and him to a bottle of champagne before they leave with the turtles: "Why do I always end up feeling like a child? I'm the big turtle humanitarian but he thinks of people as well" (130). Since George is altogether unresentful, however, William's insight into his fallibility does not make his self-confidence crumble as it did when he had no one but his own dead father to compare himself to. When William goes to see him after his clashes with Sandor, George even corrects William's too pessimistic evaluation of the outcome of the turtle adventure:

> 'You know how it is,' I said. 'Launching the turtles didn't launch me. You can't do it with turtles.' Why was I talking to him like a son to a father? He wasn't older than I or wiser. Just calmer.
>
> 'You can't do it with turtles,' he said. 'But with people you never know straightaway what does what. Maybe launching them *did* launch you but you don't know it yet.' (172)

Although William in the end perceives George as a father figure, certain of his traits actually correspond to qualities that would have characterized women in more traditional stories, e.g. his housewively complaint that he is fed up with

35 His function can be read literally: he is the one who keeps his head, while William and Neaera are never far from losing theirs.

cleaning up after the turtles in his care (47), or the way he assists William and Neaera when they carry out his own fantasy of setting the turtles free (47). Neaera likes him because he makes her feel at home in her own flat; he does not need to invade her rooms, trying to appropriate them as well as her, because he has a territory of his own: "George seemed to carry a clear space about with him that made all things plain and simple where he was" (176). Nevertheless it would be too daring to say that George is the ideal new balanced human being that the novel posits as the aim of the development William and Neaera are still involved in. Too little is known about him: we do not learn whether or not he has ever been to the edge of the abyss or for how long he will be able to work as Head Keeper at the Zoo if his desire is to set animals free. He remains a stranger like Miss Neap, relevant only in so far as he influences the two protagonists as a minor character in their story. What is certain, though, is that he brings out the best in both Neaera and William. The latter is reborn a third time in the last chapter, on his way to the Zoo during the lunch-hour, with a bottle of champagne to make up for his previous omissions and thank George for his part in the adventure: "Camden Town is the windiest tube station I know. Coming up on the escalator with my hair flying I felt as if I was coming out of a dark place and into the light, then I laughed because that's what I was actually doing" (190). He does not stay to drink the bottle with George and Neaera when invited, using the shop as an excuse to explain his haste. He may simply be tactful, but it also seems that he enjoys the swiftness of his movements that day, the sense that nothing can stop him: a contemporary, non-primitivistic form of shamanic ecstasy (191).

D. M. THOMAS: *THE WHITE HOTEL*, AND J. M. COETZEE: *FOE*

As we have seen, Hoban does not use the structural device of juxtaposing two diaries in order to contrast a male with a female perspective of the same event. William and Neaera are, as he says in the interview with Haffenden, "two aspects of one entity" (137). This entity is the action they perform together, or rather, the action that happens through these two subjects in progress, turning them into its instruments. Their sexual difference matters only in so far as it does not matter for the outcome of their undertaking: sexual desire is not part of their relationship, and there is no competition for the status of originator between them since both of them eventually agree that "It seemed to want to happen" (129) independent of their own plans. One could also say, before the action they are both feminine subjects. This is an unusual solution to the question of authorship and power that has been addressed again and again by contemporary writers, women as well as men. D. M. Thomas's

The White Hotel (1981) or J. M. Coetzee's *Foe* (1986), on the other hand, stage rivalries between male and female characters for "the truth", that is, for the (impossible) priviledge of being the absolute subject rather than the object of representation. In both novels a female protagonist, tries to persuade a famous male author, "Freud" respectively "Foe" (Defoe), that his use or interpretation of her story violates facts as well as sensibilities. *The White Hotel* imitates Freud's case histories and letters to colleagues and patients in order to emphasize the contrast between his tendentious interpretations of her hysteria and the lyrical as well as narrative (self-)representations of his patient Elisabeth ("Lisa") Erdman.[36] *Foe*, on the other hand, presupposes the reader's familiarity with Defoe's novels, especially of course with *Robinson Crusoe*.

Susan Barton's first person account of her life with Cruso [sic] and Friday on a barren island, her unread letters to Foe, and eventually her dialogues with him take up the major part of the novel until an altogether different new narrator tries to approach the blind spot in both her and Defoe's version the story of the island. The cultural constructions of both gender and subjectivity are thus highlighted; "the truth" turns out to be a hole in the story, screened by a variety of relative truths. These truths are not equivalent, however. Both novels demand moral evaluations to be reintroduced into competing discourses of power and liberation. While *The White Hotel*, with its focus on Freudian psychoanalysis and European history up to the anti-Semitic massacre of Babi Yar, limits its attention to the Western sphere, *Foe* also addresses conflicts arising between different cultures: Once Foe and Susan have stopped quarrelling over the best way of being creative,[37] their attention turns to the African Friday. He was saved from Cruso's island together with Susan, while Cruso himself died. Foe is convinced that he and Susan will eventually be able to "make Friday's silence speak, as well as the silence surrounding Friday" (142). Since Susan is concerned about respecting Friday's point of view, she tries in vain to teach Friday to write so that he can give them clues about what happened to him (145). But the very metaphors of perspective and voice, which underline the importance of the visual and of speech in Western culture, are undermined at the moment when the African fills a slate with eyes set upon feet, signalling that his culture hinges upon altogether different metaphors

36 For a detailed analysis of *The White Hotel* see Mary F. Robertson's excellent as well as critical essay "Hystery, Herstory, History: 'Imagining the Real' in Thomas's *The White Hotel*." (1984).

37 Susan, who would no doubt be categorized as a typical hysteric by Freud, repeatedly insists on being the "father" of the story Foe is to write down (123, 126, 140), while he tries to throw her back on her biological potential for maternity (125) because he himself is fed up with being a writer ("An old whore who should ply her trade only in the dark", 151). Their dispute is only settled when both recognize the equivalence of the cultural and the physical (152).

(147). He perceives with his feet, dances to express himself or to forget the present and is able to take care of himself even though slavers or Cruso have cut off his tongue and castrated him. The point is therefore not to write any further stories about or for someone else, but to explore the abyss of one's own (hi)story and *experience* the terror at the bottom. Coetzee's image of a kraken as the possible embodiment of that which might drag the exploring subject to its death (140, 156) resembles the beginning of *Turtle Diary*; moreover the Krakens in *The Medusa Frequency* come to mind. But most of the time terror terrifies because the form in which it will eventually manifest itself defies our expectations: it is usually not stranger than anything we could have expected but much too familiar. So far the essence is the same as that which can be extracted from Freud's essays on Medusa's head and on the uncanny, but Coetzee does not repeat the mistake of presenting yet another version of the myth of the maternal genitals as the alpha and omega of bliss and terror. He ends his novel by letting an anonymous new first-person narrator dive down to a wreck lying at the bottom of the sea off the coast of Cruso's island. He (or she) finds the wreck of a slave-ship. There is no kraken inside but the dead bodies of Susan, the captain and Friday. The narrator's question "what is this ship?" is answered in nonverbal language, for this is "a place where bodies are their own signs ... the home of Friday" (157); we too know this language if we dare indeed confront that which our culture has made us consider abject:

> His [Friday's] mouth opens. From inside him comes a slow stream, without breath, without interruption. It flows up through his body and out upon me; it passes through the cabin, through the wreck; washing the cliffs and shores of the island, it runs northward and southward to the ends of the earth. Soft and cold, dark and unending, it beats against my eyelids, against the skin of my face. (157)

The ship as a vehicle of slavery and colonization is related to the eyes and to the skin. The soft but cold stream emanating from Friday's body, perhaps a stream of blood, asks the narrator back: why do you feel this urge to discover, colonize, subdue and appropriate everything, first with your eyes, then by sending people of your skin all over the earth? Here inside the wreck you should open your eyes and see what you have done, but now they are closed. You pretend that my message is too dark to be understood. I'll beat against your eyelids, however, until you drop your resistance. Look at the wreck of your own abjected body, at the dead bodies of your victims as well as those of your fellow conquerors, and if you ever manage to reach the surface again, let *this* be your tale.

VLADIMIR NABOKOV: *LOLITA*

Vladimir Nabokov and Salman Rushdie have chosen a slightly different way of undermining their male narrators' authority in *Lolita* (1959) and *Midnight's Children* (1981). While Humbert Humbert explicitly seeks to immortalize his beloved Lolita, fully aware of the gap between his literary creation and the real twelve-year-old girl (62) and therefore implicitly revealing that he above all seeks to eternalize himself through his art,[38] Rushdie's Saleem Sinai explicitly tries to make sense of his own life – he speaks of "the business of remaking my life" (10) – by linking his biography to the history of the Indian subcontinent. Since he, too, needs a female character as touchstone for his narcissistic self-image, however, he tells the story of his life to his illiterate and supposedly naive narratee Padma. The pretensions and control fantasies of both narrators crumble even though there are no parallel narratives by other narrators to contradict their stories: inconsistencies and self-conscious insights sufficiently alert the readers to the narrators' fallibility. In *Midnight's Children*, Padma efficiently enforces the author's implicit criticism of his unreliable narrator, as will be shown presently. Nabokov, on the other hand, added a fictitious foreword to Humbert Humbert's "confession", in which a hypocritical "editor" justifies its publication by the "lesson" that can be learned from reading about the narrator's illegal passion for minor girls. Editor John Ray, Jr., calls H. H. "abject" and "a shining example of moral leprosy" (7). His "aesthetic" fascination with the narrative, however, which mirrors H. H.'s own fascination with literary texts on doomed seductive (child-)women, shows that the editor is of the same kind; actually he is glad that Humbert never attended "a competent psycho-pathologist" to prevent his "special experience": "... there would have been no disaster; but then, neither would there have been this book" (7). Elisabeth Bronfen's interpretation of *Lolita* in *Over Her Dead Body* focuses on the victimization of women by an insatiable art Moloch:

> I will limit myself to a discussion of the plethora of allusions to the conjunction of femininity and death.... In this narrative an excessively figural rendition of the beloved 'killed' into the trope of muse (with this gesture supported by references to other texts undertaking the same figure), inevitably also articulates the real subject position of the effaced child-bride Dolores Haze, though only uncannily, as a presence in absence. (371)

One might, however, also investigate the degree to which H. H. himself is already "(un)dead", i.e. consumed by the machinery, while still portraying himself scheming to conquer Lolita, and truly alive only at those moments when

38 This is an inference supported by the last sentence of the novel, too, as Bronfen's interpretation of *Lolita* underlines, see *Over Her Dead Body*, p. 372.

the awareness of his lack of control over his text and the body of his beloved (Bronfen 378), but also the lack of control over his own body dawn upon him. Such moments are, in H. H.'s own words, "icebergs in paradise" (283). He is only alive then, precisely because those short moments force him to see the world and his body outside the image repertoire he otherwise tries to repeat and reproduce with the obstinacy of a madman imprisoned in the vicious circle of a repetition compulsion (cf. Freud, "Jenseits des Lustprinzips"). Humbert is a Perseus figure in love with the reflection of his deeds in Athene's shield. What he wants to see there, though, is not the murder of Medusa but a love story. The girl with names as numerous as the snakes on Medusa's head, i.e. Dolores Haze, Dolly, Lo, Lola, Lolita, Mrs Richard F. Schiller, etc., only turns into an incarnation of the ancient monster in his description when her anger is at its highest pitch and she briefly succeeds in confronting him with her view of the so-called "love" story – at such moments, she openly asserts her subject position; wide awake, she does not permit Perseus to murder her:

> She said she loathed me. She made monstrous faces at me, inflating her cheeks and producing a diabolical plopping sound. She said I had attempted to violate her several times when I was her mother's roomer. She said she was sure I had murdered her mother.... It was a strident and hateful scene. I held her by her knobby wrist and she kept turning and twisting it this way and that, surreptitiously trying to find a weak point so as to wrench herself free at a favourable moment, but I held her quite hard, and in fact hurt her rather badly for which I hope my heart may rot,[39] and once or twice she jerked her arm so violently that I feared her wrist might snap, and all the while she stared at me with those unforgettable eyes where cold anger and hot tears struggled, and our voices were drowning the telephone, and when I grew aware of its ringing she instantly escaped. (203)

Her gaze does not turn him to stone. It tries, on the contrary, to send him back to the "real" world of changes, movements and other people to which he does not wish to return by his own efforts. But its effect is only short-lived: his narcissism, the true source of his and her destruction, usually proves stronger than her "monstrous" resistance.[40]

39 Like Oedipus, H. H. unwittingly pronounces his own sentence at this moment: his heart will indeed rot, but only in the figurative sense. Quite in tune with his emotional stagnation, it will be congested by a clot of blood: as the "editor" tells us, H. H. "died in legal captivity, of coronary thrombosis, on November 16, 1952, a few days before his trial was scheduled to start" (5). But his repentance and self-punishment do not cure society. On the contrary, his narrative will spread the disease further, as the editor's reaction shows.

40 The violence he develops at moments when he feels that he has lost control and is the character in a plot designed by others would fill a separate study. I will therefore add only one observation that is interesting in regard to the analogy with Perseus and Medusa: after raping and misrepresenting Lolita, both of which are figurative murders, i.e. of her bodily autonomy and her subjectivity, he seems to intend to kill her physically, too. He checks his pistol after the possibility of a rival pursuing them has begun to dawn upon him (213-214). The murder fantasies which anticipate his actual murder of Quilty at the end of the book (296ff.) are deliberately kept

Each time he "kills" Dolores into the trope of muse, he also "kills" the reality of his own body into the trope of an immortal, unsexed, or rather "maternal" poet. Centuries of literary tradition have promoted this "transformation". As long as his real male body disturbs illusions of harmony and peace, just as the uncanny returns of Lolita's effaced subject position do, his self-criticism can take effect:

> I recall certain moments ... when after having had my fill of her ... I would gather her in my arms with, at last, a mute moan of human tenderness (... her grave grey eyes more vacant than ever – for all the world a little patient still in the confusion of a drug after a major operation) – and the tenderness would deepen to shame and despair, and I would lull and rock my lone light Lolita in my marble arms, and moan in her warm hair, and caress her at random and mutely ask her blessing, and at the peak of this human agonized selfless tenderness (with my soul actually hanging around her naked body and ready to repent), all at once, ironically, horribly, lust would swell again – and 'oh, *no,*' Lolita would say with a sigh to heaven, and the next moment the tenderness and the azure – all would be shattered. (283-284)

Ultimately, though, Humbert's penitence as well as Lolita's resistance are thwarted by the way the editor kindles the readers' desire for the book:

> A desperate honesty that throbs through [Humbert Humbert's] confession does not absolve him from sins of diabolical cunning. He is abnormal. He is not a gentleman. But how magically his singing violin can conjure up a tendresse, a compassion for Lolita that makes us entranced with the book while abhorring its author. (7)

Instead of destroying the manuscript, he keeps alive a fatal literary tradition (confessions, "true" stories) despite the sacrifices it presupposes. Thus, H. H.'s failure is double. As a man, he can only offer Lolita "the parody of incest"

---

ambiguous in regard to the victim (214, 227) so that the readers must fear for Lolita's life – until, after Lolita's escape from hospital (245), he spells out his desire to kill his rival. But the desire to kill her as well shines through all his conscious attempts to repress it, most of all when he negates having ever had such a desire, i.e. the last time he sees Lolita, now pregnant Dolly Schiller, whom he has not been able to persuade into leaving her husband to live with him: "Then I pulled out my automatic – I mean this is the kind of fool thing a reader might suppose I did. It never even occurred to me to do it" (278).

The degree of aggression as well as its object (the ego or an other) is obviously related to previous feelings of self-confidence or anxiety. William G., for instance, feels frightened when Miss Neap's suicide makes him aware that he "might in fact be only a minor character in somebody else's" story rather than the protagonist of his own (TD 186). Being diffident anyway, this reminder of his personal insignificance cannot rouse his anger; it can only reinforce the sense of his lack of control. Riddley Walker's first "connexion" establishes a sense of estrangement, too (RW 58). Having planned an altogether different "reveal" (57), Riddley is overwhelmed by a message coming from his unconscious. While William G. fantasized about a shaman's initiation into power and his ecstatic journeys to a prehistoric and prelingual state (TD 61), Riddley actually experiences his trance inspiration as a complete deprivation of power, both psychic and social. But like William, he does not turn aggressive. Although Riddley is too young to understand the full implications of his revelation, he writes: "I fealt like my Luck gone from me. I fealt like I rathert not come a wake that day" (RW 59-60).

(286), noticing again and again that she does not feel sexually attracted to him at all; in her perception, his body is reduced to the aggressive features of a rapist: "... I was to her not a boy friend, not a glamour man, not a pal, not even a person at all, but just two eyes and a foot of engorged brawn – to mention only mentionable matters" (282). As a poet-"mother", on the other hand, writing in the "well-heated, albeit tombal seclusion" of a prison cell and eventually condemning himself to deliver a stillborn narrative "Lolita" because his conscience forbids him to "parade living Lolita" (307), he is cheated by his own desire for immortality – or he himself would have destroyed his manuscript instead of simply deferring its publication – and by the editor's desire to spread and consume this kind of literature. Zeuslike, John Ray lifts the book from the tomb.

Meanwhile, Nabokov is laughing about both Humbert Humbert and John Ray's inability to enjoy the "aesthetic bliss" afforded by works of art without trying to impose it onto their realities:

> I am neither a reader nor a writer of didactic fiction, and, despite John Ray's assertion, *Lolita* has no moral in tow. For me a work of fiction exists only in so far as it affords me what I shall bluntly call aesthetic bliss, that is a sense of being somehow, somewhere, connected with other states of being where art (curiosity, tenderness, kindness, ecstasy) is the norm. ("On a Book Entitled *Lolita*", 313)

With the modernist's belief that the spheres of art and life can be kept apart if art is treated appropriately, that is as a medium of transcendence, escape and invention, he mocks the two characters because for them, the purpose of art, and here especially fiction, is above all to represent life, accommodating the needs of exhibitionists and voyeurs; they thus resemble the ape which (allegedly) inspired Nabokov to begin writing *Lolita* around 1940:

> As far as I can recall, the initial shiver of inspiration was somehow prompted by a newspaper story about an ape in the Jardin des Plantes who, after months of coaxing by a scientist, produced the first drawing ever charcoaled by an animal: this sketch showed the bars of the poor creature's cage. (309)

SALMAN RUSHDIE: *MIDNIGHT'S CHILDREN*

Salman Rushdie, however, born almost half a century after Nabokov,[41] can no longer simply shift the responsibility for tragedies resulting from the abuse of art onto incompetent or perverted readers. *Midnight's Children* was written by an author who is aware that reality is the product of a complex, chaotic interaction between representations (documentary, artistic, religious,

41 Rushdie was born in 1947 while Nabokov was born in 1899, like Borges and Hemingway.

political, etc.) and the Real (that which we experience precisely when we are at a loss for words, exposed to something our representational systems either seek to repress or have not yet learned to deal with).[42] "Art" and "life" do not coexist in pure form but are inextricably involved with each other. Or, as Goodparley told Riddley Walker, "Words! Theywl move things you know theywl do things. Theywl fetch" (RW 118). This entails, on the one hand, that pure "aesthetic bliss" does not exist: depending on the context, one person's bliss may be another's vexation; on the other, it entails that those who produce art or other forms of representation are as responsible for their effect as those who receive them. I would now like to discuss how the novel's narratee Padma not only corrects Saleem's pretensions to authority but also allows the author to show by what foul means and why his narrator tries to defend his position against her criticism. Ultimately, of course, both are bound to lose their struggle for superiority: the pressures of mortality and the masses, which impose limitations on the worst of tyrants, do not spare a self-made historian and autobiographer and his bride, strong though her arms and her determination may be.

The Indian scholar Charu Verma, taking offence with the way Padma is portrayed in the novel, thinks it is necessary to rehabilitate the woman who appears to be marginalized and devalued though she is "Saleem's constant companion and audience, interlocutor and critic" (Verma 63); her essay "Padma's Tragedy: A Feminist Deconstruction of *Midnight's Children*" (1989)

> ... aims at highlighting the strategies used by Saleem, the narrator, to give Padma a short shrift. These strategies reflect certain attitudes and ideological positions which reveal this otherwise remarkable novel to be a very sexist text. A humanistic focusing on Padma involves resisting the thrust of the male text, and it enables us to notice several disturbing sexist biases both in Rushdie and his narrator-protagonist. (59)

While her essay is well-meant, it is based on an elementary error: as the quotation shows, Verma identifies the narrator with the author. While she then goes on to present a series of examples which both document Saleem's diminishing image of Padma and point to his omissions in his account of her, Verma is blind to textual details by which Rushdie has inscribed his criticism of the narrator: there are not only signals which show that Padma differs from Saleem's description, but one might also gauge the power of her presence by the fact that she manages to shine through the cracks of Saleem's story despite all his narcissistic and sexist attempts to suppress her. Moreover, Padma is not

42 See ch. 11.2. for a detailed analysis of Rushdie's interrogation of reality in *Midnight's Children*.

the only person he seeks to suppress, nor is she suppressed merely because she is a woman.

Padma appears for the first time in the second chapter, "Mercurochrome". She brings food to Saleem, harvesting in return his patronizing pity for being illiterate, ignorant, vulgar, ugly and also "named after the lotus goddess, whose most common appellation amongst village folk is 'The One Who Possesses Dung.'" (24). Only during her next visit is she established as narratee. Actually she blackmails Saleem: if he does not read out his manuscript to her, he won't get any more food (31f.) – the "intellectual" is reminded of his material needs, which make him more dependent on Padma than she will ever be on him. Of course she is offended by his description of her when he sarcastically complies with her demand. More importantly, however, she instantly begins to correct his misinterpretation of the connotation of her name, demonstrating that evaluations require a context: "'In my village there is no shame in being named for the Dung Goddess. Write at once that you are wrong, completely.'" (32). Saleem and Padma are not only separated by their sexes. Rushdie also underlines right from the beginning that their values, their views on history and their outlook on the future owe a good deal to class difference. While Saleem ironically calculates Padma's utility to his project – "perhaps our Padma will be useful, because it's impossible to stop her being a critic" (32) – he neither notices how useful she really is in the domain of story-telling in which he thinks he can "educate her" (38): she checks his Shandyan digressions (39), watches over narrative sequence (338), laughs at "typical" male fantasies (46), sympathizes with Saleem's "mothers" Amina Sinai (88), Vanita (118) and Mary Pereira (119, 281) when he craves pity for himself or his paternal ancestors, and finally, she continues to relativize his evaluations (119f.). Nor does Saleem ever take in that Padma's interest in him is perhaps based on far more pragmatic reasons than on the romantic infatuation he will keep projecting onto her: even before she knows the story of his life, she is aware that he must be a favourite of her employer Mrs Braganza, perhaps her heir, at any rate the only man admitted to the pickle factory in which she normally stirs huge chutney vats. She actually abandons him for a couple of days, when he offends her pride too much by writing that she is sitting in his "enchanted shadows, ... captivated, helpless as a mongoose frozen into immobility by the swaying blinkless eyes of a hooded snake, paralysed – yes! – by love" (121).[43] Padma's furious reply before she leaves reveals not only sexual frustration and anger at his vanity, as he thinks and

43 Incidentally, a mongoose is a catlike predator whose favourite prey are snakes, even poisonous ones. Saleem's simile is therefore not only offensive but altogether ill-chosen.

blames himself for, but also a certain disappointment that her intention to seduce and use Saleem as a means of social advancement has failed: "'Love *you*?' our Padma piped scornfully, 'What for, my God? What use are you, little princeling,' – and now came her attempted *coup de grâce* – 'as a *lover*?'" (121)[44] When she has gone, he promptly misses her, that is, he does not miss critical Padma but fantasizes about one who would reassure him in times of doubt and confusion: "... in her absence, my certainties are falling apart. (...) ... I, now, Padma-less, send these words into the darkness and am afraid of being disbelieved" (166-167). But on returning, Padma apologizes in a way that affords further glimpses of her thinking:

> 'It was my own foolish pride and vanity, Saleem baba, from which cause I did run from you, although the job here is good, and you so much needing a looker-after! But in a short time only I was dying to return.
> 'So then I thought, how to go back to this man who will not love me and only does some foolish writery? (Forgive, Saleem baba, but I must tell it truly. And love, to us women, is the greatest thing of all.) ...' (193)

She never says that she is in love with Saleem but she has obviously accepted responsibility for him; moreover, she wants to get her good job back and in addition to be loved by him. She even tries to cure Saleem's impotence with an aphrodisiac, but the herbs she administers turn him delirious. To appease Saleem, Padma echoes one of his favourite stereotypes: "'This love, mister,' Padma is wailing, 'It will drive a woman to craziness.'" (193).

Verma insinuates that Padma uncritically swallows the compliments paid her when Saleem after this crisis compensates her for his former devaluations by a series of flattering comparisons with ancient goddesses (194f.):

> All male dominant ideologies need to compensate man's actual degradation and exploitation of woman by doling out to her some imaginary, mythified space in which she is worshipped as a goddness [sic]. This mythified space is the opium of her sex. This unreal space is a device to legitimise her actual exploitation day in and day out. Padma's description as the lotus-goddess is no compliment too [sic] her, though she may think it is, because she is a willing dupe of the sexist politics of India. (63-64)

Yet, her criticism of Padma not only neglects entirely Saleem's delirious condition at the time and the fact that Rushdie fully exposes his narrator's fickle jumps from devaluation to hyperbolic praise, but it also suppresses

44 Such harsh sounds can hardly ever be heard from a female character of the Hoban universe: it is, for instance, up to Underground and a fellow busker to make Kleinzeit aware of his exploitation of Sister (100). In *Fremder*, however, Caroline Lovecraft does not swallow her disappointment with Fremder's lack of cooperation (58f.): her reproaches are a refreshing contrast to the silent withdrawals of Gretel, Sister, Harriet, or the wife in "The Devil's Kitchen".

Padma's anxiety, which replaces her embarrassed and then amused response to Saleem's flatteries as soon as his eulogy turns excessive: "'My God.' Padma is rushing for a towel to wet in cold water, 'your forehead is on fire! Better you lie down now; too soon for all this writing! The sickness is talking; not you.'" (195). To all appearances, it is Verma's criticism that is biased and sexist, not Rushdie's novel. Saleem's narrative about the supernaturally gifted children of midnight, finally, confirms Padma's fear that Saleem has turned not only ill from her love potion but crazy (200); she is certainly not the gullible and ignorant "necessary ear" (149) he fantasized about while she was absent.

The next step shows most clearly that Rushdie must not be confused with Saleem. As soon as Saleem (literally) smells that Padma and Mary Braganza try to lure him into an asylum, he takes advantage of his "education, or class-origins" (212). He summons all his rhetoric to instil a sense of his alleged mental superiority and religious vocation in the two worried but simple women until they are intimidated enough to allow him to stay in his office (211). By making Saleem lay bare his dubious strategy of persuasion, Rushdie not only undermines the authority of his narrator, but he also alerts his readers to a practice which is quite common among populists, gurus and other seducers. Fortunately, the effect of Saleem's manoeuvre is only short-lived. By the end of the chapter Padma has resumed her position as a critical listener. Smiling she points out an error in his chronology of events (222).

While Saleem keeps insinuating that she is more interested in him than in his tale, reducing her to a strong-armed comforter to whom he owes nothing (270), she persists in signalling that he cannot spoon-feed her: the information she finds interesting differs from what he would like her to be interested in. The most telling example is the episode when she infuriates him because she fails to pity him sufficiently for contracting leprosy; instead she cries about Saleem's ayah Mary Pereira, who runs away from the house of the Sinais after admitting a crime she committed eleven years earlier, when Saleem was born: in order to please her revolutionary boyfriend, Mary then exchanged the wealthy Sinais' true son Shiva for Saleem, born at exactly the same time but as the son of beautiful doomed Vanita and the poor musical clown Wee Willie Winkie (or more likely, the Englishman William Methwold, with whom Vanita had committed adultery) (280f.). If Padma is interested in Saleem, it is precisely because his tale has whetted her appetite for an alternative to the life she knows: he could take her to Kashmir in the summer, enabling her to escape from the heat of Bombay and "the sneer-lipped barbs hurled by our workforce of downy-forearmed women" (384). But narcissistic Saleem would prefer to continue profiting from her without having to honour any debts. The man whose own claim to his position in life has been called into question by his autobiography is determined not to gratify her "desire for legitimacy" (384). She does not give up, however, nor will she revert to flattery. Although he explicitly sends her to a "back seat" (385), she once more interferes with his story when he tries to blame, or even demonize, women for the entire course his life has taken:

> Too-many-women: are they all aspects of Devi, the goddess – who is Shakti, who slew the buffalo-demon, ... who is Kali Durga Chandi Chamunda Uma Sati and Parvati ... and who, when active, is coloured red?
>
> 'I don't know about that,' Padma brings me down to earth, 'They are just women, that's all.' (406)[45]

Finally, she takes her fate in hand and proposes to Saleem. He cannot reject her offer of marriage but accepts it "meekly and with every appearance of gratitude" (444). He is not only aware of his weakness but also of the fact that the future will no longer be in the hands of himself, his friends the magicians, or his personal enemy, disinherited Shiva. Women like Padma or Mrs Braganza, who turns out to be Mary Pereira, flourish, promising a future full of "new things" and "new stories" (445). By comparison, he is a sorry figure:

> ... nine-fingered, horn-templed, monk's-tonsured, stain-faced, bow-legged, cucumber-nosed, castrated, and now prematurely aged, I saw in the mirror of humility a human being to whom history could do no more, a grotesque creature who had been released from the pre-ordained destiny which had battered him until he was half-senseless; with one good ear and one bad ear I heard the soft footfalls of the Black Angel of death. (447)

On the other hand, he also expects changes from the next generation, brought up by these women. Saleem's adopted son Aadam, whose real parents are Parvati-the-witch and Shiva, belongs to "a second generation of magical children who would grow up far tougher than the first, not looking for their fate in prophecy or the stars, but forging it in the implacable furnaces of their wills" (447).

The impression that Rushdie locates hope for the future in "maternal" instincts is certainly not wrong: Mary Braganza welcomes Saleem like a long-lost son, saving him once more from destitution when he arrives at her factory

45 By making a female character contradict his male narrator, Rushdie has chosen the most straightforward way of criticizing the demonization of women. In *V.*, on the other hand, Thomas Pynchon trusted to his readers' ability to read as a satire Stencil's excessive search for a mysterious woman he could blame for every catastrophe of the twentieth century. In Hoban's novels, finally, there are again and again scenes in which male protagonists first blame their lovers, partners, wives or mothers for difficult situations they find themselves in before they eventually grow up to accept the responsibility for their lives (e.g. LN 150, TD 55, etc.)

with baby Aadam on his arm (457). Padma, on the other hand, repeatedly offers to look after him, responding to his need as much as to her own ambition. But "maternal" is only used in the figurative sense, for the propensity for solicitude and solidarity is not reserved to mothers – significantly, neither Mary nor Padma have ever had any children of their own; nor is solicitude an attribute of female biology: think of Picture Singh's "fatherly" care for both Parvati and Saleem (378, 395), or Saleem's readiness to care for his arch-enemy's son Aadam. On the other hand, real mothers and fathers can be less than maternal and paternal: Indira Gandhi, for instance, who is explicitly referred to as the mother of Sanjay and Rajiv (421) and who has violently appropriated the metaphorical title of a "Mother of the Nation" (420), becomes the model for Saleem's Black Angel of Death in his apocalyptic fantasy of his thirty-first birth, wedding and death day (463). Together with Saleem's violent alter ego Shiva, the paradigm of an irresponsible father who abandons all women who bear his children (409) and whose return Saleem has always anticipated with mortal terror (389, 406), the "Widow" Indira Gandhi seems to bring about Saleem's annihilation:

> ... I see a mythological apparition approaching, the Black Angel, except that as it nears me its face is green its eyes are black, a centre-parting in its hair, on the left green and on the right black, its eyes the eyes of Widows; Shiva and the Angel are closing closing, I hear lies being spoken in the night, anything you want to be you kin be, the greatest lie of all, cracking now, fission of Saleem, I am the bomb in Bombay, watch me explode... (463)

Yet, as his vision extends, those two figures become insignificant. Rushdie undercuts his narrator's desire for a dramatic showdown; it is the crowd, the teeming millions of India's population which will irresistibly grind Saleem's existence to dust:

> ... bones splitting breaking beneath the awful pressure of the crowd, bag of bones falling down down down, just as once at Jallianwala, but Dyer seems not to be present today, no Mercurochrome, only a broken creature spilling pieces of itself into the street, because I have been so-many too-many persons, life unlike syntax allows one more than three, and at last somewhere the striking of a clock, twelve chimes, release. (463)

To sum up: the feminist and class-sensitive deconstruction of Saleem's autobiography which is inscribed in the novel is more convincing than Verma's so-called feminist deconstruction of *Midnight's Children*, which ends up being a repetition of Saleem's sexist and class-blind description of Padma joined to an even more derogatory assessment of the figure it supposedly seeks to rehabilitate:

> Padma is reconciled to male sexual and economic domination ... We should not regard Padma as a model for Indian women. Even as it is, she is projected as a pathetic victim who does not exist as a free, self-willing actor, but only as her master's voice. (Verma 64)

RIDDLEY WALKER

From the human "bomb in Bombay" who asks us to watch him explode we can now move on to the pulsating heart of Hoban's fourth novel, his wise boy narrator Riddley Walker. In ch. 6.4, I have announced a further discussion of the seeming change in Russell Hoban's perception of sex and gender between the publications of *Turtle Diary* and *Riddley Walker*. What was said there can now be refined, that is, that Riddley's pantheistic mysticism and his final resolution not to struggle for power, but to oscillate between positions of power and powerlessness, actually exclude essentialism in a traditional or naive sense. First of all Riddley's development subsumes that of both William and Neaera in the previous novel. Although his world is characterized by a strict binary gender separation that is rigidly essentialistic because gender is derived from biology, that is, a world in which women's function is mainly to give birth or be priestesses and embodiments of the Mother Goddess while men do everything else, Riddley learns that his male body can profit from both "feminine" and "animal" ways of behaviour.[46] Even intellectual abilities are regarded as unmanly by his contemporaries. He is teased early on by a "hevvy" from his fents for being "myndy": "You ben lernt to read and write and all ways thinking on things. Trubba not nor I aint staring but I wunt want to be like that it aint no way for a man to be" (61). Intuition, perceptiveness and the ability to surrender or withdraw when a struggle would be a false struggle are invaluable additions to a "masculinity" and a rationality whose limitations he experiences but whose powers he eventually decides to use all the same, too, so as not to be victimized by his surroundings. He achieves a dynamic balance, energized and destabilized by his drives and the divine principle that "thinks us". As a consequence the oedipal pattern into which he at first seems to move, a psychic fool's circle, is called into question.

When we first encounter him, he has just reached maturity, makes love to the tel woman Lorna, the oldest woman in the fents (5), and briefly afterwards

46 That Hoban is no traditional essentialist can also be gleaned from a comparison between *Riddley Walker* and William Golding's *The Inheritors*. In the latter novel, the disruption of the "natural" gender binarity which the Neanderthals have always observed (cf. the old woman's law: "A man for pictures. A woman for Oa", 95), is a symptom of their impending extinction. Riddley's transgression of various boundaries, however, prefigures the positive breaking of fool's circles.

causes an accident in which his father is killed. He gets involved in solving the riddle of the 1 Big 1 for Goodparley, discovers that he probably unconsciously wished to kill his father (190), but by the time this insight is suggested by Granser's severed head, his first visit to Cambry has already made him change course. He need not be blinded to reform for he underwent symbolic castration when his failure with the Mother Goddess shamed him into surrendering all claims to power.[47] Goodparley, on the other hand, is an incurable Oedipus who even seeks to solve the riddle of the 1 Littl 1 when blind. David Cowart writes: "Like Oedipus, Abel Goodparley seeks to account for and deal with the plague, little realizing that his researches will bring his own downfall or that they resemble the researches that brought humanity to Bad Time" (98-99). Goodparley believes in unity like Riddley, but his "solutions" to conflicts or riddles always consist in eliminating differences and blurring distinctions: Goodparley craves sameness like the Punch in his show who kills every opponent as well as his beloved Pooty and her baby so as to indulge in the illusion that he is invincible – an illusion because he is instantly haunted by Drop John, the ghost of Mr On The Levvil (134). Riddley, though, perceives unity in the interaction of different elements and therefore need not destroy what is different. Instead he translates his newly found flexibility and his empathic ability into artistic creativity.

Getting off the oedipal track coincides, or is marked by, the discovery of Greanvine, a male figure of mortality (160ff.). This is significant for the discussion of the question whether Riddley is actually a male hysteric. The Romantic poet Novalis, whom Christina von Braun has identified as a typical example of a male hysteric in "Männliche Hysterie – weibliche Askese: Zum Paradigmenwechsel der Geschlechterrollen", profited from the experience of mortality, too. But in contrast to Riddley, it was the death of his fifteen-year-old fiancée Sophie von Kühn which fired his imagination to such a degree that his friend Friedrich Schlegel envied him for his loss (63). Even before she was dead, he treated the girl as his muse, thus disembodying her and turning her into a metaphor. Sophie was startled rather than pleased; for she was neither

47 Discussing mysticism, Lacan too stresses its incompatibility with phallic display; he speculates that mystics experience feminine *jouissance*, something radically different from phallic orgasm. Male mystics do so despite their sex; it is an experience which shatters all assumptions about identity ("God and the *Jouissance* of ~~The~~ Woman", 147). Lacan warns against confusing feminine *jouissance* with women, and woman with God: "... the more man may ascribe to the woman in confusion with God, that is, in confusion with what it is she comes from, the less he hates, the lesser he is, and since after all, there is no love without hate, the less he loves" ("A Love Letter", 160). In *Riddley Walker*, Lorna Elswint, the priestess of the Mother Goddess herself, as a matter of fact demystifies woman by positing beside the goddess (a mystification of woman by definition) an "it" which pre-exists all human distinctions, "some kynd of thing it aint us but yet its in us" (6).

self-confident nor educated enough to be able to protect herself from his cannibalistic "love" (61f.). Christina von Braun's thesis is that the male hysteric desires to give birth to his own (male) femininity rather than to encounter and accept the radical alterity or strangeness of real women (57, 64). What we see here, then, is the symptom that also characterizes Orpheus after he has lost Eurydice (cf. ch. 8.3): the male survivor seemingly appropriates the femininity and mortality of his dead beloved, while he really seeks to legitimize his own femininity and to displace his mortality; henceforth he will shun contact with other women, indulging in the illusion that he now functions as a totality that can immortalize itself through art. Riddley, on the other hand, who has seen his mother, his father, many of his childhood friends and Belnot Phist die, has never had any narcissistic illusions of immortality: on the very first page, while watching the boar die, he says to the speared animal: "'Your tern now my tern later.'" (1). And the femininity he admits (after having already admitted "1st knowing", which is coded as an animal ability in his society, i.e. a gift from the dogs) need not be derived from any of the female characters who populate the novel. It is always clear that it is his own femininity that is stimulated in the crypt of the cathedral. His femininity is alien only in so far as all ideational representatives of drives fixated in the unconscious are "other". But he need not "legitimize" its influence on his conscious personality by the excuse of seeking to revive a dead beloved: there is no hysterical compromise but an acceptance of symbolical castration. The fact that the crypt is regarded as the womb of the Mother Goddess of course suggests that the archaic mother of primal repression is the origin of a subject's femininity; by way of making Riddley find Greanvine's head rather than a representation of Medusa, however, the burden of mortality is dissociated from femininity. While Medusa was deprived of being the subject of her gaze and forced into "giving birth" (at the neck) to Pegasus and Chrysaor, personifications of the imagination and of male heroism, Greanvine is deprived of his tongue and forced to give life to a tree that is growing through his body, a figure of natural regeneration. The murder of Medusa forces her into the feminine object position and the role of a mother at the same time that Perseus usurpates the subject position, thus becoming "a man". Mortality and femininity are thus jointly repressed by the masculine subject and will also return together. Greanvine, however, is not effeminated by death but dehumanized; Riddley's thoughts clearly distinguish giving birth from growing a tree through the mouth: "A man myt get 100s of childer but the onlyes new life growing out of him wil be that dead mans vine at the end of his run" (163).

How does this fit with the fact that one aspect of the Mother Goddess is death, personified and vulgarized as Aunty, whom David Dowling has described as "a copulating mincing machine which destroys human beings" (*Fictions*, 207)? Let's take a look at the way she is described in *The Bloak as Got on Top of Aunty*:

> Every body knows Aunty. Stoan boans and iron tits and teef be twean her legs plus she has a iron willy for the ladys it gets red hot. When your time comes you have to do the juicy with her like it or not. She rides a girt big rat with red eyes it can see in the dark and it can smel whos ready for Aunty. Even if they dont know it ther selfs the rat can smel if theyre ready. (87)

Coding death as "doing the juicy" with Aunty combines sexuality and mortality as in the mythic patterns that have determined patriarchal culture, hallmark of an oedipal repression process with its specific set of anxieties. Many of Aunty's features show that she is indeed the Mother Goddess herself, whose function as death goddess had been repressed before it returned disfigured as an uncanny "aunt" equipped with a murderous dentate vagina and an iron phallus instead of a life-giving womb. In contrast to the Greek Medusa, however, Aunty is immortal like Hoban's own Medusa. She does not lend herself to appropriations which allow a "hero" like Perseus to displace his incestuous desire and his desire for death onto her by killing her. The only "triumph" allowed to the "bloak" in the seeming success story Wayman Footling once told Riddley is actually a failure, for Aunty postpones the death of her male pursuer when he tries to commit suicide; later on, when he brags about his seeming victory, she will promptly devour him. But Aunty is not the only representation of death. In Lissener's story *The Lissener and the Other Voyce Owl of the Worl*, there is a is "male" representation of death, i.e. the Other Voyce Owl: "He sat in the worl tree larfing in his front voyce only his other voyce wernt larfing his other voyce wer saying the sylents" (82): the owl is the death drive turned outwards, a representation of the (here) masculine urge to destroy the world; the laughter of the owl, like the clowns' performances in Angela Carter's *Nights at the Circus*, is a cover for the owl's work of annihilation. In *Pilgermann*, the owl will again be associated with the death drive, but both in the aggressive and the suicidal version and it is also identified as the "Jew-bird" (42); it is Pilgermann's preferred after-life shape. Later in *Fremder*, it will become the bird of depression, loss and guilt, and it will not only be one of Fremder's emblems (beside the arctic tern, which embodies being unlost) but also that of women prone to depression or terror.

PILGERMANN AND *THE MEDUSA FREQUENCY*

Pilgermann has already been discussed extensively in terms of its inscribed criticism of the protagonist's forgetting Sophia (see ch. 7.4). Yet, there are two points which I would like to address because they will provide a transition between the concerns expressed in *Riddley Walker* and those expressed in *The Medusa Frequency*: The first point is Hoban's double focus on Sophia as both Pilgermann's object of desire and as a suffering woman, more precisely, as a woman suffering because Pilgermann is more influenced by the death drive than by his desire for her: whereas *Riddley Walker* was preoccupied with destruction on a global scale, *Pilgermann* complicates and at the same time individualizes the theme. What is now examined is not merely masculine aggression in general, but the conflict between the desire for death and the desire for life (Sophia) in the psychic economy of his male protagonist. Pilgermann "fails" (actually it is his unconscious which fails him) because he eventually "forgets" to consciously maintain the hierarchy between his conflicting desires which would qualify his death as the ethical act of a death for an other; by contrast, Bembel did not fail when he had to make a choice between helping Pilgermann and being obedient to Death. Pilgermann unconsciously prefers dying through Bohemond's sword to making another attempt to leave Antioch on behalf of Sophia. The question of responsibility is discussed exclusively from his perspective because her view is altogether inaccessible to the narrator. In *The Medusa Frequency*, on the other hand, we will be presented with a female protagonist who can speak for herself and who is also clever enough to escape victimization, i.e. Melanie Falsepercy.

The second point I would like to draw attention to is related to the first: it is the curious absence of contrast between the "real" woman Sophia and the represented woman in Vermeer's *Head of a Young Girl*, which has not been discussed so far. While Pilgermann has no trouble projecting questions onto the look of the Vermeer girl and theorizing about the willing look of the painter, giving "life" to both the absent model and the painter, Sophia remains conspicuously lifeless even while she is the seductive woman whom Pilgermann cannot resist. She hardly speaks, and what she says is limited and repetitive like the words of an automaton: "She says, 'Thou Jew! My Jew!' Only one other thing does she say, her name when I ask it: her name is Sophia" (16). It is symptomatic that her view of the story is altogether inscrutable to Pilgermann. If he knew Sophia's views this would prove that a dialogue had taken place between the two lovers. But Pilgermann never wants to find out who Sophia is, what she expects from her life or from him. They make love like animals. Had he made the effort to ask her what she wanted or whether she wanted him for more than a night when her husband had left the town to go on his pilgrimage, he would no doubt have incurred the risk of being rejected by her, but he might also still be alive and with her. When the insight in his missed chance eventually haunts him, he feels tormented – but when he gets a last opportunity to go back to her, his unconscious makes another decision for him.

The "life" of the painted woman, on the other hand, is as dependent on Pilgermann's subjectivity as his treatment of Sophia. The "Vermeer girl" cannot say no to the way she is represented in the novel. She must carry the weight of all his projections like the "real" woman, even if she probably does not agree that one can always look "with the eye that is in love with seeing" (PG 97). What if Vermeer had not only looked at her but had also shown her a Boschian painting of Pilgermann's night journey to the fall of Jerusalem, with Sophia, raped and murdered, in the foreground? Wouldn't she have averted her eyes, got up and become unwilling? Pilgermann's tragedy is to be mentally constituted in such a way that he cannot treat a live woman differently from a represented one; his redeeming feature, however, is that he is conscientious enough not to hide his weakness and to show us how he failed and why.

In *The Medusa Frequency*, the focus is no longer on the Vermeer girl's eyes, or rather, the failure of Herman's projection of complementarity is being staged: suddenly he realizes that he is not seen *by* her, and a scary unforeseen element will turn out to have been waiting under her headdress. Early in the novel, Herman qualifies the Vermeer girl as "an aspect of the Mother Goddess, the female principle" (MF 47). It seems as though Herman were looking for the same as Pilgermann: the Eternal Feminine, wisdom, his muse and ideal complement. At first the Vermeer girl is therefore the representative of the "*object small a* [*objet a*]", the Eurydice figure or the repressed oedipal mother, who orients his sexual desire: "Lacan's formula for the lost object which underpins symbolisation, cause of and 'stand in' for desire. What the man relates to is this object and the 'whole of his realisation in the sexual relation comes down to fantasy'" (Rose, "Feminine Sexuality...", 72). But as I said at the beginning of my discussion, the painting finds a way of disturbing his sexual fantasy. When Herman Orff seeks comfort by looking at the Vermeer girl, he is disappointed: his print fails to gratify his desire, it seems empty, and the original painting is not to be found at The Hague. When the Vermeer girl eventually becomes "responsive" again, she shows herself as Medusa, i.e. as a representation of his vulnerability and his mortality, "flickering and friendly" because he has looked at her respectfully without any expectations.

The unruly snakes by which Broomfield has made explicit what was but a *punctum* in Vermeer's painting[48] and Herman's eventual interpretation of the figure as Medusa give evidence of a demystifying awareness that ideals which female figures have time and again been made to represent cannot hold. Something repressed and hidden under their beauty and desirability will return. Literally "sticking out", escaping from the scarf and indifferent to the spectator's fantasy of complementarity, taking up the colour of the background and of the woman's eyes, the snakes insist on the existence of something which will destroy, or at any rate, add on to, all mystifications prompted by sexual desire – mortal *jouissance.*

In Lacanian terms, Herman's encounter with Medusa would have to be interpreted as an encounter with both his repressed femininity and his mortality;[49] but as I argued in the previous chapters, the issue of sexuality is treated in this novel in terms of the complementary action cycle of Orpheus and Eurydice: Herman has already accepted the passive (or "feminine") role in relation to Melanie (i.e. his "dismemberment" through her usurpation of "his" role), before Medusa appears to him for the first time, and the destabilization of his gender identity clearly affects him less than the encounters with Medusa. They are related to his growing awareness of the general vulnerability of his body independent of his sexual potency or his role in a relationship. In *Pilgermann*, the distinction between sexuality and vitality is made, too, although the oedipal formula ("To decapitate = to castrate", cf. ch. 8.3) blurs the distinction as soon as it is being made: "What was I before I was castrated? I was already castrated, was I not, by mortality? All of us are castrated by mortality, we are unmanned, unwomaned, we are made nothing ..." (PG 200). The name "He-*R*-man"[50] captures the sexual aspect of the destabilization of his subjectivity: it designates a subject who becomes aware of the precarious split within itself which involves it in a process of permanent redefinition. Returns of *R*epressed femininity undercut Herman's being a solid and unchanging He-man (a masculine subject). The appearance of Medusa, however, specifically encodes his recognition of mortality: an experience which displaces his sexuality in importance, adding a new undertone to his writing, i.e. the "mothercode".

---

48 See above, note 1, for a definition of *punctum.*

49 See ch. 8.3: Instead of positing two types of drives, that is a sexual drive and a death drive, as does Freud, Lacan claims that there is only one type and that there is an "essential affinity of every drive with the zone of death, ... the drive ... makes present sexuality in the unconscious and represents, in its essence, death" (*The Four Fundamental Concepts of Psycho-Analysis*, 199).

50 In ch. 8.2, I read the name as "her man"; incidentally this is one of the expressions by which Lacan refers to the phallus (cf. note 16 in ch. 8.3).

Herman is fortunate that Medusa eventually adds her difference to the portrait of his ideal woman, the Vermeer girl: This is the form which allows him best to bear the unbearable. The term "mothercode" equally underlines that the oedipal pattern still colours his thinking about mortality, i.e. the semiotic is derived from the archaic mother as in Kristeva's theory of poetic language.[51] The "privilege" Herman enjoys at the end of the novel nevertheless does not go so far that he can consider himself the author of Medusa's appearances, nor that she will always be so friendly. Moreover, both the novel itself as well as Hoban's earlier and later texts abstain from stabilising the association of mortality with Medusa, or more generally with a female figure: the head of Orpheus takes that function for Gösta Kraken, Greanvine for Riddley Walker, Bohemond for Pilgermann, Dahlmann for the narrator of "The Man with the Dagger", and Izzy Gorn for Fremder. Herman would be completely deluded if he thought that he could *choose* a figure standing in for death. The substitution of Medusa for Eurydice signals precisely his perception of the difference between a traditional and a new way of representing mortality: it is no longer the woman who must die so that her lover or another male observer can familiarize himself with the subject, but he himself is exposed to the threat which manifests itself in a shape he cannot determine himself.

Melanie Falsepercy contributes to this change in several ways: for instance when she, the "real" woman who will not turn into Eurydice, interrupts Herman and the head of Orpheus conjuring up a Eurydice who is "waiting for" Orpheus to bring "the strange and many colours of death into her dream": "Just then I heard Melanie's bare feet on the floor behind me and I closed the fridge as she came into the kitchen" (72). She makes Herman see what it is like to be Eurydice and to understand why Eurydice kept weeping and protesting to Orpheus that his songs, which celebrated "loss" (119), emptied their relationship out (99). Although she, too, knows that she must confront the theme of mortality (cf. ch. 8.2), her approach is not to linger on sad subjects, as her conversation with Herman in hospital shows; she criticizes his obsession with the "thing of darkness" (127). On her farewell tape, Melanie once more spells out the difference between his preferred view of her, to which she could not correspond (Eurydice), the role she played for him (Orpheus), her self-representation (Persephone), and the I "so full of my own death that I understand nothing" (Rilke's Eurydike) (137-138). She thus enacts the contradiction between woman (the object of masculine desire) and her self-(chosen-)representations, which can never be fully her own since she is part of

51 See "Revolution in Poetic Language" or *Powers of Horror*; also see ch. 8.2, n. 3.

a culture whose mythical figures and stereotypes have left their marks on her. Being aware of contradiction, she is nevertheless unable to get away from it, as will be Caroline Lovecraft in *Fremder*. Hoban's representation of Melanie follows feminist lines. See, e.g., Teresa de Lauretis:

> Feminism has produced ... a political-personal consciousness of gender as an ideological construct which defines the social subject; ... in en-gendering the subject as political, feminism understands the female subject as one that ... is not either 'in ideology' or outside ideology ..., but rather is at once inside and outside the ideology of gender, or as I have used the terms, is at once woman and women. In other words, ... the female subject of feminism is in both places at once. (*Technologies of Gender*114).

The consciousness thus raised can become the basis for new relationships no longer merely based on fantasmatic complementarity (one cannot get away from complementarity altogether because falling in love is always a falling in love with the "object small a" the other *seems* to be and will later turn out *not* to be). Herman's reaction to Melanie's tape, at any rate, is full of respect for the strangeness that remains after a dialogue has taken place (and this is different from Pilgermann's utter ignorance about Sophia):

> This was Melanie who was a mystery to me and, as everyone is, to herself, whose thoughts I didn't know, whose being had its own spacetime and its own world line separate from mine. We had talked intimately, had been lovers briefly, yet her voice came to me as strange and distant as those many voices from far away reflected from the ionosphere and expressed digitally on my radio's frequency counter. (137)

Women do not die in this novel but the men who cannot leave behind the action cycle of Orpheus and Eurydice, that is, Gom Yawncher and Gösta Kraken. Istvan Fallok, the composer to whom Orpheus keeps returning, is not really an exception; for though he may not die physically he is paralysed by his obsession and looks haunted like death-in-life (22). Herman, however, has ceased to be an element of that cycle which subjects everyone to a fantasmatic complementarity. He takes the Kraken as his new guide into the depths of the abyss and is reborn from the egg of a snake (90).

In regard to his male protagonists and to masculinity, Hoban has done the work required by Cixous in "The Laugh of the Medusa": he has called into question the opposition between activity and passivity, criticized virility myths, possessiveness, and male protagonists shying away from a dialogue with women; above all he has restored to his men their bodies, vulnerable and mortal, but theirs all the same, freeing them from the desire to colonize women and other territories. They can be under way at night, carrying their space with them. Hoban has strengthened non-rational, intuitive and mystical sources of information against the predominance of the coldly rational, without thereby embracing primitivism. It is not *no* power, *no* language, *no* knowledge, or *no* masculinity, his male protagonists must aspire to, but the most promising ones learn *not to struggle* for these determinants of a conventionally defined subjectivity; for admitting weakness, fallibility and vulnerability, embracing the sound material of the language, welcoming intuition and emanations from the unconscious, or experiencing the "feminine" role within a relationship is not necessarily undesirable: what is undesirable is to be pressed into an iron mould and be unable to budge (and as a consequence press the other into a complementary mould). Moreover, it is always made perfectly clear that *every* position or role assumed entails its own specific set of responsibilities.

A theme Hoban will go on exploring despite his feminist sympathies is that of mortality, of the death drive, the thing of darkness in the abyss. Just as a simple role reversal cannot be enough to define the female subject of feminism, men cannot simply define their new subjectivity by blindly following the agenda of feminists. Their programmes must place the stresses elsewhere, i.e. on those facets of their subjectivity which have been neglected or overemphasized in their upbringing as men in this culture. Melanie's criticism of Herman's being attracted to the "thing of darkness" is therefore not altogether justified; her feminism, designed to rehabilitate her difference, blinds her to his difference. Of course, she knows from experience how dangerous it is to face mortality: she had to develop strategies to free herself from the mortality burdened on her by culture. But Herman must first move in the other direction before he can follow her. Rather than to go on studying death by looking at various Eurydices lost, gone or killed, he must explore abjection, that is the influence of the death drive on his own body (depression, vulnerability, mortality), on his language (silence, rupture, the poetic), or on his relationships with other people (narcissism, aggression), and while doing so, develop strategies of sublimation, survival and escape. To this extent and for this subject, Orpheus (without Eurydice) will for a while have to remain his guide, and Hoban's too:

> '... People said they heard more than one voice when I sang – they heard a strange human voice and they heard a second voice not human, voice of darkness, voice of
>
> moment under moment, world under
> world, dark under dark ...' (MF 71)

Part III:

The Two Sides of the Reality Membrane

9. The Moment under the Moment (1992)

In 1992 Russell Hoban published *The Moment under the Moment*, a compilation of stories, essays, sketches, and an opera libretto which he had written between 1977 and 1991. Three years earlier he had rejected the idea of assembling fragments and unfinished novel starts in a book.[1] Eventually, however, he did change his mind. The collection assembles autobiographical encounters with his past, definitions of his aesthetic preferences, stories, at times mere seeds and skeletons of stories, persistent images, shrewd observations and meditations attached to London and other places. The pieces have not been arranged in chronological order. Neither is there a clear distinction between the literary and the essayistic texts. The libretto "Some Episodes in the History of Miranda and Caliban", placed at the centre of the book, separates the section "Stories" from one entitled "Essays and Sketches".

Having previously encountered Hoban's distrust of linearity and too neat distinctions, his preference of process to product, and his suspicion that there would come a time "when ideas won't want to go the full distance of a novel" (Hoban and Bodmer 14), we should not be surprised at the arrangement. Indeed *The Moment under the Moment* resembles a collage of reality as it hits consciousness: only partly ordered, sometimes leading to desirable places in the mind, but more often to uncanny ones, to the "Little Black Thought" (EH 101)[2] and the terror of existence. In the Foreword, Russell Hoban warns his readers of, or prepares them for, the sense of estrangement that might result from reading the book; he himself evaluates his texts from a certain distance:

> Reading over these pages has been a humbling experience. I was shocked to find that the word *tawny* appeared fifteen times and *tawniness* twice; with a tremendous effort I managed to kill all but four of the tawnies. I feel all right about the stories but some of the essays are wetter in places than I'd like. But as I've already said, process is what I care about and this is it. (MUM ix-x)

All the same, or maybe predictably, *The Moment under the Moment* was not well received by all reviewers. Lorna Sage, for instance, wrote in her review: "... the materials collected in *The Moment under the Moment* are probably not going to win Hoban new converts. They'll act as welcome blueprints and stopgaps and footnotes for ready-made readers, however: doodles from the

1 Letter to Yvonne Studer, 14 May 1989.

2 All quotations in this chapter are from the *Moment under the Moment* edition of the stories; I will therefore simplify parenthetical references here by leaving away the abbreviation MUM. A key to the abbreviations has been placed directly after the Table of Contents.

oracle" (20). Yet the book is more than a door to a writer's junk room. In the 1987 essay "The Bear in Max Ernst's Bedroom or The Magic Wallet", one of the essays re-printed in *The Moment under the Moment*, Hoban indirectly presents the surrealistic (anti)programme underlying the compilation when he quotes Max Ernst's definition of the collage:

> 'One might define a collage', said Ernst, 'as an alchemical composite of two or more heterogeneous elements, resulting from their unexpected conjunction, due either to a will orientated – for the sake of clarity – towards a systematic confusion and the disordering of the senses or to pure chance, or perhaps to a will favouring chance.' (BB 194)

The alchemy of *The Moment under the Moment* might eventually take us to

> ... the images that live under the picture-cards that we conventionally exchange and the images that appear beyond where we ordinarily look, the occulting glimmers under the reasonable thought and beyond the ordinary range of thought, the words that twist and moan and dance and sing behind the words that go out through our mouths, and the unknown words that we sometimes almost hear from far away, the mysteries that move us, and the patterns of the dance that lives us. (BB 198)

What Hoban is trying to convey might in fact be a sense of that "modality of signifiance" which Julia Kristeva in 1974 called the semiotic "*chora*" (94),[3] borrowing the term from Plato's *Timaeus*, and illustrating her category by reference to Stéphane Mallarmé's symbolism:

> ... the *chora*, as rupture and articulations (rhythm), precedes evidence, verisimilitude, spatiality and temporality. Our discourse – all discourse – moves with and against the *chora* in the sense that it simultaneously depends upon and refuses it. Although the *chora* can be designated and regulated, it can never be definitely posited: as a result, one can situate the *chora* and, if necessary, lend it a topology, but one can never give it axiomatic form. (...)
>
> Mallarmé calls attention to the semiotic rhythm within language when he speaks of 'The Mystery in Literature' ['Le Mystère dans les lettres']. Indifferent to language, enigmatic and feminine, this space underlying the written is rhythmic, unfettered, irreducible to its intelligible verbal translation; it is musical, anterior to judgement, but restrained by a single guarantee: syntax. ("Revolution in Poetic Language", 94-97)

3 Incidentally, in *The Medusa Frequency* Hoban has parodied this language under the language in the form of the "Krakenspeak" subtitles of Gösta Kraken's films. Melanie explains to Herman why Kraken (the conceited intellectual alter ego of Herman Orff) uses them: "He likes the effect of subtitles. In his book, *The Flickering*, he says that under our ordinary speech there are always invisible subtitles in an unknown tongue. In all of his films since 1975 the actors speak in English and the subtitles are in Krakenspeak" (MF 107). What is criticized here, though, is less the idea of the chora than Gösta Kraken's self-consciousness. Each time Herman meets him in the novel, his rage is provoked by the theoretical jargon the director uses in explaining his technique (e.g. MF 86ff.). Herman would no doubt flinch from Kristeva's terminology, too.

Hoban and Kristeva agree not only in regard to the protean quality and spatio-temporal indeterminacy of the modalities they describe, Hoban as a "moment under the moment", Kristeva as a *chora*, i.e. a "place" (95) but also "an essentially mobile and extremely provisional articulation constituted by movements and their ephemeral stases" (93), they also associate it with potentially destructive energies, Hoban speaking from a mythic perspective whereas Kristeva argues as a psychoanalyst and linguist:

> So you have to let the night back in because it's the mother and the mother is where everything comes from. You have to let the night back in and you have to listen to what wants to speak to you. Maybe sometimes you even have to call up what can't be put down, you have to talk to demons and horrors private and public; you must remember that all of us collectively have called up what can't be put down, we have pre-empted Armageddon and it wants to be talked to in the night, it has many things to tell us, many things to whisper and shout and shriek in the silence of the night. Sometimes the voice is that of Beelzebub, sometimes that of Eurydice. (Hoban, BB 189)

> ... the semiotic *chora* is no more than the place where the subject is both generated and negated, the place where his unity succumbs before the process of charges and stases that produce him. We shall call this process of charges and stases a *negativity* to distinguish it from negation, which is the act of a judging subject. (Kristeva, "Revolution", 95-96)

The voices that make themselves heard to the writer are more often unpleasant than pleasant ones: most of the pieces in *The Moment under the Moment* are concerned with themes such as loss, frustration, anxiety, guilt, and death. This might be the result of the economy of drives which give rhythm to the chora: "... although drives have been described as disunited or contradictory structures, simultaneously 'positive' and 'negative', this doubling is said to generate a dominant 'destructive wave' that is drive's most characteristic trait" (Kristeva 95). The note Kristeva adds to her discussion of the ambiguity of drives explains why the play of "positive" and "negative" drives ultimately cannot result in a balance:

> Though disputed and inconsistent, the Freudian theory of drives is of interest here because of the predominance Freud gives to the death drive in both 'living matter' and the 'human being'. The death drive is transversal to identity and tends to disperse 'narcissisms' whose constitution ensures the link between structures and, by extension, life. But at the same time and conversely, narcissism and pleasure are only temporary positions from which the death drive blazes new paths [*se fraye de nouveaux passages*]. Narcissism and pleasure are therefore inveiglings and realizations of the death drive. ("Revolution", 128, n. 23)

It is not for me to decide whether or not the death drive exists; however, the possibility that it does, and what is more, that even pleasure might be a medium through which the death drive manifests itself, informs many of Hoban's images. It explains why the Vermeer girl and Medusa or Orpheus and the Kraken, his main icons of seduction and destruction, cannot really be thought of separately:

> All the lost beauties are one beauty, all of the fearsome or speaking heads are one head. The head of Orpheus is the Kraken and the Gorgon's head is the face of the young girl who looks out of Vermeer's painting. And the look in the eyes of the Vermeer girl is the look in the eyes of the unseen Kraken in the blackness of the ultimate deep, the great head looking for ever into the blackness. (CO 245)

In my discussion of *The Moment under the Moment*, I propose to take a closer look at the negativity underlying Hoban's process-oriented writing. One might of course find other conjunctions in the book, examine the way in which the short stories and sketches interact with the novels, for instance. One might also group the pieces according to their genres, subject matter, settings and so on. But with a view to the next chapters, where Hoban's fiction will be examined in regard to its affirmation of life and its magic realism, that is to the Hermetic screens he holds up to the Dionysiac vortex of the death drive, I would here like to focus on the ways in which he deliberately exposes himself and his readers to its fatal attraction. In *Powers of Horror*, Kristeva has defined the condition of the subject who faces what may destroy it as "abjection": "Abjection is a resurrection that has gone through death (of the ego). It is an alchemy that transforms death drive into a start of life, of new signifiance" (*Powers*, 15). The artist confronting the abject thereby sublimates it:

> In the symptom, the abject permeates me, I become abject. Through sublimation, I keep it under control. The abject is edged with the sublime. It is not the same moment on the journey, but the same subject and speech bring them into being. (11)

Hoban's efforts to face the abject date further back than *The Moment under the Moment*. As early as in 1972, when he published the essay "Time Slip, Uphill Lean, Laminar Flow, Place-to-place Talking and Hearing the Silence", he wrote:

> Mortal humanity is founded on an abyss, on black uncertainty. And society would rather have anything than that uncertainty, that primal unknowing. Where it cannot find usable truth, society tries to make false walls of certainty with lies. (TS 42)

What does it mean to face the abyss? In his novels, Hoban gave it a variety of shapes from the supernatural lion to the greedy Hospital and the monkey-like Death in *Kleinzeit*, the shark in Neaera's nightmare, Riddley's nightmarish adventures, the massacres witnessed by Pilgermann, Herman Orff's guilt-ridden encounters with Medusa and the Kraken, and finally Fremder's fight with Pythia. There is a development in so far as the protagonists have less often occasion to triumph over menaces because the latter are more and more shown to inhere in what the protagonists desire. *The Moment under the Moment* is part of this development, too. All that the characters in the fictional pieces can usually do is be overwhelmed by what terrifies them and accept their weakness, their frustration, and, in the worst case, their complete defeat. The essayist Hoban, on the other hand, is in a more privileged position; he has means to establish these aspects of experience as themes we had better think about early. Providing images and naming the terror are attempts to literally "come to terms" with it rather than hide it away; the terror is being partly integrated into the Symbolic universe albeit ultimately ungraspable in all its facets.[4] Kristeva has characterized its elusiveness:

4 By "Symbolic universe" I mean the Symbolic order of experience as defined by Jacques Lacan. Malcolm Bowie gives a good account of the Imaginary, the Symbolic and the Real in *Lacan*: "The Symbolic, the Imaginary and the Real are not mental forces, personifiable on the model-builder's inner stage, but *orders* each of which serves to position the individual within a force-field that traverses him" (Bowie 91).

"The Imaginary is the order of mirror-images, identifications and reciprocities. It is the dimension of experience in which the individual seeks not simply to placate the Other but to dissolve his otherness by becoming his counterpart. ... The Imaginary is the scene of a desperate delusional attempt to be and to remain 'what one is' by gathering to oneself ever more instances of sameness, resemblance and self-replication; it is the birthplace of the narcissistic 'ideal ego' [*Idealich, moi idéal*]. Lacan's 'Imaginary' thus creates a bridge between inner-directed and outer-directed mental acts, and belongs as much to the objects of perception as to those internal objects for which the word is usually reserved in ordinary speech. The term has a strong pejorative force, and suggests that the subject is seeking, in a wilful and blameworthy fashion, to remove himself from the flux of becoming.

The Symbolic order, on the other hand, is often spoken of admiringly. It is the realm of movement rather than fixity, and of heterogeneity rather than similarity. It is the realm of language, the unconscious and an otherness that remains other. This is the order in which the subject as distinct from the ego comes into being, and into a manner of being that is always disjoined and intermittent. In the Symbolic order 'nothing exists except on an assumed foundation of absence. ... Gaps have as much signifying power as plenitudes, and neither has such power without the other. Whereas the inhabitant of the Imaginary ventures into the world of others only to freeze, foreshorten and incorporate it, the Symbolic is inveterately intersubjective and social. It is a *res publica* that does not allow any one of its members to be himself, keep himself to himself or recreate in his own image the things that lie beyond him" (92-93).

The Real, finally, is characterized as follows: "Lacan's concept is separate from 'reality' as it is usually understood in psychoanalysis. For Freud 'reality' is the world external to the human mind, and the 'reality principle' lies in the individual's recognition that this world places limitations upon him as he pursues his pleasures. For Lacan, on the other hand, the Real is that which lies outside the symbolic process, and it is to be found in the mental as well as in the material world: a trauma, for example, is as intractable and unsymbolizable as objects in their materiality. ... The Real ... is the endlessly daunting power which supersedes the already very considerable power that Lacan ascribes to the Symbolic. For Lacan, the Real thus comes close to meaning 'the ineffable' or 'the impossible' ..." (94-95).

> The 'sublime' object dissolves in the raptures of a bottomless memory. ... As soon as I perceive it, as soon as I name it, the sublime triggers – it has always already triggered – a spree of perceptions and words that expands memory boundlessly. I then forget the point of departure and find myself removed to a secondary universe, set off from the one where 'I' am – delight and loss. Not at all short of but always with and through perception and words, the sublime is a *something added* that expands us, overstrains us, and causes us to be both *here*, as dejects, and *there*, as others and sparkling. (*Powers*, 12)

As this quotation also suggests, sublimation is not a harmless activity; dealing with the sublime object, the abject, the terror of existence, or with what Lacan has called the Real, can overstrain the writer or speaker. Goodparley's warning to Riddley Walker comes to mind again: "Put a name to some thing and youre beckoning" (RW 118). But attempting to escape from the terror by means of "lies", or in fictional terms, escapist fantasy and other forms of literary kitsch, might in fact be a worse method of dealing with it.[5] For lulling our awareness of the negativity it tries to negate (on behalf of narcissism and pleasure), this kind of fiction may in fact become the best accomplice of negativity, intensifying its impact once the "false walls of certainty" are shattered (Hoban, TS 42). Addressing one's powerlessness in the face of the abject, death, or the Real, is therefore still preferable to any futile form of escape, or as Malcolm Bowie points out in his introduction to Lacan:

> Death is the eventual triumph of the Real, but is already homeopathically present in speech. If analytic practice places its main stress on the Imaginary, and on the bolstering of the ego, it will find itself purging death-fears and death-desires from its activities. At worst, it will collude with the analysand in creating an empty and demeaning sense of immortality. A stress on the Symbolic, on the other hand, allows the individual's mortality to speak and be spoken; it allows him to be unillusioned in his desire, and, for a time, to fly in the face of the Real. (Bowie 100)

In *The Moment under the Moment*, Hoban makes room for the ruptures through which "It" (HT 146), "Pan" (PL 138), the "north in the mind" (NH 175), "Thing-in-Itself" (BR 181), the "soul of the universe" (PK 212),

5 See ch. 11, for a discussion of the differences between fantasy, the fantastic, and magic realism respectively. In Kristeva, "fantasy" is negatively connotated too. She refers to a psychic product, though; in her opinion, artistic practice, i.e. clothing such fantasies in language, implies a subject aware and, as her definition of sublimation shows, partly in control of the manifestations of the death drive: "... the subject must be firmly posited by castration so that drive attacks against the thetic will not give way to fantasy or to psychosis but will instead lead to a 'second-degree thetic', i.e., a resumption of the functioning characteristic of the semiotic *chora* within the signifying device of language. This is precisely what artistic practices, and notably poetic language, demonstrate" ("Revolution", 103). Indeed I will argue in ch. 11 that literary fantasy need not necessarily be escapist; it can also be used in a non-narcissistic way, that is to refer to mortality, the impossibility of omniscience and omnipotence.

"Dionysus" or the "'otherness' of the world" (BB 191), haunts and speaks to us in the voices of Beelzebub or Eurydice (BB 189). First of all, he abstains, as the choice illustrates, from giving it a consistent name. Respectfully circling around what must ultimately remain nameless, he nevertheless succeeds in drawing attention to the abyss and the energy animating it.

The most effective way of giving negativity access to the surface, though, is by building ruptures into the texts and desisting from unifying several issues in one narrative. The table of contents of *The Moment under the Moment* indicates a subdivision into eight stories, a libretto, and fourteen essays and sketches, which are preceded by a foreword. However, the ruptures continue right into the individual pieces: "Certain Obsessions, Certain Ideas" (237-254), for instance, could be regarded as a *mise en abyme*, a miniature version of the collection inside the collection; it consists of ten brief texts: essayistic meditations, stories and story fragments with titles of their own such as "The Sorcerer", "Thinking of Hermes", "Uncertainty", or, paradoxically, "Untitled". Another five-page sketch, "Word Pix" (200-204), demonstrates, and at the same time mocks, the effort of turning "word-picture[s]" (200) into a romantic quest sequence. Unforeseen elements which burst into the setting – here it is the sea (202) – must be repressed so that the surface pattern "hero-saves-lady-in-distress" can unfold. Subliminally, though, the sea is still present, as the narrator is very much aware: "... it's still there under the appearance of things, heaving the landscape and making one seasick" (203). A funnier example of interruption can be found in "My Night with Léonie", where the narrator's fantasies of transformation through his love for the sphinx Léonie are shattered by a German tourist:

> My mind was bursting with her [Léonie's] words as I walked away: 'If what you desire is actually possible then you will know when to come for me and what to say.' ... 'Yes,' I said aloud as I passed three stout German women standing by a coach and consulting their maps, 'you are the sphinx in every woman, that is your triumph and your specialness. ... I know that to make love with you would be a kind of alchemy in which the dull and leaden self of me would be transmuted to the gold required by you.'
>
> '*Quatsch,*' said one of the women. (NL 19)

The very sound of the German word for "nonsense" invokes cold and wet mud flung at a wall in the midst of love-making.

Abstaining from narrative closure is a further device Hoban has always used in his fictions; in *The Moment under the Moment*, with its great number of stories and fragments, this device becomes particularly prominent. We will never learn, for instance, what really happened to Lavinia, the painter described in "The Colour of Love" who had vanished in Venice. Whether or not the narrator of "The Man with the Dagger" will survive his fight with Dahlmann, and the narrator of "My Night with Léonie" go back to Paris in spite of his disappointment are left open. Harry Stone's encounter with his ghostly follower in "Schwartz" has just begun when the story ends. "Some Episodes in the History of Miranda and Caliban", finally, ends almost as it began, forming an endless mythical circle. Only "Dark Oliver" and "The Ghost Horse of Genghis Khan" provide closures: Ten-year-old Oliver, having been exposed to Hades's grief during his holiday in Greece, challenges and defeats his enemy Geoffrey on the playground when he is back home. And John, the little boy protagonist of "The Ghost Horse...", finishes a story for his father, who is in hospital. The ending he invents – a ghost horse carries wounded Temujin beyond the reach of his enemies – becomes the dream which saves his father's life, against all odds. Whereas children are thus encouraged to believe in the magical power of their fantasies, grown-ups must learn to accept their mortality, their vulnerability and the fact that all questions will not be answered nor all problems be resolved.

As forms of abjection repugnance, shame, terror, or nausea are the normal reactions to encounters with the abject – quite so, the protagonist of "Word Pix" is seasick from thinking about the sea. Laughing, on the other hand, "is a way of placing and displacing abjection", according to Kristeva (*Powers*, 8). It places abjection on situations, objects, and characters, thereby often revealing the aggressive potential Freud has described in *Der Witz und seine Beziehung zum Unbewussten* (e.g. 154). For placing abjection means burdening somebody with the ambiguity, violence and pain that cannot be separated from it (Kristeva, *Powers*, 9). Placing abjection presupposes its displacement. Kristeva does not specify the starting point of and the direction taken by the displacement. But since laughing according to Freud is a way of releasing the psychic energies connected to inhibitions (*Witz*, 118ff.), it seems legitimate to conclude that abjection is above all displaced away from the one who is laughing. Laughing about the abject signals the cut that separates the subject from what tempted and at the same time threatened it; it is a way of acknowledging negativity which transforms the Dionysiac impulse of jumping into the abyss into the Hermetic one of moving on to continue the journey. The fool on the brink, the figure with whom Hoban opens "The Bear in Max Ernst's Bedroom ..." knows both urges, too: "Our Fool on the brink has a strong Dionysiac element in him but he's got a lot of Hermes as well – our Fool is a wender of many ways who always finds new ways, a chance-taker who finds new dances" (BB 192).

The cheerful moments, even the wry smiles, however, are few and far between in this collection. In "Word Pix" and "The Man with the Dagger", for example, Hoban parodies romance plots, especially Western films. Laughter is directed at the protagonists, whose heroism we see being transformed into abjection no sooner than they have been involved in the action – our laughing acknowledges the failure of the romantic illusion of heroism and expresses our relief that we do not have to cope with their problems ourselves. The first-person narrator of "The Man with the Dagger" does not succeed in defeating his longtime arch-enemies but is knocked out by them (MD 13). We are far from the two types of narrative closure of Westerns Laura Mulvey has discussed in "Afterthoughts on 'Visual Pleasure and Narrative Cinema' inspired by King Vidor's *Duel in the Sun* (1946)": marriage or "a nostalgic celebration of phallic, narcissistic omnipotence" (33). In "Word Pix", the rejection of the romance pattern is even spelled out: the narrator's scepticism about his role as hero, his overly impersonal style – he mostly uses "one" instead of "I"– and the misfortunes he suffers dispel all romantic notions no sooner than they have been conjured up:

> Here's a solitary traveller crossing the etching of a grey desert maybe, under a dazzling white sun and he hears the horrid squak of the sphinks high in the white and pitiless sky and he cowers and covers his head but it's no use. Splat! A direct hit: the word QUASI. In capitals. (...)
>
> One has entered one of the pictures, the third from the left. That was how the solitary traveller (that's who one is) came to be shat upon by the sphinks. And now, covered in QUASI, this solitary traveller staggers on in the hope of performing, against all odds, a quasi-rescue. Incurable quasi-romantic. (WP 201-202)

In "My Night with Léonie" and "Dream Woman", Hoban makes his male protagonists experience the gap between the myth of the mythical woman as their, and solely their, desired object and supreme complement and her "reality": mythical figures such as the sphinx or the "dream woman" are always projections of a whole series of men.[6] Like real women, whose uncanny difference makes men seek the "comfort" of mythical women in the first place, as is to be assumed, they eventually shatter rather than confirm

6 In "Myth Today", Roland Barthes demystifies myths by pointing to their status as "second-order semiological systems": the concepts they transport are neither eternal, nor do they follow from the nature of their objects; they are historical, that is subject to change, although the mythic principle consists precisely in naturalizing and turning them into "depoliticized speech" (cf. e.g. pp. 99-101, 114-118, 130-1). Barthes also points out that, for a myth to function properly, an "I" is required who acknowledges "the body of intentions which have motivated" the mythic concept (111). This is the angle from which Hoban demystifies the myth of mythical women, i.e. by subverting the myth *reader's* position; he is *not* the only man addressed by the seductive call of the mythical woman although it is part of the myth to make him feel as if he were.

fantasies of omnipotence and ownership. We again laugh at the protagonists' disillusionment. In "Blighter's Rock", finally, laughter is the result of a strategy of linguistic indirection that is familiar from *Kleinzeit* and *Riddley Walker*, i.e. dislocution. Dislocuting "writer's block" to escape a head-on collision with the problem, Hoban here deals with the resistances attached to certain contents at the same time as the text performs the remedial "Witzarbeit" Freud has described (*Witz*, 134): by the minimal displacement of initial phonemes, "blighter's rock" continues to be an echo of "writer's block"; in addition, "block" and "rock" are semantically connected in so far as they can be read as metonyms of each other – a block hewn from a rock. Moreover, in a metaphoric sense, a blocked writer is a writer "on the rocks". Thus, there are sufficient associative links which permit an examination of the reasons and wider implications of "writer's block". But by evading any direct reference to "it", no psychic energy has to be wasted on overcoming the anxiety triggered by thoughts of the traumatic event. There is a surplus of energy which, on the one hand, causes laughter and, on the other, can be invested in the creative play of signifiers which constitute the text.

Instead of discussing any other strategies of deliberate displacement, however, I would now like to return to such examples where the readers are made to share, rather than look at, the characters' encounters with the abject, where language "tries to transform the sign back into its meaning", as Roland Barthes has described "the essentialist ambitions of poetry" ("Myth Today", 121). While to Barthes, it is only contemporary poetry which, in contrast to classical poetry and prose, "attempts to regain an infra-signification, a pre-semiological state of language" (120-121), Kristeva's concept of "poetic language" also includes prose:

> Language thus tends to be drawn out of its symbolic function (sign-syntax) and is opened out within a semiotic articulation; with a material support such as the voice, this semiotic network gives 'music' to literature.
>
> But the irruption of the semiotic within the symbolic is only relative. Though permeable, the thetic continues to ensure the position of the subject put in process/on trial. As a consequence, musicality is not without signification; indeed it is deployed within it. Logical synthesis and all ideologies are present, but they are pulverized within their own logic before being displaced towards something that is no longer within the realm of the idea, sign, syntax and thus Logos, but is instead simply semiotic functioning. ("Revolution", 113-114)

Both Barthes and Kristeva agree that language can only attempt to isolate the semiotic; words always trigger a signification process, that is, some displacement cannot be avoided. But it is interesting how Kristeva describes the emergence of the semiotic in spite of signification wherever language is musical.

In *The Moment under the Moment* there are many passages distinguished by their musicality. The mystical journey of the melancholic protagonist of "The Raven", who is taken to a place in his mind where differentiation and individuation have not yet taken place, is described in a hypnotic language characterized by paradox and repetition, alliteration, assonance and internal rhyme:

> Here, here, here. Our voice had become many voices, voices without number, tiny and great. The raven was no longer a raven, raven, raven, raven. Nor was I what I had been; we were without form, we were not yet alive: tiny, tiny dancing giants looming greatly in uncertain shapes and dwindling in the shadows; fast asleep and dancing in the dim red caverns of sleep. (RV 46)

Should there still be a need to illustrate the *chora*, this would be its image.[7] As soon as the first differentiation has taken place, which is shown to be the motor of evolution, life begins. The protagonist recognises that being alive invariably implies having always already lost something. But the question why this is the case remains unanswered. Thus, his journey ends more or less where it began, in front of a cage of the Zoo of London, where he went to ask the raven about "the black of things" (41):

> Nothing stopped us, and in time we arrived at the grey rainlight in the empty room, the sound of my footsteps under yellow streetlamps, and the unaccompanied cello from long ago where the raven stood on its well-worn and polished black feet looking at me through the chain-link mesh of the cage. (RV 47-48)

The little boy described in "Dark Oliver" undergoes a similar cognitive process: he learns to understand the idea of loss although the loss is not his own. Falling down a hollow tree like Lewis Carroll's Alice, he is surrounded by Hades's grief for Persephoneia. Even though the third-person narrative establishes a certain distance between the reader and the boy, the language giving insight into his perceptions tries to capture the insistence with which the idea of loss grabs hold of him:

> A name was roaring in him, bellowing in him: PERSEPHONEIA. He thought his skull would burst from it, he thought his bones would break from it. He was still falling, he was nowhere, there was nothing but blackness, and into the blackness there came the idea of the face that he sometimes saw in his dreams. Was he thinking it or was it thinking him? Inexplicably it was all around him as he fell. Bigger and bigger it grew, blotches of black on pale

7 Also see Kristeva, *Powers of Horror*, 14-15.

> green, like a rubbing done on green paper. But the green was more like pale cold fire. Cold, yes, it was bitter cold, icy cold and a freezing wind blowing. (DO 69)

"Some Episodes in the History of Miranda and Caliban", the libretto placed in the middle of *The Moment under the Moment*, is almost exclusively written in a language where the sound of words, their rhythm, is as important as the ideas they convey. Sometimes their content even coincides with their form, in other words, they mean nothing but the sounds they convey. Their emptiness, however, never lasts for long. In fact there is a scene where Miranda (as SHAKESPEARE) tells Caliban (as HE) that he cannot remain in his paradise of indifference; she is eager to name him. As soon as she has found his name, however, he also names her for the story cannot be held up, the myth inevitably appropriates them once their names have been pronounced:

> HE Here it comes, I can see it coming and I don't know how to stop it.
> SHAKESPEARE Punger, Ponger, Bonger, Slonger.
> HE Too simple.
> SHAKESPEARE Glimmerdim, Gleamdeep, Greenshadow, Snelg.
> HE Snelg isn't bad.
> SHAKESPEARE Belziflung, Fliskerbung, Gungifer, Noog.
> HE Noog?
> SHAKESPEARE It wants more of a slanty something to it, more of a cannibal, cabinal, banical sort of sound.
> HE What it wants is a chance to get out of this story.
> SHAKESPEARE Calical, Baniban, Caliban.
> CALIBAN That's it, I'm done for.
> SHAKESPEARE Caliban is who your are, Caliban is you.
> CALIBAN Miranda! (EH 90-91)

In his essays, Hoban has repeatedly expressed his desire for a medium that would not conjure up any memories and stories. Not even music always fulfils this condition, though. In "Mnemosyne, Teen Taals, and Tottenham Court Road", he distinguishes between music that "*seems* to live by memory", e.g. "a Chopin mazurka or even a Bach cantata" (MT 220), and music such as Bach's *The Art of Fugue* or the Indian *teen taal*, which "does not depend on memory; it is without greed, makes no demands; it doesn't ask to be remembered" (MT 221). The third type of music is Hermetic. Thelonious Monk's music, for instance, conjures up a mode of being where "anything at all may happen" (FL 205). Before his tune begins to be burdened by memories of youth – for not even this music can arrest the process – it inspires a chain of free floating associations which do not care much about syntax:

> Listening now to an effigy of Thelonious Monk, a dome of the dummy world, that midnight dome, those caves of nice. Always the slant rhyme with

> Thelonious, that was his Thelonious assault on the grey and civil devils of the ordinary. Walk tall and slanty, Thelonious; you live. (FL 206)

Like the drugs which induced Coleridge to write his "Kubla Khan", Monk's jazz stimulates energies that precede all reasoning:

> The letters on the screen of my computer are made up of a continual dancing; letter by letter I see my thoughts appear on the screen. My thoughts and the mind that thinks them are equally composed of the dancing, the dancing is there before anything else. You are in that dancing, Thelonious Monk, in that green dancing in which letter by letter my thoughts appear this midnight, round about this midnight mindnight. (206-207)

While negativity as terror must be faced, its temptation as death drive had better be resisted. Both "Portknockie" and "Mnemosyne..." are essays in which Hoban reflects on the right way to deal with the death drive: in "Portknockie" (1981) he identifies the desire for a return to the sea as a desire for death, a death "not yet welcome to me" (PK 211); yet he still insists that "the power of the one continuous rhythm of immanent change and permutation that vibrates behind the appearances of things" deserves attention: "... to tune ourselves to it feels good, gives us a sense of release from the hard bargain of the mortal contract" (PK 212). In "Mnemosyne...", written one year later, he points out, however, that the attention given to a particular moment must by no means lead to a holding on:

> In moving on towards death we lose moment by moment our lives. In trying not to move on, in trying to hold on to the present moment we lose our lives moment by moment just the same and we feel the loss even more. We want at the same time to hold on and to let go. (MT 233)

Trying to hold on to the present moment by means of technical devices such as cameras or tapes – for fear of losing them for good – interferes with "the moving on of being" (MT 231). He concludes that "we must outgrow the control fantasy" and "find in ourselves the shapes of letting go because we're not free to become what we're going to be next until we let go of what we are now" (MT 235). In *The Moment under the Moment* he has given death its due: how could he do otherwise when, as he writes in the epigraph to "Masada One Morning", the last text, "With each year what is at the centre of the self grows stronger and compels more recognition" (MM 256). But this respectful gesture ought not to be misinterpreted as a sign of resignation, a farewell to writing. There is still another idea which makes him move on: "And still I hunger for a story to tell, a story about Orpheus and Eurydice, a story about any man and woman" (CO 246), we read in the introduction to "And Still I Hunger with

Perseus and Fay Wray", one of the story fragments assembled in "Certain Obsessions..." (246-249). Not only the libretto he wrote for Harrison Birtwistle's opera "The Second Mrs Kong", which was performed by the Glyndebourne Touring Opera in October 1994,[8] shows that *that* theme had not been exhausted yet. Fremder, too, was waiting to perform his flicker jumps from this to the Fourth Galaxy.

10. Fremder (1996)

10.1. The Strange and the Familiar

> To have them boats in the air which they callit them space craf ... and going out beyont the sarvering gallack seas. Not jus singing it you know. Acturely going it acturely roading out thru space. Jus try to get it in your mynd try to happen it in your head o dint they trants hy you cud feal the thrus and the boost of it you know the jynt woosh of them liffing off and to the stations. Which they jumpt 1 station to the nex you see and til they jumpt right out beyont them gallack seas. (RW 193-194)

Erny Orfing's fantasy of a past (from his perspective) with space crafts in the air and jumps from station to station has become actualized in Hoban's novel *Fremder*. It is the second novel set in the future (from our perspective), though not one as remote as that of *Riddley Walker*, but only approximately half a century from now. Gigantic multigalactic corporations dominate public life (7), and technology has made progress: it is possible, for instance, to "flicker" from one galaxy to another. But the reality of 2052-2053 is much more dystopic than Orfing has imagined it. Technical failures, human frailty, street violence, pollution and cockroaches turn every place into a dump, whether it is a spaceport with the fairy-tale name Badr al-Budur, short Badru, in the Fourth Galaxy, run by deficient robots, or London characterized by pavements on several levels which manifest a class system not unlike that portrayed in Huxley's *Brave New World*. Outside the city, people live in conditions which resemble the myths about Bad Time in *Riddley Walker*. Dead bodies are eaten up by wild dogs on which people feed again in turn. Occasionally gangs of "Shorties" and "Clowns" (clones), the lower class made up by genetic waste "products", break through the barriers which are to keep them out of the areas reserved for members of "Class A". Usually they protest for "Fun Creds"

8 Cf. Thomas Meyer, "'You remember?'", *Tages-Anzeiger* [Zürich] 26 Oct 1994, 85.

(credits, the contemporary currency) and drugs. But being racist, sexist, and xenophobic they also assault everyone who is female or not "INGLASH" enough, as their graffiti show: "SNG HOARS OUT WOGS JEW UROTRASH OUT INGLAN 4 THE INGLASH. SHORTIS ROOL" (70). In their primitive graffiti as well as in the more comical examples of slurred "Berrwaylill" produced by intergalactic jumps (i.e. "cyberway lilt", cf. 50-51), the language comes closest to the dislocutions of Riddley's Inland dialect; otherwise it is mainly foregrounded when it parodies the jargons and abbreviations of science, technology, business, administration, and advertising.

Science fiction motifs have been used more extensively than in *Riddley Walker*. There are, for instance, satirical descriptions of the ever so familiar uses of the newest inventions, e.g. "'FANTASMO IMPLANTS FOR THE LIFESTYLE OF YOUR CHOICE'... a woman and a man, then two women, then two men, then...", etc. (103). Moreover, there are long introductions to the technology of flicker drive (8-11, 23-26). It is not only the pleasure of describing gadgets which motivates especially the latter, however. For the development of flicker drive is closely related to the protagonist's family history and linked to the central question which turns this novel into another postmodern novel with an ethical bias rather than to make it a science fiction novel "proper": the question is to what degree reality is subjective. This entails two further questions: how far can one's subjectivity contribute to altering the world, and consequently, how responsible are we for the world as it is?

To bring out the most important differences between this novel and *Riddley Walker* I have again underlined the features defining the structural pattern of *Fremder* in the table developed by Barbara Puschmann-Nalenz in *Science Fiction and Postmodern Fiction* (cf. below, Table 2; and ch. 6.4, Table 1, for the features of RW): *Fremder* contains a suspense story and is therefore less open-ended than *Riddley Walker*, although the question whether the ending is a real closure will yet have to be discussed; I have therefore marked these features with question marks. The procedure is non-teleological since the solution of the mystery is scattered all over the text, and the filtering of information through consciousness is underlined, e.g. by the quotation of texts by other characters than the protagonist. I also think that *Fremder* emphasizes the need for constructive impulses more than all of the novels written after *Turtle Diary*; it actually returns to the spirit which made William and Neaera liberate the turtles despite all obstacles. It is multivalent like *Pilgermann*, and deconstructive like *Riddley Walker* (although ethical limits were already recognizable there).

Table 2: Structural Pattern of Genre Conventions
(based on Puschmann-Nalenz, 108)

Postmodern Novel	*component*	*Science Fiction*
emphasizing consciousness non-teleological procedure open-end structure (?) multivalent, deconstructive	*1. predominant structural element*	action-dominated suspense-orientated teleological development *closure* (?)
no clear borderline between fiction and reality; reality is subjective (?)	*2. status of the fictional world*	postulate of reality (?); no questioning of axiomatic truth of an objective reality
narration is fictionalized auto-reflexive	*3. narrative situation and perspective*	narration is not thematic in the texts
introspective, reflective, dis-interested in public issues, anti-hero, vague	*4. protagonist and constellation of characters*	active and rational character, knowledge-able, a leader and individualist, possesses integrating abilities
intra-subjective "experienced time"; emphasis on narrative techniques (flashbacks, citation)	*5. use of time and space*	time-travelling motif emphasis on material of the *plot*
metaphors, connotations, parody, self-reflecting techniques or interior monologue, auto-referential	*6. narrative techniques*	"conventional" presen-tation, relatively "straightforward" story, narrative se-quence recognizable
reader is included, reflections on the reader and the audience; disruption of the reader's illusion	*7. conception of the reader and reader-response*	reader not reflected autonomous fiction willing suspension of disbelief
provocation and disorientation of the reader; highly intricate texts; ambiguities form the thematic focus; insecurity of the reader intended	*8. effect of text; objective of narrative process*	no lasting insecurity or disorientation of the reader; degree of sophistication not too high

However, it also addresses the fact that we must determine our reality ourselves if there is no "place of safety whatever" (MUM, BR 181). This is one of the lessons taught by magic realism rather than by science fiction. Herman Orff's passive armistice with Medusa is replaced by Fremder's conscious effort to establish a boundary between himself (his world) and (that of) Pythia, Medusa's psychotic revenant in this novel. As a first-person narrative modified by a destabilizing opening, with many flashbacks, quotations of poetry and songs, and several attempts to reconstruct the reasons for a traumatic accident, the narrative is "fictionalized autoreflexive" and "introspective" in Puschmann-Nalenz's terms (108); it emphasizes "experienced time" and "narrative techniques". The reader is not as much involved in deciphering the text as she was in *Riddley Walker*, but a "you" in the opening paragraph signals the narrator's awareness of an addressee. Moreover, the question of the constitution of reality challenges the readers' reality as much as it was challenged when Riddley spelled out his first "reveal". The ambiguities and intricacies of the text will be highlighted presently.

Women hold leading positions in society, but as "Top Exec", their behaviour is neither better "nor worse than the male-dominated governments before them" (73), as Fremder is thinking while the I Ching sign of femininity is being projected onto his belly during an interrogation (by contrast, Riddley's Eusa tattoo was one half of the sign of masculinity). The only visible change is that technology has become less phallic in *appearance* and more oriented on the female womb, see e.g. the shapes of spacecrafts (7). The Ziggurat, i.e. a rectangular tower of the kind the Tower of Babel is assumed to have been, is the London headquarters of Sheela-Na-Gig, one of the most powerful corporations, which is named after a Celtic pagan goddess; the building accommodates a huge computer called "Pythia" after the Delphic priestess – its official name is "Data Evaluator (Autonomous Response) but nobody called her DEAR" (72). While Pythia, a "Big Mother" instead of an Orwellian "Big Brother", seems to control everything, she actually turns out to be entangled in a master-and-slave relationship (with reversible roles) with Irene Heale, "a sweet-faced grandmotherly-looking woman in a business suit and a power haircut" who is the ambitious iron lady and Head of Research and Development of Sheela-Na-Gig (70). In the Ziggurat, deep space pilots such as the protagonist Fremder Elijah Gorn, with a special "oscillator" implanted in their brains (8), are questioned in sensor cradles in an examination room called the "Omphalos" – or the "Wank Parlour" in the deep spacers' own sarcastic jargon (72). Reducing the "flickerhead[s]" (8) to babies, after sending them on journeys from which they might not return (25), Pythia softly coerces them into divulging their most private thoughts and feelings. For every kind of information they can give on their flickering jumps will instantly be fed back into research and used to consolidate the Corporation's leading market position. Its greedy (phallic) motto is, after all, "*SEMPER LONGIUS*" (25).

A bridge from the "real" as well as the fictional twentieth century to the twenty-first century depicted in the novel is provided by means of a biological and ideational genealogy: in 1969, Elias Gorn, whose parents had been killed at Auschwitz (11) and who was to become the grandfather of Fremder, wrote to the real Russian scientist Boris Pavlovich Belousov (9-10). Belousov had discovered a chemical "pendulum", i.e. an oscillating chemical reaction. Elias and his wife Sarah thought that, being given the necessary technology, they could prove that what had been found by Belousov was a manifestation of a "universal communication pattern ... the primal impulse that drives all systems both microcosmic and macrocosmic" (9). They cannot have received an answer, though, for by 1964, when Anatol Zhabotinsky finally succeeded in rehabilitating Belousov's research, which had always been rejected by scientific journals, the latter was already dead.[1] In 2009, Elias and Sarah Gorn committed suicide, so their children Helen (Fremder's mother) and Isodor, short Izzy, continued their parents' research. They could also take recourse to the work of another scientist, i.e. Victor Lossiter. The latter had been inspired not only by real scientists of the 1970s such as Benoit Mandelbrot and Erwin Schrödinger, but also, and here is the fictional bridge, by the film director Gösta Kraken, whose unexpected death is the first information we are given in *The Medusa Frequency* (MF 7; FR 8f.). Early on then, Hoban mixes fact and fiction, the familiar and the strange, but at the same time, the importance of a "reality membrane" to separate this world from any other one (4), will be reinstated by the story. For if the strange turns out to be too familiar, as Freud's essay on "Das Unheimliche" points out too, the result will be a horror worse than the anxiety caused by strangers who are simply strange. As we will see, however, subjectivity can to a certain extent influence what belongs to "this side", respectively to the "other side" of the reality membrane.

Fremder is another first-person narrator in the series which started with *Turtle Diary*. He is thirty-one by the time he begins to tell his story but instantly throws us into "the deep chill and the darkness of the Fourth Galaxy" a year earlier, when he was floating through space on his thirtieth birthday on 4 November 2052, wearing nothing but a blue coverall. At first, we do not know that he is telling his own story: in the first paragraph, a narrator's voice is addressing a narratee ("you") and speaking about a floating figure. Moreover,

1 See Barnabas Thwaites, "Das Ballett der Moleküle", *Geo Wissen: Chaos und Kreativität*, March 1990 (reprint November 1993): 136-139.

we do not know whether this figure is alive or dead: not only is the question being raised by the narrator but the chapter has also started with an excerpt from Wallace Stevens's "The Worms at Heaven's Gate" in which the body of Badroulbadour is transferred from the tomb to heaven bit by bit. A dead woman, and a man floating through space: Sophia and Pilgermann inevitably come to mind. Only the second paragraph suggests that "I" and "he" refer to the same person. But this relation is never quite certain. It could well be that Fremder's story, or perhaps Fremders's dream of his story, is the dream dreamt by Badroulbadour while she is being eaten up by worms. The opening thus gives us not only an early hint about the themes of alienation, dismemberment, and uncertainty, but it also establishes a notable contrast to the self-confident opening of *Riddley Walker*: "On my naming day when I come 12 I gone front spear and kilt a wyld boar..." (RW 1).

Equipped with a German name like Kleinzeit, Fremder does not claim that his name means hero: "Fremder means stranger in German" (5). At the beginning, this seems to be ironical, for Fremder apparently knows a lot more about his ancestors than many other people. But at one point he suddenly interrupts his genealogy to remind us of *his* presence, like Pilgermann: "Fremder here" (11). Then he goes on to explain how his grandfather changed his name from Gorenstein into Gorn when he came to England (and the allusion to Frankenstein opens up another genealogical series: i.e. that of science fiction stories about mad scientists): "... he thought Gorn might be a better name to have if somebody came knocking on the door in the middle of the night. 'Gorn today; here tomorrow,' he's quoted as saying" (11). The family history becomes more inscrutable and mysterious the nearer Fremder gets to his own parents: until the time following his thirtieth birthday, he did not know who his father had been, and his mother Helen committed suicide even before he was born, leaving instructions about his future and a note for him in which she soberly apologized for shirking her maternal reponsibility:

> I'm sorry that I'm not going to be around to be your mother but each of us can only go so far: I've gone my distance and now you'll have to go yours. Learn the speech of ravens and they will feed you.
>
> Good luck,
> your mother,
> Helen Gorn (11)

Both Elias Gorn's pun on his name as well as Helen's foregrounded use of the verb "go" in the letter seem to tell her son that to be "gone" is the most natural "eigenstate" of members of the family, to use a term from quantum mechanics.[2] It is up to Fremder to discover that "Gorn" can as well be connected with "GO ON" (183). He is thus a stranger to himself at first (also see 120), sent on an oedipal path of solving his own riddle. Instead of being destroyed by his self-knowledge, however, he will be able to take the mental leap required to liberate himself from a fate that seems implacable (166). By the end of the story, he is closer to Riddley Walker (and also to Kleinzeit, the earlier riddle solver) than to Pilgermann. The gradual discovery of his family secrets, a heart of darkness as black as that of a Joseph Conrad or a Gothic novel, or as a film noir, is triggered by the pressure to explain what happened on his thirtieth birthday. The Corporation want to know how he managed to survive the sudden disappearance of the spacecraft *Clever Daughter*, flickering from Hubble Straits to Badru, while the other members of the crew, among them a man named Ernie Marlowe (70), were not heard of any more.

After Bill Charteris (another significant name, cf. ch. 6.2) has picked him up, he is taken to Hubble Straits where Dr Caroline Lovecraft, the Head of Physio/Psycho at Newton Centre interviews him several times. She is not related to the writer H. P. Lovecraft but nevertheless able to imitate "Cthulhu-speak" (39). A double conversation instantly characterizes their relationship: on the one hand, Caroline must find out what happened on board the *Clever Daughter* by analysing with him the records of the flight and the tape recordings as well as the brain scans made directly after he had been taken to Intensive Care; on the other, she tries to involve Fremder in talking "fragic" (41): a poetical and melancholic variation of verbal love-making rather than just flirting. He, however, repeatedly evades on both levels because her head-on fashion frightens and blocks him; it forces him to confront the traumata of his biography which the *Clever Daughter* incident has reactivated: "I was vibrant with fear at the time; I felt as if I was a puzzle of many pieces, all of them

2 See Douglas R. Hofstadter, *Metamagical Themas*: "Imagine a water faucet with two knobs, one labeled 'H' and one labeled 'C', each of which you can twist continuously. Water comes streaming out of the faucet, but there is a strange property to this system: the water is always either totally hot or totally cold; there is no in-between. These are called the two *temperature eigenstates* of the water. ... The only way you can tell which eigenstate the water is in is by sticking you hand in and feeling it. Actually, in orthodox quantum mechanics it is trickier than that. It is the act of putting your hand in the water that *throws* the water into one or the other eigenstate. Up until that very instant, the water is said to be in a *superposition of states* (or more accurately, a superposition of *eigenstates*)" (466). This is also the phenomenon at the basis of Schrödinger's (hypothetical) experiment with a cat: a cat in a box can either be killed by radiation or survive after having spent an hour in a box with a device to create either of these two possibilities. "At the hour's end, a human observer ... opens the lid to see what has happened. According to one extreme view of quantum mechanics ..., only *at that moment* will the system be forced to 'jump' into one of the two possible eigenstates – cat alive and cat dead – that are represented together as a superposition in the wave function of the system" (468). That is, ambiguities are disambiguated, and the same happens with the multiple associations of the name Gorn and with the floating figure of the opening paragraph, who will turn out to be alive when "I" and "he" can be identified as referring to the same person.

speeding outward from me in all directions. I was afraid I'd never get them back together and at the same time I was afraid that I would" (35). The mirror she holds up to him challenges his fragile stability, e.g. when she says that his first brain scan shows features typical of "autistics and ... cult believers.... It's a closed loop of self-reinforcing perception that locks out external stimuli" (43). Always oscillating between attraction and anger, unable to find out what could stabilize the chaotic pendulum of feelings between them, they eventually part ways after three weeks. Since Caroline could not find out anything substantial, Fremder must go back to the Earth for Pythia sessions. The only way for him to explain to himself what happened is to refer to a depressive disposition he seems to have inherited from his mother Helen. In other words, he is about to become a victim of the same disposition which brought on Pilgermann's guilt and death.

The novel has been arranged symmetrically around a central chapter (like *The Medusa Frequency*): chapter 12 forms a borderline, or a reality membrane, or the surface of a mirror through which Fremder passes between the time spent in the Fourth Galaxy (literally "heaven", though a troubled one at first) and the time on an increasingly infernal Earth, beginning with chapter 13 and ending with a return to Hubble Straits and Caroline in chapter 23. Since metaphors from the science of chaos are omnipresent in this novel, one might also say that chapter 12 is the middle section of a Lorenz attractor, also called a "strange attractor" (see Gleick 119ff., 133f., 140f.). In the middle section of a strange attractor two groups of loops, connected like horizontal figures 8 which will *never* intersect and *never* repeat themselves (i.e. differing from the two-dimensional symbol often used for eternity: ∞), change their direction, making the whole "magical image" resemble "an owl's mask or butterfly's wings", as James Gleick writes (29). This "emblem for the early explorers of chaos" reveals "the fine structure hidden within a disorderly stream of data" (Gleick 29). Chapter 12 fulfils the same function within *Fremder* although it seems to be disconnected from the story at first, ex-centric rather than part of the narrative (just as a strange attractor is an extrapolation from data gathered on turbulences). Vermeer's *Head of a Young Girl*, or *Girl with a Pearl Earring*, is mentioned in it once again. This time, the Vermeer girl has been equipped with a voice and a name for she is a poetry robot modelled on the painting we know from *Pilgermann* and *The Medusa Frequency*. Fremder tells us how he discovered her on the remote asteroid A373 in the Sixth Galaxy, which he visited "for an inventory a couple of years ago" (65). "Pearl", as he calls her, recited the first of Rilke's *Duino Elegies* in his mother's voice:

Wer, wenn ich schriee, hörte mich denn aus der Engel
Who, were I to cry, would hear me out of the angelic

Ordnungen? und gesetzt selbst, es nähme
order? and suppose even that one were to take

einer mich plötzlich ans Herz: ich verginge von seinem
me suddenly to his heart: I should perish through his

stärkeren Dasein. Denn das Schöne ist nichts als des
stronger existence. For beauty is nothing but the

Schrecklichen Anfang, den wir noch grade ertragen,
beginning of terror, which we only barely endure,

und wir bewundern es so, weil es gelassen verschmäht
and we admire it so, because it calmly disdains

uns zu zerstören. Ein jeder Engel ist schrecklich.
to destroy us. Every angel is terrible. (66)

Seduction and destruction, desire and anxiety, the angel of life and the angel of death, butterfly and owl are being superimposed in several layers in this chapter: not only Rilke's beautiful terrible angel signals ambivalence but also the Vermeer girl with her questioning eyes through which her terror shows, the artificial robot with the maternal voice, a voice, moreover, which is at once that of Eurydice (66) and that of twenty-one-year-old Helen Gorn recorded "three months after she was raped and Izzy crippled by the Shorties and the Clowns" (67). This is the chaotic emotional pattern, or a key to the structure of Fremder's desire, which has caused his difficulties with Caroline; from this strange attractor one can derive the conditions which must be fulfilled for him to feel "quiet" (67): a maternal voice must utter *his* anxiety whenever he needs her, regardless of her own terror; a painted or mechanical representation of a woman, whose beauty cannot suddenly turn into terror and who cannot simply leave him, is what gives him a feeling of safety.

His wishes, "gratified" so far only in a sublimated form on a pathetic little asteroid with a number instead of a name (like those of Antoine de Saint-Exupéry's little prince), suddenly seem to become gratified in reality, too, when he arrives at London. But being back "home" will be far more dangerous to his stability than the time spent with Caroline. For instead of having to face one "real" woman, with the contradictions and the strangeness which define her subjectivity, he is now exposed to a triad of "familiar women" who all personify symptoms of his narcissistic disposition. There is first the stereotypical "phallic" power (wo)man Irene Heale, whom he can easily dismiss as an enemy (she happens to be the mother-in-law of his childhood enemy Albert Stiggs); secondly, he meets the "Big Mother" Pythia, who seems to offer him a favour his own mother withheld when she invites him to return to her artificial womb; and finally, he can fall in love with a "perfect" beloved, i.e. Katya Mazur, the blue-eyed "dream woman" who reminds him of his minder (and supposedly his first love) Miranda. As is common with symptoms, however,[3] there comes a point at which Fremder must pay for the illusory comfort he has been given, and the price is always a direct confrontation with the traumatic experience which the symptom sought to hide: The three women turn out to be connected with each other, which removes the clean distinctions he thought he could make between them; then, he will discover that his worst "enemy" is not external but has long been in himself as part of his parental legacy; further, he realizes that the maternal womb is no safe place any more once one has been born; and finally, he will find out that the love which seems to renew the love for a lost beloved will inevitably engender another loss.

In the course of the analysis of his flicker accident, Pythia crashes when the anamorphotically distorted face of Izzy Gorn is eventually "ripped" out of Fremder's long-blocked memory (89f.). He saw the face stretched all over the Fourth Galaxy while flickering through space with the *Clever Daughter*. Katya, who attended the session to change sensors and semen collectors, faints. Instead of realizing that she is Pythia's puppet, Fremder feels flattered and "more intimate with her than I'd ever been with anyone before" (91). They make love after he has kissed her awake (like the prince and Sleeping Beauty or Snow White) and they decide to spend the evening together after her work. In the meantime, though, a packet from green-eyed Caroline with an "audio crystal" has arrived. There is no note but the music nevertheless reminds him of her, being a little piece of the Real in the dream, and later the nightmare, he is going to experience with the fake "goddess" (93) or "paper moon" woman Katya (108). While he is listening to a composition called *"La Terreur de Devenir"*, a mourning process sets in: Fremder weeps for the dead, and "I wept for all star-wanderers and deep-spacers for ever riding out to the blackness and back to the fading and broken green jewel of their birth. I wept for myself, afraid to ship out again" (107). He also begins to feel regret remembering the last evening out with Caroline, who was "crying that night ... because she'd given herself and I hadn't" (120).

3 See ch. 11.2, where Toni Morrison's ghost girl Beloved will be discussed as a personification of a symptom, too.

The coincidences of taste which will manifest themselves in Katya's choice of holograms and music, on the other hand, intermittently rouse his suspicion: "'Somebody's trying something on here – is it Pythia or Thinksec or what?'" (110). But Katya for a while succeeds in allaying his fears of a conspiracy, and he is ever so ready to believe that she is "the real thing", although "circles of bright emptiness had been there all through the lovemaking and they were still there" (111). She admits, though, that the words spoken by her in her sleep are actually Pythia's "overspill", not her own, for she has a "synaptic relay" implanted in her head (112). Fremder is jealous, as he was at one point in the interviews with Caroline (cf. 45): "'... Next you'll be telling me that you take the overspill from all the guys that come to the Wank Parlour as well.'" (112). But Katya can give the dialogue a turn that will make both laugh and prevent an outbreak of chaos: she is permanently instructed by Pythia while Caroline had nothing but her professionalism to take refuge from Fremder's inexplicable moodiness. Nevertheless, there are many hints that the relationship between the seemingly perfect lovers cannot last either: unlike Sister in *Kleinzeit*, Katya keeps fearfully looking ahead (she is an "active" Eurydice) and she repeatedly addresses the fact that their time together might be limited (114). On a trip to the Red Mountain Park the next day, they see an owl, the bird of loss (117, 27, 57). It will indeed turn out to have been the last-but-one day of her life.

While Katya is asleep after their return to her flat, Fremder experiences a night of revelations which sheds more light on the unknown chapters of his history than the weeks spent in analysis. Helen Gorn's former research assistant Lowell Sixe, a reincarnation of Redbeard, Erny Orfing, and Gom Yawncher, knocks at the door at three o'clock in the morning to give Fremder books, photocopies of notebooks and printouts which belonged to Helen. Because Katya's flat is bugged, they go to the roof of the house, where Lowell tells Fremder of Helen's "Elijah Project": instead of working on flicker drive, she sought Hermetic doors to alternate universes in which she could be a winner for a change, rather than the victim of anti-Semites and rapist Clowns, or a puppet on the string of the powerful Corporation (129f.). Fremder sympathizes with her desire: he has himself experienced the feeling of doing the right thing at the right moment, like Elijah running in front of Ahab's chariot (131). Lowell continues to tell him of Helen's unhappiness, how she was spied on by Irene Heale, her jealous competitor (137). She nevertheless managed to dodge her, working day and night, energized by her obsession (139). In September 2022, she insisted on doing a test run. She did not care whether her experiment with a rat would change everyone else's reality: Lowell thinks, it did, though – for he instantly had a "dropping sensation" (142). The front half of the rat disappeared while the back half stayed behind, and the same obviously happened to Izzy when he attempted a phase jump earlier that year in April: only his head disappeared while his body resisted the transfer. Helen thought that both the rat and her brother must have changed their minds while jumping (143). She wanted to jump herself as soon as possible to escape from Heale's supervision, but Lowell was afraid: Helen's Hermetic project had turned into a Dionysiac craziness (147). He went for a walk to evade her humiliating insults. By the time he came back, he was arrested to be "terminated" by Top Exec. A neurosurgeon saved his life, however, providing him with a new identity (149). Helen was reported to have committed suicide after a breakdown (149). Noticing a special nonsense code on a printout from the time after her official death, though, Lowell has come to the conclusion that she might still be alive (150). No sooner has he finished his tale and slipped a card with an address into Fremder's hand than he is shot from the air. Fremder reads the notebook entries in Katya's kitchen. They show him not only the progress of Helen's thinking on Elijah and on the transition between matter and mind, but there are also innuendos that brother and sister, huddling together in stormy nights, became lovers. The last photocopy is a Pythia printout dating from Fremder's thirtieth birthday. It was recorded six minutes before the *Clever Daughter* disappeared and shows the megacomputer determined to "SEEK HIM IN THE BLACK I WILL FIND HIM WHOM MY SOUL LOVETH WHEN THE TIME CAME HE DID NOT TASTE THE TASTE OF DEATH" (160).

Fremder is struck, but does not waste any time. He instantly takes a wirecar to the ominous address on Lowell's card: he is to seek a Marie Demska, to be found at the seedy "PICCADILLY RELIEF" club, 37 The Maze, King's Cross (151). A fifty to sixty-year-old beauty in a black kimono with a bearded drag queen (in Hermès trainers, called Zizi) as a bodyguard turns out to be the neurosurgeon (employed by Athena Parthenogen) who not only implanted Fremder's oscillator but who also saved Lowell's life when he was to be killed the first time. She tells Fremder that he has no standard oscillator in his brain but one wired by Albert Stiggs, his childhood enemy, according to Izzy's "circuitry diagram for the phase-jump oscillator" (165). Fremder feels doomed: "*keres anaplaketoi*, implacable fates, I thought, remembering my student translation of *Oedipus the King*" (166). Marie, however, dismisses him with kisses on the cheek and a description of the "Bamberger Reiter", the statue of a kingly rider who cannot fall from his horse as long as there is a "green man to hold him up" (166) – the function Lowell has performed for him. On the way back to Katya's flat, Ziggurat Authority lets him know through his wristphone that he is going to be picked up at midnight.

Katya is speaking in her sleep when he enters her flat and annoyed that he tries to ask her about the sense of her words: she does not understand them herself. Pythia no longer hides her presence but keeps repeating the words Fremder read on the printout, using Katya as her mouthpiece. When Katya desperately tries to fight her influence, trying to assure Fremder of her love and her humanity, she dies from an aneurysm in her brain. He cannot help her, however hard he tries, appealing to the "animal" in her when he has finally recognized that she did not know for what she had been used:

> I believed her then and I cursed myself for thinking what I'd thought. 'Remember how it is with us,' I whispered in her ear. 'Remember how we thought each other up, remember how the two of us are the answer for whatever question comes at us.' I dragged her over to the hologram, keyed in Plates 69 to 73, and put the machine on auto sequence. 'Look!' I said as the B-Z reaction appeared, the red involute spirals moving and changing to nodes of possibility and archipelagos of being. 'Look at the eyes of becoming and remember how it was when we saw the owl together.' I pressed my forehead against hers. 'See the grey sky over the Red Mountain, the grey air and the owl cruising low over the mountain; look at the owl, look at its ringed eyes of becoming. Feel the animal of you holding on to the owl in the grey air over the Red Mountain. Are you seeing it, Katya?'
>
> 'Yes, Fremder, I'm seeing the owl.'
>
> 'Can you feel the animal of you holding on to the owl?'
>
> 'Yes, I can feel that *and I'm deeply moved*,' she finished in her Pythia voice. (170)

There seems to be no such totemic animal for Katya, however, no reality to hold on to, or perhaps only a butterfly, emblem of the psyche and much weaker than the predatory emblem of loss – and of Athene, i.e. the owl.

Pythia is merely cynical about the demise of the "sweetie" with which she has fed him as the ravens had fed Elijah (123). She greedily tries to appropriate all Katya has been to him, like a raven feeding on corpses (124):

> *'Your little sweetie was just something I dressed up in for a while so we could get to know each other better. One shilling the box – allow me to sell you a couple.'* (...)
>
> *'... The Katya you knew never existed except in me: her words were my words, her thoughts were my thoughts, her loving was my loving. It was nice being loved by you; I never had that kind of a romance before.'* (170-171)

Fremder begins to realize how easy it has been to manipulate him because of his fear of the strange and his desire for the familiar, and the recognition brings on anger. But to no avail: immediately after his quarrel with Pythia, not over but literally through Katya's dying body, he is kidnapped, doped and taken to

Clever Daughter II for another flicker jump with Pythia on board, or rather with her as the living wall of the spacecraft into which he is locked like into a tomb (169-171, 176).

Pythia turns out to be the enlarged brain of Helen Gorn (a motif reminiscent of Joseph McElroy's *Plus*), removed from her skull after her suicide and appropriated by Irene Heale. It is quite obviously not a case of dog eat dog inside the city of London, but rather one of one bird feeding on the other, with Irene Heale, the woman with the sweetest face and the most promising name – "Irene": the goddess of peace; "Heale": suggesting wholeness – as the vulture at the end of the food chain. Heale made the brain addicted to a new drug called "Trance & Dance" (180); in return Helen had to work for her, but she always continued to pursue her own little scheme. The psychotic mother-monster-brain confirms that Izzy was Fremder's father, and she now wants them to become a real "family" at last, supposing that her brotherly lover "wants us all to be in the same world" (179) – failing to consider the fact that he probably jumped out of this world to escape from her clutches.

We have then, in distorted form but nevertheless recognizable, what Zizek described as the typical "dead end" of the "modern American family" when he analysed Hitchcock's *The Birds* in *Looking Awry*, quoting from Christopher Lasch's *The Culture of Narcissism* (and for "the birds" we can insert Pythia):

> ... the terrifying figure of the birds [Pythia] is actually the embodiment in the real of a discord, an unresolved tension in intersubjective relations. In the film, the birds are like the plague in Oedipus's Thebes: they are the incarnation of a fundamental disorder in family relationships – the father is absent, the paternal function (the function of pacifying law, the Name-of-the-Father) is suspended and that vacuum is filled by the 'irrational' maternal superego, arbitrary, wicked, blocking 'normal' sexual relationship (only possible under the sign of the paternal metaphor). The dead end *The Birds* [*Fremder*] is really about is, of course, that of the modern American family: the deficient paternal ego-ideal makes the law 'regress' toward a ferocious maternal superego, affecting sexual enjoyment – the decisive trait of the libidinal structure of 'pathological narcissism': 'Their unconscious impressions of the mother are so overblown and so heavily influenced by aggressive impulses, and the quality of her care is so little attuned to the child's needs, that in the child's fantasies the mother appears as a devouring bird.' (Zizek 99)

When Fremder asks Pythia whether his dead father is to blame for the disappearance of *Clever Daughter*, she seems to be unable to give him a precise answer but assumes that his, i.e. Fremder's, "Reality-Sustain-Factor" (179) dropped so low that the jump phase device of his oscillator became activated: implicitly she is trying to make him feel guilty; he, however, can't help feeling the irony of the situation. Eventually she must admit that his colleagues' will to life had not been strong enough either:

> '... when you let it drop below ten you found yourself confronting two incompatible realities – the reality of *Clever Daughter* and its crew and the reality of your father's face stretched out across the Fourth Galaxy. When you leant towards your father the rest of the crew and the ship went bye-bye in the great green glassy face of the up, up, upping wave. Then crash: the wave breaks on the beach of here and now. No more *Clever Daughter*. Only a stupid son, drifting neither here nor there.'
>
> That was my mother talking to me. At this moment that might well be the beginning of the end of my life I was looking for high tragedy but I seemed to have become the rear half of a Jewish pantomime horse.
>
> 'What about the seven others?' I said. 'Why couldn't they have held on to their reality and not disappeared?'
>
> 'Shit,' said Mum, 'they probably hadn't got any to hold on to – just doing their job like most job-doers. Reality is the responsibility of those who perceive it....' (180-181)

After this "showdown", Fremder is cured from his desire for the familiar. He won't allow Pythia to entangle him (the alienated offspring of her abjected body) in her Dionysiac realization of the Elijah Project (the "child" of her undead, vampiric brain); for he has recognized that she is going to abuse her invention to rejoin the dead rather than to find a world in which she can be a winner, as was her original intention. He, however, wants to live. To flee from a deluded, narcissistic, and deadly "family" reunion with his dead father's head and her monstrous brain, he repeats his Hermetic "suspended-animation trick", having been strengthened rather than paralyzed by the self-knowledge gained by looking at his history. When their journey reaches a critical point, he lets himself be Bach's *The Art of Fugue*, i.e. "the music in which there flickered, partly now and partly remembered, that one glance of Caroline's, that swift upward glance of fear and doubt" (182), sending the spacecraft and Pythia to the other side of the reality membrane, where she wants to be, while holding on to this side himself. He is picked up again by Bill Charteris and Caroline Lovecraft while drifting towards Badr al-Budur. He can hardly believe his good luck: "... is the world (lacking as it does half a rat, one human head, one very large brain, a couple of spacecraft, and seven crew) the one I started out with?" (184). Probably it isn't. But after all, Pythia did not forget to tell him that "reality is the responsibility of those who perceive it", and since he is not as stupid as she tried to make him feel he took his only chance. His desire for life has altered the entire reality-frame surrounding him. Having felt like Elijah waiting for the rain all his life, he asks himself whether he has now fully realized himself and become whole at last. But on the screen of his mind there only open up "nodes of possibility expanding in concentric circles", like those in a Belousov-Zhabotinsky reaction, or an owl's "eyes of becoming" (182). This is the opposite of closure.

10.2. A Woman's World?

"This is a man's world, ... but it would be nothing without a woman or a girl. He's lost in the wilderness..."
(James Brown, *It's a Man's Man's Man's World*)

The lyrics of James Brown's song describe, in a nutshell, and extremely simplified of course, the kind of situation feminism keeps writing against: in a world dominated by patriarchal governments, sciences, philosophies, myths, phallic sexuality, male anxieties, and so on, yet perceived to be empty and worthless, women are welcome to complement and back up the beaten heroes. They are supposed to make the wilderness a little bit more comfortable for them, but fail to be perceived as participants and subjects just as afraid and exposed, though not only to the "wilderness" and the terror of becoming, but also to the demands made on them by men. This is what Caroline is crying about and protesting against the last night she and Fremder spend at Hubble Straits before he is sent to the Earth:

> 'First Navigator Fremder Gorn,' she said, 'it just occurred to me that there might be something missing in you and that's why you didn't disappear with the ship and the others. You're the most alone person I've ever met. You know how wirecars have couplers, what they call male and female couplers – you push one car up against another and there's a clunk and they connect? Most people have couplers but you seem not to. You weren't connected to your ship or the others; when they went you stayed alone. And you never connected with me although you stuck your male part into my female one. I wanted you to give me the how-it-is-with-Fremder the same as I gave you the how-it-is-with-Caroline but you wouldn't do it and now you're going Earthside with all the how-it-is still locked up in you. OK, that's the last assessment from Dr Love-but-not-very-crafty.' (59)

The future society imagined in *Fremder* at first glance seems to be a sceptical calling into question of a world run by women. Despite Fremder's assessment that "they hadn't done any worse than the male-dominated governments before them" (73), it will become quite clear that this is a duplicitous statement. The women shown to be in power have indeed "done no worse", but also no better: they can handle the world just as little as their predecessors. Their means are subtler and softer, perhaps, their aesthetics may be slightly different – although the purple-coloured Ziggurat with the Omphalos inside, i.e. a "womb" perversely turned inside out and surrounded by greenish-grey dead male bodies, seems phallic (69)[1] – but exploitation and power games of the familiar kind have not disappeared.

The death drive has many women in its grip, particularly Helen Gorn, who *seems* again and again *responsible* for her own unhappiness, suicidal long before she commits suicide: she was raped because she and Izzy, "looking Jewish", wanted to walk on unsafe paths at night (21) – simply doing what most of Hoban's male protagonists enjoy without having to pay so dearly; she got pregnant because of her incestuous love for her brother – having been slighted by all other men except Lowell Sixe because she was neither a member of the uppermost class nor particularly beautiful (18, 134f.); she failed to honour, or even perceive, Lowell's sincere loyalty – because her obsession with the Elijah Project had made her crazy, "but it was a world-class craziness ... she could have told me the moon was made of green cheese and I'd have believed her", as Lowell says, defending her despite her ratty behaviour towards him since he is a true green man (138); and later, her isolated brain became corrupted by drugs – because her greedy competitor Irene Heale could not leave the dead woman alone but wanted to build her career on Helen's research (180).

Seeing only Helen's responsibility would be to take the position of those offenders who put *all* the blame on the victims (who often do have a share in the crime, it is true, but certainly not the greater part of it). But this does not happen in Fremder's account: he combines the description of the wrongs suffered by his mother with a reflection of his own desires and his own behaviour towards the women he has encountered, determining the outlines of his responsibility for their suffering. He learns to be with his mother, while jumping out of her tomb-womb-spacecraft when her desire to be with him acquires the totalitarian excessiveness of a psychotic. It grows more and more obvious that the "Earthside" matriarchal society portrayed in *Fremder* is actually a depiction of Fremder's oedipal desires and anxieties, haunting him in the real now rather than "merely" sabotaging his sexuality. It cannot be a woman's idea of the world if she aspires to something else than the patriarchal system with inverted signs; Helen/Pythia, Katya and Irene are male fantasies about Woman with which women must not identify and from which Fremder, too, will distance himself. He often compares himself to Hamlet, whom Freud compared to Oedipus in *Die Traumdeutung* (cf. 268-270), e.g. when he rebukes Caroline: "'Do you remember, Dr Lovecraft, in *Hamlet*, where Hamlet shows

1 The way Angela Carter's *Nights at the Circus* can be seen as a response to *Pilgermann*, *Fremder* could be seen as a response to Elisabeth Bronfen's essay "From Omphalos to Phallus: Cultural Representations of Femininity and Death" (1992).

Guildenstern a recorder and asks him if he can play it?'" (55), or when his treatment of Katya turns her into an Ophelia destroyed by his distrust (169). Hamlet, as we know, though, was doomed no less than Oedipus.

The task he must therefore fulfil by solving the riddle of his identity, is to find a way of distancing himself both from Pythia's excessive narcissistic claims on him and from a repetition of the wrongs done to her by everyone else. He cannot simply switch from the Oedipus to the Perseus pattern, for he cannot identify with the murderer of Medusa: such a switch would perpetuate the system from which he himself and also the women in the novel suffer. Interestingly, he is given presents before the showdown with Pythia, like Perseus; but the "biographical mirror" he gets from Lowell Sixe and Marie Demska's information on the dangerous jump phase oscillator in his brain make him neither invisible nor do they present a distorted image of Helen Gorn: he must solve his problems by confronting both his history and his mother directly, without cheating. He sympathizes with the suffering of Medusa when Katya puts on the hologram of her decapitated head: significantly, however, he also notices Pegasus, the winged horse representing the imagination which emerges from her bleeding neck – a Hermetic figure, actually, and an animal (117).

His solution and his salvation comes from identifying Izzy Gorn's anamorphotically distorted face in the Fourth Galaxy as the face of his dead father ("Is he gone?", a literally distorted version of Freud's Dead Father from *Totem und Tabu*). Leaning towards him, acknowledging him (182), he lets go of the world to relax in the spacecraft smelling of dead rats[2] and blocked drains (an abject place indeed, in Kristevan terms) when Pythia tries to stage her idea of a family reunion (175). Letting go activates his mind, "BE WITH ME, said my mind" (182), which in turn lends him the strength to jump out of Pythia's trajectory: "... I felt myself go and then came that feeling of being grabbed by the brain and slung against a wall when I came out of flicker" (182). It is the same kind of empowerment which Neaera felt when she identified with Kong in the cinema, an empowerment based on a trust in unconscious resources unencumbered by the oedipal ballast of our culture (cf. chs. 8.3 and 8.4). He thus succeeds in sending his mother's brain on her own errand without killing her, for her reality is her own responsibility, as it was of those members of the crew who did not survive the first *Clever Daugher* incident (181). At the same time, he asserts his own reality, Bach's music and Caroline's "swift upward

2 The motif of rats actually engenders an interesting sequence of associations: they recall Manny Rat and Freud's obsessional neurotic who became famous as the "rat man", Anne Sexton's palindrome "RATS LIVE ON NO EVIL STAR", and Helen Gorn's dislocution of it in "Evil rats on no star live" (180).

glance of fear and doubt" (182). The monstrous maternal super-ego, the archaic mother about to swallow him, has been exchanged for a new law. The Name-of-the-Father (in Lacanian terms) is being re-established, though not according to the oedipal scheme. For the dead father comes to represent mortality for Fremder, releasing his mother from the task of being included in what Bronfen calls the "unencompassable body of *materiality-maternity-mortality*", whose "failed repression" has again and again been "at stake in representations of feminine death" ("From Omphalos...", 146). The umbilical cord to the archaic mother is being cut, his body and his mortality become his.

He defines a thetic boundary or reality membrane which is to prevent his fantasies from emerging in the real again, banishing them to the other side, or the unconscious, where they can do no harm. The work of repression, for which Fremder's escape is an image, cannot guarantee, however, that there will be no more intrusions from the other side or further damages done on his own side of the reality membrane: Irene Heale is in possession of all the technological knowledge to turn herself into another Pythia. She might want to fill in the gap left by Pythia in the Omphalos and reproduce the phase jump oscillators which have catapulted half a rat, Izzy's head and Helen's brain to some other place. The terror will always have to be faced, it is immanent to life, and boundaries must be set up again and again as new challenges present themselves.

This point is also being made in Hoban's essay "Blighter's Rock", which is concerned with the central ideas of *Fremder*. Hoban discusses people's craving for horror films and horror stories and eventually turns to the film *Nightmare on Elm Street*, in which the boundary between reality and the world of nightmares has collapsed completely:

> The end ... leaves us with no clear distinction between nightmare and waking, no place of safety whatever, and the very nature of reality in question. Millions of filmgoers, and I as well, found that entertaining. Perhaps we even felt at home with it. Why is that? Rilke, in the first of his Duino elegies, said:
>
> Beauty is nothing but the beginning of terror ...
>
> There is indeed such a spectrum: look at Vermeer's *Head of a Young Girl* for example – there are reproductions of it everywhere; if you follow your mind into the look with which that girl looks out at you, you come to Thing-in-Itself and the terror at the back of her eyes. You come to what waits in the blank paper: the ungraspable isness of what is. In trying to take hold of it the mind finds only the incomprehensibility of itself and the original terror of Creation, the bursting into being of something out of nothing. And yet the mind – this one mind that we all share – is hungry for that terror.
>
> In the original terror is the vital energy that is the beginning of beauty and everything else – perhaps even a better understanding of the human situation. When it comes at you out of the blank paper it's difficult to sort out what

> wants to be put into words and it isn't always possible to look straight at it; that's why any blighter can find himself or herself rocked from time to time. But with patience, blank paper of the right kind, and a favouring road from Hermes, one gets unrocked often enough to make it worth the bother. (MUM, BR 181-182)

As for relationships between women and men, it is meaningful that Fremder is saved by means of a memory of Caroline Lovecraft's glance of fear and doubt, and not by the memory of their love-making or her beauty: it is sharing the terror which defines a "new" or "other" love that can last, not the narcissistic fantasy that a beloved can make up for the terror of being. This fantasy may make people fall in love with each other and stimulate their sexual desire, but disillusionment usually sets in rather quickly. Fremder must become reconciled to Caroline's "strange" features which frightened him at the beginning: her directness, her sarcasm, her scientific ambition, the "menacing alien voice" she adopts to recite H. P. Lovecraft (39), and probably above all her protean changes from one personality into another. Rather than to be radically different from Katya, Helen and Irene, she combines aspects of all of them, and in addition there are also facets probably not even she can explain to herself.

So far I have been presenting Caroline as the "real" woman opposed to the three personifications of symptoms of Fremder's desire in the second half of the novel. But to round off the picture, I now want to show that, like Melanie Falsepercy, Caroline is not a cultural blank. On the contrary. The terror in her eyes is not what makes her a stranger, for she has been endowed with the terror of Vermeer's *Head of a Young Girl*, or *Girl with a Pearl Earring*, i.e. the painting which defines Fremder's desire. This is the feature which distinguishes the original portrait by Vermeer from cheap adaptations (the poetry robot makes up for the missing black background by letting Helen Gorn recite the first of Rilke's *Duino Elegies*).[3] Let me conjure her up once more, to show how the terror interacts with her other features.

Highlighting draws attention to a pearl hanging from her shaded ear. It is at the same time a metonym and a metaphor of her: She is wearing a pearl

3 By contrast, Helen Gorn, who otherwise does not resemble the portrait, has the Vermeer girl's seductive pose on the photograph taken when she was seventeen: "Her body's half-turned away from the camera and she's looking back over her shoulder" (18-19); Katya's hair is coloured like the Vermeer girl's golden headdress and her accommodating manner seems to be the fulfilment of the promise implied by the young woman's movement towards the spectator and by her half-parted lips (92), but Fremder quite obviously wants her to be *more* like the Vermeer girl than she is when he tells her that her face and her blue eyes are like those of the Vermeer girl (110): actually, the painted woman's eyes are dark and the only spot of colour which can be made out is olive rather than blue; even Irene Heale is equipped with one of the portrait's agreeable features: she has a sweet face despite her age, her position, her business suit and her power haircut (70).

because she is worthy of such a precious jewel (metonymic reference); the pierced ear and the pierced pearl, suggesting that she is no longer a virgin, are linked by a barely visible gold chain or wire which hides rather than emphasizes the piercing (metaphoric reference). Jean Chevalier and Alain Gheerbrant write in their *Dictionary of Symbols* (1994) that in Persian literature, the "phrase 'to pierce the pearl of virginity' is used to mean the consummation of a marriage" (745). Like the pearl's white glimmer, the young woman's immaculate skin points to purity and absence of artifice. The pearl does not need to be supplemented by any other jewels or an elaborate setting, just as the woman's face is placed at the centre of a painting whose background is black;[4] her golden gown and the blue and gold scarf veil her body and the back of her head while the position of the pearl as intermediary between the luminous face and the white collar draws attention to the decency of her garments. Her body is turned away from the spectator, suggesting a passive, waiting posture. She must have turned her head to look at the invisible spectator, perhaps because he called her name – a gesture which signals willingness like her half-parted lips. Placed side by side, reinforcing each other, the pearl symbolises, while the young woman is the personification of, "the sublimation of instinct" (Chevalier and Gheerbrant 743): she promises "enlightenment and spiritual birth, ... the Sublime Essence hidden in the Self" (745) – in other words, Woman, a supreme fantasm. It is remarkable, then, that in Hoban's descriptions of the Vermeer girl in *Pilgermann* and *The Medusa Frequency*, the pearl is of no importance. Fremder's calling the poetry robot "Pearl" (FR 65) is the first time that attention has been drawn to the jewel, and I have already discussed what an ambivalent position the robot holds in this novel. If the uncanny darkness of the woman's pupils and her surroundings as well as the snaky shape under her headdress did not counter the symbolism of the pearl, the painting would no doubt be an example of kitsch; sublimation would then be reduced to a "restitutive function", i.e. it would be "an attempt at symbolic repair of the imaginary lesions that have occurred to the fundamental image of the maternal body" (Lacan, *Ethics*, 106). Including the terror, however, locating it in the eyes of the painted woman as well as under her headdress and in the background, the painting becomes a sublimation which fulfils an ethical function by creating "socially recognized values", i.e. it functions as an approach to the ultimately ungraspable Real by which our being is structured (Lacan, *Ethics*, 107).

4 Elisabeth Bronfen points out that according to Max Raphael's study *Die Farbe Schwarz*, "the colour black in portrait painting signifies the indeterminate, the unbounded, the immaterial, while white is determined, bounded, constant" (see *Over Her Dead Body*, 9).

But this is not all. It is not merely, as Lacan argues, the creation of "something" out of the "nothing", or absence, seen on the maternal body, i.e. an acknowledgment of the impact of the Real on her, that is at stake here; this is also Bronfen's notion of the "omphalos", the signifier of mortality which she derives from the "loss of the maternal body", following Lacan's definition of the ethic and suggesting that it become the new site of castration ("From Omphalos...", 155):

> It is precisely because the paternal threat, and its privileged signifier the phallus, is only incidental to this death-related notion of castration, while the maternal loss is endemic to it, that I suggest (reformulating Lacan) that the site of castration be relocated – at the navel – and that we read the navel in the sense of Lacan's *objet a* – as a remainder or residue, 'which harkens back to the primordial object of satisfaction, that original object in relation to which every subsequent attempt at satisfaction must be deemed a refinding of the object: the mother'. Precisely because, as Boothby explicates, castration is the detachment of desire from the imaginary other and as such part of sublimation, and the *objet a* is 'cut free from the maternal relation' so as to 'circulate in the signifying chain', it is the omphalos which is as much a 'key signifier in the unconscious' as Lacan's phallus. While in the symbolic order the phallus points the way to ever-ongoing signification and deferral of desire, the omphalos points to the real, to death, excluded from the imaginary organisation of identity. As emblem of what I have called the unencompassable body of 'materiality–maternity–mortality', the omphalos can be seen as a crucial site engendering moral law... (156)

While I agree with her that we need two distinct "key signifiers" in the unconscious, one to orient sexual desire and language, the other to orient mortality (and the semiotic, the sound of the voice, poetry?), I want to draw attention to a conceptual omission in her definition of the omphalos that also characterizes Freudian and Lacanian definitions of desire. Like Lacan, Bronfen reads the signifiers in the unconscious only as tokens of absence and castration. What needs to be affirmed more, however, and particularly in view of a definition of the omphalos as a "site engendering moral law", is the "other side" of signifiers. They not only remind us of an absence, of our being cut off from the past, but they also produce new links; "castration", whether mortal or sexual, always also gives us an impetus to liberation and to a look forward into the future.

In terms of a non-restitutive sublimation of the Real this entails the following: Recalling my stress on the *Freudian* notion of the drives, i.e. as links between the body and the psyche (ch. 8.3), I will now argue that sublimation which is non-restitutive not only foregrounds (rather than repairs in the symbolic) "the imaginary lesions that have occurred to the fundamental image of the maternal body" (Lacan, *Ethics*, 106), but it also highlights (rather than deflects attention from) the decay of the spectator's *own* body, that is the terror to which not only the represented figure is exposed. As Hoban writes in "Blighter's Rock", "You come to what waits in the blank paper: the ungraspable isness of what is. In trying to take hold of it the mind finds only the incomprehensibility of itself and the original terror of Creation" (181-182). Sublimation highlights the effects of the spectator's *own* mortality, and by that operation *entrusts* the spectator with his/her own body, it *creates* that body for him/her. While the umbilical cord with the archaic mother is being cut, subjects, who would perhaps prefer to constitute themselves entirely through language (i.e. "beyond facticity", as Bronfen writes, 155), are being reminded of their facticity and their responsibility for the Real of which they are part *themselves*, and *not only through the abjected maternal body.* Sublimation defined in this way is a creation of "something" (responsibility, ethics) out of the aging, splitting, and passing away of "something else", i.e. out of the dissolution of one's own, or no longer disowned, body (rather than out of a vague "nothing" with maternal overtones). This is the terror of creation Russell Hoban's fiction is about.

Caroline's glance also resembles that of a little bronze head of a goddess standing on her desk (40):

> ... a museum replica of a small head of a goddess, a thin shell of bronze with a dark green patina, almost a mask because there was no back to it, the edges of its incompleteness following pleasingly the undulations of the hair.
> 'Greek, second century B.C.,' said Lovecraft, 'found near Mersin, Cilicia. It's only a replica.'
> 'I know,' I said. 'I used to visit her at the British Museum.' As on the original the whites of the eyes had been painted in and the wearing-away of the paint had been duplicated: the dark and light gave the impression of an upward seductive glance when viewed from above; when I brought my face down to the level of her eyes her look changed to one of fear and doubt. The card on the plinth said, HEAD OF A GODDESS.
> 'She's got to be Aphrodite,' said Lovecraft. 'She couldn't be anyone else.'
> 'I think you're right. Sometimes it took four or five tries before I could walk away from her.' (39-40)

What if it were indeed Aphrodite's face, the Nymph-face of Athene, which Zeus did not allow her to wear, preferring the daughter born from his head to be ugly (cf. ch. 8.3)? Or is it perhaps the face which she took away from Medusa to punish her? Did she really *punish* Medusa, or rather protect the Gorgon's true face from Perseus's lust for murder and domination, so that he would never recognize the structure of his desire and remain a slave to his own blind spot? Perhaps Athene and Medusa are really good friends who sometimes meet to laugh about Zeus and the other mythical characters they fooled.

Fremder, at any rate, may look at that face. Small, incomplete, doubtful, without a back, exposed, the head of the goddess certainly poses no threat to him although it is captivating. He does not return the trust shown him at first, but after escaping from his mad mother, sparing her while going his own way, he may return to Caroline and the head of the goddess which is almost a mask, whoever they are. The circles of emptiness which once took the place of his unknown parents and which he also saw while being with Katya (14, 40, 93) are gone. They have been replaced by "eyes of becoming, nodes of possibility expanding in concentric circles" (184). Without Oedipus and Perseus, there remains only the terror of becoming, a terror that must be borne – and born – by us all. Even if the story were indeed no more than the dream frozen in the brain of a man floating through space, or that of dismembered Badroulbadour ascending from the tomb, the terror of becoming is that birthmark of the Real which pierces through every reality-frame. Paradoxically, it is, as Izzy wrote in his notebook, "In the storm a safe place and wild place. ... The forever-moment that has always been and will always be, the centre to which the universe configures itself" (159).

Lacan once described the role of the psychoanalyst as that of a "mediator between the man of care and the subject of absolute knowledge", which requires "subjective ascesis ... which can never be interrupted" ("The Function and Field of Speech and Language in Psychoanalysis", 105). He demanded that the analyst engage himself (never a "she" in Lacan) with the analysand in an interactive relationship; the mystic, on the other hand, is the one who is able to approach the moment of creation:

> For how could he [the analyst] possibly make his being the axis of so many lives if he knew nothing of the dialectic that engages him with these lives in a symbolic movement? Let him be well acquainted with the whorl into which his period draws him in the continued enterprise of Babel, and let him be aware of his function of an interpreter in the discord of languages. As for the darkness of the *mundus* around which the immense tower is coiled, let him leave to the mystic vision the task of seeing in it the putrescent serpent of life raised on an everlasting rod. (105-106)

Part IV:

Enlarging the Limited-Reality Consensus

11. Magic Realism – Realism Unrestrained

Before proceeding to discuss Russell Hoban's "magic realism" I will try to determine the approximate position of the genre in the terminological net spanned by various studies of nonrealistic fiction. I will begin by presenting some aspects of its history as discussed in empirical studies by Amaryll Chanady, Geoff Hancock, and Robert R. Wilson, then go on to relate it to Robert Scholes's term "fabulation" as well as to the concepts "fantastic", "uncanny" and "marvellous" as defined and refined in the theoretical studies by Tzvetan Todorov and Christine Brooke-Rose. What I have in mind is eventually to derive from these preliminaries a definition that will allow me to compare the forms and functions of magic realism (MR) in the works of various twentieth-century writers without foregoing the larger historical perspective. Susanna J. Sturgis's imaginative approach to MR breathes the spirit of the genre itself:

> On the peripheries of fantasy, in the heart of reality, exists a dimension where the two mingle with barely a raised eyebrow. The settings are recognizable, if sometimes unfamiliar ...
>
> And then ...
>
> Reality turns a somersault, twists and backflips and lands in an unexpected place. The artist scrapes away a bit of paint on her canvas; something covered over is revealed. ...
>
> Magic realism exists within the realm of f/sf [fantasy and science fiction], or speculative fiction; at the very least, it shares a long frontier and a common language. All the same, gates open for magic realism that would be slammed in science fiction's face. Some gates. At least part way.
>
> But magic realism is no model of decorum. It's paradoxical, shifty, rebellious, quirky, and loud. Sort of like ... science fiction? (...)
>
> ... Both magic realism and f/sf delight in stretching, transcending, toying with, and otherwise playing havoc with boundaries, political, literary, and otherwise. Dancing, as Ursula K. Le Guin put it so well, 'at the edge of the world,' between night and day, past and future, real and unreal until the demarcation line dissolves in a swirl of color. (...)
>
> These writers manage to switch off the internal editor that restrains the imagination with hydraulic brakes: 'No one would believe that! Are you crazy?' If they're walking down a city street and a paint-peeling fire hydrant grins up at them, they stop for conversation. (1-4)

Let's take a closer look now, however, and work towards a "proper" definition of this fascinating genre. Scholes's study *Fabulation and Metafiction* ends in the sentence "Fabulation lives" (218) – so does magic realism.

11.1. Towards a Definition

When MR was first defined by the German art critic Fanz Roh in *Nachexpressionismus: Magischer Realismus* (1925), it referred to a style of painting which

> ... distinguished itself from Expressionism by depicting the real world instead of distorting it in a fantastic manner. He [Roh] also believed that it expressed the magical spirituality of the external world and the miracle of existence. It did not copy nature, but was a second creation. (Chanady 49)

Apart from problems that arise if a term is transposed from one art to another, Roh's definition raises further questions, as Chanady points out:

> These ideas cannot be reconciled on a strictly logical level, since the subjective rendering of reality as magical or marvellous contradicts the assertion that one is painting the 'real world,' unless of course the 'real world' is simply defined as one's personal interpretation of reality. But in that case, the 'real world' varies from one artist to another. (49)

The problems of interpreting correctly what Roh meant by "depicting the real world" are of course nothing else but the problems raised by realism as a literary genre, that is, first, the question of *what* is part of reality, and secondly, if stylistic means which have been naturalized "so as to make the work seem a reflection of everyday reality" (Abrams 153) are any more valid than those which foreground a work of art's artificiality. Magic realism brings such problems to the fore rather than to conceal or, like fantasy, evade them.

For the implications of "magic" we had best turn to the programmes of Surrealism. There is, for instance, "André Breton's belief that sterile rationality should be rejected in favour of a search for the marvellous in dream sequences and free thought association" (Chanady 57), or Pierre Mabille's view that "the marvellous can best be found in the myth and folklore of primitive people still living in a pre-reflexive state and capable of grasping intuitively what civilized people can only partially find through artificial means" (Chanady 57). The purpose of their quest was to recover that (imaginary) wholeness of existence which had (allegedly) been lost in the process of civilization, for instance, through the moral rigidity of Christianity or the stress on rationality in Western culture since the Enlightenment (Hancock 43). These premises sufficiently explain why the Surrealists preferred the fields of magic and psychoanalysis as hunting grounds for the marvellous: "The surrealist revolution was based on the fact that new myths come from the imaginary. Using Freud as a springboard, automatic writing, and the power of love, the surrealists created an entry into the marvellous" (Hancock 37). I would like to add a longer passage from Hancock in which he discusses Breton's interest in magic:

> ... he was also attracted to magic which embodied the highest moral and intellectual aims: changing one's life. Magic was preferable to science and religion (which Breton mistrusted) because it attempted to conquer and control the natural and supernatural forces of the world. Magic was also secret and irrational, above the ordinary laws of experience. As a means of liberating the mind, the magic mentality was fundamental, stretching back into antiquity. The words *mage* and *magie* originate in a Mesopotamian phoneme meaning 'deep'. (...)
>
> Breton's concern with the magical origin of all art was published in 1957 as *L'Art magique*. This was a survey of the primal origins of magic and religion, beginning with prehistoric art, and extending through Mesopotamia and Egypt. Breton felt that art had lost its magic force in Cretan and Greek sculpture, which emphasized human and not fantastic figures. Over the centuries, magic went underground in an adversary position against Christianity. But it was accessible to those who looked at the 'magic paintings' of Brueghel the Elder and Hieronymus Bosch, to name only two.... This secret tradition extends to the Gothic works of Goya, and the magical themes found in Gauguin and Rousseau, then it becomes explicit again in the Cubists and the surrealist painters. (38)

One can summarize all these points by saying that "magic" implies an interest in the supernatural and the repressed contents of the unconscious as well as a renewed respect for intuitive knowledge and the nonrealistic products of the imagination.

A group of Latin American writers believed that derivatives of Roh's term, combined with notions from the Surrealists' programme, were particularly fit to characterize their depictions of the marvels of their continent, among them Miguel Angel Asturias and Alejo Carpentier, who had collaborated with the Surrealists during their stay in Paris in the 1920s (Chanady 57). They were thus the earliest conscious practitioners of MR as a literary genre – according to their own definitions.

> Arturo Uslar Pietri, the Venezuelan author who was perhaps the first person to apply the term magic realism to Latin American fiction, defined the mode in 1948 as a 'poetic divination or poetic negation of reality,' in which man is considered 'as a mystery.' (Chanady 52)

Uslar Pietri's indebtedness to Roh and the Surrealists is evident:

> In his own short stories, the Venezuelan author describes reality as strange, without referring to myth and magic in the anthropological sense. ... Uslar Pietri's poetic style, characterized by metaphor and personification, makes empirical reality appear magical. (Chanady 53)

Note that supernatural elements are excluded from his stories; it is merely the style which generates a magical effect.

One year later, the Cuban writer Alejo Carpentier, who called "the marvellous the subconscious of Latin America" (Hancock 36), formulated a concept that was slightly different from Uslar Pietri's magic realism in the prologue to his novel *The Kingdom of this World* (1949) – "lo real maravilloso", or the marvellous real. It is notably Carpentier's rejection of stylistic defamiliarization which distinguishes his term from Uslar Pietri's and at the same time expresses his critique of the Surrealists (Chanady 57); Mabille's influence nevertheless shows in Carpentier's turning to native lore:

> According to Carpentier, Latin American history is nothing but a chronicle of the marvellous real, because of the continent's impressive natural beauty, the legends it inspired about the spring of eternal youth and Eldorado, and the presence of the Indians and blacks who still believe in myth and magic. He believed that the New World reality is more marvellous than the artificial, fantastic creations found in Arthurian romances, Gothic literature and Surrealism. Much of Carpentier's fiction is characterized by this attitude, which is frequently identified with that of the magic realists. (Chanady 51)

Once more, the supernatural is not considered to be part of the reality described as marvellous real; the marvellous is merely intimated, here "inspired", by the exotic quality of nature and the fascination of strange rites on an outsider more familiar with Europe than with his home continent, who does not himself believe in myth and magic (Chanady 53).[1] However, simply watching, taking a voyeuristic look at the supposedly intact magic reality of the Indians and black practitioners of the Voodoo cult does not alter the rational and materialistic basis of the curious outsider's reality but on the contrary serves to confirm it. While the Surrealists tried to retrieve for themselves whatever had been lost or repressed by their own culture by cajoling information from their unconscious, practising automatic writing, composing incongruous images, and studying myths, fairy tales and magic techniques (Hancock 41), Uslar Pietri and especially Carpentier remained realists at heart. They simply defined realistic literature with a Latin American theme as new genres. Only Uslar Pietri did not altogether neglect the creative potential of fiction: Aspiring to defamiliarise reality by linguistic means, he may be called one of the fore-

1 There is a link between the incredibly real I tried to trace in Hoban's *Turtle Diary* (cf. ch. 5.1) and Carpentier's notion of the marvellous real. In both cases an onlooker's preconceived notions of reality clash with what he actually sees; he either reacts with disbelief or, in Carpentier's case, with astonishment. José Ortega y Gasset, the Spanish essayist and philosopher from whose *Meditations on Quixote* (1914) the term incredibly real has been borrowed, actually prepared the ground for both the Surrealists and the Latin American magic realists.

fathers of the French *Nouveau Roman* (cf. Brooke-Rose 291ff.). However, he might have gone beyond forms to innovate the range of themes as well. In contrast to the realists' problematic tenet that fiction ought "to present an accurate imitation of life as it is" (Abrams 152), fiction does not necessarily have to observe objective truth conditions since its medium is language and since there is no one-to-one correspondence between reality and language;[2] fiction therefore invites *magic realism*, that is the combination of natural and supernatural themes. As Hancock says:

> Magic realism raises fundamental questions. How do we know ourselves and our society? How do we deal with that knowledge in our bones? Are we in exile from our roots by choice or by necessity? How do we de-colonize our imaginations? (37)

In the years after Uslar Pietri and Carpentier, many writers, Latin American and other, have understood that their fiction is the very place to create a substitute for the *magic reality* they and their readers cannot experience themselves any more. In 1968, the Guatemalan author Miguel Angel Asturias likened the melting of the two rationalities in MR to a state of mind known to Indians:

> ... for the Indians there exists an intermediate reality between the real and the magic that is 'a melting of the visible and the tangible, the hallucination and the dream.' According to him, magic realism 'has a direct relationship to the original mentality of the Indians. ...' (quoted in Chanady 55)

Yet, since supernatural motifs are no prerogative of certain cultures or retrievable only through clever techniques for probing the unconscious, there is no need for writers to delimit the range of such motifs to a stock of myths of "primitive" people or to images straight from the unconscious; this is where MR turns out to be a category related to, but much broader than Surrealism. Moreover, it is the presence of both supernatural *and* natural elements which constitutes MR:

---

2 I do not claim that there is no correspondence between reality and language, i.e. that language is altogether self-referential or autonomous, as Todorov writes: "Les mots ont gagné une autonomie que les choses ont perdue" (*Introduction*, 177). But their relationship is complex: a word like "unicorn", for instance, clearly illustrates that language can designate things which do not exist as real objects in the outside world, it is a sign referring to other signs (the example has been borrowed from Umberto Eco's *Einführung in die Semiotik*, 71; ch. A.2.II); the opposite is true as well – for certain contents there are no words: why should there be any literary symbols if all things could be said straight? Finally, consider Gertrude Stein's "a rose is a rose is a rose is a rose" (Eco 149-150, ch. A.3.I.5): the phrase does not merely refer to a "rose in the outside world" but also to the word "rose" as a word; moreover, it alerts us to various uses of this word, as part of definitions, figure of speech, or symbol, all of which are evoked at the same time as rejected by the phrase.

> ... magic realism is also a fantastic reflection of something that once happened, however distorted it may be in the retelling. The fiction is based on 'actuality' as far as that can be understood; no symbols intrude. The writer accumulates precise details around a probable event, or a probable legend, or a likely hyperbole. (Hancock 41)

Or as Chanady concludes: "... it is easy to go one step further and consider any fictitious juxtaposition of the natural and the supernatural as belonging to the mode" (50). The term "juxtaposition", which Chanady will later on modify as "unproblematic" (56), calls for discussion. In my analysis of Russell Hoban's and other writers' texts, I hope to show that the relation between natural and supernatural elements is more complex than a mere juxtaposition, and that this relation, or rather these relations are far from "unproblematic".

Robert Scholes's term "fabulation" also refers to a complex genre but differs from MR in a number of ways. His term could not possibly be ignored – least of all because it is mentioned in connection with magic realism in M. H. Abrams's well-known *Glossary of Literary Terms*:

> The term **magic realism** has been applied to the prose fiction of Jorge Luis Borges in Argentina, as well as to the work of writers such as García Márquez in Columbia, Günter Grass in Germany, and John Fowles in England; they interweave, in an ever-shifting pattern, a sharply etched realism with fantastic and dreamlike elements. Robert Scholes has popularized the term **fabulation** to describe the large and growing class of such recent novels, which do not fit the traditional categories either of realism or of romance. These violate, in a variety of ways, standard novelistic expectations by drastic – and sometimes highly successful – experiments with subject matter, form, style, temporal sequence, and fusions of the everyday, the fantastic, the mythical, and the nightmarish, in renderings that blur traditional distinctions between what is serious or trivial, horrible or ludicrous, tragic or comic. (122)

Further features, which Abrams has omitted, are the bent of fabulation for allegory (Scholes 24), its problematizing of the concepts of history and historiography (208) and its "direct plunge back into the tide of story" (25). While Abrams's definition underscores the subversive aspect of fabulation, its *violation* of expectations, Scholes more than once points to the *delight* in form and story-telling writings of this kind imply. Although various of the enumerated features point to a similarity between the two genres, fabulation is a broader category than MR if we regard the combination of abstract features in each genre. To elaborate on this, it will be helpful to take recourse to categories defined in theoretical studies.

Theory has actually made a number of essential contributions to the study of genres. In his *Introduction à la littérature fantastique* (1970), Todorov begins by distinguishing beween historical and systematic genres. A systematic genre is deduced from a theoretical model; historical genres, on the other hand, are empirical categories derived from concrete works of fiction (18). Scholes's definition shows that he refers to historical genres and modes: "*Among all these works* we can trace the various diachronic relationships of literary genres as they evolve in time, and the synchronic relations of literary modes as they exist across time" (Scholes 107; emphasis added). Todorov is not concerned with historical genres at first but discusses Northrop Frye's influential *Anatomy of Criticism* (1957). He dismisses Frye's list of theoretical genres and modes as incoherent and unsystematic, locating as a main source of their deficiency the arbitrariness of their defining features (19-21). Having determined the constitutive elements of a work of fiction, which fall under three aspects, the verbal (style and perspective), the syntactic (plotting), and the semantic (themes) (24f.), he goes on to define three systematic genres which are essential for fantastic fiction in the widest sense: the pure fantastic, the uncanny, and the marvellous (28ff., 46ff.). His main criterion is the reader's reaction to the nature of events depicted in a story (37); the protagonists usually do but need not share this reaction (37f.). The pure fantastic implies that the reader hesitates between a natural and a supernatural explanation for the events described; the text builds up an ambiguity which cannot be resolved (37). In examples of the uncanny, a shocking, incredible or extraordinary event is given a natural explanation (51-53); the marvellous, finally, is defined by the unquestionable existence of supernatural events (46f., 59f.).[3] Todorov insists that in fantastic fiction, the events must not be given either an allegorical or a poetic interpretation (38). The latter is due to his notion of a poem as an altogether self-referential construct of no descriptive value (65) – an example of formalism in the extreme, to which I would not

3 A comparison with Freud's notion of the uncanny, as he develops it in his essay "Das Unheimliche" (1919), shows that Todorov has narrowed the scope of this term. Freud's fictional uncanny in fact includes Todorov's "fantastic": "Das Unheimliche des Erlebens kommt zustande, wenn *verdrängte* infantile Komplexe durch einen Eindruck wieder belebt werden oder wenn *überwundene* primitive Überzeugungen wieder bestätigt scheinen. ... Das Unheimliche der Fiktion – der Phantasie, der Dichtung – ... ist ... weit reichhaltiger als das Unheimliche des Erlebens, es umfasst dieses in seiner Gänze und dann noch anderes, was unter den Bedingungen des Erlebens nicht vorkommt. ... Das paradox klingende Ergebnis ist, *dass in der Dichtung vieles nicht unheimlich ist, was unheimlich wäre, wenn es sich im Leben ereignete, und dass in der Dichtung viele Möglichkeiten bestehen, unheimliche Wirkungen zu erzielen, die fürs Leben wegfallen.* (...) Der Dichter hat ... noch ein Mittel zur Verfügung, durch welches er sich dieser unserer Auflehnung entziehen und gleichzeitig die Bedingungen für das Erreichen seiner Absichten verbessern kann. Es besteht darin, dass er uns lange Zeit über nicht erraten lässt, welche Voraussetzungen er eigentlich für die von ihm angenommene Welt gewählt hat, oder dass er kunstvoll und arglistig einer solchen entscheidenden Aufklärung bis zum Ende ausweicht" (271-273; Freud's emphasis).

subscribe.[4] If Uslar Pietri's technique of the stylistic defamiliarization of reality is considered, however, it will become clear why Todorov tries to preclude poetic interpretations: a reader cannot react to the nature of events if the only "strange" thing in the text is the style. His rejection of an allegorical interpretation, on the other hand, is based on the assumption that an allegory explicitly points to its double meaning, one literal, the other ethical, with the literal meaning being more or less obliterated by the moral; an allegory can therefore exist independent of the reaction of the reader (67-69). But Christine Brooke-Rose convincingly suggests that there is more similarity than difference between allegory and the fantastic; she concludes:

> In other words, is not the fantastic as defined by Todorov a modern development (non-hierarchised levels, stronger paradox) of medieval allegory – two among various ways of writing metaphorically, or on several levels, or paradigmatically – just as the marvellous is a version of Frye's romance mode? I say 'as defined by Todorov' because clearly his constraint applies only to the 'pure' fantastic: the marvellous ... can easily tend towards encoded allegory, just as the uncanny and indeed all 'strange' fiction onto which the uncanny opens out can easily tend towards at least a moral meaning. (70)

In chapter five (80-96), Todorov discusses the discourse of the fantastic. He notices a tendency in such works to use figurative language literally (82). Moreover, a first-person narrator usually mediates the events (87).These are arranged in an irreversible order, that is, the reader ought to read the text from the beginning to the end without skipping any passages if her pleasure of reading is not to be spoilt (94f.). Brooke-Rose is quite right to point to the blurring of categories in this and subsequent chapters: while the special use of figurative language, first person narrative and irreversibility are discussed as aspects of the fantastic, Todorov's examples are from the marvellous, the fantastic-marvellous, the fantastic-uncanny, and the uncanny as well (Brooke-Rose 83). He has, in other words, begun to talk about the fantastic as a historical genre, fantastic being used "in the more generally accepted sense" (Brooke-Rose 82).

Todorov's classification of themes in chapters six through nine, actually a by-product rather than the main interest of his study, forms its most intriguing part. As a matter of fact, he cannot possibly speak about fantastic themes in particular because the discussion of themes bans the reader, whose hesitation is

---

4 "On voit maintenant pourquoi la lecture poétique constitue un écueil pour le fantastique. Si, en lisant un texte, on refuse toute représentation et que l'on considère chaque phrase comme une pure combinaison sémantique, le fantastique ne pourra apparaître..." (65). It is interesting to see that Todorov relativizes his own argument a little later by admitting, in parentheses, that there are indeed "des anthologies de 'poésie fantastique'..." (65).

constitutive for his pure fantastic, from the field of vision (109). Having criticized earlier attempts at classifying literary themes for being unsystematic, or else, for classifying according to unliterary categories (97-112), he decides first to examine what themes can co-occur in stories and then to group them according to their compatibility (113ff.). Two major groups emerge: themes of the self (*les thèmes du je*) and themes of the other (*les thèmes du tu*). Under themes of the self he subsumes such events as metamorphoses, the appearance of fantastic beings as agents of good or bad luck (115), or a sense of pan-determinism (116): everything is meaningful, nothing left to chance. The borderline between the physical and the spiritual worlds seems to have been abolished (120). Since themes of the self are tied to the perception and consciousness system, many works of this group problematize the nature of impressions, especially of vision (126f.). In interpretations denying the existence of the supernatural, unusual phenomena of this group tend to be interpreted as products of a child's mind, as mystical experiences, as symptoms of psychosis, or of drug abuse (121f.).

Themes of the other are related to the unconscious; love, especially sexual desire, perversions, violence, death and life after death, the appearance of vampires and the devil fall under this heading (145f.). Since protagonists seek to establish relationships with other people (or supernatural beings), their discourses form a central element (147). Todorov expands the analogy to psychoanalytical categories which he has established for the first group by tentatively suggesting a link between themes of the other and neurosis (155). Although he does not pursue the thought, Todorov points out that the dichotomy between themes of the self and themes of the other might as well be analogically linked to social structures, or to attitudes towards the supernatural (161). But above all, self and other, or literally "I" and "you", are categories which are both abstract and connected with language, hence with literature (164). Works which combine themes from both groups, e.g. Balzac's *Louis Lambert*, seem to disprove Todorov's classification. But since their very incompatibility is the point at issue, his classification according to the compatibility of themes remains valid (148).

When Todorov tests the theoretical genre of the fantastic against concrete examples of late nineteenth-century fiction, his examples of the pure fantastic (Todorov mentions only two, Henry James's "The Turn of the Screw" and Prosper Mérimée's *La Venus d'Ille*) prove to be in a minority (48f.); most of the texts combine the fantastic with the uncanny or the marvellous. Todorov illustrates his find in a diagram, where the pure fantastic is merely represented as a line between the two mixed genres (49):

uncanny I fantastic-uncanny I fantastic-marvellous I marvellous

Christine Brooke-Rose is right to criticise Todorov for suppressing the pure fantastic and continuing to focus on historical genres (Brooke-Rose 65-68). This is inconsistent with his own precepts: earlier on, Todorov criticised Frye's abandoning eight of the thirteen theoretical modes that are predicted by his model because he could find only five of them being realized; Todorov then insisted on the importance of setting up theoretical models which would be able to predict non-existent historical genres (19). The diagram moreover suggests that his genres form a continuum along which only neighbouring categories can combine. Note that Todorov does not say so: in his last chapter he mentions Kafka's *Metamorphosis* as an example of twentieth-century fiction in which the uncanny combines with the marvellous (180) – an example of MR. However, since the diagram may give rise to misunderstandings,[5] the systematic genres ought to be explicitly defined as separate categories.

I have to make two more objections to Todorov's theoretical genres: the first concerns the evaluative connotations of his terms, the second, the role of "the reader" in setting up the distinctions. Whereas "uncanny" has negative connotations, "marvellous" tends in the other direction. We either need more general categories (e.g. natural / fantastic / supernatural), or supplement Todorov's set with corresponding terms of the opposite value. The second option will of course increase the range of differentiations. The result is a grid of theoretical categories divided, on the one hand, into positive and negative evaluations of events, on the other, according to the nature of the events (both from the perspective of the implied reader):

	NATURAL	INDETERMINATE	SUPERNATURAL
POSITIVE	cosy		marvellous
		fantastic	
NEGATIVE	uncanny		horrific

Two new terms appear in my grid: the cosy and the horrific. The cosy, as supplement to the uncanny, needs only little explanation; it suggests ease, health, reason, the absence of lies, earthly happiness. If Swift's Houyhnhnms were not altogether marvellous creatures, the description of their uneventful lives would no doubt be an example of the pure cosy. But Swift does not believe in their snug idyll: by creating slightly ridiculous imaginary beings,

5 Cf. Brooke-Rose's ostensibly half-hearted attempt at turning the diagram into a circle by joining up its ends and inserting "Realism" between the uncanny and the marvellous. She cannot exclude the possibility that "Todorov's model supposes a linear movement on the hesitation criterion" (84).

thus adding one more example of the supernatural to Gulliver's adventures, he signals his distrust of a surplus of horse-sense. The horrific, as supplement to the marvellous, suggests horror and panic in the face of an involuntary exposure of the protagonists to malevolent supernatural forces such as devils, ghosts, vampires, dragons, etc. The stress here is on "involuntary" and "malevolent"; for there are numerous stories in which heroes set out to meet dragons (medieval romances) or ghosts ultimately prove to be friendly (Wilde's Sir Simon de Canterville) – these are examples of the marvellous rather than of the horrific. *Dracula* is horrific for the greater part until the surviving protagonists pluck up all their courage to brave the King-Vampire and his fellow creatures; as the victims turn into heroes, the story shifts from the horrific to the marvellous.

I was tempted to introduce another category as a positive supplement to the fantastic: the mystic. The following considerations were in my mind. First, all of Todorov's examples of the pure fantastic imply some danger for the protagonists, and the mixed genres, among them the so-called Gothic novels, mostly end in the discovery of mental illness or fraud (uncanny endings), or of some demonic force (horrific ending). Moreover, discussing the preference of the nineteenth century for the fantastic, he calls it the bad conscience of that period (176). That is, the historical examples which Todorov has used to illustrate his theoretical category charge the term negatively. A positive counterpart to the fantastic would have had to share with it its most important defining feature: the implied reader's hesitation between a natural and a supernatural explanation. But if the reader cannot decide between these two options, it is also impossible for him to evaluate the events. Hence, the theoretical genre is neither positive nor negative.[6]

Todorov's classification of themes actually appears to provide for two versions of the historical fantastic, however. If themes of the self are realised as sincere mystic quests and themes of the other as open quests for love, they will create a more positive variant, which tends to be resolved in a marvellous or a cosy ending; however, if themes of the other imply that unknown forces or repressed desires victimise the protagonists, or if they deny their selves and

6 Incidentally, what is true for the fantastic also applies to realizations of the natural and the supernatural. There is hardly any work of art where the uncanny is not shown to be part of the cosy, or the horrific, part of the marvellous. Hence positive and negative evaluations often collapse when the theoretical genres are put into practice. Actually, Freud's preliminary discussion of the etymology of "heimlich" brings to the fore an uncanny ambivalence of the term's two meanings: in the sense of "hidden, secret" it contradicts its other meaning "familiar, known" – in other words, "unheimlich" is always already included in "heimlich" (Freud, "Das Unheimliche", 244-250). However, Freud does not pursue the idea of evaluative, or ethical ambivalence; instead he goes on to discuss the uncanny in terms of the developmental stages of the psychic apparatus, cf. note 3 above.

embark upon their mystic quests in the wrong spirit, the fantastic will inevitably tend towards the uncanny and the horrific. Villiers de l'Isle-Adam's *Véra*, which Todorov discusses as an example of the fantastic-marvellous (73f.), may serve to illustrate this: At the beginning of the story, the protagonist aspires to a contact with the supernatural not for selfish reasons but in order to achieve a resurrection of his dead beloved; his enlarged sensitivity (theme of the self) is merely a means to the supreme end (theme of the other). His servant, on the other hand, assumes that he is mad (theme of the self), while the reader cannot possibly decide who is right. When the young woman eventually returns from the country of the dead, the fantastic turns into the marvellous. Mind that the marvellous here ultimately serves to realise a theme of the other: the protagonist's love proves to be stronger than death; but themes of the self and themes of the other are probably less incompatible in practice than in theory, conflicts between both the rule rather than the exception, the very stuff of fiction.

It would be just as wrong to consider themes of the other generally negative as to associate themes of the self with a protagonist's bliss. Sisir Kumar Ghose, the author of the *Encyclopaedia Britannica* article on mysticism writes: "The holy is not always and altogether a pleasant experience. Often shrouded in a fear that is more than fear, it is an inward dread and shuddering" (vol. 12, 789). Preferences for the darker or the brighter sides of each type of theme, and also for a genre, depend as much on a writer's individual disposition as on the function of literature and the expectations of the audience in each period. Brooke-Rose's question about general affinities between Todorov's genres and types of themes is therefore unanswerable:

> ... it would have been interesting to have some kind of link made to know for instance whether the themes of the self ... , or the themes of the other ... are more, or less, predominant in the marvellous or the uncanny or the pure fantastic. (84)

One might only, cautiously, say that Villiers de l'Isle-Adam's fantastic-marvellous story, actually a predecessor of MR, about a theme of the other is not representative of the late nineteenth century; the gloomier side of the theme clearly prevailed in the unrealistic literature of that era as a result of the many sexual taboos dominating society. But so did the negative side of themes of the self: there was no room for mystic quests in a positivistic age. Since Todorov's view of the fantastic is based on, and biased by, the evidence of the literature of that time, he associates the fantastic with nothing but the negative aspects of both types of theme. Speculating that its only function was to bring up censored topics, Todorov argues that fantastic literature could not but disappear when psychoanalysis began to deal with the darker realms of the psyche (168f.).[7] Even though the argument has its appeal, the fact remains that fantastic literature, or more generally nonrealistic fiction, continues to be written, that is, literature cannot simply be "replaced" by psychoanalysis. It definitely has more functions than the one mentioned by Todorov.[8]

My last objection to Todorov's theoretical genres concerns, as I said earlier on, the role of "the reader". Having defined a work of fiction as a linguistic structure, he bases the most important criterion for distinguishing between his categories on an elusive extralinguistic factor, the reader who is always immersed in history and subject to the social and aesthetic conventions that are predominant at a given time. The supposedly ahistorical Todorovian figure who hesitates, in the case of the pure fantastic, between a natural and a supernatural explanation for the events depicted is in fact a Cartesian subject firmly rooted in realism. Since every reader does not match this description, it would perhaps be safer to define the pure fantastic on textual grounds as a category in which certain semantic elements do raise questions about the nature of events depicted, cancelling each other out so that several mutually exclusive interpretations will result. All the same, the fantastic will remain in the realm of realistic fiction as long as its natural elements serve as the unquestioned background against which the "truth" of the supernatural ones is discussed and called into question. The borderline between the natural and the supernatural is foregrounded in the process. MR, on the other hand, combines the natural and the supernatural without giving precedence to either. Besides natural elements it may contain fantastic ones, but these alone are insufficient. The adjective "magic" signals that the borderline between the natural and the supernatural, which is still present in the fantastic, has become permeable. Both the natural and the supernatural are shown to be equivalent representations of reality which merely differ in the conventions but not in the degree of "authenticity" which link them to the object of representation, i.e. the "natural" is just as arbitrary a depiction of reality as the supernatural.

Like fabulation, MR is a historical genre originating in the twentieth century although its predecessors could probably be traced back to the oldest examples of literature. Scholes limits his term "fabulation" to prose fiction written after Borges, and especially after the mid-1960s (3, 56). These dates are also relevant

7 "... la psychanalyse a remplacé (et par là-même a rendu inutile) la littérature fantastique. On n'a pas besoin aujourd'hui d'avoir recours au diable pour parler d'un désir sexuel excessif, ni aux vampires pour désigner l'attirance exercée par les cadavres..." (168-169).

8 In "Der Dichter und das Phantasieren" Freud says that literature is entertaining because it provides relief from tension (223).

for MR: while the Surrealists frequently abandoned realism altogether, Borges was one of the first writers who systematically explored possibilities and limitations of the natural and the supernatural by bringing them into a dialectic. Without calling himself so, he became not only a fabulator in general but one of the first magic realists almost ten years earlier than his realist colleagues Uslar Pietri and Carpentier, who would introduce the term MR to South American fiction. Kafka's *Metamorphosis* (1916) could of course be discussed as an earlier twentieth-century example of MR. Moreover, it would no doubt be interesting to work out the connections between MR and predecessors such as Swift's *Gulliver's Travels*, but this would exceed the scope of this study. Beginning with Borges's short stories has the advantage that within the work of one writer, all the shades of realistic and nonrealistic literature, fantasy, science fiction, MR, the fantastic and the sceptical realism of a fabulator can be compared with and distinguished from each other. Russell Hoban's work exemplifies practically all the facets of fabulation, too; the term thus anchors him in the present, in the midst of a contemporary "movement". If I nevertheless insist on discussing his use of MR, or his specific versions of science fiction, historiographic metafiction, or the realistic novel, this is to do justice to the variety of forms he has worked with.

Fabulation as a collective term tends to blur such distinctions for its examples run the whole gamut from works without any supernatural elements – e.g. Iris Murdoch's *The Unicorn*, which contains at best fantastic hints at the existence of the supernatural – to pure examples of supernatural fiction, which are set in an altogether imaginary spatio-temporal realm – e.g. John Barth's fantasy *Giles Goat-Boy*. Robert R. Wilson's concise distinction between realism (1), fantasy (2) and MR (3) according to their handling of space will illustrate my point:

> The concept of a fictional world, in which signification generates the experience of co-presence and placing, may then be forcefully simplified into three subdivisions: 1) the fictional world in which all the deictics and descriptions operate as if they were being used in the extra-textual world and which, thus, constantly begs comparison to that world; 2) the fictional world in which all indications of distance, capacity or arrangement are generated in accordance with self-contained axioms or 'rules' (this is the space of a self-contained game); 3) the fictional world in which the indications of local place are sometimes those of the extra-textual world, but at other times they are those of another place which, if it were to exist purely, would be a closed axiomatic game of the second kind. (Wilson 68)

If MR is the combination of realism with fantasy, the result are stories like Borges's "Tlön, Uqbar, Orbis Tertius".

Analogically, the handling of time might serve to distinguish MR from science fiction, the other type of supernatural fiction mentioned in the initial quotation from Susanna J. Sturgis. If the main unrealistic element of a story is its setting in the future, and unfamiliar objects and conditions are derived from the imagined progress and/or failure of technology and human resources, we are in the realm of science fiction. Most theoreticians as a matter of fact classify science fiction as a subtype of supernatural fiction, too, e.g. Todorov, as a subtype of the marvellous (62). I do not hesitate to call it "supernatural fiction". Its conservative practitioners, though, generally do not wish to pass their works for imaginary prophecies of the future, which they nevertheless are, but for probable extrapolations based on exact scientific facts. Brooke-Rose, who supports Darko Suvin, thus underlines the close relationship between science fiction and realism (78f., 81f., 99-102). Certain other science fiction writers have gone further: until recently they have displayed a veritable contempt for colleagues with an unfirm grasp of the sciences or a disposition to abandon realistic techniques (cf. Atheling's comments on writers of the New Wave, 128ff.). All the same, science fiction is no science, nor can it be truly realistic: after all, the "reality" it pretends to imitate exists no more than the deliberately unrealistic settings of fantasy. Puschmann-Nalenz, who has so far been consulted in terms of science fiction genre definitions (cf. chs. 6.4 and 10.1) abstains from resolving the quarrel: she presents the status of reality as the "central paradox" of science fiction (109, also see 92f., 103-107). At any rate combinations of science fiction with other nonrealistic genres cannot be treated as deviations but are the rule (cf. Scholes and Rabkin 165ff.). When science fiction blends into MR, the outcome is such novels as *Fremder*.

MR appears in a great variety of shapes and fulfils diverse purposes, but it will be the task of my next chapter to illustrate these.

11.2. A Magical Mystery Tour from Borges to Rushdie

Beginning with Jorge Luis Borges, I will now take you on a magical mystery tour of the world. While Borges's short stories have been chosen with the intention of, once more, exemplifying and refining the terms presented in the previous chapter, that is, above all, "fantasy", "magic realism" and "the pure fantastic", the other works present variations of MR. They vary in the kinds of supernatural elements employed, in the ratio of, and the qualitative relationship between, natural and supernatural elements, as well as in the function of their magic realism.

JORGE LUIS BORGES: "THE CIRCULAR RUINS", "TLÖN, UQBAR, ORBIS TERTIUS", "DOCTOR BRODIE'S REPORT", "THE LIBRARY OF BABEL", "THE IMMORTAL", "THE OTHER", AND "THE SOUTH"

Borges's "The Circular Ruins" lends itself ideally for a first approach because it is not only an example of MR but a story about the creation and the effects of MR. A gray man, obviously a Zoroastrian, travels to the circular ruins of an ancient temple. "The purpose which guided him was not impossible, though supernatural. He wanted to dream a man; he wanted to dream him in minute entirety and impose him on reality" ("The Circular Ruins", 58). His first attempt fails because he does not allow sufficient time for the project. In his dream, he is a teacher who selects from an enormous group of students one who is "worthy of participating in the universe" (58). He soon realizes that he can "expect nothing from those pupils who accepted his doctrine passively" (58). Thus, he singles out one sceptical student who resembles him. Before the young man can enter reality, however, the teacher loses him because his haste has put him under too great a mental strain: he cannot dream any more. After recovering from his block, the man makes a more modest second attempt, no longer as the teacher of his creature but now as his "father". So as not to fail a second time, he seeks help from the deity of his temple. The god of fire agrees to support him but imposes a condition: The dreamer will have to send his "son" to another ruined temple after having instructed him in all the rites. Two years pass until he is "ready to be born" and sent away (61). The son is spared the knowledge that he is only a phantom even though the old man never ceases to worry that the son's ability to walk on fire will eventually lead to the discovery of his secret. It is the magician, however, who is shocked into acknowledging the truth about himself. When a fire is consuming his own temple, he resigns himself to death, but the flames cannot "bite his flesh" (63). He is somebody's projection, too; his "reality" has been an illusion like his son's.

The story's outcome can be interpreted in two ways: one formalist, the other humanist. On the one hand, it creates metafictional awareness: so-called realistic elements like the dreamer are as contrived and fictitious as explicitly supernatural ones; the distinction we make in stories between elements which seem to "imitate" reality and those which "depart" from it is only gradual, not absolute. Both are verbal constructs. Words, moreover, are never quite adequate for communicating experience, as Borges pointed out in an interview with César Fernández Moreno:

> At some point later on it occurred to me that words always presuppose a shared experience ... if a mystic has had an immediate experience of God, or of truth

> (which comes to be the same thing), he can't communicate that experience to others because for him that sound belongs to that experience, while for the rest of us it is simply a word in the dictionary, a word of rather vague sense. (Borges and Fernández Moreno 7)

And yet, as we can read in "The Immortal", "[when] the end draws near, there no longer remain any remembered images; only words remain" (148). Deficient though words, and hence our fictions, may be, they can all the same help us to understand experience once we have made it. This is the second insight offered by the end of "The Circular Ruins". Because of his knowledge of his imaginary son, because of his fiction, the old man knows how to interpret his own incombustibility – reference comes into being. Borges is no formalist, as Scholes underlines in *Fabulation and Metafiction* (9ff.); his fictions go beyond mere self-referentiality as they refer the readers to a reality that is more real than language.[1]

The fact that the magician's first attempt at dreaming a man fails can be interpreted in terms of the allegory, too: the student who knows that he is illusory cannot be "imposed" on the world. He maybe represents fiction that points excessively to its artificiality, supernatural fiction which does not even try to hide its unreality. The second dream child, on the other hand, has been shaped with greater care to make him fit for the world. He is allowed to remain unselfconscious even though the days of his ignorance may be counted as are those of his creator. He might stand for a kind of MR which uses its unrealistic elements most unobtrusively.

Throughout his career, Borges experimented with both realistic and nonrealistic stories, giving preference to neither mode even though he is more generally associated with his fabulatory output:

> ... I don't think the poet should try to be realistic or try to avoid it; whether we like it or not we are immersed ... in reality; we are a part of reality and can't leave off being real and contemporary ... what does it feel like to commit a murder? – Dostoevsky imagines a book called *Crime and Punishment*, a realistic novel, or a novel of realistic appearance; while Shakespeare imagines or re-creates the story of Macbeth and the three witches or fates. Both means are equally valid. ... In other words, the symbols we use are of very little importance. What is important is that the symbols be charged with emotion ... (Borges and Fernández Moreno 14)

1 This must be pointed out, for many readers of Borges's stories have completely overlooked that he never merely wrote about books, see e.g. Angela Carter's account of her misreading of Borges in the interview with John Haffenden: "I had spent a long time acquiescing very happily with the Borges idea that books were about books, and then I began to think: if all books are about books, what are the other books about? Where does it all stop? Borges is happy with the idea of a vast *Ur*-book, which is a ridiculous proposition" (Carter and Haffenden 79).

There may be no conflict between the various means of representation in Borges,[2] but there certainly is one between representations and the objects represented. Many of Borges's stories stage a competition between "real" life and the world of ideas, that is of philosophy and the imagination. One would assume that the sympathies of an author who said of himself that he felt as if he had never left his father's library and the world of books (Borges and Fernández Moreno 4) are clearly on the side of ideas; but in fact, he often describes a world threatened by mental constructs. Thus, "Tlön, Uqbar, Orbis Tertius", the first story of *Ficciones* illustrates the danger of ideologies. The narrator, author of an article for *The Anthology of Fantastic Literature, 1940*, begins by relating how his friend Bioy Casares quoted a heresiarch from a country that he had never heard of before, Uqbar. It was not mentioned anywhere but in Casares's obviously pirated edition of a volume of *The Anglo-American Cyclopaedia*, which differed from any other copy by the addition of an article on Uqbar on its last pages. Two years after this discovery, an English friend of the narrator's father, Herbert Ashe, dies. The narrator finds at his hotel a strange octavo volume: "The book was written in English, and had 1001 pages. On the yellow leather spine, and again on the title page, I read these words: *A First Encyclopaedia of Tlön*. Volume XI. Hlaer to Jangr" (21). Tlön, as we know from the first section of the article, is the imaginary region to which all the literature of Uqbar refers. In the years that follow, the narrator and his friends amuse themselves by trying to find out who has invented Tlön. The volume of the encyclopaedia is so rich, and sometimes also contradictory, that it cannot have been the work of one person. This thesis will prove to be right. After adding examples of Tlönist thinking – it is a planet where idealism is the norm while materialism occasions "scandal" (26) – the narrator concludes his article. However, seven years later, in 1947, he adds a postscript. This is the point at which Borges's story, written in 1941, turns into MR. It does so not only because the last section is set in the future but above all because the imaginary construct of a secret society which was founded in the early seventeenth century and counted among its members the philosopher George Berkeley and the mystic Johann Valentin Andreä has begun to influence "reality" in a significant way. Various objects from Tlön are found, inaugurating what might be termed a "Tlönization" of the world: a compass

2 Nowadays that representations are seen in conjunction with socio-political and historical contexts, which usually favour one or the other type of representation, this modernist aesthetic tolerance has lost the innocence of a self-evident truth. See, e.g. chs. 3 and 5 of Linda Hutcheon's *A Poetics of Postmodernism: History, Theory, Fiction* (New York: Routledge, 1988). I would not want to criticize Borges on these grounds, though, for that would mean to disregard *his* particular context. Also see my discussion of Nabokov's defence of artistic freedom in ch. 8.4, p. 380.

(32), a little cone "made of a metal which does not exist in this world" but which is the symbol of "divinity in certain religions in Tlön" (33), and finally, a complete forty-volume edition of the *First Encyclopaedia of Tlön* (33). There is a good deal of irony in the fact that the infiltration from the fictitious idealistic planet must take recourse to material objects; but the narrator too becomes the involuntary butt of satire. He tries to understate the seriousness of what is going on around him:

> Almost immediately, reality gave ground on more than one point. The truth is that it hankered to give ground. Ten years ago, any symmetrical system whatsoever which gave the appearance of order – dialectical materialism, anti-Semitism, Nazism – was enough to fascinate men. Why not fall under the spell of Tlön and submit to the minute and vast evidence of an ordered planet? Useless to reply that reality, too, is ordered. It may be so, but in accordance with divine laws – I translate: inhuman laws – which we will never completely perceive. Tlön may be a labyrinth, but it is a labyrinth plotted by men, a labyrinth destined to be deciphered by men. ("Tlön ...", 34)

His own footnote undermines his argument, however: "There remains, naturally, the problem of the *matter* of which some of these objects [from Tlön] consisted" (34). If Tlön is as real as reality, its laws will be as impenetrable as our own. Repressing this truth by hiding in an ivory tower, the narrator adopts an indifferent attitude: "The world will be Tlön. I take no notice. I go on revising, in the quiet of the days in the hotel at Androgué, a tentative translation into Spanish, in the style of Quevedo, which I do not intend to see published, of Sir Thomas Browne's *Urn Burial*" (35). He does not realize that the day may come when his ever so harmless activity will be considered an act of heresy or treason which may cost his life, for in a Tlönicized world, Spanish no longer exists, and to speak of an individual author's style is totally absurd when "the dominant notion is that everything is the work of a single author" (28). Since ideas are prone to actualization, and actualizations, to degeneration and corruption, it takes very little to turn the most well-meant ideas into a source of danger: this motif runs through the entire story. While he made his narrator refer to dialectical materialism, anti-Semitism, and Nazism, Borges could not even be aware of the full extent of horror and disorder these "symmetrical" systems had in store (34).

The narrator's naiveté might easily be explained away by his interest in nonrealistic fiction; but Borges also launched satirical attacks on excessively faithful realists, e.g. in his story "Doctor Brodie's Report", written thirty years after "Tlön, Uqbar, Orbis Tertius": Dr. Brodie, a Presbyterian missionary from Aberdeen, travels to "the heart of Africa" ("Doctor Brodie's Report", 91), where he tries to convert the tribe of "the 'Mlch'", whom, he says, he will "call

Yahoos so that my readers will be reminded of their bestial nature" (92). All his experiences with them are revolting: they conceal themselves while eating but all "other physical habits they perform in open view, much the same as the Cynics of old" (92); they are ruled over by a king, who nominally wields absolute power but in reality is no more than a helpless scapegoat, gelded, blinded and crippled (94). The Mlch can predict the future while their memory is totally deficient: "They convey, for example, that 'A fly will graze the nape of my neck'" (96). For a man who believes in predestination, Brodie's comments upon the discovery of the Mlch's ability are remarkably unenthusiastic; he prefers underscoring the value of memory to drawing the apposite conclusion from this newly found piece of evidence for one of the tenets of his religion (96). After his escape from the Mlch's village, he is haunted by the "essential horror of the experience" (100), but his faith in the principles of civilization is so strong that he ends by defending the Mlch:

> ... it would be unjust to overlook certain traits which redeem them. They have institutions of their own; they enjoy a king; they employ a language based upon abstract concepts; they believe, like the Hebrews and the Greeks, in the divine nature of poetry; and they surmise that the soul survives the death of the body. They also uphold the truth of punishments and rewards. After their fashion, they stand for civilization much as we ourselves do... (100)

For Brodie the abstract sense of such words as "institution", "king", or "punishments and rewards" counts more than their actualizations. Even if they have come to designate the exact opposite of their original referents, and thus are almost as remote from the reality which informed their definition as words referring to imaginary objects, he continues to build his judgment on them. Thus, he is by far the most deluded of Borges's characters. Borges reinforces his satire by making the "editor" of Brodie's report describe him as a man who was so sober and uninspired, i.e. wary of delusion, that he read "the wondrous tales of Shahrazad" (91) for no other reason than to study "the customs of the Mohammedans" (91). It is no surprise that he did not recognize miracles when they happened to him.

Borges usually encourages his readers' scepticism precisely when offering them realistic stories; it is no accident that the magic realistic "Doctor Brodie's Report" rounds off a realistic collection. In the preface to *A Universal History of Infamy*, which is a collection of stories about real criminals, he enhances the artificiality of his work so as to make the stories palpable: "The book is no more than appearance, than a surface of images; for that reason, it may prove enjoyable" (12). On the other hand, certain of his images are designed to take us closer to reality by pointing exactly in the other direction towards unreality. The degree of unreality displayed in his stories varies. In "The Library of Babel", fantasy prevails. The story is an allegory devised to illustrate concepts such as infinity and the order of the universe, but at the same time, it stages the impossibility of coming to terms with such ideas. The fictitious model universe, that is the library and its ingredients are overt simplifications: all chambers of the library – just how many of them there are is unknown to the narrator – are regular hexagons, all books are of the same length and contain texts that are permutations of twenty-five symbols. Nevertheless, the librarians fail to see through the system. All they can do is adopt certain attitudes towards the search for meaning and apply various interpretations to their finds. None of them is altogether invalid, not even the formalist view "that books in themselves mean nothing" ("The Library ...", 81), as the narrator says. Since the librarians' failure is not a simple realistic imitation of our own failure of coming to terms with the world, we must guess to what "ungraspable reality" Borges's allegory may point.[3] This might for instance be done by exploring the differences between the library of Babel and our own universe: Our world, which is negated by the fantasy, contains other objects than books, a good deal of other places than libraries, and a great number of sign systems with more or less than twenty-five symbols. How are we to make sense of such complexity if the librarians fail in their simplified model universe? Rather than to offer escape from our condition of ignorance and weakness, Borges's fantasy increases our awareness of it. Hopeless though the attempt to see through this unfathomable chaos may be, however, it is perhaps not an altogether dishonorable activity. After all there are far more questionable ways of dealing with the human condition.

Topics that are probably less beyond our mental capacities can afford more realistic presentations. Thus the magic realistic stories "The Immortal" and "The Other" emphasize our subjection to the passing of time by presenting characters who move outside the temporal laws. In "The Immortal", the antique dealer Joseph Cartaphilus describes the effects of the experience of eternity on those who are not bound to die: they are almost indifferent to the physical world, or to questions of good and evil, since longevity levels all evaluations and sensory impressions:

> There are no moral or intellectual merits. Homer composed the *Odyssey*; if we postulate an infinite period of time, with infinite circumstancs and changes,

3 Scholes discusses Borges's notion of successful allegories thus: " ... Borges suggests that allegory fails when its fictions are reducible back to single word-concepts, but succeeds when its fictions function as complex signs moving away from simple concepts toward the 'ungraspable reality.' For Borges, the language's tendency toward logic is a movement away from reality. The more precise and fixed the terminology, the more inadequate it must become. Thus allegory, at its best, is thinking in images, intuitive and open to truth" (*Fabulation*..., 11).

> the impossible thing is not to compose the *Odyssey*, at least once. No one is anyone, one single immortal man is all men. ("The Immortal", 145)

Only striving for death, an aim that centuries of thinking on their condition have eventually shown the immortals to be worth pursuing, does revive their energy, and they disperse over the earth to find the river which will end their immortality:

> Death (or its allusion) makes men precious and pathetic. They are moving because of their phantom condition; every act they execute may be their last; there is not a face that is not on the verge of dissolving like a face in a dream. Everything among the mortals has the value of the irretrievable and the perilous. (146)

In "The Other", Borges plays with the Heraclitean idea that the same moment cannot occur twice. The unrealistic element in this story is the fact that a seventy-year-old "Borges" meets his nineteen-year-old self on a bench that exists "in two times and in two places" ("The Other", 10). Just before discovering his younger self he is deluded into believing that he has lived "that moment once before" (3). The encounter with his double, however, shatters the illusion. Too many attitudes have changed, too many beliefs been abandoned in the course of a lifetime; should a later and an earlier moment coincide, one's self must split: "'Only individuals exist – if it can be said that anyone exists. "The man of yesterday is not the man of today," some Greek remarked. We two, seated on this bench in Geneva or Cambridge, are perhaps proof of this.'" (7). Borges's ironical essay "A New Refutation of Time" makes a longer detour to arrive at the same conclusion. But it also shows once more why he did not give up playing with unreality, conjuring up illusions, writing fiction in spite of his fundamental scepticism:

> *And yet, and yet....* Denying temporal succession, denying the self, denying the astronomical universe, are apparent desperations and secret consolations. Our destiny (as contrasted with the hell of Swedenborg and the hell of Tibetan mythology) is not frightful by being unreal; it is frightful because it is irreversible and iron-clad. Time is the substance I am made of. Time is a river which sweeps me along, but I am the river; it is a tiger which destroys me, but I am the tiger; it is a fire which consumes me, but I am the fire. The world, unfortunately, is real; I, unfortunately, am Borges. ("A New ...", 269)

Well-formed fictions, as we have seen before, may offer some pleasure, comfort and escape, or lend grace to our most painful experiences.

In the last story by Borges which will be discussed here, "The South", the saving illusion is not recognizable at first glance. On the contrary, we might read the story as a celebration of real life and a repudiation of fiction in general and nonrealistic fiction in particular. Like "Doctor Brodie's Report", it has been placed at the end of a collection and might be seen as the antithesis to the title of the collection, *Ficciones*. Its protagonist is a librarian of German and Argentine descent, Juan Dahlmann, who has dreamt all his life of leaving Buenos Aires to go south to a little ranch he has inherited from his "romantic" maternal grandfather, the hero Francisco Flores (167). However, his passion for books and his "indolence" (167) surpass his desire for the South until an ironical accident changes his life: reading a rare copy of Weil's edition of *The Thousand and One Nights* while going home he knocks his forehead against the edge of a door someone has left open. Little later, he must be taken to hospital: his failure to dress the wound has resulted in septicemia. In spite of a severe crisis, Dahlmann seems to survive. He decides to travel to his ranch for convalescence, carrying the copy of *The Thousand and One Nights* with him as "a kind of affirmation that his ill-fortune had been annulled" (170). But he reads very little, the "joy of life distracted him from paying attention to Scheherazade and her superfluous miracles" (170). His journey ends in a general store where he hopes to find a vehicle for the last part of the way. Instead he finds himself challenged to a knife fight which he accepts instinctively although he has no doubt that he is bound to die: "He felt that if he had been able to choose, then, or to dream his death, this would have been the death he would have chosen or dreamt" (174).

Dahlmann's evaluation of his situation is the last of a series of hints that the story of his convalescence and the journey south may never actually have taken place. Distinctive supernatural elements have not been used, but slight details that are scattered throughout the text disturb, though they never really contradict, the logic that a realistic story proper would have to observe. Why, for instance, is the railroad car in which Dahlmann wakes up "not the same" as the one he fell asleep in (171)? Why is he "travelling into the past and not merely south" (171)? How can the shopkeeper, who has never seen him before, know Dahlmann's name, and why, finally, is Dahlmann not in the least surprised at the fact (173)? Taken individually, these pieces of information would arouse no suspicion for they can always be read figuratively or given some explanation; we do, for instance, get an answer to the first question, but it does not disambiguate the interpretation of the statement about the railroad car: "... the plain and the hours had transfigured it" (171). In conjunction, such details suggest that the account of Dahlmann's journey may be the content of a dream or a hallucination during general anaesthesia, maybe the content of his last thoughts before death, or of a spiritual journey to an alternative universe where all one's desires are gratified. There, Scheherazade's miracles would indeed be superfluous. As we cannot decide which interpretation is valid, I suggest that we are in a similar situation as Todorov's reader of the pure fantastic. The interesting fact about this story is, though, that doubts about the reality of the events depicted are not supported by the story's narrative mediation: "The South" is no first-person narrative even though Todorov stresses the importance of such mediation (87).[4] Its ambiguity rests above all on the peculiar way in which textual cohesion has been established. The reality of the sanitarium is still uncannily present although the journey is supposed to be taking place after Dahlmann's discharge. Alerted to the possibility of the journey's unreality, we suddenly notice further hints for a double reading:

> ... it was as if he was two men at a time: the man who traveled through the autumn day and across the geography of the fatherland, and the other one, locked up in a sanitarium and subject to methodical servitude. (170)

> Once inside [the general store], Dahlmann thought he recognized the shopkeeper. Then he realized that he had been deceived by the man's resemblance to one of the male nurses in the sanitarium. (172)

It is no doubt a subtle way of generating a sense of undecidability, but one that is as valid as that of subjectivizing a narrative through a first-person narrator when supernatural elements have been used. One more sentence at the end of the tale would suffice to resolve it in a realistic or an unrealistic way and thus to disambiguate our reading. After the "fight", Dahlmann's body might be removed from the operating theatre or shown as mysteriously missing from the hospital. Both versions would be as believable as the "straight" reading of the story. For the details I have quoted above link its parts by what Borges called "magical causality" or "prefiguration by innuendo" in his 1932 essay "Narrative Art and Magic" (quoted in Wheelock 3). But the possible outcomes thus prefigured never become explicit – the nature of the story's events therefore cannot be determined by the readers. Earlier on, in chapters 4.2 and 6.2, I used Fritz Senn's term "dislocution" for a similar technique, and it is no surprise to read in the penultimate paragraph of Borges's essay, that to him, Joyce's *Ulysses* is the paragon of this kind of causality ("Die Erzählkunst und die Magie", 90). Both dislocution and magical causality are examples of foregrounded cohesion; for the sake of differentiation one might define dislocution, following Fritz Senn, as a foregrounding through the incongruity of cross-references, while magical causality rather builds up a network of cross-references, congruent in itself but in opposition to the predominant network, which suggests the existence of another level of reality beyond the one

---

4 "Dans les histoires fantastiques, le narrateur dit habituellement 'je': c'est un fait empirique que l'on peut vérifier facilement. ... Les exceptions sont presque toujours des textes qui de plusieurs autres points de vue s'éloignent du fantastique" (87).

apparently depicted by the text. Both techniques draw attention to the medium of language, to the textuality of a story.

Our awareness of magical causality establishes a fundamental difference between Dahlmann and us. We need to know that the journey is fictitious while he does not. The closer one is to death, the less does it matter if one is aware of the unreality of one's perceptions. In fact, Dahlmann's dream or supernatural journey lends dignity to his situation because he is not aware of its unreality. For us, however, life's reality must be reinstalled and we, be undeceived. In the process, we come to realize that the story is making the same two points we have noticed in other stories: a celebration of real life is possible only through fiction; on the other hand, this does not postulate the superiority or autonomy of fiction, for fiction is bred by our needs and our unfulfilled desires. It ought to be no less but also no more than "a mirror that reflects the reader's own features and ... a map of the world", as Borges wrote in *Other Inquisitions* (quoted in Scholes, *Fabulation...*, 12). As soon as fiction tries to replace the world and to make too many claims upon the reader, its pleasant aspects are lost – after all, Dahlmann has an accident because his copy of *The Thousand and One Nights* fascinates him too much. If one wants to live, one has to be aware of the difference between life and fiction. The narrator of the magic realistic story "The Book of Sand" is cleverer than Dahlmann. Before his mysterious book can impose itself too much upon his life, he gets rid of it in a library.

My interpretation of "The South" might point the way to a complementation of Todorov's theory of the pure fantastic. The latter is built on a model of language in which textual cohesion figures only as the condition of irreversibility of the plot. That is, only the sequence, not the quality of the pieces of information which are responsible for cohesion have been taken into account. Yet, as we have seen, ambiguity may be established at this level if a network of interrelated hints suggests the presence of a reality other than the one presented at the surface of the text. Thus, attention is drawn to the possible fictitiousness or unreality of the surface setting and events, which, all the same, from the semantic point of view, do not appear to be supernatural, hence the story cannot be qualified as MR. In order to come to terms with such a subtle strategy of textual disorientation I would like to suggest a last alteration of Todorov's definition of the pure fantastic: if a text represents several mutually exclusive realities and the readers are invited to decide which of them is "real", which "unreal", without ever being able to reach a definite conclusion, a text belongs to the pure fantastic. Historically, this leads to a "supernatural" and a "natural" variant of the fantastic with "The South" being an example of the "natural" variant.

Mediation by a first-person narrator, a feature overrated by Todorov, is only one of several means of creating this particular ambiguity, which will inevitably result in linguistic self-consiousness. I think that this *aesthetic* function of the fantastic, its creating linguistic self-consciousness, is the condition for the social function Todorov associates with it. *Because* the artificiality of at least one representation of reality in "The South", or of the supernatural elements in the older fantastic texts is offered as a means of escape from facing unpleasant or embarrassing truths head-on, the fantastic lends itself, for instance, to the treatment of taboo subjects, e.g. sexuality in many of Todorov's examples or death in "The South". Unlike Todorov, who claims that the historical fantastic lost its function when psychoanalysis began to concern itself with such subjects, I believe that there will always be a need for an imaginative approach to these; and even though many of the old taboos have lost their strength, there will always be new ones to deal with.

The distinction between Todorov's "supernatural" variant of the fantastic and MR has been sketched out earlier: both juxtapose natural and supernatural elements; but whereas the "supernatural" fantastic has been defined as that mode in which readers are invited to decide whether or not the supernatural elements are a "real" ingredient of the reality depicted, without being allowed to reach a definite conclusion, MR is the mode which entrusts the readers with the responsibility for the permeable boundary, as the discussion of *Fremder* has shown, too (cf. ch. 10.1). It creates distance not only to a particular subject matter, i.e. to certain objects of representation, but to representation in itself, by showing that the "natural" need not necessarily be taken as a more authentic representation of reality than the "supernatural". MR lays bare the conventions by which the distinction between "natural" and "supernatural" has been established, in other words, it entails a pervasive metafictional awareness.[5]

5 For the distinction between realism and metafiction see Linda Hutcheon, *Narcissistic Narrative*: "... the theoretical basis of 'traditional realism' is what could be called a mimesis of *product*. The reader is required to identify the products being imitated – characters, actions, settings – and recognize their similarity to those in empirical reality, in order to validate their literary worth. Since no codes, no conventions for this procedure are acknowledged, the act of reading is seen in passive terms. Metafictions, on the contrary, bare the conventions, disrupt the codes that now *have* to be acknowledged. The reader must accept responsibility for the act of decoding, the act of reading. Disturbed, defied, forced out of his complacency, he must self-consciously establish new codes in order to come to terms with new literary phenomena. Since product mimesis alone does not suffice to account for the new functions of the reader as they are thematized in the texts themselves, a mimesis of *process* must perhaps be postulated. The novel no longer seeks just to provide an order and meaning to be recognized by the reader. It now demands that he be conscious of the work, the actual construction, that he too is undertaking..." (38-39). Hutcheon shows that self-consciousness even exists for certain types of realistic fiction: "With Flaubert's realism, the reader's relation is primarily to language itself and this language, the reader is made to feel, can never correspond to reality" (*Narcissistic Narrative*, 150). But encouraging linguistic self-consciousness is not as radical a strategy as that of creating metafictional awareness in the reader, who is forced into taking responsibility for the kind of reality she constructs and the codes she applies.

However, a text may draw attention to its textuality elsewhere than in the nature of events presented: e.g. by means of a self-conscious first-person narrator and a narratee, various types of *mise en abyme*, or by presenting a story with more than one ending. Frequently, MR avails itself of one or more other metafictional elements to enforce the effect of the dialectic between its supernatural and its natural elements (also see Hancock 41f.).

GABRIEL GARCÍA MÁRQUEZ: *ONE HUNDRED YEARS OF SOLITUDE*

In Gabriel García Márquez's *One Hundred Years of Solitude* (1967), a mysterious pile of parchments which several members of the Buendía family have been trying to decipher for one hundred years most distinctly unites the supernatural and the metafictional; for when the last descendant of José Arcadio Buendía finally succeeds in discovering its code, it turns out to contain the very story we have been reading so far, the history of the rise and fall of the Buendías. At the moment when Aureliano Babilonia is catching up with his own present and skipping some pages to anticipate his future, an apocalyptic storm is destroying what is left of the city of Macondo; the last words he is reading coincide with the novel's last words:

> Before reaching the final line, however, he had already understood that he would never leave that room, for it was foreseen that the city of mirrors (or mirages) would be wiped out by the wind and exiled from the memory of men at the precise moment when Aureliano Babilonia would finish deciphering the parchments, and that everything written on them was unrepeatable since time immemorial and forever more, because races condemned to one hundred years of solitude did not have a second opportunity on earth. (383)

The gypsy Melquíades's prophetic manuscript is a so-called aporistic *mise en abyme*, that is an element which "is supposed to include the work in which it itself is included" (Hutcheon, *Narcissistic Narrative*, 56). It foregrounds what Robert R. Wilson called "world-interpenetration" or intertextual "spatial enfolding" in the second of the two ways described by him:

> In magic realism world-interpenetration takes place in a variety of ways ... On the one hand, the hybrid constructions of magic realism arise, in some passages ... when something different, even inconsistent, arrives. It comes from outside an already established world ... and informs it temporarily. On

---

Hutcheon's definition also allows for *covert* forms of metafiction (31-34): the detective story, fantasy (in the broad sense of supernatural fiction or fiction with supernatural elements, i.e. MR), game structures, the erotic, and texts which direct "the reader's attention to language itself, to its potential for semantic duplicity" (34) – perhaps "The South" had rather be qualified as an example of this last form of covert metafiction, not only as a linguistically self-conscious text, because its protagonist is a librarian and passionate reader, not a writer. This does not alter its status as a fantastic text, however.

> the other hand, one world may lie hidden within another. Then the hybrid construction emerges from a secret already contained within, forming an occulted and latent aspect of the surface world. This, it seems to me, is what commonly happens in the fiction of García Márquez. (72)

Whether to call the parchment horrific or marvellous is not easy to determine at this stage, though: can one call it horrific because it leaves the Buendías no choice and seals their fate? Or is it rather marvellous since it lets Aureliano know something nobody else does, namely the precise moment of his death? Maybe proceeding by an indirect route will eventually lead us to the answer.

The aporistic *mise en abyme* is not the only supernatural element used by García Márquez. He freely combines sudden manifestations of a hidden reality with intrusions from the outside: marvellous flying carpets reminiscent of the *Arabian Nights* (38), the phenomenon of levitation (86, 223) or the appearance of ghosts (80, 136, 176, 195, etc.). The most important quality of all these elements is that they unsettle or intrigue the characters less than scientific "miracles" such as electricity or the cinema do (211). A flying carpet, on the other hand, is no more than "an object of recreation" (38); José Arcadio Buendía even shows contempt for it: "'Let them dream,' he said. 'We'll do better flying than they are doing, and with more scientific resources than a miserable bedspread.'" (38). This confirms what Amaryll Chanady writes about García Márquez:

> Reality is so astonishing, that the greatest difficulty encountered by Latin American authors is making the incredible seem believable to a reader unfamiliar with their world. At least this is the opinion expressed by García Márquez, who believes that the New World is so remarkable that his best literary creations do not even approximate the prodigies he encounters in life. He claims that it is unnecessary to invent, since reality will always write better than any author. (51)

By understating the importance of the supernatural, even as a means of entertainment, attention is drawn to the novel's natural elements: the jungle with its fauna and flora, extreme meteorological conditions ranging from torrential rain to extreme drought, and above all the struggle for survival, power and love in these special surroundings.

In terms of themes, García Márquez's panoramic novel is divided between self and other in so far that it stages a conflict between the quest for the satisfaction of personal needs and the demands of society, between the need for communication and love on the one hand, and the fulfilment of an individual death drive on the other, finally, between a sense that everything is predetermined and the effort of the founders of Macondo to escape past curses and embrace something new. I do not think that death belongs to the themes of the other in this novel, as it ought to according to Todorov. Manifesting itself both as a realization of the death drive which determines the actions of the destructive characters, that is as an integral kernel of their selves, and as the fate that has always been awaiting the Buendías and Macondo, death is presented as an event that inhabits all existence rather than being its other. Solitude is associated with the ideas of fate and death; it is a punishment for those incapable of establishing vital relationships with others. This is the case for most members of the Buendía family. Time and again, they dedicate their lives to the lonely, or violent, pursuit of crazy projects. Or else, they succumb to incestuous relationships, the source of their family curse. It is impossible for the few life-affirming members of the family who seek communication with the outside world to escape the predicament. Thus fate seems to win (theme of the self): the birth and death of pig-tailed little Aureliano, the son of Aureliano Babilonia and his aunt Amaranta Ursula, testifies to the end of the family's history. Everything happens as set down in Melquíades's parchments. It still does not follow from the fate they describe, though, that the parchments themselves are unequivocally horrific.

Many of the supernatural elements serve the communication between the dead and the living (theme of the other): ghosts act as teachers (e.g. 177), and mysterious tokens foretell or announce the death of some of the characters (129, 137); since they clearly assist the characters in their struggle against the hardships of life in the jungle, they belong to the marvellous. Selfish or violent characters are barred from enjoying the effects of miracles: Melquíades's room, for instance, looks fresh and tidy only to those who enter it in the right spirit (244); while offering shelter to José Arcadio Segundo, it always looks abandoned and dirty to colonel Aureliano Buendía (244) and to the soldier who has come to search the house for José Arcadio Segundo (289). Similarly, the colonel never sees the ghost of his father under the chestnut tree where he died (227). Uncanny nature, on the other hand, aligns itself with fate; it destroys by means of a flood (291), drought (305), and an apocalyptic storm (383) all the efforts of those who have tried to establish and maintain a living community at Macondo.

Even though, as I argued earlier on, the natural is considered more remarkable than the supernatural within the magic reality of *One Hundred Years of Solitude*, both would remain altogether insignificant if they were not passed on to anyone. For the novel's ending clearly suggests that the world and its inhabitants are "alive" only in terms of the narratives about, or memories of, them. Colonel Aureliano Buendía's life documents this: While he is in love with Remedios, the only person who can stimulate his will to live, he begins to write poetry (69). After her death, however, he not only gives up writing but turns into a ruthless, misanthropic warrior. It is in line with his succumbing to the death drive that he retains hardly any memories of his life. Only his mother Ursula Iguarán's brave intervention can put an end to his destructive ways; she risks her life to prevent her cruel son from executing his former friend Gerineldo Márquez. Holding up a mirror to his heartlessness, she compares him to the pig-tailed monster whose birth will mean the end of the Buendías (163). His aggression then turns against himself: He destroys "all trace of his passage through the world" (167), burns his poetry (168), attempts suicide, but fails (170), and rejects all governmental honours (202). With only one ineffectual relapse into his old belligerence (228), he lives like a shadow up until his death (250). The one thing he thinks worth passing on to the occasional companion of his solitary last days, his great-nephew José Arcadio Segundo, are stories glorifying war. But the young man who once seemed to take after the colonel (245) ceases to respect him and believe his stories after he has experienced the reality of death himself as the only survivor of a massacre: thousands of workers of the all-powerful banana company who have assembled to protest against untenable working conditions are shot by governmental forces; having saved a child, José Arcadio Segundo is wounded, loses consciousness and hours later, comes to in a train loaded with the victims' corpses (284). Nobody believes his story when he at last finds his way home, for the propaganda spread by the government and the banana company is efficient:

> The official version, repeated a thousand times and mangled out all over the country by every means of communication the government found at hand, was finally accepted: there were no dead, the satisfied workers had gone back to their families, and the banana company was suspending all activity until the rains stopped. ... (287)

The seeds of destruction would continue to be spread, for the government, whose enemy the colonel was throughout his life, finally try to turn him into their hero. But the novel proves both the colonel and the government wrong by letting José Arcadio Segundo have the last word in this matter, giving a voice to someone who would have been silenced otherwise:

> When the door closed, José Arcadio Segundo was sure that the war was over. Years before Colonel Aureliano Buendía had spoken to him about the fascination of war and had tried to show it to him with countless examples drawn from his own experience. He had believed him. But the night when the soldiers looked at him without seeing him while he thought about the tension

> of the past few months, the misery of jail, the panic at the station, and the train loaded with dead people, José Arcadio Segundo reached the conclusion that Colonel Aureliano Buendía was nothing but a faker or an imbecile. (289)

Fiction can also alleviate the work of death. Whereas no supernatural miracle will bring back to life the dead, the novel partly undoes the threat of Melquíades's parchments. When we are reading the last sentence of the novel, which states that Macondo "would be wiped out by the wind and exiled from the memory of men" (383), an inevitable and irreversible act of destruction, we know that communication has in fact been stronger than death, fate and solitude. For in order to "revive" the characters we need only go back to the beginning of the book. Since novel and parchments are virtually identical, the obverse and the reverse sides of the same text, the cosy and the uncanny, the horrific and the marvellous become one.

The implications for writers can be derived from these givens: they must be the chroniclers of their times who form the necessary counterweight to the destructive forces in nature and society. Although these cannot be eliminated by fictional miracles, fiction can try to provide arguments against the nihilism inspired by nature, contradict the false glorification of warriors and unmask governmental lies, thus encouraging more positive attitudes. Readers, on the other hand, are called upon to take part in the communicative exchanges which turn passive experience into life proper. Their critical and perceptive participation might then enable them, contrary to the protagonists in the novel, to read the signs of warning and act before it is too late.

TONI MORRISON: *BELOVED*

García Márquez's political and social engagement clearly parallels his aesthetic interests, if it does not surpass them. But the reality he describes in his novel cannot be attributed to any particular country on the South American continent, for the conditions and personalities he has portrayed match those in his home country Colombia as well as those of several others. As we move on to Toni Morrison's *Beloved* (1987), the historical circumstances of the situation she describes become more specific since the novel is based on an actual fact which occurred in Cincinnati during the 1850s. It is an attempt to come to terms with slavery in a way that goes beyond the slave narratives written at that time. Interestingly, though, Morrison did not simply pack as many facts as she could into her narrative. In "The Re-Imagining of History in Contemporary Women's Fiction", Linda Anderson writes, quoting from an interview with Morrison:

> But whilst [Morrison] researched very thoroughly the historical background of the novel, 'Cincinnati, and abolitionists, and the underground railroad', she also refused to find out any more about Margaret Garner [the woman upon whom Sethe was modelled]: 'I really wanted to invent her life'. Leaving space to imagine her central character – Sethe in the novel – is also a way of leaving space for subjectivity, for the interiority denied by historical records. 'They "forgot" many things', Morrison has said about slave narratives. 'Most importantly – at least for me – there was no mention of the interior life.' (Anderson 138)

Instead of merely turning a slave narrative into a (realistic) psychological novel about slavery, Morrison has chosen to use magic realism. Anderson argues that the novel thus "speaks, like the characters, from within a culture which not only unquestioningly accepts the existence of ghosts but which more generally does not prioritize the rational" (138). While this cultural argument may well be true, I am convinced that Morrison was also quite conscious of that property of supernatural elements which Todorov has underlined, i.e. their providing vivid images for psychic processes. Her preference of imaginative expressivity to abstract verbal subtlety becomes clear when one reads theses such as the one put forward by the anthropologist Robert Hertz (written at the beginning of the twentieth century and translated into English in 1960):

> ... the death of a stranger, a slave, or a child will go almost unnoticed; it will arouse no emotion, occasion no ritual. ... Since society has not yet given anything of itself to the (new-born) child, it is not affected by its disappearance and remains indifferent. (quoted in Bloch and Parry 4)

His argument underlines "the social construction of emotion" (Bloch and Parry 5), positing society as an "entity acting for itself" (6); moreover, to him, it seems to be a matter of course that strangers, slaves and children are no part of society and therefore entirely negligible. The point is, however, that "society" does not exist prior to the moment when it is constituting itself, for instance, *through* the regulation of emotions in symbolic rituals (Bloch and Parry 6). This implies that precisely by *choosing* not to notice the death and the suffering of members of certain groups, a dominant group marginalizes them, depriving them of their humanity; consequently, it can exploit them without damage to their conscience.

In *Beloved*, Morrison focuses on the feelings of the African-American victims of such an ideology. For like many of "schoolteacher's"[6] racist

6 "Schoolteacher" is one of the worst racists in the novel; he has no proper name but is only referred to by his function.

definitions in her novel, Hertz's remark belongs to the definer, not the defined (*Beloved*, 190): the death of a child, a slave, or a stranger will never go unnoticed; individual psychology contradicts social anthropology. Even though so-called society may pretend to be indifferent, the emotions of the victims and their families and friends cannot be eliminated by declaring them inexistent.[7] Whatever has been repressed will return with a vengeance. In order to bring this home to her readers, Toni Morrison has made a dead slave girl the protagonist of her novel, temporarily restoring to the object of her imaginative language the power, humanity and individuality of which the analytical language of certain anthropologists and racists has deprived her.

Beloved at first only manifests herself to her family as a poltergeist, scaring away all potential visitors and eventually making her brothers Howard and Buglar move out, before she achieves bodily presence. The timing of Beloved's appearance gives us a hint as to its motivation: just when Paul D, an old friend of Beloved's mother Sethe comes to liberate the family from the poltergeist to begin a new life with Sethe and her remaining daughter Denver, Beloved interferes. The ghost girl jealously tries to sever her mother and her sister from all human company and eventually, even to kill them. She thus plays the role of an agent of death, and since she is presented as an intruder from the outside who competes against a potential lover, we are unmistakably in the realm of the themes of the other.

The beyond from which Beloved returns is described in her elliptic interior monologue in Part Two (210-213); it is an upside-down world, in many details mirroring the conditions on slave ships (Anderson 140), where bodies, piled upon each other, are suffering and taking pains to "die forever" (210). Even though being dead is presented as a laborious process, the majority of the dead remain in their graves. They make no attempt to lure the living into their world. Looking for reasons why Beloved deviates from them will reveal an enormous hunger for recognition on her part. Moreover, her reappearance is evidently rooted in the psyches of the members of her family, too.

To understand what is at stake in the novel, it will be indispensable to turn to anthropology once more and see what explanations it can offer for the return of the dead. However, psychoanalyis will be consulted as well to supplement the gaps left by the other discipline. Slavoj Zizek writes:

> Apropos of this phenomenon, let us then ask a naive and elementary question:

---

7 Dominant groups are never indifferent, of course. The atrocious perversities to which they subject "their" subjects – all the characters in the novel can tell stories of excessive brutality and sexual exploitation – testify to a surplus rather than a lack of emotional involvement on their part.

> why do the dead return? The answer offered by Lacan is the same as that found in popular culture: *because they were not properly buried*, i.e., because something went wrong with their obsequies. The return of the dead is a sign of a disturbance in the symbolic rite, in the process of symbolization; the dead return as collectors of some unpaid symbolic debt. (Zizek 23)

A proper burial, like any rite of passage, is structured as a series of three phases which affect the dead and the mourners alike (Van Gennep, Turner, and Hertz in Huntington and Metcalf 8f., 11-14): In phase one, the soul leaves the body, the corpse is removed from society (real burial), and the mourners have to confront the physical absence of the deceased. While the corpse is slowly decaying during the second phase, the soul hovers between the realms of the living and the dead. The mourners must try to settle accounts with the deceased and with each other: feelings of love or hate (or both) are withdrawn from their former objects (Freud, "Trauer und Melancholie", 210), negotiations over the dead person's belongings and his or her social position take place. The second phase is the most dangerous and unstable one because the emotional, physical and social vacuum left by the deceased has not been filled with new contents yet. Disputes over an inheritance are the rule rather than the exception.The soul may be unwilling to leave the living, the mourners, unable to withdraw their feelings from the dead. This might become apparent in their succumbing to melancholia if their disposition is narcissistic (Freud, "Trauer ...", 202f.), or their developing neurotic symptoms, e.g. when the repressed loss of the object for some reason re-emerges into consciousness (Freud, "Trauer ...", 204; or "Der Sinn der Symptome", 277); it is this phenomenon, I will argue, which is illustrated by the novel's MR, with Beloved standing for a symptom, Sethe and Denver for neurotic characters. Some mourners may even be victimized by psychotic hallucinations which make them believe that the deceased are still alive (Freud, "Trauer ...", 198), but this option can be ruled out for Sethe and Denver since they are not the only ones who see Beloved.[8] Finally, in the third phase, given that the work of mourning has been crowned by success, the mourning period is terminated by a secondary, symbolic burial. The soul has found its place in the society of the dead, the corpse, which has been reduced to an anonymous skeleton, is, in some societies, buried a second time

8 Of course there is a possibility that Beloved herself is a traumatized, schizophrenic fugitive who has assumed the role of Sethe's daughter in order to be put up by her (119, 235); this would not alter her relationship with, or symptomatic effect on, Sethe and Denver, however. Morrison pointed out in an interview that she had constructed the story in such a manner that Beloved's experience could also stand for that of the Middle Passage (L. Anderson 140). Notwithstanding this fact, the textual clues for the girl being real are never strong enough to turn the magic realistic novel into a fantastic, or even fantastic-uncanny one. Or to put it differently: the question of her reality is not being raised.

(Huntington and Metcalf 15). The mourners signal in various ways that they have overcome their loss: by ceasing to wear black clothes, for instance, but above all, by forming new attachments. They can now remember the dead person without the initial pain of loss being renewed (Freud, "Trauer ...", 199, 209).

Beloved could not possibly be properly buried for a number of reasons. First of all, she was killed by her own mother out of love, which plunged Sethe into an inextricable emotional dilemma that she had to repress in order to live on (149ff., 163, 203). Her moving monologue shows how her paradoxical act inevitably resulted in paradoxical explanations which would offer no solution to her predicament: "I'll explain to her, even though I don't have to. Why I did it. How if I hadn't killed her she would have died and that is something I could not bear to happen to her" (200). Being at the same time the person who loved and harmed her most, Sethe was weighed down with the impossible task of having to cope both with a deep sorrow and an unfathomable sense of guilt. Prostituting herself to pay for Beloved's tombstone she had to suffer abject humiliation in addition to her other burden: "... those ten minutes she spent pressed up against dawn-colored stone ..., her knees wide open as the grave, were longer than life, more alive, more pulsating than the baby blood that soaked her fingers like oil" (5). The only reason why Sethe did not give in to her suicidal impulse at the time of her release from prison was her love and sense of responsibility for Howard, Buglar and Denver. Repression had its price, however: Sethe became colour-blind and forgetful of many events of her past: "Funny how you lose sight of some things and memory of others" (201). Moreover, her traumatized sons would not let her touch them any more after witnessing the deed (183), and Denver turned into a solitary and timid child (29, 99) who even developed a temporary, hysterical deafness when a boy at school asked her about her mother's crime (103). Beloved, on the other hand, increasingly resented having been deprived of the maternal attention which was her due and enforced her haunting of the house – a symptom with which Howard and Buglar were unable to cope in the long run (104). Accounts thus could not definitely be settled, even though the remaining inhabitants of the haunted house, Sethe and Denver would get used to the compromise that the poltergeist represented, i.e. a compromise between being reminded of and diverted from the traumatic experience in which all their problems originated.

Paul D's arrival disturbs the precarious balance of this arrangement: by exorcising the poltergeist, he at once dispossesses Beloved of her right to Sethe's attention, forces Sethe to form a new relationship although her ambivalent entanglement with her dead daughter makes her far from ready for this, and finally deprives Denver of "the only other company she had" after her grandmother's death and her brothers' escape (19). The result is a revival of the old conflicts and the formation of a symptom which will turn out to be far more challenging than any of the other ones Sethe and Denver have had to deal with – Beloved's manifesting herself as a young woman (50f.).

Beloved's appearance at first means relief to everyone but Paul D, who is being driven from the house in successive stages (64, 114, 126, 165). Sethe no longer needs to mourn for Beloved, and her deed seems to have been undone; the horrific poltergeist thus turns into a marvellous helper figure. The ghost girl's arrival triggers a processing of the events that led up to the killing, for Beloved keeps asking questions about the past. Thus we learn, for instance, that killing one's unwanted children was common practice among slave women when Sethe was a child. She was herself the only child her mother had not killed because she had loved her father (62). Denver, too, benefits from listening to these stories. She, who has always been afraid of Sethe having another murderous fit, begins to understand and eventually love her mother although the stories in which she plays no role never interested her before Beloved elicited them from Sethe (62f.). Beloved goes on to transform Denver by encouraging her not only to listen to but tell the story of her birth in her own words, thus turning her into an active participant in the process of coming to terms with the past. Story-telling makes Denver empathize with Sethe, that is, identify with her in a non-narcissistic way: for the first time she perceives her as another human being and not only as her mother, whose care she can simply take for granted.[9] As a result, Denver gradually discovers that Sethe's suffering entails responsibility on her, Denver's part. At first, though, she cannot name the person she owes something to:

> This was the part of the story she loved. She was coming to it now, and she loved it because it was all about herself; but she hated it too because it made her feel like a bill was owing somewhere and she, Denver, had to pay it. But who she owed or what to pay it with eluded her. (77)

After an initial period of bliss, debts have to be honoured. Beloved begins to fulfil the more disagreeable function of a symptom, that is, of delivering "the coded message in which the subject receives its own message from the Other in reverse form" (Zizek 132), reminding Sethe of her deed instead of

9 What the *fact* of her existence and the *images* of her birth in her story suggest, namely the cutting of the umbilical cord between herself and her mother, yet awaits its accomplishment in the *Symbolic* order. Significantly, we are not told about this part of her birth (84). M(y)-other must first become an other, to whose love Denver does not have exclusive and unquestioned access and to whom she owes something.

providing the illusion that it has never taken place. Despite her adult body Beloved is far from grown-up and sympathetic; she displays the narcissistic features of the baby she was when she was killed:

> Beloved accused her of leaving her behind. Of not being nice to her, not smiling at her. She said they were the same, had the same face, how could she have left her? And Sethe cried, saying she never did, or meant to – that she had to get them out, away, that she had the milk all the time and had the money too for the stone but not enough. That her plan was always that they would all be together on the other side, forever. Beloved wasn't interested. She said when she cried there was no one. (241)

Even though Sethe's revising of her past has shown how, like Lear, she has far more been sinned against than sinning, she is not strong enough to face Beloved's reproaches without wearing herself out (242). She thus resembles the obsessional neurotic, who is subdued by a particularly cruel super-ego (Laplanche and Pontalis 281). A love-hate relationship from which Denver is excluded keeps the ghost and her mother locked in mortal combat. Sethe's guilt is translated into Beloved's aggressiveness and insatiability. Thus, the past literally feeds on the present: Beloved eats up all the food in the house until Sethe and Denver are close to starving. There are no new supplies because Sethe's infatuation with Beloved has resulted in her neglecting and eventually losing her job.

It is Denver who now finds the strength to help her mother. Watching the two women, she finally acts as an autonomous being:

> Frightened as she was by the thing in Sethe that could come out, it shamed her to see her mother serving a girl not much older than herself. When she saw her carrying out Beloved's night bucket, Denver raced to relieve her of it. But the pain was unbearable when they ran low on food, and Denver watched her mother go without ... (242)

The comparison she draws between Beloved and herself, "a girl not much older than herself", shows that the ghost is not only a symptom of Sethe's guilt but also of Denver's desire for Sethe's protection, her fear of growing up and becoming independent. The reversed message that is conveyed through Beloved is "You, Denver, must help Sethe." In fact, the novel captures the moment when the message is being reversed: "The job she started out with, protecting Beloved from Sethe, changed to protecting her mother from Beloved. Now it was obvious that her mother could die and leave them both and what would Beloved do then?" (243). It is at this moment, when she becomes conscious of her mother's mortality, that Denver is cutting the last, that is the social or

Symbolic[10] umbilical cord which has enabled her to shirk all responsibility and instead rely on Sethe for the upkeep of the family.

The first step Denver takes is to leave the hermetic circle which Sethe has drawn around their house. The girl seeks their neighbour's help, thus re-establishing the vital social bonds which began to crumble when her grandmother's spontaneous feast to celebrate her daughter-in-law's arrival with Denver "offended [the neighbours] by excess" (138). Sethe's apparent pride and self-sufficiency after her deed, her failure to ask for help rather than the neighbours' disgust at the killing, had completed their alienation (152). Paul D was in fact the last person to be driven out of the house. His example illustrates, though, that it was not pride but Sethe's lack of words for the deed at the dead center of her circles which had always prevented her from opening herself:

> Sethe knew that the circle she was making around the room, him, the subject, would remain one. That she could never close in, pin it down for anybody who had to ask. If they didn't get it right off – she could never explain. Because the truth was simple, not a long-drawn-out record of flowered shifts, tree cages, selfishness, ankle ropes and wells. Simple: she was squatting in the garden and when whe saw them coming and recognized schoolteacher's hat, she heard wings. Little hummingbirds stuck their needle beaks right through her headcloth into her hair and beat their wings. And if she thought anything, it was No. No. Nono. Nonono. Simple. She just flew. Collected every bit of life she had made, all the parts of her that were precious and fine and beautiful, and carried, pushed, dragged them through the veil, out, away, over there where no one could hurt them. (163)

Like everyone else, Paul D therefore thought that Sethe was a psychotic murderess: "This here Sethe talked about safety with a handsaw. This here new Sethe didn't know where the world stopped and she began" (164). It is clear from her thoughts, however, that her deed was a defensive reaction against schoolteacher, the root of all the evil that occurs in the novel, not a general failure to recognize boundaries between the world and herself. The sadist had indelibly imprinted his marks both on her body, in the form of a huge, tree-like scar on her back (15-17), and on her mind (70, 149ff., 193ff.). The shock she must have experienced at his appearance in a place where she had felt safe, seems to have confused her. So as not to become schoolteacher's prey again, Sethe anticipated his cruelty and directed the aggression towards herself, thus depriving him of holding sway over her once more. If she failed to differentiate at this moment, it was between herself and her little children, succumbing to an hysterical identification with them (Freud, "Trauer ...", 204). Denver is

10 See note 4 in ch. 9 for Lacan's distinction between Real, Imaginary and Symbolic.

more successful where others fail to understand Sethe because her sensitivity, intensified in the two years of her deafness, has made her more independent of words. Moreover, after months spent listening to and making up stories about the past, she is now fully able to grasp what Sethe must have been going through when she killed Beloved. Hence, she assists her as best she can:

> Denver thought she understood the connection between her mother and Beloved: Sethe was trying to make up for the handsaw; Beloved was making her pay for it. But there would never be an end to that, and seeing her mother diminished shamed and infuriated her. Yet she knew Sethe's greatest fear was the same one Denver had in the beginning – that Beloved might leave. That before Sethe could make her understand what it meant – what it took to drag the teeth of that saw under the little chin ... Beloved might leave. Leave before Sethe could make her realize that worse than that ... was what Baby Suggs died of, what Ella knew, what Stamp saw and what made Paul D tremble. That anybody white could take your whole self for anything that came to mind. Not just work, kill, or maim you, but dirty you ... And though she and others lived through and got over it, she could never let it happen to her own. The best thing she was, was her children. Whites might dirty her all right, but not her best thing... – the part of her that was clean. (251)

The crisis must be overcome by the two women, and all Denver can do is keep them and herself alive (232).

At the climax, Sethe once more acts out her drama (256ff.). Yet, the events of the past only seem to repeat themselves. Several of the conditions which led to the murder in the past have undergone change: Sethe has had sufficient time to find out that the act of aggression in which she meant to kill herself and her children should actually have been directed towards the aggressor, schoolteacher (262). Grown-up Denver is no longer a burden but can assist her mother as well as prevent her, together with neighbour Ella, from doing any more harm at the most critical moment (262, 265). The other neighbours have been appeased by Denver, too, thus Sethe is no longer isolated but protected by their solidarity (265). Finally, Mr Bodwin, the white landlord and abolitionist to whom schoolteacher's role has been transferred in the re-enactment of the scene, has always been a benefactor of Baby Suggs' family (265). He abstains from taking Sethe to court after surviving her attack although Paul D and Stamp Paid do not know if he was aware of being attacked at all; his eyes were fixed on naked Beloved, who was standing beside Sethe on the porch before the latter began to run towards him (264). The ghost, having no more reason to reproach Sethe, disappears for good.

Thus, a healing process can set in: Sethe is relieved from her obsessive attempts at justifying and making atonement for her deed. Like an ordinary mourner, Sethe must now learn to withdraw her libidinal energies from

Beloved and regain the self-confidence she lost when she penitently complied with Beloved's reproaches. Paul D, who has himself undergone change by examinig his biography and trying to understand Sethe's (235, 265ff.), gives her the clue towards final recovery: "You your best thing, Sethe. You are" (273). Her reply, "Me? Me?" (273), though a question, signals her willingness at least to consider being born again.

The willingness to suspend disbelief and the readiness to imagine what may lie *beyond* the images presented in the text will prevent readers of MR from being distracted by the irrelevant question whether or not supernatural elements are meant to be "real". MR fiction is therefore particularly apt to fulfil a cathartic function not unlike dreams. Incidentally, *Beloved* spells this connection out: "They forgot her like a bad dream. After they made up their tales, shaped and decorated them, those that saw her that day on the porch quickly and deliberately forgot her" (274). Horrors can and must be forgotten – but only *after* they have been turned into stories and made safe from dangerous repression. In the Preface of *Playing in the Dark*, Toni Morrison has underlined the parallel between the work of a novelist and that of psychoanalysis, too:

> Some years ago, in 1983 I believe, I read Marie Cardinal's *The Words To Say It*. More than the enthusiasm of the person who suggested the book, I was persuaded by the title: five words taken from Boileau that spoke the full agenda and unequivocal goal of a novelist. Cardinal's project was not fictional, however; it was to document her madness, her therapy, and the complicated process of healing in language as exact and as evocative as possible in order to make both her experience and her understanding of it accessible to a stranger. The narrative into which life seems to cast itself surfaces most forcefully in certain kinds of psychoanalysis, and Cardinal proves herself ideal in rendering this 'deep story' aspect of her life. (v)

Finding "the words to say it", documenting "the complicated process of healing in language as exact and as evocative as possible" – in *Beloved*, Morrison shows how the liberation of slaves could not possibly be accomplished merely through wars and legal alterations: its "deep story" was that physical and psychic wounds had to be healed first, the past to be faced, so that life could go on. From a wordless confrontation with the past (259) through a revival of feelings by means of music (261) to a symbolization of pain and recovery in tales that are "not to be passed on" (274f.), all stages had and still have to be gone through by all concerned. Only after this detour can the past be forgotten, most of it, for there will always be a remainder of injustice which cannot be soothed or named, "a loneliness that roams" (274), a void that shapes African-American existence – this is what Beloved stands for.

After discussing the metafictional and psychological implications of MR, merely touching on its realistic component in the works discussed, I now want to place the issue of reality – society, politics, and history – at the centre; for MR has also been used as an engaging vehicle for feminist and post-colonial literature. We will be looking at two examples, Angela Carter's *The Infernal Desire Machines of Doctor Hoffman* (1972) and Salman Rushdie's *Midnight's Children* (1981).

ANGELA CARTER: *THE INFERNAL DESIRE MACHINES OF DOCTOR HOFFMAN*[11]

Lorna Sage has quoted Anthony Burgess's praise of Carter in the introduction to "The Savage Sideshow", her much quoted interview with Angela Carter: he underlined her "capacity for looking at the mess of contemporary experience without flinching" (Burgess quoted in Carter and Sage 51). Yet, unlike Tom Wolfe or Joan Didion, Carter, who also used to work as a journalist, did not take recourse to journalistic techniques to convey her thoughts about this experience in her fiction; she preferred to take advantage of the rich fund of literary means of expression, both traditional and experimental. In its treatment of reality, *Hoffman* resembles a very old prose genre, the picaresque novel. Its first-person narrator alerts us to the similarity at the same time as he tries to divert us from the consequences this will entail for his own person – tellers of picaresque tales being notoriously unreliable: "Expect a tale of picaresque adventure or even of heroic adventure, for I was a great hero in my time though now I am an old man and no longer the 'I' of my own story..." (14). While preserving the episodic structure and the criticism of heroic postures that is typical of earlier picaresque fiction, Carter has transcended the genre, or expanded it, by adding nonrealistic elements to what is usually deemed to be one of the precursors of the realistic novel.[12] For while the old picaresque genre fulfilled the task of criticizing societies in a state of disintegration, Carter's aim was to scrutinize the no less precarious state of mind of her narrator Desiderio – that is, the nonrealistic elements are again psychologically motivated.

11 In her essay "Enthralment: Angela Carter's Speculative Fictions", Elaine Jordan half-seriously called this title "an outrageous imposition" (31) and announced that she would abbreviate it to *Hoffman*; I will henceforth follow her in this wise practice but come back to the title's suggestive complexity later.

12 See, for instance, M. H. Abrams's account of picaresque fiction: "... picaresque fiction is realistic in manner, episodic in structure ... and often satiric in aim" (118). For more detailed discussions of the genre, see Ulrich Wicks, "The Nature of Picaresque Narrative," *PMLA* 89 (1974), 240-249; or Harry Sieber, *The Picaresque* (London: Methuen, 1977).

Gulliver's Travels might be named as another ancestor of *Hoffman*. Like Gulliver, Desiderio travels through unknown regions, both as the medium and the target of criticism. Swift's satire has even been assigned a role in the third chapter, "The River People". Of all books, this is the one with which Desiderio is obliged to teach his Indian host Nao-Kurai to read and write because another one is not available (75). Even if the matter-of-fact Indian were not too old to learn the alphabet, this book would present him with further obstacles: so as to understand it, he would have to come to terms with Swift's irony and thereby learn that reading and writing skills are no protection against being cheated by white people (74). Words can have multiple meanings, hence a recognition of irony as well as an imaginative potential to detect and react to possible dangers inherent in ambiguity are indispensable for survival in their/our culture. This potential cannot be exercised by a mind caught up in traditional myths and behavioural patterns. Desiderio, whose mixed Indian and European origin has equipped him with an innate ironic double vision (16), will survive his stay with Nao-Kurai's family precisely because he is able to keep a critical distance to their myths (91); however, his journey will lead him to despair because he is not sufficiently free from other constraints, those of the culture he grew up in. For it is not only the river people who live in encrusted structures. Carter's novel lays bare how pervasive and enthralling most representations are, how they govern our perception of reality and our desire to a degree that true liberation is possible only in rare moments. Racial stereotypes such as the one about the River People's inflexibility or later, in chapter six, "The African Coast", the cruelty and sexual potency of the African chieftain, serve the same function as the gender stereotypes spread by myths and other cultural products which will be discussed further on: they do not objectively describe what the defined objects are but reflect what the definer wants them to be.

Owing to this subjective bias, it is at first impossible to situate the narrator temporally or spatially. If there were not the many cultural reminders of our own world such as references to Mozart, Marvell (12) and Lenin (13), or to the monuments of the Ancient Egyptians (12), the novel would fulfil all the conditions of a fantasy. Its setting can be derived only approximately, from the beginning of chapter three – we are obviously in a country of the South American continent, for the sardonic account of its discovery and settlement history as well as of the systematic extinction of Indians gives us rough hints about its whereabouts (67): whether we are in Brazil or Guyana, however, cannot be determined unequivocally since the country's features speak for a combination of both rather than for one of them. What is also clear is that the twentieth century has already begun (67). Yet, we soon forget this piece of information again. For the greater part of the novel, we seem to move through a timeless and fantastic, then again rather nineteenth-century set of landscapes – according to the subjects who desire them to come into existence. The sudden appearance of modern helicopters at the end of the book, which situate the novel's main action sometime in the later twentieth century is therefore as unsettling for us as for Desiderio (192f.). Since the story is told fifty years later, that is probably early in the twenty-first century, realism, though at first almost imperceptible, blends with science fiction as well as fantasy.

Gerardine Meaney attaches considerable importance to the fact that Carter did not indulge in producing pure fantasy.[13] The grounds upon which she has based her evaluation, however, are questionable:

> ... speculative fiction asks, 'What if ...?' Its relation to perceived 'reality' is one of interrogation. Fantasy's relation to reality, however, is one of negation. ... If a simple opposition between fantasy and reality is established then the fantasy is not even escapist, but reactionary. It becomes no more than a fit of freakishness which reinstitutes the norms on which it depends to define it by opposition. (Meaney 85)

Meaney here implicitly perpetuates a popular prejudice against fantasy and a misconceived notion of realism. The prejudice, i.e. that fantasy is intrinsically "escapist" or "reactionary", hinges on the faulty assumption that realism *equals*, or at least directly confronts, reality. According to this view, then, avoiding realism coincides with evading, or even negating, reality. Realism, however, may be as "reactionary", "escapist" or "subversive" as fantasy; for it is the degree to which each literary genre hides or flaunts the distance that separates it from reality, moreover the kind of reality it explicitly or implicitly refers to which makes it more or less "reactionary", "escapist" or "subversive". MR flaunts its artificiality more clearly than any of the other genres because, as we have seen, it juxtaposes two standards of referentiality. This is the reason why it is indeed important that Carter has not taken recourse to fantasy: In MR realism and fantasy (or, more generally, the natural and the supernatural) interrogate each other in such a way that the readers are in turn encouraged to interrogate their reality. However, the process does not take

13 She calls *Hoffman* an example of "speculative fiction" (85), a term borrowed from Suvin's *Metamorphoses of Science Fiction* and Scholes's *Structural Fabulation* (Meaney 228, n. 4): "The presence of familiar elements gives plausibility to the 'What if ...?' and gives the reader a framework of references to work with. The cognitive elements are also there to be made strange, however, and the interaction of familiar and alien is, in truly speculative fiction, a mutual putting-into-question" (85). Though "speculative fiction" roughly corresponds with MR, the term itself gives no hint about the genre's double inscription. I will therefore persist in using the term MR.

place automatically. It therefore can happen that even MR is interpreted as escapist.

Carter was aware of possible misreadings of her fiction as escapist, but her answer to John Haffenden's respective question shows that this could only happen if the readers' concept of reality was too narrow:

> [Haffenden] *I know that you find it fundamentally important to have an intelligent awareness of society, and yet the highly stylized and decorative apparatus of your novels might appear to be disengaged from the social and historical realities you want to illuminate.*
> [Carter] Yes, this is a very real risk, really tricky. Obviously the idea that my stories are all dreams or hallucinations out of Jung-land, or the notion that the world would be altogether a better place if we threw away our rationality and went laughing down the street, or even the one that schizophrenia is an enriching experience, that's all nonsense. I *can* see how it must look to some readers, but the point is that if dreams are real as dreams, then there is a materiality to symbols; there is a materiality to imaginative life and imaginative experience which should be taken quite seriously. (Carter and Haffenden 85)

This is a far cry from the lack of commitment of which some critics would accuse Carter.[14] The materiality of symbols, their being not merely a medium between reality and a subject but an *ingredient* of reality, has to be taken seriously because they can be used as a hostile or inhibiting social instrument by means of which some of the members of a society, workers, slaves, colonized peoples, or women, are being held down. We have already come across this phenomenon in "Tlön, Uqbar, Orbis Tertius", *One Hundred Years of Solitude* and *Beloved* and we shall encounter it once more after *Hoffman* in *Midnight's Children.* I will now go on to examine in what ways the symbols of the imaginative life of the early 1970s interact with fantasy and science fiction in *Hoffman*.

The grotesque title of the novel provides us with many clues to begin with: "Infernal" points to a demonization, that is a delegation of responsibility to supernatural powers, of phenomena which are usually all too human and probably related to the unconscious – the familiar device of Gothic fiction, as Todorov has shown, but also of the Satanist cult which would flourish since the late 1960s, the uncanny twin of the Flower Power movement. "Desire Machines" conveys a mechanistic image of humanity: Gilles Deleuze and Felix Guattari, who coined the term "desiring-machines" in *Anti-Oedipus: Capitalism and Psychoanalysis* (1972), would refer in this way to (schizophrenic) subjects who are productive through desire. They rejected the Freudian

14 See for instance Robert Clark's criticism, quoted in Jordan 26f.

notion of desire as lack because according to this notion, "what is represented is always what is absent", as Adams and Searle write in their headnote to the excerpt from *Anti-Oedipus* (284). While "desiring-machine" is positively connotated in *Anti-Oedipus*, the "desire machines" of Carter's title are obviously subject to criticism. Apart from echoing Deleuze and Guattari's "desiring-machines", this expression might also refer to all those artificial devices by which our thinking and our unconscious are influenced: the mass media, art, commercials, drugs, in short, whatever makes us susceptible or vulnerable to symbols, which thereby become material. "Doctor Hoffman", finally, besides referring to Desiderio's antagonist conjures up the image of two men who have invented such devices: the first is Albert Hofmann, the Swiss inventor of LSD, the hallucinogenic drug notorious for its property of causing euphoric as well as frightening schizoid states of mind, the other, the German romantic writer E. T. A. Hoffmann, echoes of whose magic realistic tales can be made out in the novel whenever Albertina Hoffman, the doctor's daughter, significantly absent from the title, assumes the shape of one of E. T. A. Hoffmann's romantic heroines to comply with her father's or Desiderio's wishes. Hoffmann's tales, like a great number of other subtexts which inform the novel, represent the literary and philosophical past which, as a powerful desire machine, still dominates the present; Elaine Jordan has listed some of the other subtexts: "*Hoffman* explores pornography, the Gothic, fairy tales, horror films, boys' imperial adventure stories, anthropological idylls according to Rousseau or Lévi-Strauss, and the fantasies of philosophy, the world as Will and Idea" (34). The title both opens up an entire network of tensions and also leaves some significant gaps which will now be looked at in greater detail.

The novel's publication date 1972 is also that of Fredric Jameson's study *The Prison-House of Language*. The two authors appear to have reacted to the same aspect of the *Zeitgeist*. The status of reality and its representations was being intensely questioned, no doubt as a consequence of a growing awareness of the manipulative effects of the mass media and the changes brought about by the psychedelic and protest culture of the "crazed obscene uproarious Mammon-faced drug-soaked mau mau lust-oozing Sixties" (Tom Wolfe in Malcolm Bradbury, *The Modern American Novel*, 159). Thus, one way of interpreting *Hoffman* would be in terms of its staging a war between absolute formalists and positivists, embodied in Dr Hoffman and the Minister. Jameson does not conceal his anxiety about a culture that presents itself as a "systematized and disembodied nightmare" where linguistics and the theories derived from it cannot be ignored because they offer tools to come to terms with "a world from which nature as such has been eliminated, a world saturated with messages" (ix). Carter's fictional world is even more radically challenged, because fantasies have begun to invade the world of substances as physical manifestations. It would nevertheless be wrong to read the novel as an anti-formalist cautionary tale. Carter must not be confused with her narrator.[15] For Desiderio, as has already been pointed out, is a far from reliable source, and his ending the war in the Minister's sense, that is for the positivists' party, is by no means the best possible outcome. After all, there are victims to mourn over, foremost the woman to whom he has self-pityingly dedicated his autobiographical account, Albertina.

Hoffman is the first part of a planned trilogy of MR fictions in which Carter intended to examine the conditions of womanhood in different contexts (Jordan 31). For her, the 1960s raised urgent questions as to the conditioning effect of culture in terms of gender definitions, as she writes in her "Notes from the Front Line":

> I can date to that time and to some of those debates and to that sense of heightened awareness to the society around me in the summer of 1968, my own questioning of the nature of my reality as a *woman*. How that social fiction of my 'femininity' was created, by means outside my control, and palmed off on me as the real thing. (quoted in Jordan 21)

Albertina, whose very first name is derived from a masculine one, is the purest embodiment of a woman defined by men only: her father, Desiderio, the Minister, the Count, and even the male centaurs (though it is not impossible that they are in fact manifestations of Desiderio's sick mind). She undergoes the most miraculous transformations to match their desires: whether she appears as a black swan (30), a Victorian romantic heroine (201), an androgynous ambassador (32) or as a beautiful but crippled hermaphrodite (214), to name just a few of her shapes, she is never shown as living up to her own desire – it seems that she does not have a desire of her own, except the one of identifying with that of the men and male creatures who exploit her, as becomes clear after her rape by the centaurs (186). Even when Desiderio feels most estranged from her, when she is a soldier, "the absolute antithesis of my

15 For Freud, of course, the case is clear; he writes in "Das Unheimliche": "Tragen wir noch etwas Allgemeines nach ... , dass es nämlich oft und leicht unheimlich wirkt, wenn die Grenze zwischen Phantasie und Wirklichkeit verwischt wird, wenn etwas real vor uns hintritt, was wir bisher für phantastisch gehalten haben, wenn ein Symbol die volle Leistung und Bedeutung des Symbolisierten übernimmt und dergleichen mehr. Hierauf beruht auch ein gutes Stück der Unheimlichkeit, die den magischen Praktiken anhaftet. Das Infantile daran, was auch das Seelenleben der Neurotiker beherrscht, ist die Überbetonung der psychischen Realität im Vergleich zur materiellen, ein Zug, welcher sich der Allmacht der Gedanken anschliesst" (266-267). Russell Hoban, as we have seen in the analyses of his fiction and shall see again in chapter 11.3, calls into question the Freudian devaluation of psychic reality.

black swan and my bouquet of burning bone" (193), we cannot take this persona to be a manifestation of her own free will for she instantly points out that her father is her superior when Desiderio offers to be her batman (193). Being totally dependent on those whose "idea" she is (142), she is condemned to perish from the beginning. Her father's plans are to sacrifice her and Desiderio for his absurd project of reducing, as she tells him, "' ... everything in the world to the non-created bases from which the world is built. And then he will take the world apart and make a new world.'" (203). When her father is dead, she is left at Desiderio's mercy. Dying, of course, she cannot but approve of her death: " ... she spoke to me before she died. She said: 'I always knew one only died for love.'" (217). The reality thus criticized through her is one in which women are completely barred from physical and psychic autonomy, or as Elisabeth Bronfen states the case in *Over Her Dead Body*, the novel provides "a feminist re-reading of the cultural cliché that woman is man's symptom, the phantom of his desires" (420).

The picture of women in pornographic fiction as well as in Freudian symbols of the unconsious does not escape Carter's scrutiny, either. In "The Erotic Traveller", when Desiderio and the Count visit a brothel, the prostitutes are described with scathing irony:

> ... when I examined them more closely, I saw that none of them were any longer, or might never have been, woman. All, without exception, passed beyond or did not enter the realm of simple humanity. They were sinister, abominable, inverted mutations, part clockwork, part vegetable and part brute. (132)

Freudian imagery, on the other hand, is parodied in "The Acrobats of Desire" when Desiderio, against the peep-show owner's explicit prohibition (a little side-hint at the oedipal conflict) peeks in his bag with samples: "These sets usually consisted of six or seven different aspects of the same scene which might be, typically, a nursemaid mutilating a baby, toasting him over a nursery fire and then gobbling him up with every appearance of relish" (107).

However, Carter's criticism is not restricted to traditional clichés but also extends to the notion of an allegedly redeeming anti-rational mother cult forwarded by certain feminists to challenge patriarchal myths. Time and again, for instance in the second novel of the trilogy, *The Passion of New Eve* (1977), as well as in the third chapter of *Hoffman*, she debunks such nostalgic fantasies. A woman's life in the "theoretically matrilinear" society of the river people (80), where language is still predominantly semiotic in Kristeva's sense – "... their words depended not so much on pronunciation as intonation"

(*Hoffman*, 70)[16] – and where the gratification of sexual desire does not provoke any oedipal conflicts (83), forms no viable alternative to Albertina's heteronomous identity. Even though the Indian women's down-to-earth physical presence is the sheer opposite of Albertina's characteristics (70-73, 80), Desiderio depicts them as rather ridiculous creatures. They are by no means any more liberated from stereotypes than Albertina but merely caught up in another set of them – which of course does not prevent *him* from feeling utterly at home and happy with them at first (77); that is, he feels happy until Nao-Kurai, in his greed for literacy, turns them into instruments for incorporating Desiderio's knowledge according to the cannibalistic pattern of an old myth (91). But Carter's project is to break *all* fetters, and if she writes myths, as in this episode, it is to turn them against themselves, according to Roland Barthes's sentence "the best weapon against myth is perhaps to mythify it in its turn, and to produce an *artificial myth*" ("Myth Today", 123).

Women who do live up to their desires, who reject being turned into living manifestations of masculine desire or instruments of questionable cults, actually do exist in the novel too; significantly, though, these women are forced to earn a living at the circus, with other outcasts, by exposing their "difference" to voyeuristic eyes which violate their dignity no less than the stereotypes and myths inscribed on the real and supernatural bodies of the other women in this novel (106). While they give living proof of a kernel resistant to the machinations of Hoffman's desire machines – see Mamie Buckskin's envy at Madame la Barbe's beard (109) – Carter dialectically juxtaposes the fact of their existence with Hoffman's formalist "theory", derived from shamanic traditions and "antique pseudo-sciences" (97) and forwarded by the peep-show proprietor, who used to be a professor of physics and Hoffman's teacher, once (48, 95): According to the three "hypotheses" of the "theory of Phenomenal Dynamics, ... [t]he universe has no fixed substratum of fixed substances and its only reality lies in its phenomena ... only change is invariable ... [and] the difference between a symbol and an object is quantitative, not qualitative" (96). It is due to Phenomenal Dynamics, which the old man defends with the zest of an "old, blind evangelist" (100), that "physical objects and real events may be evolved" from the samples in his sack (96). Desiderio cannot refrain from commenting on the peep-show proprietor's literal and figurative blindness, which should actually alert the professor to the problems and limitations of his former student's tenets (98, 100). But otherwise, Desiderio admits that he does not understand a great deal except that "Hoffman's Phenomenal Dynamics

16 See "Revolution in Poetic Language", pp. 89-136.

involved a hypothetical dialectic between mutuality and transformation" (104). A synthesis between the two parties presented in this episode, that is a mutual transformation cannot take place because all of them, Madame la Barbe, Mamie Buckskin, the peep-show proprietor and the other freaks of the circus world presently die in an earthquake. It no longer matters whether it has been caused by Desiderio's playing around with the peep-show proprietor's sack of probability samples, thereby confirming Hoffman's theories, or else by pure contingency, proving that the fact of mortality is one of the "boundaries of nature" from which even Hoffman must retreat, as Albertina tells Desiderio (108). What does matter, however, is how death alters Desiderio's attitude towards the victims. Bored with their care and interest while they were alive, he suddenly finds them interesting and endearing (106f.). The circus women's death eventually deprives even them of the subjectivity they have maintained throughout their lives for it allows Desiderio to portray them as he likes.

Desiderio's revealing remarks display a supreme will to control, to absolute authorship. As Bronfen writes:

> The duplication of event with explicit commentary is, in fact, a reduction of semantic freedom and mirrors rhetorically the impasse which is the novel's theme: woman can only exist as and in the meaning her lover, as author of her, intends. A move on her part into articulating alterity, into signifying a meaning beyond the one he narcissistically constructs, is fatal. (*Over Her Dead Body,* 421)

But his authorial gesture is paralleled, and in a certain sense also contradicted, by his childlike irresponsibility and his cunning. He shirks responsibility for the events described throughout his narrative by constantly referring himself to the "masters" for or against whom he is working; even the writing of his autobiography is an apparent act of obedience: " ... they have told me that I must write down all my memories of the Great War, since, after all, I remember everything" (11). Far from being a loyal servant like Albertina, however, he confesses: " ... perhaps the whole history of my adventure could be titled 'Desiderio in Search of a Master'. But I only wanted to find a master, the Minister, the Count, the bay, so that I could lean on him at first and then, after a while, jeer" (190). Another of his strategies is to look for scapegoats; in the title, for instance, he demonizes the desire machines instead of calling into question the characteristics of his desire, which makes them dangerous – incidentally, such "scapegoatism" is also popular with the masters: the peep-show proprietor calls Desiderio Satan, after he has himself betrayed Hoffman (49), or the Minister thinks Hoffman satanic while Desiderio is aware of his "envy for the very power the Doctor abused with such insouciance" (28).

Exactly like these masters, he has a sado-masochistic disposition which is founded on an altogether narcissistic personality. All those who challenge his identity seriously, who try to make him love them more than he loves himself, are exposed to his sadism, which he uses as a defence. For what would happen if he followed the peep-show proprietor's instructions, i.e. "To express a desire authentically, ... is to satisfy it categorically" and "Objectify your desires!" (110)? He, who is just as pure a subject of desire as Albertina is the pure object, would lose his subjectivity in exchange for the hierarchy-free mutuality of love, which creates "phenomena through an interplay of elemental aspects of maleness and femaleness" (97).

Instead of letting this dialectic come into play, he destroys what could trigger the process. Killing Albertina is the last of many instances in which Desiderio's morbid fantasies, which always involve a master-and-slave dichotomy, have found an expression (e.g. 56, 107, 115). The Minister is safe because he is so self-sufficient and efficient that Desiderio can live idly beside him, passive, uncreative and parasitic (15); also the peep-show proprietor's demands do not challenge his narcissism: "My tasks were simple and housewifely, for he did not allow me to meddle with the set of samples" (100). A true picaro, Desiderio draws pleasure from transgression of laws, therefore helps his various masters to preserve them; he is nothing but the handyman of the romantic hero or the villain. Hero and villain both actively strive for an actualization of their desire, their creative respectively destructive aims, even though they might die on the way. By contrast, Desiderio would never risk his life for anything (57). The closest he gets to losing himself is while he is being raped by the – apparently supernatural – Moroccan Acrobats of Desire (115-118), who earlier roused in him a strong homoerotic desire (112). Although he admits having been warned before they assault him, he chooses to stay with them, like their little musician (117). The castrated black boy, who "seemed to go in almighty fear of his protectors" but nevertheless "lay in an attitude of utter submission" instead of striving for freedom (116), most perfectly mirrors Desiderio's preferred position in life: that of being the masochistic party in an inhumane sado-masochistic masculine world which subjects, castrates and freezes the roles of all its members (e.g. defining femininity as castrated masculinity) to uphold its illusions of power rather than to become humane, open to improvisation, change, difference and love. The shock of recognition is so strong that Desiderio has "a great need to leave humanity behind for a while" (118). Carter ironically complies with his wish: all the other characters of this episode, whether free within the boundaries of the circus ring or fettered by Puritan conventions, perish in an earthquake.

Accentuating Desiderio's confrontation with himself, the earthquake occurs right after his initiation into the truth, which he forecloses at once:

> A blubbered wreck, I lay on the coverlet and I think that I was calling for my mother, though it was probably Albertina. After a time, Mohammed came, fed me more coffee and, I think, a little arak and held me in a fairly warm and comforting embrace, murmuring to me in his vile French that I had been initiated – though into what I had no idea. (117-118)

All these givens are the reason why I do not agree with one of Bronfen's last arguments in her analysis of *Hoffman*, i.e. that "what is never disclosed as an illusion is Desiderio's romantic text" (*Over Her Dead Body*, 424). By the time he wants to make us believe that Albertina indeed returns from the dead to comply with his last wish, we have learned to distrust him. If we do not see through his picaresque lies, we will deliver ourselves to a man who says of himself, on the very last page: "The shrug is my gesture. The sneer is my expression. ... I am the check, the impulse of restraint" (221).

In this novel, it is not one of the supernatural creatures but the narrator *himself* who prevents change and brings death. He can neither whole-heartedly identify with the Minister's positivist sternness and struggle for perfect propriety; after all, the Minister only defends his "thickly, obtusely masculine" city (15), from which "freaks", male or female, and the imagination have been banished (101). Nor can Desiderio identify with Hoffman's equally totalitarian formalist abnegation of reality for the sake of an unlimited play of realized desires; for Hoffman is too prim and intellectual to be trustworthy: "I could not see how he could have got that notion of liberation inside his skull. I was sure he only wanted power" (209). Moreover, by "the liberation of the unconscious" Hoffman above all "liberate[s] man", as he points out himself (208): woman's liberation indeed requires other measures. Sceptical Desiderio would therefore be an ideal ally for those women who feel uncomfortable with these polarities too.[17] Because he is too uncreative to develop strategies which

17 See Linda Anderson's description of the problems many feminists have in taking sides with both realism and poststructuralism, and their attempts to find ways in between: "The fear that post-structuralist theory could be disabling for women, making history disappear even before we have had a chance to write ourselves into it, needs to be set against another danger: the constant danger that by using categories and genres which are implicated in patriarchal ideology we are simply re-writing our own oppression. ... One of the paradoxes that we face is that even as post-structuralist theory frees us from paradigms which underwrite the (masculine) subject, it catches us back in theoretical toils in which we can also lose ourselves and thus renews our need to reach beyond texts into the materiality of our lives. Describing her attempt to situate her own thinking about history in an unthought-of space between fact and fiction, Linda Gordon finds that her critical poise is uncomfortably put in question: 'I would like to find a method in between. This in-between would not imply resolution, careful balance of fact and myth, or synthesis of fact and interpretation. My sense of a liminal method is rather a condition of being constantly pulled, usually off balance, sometimes teetering wildly, almost always tense. The tension cannot be released.'" (134-135).

might undercut this opposition, however, his indifference, lack of passion and dedication turn him into women's worst enemy. As little as Albertina could ever be the model of a new woman, Desiderio in no way proves to be an active agent of positive change.

In *The Passion of New Eve*, a post-apocalypse novel, Carter does not satisfy her readers' need for a more optimistic outcome yet. Having attacked the stereotypes of femininity as defined by men in *Hoffman*, she now particularly sets out to demolish myths of the Mother which opt for an inversion of power, and she also "mounts a critique of women's 'feminine' behaviour" (Jordan 36). If love and happiness are possible in this novel, they are short-lived. Moreover, they ironically take place between an originally male transsexual, Evelyn/Eve, and a Garbo-like transvestite, the actress Tristessa, who will turn out to be a man. Only in *Nights at the Circus* (1984) do a man and a woman finally achieve happiness (cf. ch. 7.4). I take this novel to be the third part of the trilogy in the absence of any explicit other candidate (Jordan 31) because it sets off from one of the environments we have encountered in *Hoffman* as does *New Eve*. But as Elaine Jordan rightly points out, not even in *Nights at the Circus* does the happy ending really stand a realistic chance:

> Carter offers a love story with a romantic ending, in bed not marriage... (...) 'True love', till death, the real romantic thing, can triumph because the nineteenth century and its confining institutions, as well as the pieties of nostalgic peasant resistance, have been blown away, fantastically. (38f.)

SALMAN RUSHDIE: *MIDNIGHT'S CHILDREN*

This survey of contemporary forms of MR will now be brought to a close by a second look at Rushdie's *Midnight's Children*, a novel, as Malcolm Bradbury writes, which "was and was not about India" ("Rushdie's Empire", 361), written in response to and as a criticism of a certain nostalgia for "Indian" themes. Clement Hawes writes that it is "the attempt by Rushdie ... to imagine an India beyond the stifling stereotypes recyled in the fiction and films of contemporary Raj nostalgia: *The Jewel in the Crown, Indiana Jones and the Temple of Doom, Heat and Dust, Gandhi, A Passage to India*, and so on" (158). He does not simply revert to a celebration of primitivism and the "true" values of an indigenous culture to oppose the Raj nostalgia, though. He is too much of a postmodern and post-colonial writer to adopt such a naïve strategy.[18] In *Midnight's Children*, Rushdie engages in the encyclopedic

18 Linda Hutcheon has sketched out the main features of this allegiance in "Circling the Downspout of Empire": "While I want to argue here that the links between the post-colonial and the postmodern are strong and clear ones, I also want to underline from the start the major

enterprise of subverting assumptions about India and Europe, historiography, "realism" and nonrealistic fiction, narrative unity, originality, gender, the "imperialist subject" and the "subject of humanism" (Hutcheon, "Circling the Downspout of Empire", 150). It is not for him to respect any restrictions to expressive freedom as Hutcheon makes them out in some forms of feminist and post-colonial writing:

> The current post-structuralist/postmodern challenges to the coherent, autonomous subject have to be put on hold in feminist and post-colonial discourses, for both must work first to assert and affirm a denied or alienated subjectivity: those radical postmodern challenges are in many ways the luxury of the dominant order which can afford to challenge that which it securely possesses. ("Circling...", 151)

When Rushdie uses supernatural elements, he does so with the irony, self-consciousness and critical awareness of their implications that is due to the complexity of his subject matter.

The very first page of the novel invokes echoes from *Grimm's Fairy Tales* and *The Thousand and One Nights* – no Indian fairy tales but German ones respectively Arabian tales about the Persian court of Shahryar, altered and varied in innumerable translations and special editions; the latter collection, to which many MR stories allude, is a veritable cipher for cross-cultural projections. Saleem Sinai, the narrator is tempted to begin his autobiography by using the formula forever associated with fairy tales: "I was born in the city of Bombay ... once upon a time" (9). But no sooner has he uttered the magic words than he revokes them again; history's clutches are stronger than magic charms: "No, that won't do, there's no getting away from the date: I was born in Doctor Narlikar's Nursing Home on August 15th, 1947" (9). Throughout his narrative, fairy tales are associated with escape from a life which is both frightening and maybe less meaningful than the coincidence of his birthdate with the date of India's Independence might suggest. Thus, he tells us that whenever the fear of purposeless existence overcame the boy Saleem, he hid in his mother's washing chest (a nice image for regression), where, he says, using a telling verb to describe the action, "I buried myself in fairy tales" (152-153). Yet, his adult narrative is motivated by the same impulse: "I must work

difference, a difference post-colonial art and criticism share with various forms of feminism. Both have distinct political agendas and often a theory of agency that allow them to go beyond the postmodern limits of deconstructing existing orthodoxies into the realms of social and political action. (...) ... cultural dominants, however, are shared by all three forces. As Gayatri Spivak notes: 'There is an affinity between the imperialist subject and the subject of humanism' (202). While post-colonialism takes the first as its object of critique and postmodernism takes the second, feminists point to the patriarchal underpinnings of both" (150-151).

fast, faster than Sheherazade, if I am to end up meaning – yes, meaning – something. I admit it: above all things, I fear absurdity" (9).

Saleem, aged no more than thirty-one years, is falling apart. Though he is never altogether explicit about the reason for his early decay, we must assume, from several hints that he has contracted leprosy (37, 65, 280). In the attempt to make sense of his disastrous life he avails himself of two narrative strategies: one of them is the attempt to turn his own biography into an allegory for the development of India since its coming into independence, the other, his underscoring crucial moments by introducing supernatural elements, as Jean-Pierre Durix's study of MR in *Midnight's Children* shows (58). However, both his "chutnification of history" (459) and the "fantastic heart" (195) of his own story, the introduction of the thousand and one children, all gifted with supernatural powers like himself and born, with him, "between midnight and one a.m." on Indepencence Day (195), are infected by his general incredibility. Not only is his story inconsistent, he for instance twists facts such as the date of Gandhi's death in order to make the date match the première of his uncle Hanif's first feature film and only success (142), but our doubts are kindled and nourished by his open display of a megalomaniac wish for omnipotence over his life, that of other people (126), and especially over his listener Padma (121); further obstacles to his credibility are his delirious condition while telling her and us the most marvellous part of his story (195), and also his own admissions of doubt, e.g. "Am I so far gone, in my desperate need for meaning, that I'm prepared to distort everything – to re-write the whole history of my times purely in order to place myself in a central role?" (166). Credibility, though, is not a good narrator's most essential feature, as Saleem knows from Tai, the boatsman who is the first story-teller we encounter beside Saleem (15f.). Although he tells such paradoxical stories as the one of seeing "old and fagged out" Jesus (16), he fascinates Aadam Aziz, Saleem's far from superstitious grandfather, "because of the endless verbiage which made others think him cracked. It was magic talk ..." (15). Saleem, on his part, is often desperate to captivate Padma "with her down-to-earthery and her paradoxical superstition, her contradictory love of the fabulous" (38). Supernatural elements procure pleasure, whereas realistic fiction and films, this is the lesson he has learned from his poor uncle Hanif, may well occasionally be true, even, ironically, prophetic (244) but they can attract no audiences.

Are we in the realm of Todorov's fantastic rather than in the realm of MR, since we do not know for sure how to interpret Saleem's use of supernatural elements? My contention is that the "supernatural" fantastic becomes obsolete at the moment when not only the supernatural is called into question, but also the natural; in other words, there can no longer be a "supernatural" fantastic when the natural, historical parts of a story are unmasked as no more reliable a depiction of reality than the supernatural ones. This is the case in *Midnight's Children*.

Saleem does not always want us (and Padma) to be lulled by the marvellous. Besides subverting his credibility by self-reflexive comments on his narrating, he also points to the political dimension of the irrational. Neither assuming an iconoclastic Marxist pose of denunciating religion, myths and other forms of the supernatural as opium for the people nor simply laughing like his uncle Hanif, who does not take it seriously at all, Saleem explains how the "supernatural invasion" of India after the euphoric and progressive beginnings of the state has in fact served a conservative backlash:

> ... I remain, today, half-convinced that in that time of accelerated events and diseased hours the past of India rose up to confound her present; the new-born, secular state was being given an awesome reminder of its fabulous antiquity, in which democracy and votes for women were irrelevant ... so that people were seized by atavistic longings, and forgetting the new myth of freedom reverted to their old ways, their old regionalist loyalties and prejudices, and the body politic began to crack. (245)

Repressed fears and aggressions manifest themselves as superstitions which turn people into an easy prey for fanatics aspiring to absolute power. In fact, what is at work here is the same concern with the materiality of symbols and repressed contents of the unconscious that was discussed in Borges, Morrison and Carter. Propaganda works in a similar fashion but instead of merely declaring the unreal real, it also does the opposite by trying to turn real atrocities into "impossible hallucinations" (317), as the episode on the Pakistani's invasion in Bangladesh shows. Parallels to the massacre described in *One Hundred Years of Solitude* (282ff.) are obvious. Like García Márquez, Rushdie in such passages uses MR as a medium for bitter political satire. Shamsul Islam calls Rushdie's work "a dark allegory of the post-independence situation in the Indo Pakistani subcontinent", this "*despite* its fantasy and playfulness" (125; emphasis added): The preposition shows that for him, there is an opposition between the serious moral concern of satire and the "comic exaggeration, laughter, and non-seriousness" of nonrealistic fiction, and he goes on to discuss how Rushdie manages to "reconcile" these "contradictory impulses" (125). However, this view overlooks the fact that the supernatural, by virtue of its metafictional distancing the readers from the subject matter, is often the precondition for a detached discussion, or for satire. Rushdie writes in his defence of *The Satanic Verses*, where the device unfortunately failed:

> I genuinely believed that my overt use of fabulation would make it clear to any reader that I was not attempting to falsify history, but to allow a fiction to take off from history. The use of dreams, fantasy, etc. was intended to say: the point is not whether this is 'really' supposed to be Muhammad, or whether the satanic verses incident 'really' happened; the point is to examine what such an incident might reveal about what revelation is, about the extent to which the mystic's conscious personality informs and interacts with the mystical event; the point is to try and understand the human event of revelation. The use of fiction was a way of creating the sort of distance from actuality that I felt would prevent offence from being taken. I was wrong. ("In Good Faith", 20)

According to Silvia Albertazzi, nonrealistic elements also add new perspectives to other representations of the world; they can thus describe utopias: "... dreaming is a political act. The migrant who has been robbed of his roots, language and habits *dreams* a new reality for himself..." (13). Saleem himself invites a plurality of interpretations of the midnight's children that is less optimistic, or more ambivalent:

> ... they can be seen as the last throw of everything antiquated and retrogressive in our myth-ridden nation, whose defeat was entirely desirable in the context of a modernizing, twentieth-century economy; or as the true hope of freedom, which is now forever extinguished; but what they must not become is the bizarre creation of a rambling, diseased mind. (200)

Of course, he cannot stop us from considering even the last option, as Padma does. Earlier on he gave us a very similar lesson on reality: "Reality is a question of perspective; the further you get from the past, the more concrete and plausible it seems – but as you approach the present, it inevitably seems more and more incredible" (165). Thus, by providing new insights, the novel fulfils its purpose as Rushdie defined it in the essay quoted earlier: "The [novels] I care most about are those which attempt radical reformulations of language, form, and ideas, those that attempt to do what the word *novel* seems to insist upon: to see the world anew" ("In Good Faith", 18).

Islam's "despite" also excludes the possibility that the supernatural is precisely what is attacked by the satire. We have already come across its ambiguous status as a means of escape or as an expression of the desire for omnipotent control. Durix adds another aspect:

> Too much magic leads to paranoia in the characters that possess the special powers. Too many dreams mean the gradual disappearance of all social identity and existence, as we see with the expedition into the Sundarbans when Saleem and his companions eventually become transparent. The journey to the end of dreams opens out onto the void. (62)

Saleem's story illustrates the instability of a subject that must try to establish itself somewhere between the narcissistic belief in holding a "place at the centre of the universe" as "the Blessed One" (126) and a state of absolute dissolution in which "I" and consciousness no longer exist because existence has been reduced to instinctual reflexes (350). The supernatural underlines the transformations of Saleem's subjectivity in so far as it makes psychic processes visible (a function it possesses in most of the texts discussed): the challenge to his narcissistic illusion of centrality, by means of a choir of voices which say no more than "I" at first (168), a dreamless and desireless condition, as transparency, etc. Only towards the end of his life does he get reconciled to the impossibility of wholeness and unity:

> I no longer want to be anything except what who I am. ... I am everyone everything whose being-in-the-world affected was affected by mine. I am anything that happens after I've gone which would not have happened if I had not come. Nor am I particulary [sic] exceptional in this matter; each 'I', every one of the now-six-hundred-million-plus of us, contains a similar multitude. (383)

As Carter attacks myths, Rushdie repeatedly attacks the supernatural where it assumes real power through religion. It is for instance in the chapters about Saleem's exile in Pakistan, "Jamila Singer" and "How Saleem achieved purity", that Saleem, having lost his telepathic gifts but equipped with a hypersensitive nose, smells hypocrisy and falsehood behind pious façades: Karachi to him is a "city of mirages" (like Macondo):

> ... Karachiites had only the slipperiest of grasps on reality, and were therefore willing to turn to their leaders for advice on what was real and what was not. Beset by illusionary sand-dunes and the ghosts of ancient kings, and also by the knowledge that the name of the faith upon which the city stood meant 'submission', my new fellow-citizens exuded the flat boiled odours of acquiescence... (308)

Earlier, before he was able to identify the voices of the midnight's children for what they were, he linked his experience to that of Muhammad, who "heard a voice saying, 'Recite!' and thought he was going mad; I heard, at first, a headful of gabbling tongues, like an untuned radio" (163). Although Saleem hastens to add a pacifying bracket to the name of the prophet (163), Rushdie undermines the foundations of Islam no less than in *The Satanic Verses* by suggesting ever so indirectly that the prophet's voices probably were of the same fictive or insane quality as those of the narrator. Besides, Christian tenets and Hindu fanaticism are no safer from his questions but in their case, supernatural elements are less relevant for the satire. Finally, though Rushdie has never made a secret of his Marxist sympathies (Albertazzi 12), his association of Communism with the magicians' community in Delhi (397) is no less ambivalent than the association of the supernatural with other real phenomena. Albertazzi's evaluation captures once more only the positive aspect:

> [The magician's] slum is a domain where fantasy has finally come to power. Their openness, their courage and their magic are metaphors for the optimism of Rushdie's politics, the stubborn will to keep on believing in the Godot-like revolution his whole generation was expecting during their youth. (13)

As we turn to the novel itself, clues for a more critical view of the magicians' commitment are numerous. Parvati-the-witch, for instance, complains to Saleem, "in our colony I can't tell anyone about my real magic, ... because they don't believe in such things" (395) – in other words, the magicians are taken to be fakes, producers of attractive political illusions in whose actualization they do not believe. Moreover, they are not sufficiently steadfast to meet all the various challenges to their community and solidarity. While they are "Communists, almost to a man" (397) when Saleem gets to know them, internal quarrels (399), Indira Gandhi's repressive politics during the Emergency (427), the country-wide sterilization campaign (421) and Sanjay's "civic beautification programme" for poor districts (429) effect irretrievable changes:

> Nor did they notice that they had changed; they had forgotten that they had ever been otherwise, Communism had seeped out of them and been gulped down by the thirsty, lizard-quick earth; they were beginning to forget their skills in the confusion of hunger, disease, thirst and police harassment which constituted (as usual) the present. To me, however, this change in my old companions seemed nothing short of obscene. (444-445)

Just as the midnight's children lose what is left of their magic (439), the magicians lose all their spirit.

It would be easy and comfortable for a European reader to read the novel as no more than an allegory about post-independence India. Richard Cronin writes:

> We shall never know how much of its popularity in Britain *Midnight's Children* owes to its capacity for generating the kind of indignant satisfaction with which, even now, many Britishers like to contemplate the political difficulties of their former colonies. But their view is unconvincing. The version of empire offered in *Kim*, ... and Rushdie's version of India since 1947, ... are both of them children's histories of India, the products of fantasy rather than historical research. (210)

Even though I agree that such readers are altogether wrong, I do not share Cronin's reasons for his evaluation. For he does not sufficiently take into account Saleem's role as intermediary. It is not Rushdie whose historical research is deficient, but Saleem's, and Saleem is neither a child while telling the story nor is he one hundred percent Indian.[19] In the course of the novel we learn that he is a changeling, not the Sinai's natural son but that of a, probably, Indian woman called Vanita, and of the old English imperialist William Methwold, whose Englishness is no sooner established than demolished, for we learn that his grandmother, from whom he inherited his big nose, was from Bergerac (95, 103, 117). If Saleem were the son of Vanita's husband, the clown Wee Willie Winkie, his identity would be even more uncertain for we never get a hint about his nationality – not even his real name is known and his pseudonym points to a story by Kipling (101f.). Rushdie permanently undercuts neat distinctions to celebrate hybridity:

> Throughout human history, the apostles of purity, those who have claimed to possess a total explanation, have wrought havoc among mere mixed-up human beings. Like many millions of people, I am a bastard child of history. Perhaps we all are, black and brown and white, leaking into one another ... ("In Good Faith", 18)

While this should indeed be reason enough to rethink such unreliable categories as nationality, ethnicity, race, class, religion and family, most people remain indifferent, even repress the difference it should make as the Sinais do when Mary's fraud is disclosed:

> I was still their son: they remained my parents. In a kind of collective failure of imagination, we learned that we simply could not think our way out of our pasts ... if you had asked my father ... who his son was, nothing on earth would have induced him to point in the direction of the accordionist's knock-kneed, unwashed boy. (118)

The imaginative failure consists in the inability to define something new on the basis of hybridity. Indians prefer to cling to the half-European changeling rather than to seek, reinstate and respect their own son, who might have been degraded by a lower-class life. The Europeans, on the other hand, are not in the least in a better position; for it is their own bad example, their own inability both to recognize their mixed origins and revise the repressions upon which they have based their self-definitions which is imitated in their former colonies, in India no less than in the rest of the world. The mirror metaphor, by which Saleem's fate is likened to that of India in Nehru's letter (122) and which he later explains (238) and varies (447), inextricably implicates us: if Europe repeats itself in India (185), and Saleem's fate mirrors that of his home

---

19 Yet, what does "Indian" mean? The novel constantly subverts the notion of the subcontinent's unity too, e.g. when Aadam Aziz attempts to define his allegiances (40).

country, then he also mirrors the fate of Europe. The last time he is looking into a mirror, that is into "the eyes of a child who was simultaneously not-my-son [i.e. Shiva's son, the second Aadam in the novel] and also more my heir than any child of my flesh could have been" (447), he sees that his time is over, that the dispossessed for whom Shiva stands, whom he has banished from his thoughts and his narrative, while always aware of his uncanny presence (299), will return to assume power:

> ... from now on, mine would be as peripheral a role as that of any redundant oldster: the traditional function, perhaps, of reminiscer, of teller-of-tales ... I wondered if all over the country the bastard sons of Shiva were exerting similar tyrannies upon hapless adults, and envisaged for the second time that tribe of fearsomely potent kiddies, growing waiting listening, rehearsing the moment when the world would become their plaything. (447-448)

Saleem's hysterical fears, which are not unlike the fears that everywhere prompt xenophobia and the conflict between the generations, seem to be dispelled when little Aadam utters his first word, which seems to point to the boy's respect for Saleem's authority: "Aadam, very carefully: 'Abba...' Father. He is calling me father" (459). But Rushdie will not comply with Saleem's whishful thinking: "he has not finished, there is strain on his face, and finally my son, who will have to be a magician to cope with the world I'm leaving him, completes his awesome first word: '... cadabba.'" (459). While some critics interpret Aadam's birth as an optimistic "expression of Rushdie's notion of new Indian social and national attitudes, existing despite the venality or stupidity of the post-Emergency politicians" (Goodwin 20), others argue for the exact opposite: "Saleem's elephant-headed son ... unlike the god of wisdom [Ganesh] whom he resembles, fails to bring any promise of dawn – his birth coincides with the beginning of the long night of the state of Emergency" (Islam 131). Both readings are blind to the multiplication of ambiguity which Rushdie not only installs by means of Aadam's first –magical – word but also by making Saleem interpret it: "Abracadabra: not an Indian word at all, a cabbalistic formula derived from the name of the supreme god of the Basilidan gnostics..." (459). Everything is open; Rushdie's magic realism neither serves to affirm nor to negate reality but to interrogate it and stimulate the imagination.

By simply banishing difference from cultural representations such as histories, fictions or paintings, a dominant culture cannot eliminate uncanny elements for good, as we have also seen in Carter's novel *Hoffman*; if the autobiographer Saleem believes that "it is possible to create past events simply by saying they occurred" (443), he succumbs to an illusion, as he is very much aware in the end. Clement Hawes calls this disillusionment of the narrator as well as the readers an "unmasking of the trope of metalepsis, by which effects are retrospectively constituted as origins and causes" (148). Far from being merely a postmodern ironical flaunting and subverting of narratorial powers, this unmasking undermines the very strategy by which "the West" has constituted itself, its own myths and ideologies of cultural superiority since the late eighteenth century, e.g. in the form of a "fabrication of Ancient Greece as the origins of the 'West'" (148). Art, especially literature, has helped to transport these ideologies to all the places where the conquerors wished to establish their cultural superiority:

> ... the canon, in the case of English literature, was first developed and institutionally defined, as Gauri Vishwanathan [sic] demonstrates, precisely in the crucible of colonial administration in India ....
> The canon-making process, essentially an experiment in socio-political control in India, began as early as the 1820s: the result, as Viswanathan shows, was only 'imported' some fifty years later for home consumption. ... it was ultimately a grand strategy ... that in 1835 impelled Thomas Babington Macaulay, the East India Company's arrogant promoter of English literature over Indian classics, to write his infamous Minute on education. According to Viswanathan's analysis, the canon of English authors functioned in India precisely to aestheticize domination, to transmit 'Christian culture' and displace indigenous cultures without the controversial appearance of overt religious indoctrination. (Hawes 157-158)

Saleem, of course, is not immune to the "masks of conquest" (Viswanathan's title),[20] that is the cultural influence of the West:

> In India, we've always been vulnerable to Europeans ... Evie had only been with us a matter of weeks, and already I was being sucked into a grotesque mimicry of European literature. (We had done *Cyrano*, in a simplified version, at school; I had also read the *Classics Illustrated* comic book.) Perhaps it

---

20 See Viswanathan's introduction to her study: "This book sets out to demonstrate in part that the discipline of English came into its own in an age of colonialism, as well as to argue that no serious account of its growth and development can afford to ignore the imperial mission of educating and civilizing colonial subjects in the literature and thought of England, a mission that in the long run served to strengthen Western cultural hegemony in enormously complex ways. It is not enough, as D. J. Palmer, Terry Eagleton, Chris Baldick, Peter Widdowson, and Brian Davies, among others, seem to believe, to provide token acknowledgement of the role of empire by linking the Indian Civil Service examinations, in which English literature was a major subject, to the promotion of English studies in British schools and universities. Important as these examinations were, they do not indicate the full extent of imperialism's involvement with literary culture. The amazingly young history of English literature as a subject of study (it is less than a hundred and fifty years old) is frequently noted, but less appreciated is the irony that English literature appeared as a subject in the curriculum of the colonies long before it was institutionalized in the home country. As early as the 1820s, when the classical curriculum still reigned supreme in England despite the strenuous efforts of some concerned critics to loosen its hold, English as the study of culture and not simply the study of language had already found a secure place in the British Indian curriculum" (Viswanathan 2-3).

> would be fair to say that Europe repeats itself, in India, as farce ... Evie was American. Same thing. (185)

Certain Europeans, however, succumb no less to their own representations. Besides glorifying their superiority and banishing, at the same time as kindling a desire for, the unknown regions of the world (see the picture of young Raleigh above Saleem's crib, 15, 122f.), these representations could also vilify or domesticate the colonized cultures; think of Caliban, whose model informs Saleem's description of Tai the fisherman (15), or of the Oriental fairy tales and myths which were translated and edited at a time, i.e. in the eighteenth and throughout the nineteenth centuries, when "even the most seemingly 'domestic' novels [by English women writers] had become saturated by the racial ideologies of British imperial rule" (Hawes 155). Saleem at one point makes us aware how much transliterations can change the sense of a word:

> O fortunate ambiguity of transliteration! The Urdu word 'buddha', meaning old man, is pronounced with the Ds hard and plosive. But there is also Buddha, with soft-tongued Ds, meaning he-who-achieved-enlightenment-under-the-bodhi-tree... (349)

Translations of course allow for an even greater interpretative, or manipulative, scope.[21] It is therefore not astonishing that they did not only fail to redress the balance of cultural exchanges, but on the contrary contributed to assert "Western superiority":

> ... the translation of texts such as the *Arabian Nights* and the *Mahabharata*, as Tejaswini Niranjana shows, was a central aspect of the Orientalist project of textualizing the Asian cultures under the 'indirect rule' of European domination: it was, indeed, 'a significant technology of colonial domination' (21). The epics and legends of Indian antiquity, therefore, have less oppositional force than a nativist reading might suppose. (Hawes 164)

This will take us back to the beginning of the discussion of *Midnight's Children*. Rushdie once deliberately simplified the kinds of naïve reader responses he expected for his novel by saying "in England people read *Midnight's Children* as a fantasy, in India people read it as a history book" (quoted in Todd 73). He was not wrong; one can indeed find instances of such readings (e.g. Sushila Singh or Richard Cronin). However, it is precisely the cross-breeding of both genres, one subverting the foundations of the other, which lends this novel its irresistible power – and magic. Rushdie abstains

21 Just consider, for instance, the difference it will make if a word in a myth or fairy tale is translated as slave instead of vassal; consider how much easier it will be to demonstrate the "inferiority" of a culture exploiting slaves instead of one built on a complex system of mutual obligations.

from simply inverting strategies of cultural domination by glorifying the "East" and demonizing the "West" in turn. Non-Indian readers who expect a fantasy full of the charms and mysteries of a stereotyped and domesticated Orient, will find a text which implicates them and which is saturated by dozens of implicit and explicit allusions to their own literatures and films, from *Tristram Shandy* to the *Tin Drum*, from Shakespeare to Wilde, Kipling or García Márquez. Indian readers expecting to read a history of their country from their own point of view, on the other hand, will find that both the narrator's unfathomable biographical background and his fallibility preclude such an option from the beginning; they are referred back to themselves: "... no sane human being ever trusts someone else's version more than his own" (211).

In contrast to Angela Carter, who trusts to her readers' ability to read the signals which point to Desiderio's unreliability, Rushdie supplements his narrator by a narratee, Padma. Her role has already been discussed in detail in chapter 8.4. Nevertheless, I would like to end by highlighting once more her contribution to the "proper" reception of Rushdie's MR. I have already quoted a passage in which Saleem explains his use of supernatural elements as a concession to her "contradictory love of the fabulous" (38). There are several passages in the book, however, in which she corrects not only his evaluations of Indian subject matter (e.g. 32, 120, 222, etc.) but also checks his attempts at spellbinding her. Her reaction to the story of the midnight's children is characteristic: "Padma is looking as if her mother had died – her face, with its opening-shutting mouth, is the face of a beached pomfret. 'O baba!' she says at last. 'O baba! You are sick; what have you said?'" (200). Although he bullies her and Mary Pereira into believing him so as to escape being taken to an asylum, he self-critically analyses the way in which he has taken advantage of their lack of education:

> By my show of erudition and by the purity of my accents, I shamed them into feeling unworthy of judging me; not a very noble deed, but when the ambulance is waiting round the corner, all's fair. (It was: I smelled it.) Still – I've had a valuable warning. It's a dangerous business to try and impose one's view of things on others. (212)

He goes on to comfort Padma: "... if you're a little uncertain of my reliability, well, a little uncertainty is no bad thing. Cocksure men do terrible things. Women, too" (212). But he need not have worried about her powers of discernment; by the end of the novel, she has not only regained sufficient self-confidence to propose marriage to him but also to dismiss his artistic endeavours with a sovereign gesture: "You listen to me, mister – but me no buts! Never mind all that fancy talk any more. There is the future to think of" (444).

Whereas Rushdie's MR runs the whole gamut of expressive possibilities offered by MR to comment on historical, political, psychological, sexual, and aesthetic issues, Russell Hoban's novels and short stories are more modest and restrained. With few exceptions, all of his fictions can be classified as MR. In the next chapter, I will examine what purposes are served by the genre and what allegiances and differences can be established between him and the writers presented in this chapter.

11.3. Certain Obsessions: The Semi-Transparent Screens of Russell Hoban's Magic Realism

"... the magical thing about magic is that what lies behind it is always *non*-magical."
(Douglas R. Hofstadter, *Metamagical Themas*, p. 6)

Russell Hoban's writing is based, as we have seen earlier, on an awareness of the Real, i.e. "that which lies outside the symbolic process", the "permanent agent of disharmony" (Bowie 94; also see ch. 9, n. 4). By speaking of certain aspects of the Real, Hoban tries to transform them into reality. In this sense, the essay "The Bear in Max Ernst's Bedroom or The Magic Wallet", which he first read as keynote address to the Manitoba Writers' Guild in 1987 (MUM, BB 183), is not only programmatic for *The Moment under the Moment* but for his entire writing: "... what do I want from you? I want to encourage you, if you're not already doing it, to help enlarge the limited-reality consensus" (MUM, BB 198). Since the Real is the order of experience which surpasses reality, magic realism appears to be the perfect mode for symbolising those aspects of the Real which are not (yet) part of the reality consensus. It is precisely by symbolizing them as supernatural elements, along with natural elements which are coded as "realistic" (i.e. linguistic elements for which we will find referents in reality, as we are assured by the consensus), that MR invites us to rethink reality: MR does not simply smuggle unfamiliar elements into a realistic representation, but by choosing the supernatural, i.e. the mode which marks the represented elements as inexistent, it brings them up for discussion. This does not imply that these newly symbolized aspects of the Real have, in reality, the same status as the "realistic" elements – dreams and ghosts will remain dreams and ghosts. But it implies that they probably cannot be ignored or dismissed. They influence reality in so far as they influence those who perceive them.

As Hoban points out in "Household Tales by the Brothers Grimm", we still need to know where the ordinary reality-frame ends and the extraordinary one begins, even if the project is that of expanding the reality consensus, the ordinary reality-frame, by including aspects of the Real:

> ... reality does not end at the limits of society's frail consensus; the unknowable thingness of things and the ideas that emanate from it are equally real with all things else. Myth and story have the practical function of keeping us in touch with the unknown and unknowable in ourselves and in the universe. The more awareness we have of the other-than-rational in us, the better able we are to be reasonable in our actions.
>
> Goya wrote – I think it was on the title-page of *Los Caprichos* – 'The dream of Reason produces monsters'. I don't think that's how it is. I think it's when reason is *not* allowed to dream that it acts out its dreams while awake, and then it is that monsters are produced.... I believe that both as individuals and as a society we can find a healthy balance only when our minds (or mind) can move freely from the ordinary to the extraordinary reality-frame. The healthy mind knows where it is and draws its sustenance from different realms for dream and waking action. The danger of those fictions current now in television, films, and government is that violent and uncontrollable dreams have moved out of the realm of the extraordinary and into the ordinary, there to become part of our stock of usable action. (MUM, HT 152)

As we have seen in chapter 11.2, all magic realists in one form or another emphasize the existence of the Real, at the latest when they deal with that universal intrusion of it which as a bare fact cancels all ideological, religious or philosophical differences: death. It is the degree to which an awareness of the Real shows through his fictional screens which distinguishes Russell Hoban's MR from that of other writers. David Punter, who has compared the novels of Angela Carter and Russell Hoban in his contribution to *The British and Irish Novel since 1960*, thinks that both of them are more aware of "the real world transformed" (and I take this to mean both reality and the Real) than other contemporary writers:

> Carter and Hoban, I think, are important writers because they are able to use techniques which are frequently referred to as postmodernist without losing sight of the real world. Both writers are fascinated by story as such, but this fascination does not in the end deflect them into the kind of all-embracing relativity which pervades so much postmodernist writing, and it is because of this return to the real world transformed that I take the label of 'magic realism' to be a useful one. (Punter 156-157)

On the other hand, magic realists also differ in the ways in which they define the Real, apart from its manifestation in death, and in the ways in which they code it in their narratives, for instance as natural or supernatural elements. Whether it is pure contingency, the drives, God, cosmic entropy, an inflexible pattern which subjects us to iron laws, or a universal transmission which broadcasts us does indeed make a difference. As we have seen especially in *Pilgermann*, but also in the quote at the beginning of this chapter, for Russell Hoban there exists a dynamic pattern constituted by the way in which we live our lives from one burst of being to the next. The pattern is both inside us, like a genetic code, and beyond us. We are not absolutely free in our actions since our spatio-temporal position in the pattern, i.e. our sexual, social and historical identity, imposes certain limitations on us, but to a certain extent we can change the pattern by the way we live, the decisions we make, and our openness to change.

Wilkie has called a consciousness such as Hoban's "mythological":[1]

> The mythological consciousness is a timeless consciousness. It has transcended the limitations of its ego and has confronted the 'shadow' of itself. And the 'shadow', according to Jung, is the narrow gate through which it must pass to go beyond even its personal unconscious, to touch the preconscious experience of the psyche. Here, in this state that Neumann has called the 'uroboros: the psychic state of the beginning' – that is as much the experience of the individual as it is of the race – it meets the mythical time of origins, the 'paradisal time'.... It is the time that is indifferent to objective chronology.... (13)

As I showed in chapters 7.4 and 8.3, however, certain notions of the Real may become problematic, e.g. at the moment when individual subjects cannot, or do not want to, recognise themselves as subject to mythical patterns because myth is seen as constructed and not given, temporal and not eternal; the transcendental may be categorically dismissed as a delusion or called into question in some aspects, or else the quest for it is subordinated to, and truly actualised only as, a genuine care for an other: striving for the recovery of "paradisal time" must not lead to the unethical neglect of one's fellow human beings, who are "impaled on history" (PG 222). Rather than to let his protagonists abandon themselves completely to mythological and metaphysical thinking, Hoban always makes them aspire to a dynamic balance between the

1 Unfortunately, she has not derived this term from Barthes's redefinition of the "mythologist" in the essay "Myth Today" (1956): "If I focus on a full signifier, in which I clearly distinguish the meaning and the form, and consequently the distortion which the one imposes on the other, I undo the signification of the myth, and I receive the latter as an imposture. ... This type of focusing is that of the mythologist: he deciphers the myth, he understands a distortion" (115). For Wilkie, "mythological consciousness" is linked to Jungian archetypes as the quotation below will show, i.e. to the questionable claim that certain representations are closer to the Real, or "truer" than others. As the discussion of the pattern in *Pilgermann* has shown, however, Hoban actually problematizes such assumptions. He "understands a distortion", although he is also aware that it is often preferable to distort rather than to abstain from representing the Real.

requirements of historical reality and those of the atemporal Real, be it psychic or transcendental.

In this chapter, I will first briefly group Hoban's texts according to their genres and discuss those which do not fall under the heading of MR. Occurrences of the words "magic" and "magical" will then be examined as a preliminary to Hoban's use of supernatural elements in MR texts. A comparison with the writers presented in chapter 11.2 will conclude my analysis.

MR is the mode Russell Hoban has preferred throughout his career. Even *Riddley Walker* and *Fremder*, so far treated as postmodern novels which make use of science fiction motifs, are magic realistic precisely in the dominant feature in which they deviate from the science fiction paradigm. Their postmodernity is magic realistic: both novels call into question the borderline between fiction (or subjectivity) and reality while also insisting on our responsibility for establishing such a borderline, or reality membrane, time and again. There is one more text which follows this pattern, i.e. the fragment titled "Untitled", which forms the last part of "Certain Obsessions, Certain Ideas" (MUM, CO 249ff.).

"Some Episodes in the History of Miranda and Caliban", the opera libretto with its dreamlike supernatural transformations of the main characters from one shape into another is a fantasy about the Real of desire. There is no "natural" counterpoint to interact with the endless circles of desire experienced by Miranda and Caliban. The short story "Dream Woman", on the other hand, is magic realistic in so far as it addresses the status of dreams in reality. The dream woman sends the "realy" back to his world although he would like to stay with her; it is she, then, who rejects an expansion of consensus reality in such a way that dream and waking experience would become equivalent (MUM, DW 60).

The scope of consensus reality is also addressed in the realistic texts, i.e. in *Turtle Diary* and "The Colour of Love". They dramatize intrusions of the Real into everyday reality without openly transgressing the representational codes which separate natural from supernatural elements. Dreams are dreams: although Neaera thinks she must act after dreaming of the shark, she knows that reality and dreams belong to different reality-frames. Short-lived magical moments are described without the assistance of supernatural elements: a particular colour of the sky at dusk (MUM, CL 55) or the model of Port Liberty (TD 40) intimate a reality behind all appearances. Lavinia Haworth in "The Colour of Love" even quotes from a *Scientific American* article on quantum mechanics to underline her feeling that there exist other realities beside the "received world" (MUM, CL 54). This is the theory from which Helen and Izzy Gorn will develop their phase-jump oscillators in *Fremder*.

Normally, though, Hoban uses the supernatural to represent the Real, as his protean transformations of the characters of Shakespeare's *Tempest* in "Some Episodes in the History of Miranda and Caliban" show. While the juxtaposition of realistic and nonrealistic elements and characters in Shakespeare's play invites us to consider the supernatural as hitherto unaccounted-for aspects of reality (e.g. in a magic realistic reading, Caliban might be regarded as Prospero's unconscious desire), Hoban's libretto does not refer to reality at all. Its aim is to represent the pattern which orients the characters of Shakespeare's play, the *ideas* of Miranda and Caliban. For Hoban, they are complements involved in an endless and timeless action cycle of gain and loss. "Miranda" and "Caliban" are merely two of many roles they play somewhere on the way, besides "She" and "He", "Shakespeare" and "Freud", the "Sphinx" and a "Traveller", or "Terror" and "Boredom". Ultimately, though, they will return to the beginning: their pattern thus is no "strange attractor" (cf. ch. 10.1) but a circle of a higher order, or a three-dimensional helix whose beginning and end meet. The MR stories, on the other hand, especially those with science fiction elements, usually address the need for change as well as the difficulty of introducing it into established patterns and seemingly closed systems. Hoban shows how easy it is for characters to lapse into their old ways even after apocalyptic catastrophes, which might otherwise be associated with fresh starts. Thus Riddley inadvertently contributes to the rediscovery of gunpowder, and the three tragi-comical protagonists of "Untitled" go and seek a woman although they have never seen one (MUM, CO 254). Fremder's leap out of his seemingly ineluctable fate is the most emphatic affirmation of change.

The distinction between Hoban's fantasy and his realism might be sketched thus: while fantasy (the pure supernatural mode) can be (mis)read as claiming to represent the Real as it is (though Hoban himself would never affirm such finality),[2] the realistic fictions openly negotiate about aspects of the Real. My thesis is that his MR texts imaginatively reinforce points made in the realistic texts. Where supernatural elements are juxtaposed with natural ones, the former heuristically personify, embody, or materialize aspects of the Real so as to give a temporary shape to what is really ungraspable. Since some of these elements appear in several texts, but are never altogether identical with earlier appearances, his MR texts, these semi-transparent screens, make the Real flicker through surface appearances (words conjuring up

2 This is the reason why the tile pattern in *Pilgermann* is presumptuous and dangerous; it fixes the Real in a way that falsifies it: "'... Do I not know how far I have overstepped the bounds of what is permitted in one's approach to the Unseen?'", Pilgerman meditates on his responsibility (PG 180).

images) precisely at that moment in-between, when one image is fading and the next has not yet taken shape.

Before focusing on the texts' supernatural elements, I would like to approach the supernatural from a linguistic angle, by way of tracing places in which the words "magic" or "magical" have been used in Hoban's texts: Frog in *The Mouse and his Child* offers useless "LOVE POTIONS AND MAGIC CHARMS" (MC 37). In the final showdown with the lion, on the other hand, Jachin-Boaz experiences "No magic. Reality unbearable, inescapable" (LN 188). The yellow paper of the next novel, *Kleinzeit*, flatters the presumptuous would-be hero and writer on his writing: "It's like magic with you, said the yellow paper" – and goes on to shake off all he has written immediately after her compliment (166). Neaera from *Turtle Diary* is less generous with praise: she finds that the aquarium at the zoo is "not magical" (TD 26). But she hopes that setting the turtles free will give back to the world some of the turtle's "magical reality, juice of life in a world gone dry" (TD 50). A little later William reflects on the "magical transformations" that shamans undergo, wondering whether he could be a turtle (TD 61). Both will eventually find out that it is up to themselves to alter their reality. In *Pilgermann*, the protagonist must face the anti-Semite Konrad's prejudices: "Everybody knows about Jew magic" (PG 82). Pilgermann himself does not use the word in a derogatory sense: he looks forward to the coming of "Elijah fed by angels, fed by ravens, Elijah the magical" (PG 213), and he admires the ghosts of his dead fellow-travellers because they have "acquired not only merit but magical power by completing the journey to the end of themselves" (PG 218). But magic is thereby associated with mortality. Tension also comes to light in *The Medusa Frequency*, where magic is on the one hand part of a slogan for an aftershave, "CLASSIQUE: ETERNAL MAGIC BY ORPHEUS" (MF 49), and on the other hand the attribute of a valuable terracotta dancer:

> Let us say that I put into your hands this little terracotta dancer, and the beauty and the tragedy of it become the whole world to you, become all that is precious and to be enshrined in your heart, take on even a magical significance so that you know in your heart that if ever this little dancer is broken then the world is lost. And in you a devil stirs, a devil with a hammer in its hand. (MF 79)

The sphinx Léonie's sexuality *is* of "magical power" (MUM, NL 17) whereas Chinese radicals merely *seem* "magical, as if the physical act of making the strokes in black ink on white paper had the power of calling up the physical being of what the character represented" (MUM, SZ 31). At Paxos, it is a goat's eyes, a donkey's bray, olive trees and stones which convey a sense of magic (MUM, PL 135). Back home, night itself "crouches magically with the fire reflected in its eyes" around a story-teller and her listeners (MUM, HT 148). The three last "magical" items seem as diverse as the preceding list: they are Whitman's lyric "Out of the Cradle Endlessly Rocking" (MUM, IC 161), the wallet of the Fool from the Waite and Smith Tarot deck, "heavy with the past, present, and future of the universe" (MUM, BB 197), and Thelonious Monk's hat (MUM, FL 206).

Some trends can be derived from this haphazard survey: what is called "magic" or "magical" need not be supernatural, for a distinction must be made between blunt debasements of the concept, figurative usages (similes and metaphors), and instances where what is meant is indeed the effect of a communication between reality and the Real. Unless the concept has been grossly abused, magic is always a matter of life and death, both individual and cosmic. Animals, mythical and fabulous beings, and works of art appear to be its ideal media. Human beings who transmit magic are either shamans or special artists. Some of the items that appear on the list are traditionally associated with magic, e.g. charms, the night, or shamanic transformations, while others become so in Hoban's perception and presentation.

The bridge from the expression "magic" to magic realism is built by that mythical figure which does not appear on the list because it embodies the essence of all that is magical and therefore need not be qualified by the adjective: Hermes.[3] MR is a Hermetic genre, as will become clear from the

---

3 I would like to quote some passages from Kerényi's study *Hermes: Guide of Souls* to illustrate in what sense Hermes is related to the magical items listed above: "... we must be prepared not only for what is immediately intelligible, but also for what is strangely uncanny" (5; contradictory traits: positive and negative evaluations collapse as in Freud's "heimlich/unheimlich" opposition); "Hermes is deliberately kept at a distance from every heroic happening" (7; anti-heroism of characters, weakness of shamans); "This youthfully handsome, friendly, and thievish guide, who possesses magical golden shoes which transport him over earth and sea and a magical staff with which he puts people to sleep and awakens them again – has he not all the characteristics and attributes of a seductive and lethal guide of souls ... ?" (9; seduction, transport from one realm to the other, Elijah, ghosts); "We are faced with the skilled highwayman and bandit, as well as the flattering deceiver" (21; false compliments, the language of ads); "Meeting and finding are revelations of Hermes' essence" (23; the Fool's wallet contains such finds); "... out of his victim's death he conjures music..." (26; this is why the terracotta dancer will be broken, and with it the world will be lost); "This is not Apollonic music....: '... fair sang the / God to the notes, improvising his chant / as he played, like lads exchanging taunts / at festivals'" (27; Thelonious Monk and Walt Whitman); "... is not then Night the very stuff of Hermes? that which gives him reality? Yes, if one knows the God beforehand and brings his image along, then one recognizes in him the familiar characteristics of the night and vice versa" (50); "The original Hermes had no special need of a love affair with Aphrodite in order to beget Eros with her: he possessed her as his feminine aspect, and perhaps the latter was even the more prominent part before the masculine nature in him became aroused." (63; power of the Sphinx, unstable sexuality); "... the word for the simplest mute stone monument, ***herma***, from which the name of the God stems, corresponds phonetically to the Latin *sermo*, 'speech'... Hermes is ***hermeneus*** ('interpreter'), a linguistic mediator, and this not merely on linguistic grounds" (88; stones, the idea of mediation).

attributes Karl Kerényi attributes to him in *Hermes: Guide of Souls*, the book that Hoban, too, quotes in "'I, that was a child...'":

> For the great mystery, which remains a mystery even after all our discussing and explaining, is this: the appearance of a speaking figure, the very embodiment as it were in a human-divine form of clear, articulated, play-related and therefore enchanting language – its appearance in that deep primordial darkness where one expects only animal muteness, wordless silence, or cries of pleasure and pain. Hermes the 'Whisperer' (*psithyristes*) inspirits the warmest animal darkness. (Kerényi 88; or MUM, IC 166)

We find in Hermes as in MR the juxtaposition of two realms, the human and the divine (or natural and supernatural), linguistic playfulness as well as clear language, and the dangerous proximity of what I have called the Dionysiac vortex of the death drive in chapter 9.

With such a wide-spanned underlying analogy it is clear that Hoban's MR can fulfil all the functions we saw it fulfil in the novels and stories examined in the previous chapter: it is metafictional, dramatizes the Real of desire and tries to come to terms with political aspects of reality. But besides having these properties it also establishes a metaphysical dimension that most of the novels and stories discussed so far either contest or call into question. While the Hermetic consists in giving language to the unknowable, or more generally, in energizing processes, Hermes as a figure does not appear among the supernatural characters which populate the MR texts. The principle of naming always remains but a name.[4] As the title of chapter 6 of *The Medusa Frequency* points out, "We're not Talking about a Bloke with Winged Sandals" (MF 42) but about a "frequency of probability when complementary equivalents offer and anything can be anything" (MF 44). In my analysis of the character constellations of this novel in chapter 8.2, I called Hermes a catalyst. A catalyst requires material to work on and characters that will respond to its influence. In *Pilgermann*, Hermes corresponds to the will of God, which "was simply that everything possible would indeed be possible" (PG 182). Pilgermann thinks that "only humans would bother to play" God's game, in which the "possibilities of choice were beyond all calculation and the probability of wrong choice so high as to be almost a certainty" (PG 182). But in the overall view of Hoban's texts it is quite clear that the frequency of

4 Is it too daring to associate Hermes, "the ithyphallic" (MUM, CO 244), with Lacan's privileged "signifier", i.e. the "phallus"? See for instance Jacques Lacan's "The Agency of the Letter in the Unconscious": "... the structure of the signifier is, as it is commonly said of language itself, that it should be articulated" (152). Hermes is articulated at the moment when a shift occurs, something inert begins to move and the nameless acquires a name. His function is to effect a transfer; the signifier's analogous function is to effect "transference" ("The Agency...", 170).

probability is not limited to the human sphere but stretches from the interaction of the tiniest particles to the generation and destruction of universes.[5]

At the beginning of his writing we find two clockwork mice who become self-winding and a whole host of speaking animals, among them, foremost, Manny Rat. The distinction between the marvellous and the horrific causes difficulty right from the beginning. One cannot say that the mice are marvellous creatures because they reach the goal of their quest while Manny Rat, their opponent, is thoroughly horrific. What is interesting is that the pair of heroes are and remain *clockwork* toys and the rat, a deeply *ambivalent* figure, not simply a villain. Self-winding though father and son may be in the end, they remain mechanical creatures who have nothing new to expect: "'Your fortune has been made,' said Frog, 'and needs no more telling.'" (MC 198). Their happiness is a kind of stagnation. Manny Rat, on the other hand, still has a potential for change in him. He nearly therefore became the protagonist of a sequel, as I showed in chapter 2.4. It is often in the particulars of supernatural elements, in the details rather than the main characteristics, that we find something that is analogous to what Freud has described as "the navel of the dream": the Real that makes itself known in spite of predominant images.[6] Even the dead Nazi rats, who rape the narrator of "The Devil's Kitchen" after he has shrunk to their size (DK 169), do not altogether match the definition I gave of the horrific in chapter 11.1: something that suggests horror and panic in the face of an involuntary exposure of the protagonists to malevolent supernatural forces. For the rats would have been "powerless" like Dracula, had the narrator not cooperated (DK 170). His transformation into a "Töchterchen" is prefigured by his ambivalent feelings: he buys the dolls' kitchen although he feels uneasy about it (DK 164). And even though the rats disgust him, he accepts all their conditions in order to get a story out of them (DK 168). The story can take place because his disposition prompts him to be open to any chance that might offer itself. What applies to the clockwork mice and Manny Rat is therefore also true for human characters: as long as there is an inner split, they move and develop, they are, as Riddley Walker would say, "ready for any thing" (RW 199).

Orpheus, who is first mentioned in *Kleinzeit* (e.g. KL 146-150) but only appears – not in person, but in pieces, i.e. as a rotting head – in *The Medusa*

5 See for instance the narrator's mystical visions in the short story "The Raven" (MUM, RV 44-48)

6 In *Die Traumdeutung*, Freud writes: "Jeder Traum hat mindestens eine Stelle, an welcher er unergründlich ist, gleichsam einen Nabel, durch den er mit dem Unerkannten zusammenhängt" (130, n. 2)

Frequency, is the archetypal image of the element that yields to the influence of Hermes. To Hoban this is so crucial a feature that he has altered the mythical genealogy: both in *The Medusa Frequency* and in "Certain Obsessions, Certain Ideas" Orpheus is Hermes's son, not Oeagrus's or Apollo's (MF 36; MUM, CO 243). He tells Hermes that he is "the first singer, ... the one to whom Hermes brought Eurydice and perpetual guilt" (MF 33). Dissolution and decapitation form the last Dionysiac part of his way (MF 120). As before, these attributes point the way to the ideas behind him, but what is essential is the last self-characterization with which he prefaces his story: "I may be lying or I may even be making it up as I go along. I was a good musician but I'm not reliable in any other way" (MF 36). It is this feature through which the entire myth of Orpheus and Eurydice offers itself to its Hermetic dislocution, as I showed in chapter 8.3.

In *The Lion of Boaz-Jachin and Jachin-Boaz*, the supernatural lion complicates the picture. He, and not just one of his features, is the navel of the novel, for he is ungraspable in his totality. The movement of the two protagonists is not the result of a simple dialectic between oppositional poles such as good and evil (Manny Rat) or slavery and freedom (the clockwork mice) but, as I tried to show in chapter 3.2, of an intricate web of feelings in which fear, courage, weakness, defiance, guilt, solidarity, dependence, responsibility, impotence, a suicidal urge, rage and ambition are inextricably mixed. The lion embodies all of them, and more; he is "Being unbounded, terrifying, violent medium of death and life, indifferent to both, contemptuous of mortal distinctions" (LN 188). He is indeed "No magic" (LN 188) but the Real itself, the complex field of forces which prompts different responses from different percipients: "magic" as creative Hermetic response (Jachin-Boaz and Boaz-Jachin's quest for a new life), "realism" as a more passive response (Gretel's accepting the challenge of a life with Jachin-Boaz), "romance" as a narcissistic attempt to stop any further development, and/or redress losses effected by the development (the lion initially makes Jachin-Boaz feel like an "exiled king", LN 50), or "silence" as Dionysiac disruption, as death (the attempted suicide of Jachin-Boaz's wife). Lions will reappear in different guises in later stories, e.g. as the "Hidden Lion" pattern and Christ in *Pilgermann* (23, 123), as a black Chinese lion sculpture in "Schwartz" (MUM, SZ 32), or in the name and body of the sphinx Léonie (MUM, NL 17). But only in *Pilgermann* does the complexity of this supernatural element amount to that of the lion of Boaz-Jachin and Jachin-Boaz. While the latter establishes the equivalence of psychic and external reality, both the pattern and the Christ-lion in *Pilgermann* underline the immanence of the metaphysical in physical reality. Hoban's essay "Pan Lives" provides the synthesis between all these realms:

> Can God and word and reason be thought of separately? Obviously not. (When I talk of God here I don't mean any particularised denominational God, I mean the primal force and mover of the cosmos, I mean the universal mind, I mean whatever it is that pervades the universe and requires us to take notice of it.) If God is the origin of all things then word and reason along with everything else must come from God. (MUM, PL 127-128)

The raven from the eponymous story (traditionally a magical bird) comes closest to the lions in terms of giving a human character a sense of the connectedness of everything. For as a response to the narrator's question what "the black" in the expression "a black time" (MUM, RV 41) might be, the raven takes him, as I have pointed out in chapter 9, on a mystical journey that connects the mundane with the microcosm of particles and the macrocosm of the universe:

> Up we flew, high, high into the blue dome, when whistling down in a dizzying black-winged rush we shot the long, long curve past faces huge and tiny on the flickering screen of memory, faces in the shadows, in the light, lips shaping words remembered and forgotten in the moving gleams of time, the wavering of candlelight, the whispering of gold watches, the boom of tower clocks, the fading ink of letters tied with faded ribbons; faces wheeling with horsemen and battles and cannon, marching with armies, screaming in burning cities, drowning in shipwrecks and the thunder of the wild black ocean; palimpsested voices, distant figures and the changing colours of processions, plagues, migrations, ruins, standing stones, cave drawings, jungles, deserts, dust, meteorites, dinosaurs, giant ferns, volcanoes, floods, blue-green algae, silence, the grey rainlight in an empty room, the sound of my footsteps under yellow streetlamps, and an unaccompanied cello from a long time ago. (MUM, RV 44-45)

In *Fremder*, Elijah's having been fed by ravens is addressed again and again. Fremder, though, eventually finds a way to free himself from that kind of dependence on "the black". In other novels and stories, the field of forces within which the human protagonists move is usually spanned by separate elements. In *Kleinzeit*, for instance, God, Shiva, Hospital, Death, Word, Memory, and Underground are all "characters" who compete for Kleinzeit's attention, alleviating or encumbering his life with their presents and demands. They are as real as the Creative Director, the doctors, Sister and Kleinzeit's fellow patients.

Death, which was merely one aspect of the lion of Boaz-Jachin and Jachin-Boaz, acquires more and more shapes in the course of Hoban's writing. In *Kleinzeit*, it is one among many other personified supernatural figures; at the same time, it here also appears in its funniest shape, as a monkey that can be kept at bay with a frying-pan, but not for good (KL 122). Death is also represented in *Turtle Diary* and *Riddley Walker*. These representations, Miss Neap's suicide (TD 181), the shark in Neaera's nightmare (TD 77), Brooder Walker's death (RW 10) and the mythical figure of Aunty (RW 87), follow the usual strategies of displacement: death is represented by contiguity or comparison as either someone else's death or an allegory for death. As Elisabeth Bronfen writes in *Over Her Dead Body*, "any representation of death necessarily works over a constantly receding, ungraspable signified" (12). In Hoban's MR, the personifications of death enact their ungraspability. Although it is *their* death that the characters encounter, they are not in control of it (see e.g. PG 44, 57, 217). Like the lion of Boaz-Jachin and Jachin-Boaz (LN 130), or Hospital in *Kleinzeit* (KL 150), death is what it is: symbolization fails. Barbara Herkommer's diligent analysis of death in *Pilgermann* brings this aspect out very clearly (Herkommer 206). Pilgermann himself has to learn this uncanny lesson on his second encounter with Death: believing himself the subject of representation in control of Death's appearances, he is doomed to fail (PG 59).

In the most recent stories, figures of death and places associated with dying are never steady before the actual moment of death. Medusa, for instance, never appears as a clear-cut character: she is "quivering", a body in the process of becoming a face, when she first appears to Herman (MF 90), "flickering and friendly" when he sees her last emerging from Vermeer's *Head of a Young Girl* (MF 143). "The Man with the Dagger", on the other hand, is set in a flickering black-and-white Latin American town populated by skeletons. The narrator himself feels how he is "flickering into black-and-white" at the beginning of the story (MUM, MD 5). Various skeletons offer him easy ways of dying: the hotel keeper suggests that he "check in" at Hotel Death prematurely to "beat the rush" (MUM, MD 7) whereas Noir, the skeleton whore who has got his "skeleton cherry", is disappointed that she cannot get any more of him (MUM, MD 8f.). The narrator declines their offers because it is Dahlmann, the protagonist of Borges's short story "The South", that he has come to see. Immediately before Dahlmann appears, the flickering stops (MUM, MD 14). The narrator feels a strong urge to go home, but when Dahlmann throws his dagger in the air and Whitey provides him with a long knife, he accepts Dahlmann's challenge to a fight. The story stops – and death is "rendered"[7] in one of the ways I discussed in chapter 9, that is, by means of rupture and silence.

Significantly, *Fremder* once more embraces life: instead of joining Helen and Izzy Gorn in another reality that could well be the realm of the dead, Fremder sabotages the last phase-jump experiment of Pythia. He tunes to a frequency that will take him back to a drab reality but one he knows and one, too, he knows to be inhabited by people as doubtful and frightened as he normally is himself.

Is there a distinction between the protagonists and the readers, between the inside and the outside of the texts? If an element can be the navel of the narrative, which calls into question the distinction between psychic and exterior reality, and between the physical and the metaphysical within the fiction, is not then a magic realistic narrative, which interrogates reference (i.e. the relation between material and linguistic reality), a navel of reality? We might be so much used to MR texts, as a matter of fact, to all kinds of texts, that we do not even regard them as something special, something that sticks out from reality, or perhaps I had rather say something that probes into reality in search of the Real.[8] The prefix "meta-" in metafiction actually can be understood precisely as such a "transcending" of boundaries, fiction which is not merely self-conscious or self-referential[9] but which transcends itself as it involves the extratextual reader in the process of its creation, inviting him or her to rethink reality and the norms by which it is linked with fiction.[10] Russell Hoban's fiction shows that works of art always transcend themselves to interfere with reality. While *The Lion of Boaz-Jachin and Jachin-Boaz* only reluctantly creates metafictional awareness of this kind,[11] Hoban's later novels

---

7 See Zizek's distinction between symbolic representation, imaginary imitation and immediate 'rendering' (40).

8 See Zizek on the "phallic anamorphosis" at work in Hitchcock's films: "'Phallic' is precisely the detail that 'does not fit,' that 'sticks out' from the idyllic surface scene and denatures it, renders it uncanny. It is the point of *anamorphosis* in a picture: the element that, when viewed straightforwardly, remains a meaningless stain, but which, as soon as we look at the picture from a precisely determined lateral perspective, all of a sudden acquires well-known contours" (90). I prefer Bronfen's "omphalic" to the "phallic" metaphor where the Real is concerned. Incidentally, navels actually stick out, too, before they withdraw into the body.

9 Hoban's view of language as Logos, which he develops in "Pan Lives", and of literature which can at best "make a space in which the silence can speak, in which the language of the everything can be heard" (MUM, PL 138-139), is opposed to the notion of self-referentiality that, for instance, William H. Gass sees as the basic feature of any work of art: "A work of art is made to last as a valuable being in the world. As such it may develop, over time, useful relations to the world; but just as human beings ultimately must find their values in themselves, so works of art must *be relevant by being*" (Gass and McCauley 40).

10 See Hutcheon's definition of metafiction as "mimesis of process" in ch. 11.2, note 5.

11 For instance at the moment when Boaz-Jachin's magic ritual conjures up the lion from a relief (LN 43), or in a brief and unobtrusive passage where Jachin-Boaz is nonplussed by the assumption of his employer that supernatural and horror stories are a harmless means of "escape" from reality (LN 161f.).

and stories more and more emphasize the interaction between "art" (and this refers to all media: fiction, painting, sculpture, architecture, or music) and "life"; they are inseparably entangled and mutually productive. In *Kleinzeit*, for example, we find among the supernatural elements Word and the yellow paper, who leave Kleinzeit no choice: either he struggles to become a writer or he will have to die – they massively alter his reality. Riddley Walker's trance "reveal", "EUSAS HEAD IS DREAMING US" (RW 58), clearly implicates the readers, and so does the opening of *Fremder*. The narrator of "The Man with the Dagger" literally enters a story by Borges (MUM, MD 4), the narrator of "Word Pix", a series of etchings (MUM, WP 201). In *The Medusa Frequency*, finally, the media through which supernatural characters talk to Herman stretch from myth (the head of Orpheus, MF 31) to paintings (the Vermeer girl, MF 79; Medusa, MF 90) to the computer screen (the Kraken, MF 8), that is, from the most ancient to the most recent.[12]

Literature which wants to be more than literary, which is written with the aim of enlarging "the limited-reality consensus" (MUM, BB 198) is no doubt political. But in contrast to literature which tries to encourage readers to change their material conditions, e.g. post-colonial fiction, Hoban's fiction relativizes the importance of everything material. In *Riddley Walker*, he has contrasted the two forms of political intervention in a scene where Riddley compares his father's activity as connexion man to his own: While Brooder Walker in a difficult situation encouraged his audience to move from one settlement to the next, Riddley finds himself unable to produce a "reveal" that is reasonable, solid and oriented towards the audience's needs; he cannot help condensing the content of a mystical vision that has taken hold of him in the sentence quoted above (RW 58). From *The Mouse and his Child* to *The Moment under the Moment* we see characters becoming conscious of powers beyond their immediate grasp and control. Irruptions of the Real time and again disturb their planning. In *Fremder*, however, subjectivity is shown to have a certain influence on the outcome of the story: but subjectivity might be split and can lead to death, too, as the fates of the rat and Izzy Gorn show. In the fabulous world of *The Mouse and his Child*, where the animals and clockwork toys take the position usually reserved for human characters, it falls to the tramp to play the role of fate, as I argued in chapter 2.5. Frog's involuntary prophecy of the two mice's future moreover shows that the Real also inhabits them, as it does the human characters of the later texts: "All else

12 Brian McHale has coined the term "interface fiction" for "postmodernist fiction of the cybernetic interface, that is, texts which register the first, often traumatic encounters between 'literary' culture (high culture generally) and the transformative possibilities of computer technology" (*Constructing Postmodernism*, 236).

beyond the pattern in the snow departed from his vision; his ears hummed, and other sounds all vanished, leaving him alone with the voice of his mind and the dark seeds dancing in the stillness of their mystic changes" (MC 41). In this perspective, wars, pogroms, ecological catastrophes, or personal problems like illnesses or difficult relationships acquire another significance than in the human perspective. Especially in *Pilgermann* Hoban explores the limits of freedom and the share of responsibility every individual must bear. Since Pilgermann consists of waves and particles, he can comment on events that took place after the time of the crusades; on the Holocaust he writes:

> ... I must say, though lightning strike me as I speak, that there are moments when I begin to wonder whether God really is omniscient; I begin to think that it may be with him even as with some lowly mortal novelist who, having written a tremendous later scene, must perforce go back to insert an earlier one to account for it. Here of course I'm being arrogant, and maybe that's why God keeps writing slaughter scenes: the character gets out of hand; X, having been called the chosen, presumes too much, grows excessively familiar, requires too much of God, becomes like the relative who turns up uninvited on the doorstep to stay for a month. Maybe it's that simple – God is omnipresent but not omnipatient. He sometimes needs to make a little space around himself and Pffft! there go a few hundred or a few million X. (PG 40)

The temptation of blaming God, or the frequency of probability, for human affairs is overwhelming; a great number of crimes have already been justified in this way. But Hoban does not embrace moral relativism. There may be "no Heaven and Hell as what could be called places" (PG 68) to reward the good and punish sinners, yet judgment takes place every moment, as Bembel Rudzuk emphasizes (PG 173, 179f.).

Even though his main concern is to enlarge the limited-reality consensus, Hoban does not avoid addressing contemporary "issues" in his MR texts: In *The Lion of Boaz-Jachin and Jachin-Boaz* he points out the importance of self-realization; in *Kleinzeit*, he attacks the degradation of patients in the medical machinery; the relation between religion and violence is considered in *Pilgermann*, artistic ambition in *The Medusa Frequency*; and relationships between men and women in almost every text. In *The Medusa Frequency*, he actually corrects the imbalance of an approach to life that no longer respects the material world at all: Gom Yawncher's death reminds Herman of the reality of bodies (MF 125), Orpheus's and indirectly also his own, see chapter 8.1. *Fremder* is a clear affirmation of drab reality to an oedipal "paradise". What is noticeable, though, is how Hoban usually "tones down" the natural to signal that it is not necessarily more real than the supernatural.

While the mediation of the external world through various characters' consciousness, a simple form of psychological realism, was responsible for the effect of unreality in *The Lion of Boaz-Jachin and Jachin-Boaz*, see chapter 3.1, the MR novels from *Kleinzeit* to *Fremder* and the short stories undermine realism by means of another technique: its characteristics are economy of description in regard to setting, distrust of the well-made plot which suggests authorial omnipotence, and the use of types rather than complex characters, caricature combined with a concise and dislocutionary style that is reminiscent both of Hemingway's iceberg technique and Joyce's language games. Ever since *Turtle Diary* Hoban has also preferred first-person narrators for his narratives to emphasize the process of story-telling. The only exceptions are "Dark Oliver" and "The Ghost Horse of Genghis Khan", the two stories about boys which also differ from the other stories collected in *The Moment under the Moment* because they are closed narratives, see chapter 9. "Certain Obsessions, Certain Ideas", which gives partial insight into the early stages of *The Medusa Frequency*, captures interesting shifts of perspective: The first paragraph of "The Raging of the Head of Orpheus" (MUM, CO 239) invokes a synaesthetic primal scream in which sound, sight, taste, chronology and space are engaged in a carnivalesque, delirious dance indifferent to syntax and logic. The subsequent, humorous third-person section with the title "Interviews with the Head of Orpheus" (MUM, CO 239-240) establishes the greatest possible distance between the readers and the head. An eleven-year-old protagonist, John Orf, finds the head of Orpheus, and Police Constable Orson Footer records Orpheus's monosyllabic answers to his questions. Only the next section, "The Finding of the Head" (MUM, CO 240-243), reverts to first-person narration. Its narrator experiences the instability of boundaries between inside and outside that has become the hallmark of Hoban's MR. "Thinking about Hermes" (MUM, CO 243-245), finally, derives such epiphanies from the Hermetic aspect of the Real, which underlies, inheres in, and transcends reality.

On the basis of this survey it should now be possible to compare Russell Hoban's MR with that of the writers presented in chapter 11.2. If a graduation according to affinity were to be established, the order in ascending degrees of affinity might look thus: Rushdie, García Márquez, Carter, Morrison, Borges. In Rushdie's *Midnight's Children*, the Real of history, i.e. a permanent process of decay ungraspable in its details, crushes post-independence India. The individual with its particular subjectivity is swallowed by the masses. Neither language nor the supernatural can fulfil a restorative or constructive function because they do not give access to the Real. Saleem's telepathic powers as well as the supernatural talents of the other children of midnight are too weak to hold up the process. Universal entropy affects not only everything material but also Saleem's narrative attempt to restore logic, causality and, through them, meaning. There is a postmodern distrust of all attempts to impose order on the chaos of experience. Technically *Midnight's Children* resembles Hoban's novels from *Kleinzeit* onward, with their resistance to linearity, coherence and closure. But here the similarity ends. Rushdie's first-person narrator is unreliable because he overestimates his role on the stage of history. His "chutnification of history" in his "long-winded autobiography" tries to preserve everything from oblivion (*Midnight's Children*, 459) although this is a hopeless undertaking. By contrast, Hoban's characters tend to underestimate their abilities and to revert to verbal economy as narrators. At mystical moments, which are always ethical moments, they perceive the dynamic pattern underlying their existence: they are shaped by the pattern but also able to change it. Their subjectivity and their material being are intimately linked. Whereas Rushdie dismisses mysticism suspecting that "the mystic's conscious personality informs and interacts with the mystical event" ("In Good Faith", 20), Hoban's mystics act more responsibly once they know that they are part of something larger than themselves. Mysticism does not endow them with supernatural powers, it only affords those glimpses of the other side of the reality membrane which the characters of *Midnight's Children* are denied. To sum up, one can say that Rushdie uses MR to entertain his readers and to subvert postures of mastery; his project is not to enlarge the limited-reality consensus but to engender scepticism by drawing attention to the multiple ways in which people seek to impose their view of reality on the world. The only undebatable fact is mortality.

García Márquez is closer to Hoban because he, too, believes in a hidden reality underlying the limited-reality consensus; moreover, he, too, believes that it is possible to influence that hidden reality. On a superficial level, *One Hundred Years of Solitude* seems to work on the assumption that the Real, as implacable fate, is predetermined and cannot be escaped. Melquiades, who appears to "know what there was on the other side of things" (15) – a formula that resembles those Hoban has used to characterise the Real –, is therefore able to predict the future of the Buendía family. In his parchments he "concentrated a century of daily episodes in such a way that they coexisted in one instant" (382) – here Hoban's definition of the moment under the moment which is always now comes to mind. But the Buendías' fate is above all sealed because Melquiades fails as a translator between the hidden reality and the limited reality in which they live. His prophetic parchments are useless because nobody can read them before it is too late. Had they been more legible, the family tragedies might have been prevented. The natural disasters which finally destroy Macondo would of course have occurred all the same. The inhabitants of Macondo could have taken precaution, however. The parchments are not only useless but also wrong in so far as they predict that Macondo will be "exiled from the memory of men" (383) as soon as Aureliano Babilonia has deciphered the last page of the script. The very existence of the novel contradicts the prophecy, underlining García Márquez's humanistic trust in the power of language to create realities and preserve memories. Whereas for Hoban even an altered subjectivity can effect a transformation in the Real, García Márquez puts faith only in communication. His MR therefore does not aim to enlarge the limited-reality consensus, but to bring out the means which are already at our disposal in our limited reality.

Angela Carter holds a middle position. While *The Infernal Desire Machines of Doctor Hoffman* demonstrates the power of desire in influencing reality, a point on which she would agree with Hoban, she is pessimistic about the overall effect of its influence. For desire and therefore also the imagination are formed by cultural inscription. For Carter desire is not the expression of a metaphysical pattern which precedes humanity, but, in Europe, of a predominant patriarchal culture which supports hierachies and requires the elimination or marginalization of everybody who resists appropriation. As a consequence most subjects would not be liberated or revitalized by simply living up to their alienated desire. Like Hoban, though, Carter would reject turning away from the imagination in favour of a cold rationality. But before the imagination can set people free and enrich their experience, the scraps from the past with which it is filled need to be scrutinized and put to new uses – since it is unlikely that they can be discarded, as the ending of *Nights at the Circus* shows (cf. ch. 7.4). MR allows Carter to initiate the necessary process of interrogation. Moreover, in her view there are limits to what is possible. Hoffman's main principle, that "everything it is possible to imagine can also exist", which he finds confirmed in "mythological references" (*Hoffman*, 97), is refuted in the novel by the presence of a great number of characters who cannot alter their conditions and dispositions much as they would like to. Moreover the dead stay dead. There is a resistance in the material as well as in the psychic realm that no (supernatural) invention can affect: it is in the representation of these resistances rather than in any of the phenomena depicted that I would locate Carter's most valuable contribution to the symbolization of the Real.

I have placed Toni Morrison as next in affinity to Hoban because she shares his belief in the beneficial effect of a deliberate confrontation with the Real, especially with the Real of trauma. The complexity of the ghost girl Beloved and the way in which her influence alters those involved with her corresponds to that of the lion of Boaz-Jachin and Jachin-Boaz. Of course, the backgrounds of both novels are different: Morrison's novel is an attempt to come to terms with the psychic consequences of slavery while Hoban's is concerned with the trauma of separation. But both make that use of MR which to my mind is the most helpful, that is, they clothe elusive mental processes into vivid images. There is another difference between the two novels, though, that I do not want to conceal. While Hoban's lion disappears in the end, Beloved continues to haunt Sethe's house, even though less and less perceptibly. Morrison's ending is wiser in that it acknowledges the impossibility of a complete healing of trauma. There will always be some remainder that can neither be named nor healed. More than two decades of thinking about the Real have led Hoban to more refined ways of presenting it, too: from Death-as-monkey in *Kleinzeit*, who leaves the protagonist with a "See you" (KL 190) rather than a farewell, to the "flickering" figures in *Pilgermann*, *The Medusa Frequency*, "The Man with the Dagger", or *Fremder*, the threats and dangers, i.e. aspects of the Real dealt with for the time being, might return any time.

Borges, finally, is closest to Hoban. Like Hoban, he experimented with various forms of realistic and nonrealistic fiction. One motive for his writing was to probe the limitations of knowledge: What can we know about the world? Where and why do our senses fail us? In what sense are meaning and reference always in danger of slipping? In other words, his focus was philosophical and epistemological. Hoban is interested in consciousness, too. Especially in *The Lion of Boaz-Jachin and Jachin-Boaz* and *Turtle Diary* he juxtaposed different ways of perceiving the world. From the beginning, however, he has mainly focused on ontology: What reality is this? Should we expand the limited-reality consensus? In what sense do our fictions and our subjectivity interact with the world? Although Borges has asked similar questions, his answers are more evasive. His stories and essays create the impression that he never really stops being a sceptical experimenter who tries out various ways of model-making. By contrast, Hoban emerges from his fiction as a writer who takes a position. So do his characters: "Reality is the responsibility of those who perceive it", says Pythia in *Fremder* (181); and while Pilgermann only learns this lesson when it is too late, Fremder takes his chance and thus saves his life.

CHRONOLOGY

CB: children's book; E: essay; N: novel; OL: opera libretto;
SS: short story or sketch

1959: *What Does It Do and How Does It Work* (CB)
1960: *Bedtime for Frances* (CB)
1964: *A Baby Sister for Frances* (CB)
1966: *Tom and the Two Handles* (CB)
1967: *The Mouse and his Child* (CB)
1971: "Thoughts on a Shirtless Cyclist, Robin Hood, Johann Sebastian Bach and One or Two Other Things" (E);
A Bargain for Frances (CB);
Best Friends for Frances (CB)
1972: "Time Slip, Uphill Lean, Laminar Flow, Place-to-place Talking and Hearing the Silence" (E)
1973: *The Lion of Boaz-Jachin and Jachin-Boaz* (N);
Harvey's Hideout (CB)
1974: *Kleinzeit* (N);
How Tom Beat Captain Najork and his Hired Sportsmen (CB)
1975: *Turtle Diary* (N);
"Thoughts on Being and Writing" (E);
A Near Thing for Captain Najork (CB)
1976: Introduction to *Household Tales* by the Brothers Grimm (E; rpt. in MUM as "Household Tales by the Brothers Grimm")
1977: *Dinner at Alberta's* (CB)
1979: *La Corona and the Tin Frog* (CB)
1980: *Riddley Walker* (N);
The Twenty Elephant Restaurant (CB); *Ace Dragon Ltd.* (CB)
1981: "Portknockie" (E)
1982: "Footplacers, London Transport Owls, Wincer-Boise" (E);
"Mnemosyne, Teen Taals, and Tottenham Court Road" (E)
1983: *Pilgermann* (N);
"Pan Lives" (E); "Fragments of a Lament for Thelonious Monk" (E)
1984: "'I, that was a child, my tongue's use sleeping...'" (E)
1985: "Dream Woman" (SS); "Certain Obsessions, Certain Ideas" (SS; containing 'The Sorcerer', 'The Burlesque Altar', 'The Raging of the Head of Orpheus', 'Interviews with the Head of Orpheus', 'The Finding of the Head', 'Thinking about Hermes', 'Faces and Heads', 'And Still I Hunger with Perseus and Fay Wray', 'Uncertainty', 'Untitled')
1986: *The Marzipan Pig* (CB)
1987: *The Medusa Frequency* (N);
"The Ghost Horse of Genghis Khan" (SS);
"The Bear in Max Ernst's Bedroom or The Magic Wallet" (E)
1989: "The Man with the Dagger" (SS);
"The Raven" (SS);
"Dark Oliver" (SS);
"North" (E); "Blighter's Rock" (E)
1990: "Schwartz" (SS);
"The Colour of Love" (SS);
"Masada One Morning" (E);
"Some Episodes in the History of Miranda and Caliban: An Entertainment in Two Acts" (OL);
1991: "My Night with Léonie" (SS);
"Word Pix" (SS);
"With a Choked Cry" (E)
1992: *The Moment under the Moment* (SS, OL, E);
"The Devil's Kitchen" (SS)
1994: "The Second Mrs Kong" (OL)
1996: *Fremder* (N)
1997: *The Trokeville Way* (CB)
1998: *Mr Rinyo-Clacton's Offer* (N);
Riddley Walker. Expanded Edition. Afterword, Notes, and Glossary by Russell Hoban. (N)

BIBLIOGRAPHY

1. Russell Hoban

1.1. Primary Sources

NOVELS

Fremder. London: Jonathan Cape, 1996.

Kleinzeit. 1974. London: Picador-Pan Books, 1976. (first publ. by Jonathan Cape)

The Lion of Boaz-Jachin and Jachin-Boaz. 1973. London: Picador-Pan Books, 1974. (first publ. by Jonathan Cape)

The Medusa Frequency. London: Jonathan Cape, 1987.

Mr Rinyo-Clacton's Offer. London: Jonathan Cape, 1998.

Pilgermann. 1983. London: Picador-Pan Books, 1984. (first publ. by Jonathan Cape)

Riddley Walker. 1980. London: Picador-Pan Books, 1982. (first publ. by Jonathan Cape)

Riddley Walker. Expanded Edition. Afterword, Notes, and Glossary by Russell Hoban. Bloomington and Indianapolis: Indiana University Press, 1998.

Turtle Diary. 1975. London: Picador-Pan Books, 1977. (first publ. by Jonathan Cape)

SHORT STORIES, SKETCHES, OPERA LIBRETTO

"Certain Obsessions, Certain Ideas." 1985-1986. *The Moment under the Moment* 237-254.

"The Colour of Love." 1992. *The Moment under the Moment* 49-59.

"Dark Oliver." 1989. *The Moment under the Moment* 63-73. (first publ. in the Observer Magazine)

"The Devil's Kitchen." *Granta* 42 (1992): 164-170.

"Dream Woman." 1985. *The Moment under the Moment* 60-62. (first publ. in *Fiction Magazine*)

"The Ghost Horse of Genghis Khan." 1987. *The Moment under the Moment* 74-80. (first publ. in the *Listener*)

"The Man with the Dagger." 1989. *The Moment under the Moment* 3-16. (first publ. in *Granta*)

The Moment under the Moment. Stories, a Libretto, Essays and Sketches. London: Jonathan Cape, 1992.

"My Night with Léonie." 1991. *The Moment under the Moment* 17-29. (first publ. in *Sphinx*)

"The Raven." 1992. *The Moment under the Moment* 41-48.

"Schwartz." 1990. *The Moment under the Moment* 30-40. (first publ. in *Encounter*)

"Some Episodes in the History of Miranda and Caliban: An Entertainment in Two Acts." *The Moment under the Moment* 81-122.

"Word Pix." 1991. *The Moment under the Moment* 200-204.

ESSAYS

"The Bear in Max Ernst's Bedroom or The Magic Wallet." 1987. *The Moment under the Moment* 183-199. (first publ. in *Brick*)

"Blighter's Rock." 1989. *The Moment under the Moment* 178-182. (first publ. in *The Pauline*)
"Footplacers, London Transport Owls, Wincer-Boise." 1982. *The Moment under the Moment* 214-216. (first publ. in *Granta*)
"Fragments of a Lament for Thelonious Monk." 1983. *The Moment under the Moment* 205-207. (first publ. in *Granta*)
Introduction. 1976. *Household Tales*. By the Brothers Grimm. London: Pan-Picador, 1977. 7-19. Rpt. as "Household Tales by the Brothers Grimm." *The Moment under the Moment* 141-155.
"'I, that was a child, my tongue's use sleeping...'." 1984. *The Moment under the Moment* 156-170.
"Masada One Morning." 1990. *The Moment under the Moment* 255-260.
"Mnemosyne, Teen Taals, and Tottenham Court Road." 1982. *The Moment under the Moment* 217-236. (first publ. in *Granta*)
The Moment under the Moment. Stories, a Libretto, Essays and Sketches. London: Jonathan Cape, 1992.
"North." 1989. *The Moment under the Moment* 175-177.
"Pan Lives." 1983. *The Moment under the Moment* 125-140. (first publ. in *Granta*)
"Portknockie." *Places*. Ed. Ronald Blythe. Oxford: Oxford University Press, 1981. 57-61. Rpt. in *The Moment under the Moment* 208-213.
"Thoughts on Being and Writing." *The Thorny Paradise*. Ed. Edward Blishen. Harmondsworth: Kestrel Books, 1975. 65-76.
"Thoughts on a Shirtless Cyclist, Robin Hood, Johann Sebastian Bach and One or Two Other Things." *Children's Literature in Education* 4 (March 1971): 5-23.
"Time Slip, Uphill Lean, Laminar Flow, Place-to-place Talking and Hearing the Silence." *Children's Literature in Education* 9 (November 1972): 33-47.
"A View from the Soup." *Book Window* 3.1 (Winter 1975): 1-7.
"With a Choked Cry." 1991. *The Moment under the Moment* 171-174. (first publ. in the exhibition catalogue *Box of Delights*)

CHILDREN'S BOOKS (SELECTION)
Ace Dragon Ltd. 1980. London: Random Century Children's Books, 1992.
Arthur's New Power. London: Gollancz, 1980.
The Atomic Submarine: A Practice Combat Patrol under Water. New York: Harper and Row, 1960.
A Bargain for Frances. 1970. London: Mammoth, 1992.
Bedtime for Frances. New York: Harper and Row, 1960.
The Dancing Tigers. London: Jonathan Cape, 1979.
Dinner at Alberta's. 1975. Harmondsworth: Puffin, 1980.
Egg Thoughts and Other Frances Songs. New York: Harper and Row, 1972.
The Flight of Bembel Rudzuk. 1982. London: Walker, 1990.
Herman the Loser. 1961. Tadworth: World's Work, 1972.
How Tom Beat Captain Najork and his Hired Sportsmen. London: Jonathan Cape, 1974.
Jim Hedgehog's Supernatural Christmas. Harmondsworth: Puffin, 1991.
The Little Brute Family. 1966. London: Pan Books, 1973.
The Marzipan Pig. London: Jonathan Cape, 1986.
The Mole Family's Christmas. 1970. London: Red Fox, 1992.
M.O.L.E.: Much Overworked Little Earthmover. London: Jonathan Cape, 1993.
Monsters. London: Gollancz Children's Paperbacks, 1989.

The Mouse and his Child. 1967. London: Faber and Faber, 1974.
The Pedalling Man and Other Poems. 1969. London: Heinemann, 1991.
The Rain Door. 1986. London: Macmillan Children's Books, 1987.
The Sea-Thing Child. London: Gollancz, 1972.
The Serpent Tower. London: Walker, 1981.
They Came from Aargh! London: Walker, 1981.
The Trokeville Way. London: Jonathan Cape, 1996. New York: Knopf, 1997.
The Twenty Elephant Restaurant. 1978. Harmondsworth: Puffin, 1987.
Ugly Bird. New York: Macmillan, 1969.
What Does It Do and How Does It Work? New York: Harper and Row, 1959.

1.2. Interviews

Hoban, Russell, and Michel Bodmer. "A Conversation with Russell Hoban." Private interview. Zürich, 10 November 1983.
Hoban, Russell, and David Brooks. "Russell Hoban. An Interview Conducted by David Brooks in Adelaide on 5th March 1984." *Helix* 21-22 (Spring 1985): 71-85.
Hoban, Russell, and Ned Chaillet. "Strange Sacraments." *Time Out* 2 to 8 April 1986: 95.
Hoban, Russell, and John Haffenden. "Russell Hoban." *Novelists in Interview.* London: Methuen, 1985. 121-144.
Hoban, Russell, and Alex Hamilton. "Maps of Chaos." *Guardian* 24 March 1975: 8.
Hoban, Russell, and Valerie Jenkins. "Happiness Is a Second Family that Talks to You." *Standard* 30 March 1979: 1.
Hoban, Russell, and Paul Kincaid. "The Mouse, the Lion and Riddley Walker." *Vector* 124/5 (1984): 5-9.
Hoban, Russell, and John McEntee. "The Craftsman who Makes Novels." *Irish Press* 26 April 1977.
Hoban, Russell, and Edward Myers. "An Interview with Russell Hoban." *Literary Review* 28. 1 (1984): 5-16.
Hoban, Russell, and Paul Shand. "That's the Way to Do It." *City Life* [Manchester] 7 to 21 February 1986: 36-7.
Hoban, Russell, and Philippa Toomey. "An Explorer who Maps the Continents of His Imagination." *Times* 15 November 1974: 20.

1.3. Secondary Sources

Alvarez, A. "Past, Present, & Future." *New York Review of Books* 19 November 1981: 16-8.
Anonymous. "In Jugular Vein." *Times Literary Supplement* 29 March 1974: 345.
Anonymous. "Paperbacks: New and Noteworthy." *New York Times Book Review* 22 August 1982: 31.
Anonymous. "What Toys Endure." *Times Literary Supplement* 3 April 1969: 357.
Bailey, Paul. "Unwisecracks." *Observer* 16 August 1987: 23.
Bell-Villada, Gene H. "A Narrative Still-Life." *Commonweal* 7 October 1983: 538-540.
Bowers, A. Joan. "The Fantasy World of Russell Hoban." *Children's Literature* 8 (1980): 80-97.

Branscomb, Jack. "The Quest for Wholeness in the Fiction of Russell Hoban." *Critique* 28.1 (Fall 1986): 29-38.

Butts, Dennis. "Riddley Walker and the Novels of Russell Hoban." *Use of English* 33.3 (Summer 1982): 20-27.

Cowart, David. "The Terror of History: *Riddley Walker*." *History and the Contemporary Novel.* Carbondale and Edwardsville: Southern Illinois University Press, 1989. 83-105.

Cunliffe, Marcus. *The Literature of the United States. Fourth Edition.* London: Penguin, 1986.

DeMott, Benjamin. "2,000 Years After the Berstyn Fyr." *New York Times Book Review* 28 June 1981: 1-25.

Dewey, Joseph. *In a Dark Time: The Apocalyptic Temper in the American Novel of the Nuclear Age.* West Lafayette, Indiana: Purdue UP, 1990.

Dipple, Elizabeth. "Russell Hoban: This Place Called Time." *The Unresolvable Plot. Reading Contemporary Fiction.* London: Routledge, Chapman and Hall, 1988. 160-181.

Dorris, Michael, and Louise Erdrich. "Bangs and Whimpers: Novelists at Armageddon." *New York Times Book Review* 13 March 1988: 1, 24-25.

Dowling, David. *Fictions of Nuclear Disaster.* London: Macmillan, 1987.

-----. "Russell Hoban's *Riddley Walker*: Doing the Connections." *Critique* 29.3 (Spring 1988): 179-187.

Granofsky, Ronald. "The Contemporary Symbolic Novel." *Dissertation Abstracts International* 47.2 (Aug 1986): 526 A.

Gray, Paul. "Shell Games." *Time* 16 February 1976: 72.

Herkommer-Körfgen, Barbara Maria. *Das Muster in Bewegung. Die Romane Russell Hobans.* Bern: Peter Lang, 1994.

Hildick, Wallace. "Few Laughs." *Listener* 6 November 1969: 640-642.

Horne, Philip. "Maids." *London Review of Books* 1 to 20 April 1983: 14-15.

Korn, Eric. "A Map of the Underground." *Times Literary Supplement* 4 September 1987: 949.

Lake, David. "Making the Two One: Language and Mysticism in *Riddley Walker*." *Extrapolation* 25.2 (Summer 1984): 157-170.

-----. "Riddley Walker. Pilgermann." *Foundation* 29 (November 1983): 96-98.

Lehman, David. "Pilgrim's Progress." *Newsweek* 30 May 1983: 92.

Lively, Penelope. "Five of the Best." *Encounter* 56 (January 1981): 58-59.

MacKillop, Ian D. "Russell Hoban: Returning to the Sunlight." *Good Writers for Young Readers.* Ed. Dennis Butts. St. Albans: Hart-Davis Educational, 1976. 57-66.

Maclean, Marie. "The Signifier as Token: The Textual Riddles of Russell Hoban." *AUMLA* 70 (Nov 1988): 211-219.

Maynor, Natalie, and Richard F. Patteson. "Language as Protagonist in Russell Hoban's *Riddley Walker*." *Critique* 26.1 (Autumn 1984): 18-25.

McHale, Brian. *Constructing Postmodernism.* London: Routledge, 1992.

-----. *Postmodernist Fiction.* New York: Methuen, 1987.

McMahon-Hill, Gillian. "A Narrow Pavement Says 'Walk Alone': The Books of Russell Hoban." *Children's Literature in Education* 20 (Spring 1976): 41-55.

Meyer, Thomas. "You remember?" *Tages-Anzeiger* (Zürich) 26 October 1994: 85.

Morrissey, Thomas J. "Armageddon from Huxley to Hoban." *Extrapolation* 25.3 (Fall 1984): 197-213.

Mustazza, Leonard. "Myth and History in Russell Hoban's *Riddley Walker*." *Critique* 31.1 (Fall 1989): 17-26.

Porter, Jeffrey. "'Three Quarks for Muster Mark': Quantum Wordplay and Nuclear Discourse in Russell Hoban's *Riddley Walker* ." *Contemporary Literature* 31.4 (Winter 1990): 448-469.
Punter, David. "Essential Imaginings: the Novels of Angela Carter and Russell Hoban." *The British and Irish Novel since 1960*. Ed. James Acheson. New York: St. Martin's Press, 1991. 142-158.
Sage, Lorna. "Doodles from the Oracle." *Times Literary Supplement* (10 April 1992): 20.
Schwenger, Peter. "Circling Ground Zero." *PMLA* 106.2 (1991): 251-261.
-----. *Letter Bomb. Nuclear Holocaust and the Exploding Word*. Baltimore: Johns Hopkins University Press, 1992.
-----. "Writing the Unthinkable." *Critical Inquiry* 13.1 (Autumn 1986): 33-48.
Shippey, Tom. "Fun with Flickers." *Times Literary Supplement* (8 March 1996): 24.
Swanson, Roy Arthur. "Versions of Doublethink in *Gravity's Rainbow, Darkness Visible, Riddley Walker* and *Travels to the Enu*." *World Literature Today* 58.2 (Spring 1984): 203-8.
Taylor, Nancy Dew. "'... you bes go ballsy': *Riddley Walker's* Prescription for the Future." *Critique* 31.1 (Fall 1989): 27-39.
Thornber, Robin. "A Bomb in the Myth of Time." *Guardian* 20 February 1986: 10.
Thwaite, Anthony. "Bad Time and After." *Observer* 19 October 1980: 28.
-----. "Chapters of Accidents." *Observer* 24 March 1974: 39.
-----. "Fathers and Sons." *Observer* 1 April 1973: 37.
-----. "Pilgrim's Progress." *Observer* 13 March 1983: 33.
Tonkin, Boyd. "Notes from Underground." *New Statesman* 14 August 1987: 27.
Traugott, Maggie. "Hoban's Choice: a Bit Grimm." *Independent on Sunday* 3 May 1992.
Waugh, Auberon. "But First, Life with the Lions." *Spectator* 10 March 1973: 301-2.
Weart, Spencer R. *Nuclear Fear: A History of Images*. Cambridge, Mass.: Harvard UP, 1988.
White, Edmund. "*Turtle Diary* by Russell Hoban; *Getting Into Death* by Thomas M. Disch." *New York Times Book Review* 21 March 1976: 6.
Wilkie, Christine. *Through the Narrow Gate. The Mythological Consciousness of Russell Hoban*. London; Toronto: Associated University Presses, 1989.

2. Other Authors

2.1. Literary Sources and Sacred Books

Aldiss, Brian W. *Barefoot in the Head. A European Fantasia*. London: Faber and Faber, 1969.
The Revised English Bible. With the Apocrypha. Oxford, London, New York, Toronto: Oxford University Press, 1989.
Borges, Jorge Luis. *The Book of Sand*. 1972-1975. Trans. N. T. di Giovanni and A. Reid. London: Penguin, 1979.
-----. "The Circular Ruins." 1941. *Ficciones* 57-63.
-----. "Doctor Brodie's Report." *Doctor Brodie's Report*. 1970. Trans. N. T. di Giovanni. London: Penguin, 1976. 91-100.

-----. *Ficciones*. 1956. Ed. A. Kerrigan. Trans. A. Kerrigan et al. New York: Evergreen-Grove Weidenfeld, 1963.
-----. "The Immortal." *Labyrinths* 135-149.
-----. *Labyrinths. Selected Stories and Other Writings*. Eds. D. A. Yates and J. E. Irby. Preface by A. Maurois. Trans. D. A. Yates, J. E. Irby et al. London: Penguin, 1970.
-----. "The Library of Babel." 1941. *Ficciones* 79-88.
-----. "A New Refutation of Time." *Labyrinths* 252-270.
-----. "The Other." *The Book of Sand* 3-10.
-----. "The South." 1944. *Ficciones* 167-174.
-----. "Tlön, Uqbar, Orbis Tertius." 1941. *Ficciones* 17-35.
-----. "Ulrike." *The Book of Sand* 11-14.
-----. *A Universal History of Infamy*. 1954. Trans. N. T. di Giovanni. London: Penguin, 1975.
Burgess, Anthony. *A Clockwork Orange*. 1962. Harmondsworth: Penguin, 1972.
Carter, Angela. *The Infernal Desire Machines of Doctor Hoffman*. 1972. London: Penguin, 1982.
-----. *Nights at the Circus*. 1984. London: Picador-Pan Books, 1985.
Coetzee, J. M. *Foe*. 1986. London: Penguin, 1987.
Conrad, Joseph. *Heart of Darkness*. Harmondsworth: Penguin, 1983.
García Márquez, Gabriel. *One Hundred Years of Solitude*. 1967. Trans. G. Rabassa. New York: Avon Books, 1971.
Goethe, Johann Wolfgang. *Faust II*. Frankfurt am Main: Insel Verlag, 1985.
Golding, William. *The Inheritors*. 1955. London: Faber and Faber, 1961.
Hemingway, Ernest. *A Farewell to Arms*. 1929. Frogmore, St. Albans, Herts.: Triad/Panther Books, 1977.
-----. *The Short Stories of Ernest Hemingway*. New York: Charles Scribner's Sons, 1938.
Joyce, James. *Ulysses*. 1922. Harmondsworth: Penguin, 1968.
The Koran. Translated with notes by N. J. Dawood. Harmondsworth: Penguin, 1974.
The Message of the Qur'an. Translated and explained by M. Asad. Gibraltar: Dar al-Andalus, 1980.
Miller, Walter M., Jr. *A Canticle for Leibowitz*. 1959. New York: Bantam Books, 1976.
Morrison, Toni. *Beloved*. 1987. London: Picador-Pan Books, 1988.
Nabokov, Vladimir. *Lolita*. 1955. London: Penguin, 1980.
Pynchon, Thomas. *The Crying of Lot 49*. 1966. London: Picador-Pan Books, 1979.
-----. *V*. 1963. London: Picador-Pan Books, 1975.
Rushdie, Salman. *Midnight's Children*. 1981. London: Picador-Pan Books, 1982.
Shakespeare, William. *King Lear*. Ed. Kenneth Muir. The Arden Shakespeare. London: Methuen, 1978.
Sophocles. *Oedipus the King. Oedipus at Colonus. Antigone*. Trans. F. Storr. Loeb Classical Library 20. London: William Heinemann, 1912. Vol. 1 of *Sophocles in Two Volumes*.
Thomas, D. M. *The White Hotel*. London: Penguin, 1981.
Vonnegut, Kurt. *Cat's Cradle*. 1963. London: Penguin, 1965.
Wilde, Oscar. "De Profundis." *Complete Works of Oscar Wilde*. Introduced by Vyvyan Holland. London and Glasgow: Collins, 1977. 873-957.

2.2. Further Sources

Abrams, M. H. *A Glossary of Literary Terms*. 5th edition. Fort Worth: Holt, Rinehart and Winston, 1988.
Adams, Hazard, and Leroy Searle, eds. *Critical Theory since 1965*. Tallahassee, Fla.: University Presses of Florida and Fla. State UP, 1990.
Albertazzi, Silvia. "In the Skin of a Whale: Salman Rushdie's 'Responsibility for the Story'." *Commonwealth* 12.1 (Autumn 1989): 11-18.
Aldiss, Brian W. *Billion Year Spree. The True History of Science Fiction*. London: Weidenfeld and Nicolson, 1973.
Anderson, Linda. "The Re-Imagining of History in Contemporary Women's Fiction." *Plotting Change. Contemporary Women's Fiction*. Ed. Linda Anderson. London: Edward Arnold, 1990. 129-141.
Anonymous. "Proposal for a *Diacritics* Colloquium on Nuclear Criticism." *Diacritics* 14 (Summer 1984): 2-3.
Armstrong, Isobel. "Woolf by the Lake, Woolf at the Circus: Carter and Tradition." *Flesh and the Mirror. Essays on the Art of Angela Carter*. Ed. Lorna Sage. London: Virago Press, 1994. 257-278.
Atheling, Jr., William (alias James Blish). *More Issues at Hand*. Chicago: Advent Publishers, 1972.
Babb, Howard S. *The Novels of William Golding*. Ohio: Ohio State UP, 1970.
Barthes, Roland. "Introduction to the Structural Analysis of Narratives." 1966. *A Roland Barthes Reader*. Ed. Susan Sontag. London: Vintage, 1993. 251-295.
-----. "Myth Today." 1956. *A Roland Barthes Reader*. Ed. Susan Sontag. London: Vintage, 1993. 93-149.
Bartter, Martha A. *The Way to Ground Zero. The Atomic Bomb in American Science Fiction*. New York: Greenwood Press, 1988.
Bloch, Maurice, and Jonathan Parry. "Introduction: Death and the Regeneration of Life." *Death and the Regeneration of Life*. Eds. M. Bloch and J. Parry. Cambridge: Cambridge University Press, 1982. 1-44.
Bloom, Harold. *The Anxiety of Influence*. London: Oxford University Press, 1975.
Borges, Jorge Luis. "Die Erzählkunst und die Magie." 1932. *Essays 1932-1936*. Bd. 5.1 von *Jorge Luis Borges: Gesammelte Werke*. Übs. K. A. Horst. München: Carl Hanser Verlag, 1981. 80-90.
Borges, Jorge Luis, and César Fernández Moreno. "Weary of Labyrinths. An Interview with Jorge Luis Borges." *Encounter* 32.4 (April 1969): 3-14.
Bowie, Malcolm. *Lacan*. Cambridge, Mass.: Harvard University Press, 1991.
Bradbury, Malcolm. *The Modern American Novel*. Oxford: Oxford University Press, 1983.
-----. "Rushdie's Empire." *No, Not Bloomsbury*. London: André Deutsch, 1987. 359-362.
Bronfen, Elisabeth. "From Omphalos to Phallus: Cultural Representations of Femininity and Death." *Woman: A Cultural Review* 3.2 (1992): 145-158.
-----. *Over Her Dead Body. Death, Femininity and the Aesthetic*. Manchester: Manchester University Press, 1992.
Brooke-Rose, Christine. *A Rhetoric of the Unreal. Studies in Narrative and Structure, Especially of the Fantastic*. Cambridge: Cambridge University Press, 1981.
Butler, Judith. *Gender Trouble. Feminism and the Subversion of Identity*. New York: Routledge, 1990.

Carter, Angela, and John Haffenden. "Angela Carter." *Novelists in Interview*. By John Haffenden. London: Methuen, 1985. 76-96.

Carter, Angela, and Lorna Sage. "The Savage Sideshow." *The New Review* 4.39-40 (June-July 1997): 51-57.

Chambers, J. K., and Peter Trudgill. *Dialectology*. Cambridge: Cambridge University Press, 1980.

Chanady, Amaryll. "The Origins and Development of Magic Realism in Latin American Fiction." Hinchcliffe and Jewinski 49-60.

Chevalier, Jean, and Alain Gheerbrant. *A Dictionary of Symbols*. Trans. J. Buchanan-Brown. Oxford: Blackwell, 1994.

Cixous, Hélène. "Castration or Decapitation?" Trans. A. Kuhn. *Signs: Journal of Women in Culture and Society* 7.1 (Autumn 1981): 41-55.

-----. "The Laugh of the Medusa." 1976. Trans. K. Cohen and P. Cohen. *New French Feminisms*. Eds. E. Marks and I. de Courtivron. New York: Schocken, 1981. 245-264.

Clarens, Carlos. *An Illustrated History of the Horror Film*. 1967. New York: Paragon Books, 1979.

Coale, Samuel. *Anthony Burgess*. Modern Literature Series. New York: Frederick Ungar, 1981.

Cohen, Sarah Blacher, ed. "Introduction: The Varieties of Jewish Humor." *Jewish Wry. Essays on Jewish Humor*. Bloomington: Indiana University Press, 1987. 1-15.

Collins Dictionary of the English Language. London and Glasgow: Collins, 1983.

Cowart, David. *History and the Contemporary Novel*. Carbondale and Edwardsville: Southern Illinois University Press, 1989.

Cronin, Richard. "The Indian English Novel: *Kim* and *Midnight's Children*." *Modern Fiction Studies* 33.2 (Summer 1987): 201-213.

Dawood, N. J., trans. Introduction. *The Koran*. Harmondsworth: Penguin, 1974. 9-12.

De Lauretis, Teresa. *Alice Doesn't. Feminism, Semiotics, Cinema*. London: Macmillan, 1984.

-----. *Technologies of Gender. Essays on Theory, Film, and Fiction*. 1987. London: Macmillan, 1989.

Deleuze, Gilles, and Félix Guattari. *L'Anti-Oedipe*. Paris: Les Editions de Minuit, 1972.

-----. "[Excerpts from] *Anti-Oedipus: Capitalism and Psychoanalysis*." *Critical Theory since 1965*. Eds. H. Adams and L. Searle. Tallahassee, Fla.: University Presses of Florida and Fla. State UP, 1990. 285-307.

Derrida, Jacques. "No Apocalypse, Not Now (full speed ahead, seven missiles, seven missives)." *Diacritics* 14 (Summer 1984): 20-31.

-----. "Structure, Sign and Play in the Discourse of the Human Sciences." *Modern Literary Theory: A Reader*. Eds. P. Rice and P. Waugh. Trans. A. Bass. London: Edward Arnold, 1989. 149-165.

Durix, Jean-Pierre. "Magic Realism in *Midnight's Children*." *Commonwealth* 8.1 (Autumn 1985): 57-63.

Eagleton, Terry. *Literary Theory. An Introduction*. Oxford: Blackwell, 1983.

Eco, Umberto. *Einführung in die Semiotik*. Trans. J. Trabant. UTB 105. München: Wilhelm Fink Verlag, 1972.

Einstein, Albert. *Einstein on Peace*. Eds. O. Nathan and H. Norden. New York: Simon and Schuster, 1960.

Eliade, Mircea. *Schamanismus und archaische Ekstasetechnik*. 1956. Übs. I. Köck. Zürich und Stuttgart: Rascher Verlag, 1957.
Fetterley, Judith. *The Resisting Reader. A Feminist Approach to American Fiction*. Bloomington: Indiana UP, 1978.
Foucault, Michel. "The Subject and Power." *Critical Inquiry* 8 (Summer 1982): 777-795.
Frazer, Sir James George. *The Golden Bough. Abridged Edition*. London: Papermac, 1987.
Freud, Sigmund. "Bemerkungen über einen Fall von Zwangsneurose." 1909. *Zwang, Paranoia und Perversion. Studienausgabe, Bd. 7*. Frankfurt/M.: S. Fischer, 1973. 31-103.
-----. "Der Dichter und das Phantasieren." 1908. *Gesammelte Werke, Bd. 7. Werke aus den Jahren 1906-1909*. Frankfurt/M.: S. Fischer, 1941. 213-223.
-----. "Erinnern, Wiederholen, Durcharbeiten." 1914. *Schriften zur Behandlungstechnik. Studienausgabe, Ergänzungsband*. Frankfurt/M.: S. Fischer, 1975. 205-215.
-----. "Female Sexuality." 1931. *Freud on Women. A Reader*. Ed. E. Young-Bruehl. New York: Norton, 1990. 321-341.
-----. "Femininity." 1932. *Freud on Women. A Reader*. Ed. E. Young-Bruehl. New York: Norton, 1990. 342-362.
-----. "Hemmung, Symptom und Angst." 1926 (1925). *Hysterie und Angst. Studienausgabe, Bd. 6*. Frankfurt/M.: Fischer Taschenbuch Verlag, 1982. 227-308.
-----. "Das Ich und das Es." 1923. *Psychologie des Unbewussten. Studienausgabe, Bd. 3*. Frankfurt/M.: S. Fischer, 1975. 273-330.
-----. "Jenseits des Lustprinzips." 1920. *Psychologie des Unbewussten. Studienausgabe, Bd. 3*. Frankfurt/M.: S. Fischer, 1975. 213-272.
-----. "Medusa's Head." 1940 (1922). *Freud on Women. A Reader*. Ed. E. Young-Bruehl. New York: Norton, 1990. 272-273.
-----. "Der Sinn der Symptome." 1917. *Gesammelte Werke, Bd. 11. Vorlesungen zur Einführung in die Psychoanalyse*. Frankfurt/M.: S. Fischer, 1944. 264-281.
-----. "Some Psychical Consequences of the Anatomical Distinction Between the Sexes." 1925. *Freud on Women. A Reader*. Ed. E. Young-Bruehl. New York: Norton, 1990. 305-314.
-----. "Trauer und Melancholie." 1917. *Psychologie des Unbewussten. Studienausgabe, Bd. 3*. Frankfurt/M.: S. Fischer, 1975. 193-212.
-----. *Die Traumdeutung. Studienausgabe, Bd. 2*. 1900. Ungekürzte Lizenzausgabe für den Buchclub Ex Libris Zürich, 1976. Frankfurt/M: S. Fischer, 1972.
-----. "Triebe und Triebschicksale." 1915. *Psychologie des Unbewussten. Studienausgabe, Bd. 3*. Frankfurt/M.: S. Fischer, 1975. 75-102.
-----. "Das Unbehagen in der Kultur." 1930 (1929). *Fragen der Gesellschaft, Ursprünge der Religion. Studienausgabe, Bd. 9*. Frankfurt/M.: S. Fischer, 1974. 191-270.
-----. "Das Unheimliche." 1919. *Psychologische Schriften. Studienausgabe, Bd. 4*. Frankfurt/M.: S. Fischer, 1970. 241-274.
-----. "Die Verdrängung." 1915. *Psychologie des Unbewussten. Studienausgabe, Bd. 3*. Frankfurt/M.: S. Fischer, 1975. 103-118.
-----. *Der Witz und seine Beziehung zum Unbewussten*. 1905. Frankfurt/M.: Fischer Taschenbuch Verlag, 1975.

Friedan, Betty. *The Feminine Mystique. Tenth Anniversary Edition.* New York: Norton, 1974.
Gass, William H., and Carole Spearin McCauley. "William H. Gass." *The New Fiction. Interviews with Innovative American Writers.* Ed. J. D. Bellamy. Urbana: University of Illinois Press, 1974. 32-44.
Ghose, Sisir Kumar. "Mysticism." *Encyclopaedia Britannica: Macropaedia, Vol. 12.* 1974 ed. 786-793.
Gleick, James. *Chaos. Making a New Science.* New York: Viking, 1987.
Golding, William. "Fable." *The Hot Gates.* London: Faber and Faber, 1965. 85-101.
Golding, William, and John Haffenden. "William Golding." *Novelists in Interview.* By John Haffenden. London: Methuen, 1985. 97-120.
Goodwin, Ken. "The Image of the National Child in the Work of Atwood, Rushdie, Soyinka and White." *Literature and Commitment.* Ed. G. Narain Sharma. Toronto: Tsar, 1988. 15-25.
Graves, Robert. *The Greek Myths. Combined Edition.* 1960. London: Penguin, 1992.
Halliday, M. A. K. "Linguistic Function and Literary Style: An Inquiry into the Language of William Golding's 'The Inheritors'." 1971. *Essays in Modern Stylistics.* Ed. D. C. Freeman. London; New York: Methuen, 1981. 325-360.
Hamburger, Käte. *Die Logik der Dichtung.* Frankfurt/M.: Ullstein, 1980.
Hancock, Geoff. "Magic or Realism: The Marvellous in Canadian Fiction." Hinchcliffe and Jewinski 30-48.
Hawes, Clement. "Leading History by the Nose: The Turn to the Eighteenth Century in *Midnight's Children.*" *Modern Fiction Studies* 39.1 (Spring 1993): 147-168.
Hawking, Stephen W. *Eine kurze Geschichte der Zeit.* Übs. H. Kober. Hamburg: Rowohlt Taschenbuch Verlag, 1991.
Hinchcliffe, Peter, and Ed Jewinski, eds. *Magic Realism and Canadian Literature: Essays and Stories. Proceedings of the Conference on Magic Realist Writing in Canada.* Waterloo, Ontario: University of Waterloo Press, 1986.
Hofstadter, Douglas R. *Metamagical Themas: Questing for the Essence of Mind and Pattern.* London: Penguin, 1986.
Huntington, Richard, and Peter Metcalf. "Introduction: The Anthropology of Death Ritual." *Celebrations of Death: The Anthropology of Mortuary Ritual.* Cambridge: Cambridge University Press, 1979. 1-20.
Hutcheon, Linda. "'Circling the Downspout of Empire': Post-Colonialism and Postmodernism." *ARIEL* 20.4 (October 1989): 149-175.
-----. *Narcissistic Narrative: The Metafictional Paradox.* 1980. New York: Methuen, 1984.
-----. *A Poetics of Postmodernism: History, Theory, Fiction.* New York: Routledge, 1988.
Irwin, Robert. "Islam and the Crusades." *The Oxford Illustrated History of the Crusades.* Ed. J. Riley-Smith. Oxford: Oxford University Press, 1995. 217-259.
Islam, Shamsul. "Rushdie and Political Commitment: A Study of *Midnight's Children* and *Shame.*" *Literature and Commitment.* Ed. G. Narain Sharma. Toronto: Tsar, 1988. 125-131.
Jakobson, Roman. "Linguistics and Poetics." *Style in Language.* Ed. T. Sebeok. New York: Technology Press of M. I. T. and John Wiley, 1960. 350-377.

Jameson, Fredric. *The Prison-House of Language. A Critical Account of Structuralism and Russian Formalism.* Princeton, N.J.: Princeton University Press, 1972.

Jordan, Elaine. "Enthralment: Angela Carter's Speculative Fictions." *Plotting Change. Contemporary Women's Fiction.* Ed. L. Anderson. London: Edward Arnold, 1990. 19-40.

Jung, Carl Gustav. "Approaching the Unconscious." *Man and his Symbols.* Eds. C. G. Jung and M.-L. von Franz. London: Aldus Books, 1964. 18-103.

-----. *Selected Writings.* Selected and introduced by A. Storr. London: Fontana Paperbacks, 1983.

Kerényi, Karl. *Hermes: Guide of Souls. The Mythologem of the Masculine Source of Life.* 1944. Trans. M. Stein. Zürich: Spring Publications, 1976.

-----. *Die Mythologie der Griechen, Bd. 2: Die Heroen-Geschichten.* München: Deutscher Taschenbuch Verlag, 1966.

Kinkead-Weekes, Mark, and Ian Gregor. *William Golding. A Critical Study.* Rev. ed. London: Faber and Faber, 1984.

Kofman, Sarah. "The Narcissistic Woman: Freud and Girard." *French Feminist Thought. A Reader.* Ed. T. Moi. Oxford: Basil Blackwell, 1987. 210-226.

Kristeva, Julia. *Powers of Horror. An Essay on Abjection.* 1980. Trans. L. S. Roudiez. New York: Columbia University Press, 1982.

-----. "Revolution in Poetic Language." 1974. *The Kristeva Reader.* Ed. T. Moi. Oxford: Basil Blackwell, 1986. 89-136.

Lacan, Jacques. "The Agency of the Letter in the Unconscious or Reason since Freud." *Écrits. A Selection.* 1977. Trans. A. Sheridan. London: Routledge, 1989. 146-178.

-----. *The Ethics of Psychoanalysis, 1959-1960. The Seminar of Jacques Lacan: Book VII.* Ed. J.-A. Miller. Trans. D. Porter. London: Routledge, 1992.

-----. *The Four Fundamental Concepts of Psycho-Analysis.* Ed. J.-A. Miller. Trans. A. Sheridan. London: Penguin, 1979.

-----. "The Function and Field of Speech and Language in Psychoanalysis." *Écrits. A Selection.* 1977. Trans. A. Sheridan. London: Routledge, 1989. 30-113.

-----. "God and the *Jouissance* of ~~The~~ Woman." *Feminine Sexuality.* Eds. J. Mitchell and J. Rose. Trans. J. Rose. New York: Norton, 1985. 137-148.

-----. "A Love Letter. (Une Lettre D'Âmour)." *Feminine Sexuality.* Eds. J. Mitchell and J. Rose. Trans. J. Rose. New York: Norton, 1985. 149-161.

-----. "The Meaning of the Phallus." *Feminine Sexuality.* Eds. J. Mitchell and J. Rose. Trans. J. Rose. New York: Norton, 1985. 74-85.

Laplanche, J., and J.-B. Pontalis. *The Language of Psycho-Analysis.* Trans. D. Nicholson-Smith. London: Karnac Books and the Institute of Psycho-Analysis, 1988.

Lee, David A. "*The Inheritors* and Transformational Generative Grammar." *Language and Style* 9.2 (Spring 1976): 77-97.

Leech, Geoffrey N., and Michael H. Short. *Style in Fiction. A Linguistic Introduction to English Fictional Prose.* London: Longman, 1981.

Lyons, John. *Chomsky.* Glasgow: Fontana-Collins, 1977.

Malouf, Amin. *The Crusades through Arab Eyes.* Trans. J. Rothschild. London: Al Saqi Books, 1984.

Meaney, Gerardine. *(Un)Like Subjects. Women, Theory, Fiction.* London: Routledge, 1993.

Mitchell, Juliet. "The Question of Femininity and The Theory of Psychoanalysis." *Women: the Longest Revolution.* London: Virago, 1984. 295-313.

Montrelay, Michèle. "Inquiry into Femininity." *French Feminist Thought. A Reader*. Ed. T. Moi. Oxford: Basil Blackwell, 1987. 227-249.

Morrison, Toni. *Playing in the Dark. Whiteness and the Literary Imagination*. 1992. The William E. Massey Sr. Lectures in the History of American Civilization 1990. New York: Random-Vintage, 1993.

Mulvey, Laura. "Afterthoughts on 'Visual Pleasure and Narrative Cinema' inspired by King Vidor's *Duel in the Sun* (1946)." 1981. *Visual and Other Pleasures*. Bloomington: Indiana University Press, 1989. 29-38.

Nabokov, Vladimir. "On a Book Entitled *Lolita*." 1956. *Lolita*. London: Penguin, 1980. 309-315.

Norris, Christopher. *Deconstruction. Theory and Practice*. Revised Edition. London: Routledge, 1991.

Ortega y Gasset, José. *Meditationen über "Don Quijote"*. 1914. Übs. U. Weber. Stuttgart: Deutsche Verlags-Anstalt, 1959.

Peitgen, Heinz-Otto, and Peter H. Richter. *The Beauty of Fractals. Images of Complex Dynamical Systems*. Berlin: Springer-Verlag, 1986.

Puschmann-Nalenz, Barbara. *Science Fiction and Postmodern Fiction. A Genre Study*. New York: Peter Lang, 1992.

Riley-Smith, Jonathan. "The State of Mind of Crusaders to the East 1095-1300." *The Oxford Illustrated History of the Crusades*. Ed. J. Riley-Smith. Oxford: Oxford University Press, 1995. 66-90.

Riley-Smith, Jonathan, ed. *The Atlas of the Crusades*. London: Times Books, 1991.

Robertson, Mary F. "Hystery, Herstory, History: 'Imagining the Real' in Thomas's *The White Hotel*." *Contemporary Literature* 25.4 (1984): 452-477.

Rose, Jacqueline. "Feminine Sexuality: Jacques Lacan and the *école freudienne*." *Sexuality in the Field of Vision*. London: Verso, 1986. 48-81.

Rushdie, Salman. "In Good Faith." *The Independent on Sunday* 4 February 1990. 18-20.

Sage, Lorna. *Angela Carter*. Plymouth: Northcote House Publishers, 1994.

Scheick, William J. "Nuclear Criticism: An Introduction." *Papers on Language and Literature* 26.1 (Winter 1990): 3-12.

Scholes, Robert E. *Fabulation and Metafiction*. Urbana: University of Illinois Press, 1979.

Scholes, Robert E., and Eric S. Rabkin. *SF. Science Fiction: History, Science, Vision*. London: Oxford University Press, 1977.

Schwenger, Peter. *Phallic Critiques*. London: Routledge and Kegan Paul, 1984.

Sebeok, Thomas A., and Jean Umiker-Sebeok. "'Sie kennen ja meine Methode.' Ein Vergleich von Charles S. Peirce und Sherlock Holmes." 1979. *Der Zirkel oder Im Zeichen der Drei. Dupin, Holmes, Peirce*. Hrsg. U. Eco und T. A. Sebeok. Übs. C. Spelsberg und R. Willemsen. München: Fink Verlag, 1985. 28-87.

Senn, Fritz. *Joyce's Dislocutions. Essays on Reading as Translation*. Ed. J. P. Riquelme. Baltimore and London: Johns Hopkins University Press, 1984.

Singh, Sushila. "Salman Rushdie's *Midnight's Children*. Rethinking the Life and Times in Modern India." *Panjab University Research Bulletin (Arts)* 16.1 (April 1985): 55-67.

Stace, W. T. *Mysticism and Philosophy*. London: Macmillan, 1961.

Stanzel, Franz K. *Theorie des Erzählens, 3. Auflage*. UTB 904. Göttingen: Vandenhoek und Ruprecht, 1985.

Steiner, George. *In Bluebeard's Castle*. New Haven: Yale University Press, 1971.
-----. "Silence and the Poet." 1966. *Language and Silence. Essays 1958-1966*. London: Faber and Faber, 1967. 55-74.
Stephens, John, and Ruth Waterhouse. *Literature, Language and Change: From Chaucer to the Present*. London: Routledge, 1990.
Storr, Anthony. Introduction. *Selected Writings*. By C. G. Jung. London: Fontana Paperbacks, 1983. 13-27.
Sturgis, Susanna J. "Magic Realism: What's in a Name?" *Tales of Magic Realism by Women. Dreams in a Minor Key*. Ed. S. J. Sturgis. Freedom, California: The Crossing Press, 1991. 1-5.
Theweleit, Klaus. *Buch der Könige. Band 1: Orpheus und Eurydike*. Basel: Stroemfeld/Roter Stern, 1988.
-----. *Männerphantasien, 1. Bd.: Frauen, Fluten, Körper, Geschichte*. Frankfurt am Main: Verlag Roter Stern, 1977.
Todd, Richard. "Worlds Apart: Salman Rushdie's 'Privileged Arenas'." *Shades of Empire*. Eds. C. C. Barfoot and T. D'haen. Amsterdam: Rodopi, 1993. 65-82.
Todorov, Tzvetan. *Introduction à la littérature fantastique*. Paris: Seuil, 1970.
-----. "The Typology of Detective Fiction." 1966. *The Poetics of Prose*. Ithaca: Cornell University Press, 1977. 42-52.
Verma, Charu. "Padma's Tragedy: A Feminist Deconstruction of *Midnight's Children*." *Panjab University Research Bulletin (Arts)* 20.2 (October 1989): 59-65.
Viswanathan, Gauri. *Masks of Conquest*. 1989. London: Faber and Faber, 1990.
Von Braun, Christina. "Männliche Hysterie – weibliche Askese: Zum Paradigmenwechsel der Geschlechterrollen." *Die schamlose Schönheit des Vergangenen. Zum Verhältnis von Geschlecht und Geschichte*. Frankfurt/M.: Verlag Neue Kritik, 1989. 51-79.
Weedon, Chris. "Language and Subjectivity." *Feminist Practice and Poststructuralist Theory*. Oxford: Basil Blackwell, 1987. 74-106.
Wenzler, Ludwig. "Nachwort: Zeit als Nähe des Abwesenden." *Die Zeit und der Andere*. Von E. Levinas. Hamburg: Felix Meiner Verlag, 1989. 67-92.
Wexler, Joyce. "E.R.A. for Hemingway: A Feminist Defense of *A Farewell to Arms*." *Georgia Review* 35 (1981): 111-123.
Wheelock, Carter. "Borges, Cortázar, and the Aesthetics of the Vacant Mind." *International Fiction Review* 12.1 (Winter 1985): 3-10.
Wilson, Robert R. "The Metamorphoses of Space: Magic Realism." Hinchcliffe and Jewinski 61-74.
Zizek, Slavoj. *Looking Awry. An Introduction to Jacques Lacan through Popular Culture*. Cambridge, Mass.: MIT Press, 1991.

INDEX